THE ROCK YEAR BOOK 1981

EDITED BY
Michael Gross &
Maxim Jakubowski

DESIGN BY
John Gordon

DESIGN ASSISTANTS
Alex Evans
Mandy Ollis

PHOTO CO-ORDINATOR
Chalkie Davies

US EDITORIAL ASSISTANT
Drew Moseley

CONTRIBUTORS
Tony Bacon
Adam Barnett-Foster
Julie Burchill
Linnet Evans
Pete Frame
Colin Irwin
Paul Kendall
Nick Kimberley
Barry Lazell
Philippe Manoeuvre
Phil Newell
Dan Nooger
Alexei Panshin
Rob Partridge
Tony Russell
Steve Taylor
John Tobler
Mark Williams
Bob Woffinden
Richard Wootton

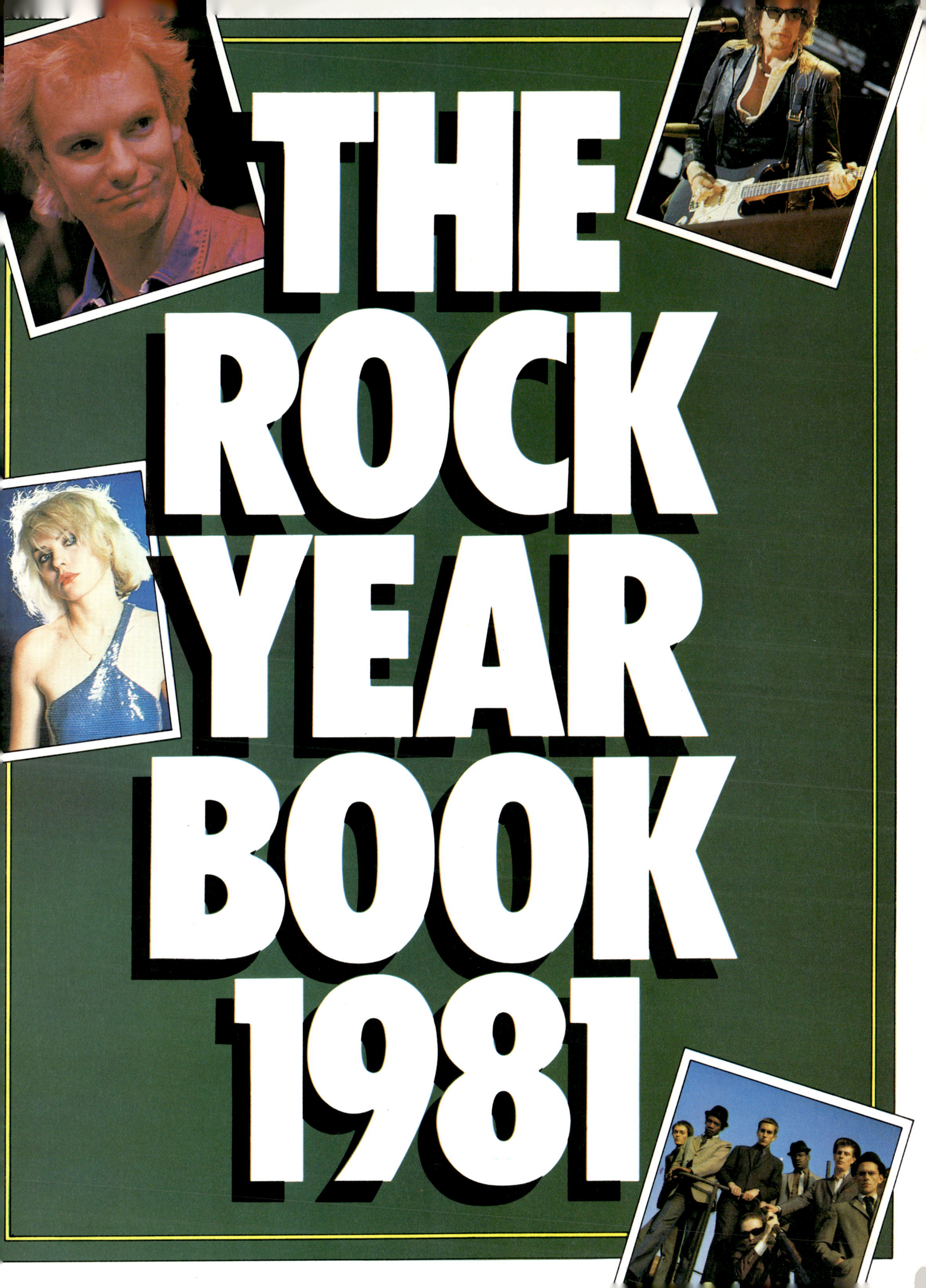
THE
ROCK
YEAR
BOOK
1981

The Original No.1.
Coca-Cola
Coca-Cola
1220
CALIFORNIA
957 XPQ
Levi's
quality never goes out of style.

CONTENTS

First Published in Great Britain in 1980 by Virgin Books,
61-63 Portobello Road, London W11 3DD

ISBN 0-907080-06-5

Printed in the USA by Connecticut Printers

First Edition

THE YEAR

SEP 1979

1. Jimmy Pursey reforms Sham 69 after brief abortive alliance with stranded Pistols Steve Jones and Paul Cook.

1. *Superior Court in Los Angeles orders Clayton Moore, star of Lone Ranger TV series, to stop wearing famous black mask trademark. Moore admits to 64 years of age. The copyright owning company, planning newer films with a younger man, had filed a civil suit.*

1. *We don't talk anymore* by Cliff Richard displaces the Boomtown Rats' *I don't like Mondays* as Britain's best selling single.

5. *Funeral of Earl Mountbatten of Burma.*

7. Guitarist John Mackay and drummer Kenny Morris abandon Siouxie and the Banshees after the start of a major headlining tour of Britain.

Musicians United for Safe Energy (MUSE) concerts span 5 nights at Madison Square Garden, netting over a quarter of a million dollars to help finance anti-nuclear groups. (Springsteen, Jackson Browne, James Taylor etc).

7. Led Zeppelin's *In Through the Out door* enters UK album chart at No. 1, Bob Dylan's *Slow Train Coming* enters at No. 2. Within a month of release, the album sells almost 3 million copies in US, temporarily stemming fears of a prophesied slump in record sales.

9. *Jody Schekter wins Italian GP at Monza to ensure 1979 World Drivers Championship.*

Cat Stevens, now known as Yusef Islam, marries Fouzia Ali at Kensington Mosque.

11. *Police in UK discover cache of £5m worth of LSD tablets.*

12. *400,000 are evacuated as 130mph Hurricane Frederick sweeps through Southern USA.*

CLIFF RICHARD

15. *An exhausted President Carter was stopped by doctors from completing a hilly six mile cross country run near Camp David.*

16. *Two circus elephants plod into Alpine town of Susa in NW Italy after retracing the march of Hannibal, his army and 57 elephants 2197 years earlier.*

18. *Leonid and Valentina Kozlov, principal dancers with Bolshoi Ballet, defect while in Los Angeles on tour. The previous month, leading ballet star Aleksandr Godunov had also been granted asylum in United States.*

ROGER DALTREY/THE WHO

The Who return to US stage for 5 sold out nights at Madison Square Garden.

The Tennessee Medical Examiners Board files official charges of "gross malpractice in the indiscriminate prescribing of prescription drugs" against Dr George Nichopolous of Memphis, who was Elvis Presley's personal physician. Apparently, massive amounts of powerful drugs had been prescribed for Presley — including a total of 95 prescriptions during the period from January 1st 1977 to August 16th 1977, the day Elvis died.

18. *California appoints its first openly homosexual judge Steven Lachs.*

20. *Bokassa I, Emperor of Central African Republic overthrown in bloodless coup.*

23. *Anti nuclear rally draws over 200,000 to New York's Battery Park. Jane Fonda and Tom Hayden subsequently tour 50 cities in opposition of nuclear power — starting at 3 Mile Island, scene of accident earlier this year.*

26. *American ABC-TV pays record $225 million to cover 1984 Olympics in LA.*

28. *Message in a Bottle* by Police tops UK singles charts.

28. Guitarist Jimmy McCulloch, former member of Wings, Stone the Crows and Thunderclap Newman, found dead in his Maida Vale flat. He was 26. His new group The Dukes was just about to be launched.

29. *Pope arrives in Ireland for 3 day visit. In speech at Drogheda, near the Ulster border, he appeals for peace between Catholics and Protestants.*

OCT

1. Pope arrives in US for 7 day visit.

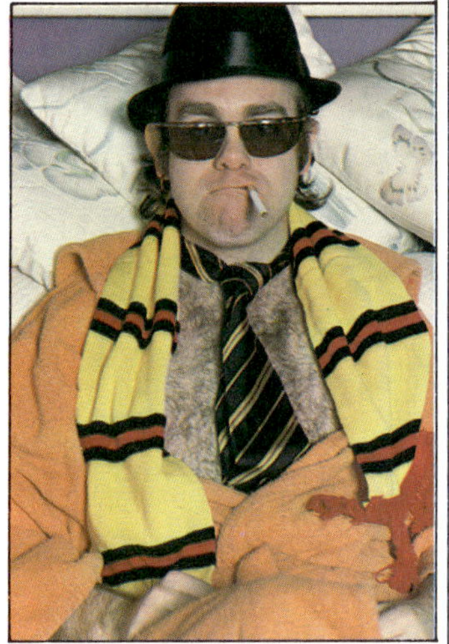
ELTON JOHN

Elton John plays 8 nights in New York.

3. *DPP says no-one is to be prosecuted over death of Blair Peach, who died as a result of injuries received at Southall National Front rally on April 23.*

6. The Knack's *My Sharona* ends its record breaking run at the top of the American singles charts.

The Eagles and Fleetwood Mac embark on world tours to promote new albums. Warner Bros. Records simultaneously unveils its largest promotional campaign ever — to accompany the release of *Tusk* by Fleetwood Mac.

13. Blondie's *Eat to the Beat* enters UK album chart at number one.

DEBBIE HARRY

18. *Bianca Jagger loses battle to have her divorce petition heard in California, where wives win more generous settlements ..... faces costs bill of £30,000. (Decree nisi granted in London on November 2).*

Pioneer punk band Penetration, from Newcastle, break up, as do the Adverts.

18. *More than 53,000 Kampuchean refugees driven into Thailand in a week of fighting against guerillas supporting Pol Pot.*

BIANCA JAGGER & RINGO STARR

20. *Pravda fiercely criticises Margaret Thatcher for her speech about the need to strengthen western defences, calling her a "bellicose lady" who had "tried on the trousers of Winston Churchill in the hope of impressing her American allies".*

20. *The Long Run* by the Eagles enters US chart at No. 2 — failing to depose Led Zeppelin who have already dropped out of the Top 10 in Britain.

22. *Confessed murderer Jesse Bishop dies in Nevada State gas chamber — the first Nevada execution since 1961.*

24. *ITV resume broadcasting after strike lasting nearly 11 weeks.*

27. *The Voluntary Euthanasia Society vote to publish controversial 'How to do it' suicide booklet.*

30. *It is disclosed that Chrysler UK (to be renamed Talbot on Jan '1 1980) lost £37,630 million in 18 months to June 30, 1979.*

LED ZEPELIN

THE EAGLES

NOV

3. Two Tone enthusiasm reaches new heights as the Specials album enters UK chart at No. 4 and the Madness album at No. 16. *Tusk* by Fleetwood Mac enters US album chart at No. 7.

4. *Several hundred students occupy American Embassy in Tehran, holding US personnel hostage. Their action is fully supported by the Ayatollah Khomeini.*

8. *Newscaster Reginald Bosanquet makes last appearance on ITN.*

9. *A full scale alert of a Soviet nuclear attack caused panic — a warning had flashed to US bases around the world and several squadrons of aircraft scrambled.*

MARILYN MONROE

12. *A pair of white gloves and an ivory fan used by Marilyn Monroe in 'Some Like It Hot' were sold for £400 at Sothebys.*

Snowy White joins Thin Lizzy and John Sloman joins Uriah Heep.

MADNESS, SELECTER AND THE SPECIALS ON BRIGHTON BEACH

12. *Death of Dimitri Tiomkin, composer of High Noon, Rio Bravo and other movie soundtracks.*

13. *The Times, last published on Nov 30, 1978, reappeared after 11½ month dispute.*

15. *Miss World title won by 21 year old Gina Swainson, Miss Bermuda.*

17. John Grascock, 27, former bass player with Jethro Tull, dies in London. He had quit the band following heart surgery from which he never recovered.

CHUCK BERRY

19. Chuck Berry is released from Lampoc Prison Farm, California after serving two thirds of his four month jail sentence for income tax evasion. Whilst inside, he entertained fellow felons with a special concert.

23. *Death of Hollywood actress Merle Oberon.*

Marianne Faithfull is arrested at Oslo Airport and charged with marijuana possession. After signing a confession she is allowed into the country to proceed with her promotional tour.

MARIANNE FAITHFUL

29. *British Steel Corporation announce a loss of £145.6 million for the first half of 1979.*

Anita Pallenberg, former girlfriend of Keith Richard, is cleared of any complicity in the death of Scott Cantrell, who shot himself in the head in Richard's New York house last July. Cantrell's father had claimed that Pallenberg lured him to the house with promises of sex and drugs.

30. *Death of Joyce Grenfell, comedy actress and writer, and of Zeppo Marx, last surviving member of the Marx Brothers.*

DEC

4. Eleven people were trampled to death in the rush to obtain good seats for The Who's concert in Cincinnati, Ohio. An £11.25 million lawsuit of negligence was brought against the group.

6. *BBC-TV children's programme 'Blue Peter' raises over £2m to help the hungry in Kampuchea.*

PETE TOWNSHEND/THE WHO

8. *Walking On The Moon* by Police jumps to No. 1 in UK.

8. *The Wall* by Pink Floyd enters UK album chart at No. 3. Pink Floyd close the decade at the top of the UK singles chart with *Another Brick In The Wall.*

18. *Stuntman Stanley Barrett, aided by a sidewinder missile in his rocket car, becomes the first person to exceed sonic speed on land clocking 739.666 mph on Rogers Lake, California.*

24. *Death in Denmark of Rudi Dutschke, West German radical student leader of the sixties.*

25. *Soviet Union begins a massive two-day airlift of troops and military equipment into Afghanistan, with a further five divisions on the border. On 27th, President Hafizollah Amin, who came to power in September, is executed.*

21. *In Kampuchea, Khmer Rouge leaders oust Pol Pot as President and appoint Khieu Samphan to the post. Despite his replacement, Pol Pot remains effective leader of the deposed Khmer Rouge regime.*

22. *Death of Darryl F. Zanuck, the last of the flamboyant Hollywood film moguls.*

22. Clash double album *London Calling* enters charts at No. 9.

IAN DURY AND THE BLOCKHEADS

Stars and audiences converge on Hammersmith Odeon for 4 nights of benefit concerts to aid the refugees of Kampuchea. Among those appearing are Queen, Ian Dury and the Blockheads, The Clash, The Who, The Specials, The Pretenders, Elvis Costello and The Attractions, Wings and Rockpile.

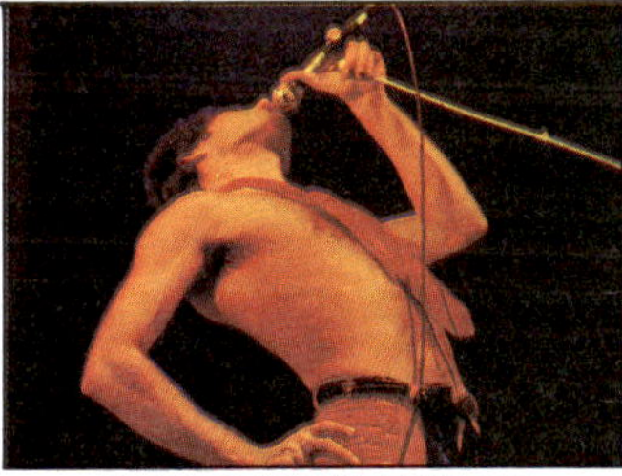

FREDDIE MERCURY/QUEEN

26. *Gold prices break the £500 per ounce barrier for the first time. Gold fever breaks out as price begins to rise steeply.*

29. *Plans for a secret trial of the Gang of Four, the ousted Chinese radicals who included Mao Tse Tung's widow, are announced in Peking. They were arrested on a charge of plotting to seize power soon after Mao's death in September 1976.*

Through the success of the album *Parallel Lines* (the year's best seller) and singles *Heart of Glass*, *Sunday Girl* and *Dreaming*, Blondie become the top selling album and singles act of the year in Britain.

30. *Death of Richard Rogers, composer of music for 40 stage shows.*

ELP finally announce their official dissolution as all 3 seek solo deals.

THE CLASH

EMERSON, LAKE, & PALMER

JAN 1980

2. Fifties rock star Larry Williams, whose songs were recorded by the Beatles and the Stones, is found dead at his Los Angeles home. His body, with a gunshot wound in the head, was discovered by his mother. A verdict of suicide was recorded.

4. *Naturalist Joy Adamson is found dead at her remote home at Shaba Game Park. At first a lion is blamed for the attack, but a herdsman is subsequently charged with her murder.*

7. Hugh Cornwell, guitarist/singer with The Stranglers, is sentenced to eight weeks in prison and fined £300 for possession of cannabis, cocaine and heroin. He had admitted the charges and pleaded guilty.

9. *In Mecca, 63 people are beheaded by sword for attacking the Great Mosque in November.*

15. *The UN General Assembly calls for an immediate withdrawal of foreign troops from Afghanistan. A day later NATO and the European Community make the same demand. Soviet troops remain unmoved.*

16. Paul McCartney is jailed in Tokyo after half a pound of marijuana is discovered in his suitcase. He spends 10 days in jail before being flown back to Britain after the authorities decided not to prosecute. Wings' tour, however, was unavoidably cancelled.

18. *The Wall* by Pink Floyd moves to No. 1 in the US album chart, remaining there throughout February, March and April.

18. The Pretenders début album enters the UK chart at No. 1, as their single *Brass in Pocket* moves to the top of the singles chart.

18. *Inflation and political unrest continue to push up the price of gold, which today reaches a record $1000 per ounce in US. Due to restrictions in New York and West Germany, the price then begins to collapse, closing at $650 per ounce at the end of the month.*

Following exploratory dates in San Francisco, Bob Dylan embarks on 24 date US tour. Reaction to his San Francisco dates was reflected in local newspaper headlines: 'Born Again Dylan Bombs' and 'Bob Dylan's God-Awful Gospel'.

DAVE GILMOUR/PINK FLOYD

Rhythm 'n' blues hit maker of the late 1940's and early 1950's, Amos Milburn, dies in Houston, aged 52, on Jan 3. His most celebrated recording, *Chickenshack Boogie*, cut in 1947, dominated US R&B charts for almost a year.

27. *Robert Mugabe returns to Zimbabwe Rhodesia after 5 years in exile.*

Capricorn Records, the flagship of Southern Boogie in the seventies, files for bankruptcy in Macon, Georgia.

27. *The US Olympic Committee decides by a unanimous vote to ask the International Olympic Committee to move, cancel or postpone the Olympics. The US House of Representatives and the Senate had already voted to boycott the games.*

30. Professor Longhair, the New Orleans pianist and singer who helped transform rhythm 'n' blues into rock 'n' roll, dies in his home city, aged 61. His 1977 album, *Live On The Queen Mary*, was recorded at a party thrown by Paul McCartney.

SECTOR 27

Tom Robinson, who disbanded his TRB last summer, announces the formation of a new outfit to be known as Sector 27.

BOB DYLAN

FEB

1. *Too Much Too Young* brings the Specials their first No. 1 single in the UK.

2. About 1000 Sid Vicious fans march from Sloane Square to Hyde Park to honour the first anniversary of their hero's death. His mother Ann Beverley, 48, was to have taken part in the march but was admitted to hospital with a drug overdose the previous evening.

SID VICIOUS

3. *State police and National Guard troopers storm the New Mexico State prison at Santa Fé to end a two-day riot that had turned into a bloodbath of convict reprisals, mutilations and burnings, with up to 35 inmates dead.*

3. *Mohammed Ali begins a tour of Africa as President Carter's envoy, to drum up support for the US-backed boycott of the Moscow Olympics.*

MOHAMMED ALI

BON SCOTT OF AC/DC

7. *Police wind up the £1m publicity campaign to net the Yorkshire Ripper, who has killed 12 women. No useful information had been forthcoming from the public.*

13. After smashing his front door with an axe, police invade John Lydon's house for the second time in a month. Lydon meets them at the top of the stairs, wielding a ceremonial sword. After causing considerable disruption, the police removed the only illegal object they can find — a miniature tear gas container for self defence in case of attack.

18. Rolling Stone Bill Wyman announces that he intends to leave the group in 1983, the 20th anniversary of his joining. "I only got into rock 'n' roll for a bit of fun and to see the world for a couple of years," he says.

19. Bon Scott, 33, lead singer with Australian heavy metal band AC/DC dies of alcohol poisoning in London.

22. In UK album charts, Elvis Costello's *Get Happy* enters at No. 2 whilst the Selecters' début *Too Much Pressure* comes in at No. 5.

ELVIS COSTELLO

22. Queen's *Crazy Little Thing Called Love* tops the US singles chart, remaining there for 4 weeks.

22. *US is gripped by inflation panic as the mounting economic crisis forces bank interest rates to a record 16½%.*

22. *Astrid Proll, former West German urban terrorist, is sentenced to 5½ years in gaol for bank robbery — but as she has already served 4 years, the remainder of her sentence is suspended.*

Pink Floyd play 7 dates at the Los Angeles Sports Arena followed by 5 at the Nassar Coliseum in Long Island, New York.

29. Buddy Holly's glasses, those he was wearing when he was killed on Feb.3, 1959, are allegedly found by a local sheriff searching through the old court records (The Big Bopper's wrist-watch is also discovered) in Mason City, Iowa.

BUDDY HOLLY

MAR

PATTI SMITH

1. Patti Smith marries former MC5 guitarist Fred 'Sonic' Smith in Detroit.

3. *Robert Mugabe wins landslide victory in Rhodesian election. His ZANU-PF party polls an absolute majority in the 100 seat parliament.*

3. A paper napkin from the Riviera Hotel, Las Vegas, signed "Thank you, Elvis Presley" fetches £500 in auction at Sotheby's. Among other rock-oriented items were 4 US dollar bills signed by the Beatles and a batch of letters and signatures by the Rolling Stones. Each lot went for £220.

5. *Jay Silverheels, the Mohawk Indian who played Tonto in the Lone Ranger TV series, dies in Los Angeles, aged 60.*

19. The secret autopsy report on Elvis Presley is subpoenaed by a Shelby County grand jury investigating the practices of Presley's personal physician Dr. George Nichopoulos.

20. *28 year old Texan truck driver Joseph Riviera enters the New York office of Elektra/Asylum Records, draws a gun, takes the office manager hostage and demands to see either Jackson Browne or The Eagles. Under the impression that they would appear and hand over enough money to finance his trucking operation, Riviera was talked into submitting quietly to police when he realised the folly of his demands.*

THE JAM

21. The Jam's *Going Underground* enters UK singles chart at No. 1 — the first record to do so since Gary Glitter's *I Love You Love* in Nov. 1973.

23. *Jacob Miller, vocalist with Inner Circle, dies in Kingston, Jamaica, the victim of a car crash.*

THE POLICE

20. *Radio Caroline, the original British pirate radio station, goes off the air permanently when the ship from which it broadcast, the MI AMIGO, sinks. Lashed by gales, she snapped her moorings and drifted onto the sandbank in the Thames Estuary.*

26. The Police play a concert in Bombay — the first rock band to do so since Hawkwind, ten years earlier.

Seven years after its release, Pink Floyd's *Dark Side of the Moon* becomes the longest charting pop album in the history of Billboard magazine. In mid-March, the album logged 303 weeks on the trade magazine's chart — eclipsing the previous record holder, Carole King's *Tapestry*, which charted for 302 weeks between April 71 and Jan 77.

27. *The 10,105 ton Alexander Kieland, a huge floating hotel and accommodation rig in the North Sea Ekofisk oilfield, overturns after one of its 5 legs shears off in a violent storm. 137 are dead or missing.*

28. *Big band era crooner Dick Haymes dies of lung cancer in Los Angeles.*

30. *Violinist and bandleader Mantovani dies in Tunbridge Wells, Kent, after a long illness. He was 74.*

In annual US Grammy Awards, Bob Dylan is voted Best Male Rock Vocalist. "The first person I want to thank is the Lord," said the grateful Bob. Rickie Lee Jones won the Best New Artist category and the Doobie Brothers took 4 awards, including "Record Of The Year" for their single *What a Fool Believes.*

31. *Legendary black American athelete Jesse Owens, hero of the 1936 Berlin Olympics, dies of cancer at 66 in Tuscon, Arizona.*

31. *Gay priests should be removed from their jobs according to outspoken Anglican churchmen. "To be a practising homosexual is wrong in the eyes of God," says their report.*

31. *An outbreak of fighting by left and right wing extremists leaves 40 dead and 450 injured at the funeral of murdered Archbishop Oscar Romero in San Salvador.*

APR

1. *Since radiation leak at 3 Mile Island nuclear power plant in Pennsylvania, deaths of children aged one and under are said to have more than doubled.*

A 180-yard stretch of Brighton Beach is opened to nudists. Only a handful brave the chilly winds and myriad gawkers, but a few days later the proliferating naked bathers become a massive tourist attraction.

Citizens of St. Paul's district of Bristol go on rampage following heavy-handed police swoop on Black and White Café. 16 police injured; thousands of pounds' worth of damage done.

5. *Castro sanctions mass exodus of Cuban dissidents wishing to escape Communist régime.*

EMI, "the greatest recording organisation in the world", announces a loss of £2.8m in the half year to Dec. 31, 1979 compared with profits of £18m a year earlier.

IPC, the publishing empire, give notice to the entire staff of Melody Maker and New Musical Express over their support of striking colleagues.

6. *San Diego schoolgirl Brenda Spencer, who killed 2 and wounded 9, starts her 25 year jail sentence. Her explanation, "I don't like Mondays, I wanted to liven up the day", inspired the Boomtown Rats' smash hit.*

6. *217 Mods are arrested at Scarborough after reintroducing the mid-60s practice of terrorising holidaymakers. Mod brawls also break out in Great Yarmouth, Brighton, Southend and Margate.*

The Osmonds, touring Britain with an entourage of 126, appeal to fellow Mormons to attend their concerts, which are an abysmal failure. Tour later ends in embarrassed shambles.

7. *President of National Hairdressers Federation urges members not to deplore the punk style, which "will certainly go down in history along with beehives for women and mohicans for men".*

'Kramer vs Kramer' wins 5 Oscars at Academy Award presentations in Hollywood. Sir Alec Guinness wins a special Oscar for "an outstanding life achievement in the cinema".

ATV film, 'Death Of A Princess', based on 1977 public execution of 19 year old Saudi Arabian Princess Misha'al for adultery, angers Saudi Arabian government. Foreign Secretary Lord Carrington is called in to smooth out the situation.

12. *President Tolbert of Liberia is assassinated in a coup staged by a group of non-commissioned army officers.*

THE OSMONDS

14. A 45-minute concert by Gary Numan becomes first publicly available rock video cassette, preceding Blondie's *Eat to the Beat* by several weeks.

15. *Jean Paul Sartre, prolific French novelist and playwright, dies of a lung disease at 74.*

17. *Independence Day in Zimbabwe. Prince Charles represents Britain; Premier Robert Mugabe assumes control. Bob Marley officiates.*

19. Annual comedy spectacular, the Eurovision Song Contest is won by Eire's Johnny Logan singing *What's Another Year?* British representatives Prima Donna finish third with *Love Enough For Two.*

Film director Alfred Hitchcock dies in California, aged 80.

22. *Unemployment in UK soars to 1,522,921 — the highest April figure since World War II.*

24. *Attempt to rescue US hostages in Tehran is bungled by crack American anti-terrorist squad.*

25. Strangler's guitarist/vocalist Hugh Cornwell is released from Pentonville Prison after serving 6 weeks for heroin possession. "It's the most depressing, demoralising, inhuman place I have ever spent any time in," he says.

26. The Beat release *Mirror in the Bathroom,* the first British single to have been recorded digitally.

THE BEAT

28. *US Secretary of State Cyrus Vance resigns over the President's decision to send a rescue squad to free the hostages in Iran. Carter appoints Senator Ed Muskie as his replacement.*

29. *Geno* by Dexy's Midnight Runners becomes best selling UK single, while Bob Seger's *Against the Wind* displaces *The Wall* by Pink Floyd at the top of the US album chart.

30. *Terrorists take over the Iranian Embassy in London, threatening to blow up the building and 20 hostages if their demands are not met.*

MAY

The film of 'The Great Rock 'n' Roll Swindle', chronicling the rise of The Sex Pistols, enters cinema top ten at No. 3 in UK, despite critics calling it "tasteless tat" and "garbage".

2. Pink Floyd's *Another Brick in the Wall* is banned in South Africa. The song had been adopted by black children boycotting school in protest of their inferior standard of education. It was now considered "prejudicial to the safety of the state".

4. *President Tito of Yugoslavia dies after a long illness.*

4. *A Special Air Services squad storms the Iranian Embassy in London freeing all the hostages and killing 4 of the 5 terrorists who had held the building for 6 days.*

PAUL McCARTNEY

14. *The Trades Union Congress Day of Action — a general strike called to show contempt for Government policy — is a washout. Most union members prefer to work.*

18. Ian Curtis, singer with Joy Division, is found dead in his Manchester home. He is believed to have committed suicide.

18. *Race riots break out in Miami, Florida, after an all-white jury clear 4 white policemen of beating a black prisoner to death. This was the first such major disorder since the long hot summers of the mid-sixties.*

Peter Criss, drummer with heavy metal megastars Kiss, leaves the band to pursue a solo career.

18. *Mount St. Helens, a volcano in Washington State, erupts with an explosion 2500 times greater than the Hiroshima bomb. Several million tons of volcanic ash are hurled into the air — as much as that from Mt. Vesuvius in AD 79. Estimates of the damage caused run into billions of dollars, and President Carter declares the region a disaster area.*

Paul McCartney solo album *McCartney II* enters chart at No. 1 within days of release.

In one of the most surprising mergers the rock world has ever seen, The Buggles — Trevor Horn and Geoff Downes — join Yes to replace departed members Jon Anderson and Rick Wakeman.

MICK JONES/THE CLASH

DEBBIE HARRY

21. Joe Strummer is arrested after a fan has a guitar smashed over his head in a fracas between The Clash and part of their audience at a gig in Hamburg.

22. Englebert Humperdinck is named father of a 3 year old illegitimate child. The judge orders him to pay £2500 to the 24 year old mother and £50 a week maintenance. The mother, Kathy Jetter, told the court that the relationship started at a concert 4 years ago when the star invited her on to the stage to sit on his lap.

29. *Bionic man Lee Majors admits defeat in attempts to woo home his errant wife Farrah Fawcett. He files for divorce citing "irreconcilable differences".*

30. After 6 weeks as America's best selling single, Blondie's *Call Me*, originally recorded for the movie *American Gigolo*, is displaced by Lipps Inc's thoroughly abysmal *Funky Town*.

Marshal Tucker bassist Tommy Caldwell dies in a car accident in his home town, Spartanburg, South Carolina.

2. Glen Matlock is fined £100 and banned from driving for a year for driving while unfit through drink.

6. *The Rank Organisation announces that it plans to make no more films. "Economic factors made it necessary", says a spokesman.*

Backed by right-wing US businessmen, former bulldozer driver Jimmy Stevens leads a bow and arrow revolt to assume control of Espiritu Santo, an island in the New Hebrides. Currently administered by Britain and France, the island was to have become independent in July — but the rebels opposed the new government.

6. Peter Gabriel's third solo album (titled *Peter Gabriel*, as were both its predecessors) enters UK album chart at No. 3. Heavy metal heroes Whitesnake enter at No. 9 with *Ready and Willing*.

6. *For the second time in one week US military forces are put on nuclear alert when computer malfunction report Soviet missiles heading for America. After 3 minutes, the error is discovered and the alert aborted.*

7. *Henry Miller, the American novelist whose 'Tropic of Cancer' and 'Tropic of Capricorn' were widely banned as pornographic, dies in California aged 88.*

10. *Comedian Richard Pryor is said to have only a 30% chance of survival after setting fire to himself whilst concocting a 'cocaine cocktail'. An explosion during the purifying process had engulfed him in flames.*

12. *Millions of young Americans are ordered to register for possible military call-up as President Carter steps up his war of nerves with the Russians over their invasion of Afghanistan.*

12. *Japanese Premier Masayoshi Ohira dies of a heart attack, aged 70.*

PETER GABRIEL

12. *The House of Lords rules that the £750,000 profits confiscated from the Operation Julie LSD raid should be returned to the convicted drug manufacturers/distributors as its seizure was illegal. The Inland Revenue is thought likely to end up with most of the money.*

12. *Presidential candidate Ronald Reagan says that, if elected, he would submit himself to periodic medical examinations and resign the Presidency if serious evidence of senility or mental deterioration were detected.*

13. Billy Joel's *Glass House* album displaces Bob Seger at top of US chart.

18. *60 people are reported dead after South African police charge into riot mobs with guns blazing in a predominantly black suburb of Cape Town. The police attack was the culmination of several days of arson and looting by disgruntled black protesting their repression by the authorities.*

20. After 3 weeks as UK's best selling single, *Theme from M.A.S.H.* is deposed by Don MacLean's revival of the Roy Orbison hit *Crying*. MacLean last reached No. 1 with *Vincent* in 1972.

20. Bob Dylan releases a new album, *Saved*, which is decimated by the critics.

20. *A shock report on drug use in America concluded that at least one in three Americans have tried either cocaine or heroin. Nearly 70% of 18-25 year olds are said to have taken marijuana. America's Health and Welfare Secretary, Patricia Harris, orders the National Institute on Drug Abuse to step up its drive "to help youngsters kick the habit".*

20. After sacking drummer Martin Atkins, Public Image Ltd. announce that "it is unlikely the band will ever perform again". The split occurred at the end of Pil's "chaotic" American tour.

21. Three members of the Stranglers are taken to jail in handcuffs following a riot, which they were said to have instigated, at Nice University. After an inadequate power supply had failed for the third time, the frustrated Stranglers were said to have told their fans to "take it out on the university, not us". After a perusal of evidence, the others were released unconditionally while Jean-Jacques Burnel was allowed out on £10,000 bail.

21. The Beach Boys and Santana headline the annual Knebworth festival.

24. *Britain's jobless soars to 1,659,676 — the worst figure since the war.*

27. *Hundreds flee from their homes after ten thousand gallons of radioactive water are accidentally spilled at the notorious Three Mile Island in Pennsylvania. Families refused to be consoled by the official announcement that contamination was confined to the plant and that no radiation had been released into the atmosphere.*

BRYAN FERRY/ROXY MUSIC

28. Roxy Music head the UK album chart with *Flesh and Blood* while Paul McCartney's *Coming Up* moves to No. 1 in the US singles chart.

JUL

4. *Emotional Rescue* by the Rolling Stones enters the UK album chart at number one during its first week of release. Three weeks later, it climbs to the top in US.

BJORN BORG

5. *Bjorn Borg defeats John McEnroe to win Wimbledon lawn tennis championship for fifth consecutive year.*

9. *Seven die in a stampede to see the Pope at a soccer stadium in Fortaleza, Brazil.*

10. *Alexandra Palace burns down when sparks from a blowtorch set fire to paintwork during preparation for a jazz and blues festival the following day. The building had housed many rock events over the years.*

11. *The Game* by Queen enters UK album chart at number 2, whilst *Xanadu* by Olivia Newton John edges up to become the top selling single.

14. Malcolm Owen, lead singer with the Ruts, is found dead in his bath. His death is ascribed to a long and continuing problem with drug addiction.

16. *Former cowboy actor Ronald Reagan is chosen as Republican candidate in November's presidential elections. He chooses former CIA director George Bush as his running mate.*

18. Billy Joel tops US album and singles chart — with *Glass Houses* and *It's still rock 'n' roll to me* respectively.

19. *Soviet leader Leonid Brezhnev opens 22nd Olympiad in Moscow. Official TV coverage fails to reveal the extent of protest over Russian invasion of Afghanistan.*

DAVID BOWIE

David Bowie makes his stage debut in lead role of Bernard Pomerance's *The Elephant Man* in Denver. The play is set in Victorian England and Bowie plays a hideously deformed man who is taken into the care of a London surgeon and becomes a celebrated society figure.

28. *Critic and author Kenneth Tynan, a pioneer of the permissive age, dies aged 53. He had the distinction of being the first man to utter a 4 letter word on British television.*

23. *President Carter's brother Billy admits accepting over £92,000 from the Libyan government. The disclosure is considered a major blow to Jimmy's chances of re-election. The incident becomes known as the Billygate scandal, and senior democrats lobby for Carter's removal from the Presidential stakes.*

PETER SELLERS

24. *Film star Peter Sellers dies from heart attack in London.*

27. *The Shah of Iran dies in exile in Cairo, aged 60. His death is greeted with rejoicing in Iran.*

28. *The Atlantic air war hots up as TWA and British Airways reduce fares to New York. One way standby fare is now £82.*

AUG

1. *Sebastian Coe wins the Olympic Gold Medal for the 1500 metres.*

SEBASTIAN COE

1. *17 die and more than 50 are injured when a train is derailed in Co. Cork, Ireland.*

2. Deep Purple reach top of UK chart with TV-advertised compilation album four years after splitting up.

4. *Queen Elizabeth, the Queen Mother, receives tributes on her 80th birthday.*

Pink Floyd play a week of gigs at Earls Court, in London — their first British concerts for some years.

PINK FLOYD

4. *Fifty Iranians are arrested after trying to storm the American Embassy in London. In New York, 200 Iranians are arrested during demonstrations and are expected to be deported.*

4. *76 are killed and over 200 injured in a right-wing terrorist massacre at Bologna railway station in Italy.*

7. *Hurricane Allen, which has already killed at least 50 people in the Caribbean, heads towards Brownsville on the Texas coast, precipitating winds of over 150 mph. Residents lock up their properties and prepare to evacuate the town.*

11. *President Carter and Senator Edward Kennedy square up for presidential nomination at the Democratic convention in New York City. Kennedy acknowledges defeat and withdraws.*

Time Out

ROCK

It was in many ways a jubilant and zestful year for rock 'n' roll, but it was also a tragic one, and it would be invidious to start a survey of the year anywhere but Cincinnati.

It was there, on December 3 1979, that The Who played the second date of their US tour at the Riverside Coliseum. Only after the gig were the group informed that 11 people had been killed in a horrific scramble through the turnstiles earlier in the evening. It was the most serious catastrophe in the history of rock 'n' roll.

Over 14,000 of the 18,000 tickets had been sold as 'unreserved' seating — a standard procedure, and yet one which had always invited trouble since it obviously precipitated a general rush for the most advantageous places. Indeed, nasty incidents had nearly occurred at this venue on previous occasions. In this case, the crowd thronging outside before the gates were opened had even been aroused to urgent action since they could plainly hear the group on stage (going through their sound-check, as it happens). Further, when the people were finally admitted, an insufficient number of gates were opened — for an audience that, as the organisers subsequently admitted, was slightly over-capacity.

Blame was naturally apportioned in various directions, and it seems inevitable that legal liabilities will be thrashed out in the courts for years to come. Of one fact, though, there is little doubt — the whole sad episode was attributable to shortcomings in administration and organisation.

Those who had survived that fatal human maelstrom were saddened and angered by some of the subsequent news reports — in particular, one on CBS television which portrayed the audience as a "drug-crazed mob", who'd somehow invited their own destruction. In fact, the later evidence of the coroner revealed that death in all cases was due to asphyxiation; traces of alcohol and/or drugs had been discovered in two of the victims, but only of "insignificant amounts".

It was nevertheless the "drug-crazed mob" angle which the British press, in its patronising and ignorant way, chose to develop. It even introduced its own drugs for the purpose. "Angel Dust Rock Horror" proclaimed the DAILY EXPRESS, for good measure appending a gruesome litany of horrors supposedly induced by this drug ("a student gouged out his own eyes", et cetera). In fact, the EXPRESS had not a sliver of evidence that this drug was to blame for the disaster — indeed, they couldn't possibly have had, since it wasn't. The SUN also carried a similar story, repeating that the cause of the "drug-crazed stampede" was angel-dust.

DIANA ROSS

The fact of the tragedy — 11 lives lost — seemed of little significance to Fleet Street beside this golden opportunity to push home one of its favourite prejudices — that rock fans are some kind of palaeolithic species. For a British audience, such journalism could only have compounded the tragedy. Rock music is clearly a culture apart, one which passes Fleet Street's understanding.

Even so, the rock music ethic is not entirely blameless in the Cincinnati affair. Rock 'n' roll, like the Romans, honours its dead above its living, and no-one could deny that it frequently wills its own corpses. Even more reason therefore why those in the eye of the hurricane — the rock stars — should try to defuse fatal incidents of their glorification potential. In this context, Roger Daltrey's post-concert statements were misjudged. he referred to the victims as "the kids" (in fact, one was the mother of two children), and affirmed that The Who tour would continue because "we owe it to rock 'n' roll and the 11 dead". The point is that people don't have to live and die for rock 'n' roll — it just isn't that important. No-one owes it anything.

It was, thankfully, a point that did reach home during the year — a sense of perspective was introduced. This was largely due to the efforts of the 2-Tone stable of artists, who ensured that rock music lost much of its encumbering self-importance and regained an uninhibited sense of fun. The bands in question — The Specials, Madness, The Selecter, The Beat — all debuted on the 2-TONE label, and all looked for inspiration to the Jamaican ska and rock steady music of the '60s, while another band who toured with most of them during the autumn,

Dexy's Midnight Runners, used the US soul and R'n'B music of the same period as their source.

The entire movement not only seemed healthy musically — it even appeared benign in a business sense, since the bands had achieved all they had by ignoring the traditional paths to commercial success in the music industry.

It was noticeable, nevertheless, how quickly they all became embroiled in it, however unwillingly. Once Madness had quit 2-TONE for STIFF, they were promoted with the standard gimmicks — double-page press ads, picture disc singles, 12″ singles with collectors' B-sides, unavailable elsewhere. In a final ironic move, their album was TV-advertised. If this represented some kind of perversion of the original aims of the movement, it nerverthelss enabled Madness' debut album to outsell that of The Specials' — to whose initial encouragement they owed their breakthrough.

By the summer, total disharmony had broken out in the ranks of 2-Tone, with The Selecter, one of the label's original names, baling out on the grounds that 2-Tone had suffered a debilitating surfeit of success.

There was indeed a thin line which separated the commercial success that beckoned every talented rock band from the betrayal of original objectives that it so often entailed. The Who had walked this razor's eged for years. Their mighty success was only further emphasised at the start of 1980 when they signed a new $15 million contract with WEA; yet they continued to wrestle with the implications of this and, so far, have come out on top. A solo album, 'Empty Glass', only confirmed that Pete Townshend's aesthetic sensibilities were as finely-honed as ever, the $15 million notwithstanding.

A film of The Who's 'Quadrophenia' had been expected to spark off a major revival. Well, it nearly did. The film itself enjoyed

THE JAM

considerable commercial success. Mod gangs duly appeared (and swarmed Scarborough over the Easter bank holiday period), and the fashion houses fell in step. Yet the revival never quite became pre-eminent, largely because UK popular music was at this time vigorously diversified, and also because there was no one instant new star, a Travolta-type figurehead, around whom the movement could coalesce.

This was despite the efforts of The Jam, the band who had anticipated any potential mod revival by at least two years. For them, this period was one of flowering success, as they finally fulfilled the promise they had shown from the start. Apart from 'Setting Sons', their best-selling album which was highly rated by the critics, they had two No. 1 singles — 'Eton Rifles' in the latter months on 1979, and, in March 1980, 'Going Underground', which indelibly registered their soaring popularity by topping the charts in its first week of release. It was a feat no-one had managed since the heady days of Gary Glitter in 1973. The Jam's record company, POLYDOR, speedily made all nine of their singles re-available, and most re-appeared in the charts. It was proof positive that the band which had initially seemed moulded in the image of the early Who had now firmly established their own identity and were beginning to create their own legacy.

Otherwise, mod bands were not quite able to kindle the flame, for all that two of them — the Secret Affair and The Lambrettas — achieved quite respectable chart success. The others who might have been expected to infiltrate the charts — the Merton Parkas, The Chords, the Purple Hearts — seemed unable to capitalise both on the spirit of the moment and the initial publicity they had enjoyed.

Thus, a mod revival did happen, but not to the extent that it became the single fount of rock fashion. There was one other revival of considerable importance. This, depending on your point of view, was either a healthy manifestation of rock's new-found heterogeneousness, or a distrubing measure of the hopelessly retrogressive tendencies of many adolescents. It was the Heavy Metal Revival.

'Revival', certainly, it appeared to be; some, though, maintained that the music had never been away, it had simply become unfashionable and therefore under-publicised. Well, unfashionable it was always likely to remain. However buoyant its popularity, its articles of faith were determinedly obscurantist. Its life-blood was its anti-metropolitanism. Its unfashionability was its very quintessence.

The rejuvenated heavy metal heroes tended to be of three varieties: those who had perhaps had their day and could scarcely have imagined that it would ever come round again; those who had never made it in the first place, and who had slogged away for years, appreciating that the music had a sizeable underground audience; and those younger bands who were now offered an opportunity to exploit the music's renewed prominence.

The first group consisted mostly of Deep Purple alumni — Rainbow, the band led by Ritchie Blackmore, which recruited a very good vocalist indeed in Graham Bonnet, and hit the Top 10 on two occasions; David Coverdale's Whitesnake, and Ian Gillan's band called, er, Gillan. At the head of the second category were Judas Priest and Motorhead. The former presumably deserved some kind of reward for sheer pertinacity — and got it, with chart albums in 'Unleashed In The East' and 'British Steel'. They were also the victims of a curious piece of business enterprise, when the finished tapes of the latter album were stolen and held to ransom. Judas Priest paid up, the tapes were returned and the album released. Of course, one shouldn't encourage such behaviour, but it did seem a delightfully ingenious wheeze.

The suddenly-sprouting newer bands were Def Leppard, Saxon, Iron Maiden, et al. The Reading Festival organisers, knowing well their audience, virtually turned their August bank holiday gathering into a heavy metal fans' convention (i.e. a danger zone for all citizens of sound mind and limb). Bands on the bill there included most of those listed

WHITESNAKE

above — Rainbow and J. Priest excepted — as well as stalwarts such as Rory Gallagher, UFO and Wishbone Ash.

No doubt British heavy metallers had been sustained by the situation in America, where heavy metal had never been away. During the year, however, Aerosmith did go away. (When asked his opinion on the break-up of Aerosmith, Shakespeare is reported to have said, "For this relief, much thanks.") Also, the first cracks in the Kiss facade began to appear, when drummer Peter Criss opted out. Boston carried on, but at least refrained from releasing any albums.

Other American bands — Van Halen for example — further confirmed their growing support, while the popularity of heavy metal was unarguably proved by Rush who, on their UK 1980 summer tour, mananaged to sell out a gig at Portsmouth Guildhall on June 2, despite the fact that they were playing in Southampton that night.

There were of course those who achieved their prominence in more individual ways. The Police and Gary Numan, for example, both of whom achieved consecutive No. 1's, and also The Pretenders, who reached those giddy heights for the first time. Elvis Costello managed to fit 20 songs on to one new album, but it was The Clash who really showed their peers what could be done by releasing an excellent double-album, 'London Calling', which retailed at just £5.00.

VAN HALEN

The Lowe-Edmunds-Rockpile caucus flourished as never before, with individual hit singles for both Edmunds ('Queen Of Hearts', 'Singing The Blues') and Lowe ('Cruel To Be Kind'). Additionally, Lowe won still wider fame by marrying Carlene Carter, and thus becoming Johnny Cash's son-in-law. He was then listed by ROLLING STONE as one of the 'Heavy Hundred' of the music industry.

News of other acts who had emerged in latter years was less heartening. Graham Parker's elusive breakthough remained elusive, his seemingly-promising label switch from PHONOGRAM to STIFF notwithstanding; and Tom Robinson, having disbanded the Tom Robinson Band, announced the formation of a new unit, Sector 27, and was promptly dropped by EMI. However, Wilko Johnson, a displaced talent for too long, was offered new accomodation in the Blockheads (a natural home for him, after all) by Ian Dury.

TOM ROBINSON

For others, the year was far more turbulent. Siouxsie and The Banshees embarked on a UK autumn tour to tie in with the release of their second album, 'Join Hands'. The tour transpired to be an especially fateful one. Half the band walked out just before the first gig in Aberdeen, and Siouxsie herself was rushed to hospital immediately after the last one in London. All very newsworthy of course, but Siouxsie, who spent two months recovering from hepatitis, probably had something a little less traumatic in mind.

Even so, The Stranglers could trump that. At the beginning of 1980, their guitarist, Hugh Cornwell, was given a three-month prison sentence for possession of harmless amounts of marijuana and other drugs. Harsh and disgraceful as this verdict was, it was confirmed on appeal, and Cornwell duly entered Pentonville prison in March.

Unfortunately, the band, presupposing a successful outcome of his appeal, had gone ahead and arranged gigs. So a two-day date at the Rainbow in Finsbury Park (part of that venue's fiftieth anniversary celebrations) took place without Cornwell, but with various sympathisers — Robert Fripp for example — deputising. Another result of the bust was that it caused The Stranglers to be scooped in their ambition to play concerts in India — The Police got there first.

Cornwell, who had been denied use of his guitar while in prison ("We've got a bus driver in here, and he can't have his bus") was released in April, having earned full remission for good behaviour. The Stranglers immediately went ahead with revised plans for their world tour, and thus it came to pass that by June Cornwell was back in prison, this time in France. Three of the band had been accused of inciting a riot at Nice University after they had abandoned their concert because of persistent power failure. The local authorities alleged that riot damage amounted to £10,000, and the group members were all released pending charges once this amount had been arranged. Their internment had obliged them to cancel just one date in Athens (somewhere else The Police had just played), but all other scheduled dates went ahead as planned.

The triumphant success of 2-Tone had provided CHRYSALIS with their second major business coup of the latter half of the '70s. Their first had occurred some three years earlier when they had scooped the world by snapping up the contract of Blondie.

Debbie Harry and co. pursued a strangely erratic course throughout 1979/80. For example, where their 1978 album, 'Parallel Lines', had been far better than anyone had a right to expect, their 1979 offering, 'Eat To The Beat', was far worse than could have been anticipated. It nevertheless safely provided them with another No. 1 hit, 'Atomic', the single version of which was, unusually, longer and better than that on the album. They were able to follow this with 'Call Me', a powerful Giorgio Moroder song that was used over the credits to American Gigolo. This gave them a single that alighted on the No. 1 spot in Britain, and wrapped tentacles around it in the US. The band did not appear in American Gigolo, though they did appear in another film, Roadie, performing 'Ring Of Fire', the song written by June Carter – Nick Lowe's mother-in-law.

GRAHAM PARKER

Debbie Harry remained one of the most captivating personalities in rock music, even if some of her activites caused bewilderment, and perhaps consternation, in her fans. She helped raise funds for Senator Edward Kennedy during the 1980 Presidential campaign, advertised Murjani jeans on US television, and donated the proceeds of one New York concert to the local Police Department to finance its purchase of bullet-proof vests.

Of those stars who had been around longer than Ms. Harry, Elton John had an unusually busy year, with three album releases to his credit. One of these, 'Lady Samantha', a compilation of mildewed and not especially memorable material issued by his former company, was something he probably wished had never happened. He might even have felt the same way about 'Victim Of Love', a disco album produced by the much-rated Pete Bellotte, with a cover photograph by the much-rated David Bailey, which did nothing for either his credibility or his bank account. By this time the latter was probably in need of some succour, since auditors at Watford Football Club, of which he was chairman, revealed that he had personally provided over £600,000 to purchase half the team for the club. One could only hope therefore that the due success of 21 at 33 (no messing here, a proper Elton John album) gave him the wherewithal to buy the other half.

Eric Clapton became yet another to have released a double-live album recorded at the Tokyo Budokan (he called his 'Just One Night'), and backed it with a successful UK spring tour. Of the other old-stagers, the Rolling Stones came up with their first new album in two years – 'Emotional Rescue' – the success of which fuelled rumours that they would shake off their lethargy and tour again; and Paul McCartney, whose year was a particularly eventful one, released his annual album (though one which was credited as his first solo recording in a decade), which drew the by-now customary response – the clatter of cash-registers and the contumely of the critics.

Other '60' stars reported back for duty, fit and healty. The Kinks were resurgent, with 'Low Budget' – a US Top 10 album. The Searchers simply reappeared – and so did Brian Wilson, turning up at the Beach Boys' Wembley concerts in June for his first UK public appearance in 15 years. By comparison, Bob Marley, who was simultaneously making his first London appearance for three years at the Crystal Palace Bowl, never goes away.

Yes became 'Maybe' for a while, and then were suddenly 'YES' in flashing neon lights. What had happened was that vocalist Jon Anderson, having released a successful album with Vangelis, opted to leave the group, at the same time as Rick Wakeman, who thereby departed for the second time. The remaining group members conferred, and then decided to replace them with Geoff Downes (keyboards) and Trevor Horn (vocals), a duo together known as Buggles who had enjoyed huge pop hits with 'Video Killed The Radio Star' and 'Living In The Plastic Age.' The results of this collaboration were awaited, if not with keen interest, then certainly with idle curiosity.

'The Wall' was the title of Pink Floyd's first album in almost three years, and it brought them chart success that even they couldn't have anticipated. In Britain the album's hit single (which didn't quite exist as a track on the album) 'Another Brick In The Wall' became one of the most-publicised records of 1979, featuring as it did a group of Islington schoolchildren cheerfully

ELTON JOHN

intoning "We don't need no education". Nevertheless, choruses of chanting children are the *sine qua non* of Christmas hits, and so the songs stayed at No. 1 throughout the holiday period, and long afterwards as well.

In the US 'The Wall' achieved even greater success, staying at No. 1 throughout the opening months of 1980, and helping to renew interest in 'Dark Side Of The Moon', the multi-platinum album that the Floyd had released several decades earlier. 'Dark Side Of The Moon' swept back up the charts, and took over from Carole King's 'Tapestry' as the rock album which had stayed in the lists for the longest continuous period: 304 weeks, and still going strong.

Coincidentally, 'The Wall' was joined as putative album-of-the-year by 'Off The Wall', a Michael Jackson solo album that was, to quote NEW MUSICAL EXPRESS, "near-perfect". With hit singles like 'Don't Stop Til You Get Enough' and 'Rock With Me' taken from it, the album stayed on the UK charts for an entire year. Michael showed that the ebullience of the Brothers Jackson which had been displayed only fitfully since their split with Motown was at last restored; at the age of 21, he embarked upon his third decade as one of rock music's outstanding vocalists. And now the bad news: it was announced during the year that The Jacksons had lost their long-running legal feud with erstwhile employers TAMLA MOTOWN, which might accordingly leave them $600,000 out of pocket.

Otherwise, the most inventive soul music of the year was delivered by Bernard Edwards and Nile Rodgers, the team behind not only the success of their own group, Chic, but also the emergence of Sister Sledge and the re-emergence of Diana Ross. The latter, with a song called 'Upside Down', was restored to the No. 1 spot in the UK — a position she hadn't occupied since 1971.

Early in the autumn Kurt Waldheim, the UN Secretary-General, wrote to Paul McCartney, suggesting that perhaps he might like to arrange some form of concert in aid of the Vietnamese boat-people. At that time several promoters had blithely been mooting the possibility of a Beatles reunion to generate funds for the South-East Asians. Waldheim's letter was a gentle hint that interest in the matter was official as well as unofficial. McCartney accordingly helped to instigate a series of Christmas shows at London's Hammersmith Odeon, under UN auspices; by this time, they were charity concerts for relief in Kampuchea.

The final line-up of artists was a fascinatingly disparate one featuring not only McCartney's Wings, but also The Clash, The Who, Queen, The Specials, Rockpile, The Pretenders, Ian Dury, Elvis Costello and bits of Led Zeppelin. Eric Clapton might have been there as well, but he was away watching West Bromwich Albion.

Needless to say, the other three ex-Beatles were not there either, and the fact that the 'Beatles-to-reform?' rumours had been allowed to flourish unchecked reflected no credit on the organisers. Funds, nevertheless, were indeed raised, but they were expected to have been swollen by a television special and an accompanying live album — neither of which appeared to be forthcoming.

Of far more immediate financial benefit, therefore, were parallel concerts organised in San Francisco in January by Joan Baez' human rights organisation, Humanitas.

These featured the usual cluster of West Coast star names — the Grateful Dead, the Jefferson Starship, the Beach Boys, James Taylor, as well as Linda Ronstadt and Baez herself. It is estimated that the shows raised over £50,000, a sum which could be set alongside the £450,000 that Baez' *ad hoc* charity — the Cambodian Emergency Relief Fund — had raised in previous months.

The single most considerable fund-raising event sponsored by rock musicians, however, was the series of Madison Square Garden concerts of September 1979 organised by MUSE (Musicians United for Safe — i.e. non-nuclear — Energy). A host of celebrities took part — the Doobie Brothers, James Taylor, Crosby, Stills and Nash, Ry Cooder, Jackson Browne, Peter Tosh, Bruce Springsteen et al. Although only the concerts featuring Springsteen were sell-outs, they altogether raised over $300,000 — and a triple-album of the event, which appeared commendably quickly in time for Christmas, was expected to swell the fund vastly. A feature film was also in preparation.

BRUCE SPRINGSTEEN

One can only say that raising large funds of money seems second-nature to Americans. Throughout the year, anti-nuclear benefits in the UK tended to be arranged on a desultory and irregular basis — and thus never attracted top performers, and never raised substantial sums — for all the provocation that the policies of the Conservative government had given anti-nuclear sympathisers.

Mention of Springsteen reminds one that, throughout the year, much was promised on his behalf, but nothing was delivered. There would be, a reliable source said, a new album before the end of 1979; European dates were definitely being arranged for early in 1980...et cetera. In the event, rock's other most notorious procrastinator, Stevie Wonder achieved more — even if his 'Journey Through The Secret Life Of Plants' was marketed without the specially-impregnated scent we had been promised.

It should also be noted that Joan Armatrading released a powerful, semi-comeback album called 'Me, Myself, I'; and on that very theme, George Harrison published 'I, Me, Mine', an autobiographical set of books which, at a retail price of £148, only ex-Beatles could afford. Talking of which, the last Beatles album, positively the very last Beatles' album ever, Rarities, was released in October 1979.

So finally one returns with sadness to the mortality rate in rock music. During the year, several people died who had made lasting contributions in the '50s — Professor Longhair, Amos Milburn and Larry Williams. Obituaries were also written for Ian Curtis (of Joy Division) and Jacob Miller (Inner Circle); their deaths were literally untimely — both should surely have made their mark in the '80s. BOB WOFFINDEN.

REGGAE

At times during 1980, you'd have been excused for thinking that the Kingston reggae scene had moved en bloc to London: Bob Marley, Sugar Minott, Prince Lincoln, Mikey Dread, Dennis Brown, Gregory Isaacs, Vin Gordon and Prince Far I were only some of those who began to look like semi-permanent fixtures. The basic reason was simple enough: money; while Jamaica juggled with its dwindling resources and imposed stringent foreign exchange restrictions, London and New York became the major sources of income — it's probably true to say that it's easier to get hold of reggae records, including Jamaican pre-releases, in London than in Kingston. That may not be entirely healthy for the music, but it's hardly surprising that so many artists and producers thought they'd be better off here, performing, recording or simply setting up deals. As the market in England was more than a little depressed in its own right, it's doubtful that anybody got very rich, and under the circumstances it's perhaps a small miracle that any decent music came out at all. In fact the year was reggae's best for some time, and most of the credit goes to those who ignored passing trends and got down to business. Four men in particular stood out: Burning Spear, Sugar Minott, Dennis Brown and Gregory Isaacs.

Burning Spear used Marley's Tuff Gong studios to cut 'Hail H.I.M.' (BURNING SPEAR); he's often been taken to task for merely recutting his old records, but here only one tune, 'Foggy Road', was dredged up from his past, and that fitted perfectly. His absolute seriousness made some of the lyrics a bit hard to swallow, but he's a committed man who just won't treat his subjects lightly. Apart from the album, the only other new Spear music we had was a single 'Getting From Bad To Worst', but ISLAND reissued 'Social Living', and finally got round to making available the dub version of that album, 'Living Dub'. So Burning Spear left his mark with a minimum of new music; by contrast, Sugar Minott had no trouble turning out records at a moment's notice, without diluting his strength: quantity almost for its own sake. A mere three albums of Minott music appeared: the first, 'Sugar Minott Showcase' (STUDIO ONE) was a new presentation of tracks left over from his years working with Coxsone Dodd, who clearly taught Sugar a lot. 'Black Roots' (ISLAND) and 'Music For Black Roots Lovers' (BLACK ROOTS) were all Sugar's own work; the latter gave us a new mix of his biggest hit, 'Lovers' Rock', featuring extra horns — Minott showing the UK lovers market how it should be done. As if three good albums wasn't enough, there were plenty of 45s to choose from: 'Sometime Girl' (WACKIES), 'You've Lost It' (BLACK ROOTS) and 'African Girl' (LIVE & LOVE) gave us the best of Sugar's half-sentimental, half-roots approach to his music. Dodd wasn't afraid to make full use of his Minott archives either — the best 45 was 'Give Me Jah Jah' (STUDIO ONE), largely thanks to a toasting section from King Stitt, the legendary DJ who hadn't been in the studio for nearly ten years. Stitt showed he hadn't lost his touch, although he had to stretch himself to meet the requirements of a discomix.

BURNING SPEAR

Dennis Brown couldn't quite keep up with Minott's breakneck pace: only one album, 'Joseph Coat Of Many Colours' (LASER), and that consisted mostly of tracks that had already been on 45 — still, a good album for all that. It was definitely the 45s that did it for Dennis: none came anywhere near the pop success of 'Money In My Pocket', though most were equally successful in the reggae shops. 'Slave Driver' (LASER), 'Want To Be No General' (DEB), 'Your Man (JOE GIBBS) and 'Let Me Love You' (CRAZY JOE) demonstrated Dennis' winning ways with fairly minimal tunes, while 'Sitting And Watching' (TAXI) was a cut above the rest by virtue of a really strong tune. The right promotion would have pushed it into the charts, but Dennis wasn't worried about that. Gregory Isaacs, usually one of Ja's most prolific singers, kept himself pretty much to himself; after a disagreement with Virgin Records over financial matters, he severed his ties with the company and established a UK outlet for his own AFRICAN MUSEUM label. His best records were 'Poor And Clean' with its unusual double-time drumming, and particularly 'Next To You', which made highly original use of the syndrum to support Gregory's plaintive voice.

Isaacs' move away from VIRGIN effectively marked the end of the company's interest in reggae; they still had the Gladiators, Twinkle Brothers and I Roy, but performing well below their best: I Roy's highspot, for example, was his toast of Matumbi's 'Point Of View', and that appeared on Matumbi's own label. With import restrictions drastically reducing the size of the

Nigerian market for reggae, Virgin were no longer able to dangle such juicy carrots in front of their artists, and with additional complications along the way, they parted company with Isaacs, Culture, the Abyssinians, Tapper Zukie and more. To a certain extent, of course, both label and artists were victims of the idea that reggae can consistently make an impression outside the closed world of reggae shops; this has never happened on a significant scale, and probably never will, but while everyone thinks it can the music is bound to suffer.

Sugar, Dennis and Gregory, then: the triumvirate, with help from Spear, made sure there was plenty to listen to, even if others had difficulty keeping up. Augustus Pablo for one had his quietest year to date, although he did produce Asher and Trimble's 'Humble Yourself' (ROCKERS INT'L), one of the year's best vocal records, and notable for its extensive use of dub technique on the vocal cut. Otherwise Pablo took a back seat, leaving it to reissues to show off his best: 'Oregan Style/Classical Illusion' (DUB VENDOR) represented his best work for Gussie Clarke, while GREENSLEEVES gave us 'Original Rockers', a collection of tracks he'd produced himself, and 'El Rockers', a discomix of Pablo's four cuts to "Real Rock", the year's most popular rhythm, taking up where 'My Conversation' left off. The 'Real Rock' revival was started at Studio One by Papa Michigan and General Smilie's 'Nice Up The Dance'. After that almost everyone fell into line; away from Studio One, Michigan and Smilie even came up with another version themselves, 'One Love Jam Down' (ISLAND, their first UK release), but it was the Pablo cuts which made best use of "Real Rock", and they'd been recorded in 1972.

SUGAR MINOTT

Sly Dunbar still manages to ring the changes on his basic rockers style of drumming, and still his ideas are copied by all the drummers in Kingston. This year, his best work appeared on TAXI, the label he started with bassist Robbie Shakespeare: apart from 'Sitting And Watching', we got Jimmy Riley's 'Love And Devotion', the Tamlins' 'Baltimore', and Black Uhuru's 'Stalk Of Sensimillia' (released in the UK on ISLAND). Not everything Sly and Robbie did was as good, but these at least displayed good singing, good songs, and crisp production, and the percussion lifted them all, not least by restrained use of the syndrum, which a year earlier had threatened to sweep everything creative aside.

It wasn't a particularly good year for dub, either on album or 45. 'African Anthem: The Mikey Dread Show Dubwise' (CRUISE) was a collection of Mikey's hardest rhythms, dubbed up to the hilt and embroidered with all manner of silly sound effects and vocal interruptions, designed to recreate Mikey's Ja radio show — successful but a bit exhausting. Some re-released dub albums also struck home: Rupie Edwards' 'Yamaha Skank' (SUCCESS), originally issued in 1972, consisted of twelve cuts to 'My Conversation', made available again to belatedly catch the craze for *that* rhythm; while Lee Perry's 'Cloak & Dagger' (BLACK ART), also from 1972, reappeared in a mix different from either the original JA or UK issues. Otherwise it was a toss-up between Yabby Yu's 'Michael Prophet In Dub' (PROPHETS) and the Aggrovators' 'Rockers Almighty Dub' (CLOCKTOWER) — but even that was 1975 King Tubbys' dubs only now issued for the first time. At the beginning of the eighties, it's time to ask if dub has played itself out, leaving us with just a succession of electronic practical jokes.

Records apart, reggae has usually failed to provide much in the way of spectacle, and 1980 was no exception: Marley appeared at the Crystal Palace Garden Party, and didn't manage to penetrate the sunshine-and-blue-skies torpor that characterises the event. The 'Rockers' film, which came out at the end of 1979, had one or two entertaining cameos (Burning Spear, Gregory Isaacs), but otherwise amounted to little more than 'Carry On Dreadlocks'. When the Royal Rasses played the Rainbow, only Prince Lincoln seemed able to make sense of the size of the place, although Mikey Dread, on tour with the Clash, managed to win himself some new fans. Jacob Miller was killed in a car crash in March; a sad and premature death certainly, but the inevitable cult which built up around him was based on a succession of mediocre records — his best work is still mostly unknown.

A year in reggae: in many ways it's depressing to look back at it. For the most part the music is sinking beneath endless reiterations of faith in Jah, hymns to ganja, whining misogyny and denouncements of Babylon. Unless reggae can come up with something worth saying, it may be done for; and the sad state of the music was only emphasised by the enormous number of reissues (partly an attempt to tap the mod/skinhead market) which made available some great music (and more than a little not so great) from times when reggae wasn't composed by rote. Still, musically there were signs of life in the old body, and after three depressing years it's safe to say that reggae is beginning to pull up its red, gold and green socks. But what if Sugar Minott takes a vow of silence all of a sudden? Not only will the record presses have only half as much work to do, but the rest of us will be hard put to find anything to listen to.
NICK KIMBERLEY

SOUL/DISCO

Possibly it's something to do with the innate dogged determination of black-based culture, developed through its long history of hangin' in there against prejudice, rip-offs and unequal opportunity; whatever, black music is demonstrably resilient both to record industry gloom and recession, and to the confused state of popular music generally as it restlessly casts around for a new Presley/Beatles-type catalyst to spark the boom of the eighties. While rock rises, falls, mutates and rises again, black music just grows, consolidates, grows a little more and keeps on consolidating.

And so, in microcosm, did it go through the later months of 1979 and the first half of 1980. The consolidation in this case came about through the redefining of the general public's taste in black musical forms – particularly in Britain – following the bursting of the ephemeral 'Saturday Night Fever' bubble which had forcibly rubber-stamped its definition of disco across so much of the musical spectrum some eighteen months earlier.

Black music, traditionally the staple of dance through its inherent rhythmic nature and celebratory style, was sucked almost wholesale into the 'Saturday Night Fever' machine in 1978, to the point where it became almost an economic necessity for many artists and producers to toe the closely-defined disco line rather than follow more creative paths.

By mid-'79, however, the disco culture in the USA had tightened itself into a predominantly white, predominantly gay club scene feeding off the music of only those artists whose discs happened to be producer-honed to the right sort of sound and tempo to fit into the endless DJ games of segue and mix. In the process, the disco scene became merely tangential to the mainstream field of black music once again, instead of dragging it by the scruff. A comparison between the disco charts and the R&B or black-oriented charts of any issue of one of the American music trade papers will demonstrate the point.

CHIC

In Britain, where the indigenous music of the black population is reggae, by virtue of most of this population's West Indian roots, the imported black music of America is still associated first and foremost with dancing and with discos – a tradition which stretches back far beyond the dreaded 'Fever' to the days in the early sixties when MOTOWN sounds and early soul sides from ATLANTIC, STAX and CHESS ruled the dance floors of the mods and their successors. That redefining of public taste I mentioned earlier has been developing because of a club scene which is almost a mirror image of that in America. Far from DJs trimming their record choices down to those tailored for the standard gay club mix, those in Britain soon tired of the 'Night Fever' fare and began ranging further into black repertoire for their music, leading and gently educating their audiences as they went along. The direction taken, by and large, was that of jazz-funk – which, while it represents a sizeable and flourishing chunk of present-day recording activity in the US, is certainly not regarded there as all-market dance music, and rarely translates into hit records. In Britain, by contrast, disco prime movers have educated the record-buying public at large to a sufficient degree that jazz-based acts like Spyro Gyra, Azymuth, Lonnie Liston Smith and Bill Summers have been scoring hit singles as well as huge dancefloor successes.

The net result of two rather different sets of circumstances on either side of the Atlantic is that soul, black contemporary music, R&B, whatever you care to name it (the three US industry magazines all tag it differently, while the British characteristically compromise with Disco/Soul – even if the music in question is straight jazz!) has had another year of growth and consolidation. Ask Michael Jackson, who recorded an album which has sold some five million copies *and* had four hit singles in a row taken from it – two of those million sellers in their own right. Ask Motown Records, which in the year leading up to its 20th Anniversary has seen a revival of its phenomenal success rate of old, with both long-established talents like Diana Ross, Smokey Robinson and the Commodores, and new pacemakers like Rick James, Teena Marie and Jermaine Jackson, the brother who quit the Five to marry the Boss's daughter. Ask Nile Rodgers and Bernard Edwards, whose string of successes with Chic led them to further writer/producer honours on behalf of Sister Sledge, Sheila B. Devotion, and Diana Ross. You could also ask a young and flourishing black-oriented record company like SOLAR RECORDS, which has enjoyed a banner year with hit acts like the Whispers, Dynasty, Shalamar and Lakeside. Or even an old but revitalised company like 20th Century Fox, scoring hits with equally long-established but now equally strongly revitalised talents like Edwin Starr, Gene Chandler and Leon Haywood.

The individual events and achievements in black music can probably best be summarised in the form of a month-by-month overview, kicking off from September 1979. The month saw Earth, Wind & Fire in top form with a top 10 hit in both American and Britain in 'After The Love Has Gone', taken from the album 'I Am', which held a similar chart rung in both countries. Even bigger in the UK were the Crusaders with their 'Street Life' single and LP, aided by the vocals of Randy Crawford, 'Street Life' was Britain's No. 1 disco/soul single for the entire month, which Michael Jackson's 'Don't Stop ('Til You Get Enough)' held the same spot on the US black music charts while it waited for pop sales to catch up. Trumpeter Herb Alpert's funk opus 'Rise', aimed squarely at the black marketplace, also brought him back into the American top 10 for the first time in years, and made a debut in the British charts. Other US biggies were Dionne Warwick and 'I'll Never Love This Way Again'; the Commodores with 'Sail On'; and Maxine Nightingale's 'Lead Me On' on the pop listings, while over on the black charts were Mass Production and 'Firecracker', Cameo with 'I Just Want To Be', and Ashford & Simpson on 'Found A Cure'. Britain saw Canadian jazz-funk guitarist David Bendeth crashing the disco/soul top 5 with 'Feel The Reel', in company with 'Lookin' For A Love Tonight' from Fat Larry's Band, Frantique's 'Strut Your Funky Stuff', and 'You Can Do It' by Al Hudson & The Partners.

In October, the Commodores and Herb Alpert both took turns at America's No. 1 slot. Donna Summer went into the top 3 with 'Dim All The Lights' (the third single from her 'Bad Girls' album to achieve this), and her one-off teaming with Barbra Streisand on 'No More Tears (Enough Is Enough)' also made its debut. Funkadelic topped the black music chart with 'Not Just Knee Deep', while GQ's revival of the old Billy Stewart R&B hit 'I Do Love You' also went into the top 5 on this listing. In Britain, Michael Jackson topped the disco/soul chart and held at No. 2 on the pop listings, while ace session man Paulinho Da Costa sold hugely with 'Déjà Vu', and Earth, Wind & Fire were back in the top 10 with 'Star'.

November saw Michael Jackson's 'Don't Stop' as America's No. 1 pop single two months after its black music chart-topping run. The latter chart fell to the major return of veterans Kool And The Gang with 'Ladies Night', which also topped the UK disco/soul chart almost simultaneously. The Commodores' 'Still', Smokey Robinson's 'Cruisin' and Prince's 'I Wanna Be Your Lover' were huge in the US; the Gibson Brothers' 'Que Sera Mi Vida', Lowrell's 'Mellow Mellow Right On', the Isley Brothers' 'It's A Disco Night' and 'Dancing In Outer Space' by the home-grown disco/funk outfit Atmosfear were UK biggies.

The year's distinctive black music phenomenon also arrived in November — the rapping record. The 'rap', or quickfire chat over a funky backing track, was hardly a new idea, but in the hands of the Sugarhill Gang, exchanging vocal gymnastics over a riff blatantly lifted from Chic's 'Good Times' (actually a short-sighted blunder which in the end cost the Gang all their not inconsiderable royalties and swelled the Rodgers/Edwards coffers instead), it was an almost universal ear-catcher. It also turned out to be the vanguard of a staggering flood of rap records which appeared from all quarters over the next three months or so, achieving various degrees of success, usually commensurate with their quality. By mid-1980, the fad had passed and people were generally singing on their records again.

As December ushered out the 1970s, 'Rapper Delight', as the Sugarhill Gang's concoction was titled, became America's No. 1 black music disc while it was achieving the amazing feat of selling one million 12-inch copies in the New York area alone. Over on the pop charts, the Summer/Streisand duet held off all comers until Christmas time. Other US biggies were Rufus & Chaka Khan's 'Do You Love What You Feel' and the Bar-Kay's 'Move Your Boogie Body', while Michael Jackson's 'Rock With You' quickly replaced its album-mate across the board. Britain begged to differ by releasing his 'Off The Wall' title track instead; this cruised the top 10 in both pop and disco/soul charts, in company on the latter with Rose Royce's 'Is It Love You're After', 'My Simple Heart' from the Three Degrees, Shalamar's 'The Second Time Around', and 'Christmas Rappin'' by Curtis

COMMODORES

Blow, the second, second-best, and second most successful 'rap', benefiting strongly from a seasonal lyric and an expatriate UK music journalist handling the plummy intro. It lined up at No. 2 behind the Sugarhill Gang on the disco/soul chart as the old year went out.

In January, Michael Jackson topped US pop and black music charts simultaneously with 'Rock With You', whilst the O'Jays' 'Forever Mine', 'Peanut Butter' by Twennynine featuring Lenny White, 'You Know How To Love Me' by Phyllis Hyman, and 'The Second Time Around' from Shalamar all soared high. In Britain, Billy Preston & Syreeta's duet on 'With You I'm Born Again' reached No. 1 on the disco/soul chart, and No. 2 pop. Booker T & The MGs' 17½-year old R&B instrumental 'Green Onions', riding high on the mod revival and a slot in the film 'Quadrophenia', also made the top ten, as did the Brazilian group Azymuth with 'Jazz Carnival', and Positive Force with 'We Got The Funk'. The biggest black music hit of early 1980, however, was to be the Whispers' 'And The Beat Goes On', an immediate disco/soul No. 1 which was also to climb to No. 3 on the pop chart shortly afterwards.

February took Shalamar's 'The Second Time Around' to the US black music pole position, holding off Ray, Good Man & Brown's 'Special Lady', Slave with 'Just A Touch Of Love', Narada Michael Walden's 'I Shoulda Loved Ya', and 'Too Hot' from Kool & The Gang. The latter was equally big in Britain, while Walden had an alternative top-tenner in 'Tonight I'm Alright', Michael Jackson took 'Rock With Me' to No. 2, and Tony Rallo from the Continent made it with a double-sider in 'Holding On'/'Burnin' Alive'.

March belonged to the Whispers, who held the US black music No. 1 against all comers, and to the Brothers Johnson, who had an immediate smash on both sides of the Atlantic with their 'Stomp'. 'Bounce, Rock, Skate, Roll' was a US top-fiver for Vaughan Mason & Crew, while in Britain Fern Kinney topped both the pop and disco/soul charts with 'Together We Are Beautiful'.

Leon Haywood, a name from the sixties, returned in April with the transatlantic smash 'Don't Push It, Don't Force It', while the Spinners (Detroit Spinners in Britain) also went back to the chart-top in both countries with their revival of 'Working My Way Back To You'. The Isley Brothers had a US No. 1 on the black singles chart with 'Don't Say Goodnight (It's Time For Love)', while in Britain a domestic outfit named Liquid Gold offered a straight disco outing in 'Dance Yourself Dizzy' and took it to No. 2. 'Groove' became the 'in' British disco word as newcomer Bobby Thurston scored a smash with 'Check Out The Groove', and jazz pianist Rodney Franklin did likewise with 'The Groove'. Blondie's overtly disco-styled Giorgio Moroder production 'Call Me', from the 'American Gigolo' film, was also a predictable chart-topper across both formats; it was already topping the American pop charts at the time, though it made only minor inroads into the black music charts — an indication of the widening gulf between the American audiences for R&B-oriented dance music, and Euro-styled disco as represented by the Blondie record.

May saw 'Funky Town' by newcomers Lipps Inc. sweep to the top of the US black music charts and then the pop chart with just two weeks in between. The record was hotly pursued by Jermaine Jackson's 'Let's Get Serious', the Whispers' follow-up 'Lady', and Smokey Robinson's 'Let Me Be The Clock'. In Britain, Rodney Franklin held the disco/soul chart top, followed by Narada Michael Walden with 'I Shoulda Loved Ya', 'Just Can't Give You Up' from Mystic Merlin, and 'Keep In Touch' by Freeez (a local group with a tailor-made jazz-funk production). Erstwhile Motown star Jimmy Ruffin also returned to the top ten with 'Hold On To My Love'.

THE CRUSADERS

During June, Jermaine Jackson's brief sojourn at the chart-top in the US was broken by what was to be the biggest black music disc of the mid-year period in the States, 'Take Your Time (Do It Right)' by the SOS Band, which was destined to hold off all comers for several weeks before breaking across into the pop charts too. Stephanie Mills climbed high with 'Sweet Sensation', while Gladys Knight enjoyed her first major hit of the year with 'Landlord'. The Manhattans, another long-pedigree act, also broke through once again with their 'Shining Star', while newcomers Change made an immediate big impression with 'A Lover's Holiday'. Britain, meanwhile, saw a veritable rush of pacemaking hits: Lipps Inc.'s 'Funkytown'; 'Back Together Again', which teamed Roberta Flack and Donny Hathaway, and had been recorded only shortly before Donny's untimely death earlier in the year; 'Behind The Groove' from Teena Marie, and 'The Scratch' by Surface Noice. Once again, this last-named was a homegrown production — a hot jazz-funk instrumental tailor-made for the progressive breed of UK disco DJs and their audiences.

July saw the (Detroit) Spinners back in action in all charts on both sides of the Atlantic with a revival of the Sam Cooke oldie 'Cupid'. In the US, Larry Graham from Graham Central Station had a solo monster with 'One In A Million You', G.Q. scored with a second Billy Stewart song in 'Sitting In The Park', and Cameo returned with 'We're Going Out Tonight'. Britain was taken by storm by Narada Michael Walden's teenage protégé Stacy Lattisaw, whose 'Jump To The Beat' jumped to the top slot on the disco/soul chart and No. 3 on the pop listings. A Japanese group, the Yellow Magic Orchestra, also scored in both areas with their 'Computer Game (Theme From The Invaders)', after the record had slept since its release in early Spring. Odyssey had a top-tenner with 'Use It Up And Wear It Out', and another funk-tinged jazz artist, Tom Browne, became the latest of his genre to strike the pulse of a peculiarly British taste in black music. BARRY LAZELL

FOLK

If rock is the one-arm bandit of the music industry, then folk just has to be the contraceptive machine.

Functional, vital, worthy, occasionally even innovative, it nevertheless occupies a shadowy corner, arbitrarily shunned by the dictators of style, and thus suffering waves of scorn and indifference based on myth and misunderstanding.

Yet while the fickleness of fashion has comprehensively consigned folk to the garbage can, and the media has collectively dumped on it from all angles, there's still an awful lot that's right about the folk scene and wrong about the rest of the industry. Even with its current ignominious image and its parlous financial plight, folk still offers enough taste and integrity to shame the increasing narrowness and obsession with commercial formula that bedevils most other factions of music.

Many of the ideologies of the punk revolution were long before embraced by the folk scene: the rejection of the concert hall syndrome syndrome in favour of the intimacy of a room in a pub; the practice of artists producing their own independent albums; the despisal of sophistication and the big business wheels...Artists like Leon Rosselson, Bob Davenport, and Peter Bond have even been fighting quite vigorously for a restoration of the left wing political values on which much of the sixties folk revival was originally founded, but which has largely subsided under middle-class encroachment. When music of social awareness became badly devalued during the seventies and songs which asked questions became associated with pretentiousness, folk clubs themselves were badly damaged in terms of public image.

Leon Rosselson, still the most radical songwriter on the scene (he has a song of terrifying vitriol against the Queen included on the most recent album with Roy Bailey), claims with some justification, that the relative disinterest of young people in folk clubs is due to the clubs' lack of awareness of in politics and social issues.

There are signs that this is changing. Certainly in Ireland, and to a lesser extent Britain, the folk scene has adopted a vehement campaign against nuclear power; feminism has gained a strong ally in folk; and the astonishing rise in popularity of Eric Bogle's work suggests that modern 'protest' and satirical songs may not only be once more acceptable, but *necessary*. Bogle has a string of anti-war songs that have become folk club classics of the last year or two; and while Bogle, a Scots emigré to Australia, is an unassuming performer, the overwhelming success of his British tour through the summer of 1980 has further accelerated his own reputation and the idiom of his music.

Roy Harris, one of the scene's most popular traditional singers, states that folk is now the genuine underground, the one real alternative to the whims and cellophane pap that afflicts all the other musical art forms. It's the one place where *anybody* can get up and play and develop in front of an audience; and while this attracts its own huge problems (audiences do get inflicted with utterly dreadful floor singers at times) some major talents are spawned in this way. David Bowie, Marc Bolan, Elvis Costello, and Billy Connolly are among those who gleaned early experience from the folk club ideal. It should also be added, however, that it's much more than a useful grounding or launching pad — however much the concept of folk being an end in itself has been demeaned, it remains admirably valid. Martiln Carthy is the ultimate example of somebody who's had opportunities to pursue more lucrative fields, but while no way stick-in-the-mud has never wavered from folk roots.

Perhaps the idea of compartmentalising specialist musics should be abandoned altogether — the variety of music accepted within the nebulous umbrella of folk is astonishingly broad. As Dick Gaughan acutely commented recently: you couldn't sing a Scots ballad in a jazz club, but you could play jazz in a folk club. Sure there are prejudices; there are still a few clubs that pursue a rigorous traditional-only policy; but Cosmotheka recreate the music-hall; Spredthick play Gershwin; New Victory Band perform English dance music; Hot Vultures belt out the blues; Noel Murphy tells jokes; Les Barker reads silly poems; the Albion Band have explored jazz rock; Andrew Frank might be something out of Gilbert and Sullivan; Earl Okin does Bossa Nova; Battlefied mix bagpipes and synthesizer. All have firm followings and are accepted without question as a perfectly valid part of the folk scene. Lea Nicholson, for godsake, has even formed a band of concertina players performing the 'Dambusters March' and 'Tubular Bells'.

The erudite Geordie Bob Davenport takes it a step further, singing anything from Bob Marley' 'Get Up Stand Up' to 'Memphis Tennessee' to 'Won't You Come Home Bill Bailey'...unaccompanied! Davenport's contention that the real folk music and the artsy scholarly approach of the folk revival are worlds apart has much credence. A wider adoption of Davenport's delightfully loose and informal attitude to performing, and the growth of freewheeling English country bands like the Old Swan Band and Flowers and Frolics (who even do Tom Robinson's 'Blue Murder') indicate his ideas are gaining ground.

Yet while there remains a vigorous undercurrent of activity, folk has such an appalling public portrayal that the mass populace can be excused for being ignorant of its existence at all. Steeleye Span split in March, 1978; and Fairport Convention finally concluded their long and erratic career at a field near Oxford in August, 1979. Both had major shortcomings in their later days, but with their demise went the main public face of folk music; and since they went there has been a return to the awful image of haystacks and fol-de-rol choruses, which naturally instantly alienates young audiences. It's getting to be as bad as the cowboy image dragged around by country music — the difference being that country music mostly deserves it.

The scene's own unassuming, protective nature, fuelled by its own occasional bigotry, contribute to this public ignorance. The early pioneers of the folk revival necessarily had to be protective and strict about the music because it was on a survival course at the time. But there's been a hangover of this isolationist attitude that sometimes creeps into elitism, and there does seem an earnest desire from within to have as little to do with other musical idioms as possible and to keep its own existence a secret.

This is all very fine and

DAVE SWARBRICK

laudable, except that's it's an attitude which has clouded folk clubs to realism. Artistic progress has been stunted and the failure of the club circuit to keep pace with the harsh realities of the financial world has forced several outstanding singers into day-jobs. Chris Foster, one of the most imaginative young interpreters of traditional songs, recently announced his retirement from performing for this very reason.

The collapse of the folk scene has been freely predicted for the last ten years, and whilst it would be a foolish man who'd suggest that it was thriving in the present difficult circumstances, it's an ill-informed one who'd claim it's on the verge of collapse. Record sales are undeniably heavily down this year and money is scarce, but then neither situation is exclusive to folk; and against that, the current edition of the English Folk Dance and Song Society's Folk Directory lists 500 folk clubs while there are around 70 folk festivals in Britain this year. Admittedly it's not representative of the scene as a whole, but the Cambridge Festival annually locks its doors when it counts to 30,000.

The scene is certainly changing, with a sharper split between the most basic pub singaround and the serious showbiz-orientated promotion. But then maybe that's because the folk scene has run its course under its original brief of preserving a country's national music heritage. In that, it's succeeded magnificantly: now it should be strong and confident enough to withstand absorbtion in the real world without its usual tandem paranoia. Davenport and his ilk are hellbent on doing just that, taking folk music out of the clubs, back into the pubs, and if they can destroy the curse of the juke box they might just succeed.

It's patently a mistake to look for a sudden boom. There was a flutter of excitement from America when Steve Forbert started streaking up the charts with a very bare, folkie-flavoured album, and when it was followed at a more sedate pace by the extraordinary Roches' debut album...well, the whole scene was buzzing like crazy and everyone thought their number had come up. The experience of the hype and fraud that accompanied the events of Greenwich Village in the early Sixties have taught us to avoid booms.

Nobody at least was fooled into too many illusions by Fiddler's Dram's dramatic bid to end the Seventies on top of the British singles charts with their buoyant singalong 'Daytrip To Bangor'. It was originally a track on their excellent innovative album 'To See The Play' (which has been roundly ignored by all and sundry) but Dram blew it with their second, hastily produced album and any bubbles that may have been arising were quickly pricked.

'Bangor' may have been a fluke, but in the last year there has been sounder ground-level evidence that may reassert folk as a potent force to pundits, and therefore to punters. The work of people like Peter Bond, Bill Caddick, Allan Taylor, Harvey Andrews, Bernie Parry, Richard Digance, and, of course, Eric Bogle has restored respectability to the singer-songwriter, an art long banished to oblivion as a result of nurds who flooded the scene in the wake of Mr. Dylan's early efforts. Dave Cousins even re-emerged as a folkie to help the cause and then announced his retirement from music. There have been other upsurges – the rise of informal English country bands (and I ain't talking about 'country' as in Poacher or other pretend-Americans) is an obvious highly positive development of the last couple of years. The continuing momentum of Celtic music is another. The Irish still lead in the field here – Planxty resurrected in 1979 surprisingly effectively, and while the Bothy Band collapsed, Stocktons Wing, Oisin, Scullion, Clannad and De Danann have all emerged as major forces. But Scotland is catching up with Silly

Wizard, Tannahill Weavers, Ossian, Bully Wee Band, Jock Tamson's Bairns and most excitingly Battlefield leading the throng. Wales has even belatedly entered the fray with Ar Log and their Celtic harps establishing themselves soundly.

Yet more than that, optimism for the future lies in the hands of the artists taking risks, creating daring and challenging music, usually without much support from the scene itself. It's a notoriously difficult scene to crack for new artists, and its introspection gives it an instinct to be wary of startling change (note the arguments that raged when the electric folk bands first started to emerge.)

Yet, despite this resistance, work of real boldness and excitement is being explored. The new June Tabor/Martin Simpson album, 'A Cut Above' has been roundly slagged but in time may come to be seen as an album of foresight for its faintly futuristic arrangements and its cross-fertilization of styles. There is in fact, a whole mafia of renegade musicians revolving around Martin Simpson, Andrew Cronshaw (who invented the electric zither), and Ric Sanders (generally associated with jazz violin), who are experimenting with electronics and folk songs and may just come up with something that will blow a few heads off fairly shortly.

Battlefield, too, are moving into brave new areas, exposing the theory that the limits of Scottish music had already been reached; and while they seem to have become exclusively engrossed in the theatre recently, the Albion Band can never be written off as innovators. their last album, 'Rise Up Like the Sun' was refreshingly demanding, and Ashley Hutchings is such a wily character that you always suspect that he's plotting some astounding new direction, even when he isn't. The other big guns, Five Hand Reel momentarily looked like stepping into Steeleye's spotlight, but lost their most identifiable member, Dick Gaughan at a crucial stage and have quietly wound down in the last year. In the current financial situation which makes it almost impossible for a big band to survive on the folk scene alone, the Albion way of using a flexible line-up — also a policy much in vogue in Ireland — is likely to be the way of the future. John Kirkpatrick and Martin Carthy have formed an occasional duo with great effect; Bill Caddick, Tim Laycock, and Peter Bond sometimes work as a trio.

Even more bizarre are the areas Hot Vultures have been reaching lately. Once recognized as the ultimate frustrated negroes they've not only taken to singing American blues in English accents, they rowed in traditional musicians Pete & Chris Coe on their last album, and at this year's Norwich Festival even joined forces with Rod and Danny Stradling, doyens of the English country network.

Coupled with the uncompromising quality of the scene's main attractions, notably Carthy, Garbutt, and Nic Jones, there is vigorous grounds for optimism. The most lethal enemy of them all, the public image, may yet be overcome. British radio has rarely done folk any favours, particularly since John Peel became disenchanted with the music, but the BBC finally dumped the goddawful 'Folkweave' programme and replaced it with 'Folk On Two', a programme that's substantially more aware, and the telly has been taking an unexpected interest in the field with a whole series of programmes from the Cambridge Festival and a Jeremy Taylor series.

Frequent exchanges between Britain and the States help to inject both scenes with energy. The Cambridge Festival is much maligned for propagating the star system and no reflecting the real folk scene; but as it was still the only place you would have got to see Ry Cooder and Doc Watson in Britain in 1979, or Rambling Jack Elliot, Don McLean, and Leo Kottke in 1980, then the accusations lose a lot of their sting. Cambridge gets more and more like a rock festival with its 50p hamburgers and its half mile queues for the loos, but there are still a never-ending supply of intimate festivals to appease the weak bladders. Organising good festivals is the one thing the English Folk Dance and Song Society seem able to do without too much pain: the week-long Sidmouth Festival in Devon in August remains a winner all the way and a surprising hotbed of adventure and experiment, while the Loughborough Festival in July is still the prime showcase of traditional music adhering admirably to its policy of presenting the old trad singers and musicians alongside the bright young sparks of the revival.

It's a bed of roses that pricks a bit, but it should still provide us with some songs of comfort while we cower in our fall-out shelters. Fear not, Steeleye Span are rising from the dead in our hour of need. Dylan's found the Lord. We'll all be saved.

COLIN IRWIN

THE YEAR IN MUSIC

BLUEGRASS

In the last five years a kind of post-bluegrass music has emerged in California, chiefly from a clique surrounding the mandolin-player David Grisman and guitarist Tony Rice. It resists classification, but could reasonably be called a sort of acoustic jazz, about equally rooted in the newgrass of the earlier '70s and the chamber jazz of the Quintet of the Hot Club of France, 40 years before. Its latest and most refined works are The Tony Rice Unit's 'Acoustics' (KALEIDOSCOPE) and Grisman's 'Hot Dawg' (HORIZON), both exceptionally well-played, if cerebral, recordings. Fiddler Richard Greene, also from the caucus, made an exceedingly uneven album, 'Ramblin'' (ROUNDER): the title track, Ornette Coleman's tune, is wonderfully done, and there is a near-miraculous 'New Orleans' by Maria Muldaur.

Back in the mainstream, the best new band playing incontrovertible bluegrass is Hot Rize, headed by fiddle and mandolin-player and lead singer Tim O'Brien (FLYING FISH). An old-time as much as a bluegrass unit, the Hot Mud Family from Ohio came up with their fifth LP in 'Live, As We Know It' (FLYING FISH) — notable chiefly, as always, for the singing of Suzanne Edmundson, the most gifted voice in country music. Without her the HMF would be just another jolly stringband; as it is, Edmundson's feature-spots are moments of emotional accuracy tht transform everything around her.

Recordings of original, founding bluegrass are beginning to reappear in decent forms. Bill Monroe's 'The Country Hall of Fame' (MCA CORAL) is an absolutely basic collection, full of standards like 'Uncle Pen' and 'Blue Moon of Kentucky' Flatt & Scruggs' 'Don't Get Above Your Raisin'' (ROUNDER) is early '50s material· exemplary bands playing backbone bluegrass repertoire.

TONY RUSSELL.

EUROMUSIC

Writing a report on the European scene is no easy task anyway. First, you have to catch the reader's attention, with no tricks or strings. Then the passing months have not been very exciting, have they? Like, for instance, September '79. Do I remember September 1979? Yeah. And what a bummer. I returned from Los Angeles with a Devo exclusive interview, only to discover that their French tour was nixed, as well as all other European dates. Recession. Economy. Americans kept a surprisingly low profile all year long. Very few tours, records quiet and sweet. It all seemed like 1974, 1975; well you know the story. Strange as it may seem, this gave old Europe a brand new energy. If they don't come knocking around no more, we'd better take care of it ourselves!

And France seemed alive again. Germany had Nina starring bright, and Italy had those incredible pirate TV stations.... Belgium was burning and even Switzerland seemed to shake to a brand new beat!

Hold it. I'm beating about the bush, and nothing is revealed. Let's do it carefully and put some order there:

<ins>September</ins>

September 8th to be more correct. Yes indeed. By that time nobody in France but Telephone seems to realize that summer's definitely over. This four-piece young, French band, fresh from a best-selling second LP and a megamoth tour of the country, plays La Fête de l'Humanité. The Communist Party annual festival! Imagine an open air gathering that (in the past) gave froggies the opportunity to check the likes of The Who, The Kinks, Chuck Berry and other superstars.... this very year, for the very first time indeed, 'La Fête de l'Huma' (as we call it) is topped by a *French Rock Band*. (Scattered as hell, shaking like leaves on a tree, Telephone went on stage the Saturday afternoon, cheered and welcomed by an estimated crowd of 200,000....). Telephone delivered. The kids went wild, and so did the rain, but nothing could control the riot going on. After three encores, they smashed their equipment and retired, definitely winners.

SERGE GAINSBOURG

Telephone don't dress funky and sing in French. So much for the trends. Any other French band could have been more funny/punk/funky/novo/cool/à la mode. Still, backstage, I raised the only important question: what other French (or Italian, or German or European) band could put on this monster winner show? None, I'm afraid. Just about that time, the Rolling Stones came back from holidays to complete their 'Emotional Rescue' sessions in Paris. A bearded Jagger refused all interviews, all encounters.

<ins>October? Nothing ever happens in October!</ins>

The Members, though, did play a set on French TV and got horrible reviews from middle-aged conservative critics. "Go back to your suburbs, lousy wankers,' writes Wolinski in leftist rag 'Charlie Hebdo'. Now we see why rock 'n' roll still has a long way to go in France! Linton Kwesi Johnson deceives at The Palace (*the* concert place in Paris), and I-Roy attracts even less patrons at the Bataclan. What's the matter? Is reggae losing its grip? Johnny Halliday, our famous Elvis impersonator, issues a souvenir book full of his memories. His new single ('Good Old Rock 'n' Roll Times') is quite awful, but the radio stations play it every five minutes.

Is there any hope, we ask? Yup. Hopes called the B52s, Rickie Lee Jones, Boomtown Rats, Joe Jackson, Police.... Still all European eyes are glued on Britain, and everybody's wondering: what are they going to do next? Will Yes and Genesis make the cover of 'NME'? What is this 'new wave'? Nobody knows. European kids go back to short hair and heavy booze. They drink socially in their favourite clubs. Places that look like 1984 on coke, places called Les Bains Douches (Paris) or Plan K (Brussels). Places where comic-strip illustrators and would-be rock stars hang around, looking for something 'exciting'. Where's Sid Vicious, now that we all need him?

<ins>December is the month</ins>

No doubt about it: a French rock critic's convention singles out Police's 'Reggata De Blanc' as LP of the year. Talking Heads' 'Fear Of Music' came close, but the blonde trio made it. Pockets full of money, European kids cruise in supermarkets, looking for strange records and bewildering sounds. Do they buy French? Is there a common market of rock? In fact, we see very few Belgian or Swiss records. In Brussels they sing in English and look to London. In Paris and all over France, a whole market of youngsters is growing. Telephone, by the way, announce sales of 400,000 copies, and a metal combo called Trust (heavily sponsored by CBS) comes close to 60,000 in two months! On the novo side, a Breton group is rising fast too. Marquis de Sade, however, wish to be *European*. They sing in French, German or English and issue an album as good and surprising as Joy Division's. But December is full of other events! French anarchist singer Serge Gainsbourg (whose reggae cover of 'La Marseillaise' provokes nothing but scandal) returns to the stage after ten years of silence. For a sell-out week at Le Palace, he is backed by Peter Tosh's band.

Still, this truly new wave exploit (Serge is 55 and outrageous) is slightly eclipsed by a triumphant Supertramp tour. Sold out. Everywhere, in France and Germany. In Bordeaux, they are even given the keys to the city by the mayor, while as in Paris they merely recorded a live LP.

Christmas Time to bury the Seventies. Fashion setters and trendy poseurs are running amok: what did we do during all those years? Adore the Stones? Half vomit punk? Poor old Seventies! What did Europe contribute?

French groups barely came to life in 1978. French cinema is as dead as Hitchcock. French people slowly sunk into a very bourgeois way of life, scarcely capable of licking the wounds of May '68. Take radio, for instance. It took ten years to impose rock 'n' roll shows on each of our three stations. "Now," sadly predicts one famous DJ, "all we've got to do is fight another ten years to be allowed rock during the day."

Novo vision

For rock is still a thing of the night. For students, lovers and truckers. The general feeling in the whole of Europe was by now crystal clear: let's not allow the 80s to be as dull-boring-blank as were the 70s. Let's care. Let's go.

By January the eleventh (a carefully-chosen date) Yves Adrien released his first book, 'NovoVision'. Yves, who used to be a rock writer, truly delivers here the strangest of modern manifestos. A new man, he writes, is born. Atomic child, the Novo man wanders through big cities ready to experiment with anything they have to offer: the strangest of drugs or even Throbbing Gristle. The Novo man is cool as ice. Me is somebody else. The Novo is a schizophrenic rocker. But right then England seems to be rising from its ashes. The whole ska thing is closely watched and discussed. Are they for real? Fake? A step beyond? Two-tone venture? Revival? Fad? Next big thing? All these questions are answered during a brilliant Specials and Madness tour. And here we go: all the European kids switch to ska, like sheep. I remember a conversation between an English skinhead and a brand new French skinhead before the Specials show. "Say, mate, do you like football?" You should have seen the French imposter! Football! Football??

A week later, I get to interview a very friendly John Lydon. "Rock 'n' roll is dead," he tells me, and Public Image prove that on stage half an hour later.

March / One sunny morning

One sunny morning in March, your humble scribe wakes up in a heavily damaged hotel room. The place is Italy. I was on the road with a French group. Being one of the first to dare the trip and take the chance to go to spaghetti land, I wanted to be with them and check out what would happen. Would the bass player be kidnapped? Equipment stolen? Too much paranoia. Every night, they played a new city. Although their records were absolutely unknown and unreleased over there, each and every pirate radio station made sure the listeners had heard them. They played under a 1,200 seat tent. The show was tight rock 'n' roll, in the Rolling Stones style. But this Italian public! Schoolgirls, students, leftists: they just loved it. For Italy has a rock public. Although the whole country is definitely out (of order) you could see some 5,000 Romans gather in a Roman antique theatre and go bananas to a French band's raw sound. In Milan, a second gig had to be added. But rock over there is no real challenge to the burgeoning of alternative free media. Yes? Every big city has its ten or twelve pirate television channels. Just imagine: every show is in fact recorded by adventurous young directors who often rush the stage with their cameras (and get beaten up in the process). All these stations are unprofessional, wild, full of mistakes and blanks. Still, they exist and broadcast, without any trouble. After the spaghettis and chianti wine, we went to the singer's room and watched porno programmes and amateur strip-tease on the tube. That's Italy.

Jailhouse metal

Why do pictures fascinate us so much? Hip French people all have their own video equipment and polaroid cameras. Every day, books are published. Books full of images, pictures, photos. Why is our civilisation so fascinated with sightseeing? Why is Helmut Newton better known than Hundertwasser? What are they in fact looking for? Look is so important out here! Of course, we are not talking about forgotten countries like Austria, where every kid seems to wear his parka and care about solar energy. But look at Paris, Brussels, Berlin! The rock world is now carefully watched by old whores and new managers. The ongoing rise and success of the media is definitely bewildering. And everybody follows. Short hair is now definitely in, like the novo look: just plain ordinary clothes and shoes. No leather jackets, no buttons. Just ordinary chic.

But outside the big cities? They don't know, and they don't care, for sure! Our friends Trust play Fleury Merogis (the Paris borstal). Their heavy metal rocks the jailhouse for the benefit of 200 carefully-selected inmates (most of them are there on drug charges). Trust plays, but no one escapes. What a publicity trick! The audiences go to pieces. Oh sure, Stiff Little Fingers sells out the Palace for the benefit of a last punk battalion. But the question is: are you novo-common or just plain modern? Are you heavy metal or hard rock? Are you disco-synthetic or plain sixties-revivalist? Let me choose my own little paradise. Even The Clash cannot pick up the pieces. Their fanatical following buys only 30,000 of the LPs in France. Will London call in vain?

April / Belgium is so hip now!

That's right. Belgium. Fatherland of Tintin and French Fries is definitely red hot. In Brussels, 80 groups (at least) try to break through. Belgium is a strange country, with a language problem. So groups sing in English rather than French to keep the anti-French Walloons happy. Brussels has famous clubs, like the Plan K (an ex-factory), the Klacik, l'Entrepot. Groups oscillate between a very novo pop music (Telex, Lio) and punk bands with synthesizers (Jo Lemaire + Flouze). Many others are waiting. Belgium is a perfect example of the European scene: keep an ear on England (just in case), keep an eye on graphics (for they are our true background out here).

Now we see 1980. The dinosaurs are truly forgotten (or so we want to believe). New Wave. New Wave. The words ring out on every lip. New. Wave. A high tide? Me, I get to spend a night in gay Paree with Nina Hagen.

My night with Nina

"I touch Nina! I touched Nina!" yells a small Parisian kid running away in a back alley. Wait, wait. Let's say I just followed her with a friend of mine. My friend's goal was very simple: to make sure that Nina would play a gig in Paris. But Nina says Nein. Nina is in fact quite an enigma. We have heard all those incredible stories about her, and now she's here, and it all seems.... true. She is a little bit on the fat side and you can recognize her ten miles away. Her hair is dyed red like a witch. So we go from club to bar with her, provoking near riots everywhere. Nina is hip. She is well known. She is the true essence of rebellion and poetry and she's old Europe gone mad after a Sex Pistols shoot. Back at her hotel, I try abortive interviews. How interesting! Nina takes a bath and then a piss. Then she dresses. But when the tape is on, it's a whole different story. She screams and yells and cries. She wants every journalist to advertise a German hospital where her junkie boyfriend is being cured. More crying. She is on her way to Hollywood where CBS are giving her six months to recruit a *real* band. "I hated my German musicians so much! They were always on hashish, you know". More silence. Long ones. We watch TV. The next day, Nina is supposed to sign her brand new LP in Paris's biggest record store. She runs away crying: "I am like a monkey in a zoo". Then I ask: "Are there any German groups we should know?". "No. It's all ze same English carbon copies, you know...." Believe it or not, Nina Hagen

NINA HAGEN

is the first German star since Marlene Dietrich. That's all they've got, and all I can find on her second LP is one good song. But I won't tell you which, cause I'm so hip, baby.

Meanwhile, in Munich, Kraftwerk is carefully preparing a long-awaited new effort that might change everything, again.

May / Do what you like
May is a new wave fiasco. A French radio station, Europe No. 1, has organized and financed a huge *New Wave Festival* that will run three weekends and be called 'Europe Rock 80 Festival'. The idea appears great at first: imagine a brand new mix of Anglo-French bands in an attempt to prove that new wave is both serious and commercial. From the first night, it became as clear as a river full or trout that new wave is not hunky dory. First, the festival was located in a far away suburb, right in the middle of nowhere. Second, tickets were outrageously expensive. Third, the new wave public does not (repeat *not*) enjoy the idea of a French Woodstock, even with cheese and red wine replacing acid and hot dogs. The whole thing went quickly nuts. The only real winners were The Specials, Starshooter (a punk French combo gone pop), Madness, Joe Jackson.... But Cure got no encore, The Dogs, Shakin' Street and many others battled against the punters' apathy. The Only Ones were bottled off stage during their third song.... even the fun Revillos had trouble obtaining an encore while fighting a bad PA. By the second weekend, anyone pronouncing the words "new wave" in the radio station's corridors was guaranteed to be fired within the next five minutes.

June is Jacno month
This is it! France has a new sound! Guitarist and moog-strategist Jacno (of Stinky Toys fame) records a solo single, full of instrumentals. One of them, 'Triangle', enters all the charts and climbs to the top with science-fiction rocket ease. Jacno is cool. He has no pretentions but to play modern French soundtracks. And how it works! Number one in six weeks, this nice blonde guy makes sure everyone understands: All you need is a Rickenbacker guitar, a synthesizer, a tape recorder and you too can be number one. Just like me. Just like The Flying Lizards. Still, straggling fans keep crowding in front of Pathe Marconi Studios hoping to see "Keith and Mick, y'know...."

1980 is now well advanced and we all know where we are heading for. Disco slips away even the nightclubs won't play it, they are now pushing the Pretenders or Madness. Heavy Metal is making a come-back. The European scene is like that: either you try to reach number one with sarcastic little songs and exciting melodies (Lio, Jacno, Telex) or you attempt a brand new mixture of punk energy and synthetic avant-garde. But the two sides communicate, more than once! But who remembers why Jacno reached number one?

The only country out of step is Switzerland. Just imagine: this small banker's paradise has almost 80 bands, none of them wishing to record! 80 bands changing names and exchanging musicians every week.... These groups desire only one thing: play, play and play. Some of them are incredibly funny (like one called Edgar Funkel, famous for their 'Brand New Cadillac' 20-minute cover). Some of them are also very political, like an all-women group called Lili Pute.

Opera
Hell! Even Spain has its new wave band, by the name of Viva Tequila! But the main thing here is this brand new attitude towards music. Three years ago, Europe had absolutely no rock tradition. Groups or records had to be English or American to be worth checking out. If a kid tried to start a band, he had to be either a millionaire or a strange kind of maniac. Gee! Didn't we have novels, opera, théâtre d'avant garde, comics or movies? That situation has now completely changed. Can you imagine ska bands playing in Lyons or Alicante? They do! The obligatory barren years are nothing but strange memories of a forgotten age. Leave it all to Magma or Stravinsky! Let me go on stage and do my thing too.... European bands are often incredibly naïve (except Nina Hagen who's been around with The Slits). But all the others: give them an interview, print their name in a magazine and they almost immediately break up. Egos. Still, something ought to rise out of this strange situation. They're all like mad scientists, pushing every button in front of them, in the hope of a final solution.

Of course, these brand new bands won't be a threat to England, a country that has it all sussed out (and in, and up, and down) since way back when.... Will they ever cross the Channel? But after all, who knows if there will be a 1981? PHILIPPE MANOEUVRE

ELECTRONIC

The year in Electronics? Well, I suppose the empire of the dreaded microchip just went on growing like a cancerous offshoot of technology gone wild, putting yet more people out of jobs on one hand and miniaturizing even more useless contraptions on the other; pocket calculators became even flatter and we even witnessed pocket Space Invaders ...

As far as the music is concerned, well, it got better or worse depending on the angle at which you peered at the scene. Synthesizers, ARPs and Moogs and other sound-bending toys became more accessible and it was very soon a case of vinyl synthetic gluttony after Gary Numan's meteoric success. Single-handed, this dubiously-gifted non-entity put synthorock on the map by cleverly integrating all his major influences: Ultravox, Bowie, Kraftwerk, etc.... into an easily recognizable sound rendered amiably bland by its sheer lack of commitment and originality. Would Numan have risen so fast to the top of the pile had the record market not been so depressed? I doubt it, but the fact remains that his autumn 1979 blitz was quite simply staggering. And, soon after Numan, the floodgates opened.

Most sorry of all must have been aquiline-looking John Foxx who had ploughed the same barren field for a number of frustrating years with his group Ultravox and charted the unknown territory which lay beyond the more classically-oriented realm of electronic music as typified by Pierre Henry or Schaeffer, blending it with rock imagery partly funded by the German pseudo-psychedelic experience of the early 70s (Neu, Tangerine Dream, Klaus Schulze, later

KRAFTWERK

La Dusseldorf). To no avail. Ultravox, particularly in their ultimate album produced by Connie Plank, 'Systems of Romance', were just that little bit ahead of their time.

Of course, Numan borrowed it all. Even to the point where he quite openly confessed his open admiration for the work of John Foxx and the ever-pioneering David Bowie.

Having abandoned Ultravox, John Foxx did release his 'Metamatic' album to muted acclaim and minor chart success in the UK just to see most people exclaim that it was just more Gary Numan imitations! And, adding insult to injury, Ultravox, his old group, added Midge Ure and saw their own album Vienna reach new heights that the previous incarnation of the combo had never scaled. It seems there's no justice in this world ...

Bring on the clones. Electronic music soon became electronic muzak. Must we name names? What's the point of being a critic if you can't knock a few harmless targets down. Here goes: New Muzik, Telex, Yellow Magic Orchestra (from Japan). Enough. Charge: adhering to non-innovative patterns and prostituting the potential of the genre. If we have to be commercial, let us at least have the quality electronic/symphonic rocksters like Jean-Michel Jarre, Vangelis, the joking Silicon Teens, Giorgio Moroder's and M's of this fading disco world. At least, they put the enjoyment back into the beat and you can dance (or try to) to it.

But then, is that the point of electronic music? Aren't we straying from the chosen path?

Shouldn't music equal feeling and emotion?

Isn't electronic music a misnomer? The essence of music is emotion, what hits you in the gut, while electronic hardware brings metal, cold images to the mind. How shall/do the twain meet? How do you reconcile warmth and cold? A strange and difficult equation for what is still an uncomfortable genre, stretched like all the rest of contemporary music between the opposite poles of experimentation and commercial endeavour.

Ralf Hutter of Kraftwerk one day asked Eno "What music isn't experimental?" and makes a valid point and convenient truism.

Parenthesis: note the mushrooming number of publications on both the recording and live performance of music and on the electronics involved in these processes (SOUND INTERNATIONAL; INTERNATIONAL MUSICIAN AND RECORDING WORLD; STUDIO SOUND; CONTEMPORARY KEYBOARD; SYNAPSE; BYTE MAGAZINE; COMPUTER MUSIC JOURNAL; PRACTICAL ELECTRONICS).

So, if it's not experimental, what shall we then call it? Some say "modernist". Others, "industrial". In a way they do characterize the genre, but never in its entirety.

The modernists are the grandsons of Stockhausen and "concrete music" mapping the interface between aural and visual experiences. Stockhausen concocted his earlier works within the hallowed premises of North-West Radio in Cologne and it's indeed in Germany that the movement flirted for the first time with rock with groups like Tangerine Dream, Amon Duul II and others, taking a leaf from both the more formal realm of "elektronische musik" and psychedelia as expressed by Anglo-American proponents such as Jefferson Airplane or Pink Floyd.

Landscapes made out of sound and primeval repetitive beats: Tangerine Dream (mostly Edgar Froese) continue unabated in the style, while others have faded and gone. Neu splintered, although Michael Rother is still active with highly melodic solo efforts; La Dusseldorf are no longer and the same fate befell Can (mainman Holger Czukay re-emerged recently with a curious record called 'Movies', displaying a large range of influence, but little actual electronics amidst the collages). Ash Ra, Joachim Roedelius and Cluster battle on, as does the uneven Klaus Schulze, most of them orbiting around the reputed SKY and BRAIN German labels. French innovators Magma have fragmented and only the tenacious Richard Pinhas endures after breaking up his group Heldon and his intuitive, if meticulously planned albums just get better and better.

In England, of course, there was the incomparable King Crimson. Robert Fripp reappeared this year after a long silence and greeted his faithful audience with a

KLAUS SCHULZE

couple of ambitious, though often obscure, albums where theory at its most abstruse tends to overshadow the brilliant playing. He has now put together a new group, The League of Gentlemen, who have yet to record.

Along the same axis, the mercurial Eno shies away from the definitive Eno album and dabbles in curious collaborations with other, similarly intellectual musicians, David Byrne of Talking Heads, Jon Hassell, Harold Budd, Laaraji and extends the ambient uses of the music to the industrial area, where technology blends with life (Music for Airports, Music for Films).

"Electronic music is a generic term describing music that uses electronically generated sound or sound modified by electronic means, which may or may not be accompanied by live voices or musical instruments, and which may be delivered live-or through speakers."
(Otto Luening)

The industrial zone is without doubt Kraftwerk territory inviolate. They have reputedly recently completed their first album in many years and are rumoured to be preparing a tour where the music will in fact be performed by robots. Should anyone be looking for someone to blame for the phenomenon, Kraftwerk would have to answer for their hordes of imitators: Ultravox, Foxx, Numan; to a lesser extent, the Liverpudlian Orchestral Manoeuvres in the Dark, who temper their technological aridity with uncommonly emotional delivery of lyrics and richer sound textures.

An interesting sideline has been the industrial minus emotions enclave; musicians working away at minimalism in a forced attempt at rendering in musical terms the bleakness and despair of many areas of modern society: Throbbing Gristle, Cabaret Voltaire, Tuxedo Moon, Suicide, Wire, Chrome, Dome. Some minimalists often neglect the heavy-

DAVID BOWIE

handed industrial connotation altogether and manage to inject a welcome note of humour into the proceedings: Flying Lizards (hiding the sardonic figure of David Cunningham) and Residents, Deutsche Amerikanische Freundschaft.

But hell, these are all only facile categories.

Where do you put the anarchistic pirates of repentant Sex Pistol John Lydon, Public Image Limited? Or the lushly romantic (and deservedly successful) Human League whose dabblings with science fiction imagery coalesce so well with the strictures of fun rock 'n' roll (they even covered the old Gary Glitter song of the same name)?

What about the ever-present and unique David Bowie?

The never-aging Terry Riley?

All active during the period under consideration and going nowhere and everywhere.

Electronic musicians all.

And electronic dabblers never die.

And electronic dabblers never say die.

Viz. the surprise production appearance of Robert Margouleff on the new Devo album, 'Freedom of Choice'. How many readers now remember Tonto's Head Band?

Or United States of America, another early pioneer?

So electronic music is still rock, first and foremost. An area where the shaping of the sound, often allied with a mechanized form of beat (although this can sometimes be dispensed with) allows an immediacy of feeling that normal instruments and voice can seldom attain without treatment or manipulation.

It's not just eerie or modernistic SF workshop effects or a rough approximation of the everyday sounds of industrial life. Although sometimes it can be all that and more.

As digital recording, sound synthesis, computer technology and signal processing become more widespread, so-called electronic music will in fact move nearer to the main body of rock, a live causeway irrigating the central organism and providing the music with even more exciting possibilities for development.

ADAM BARNETT-FOSTER.

BLUES

Despite a few signs in the '60s, the promise of a blues renaissance in black America seems to have gone largely unfulfilled. Live blues takes place mostly on campuses or in student-patronised clubs and festivals, but in either case to mainly white audiences. Blues records, except for an occasional single that makes a local splash, go likewise to a market nine-tenths white. Recordings of acoustic country blues, in fact, are much more likely to appear in Britain, or Italy, than at home.

But country blues is an idiom almost a century old, and few but the elderly play it. In some cities, preeminently Chicago, there are signs of the blues tradition in action rather than decline. The legatees may not be numerous, and they may often belong to 'blues families', but their records will at least be made and released in their own territory. Whites will buy most of them, all the same, and it will be white critics, almost exclusively, that write about them. Jimmy Johnson, the Chicago singer and guitarist, may have been playful when he said (on a recent recording), "the cover of LIVING BLUES(magazine) is where I hope to be", but after all, LIVING BLUES is a good deal more realistic goal for someone like him than EBONY or JET.

Yet even if blues has not returned to, or been reclaimed by, the black community, to a national extent, it survives in a great many places. The college circuit has brought it to such relatively exotic regions as New England and the Pacific Northwest. But if its heartbeat can be said to be anywhere, it is in Chicago. The sheer number of musicians there is remarkable. The concentration of activity that 25 years ago was nourishing the music of Muddy Waters, Howlin' Wolf and Little Walter seems equally productive today; not always so enterprising or diverse, perhaps, but far from stagnant or barren.

The city's foremost blues label at present is ALLIGATOR, a carefully run independent, which keeps a small roster but develops it with vigour and sense. Its best recent releases have been Albert Collin's 'Frostbite' and a three-volume set called 'Living Chicago Blues', a sort of gazetteer of the coming men. DELMARK, an older company, one of the pioneers of blues (and jazz) recordings in the city, has been quieter

B.B. KING

PINETOP PERKINS

lately, but it produced Jimmy Johnson's fine LP, 'Johnson's Whacks'. RAZOR, is a new label, with an LP by Johnny & Sylvia Embry, the latter a fine singer. On MR BLUES, which had previously recorded singer/harp-player Good Rockin' Charles and singer/guitarist Eddie C. Campbell, there was a new album by Mojo Buford, who has often played with Muddy Waters and had some Waters alumni with him for the date. In Britain this is available through ROOSTER, a new label jointly owned by two Londoners and two Chicagoans, which has also issued an unpredictably heavyweight LP by singer/guitarist Eddy Clearwater, 'The Chief'. One reason for taking note of this record is the presence of Lurrie Bell, son of the well known harp-player Carey Bell. The word around Chicago is that Lurrie Bell is the new guitar star, and the few recordings that have leaked out — some tracks on ALLIGATOR,s 'Living Chicago Blues Vol. 3' and, notably, his solo on Clearwater's 'Blues for a Living' — indicate that this is no frivolous rumour.

Also on ROOSTER are some EPs and 45s by, among others, Billy 'The Kid' Emerson, an entertaining and individual singer/pianist, whose early work, well known to collectors, is on a CHARLY LP. Emerson, Good Rockin' Charles and Eddie C. Campbell happened also to perform on a loose but enjoyable "Blues Legends" tour of Europe, late in 1979.

Work in Europe, though few could make a living by it, is still an opportunity that falls many musicians' way. Jimmy Rogers - celebrated amongst enthusiasts for his work in past Muddy Waters bands - and guitarist Left Hand Frank Craig were well received, and Albert Collins' single London concert in May 1980 was superb. Rogers and Craig made a decent record while in England for the JSP label, 'Chicago Blues'. Otis Rush, who was billed for the Camden Jazz Festival but failed to show, had no new record, but his famous COBRA sides of the '60s - once reissued on BLUE HORIZON, but

ALBERT COLLINS

unavailable for years - were reinstated again by FYLRIGHT, as were Magic Sam's contemporary work for the same label. This material, the first flowering of the "West Side sound", continues to be subtly influential upon much of Chicago's music.

Reissue programmes which don't require the agility, or the risk, involved in the recording of active musicians, have traditionally been a European forte. The major project of that kind recently has been the series The Piano Blues on the English MAGPIE label, 13 albums long and still proceeding, which is attempting to do for the pianos blues idiom of the prewar years what Gibbon did for the Roman Empire.

The records are well researched, meticulously presented and consistently enjoyable: overseas blues scholarship at its most creative.

Another English company, CHARLY, having basked long and usefully in the SUN catalogue, has acquired the rights to VEE JAY, the label that recorded John Lee Hooker and Jimmy Lee in the '50s and '60s. FLYRIGHT, as well as the COBRA material, has picked up the small but valuable JOB catalogue, which includes the best work by J B Lenoir and other Chicagoans. When first issued in Europe in the '60s, such music as this became the basic repertoire of R&B. It can be hardly accidental that it reappears now, when R&B of the Flamingo/Marquee/Ricky Tick/middle '60s style is experiencing a sudden revival in Britain. The optimist can argue that this simply proves R&B's innate strength and durability, and that we can look for this cyclical revival about every 15 years. The pessimist can counter that some of the 1980 players are not just patterned after their predecessors but actually *are* them (such as the Blues Band). How artificial a resuscitation this Second R&B crusade is it is hard to say; the records it has produced so far are not exceptionally distinctive, but that was true on the first time round, and to some extent irrelevant.

A favorite source of material for original R&B was the songs of harp-player Billy Boy Arnold, like 'I Wish You Would' and 'I Ain't Got You'. Arnold has been making some impression himself lately, as when touring with Tommy Tucker — whose 'Hi Heel Sneakers', another obligatory song of the '60s has been reissued on a RED LIGHTNIN' 45. Arnold's recent LP Checkin' It Out, also for RED LIGHTNIN' and featuring an English R&B veteran guitarist T S McPhee (playing very well, too), is a boisterous addidition to that inventive catalogue. The same company also revived the spirit of blues lunacy with a compilation of early and highly eccentric sides by Screaming Jay Hawkins.

Reissues of early ('20s and '30s) blues are more infrequent nowadays than they used to be; the stock, after all, is not unending. Mississippi John Hurt's original recordings, which have a unique and fragile grace, became available again (YAZOO), and a Dutch collectors' label, ANGRAM reissued the extraordinary gospel songs and homilies of Washington Phillips, originator of 'Denomination Blues'. Also on ANGRAM was a collection of the superbly raunchy singer Lucille Bogan. The idiosyncratic New York label STASH ran merrily on with its lighthearted compilations of low-life blues and jazz songs like 'Street Walking Blues' and 'Reefer Madness'. The French division of RCA has done some efficient work on the old BLUEBIRD material of the '30s and '40s by Big Bill Broonzy, Sonny Boy Williamson and their peers.

Nonetheless, for those who think of blues as flourishing not 25 but 50 years ago, apart from the dutiful selecting of reissues little remains but the observation of funeral rites. The original generation of the blues musicians known from records has all but passed. It is impossible to frame even in ones' imagination an event like the blues festival — not all that long ago — that brought to Europe, all at once, Son House, and Skip James and Bukka White. In October 1979 Gus Cannon died, and with the passing of that rare old banjo-player and songster went virtually the last firsthand memory of the Memphis jugband era. Beale Street's tacky rejuvenation is scant tribute to him and his kind.

And then Robert Johnson almost got his dues, though almost a lifetime too late. There was planned a three-record set of all his work, issued and unissued, with photographs and a biography, material scarcely anybody has ever seen or heard. The one blues-singer who significantly shaped something in rock music; the one who, if all other blues records were suddenly and irretrievably lost, would still hold the essence of it all, was finally going to emerge from obscurity, become something more to us than an enigma. But there was some tawdry squabble among researchers, wrangling between lawyers, and the project has been returned to darkness.

ROBERT JOHNSON

As for the leading bluesmen of today — and unfortunately they *are* all men; the times, or the audience, seem not right for a Bessie Smith — they carry themselves with great, if unchallenged, distinction. Muddy Waters continues to run a fine band, and by no means from the sidelines. B B King, astutely holding a middle-ground market with records like 'Take It Home' (MCA), deftly reaches back for his more cautious admirers with the old favorites medleys of 'Now Appearing At Ole Miss' (also MCA). They have become ambassadors, these two, but you might feel there was room for a few more. The gulf — an unnecessarily wide one — between these that can command international festivals and the rest, who have to be content with small clubs, meagrely financed tours and the inattention of all but the specialist press, is a product of play-safe booking policies rather than a true reflection of differences in ability. Muddy gives a great show, but it isn't matchless; Albert Collins is as hard a man to follow. Son Seals, Jimmy Johnson and the distressingly little-known Philip Walker are just three artists whose status outside their own territories is quite unjustifiably modest. Tough enough for them to be fighting the playlist mentality when they try to get airplay, or interest a major record-company; must they run up against it everywhere?

Every working blues musician knows the answer to that one: given luck, stamina, a good constitution and a sharp agent, he has some chance of a decent working life and a long shot at a circumscribed kind of fame. As a prospect, this may not be much, but at least it deters the dilettante and leaves the ground clear for musicians who are doing the only thing they think worth doing; the ones who can say with Eddy Clearwater, "I play the blues for a living — but I live to play the blues".

TONY RUSSELL

WESTERN SWING

Western Swing is an idiom in some danger of being misunderstood, so it's encouraging that the first-generation recordings continue to appear on reissue compilations. The unhedged message of 'Western Swing Volumes 4 and 5' (OLD TIMEY) and 'Operators' Specials' (STRING) is that there was always plenty more to the music than Bob Wills' dream (fruitful though that was). Each album reveals the diversity of Southwestern small-group music in the '30s and '40s, from the rural jazz of the Modern Mountaineers to the proto-honkytonk of Buddy Jones and Johnny Lee Wills.

A single WS originator, Adolph Hofner, from San Antonio, embodies on 'South Texas Swing' (ARHOOLIE) the cultural conjunction of swing and Texas polka music. Included on the LP is a '50s broadcast, loose almost to the point of chaos, but highly suggestive: had this union of vernacular music, local industry (Hofner was sponsored by Pearl beer) and radio been tolerated in Britain, the present state of British music, at least, would be unimaginably different. (Business and broadcasting would probably be a lot more fun, too).

ASLEEP AT THE WHEEL

Attempts to reunite original WS musicians have tended to turn out rather over-relaxed, but Johnny Gimble & the Texas Swing pioneers' 'Still Swingin'' (CMH) is somewhat more than a jog back up Memory Trail, and besides was recorded as Western Swing ought always to be recorded, to give the sound of a band playing WS of any substance is, still, Asleep At The Wheel; Alvin Crow's promise has gone on ice, and other contenders have virtually disappeared. The Wheel's 'Served Live' (CAPITOL) is no great advance on earlier work, but noisy, activating and fine to be going on with. TONY RUSSELL.

CAJUN & ZYDECO

Like Big Bands and the British Liberal Party, cajun music has friends convinced of the imminence of its revival. Not that, at home, it needs it, for in southern Louisiana it enjoys a communal acceptance and use that you would hardly find anywhere for, say, country blues. But the response in Europe lately to the tours of black accordionist Rockin' Dopsie has kindled in at least one record company, SONET, a great optimism, and it is promoting cajun music with bravado.

In its own territory cajun music gets quite a deal of airplay, and to some extent the most atmospheric of SONET's releases are those taken from, or as if from, local stations: 'This Is Mamou Cajun Radio', with fiddler Sady Courville's band, and two volumes of 'Cajun Cruisin'', compilations of '70s singles by popular younger groups. The LPs by individual bands are less successful, and that by the usually reliable Balfa Brothers 'Cajun Days', showing them for once as a dance-hall rather than an old-time band — is untidy and mostly regrettable. What a club group sounds like is much better displayed by Wayne Toups' Crowley Aces on 'Cajun Paradise': a punchy and youthful band, almost — in the context — new-wave, certainly not much burdened by respect for the old ways.

ROCKING DOPSIE & THE TWISTERS

Zydeco, the music of black French Louisiana, is most widely known from the gumbo-soul music of Clifton Chenier, whose 'Boogie & Zydeco' (SONET) is no bad introduction. Rockin' Dopsie himself is not best heard on record — 'Hold On!' (SONET) is the latest — but it's arguable that zydeco music can scarcely be heard satisfactorily outside its natural context of Louisiana and South Texas bars. For anyone interested in its stylistic development, 'Zodico: Louisiana Créole Music' (ROUNDER) is an informative guide. As for its future, the Sam Bros. 5, a teenage family band (ARHOOLIE), could be worth watching. TONY RUSSELL.

ROCKING DOPSIE

COUNTRY

Once again country music has managed to throw up more truly awful records than any other section of the industry thanks to the hard core of dedicated country fans who love an overdosing of sentiment, corn and born-again Christians, and blindly keeps the faith with artists long past their creative best and sometimes well into senility. Almost worse than the bad records are those that are bland, created by the 'crossover' artists (so called because of their desire to cross into other musical market places) who've smoothed their distinctive country sounds and avoided lyrics that might upset the substantial middle-of-the road audience that are their main target. Fifteen years ago the 25-45 age group in the US were buying Andy Williams, Frank Sinatra and their ilk but today it's the watered down country of Kenny Rogers, Anne Murray and Dolly Parton.

Little wonder really that so many rock fans hold country in contempt and won't accept that any of it can be good. They hate the sound of high-pitched nasal vocals, whining steel guitars, flashy clothes and dumb lyrics about 'crying in my beer' – 'Country is ignorance set to music' as a friend of mine delights in saying. Yet country isn't all bad or boring, it's full of talented writers and musicians, many of whom seem happy to wait on the edges waiting for the chance of fame and fortune which once achieved can last for decades. This year has provided more good music than the last two or three and it really has been worth wading through the marshmallow swamps of 'easy listening' material to find the inspired songs and music of people like Rodney Crowell, Joe Ely, the revitalised Johnny Cash, Bobby Bare, Hank Williams Jnr., and Emmylou Harris.

The country charts have been dominated all year by Kenny Rogers, an astute business man who has packaged his limited singing talents and easy-going personality with phenominal success. 'Coward of the County' was the year's biggest single and 'The Gambler', 'Kenny', and 'Gideon' (UNITED ARTISTS) seem to have taken up permanent residence in the album charts. Waylon Jennings also had three albums that sold well all year, most notably his 'Greatest Hits' package (RCA), a wonderful compilation of some of his best work including the recent 'Amanda' a good record to use when converting people who think they don't like country. Waylon's strong performance of a song with mature and intelligent lyrics written in a deceptively simple and direct style contains honest lines of the kind one can't imagine aging rock stars like McCartney or Jagger daring to sing – 'I got my first guitar when I was fourteen/Now I'm over thirty and still wearing jeans'. 'Amanda' apart Waylon seems to have peaked and much of his material is now dangerously close to self-parody as he tries to satisfy the enormous audience that still want 'outlaw' songs. His comrade Willie Nelson had also peaked, one of the all time great songwriters he's hardly written anything for five years and now revives old songs and friends – this year 'Willie Nelson Sings Kristofferson' and a duet LP with his old boss Ray Price 'San Antonio Rose' – pleasing, but in no way remarkable.

Others who've done well in the charts include several artists who made the elusive 'big break' in the late seventies, the time when they also made their best and most imaginative records. They're now playing safe with easy listening sounds and seem destined for further success throughout the eighties – Crystal Gayle, Eddie Rabbitt, T. G. Sheppard (whose initials stand for the 'The Good') and Larry Gatlin a star despite regularly committing the worst sin in country music – refusing to sign autographs.

The most important development all year has been the big breakthrough into TV and films for country acts. American television had always considered it only suitable for small stations or to be stereotyped in comedy shows like 'Hee Haw' where country singers wore straw hats and sat on bundles of hay, but the success of personalities like Dolly, Freddy Fender and Hoyt Axton on prime time talk shows and TV specials like the spectacularly successful Kenny Rogers show based on 'The Gambler', has sent producers into a frenzy to make country shows.

Country themes and soundtracks have grown popular with film makers since the considerable commercial success of Clint Eastwood's 'Every Which Way But Loose' which featured music from Eddie Rabbitt and others. The critics hated it but the public loved it and a follow up called 'Every Which Way You Can' has been made. The critics were kinder to 'Coal Miner's Daughter' which features Sissy Spacek's moving portrayal of Loretta Lynn in her rags-to-riches story. Willie Nelson contributed to the soundtrack of 'The Electric Cowboy' and had a small supporting role which revealed he had a real ability to act and led to the starring role in 'Honeysuckle Rose' opposite Dyan Cannon, and there are now plans for him to star in the film of his successful 'Red Headed Stranger' album. The most touted film of the year was 'Urban Cowboy' filmed in Mickey Gilley's enormous Houston honky-tonk with John Travolta, The Charlie Daniels Band and others, and the inspiration for a string of country discos across the US with mechnical Bulls. Dozens more country orientated films have been made during the year including 'The Best Little Whorehouse In Texas' which features Dolly Parton's acting debut.

Anyone looking around for good future film projects should consider Hank Williams Jnr's remarkable biography 'Living Proof' (PUTNAM) that was published this year and recounts his problems as the child of a country music legend, an appalling accident in 1975 when he fell hundreds of feet down a mountain and smashed his face, the long months of recovery and now his remarkable rise in popularity. Before the accident his material was no more than average but his new Waylon-influenced progressive style has brought deserved success and with his Bama Band he's probably one of the best live country acts to be seen anywhere.

Bobby Bare has long deserved recognition as a major country artist and the last year has witnessd a return to form and a high chart placing with 'Down and Dirty' (CBS) featuring a strong collection of songs by Shel Silverstein that ranged through witty anecdotes, gritty realism and biting satire – a welcome relief from the banal pop ditties of so many of his contemporaries.

Johnny Cash's work has been slipping further and further into mediocrity but he's recently celebrated his 25th year in the business and

'Silver' (CBS) is his best album in ages. The revitalisation of his career has come at the same time as his daughter Rosanne and step-daughter Carlene (both born around the time he was working alongside Elvis and Carl Perkins at Sun studios in Memphis) have come into the limelight with highly praised solo albums — 'Right Or Wrong' (CBS-USA, ARIOLA-UK) and 'Musical Shapes' (F-BEAT) respectively. Both have been considerably helped by the Cash connection, outstanding backing musicians, and talented songwriter husbands: Carlene married Englishman Nick Lowe and Rosanne married Rodney Crowell. Cash seems to have drawn new energy from the youngsters and includes at least one number apiece from his son-in-laws.

Rodney Crowell is one of the best of the new breed of country writers from Texas who've followed in the wake of Kris Kristofferson, and the first to achieve success in the mainstream of country music, writing major hits in the past few months for The Oak Ridge Boys, The Dirt Band and Waylon Jennings. He's also producer of Rosanne's album and has scored success in the rock charts with an album of his songs titled 'But What Will The Neighbors Think' (WARNER BROS.).

Other Texans showing promise include three from Buddy Holly's home town of Lubbock, Joe Ely toured with the Clash in England where he recorded 'Live Cuts' (MCA) which features many of his best songs. Many were written by his friend Butch Hancock who's released two idiosyncratic albums 'West Texas Waltzes' and 'The Wind Dominion' on his own Rainlight label in a style which evokes memories of Woody Guthrie and early Dylan and has won unanimous praise from critics in the UK and the USA. Terry Allen is the latest super-talent to emerge from the West Texas plains though his remarkable 'Lubbock On Everything' (FATE) is on an equally obscure record label and isn't easy to find.

JOE ELY

Emmylou Harris came to prominence singing with Gram Parsons and her first solo album followed his formula of mixing rock with country but with each release she's gone further back to the roots of country. Against the wishes of the record company she recorded a bluegrass album 'Roses In The Snow' (WARNER BROS.) which has become her biggest seller to date. It's done more for bluegrass than any record before or since and encouraged new interest in the young musicians who are still making the music for little labels like Sugar Hill.

Country is the hardest musical genre to 'break into' but two who've succeeded this year are Lacy J. Dalton who's been trying for fifteen years but finally hit on the right formula of combining her Janis Joplin style vocals with agressive country songs, then sent her home-made demo tape to an influential friend in Nashville; and Joe Sun a former country DJ who found out what country fans wanted to hear and decided to give it them himself — a new working of the old formula of Memphis rock 'n' roll and stone country.

In Britain the sensation of the year was Boxcar Willie, half man and half train, whose new versions of songs by his heroes Jimmy Rodgers and Hank Williams has led to a phenomenal following. Now American fans are showing an interest in his nostalgic sounds. Even more extraordinary in England has been the discovery of a man named Wes McGee who's recorded one of the best modern country albums of recent years in the attic of his home in London's St. John Wood. No one has ever believed British country music could ever be good so McGee has recorded, released and promoted the record himself, selling all his studio equipment to pay his bills. Like the others recommended here, McGee proves country music needn't be soft and soggy — it's well worth investigating.

RICHARD WOOTTON

ROCKABILLY

What I'd really like to do is bring you into my living room, sit you down, and play records for you. Then I wouldn't have this awful problem of trying to tell you about rockabilly.

If I had you here with me on this farm in Elephant, Pennsylvania, I could let you listen for yourself. Then the important questions would all be answered and I wouldn't have to fill you in with confidently uttered maybes and half-truths. As it is, I don't even know if you've heard rockabilly.

If you are European or English, you may have. In Britain and on the Continent, there's a rockabilly cult. There's audience enough to fill the Rainbow Theatre in London or the Paradiso in Amsterdam. Every now and then, a rockabilly record may even be a Top Ten hit.

If you're American, you may remember Elvis singing 'Jailhouse Rock' or Gene Vincent's 'Be-Bop-A-Lula' or Carl Perkins singing 'Blue Suede Shoes', but the probability is that you don't know rockabilly for itself. One of the paradoxes of rockabilly is that it is American in origin — purely American, quintessentially American, mythically American — but in America today it is all but totally invisible.

In the US in 1980, there are individually rockabilly artists and little hot pockets of rockabilly enthusiasm here and there. But rockabilly music is not played on the radio. And if you want to find rockabilly records, you have to look around for them. You've got to dig, boy, dig.

But rockabilly music is simple. (Some would say primitive — but then, so is a heartbeat primitive). Let me see if at a distance and even through the medium of print, I can pass on a touch of the spirit. As a warm-up exercise, run through a little of 'Heartbreak Hotel' in your mind. Now a little of 'Be-Bop-A-Lula'. Finally aloud and explosive as you can say "A-wop-bop-a-lu-mop, a lop-bam-boom!"

Now, say, "I'm feelin' right tonight." Pop those tees. "I'm feelin' right tonight". Syncopate it a little. "I'm feelin' right tonight. Gonna boogie like cra-a-zy. Gonna tear the dance floor up. Gonna roll on the floor and do it some more, do the bop, do the bop, do the bop."

That's rockabilly. If you've got a couple of guitars, a set of drums (optional) and an old-fashioned stand-up bass to slap a backbeat out of, you're ready to play rockabilly. That is, if you've caught the spirit.

It's none of that "get down stuff". As the current American group, the Memphis Rockabilly Band out of Boston, has it: "We don't play no 'Disco Duck'/ If you want that kind of music, you're out of luck".

Rockabilly is up music. It's hot medicine. It's music to make you throw your crutches down and do the boogie, music to set gran'daddy to rockin' in his rockin' chair. It's feel-good music. It's can-do music.

I needed a shot of that. I first got into rockabilly music three years ago. About the time that Elvis died in '77, a friend of mine ran his motorcycle into the side of a turning car. It was his second chance, and this time he didn't survive. It hit me hard. It took music to bring me up again. And coincidentally, in the wake of Elvis's death — almost as though Elvis's bloated body had become a dam blocking up the rockabilly channel — with the dam suddenly removed a great rush of rockabilly energy was released. Records that as 45's had been selling at auction in Europe and England for $50 or even $100, records unheard by the general public in twenty years, even music never ever released on record before, suddenly became available. For the first time, a person like me without great gobs of money to spend and living in the back of beyond could hear what I'd never heard before.

It did me a lot of good. I mean, Doctor, I can *bop* again.

But what a process of discovery this rockabilly revelation has been. I started with Buddy Holly. Holly was not exactly a rockabilly artist, although he did have a rockabilly phase. But he's not exactly not rockabilly, either. Holly was an original, and let's let it go at that. But through hunting for Buddy Holly records and attempting to piece together the size and shape of his short brilliant career, I stumbled across the first of the new rockabilly releases.

What I found was Johnny Burnette and the Rock 'n' Roll Trio, seventeen original period cuts on SOLID SMOKE RECORDS out of San Francisco. In the days before he got turned into a wimp and was set to singing 'You're Sixteen' and 'Dreamin'', Johnny Burnette — the father of contemporary rock 'n' roller Rocky Burnette — was a wild-ass rockabilly singer. And lead guitarist Paul Burlison, still playing today in Mississippi, was a fuzz-buster whose distinctive style can be heard today resurrected on songs like 'Hurricane' by the current British rockabilly group, Matchbox. This album was hot and heavy stuff. Even better, its extensive interior liner notes offered clues to other records, to specialty dealers and to fan publications with an interest in rockabilly.

Shortly after that, in a small bin in a record store in a small in Allentown, Pennsylvania, I found a treasure-trove of rockabilly compilation albums imported from England. The files of one American record company after another have been ransacked by assiduous British rockabilly freaks like Bill Millar, Martin Hawkins and Stuart Colman. For record label after record label — SUN, of course, and COLUMBIA, and M.G.M., and CAPITOL, and DECCA, and on and on, label by label — with varying results depending on the actual strength of material recorded in the Fifties, rockabilly compilation albums have been released in the last several years. And in the case of some labels, there have been two, or three, or four such albums.

I talked to the son of the owners of the record store. He had ordered these rockabilly albums as an adjunct to his developing taste for punk/New Wave music — which has been influenced to some degree by rockabilly's simplicity and power. I pointed to the first COLUMBIA rockabilly compilation. I'd just read an interesting description of it in the Jem imports flyer. I said, "Should I try that one?"

He said, "You wouldn't like it. It's too country."

I tried it anyway. It was country. I loved it.

And that's a whole other story for you. At the outset, rockabilly was country music, no question — jumped up country music, a hot crossbreeding of country boogie, Western swing, and r&b, with influence from the emerging New Orleans school of rock 'n' roll. For five years, from 1954 to 1959, with hints beforehand and trail-off after, somnolent old country music, just recovering from the impact of the life and death of Hank Williams, got up and rocked. It plain freaked out.

This rockabilly was a regional and minority

interest. It didn't get national attention in the U S. But everywhere during this period, in the South and in country America, young men got the idea that it was possible to bust free of all inhibition, to live fast and die young, to *be* Hank Williams. You could yell and scream, you could jump up and down, you could paint yourself red. Just do the romp-stompin' boogie.

And for awhile, a lot of rockabilly got recorded. Some of it appeared on national labels in regional release. Some of it appeared on one or another of the tiny record labels that flowered and died during the Fifties. Much of it never got issued at all.

Eventually, by the early Sixties, this storm had blown itself out. Country music went back to sleep again, back to shuffle beats and cry-in-your-beer ballads. It even added strings. And the country rockabilly performers by then were dead, or grown up, or had gotten religion. They quit the business, turned to more conventional country music, moved to Canada, or retired to roadhouses to play their music for the small audience that continued to care.

That's one Fifties rockabilly story, but there is another. During the Fifties, country music and urban music ran closer together than they have at any time since. Some few rockabilly songs became nationally popular. Elvis Presley, beginning as the original rockabilly star, made the transition to rock 'n' roll and carried rockabilly along, a part of the synthesis of styles that became rock 'n' roll. Rockabilly was never a large factor in rock'n'roll, but it was an important factor. It contributed purity and heat. It contributed the strong beat. Along with Little Richard and Chuck Berry — who might even be called Black rockabilly — this was the music that made mothers fear for their daughters, the music that was inveigled against from the pulpits and in the newspapers. Perhaps most of all, what rockabilly contributed to rock'n'roll was image, stance, the myths of the black-leather jacketed rebel with a ducktail haircut striking angular poses with a machine-gun guitar.

But rockabilly and the other hot strains of rock'n'roll got pushed aside before the end of the Fifties to make room for the likes of Frankie Avalon and Fabian, teen idols without the power, mystery or danger of Gene Vincent and Jerry Lee Lewis. Elvis was drafted into the Army, got his hair cut, and was never the same again. If country rockabilly dried up at the end of the Fifties, it was partly because the door to national exposure became closed to it.

Through the Sixties — the last days of rock 'n' roll, the folk boom days, the days of the coming of rock — rockabilly was forgotten in the United States. And yet, there were those who still cared for it.

If rockabilly has been rock therapy for me, there were those in Britain and in Europe to whom rockabilly has meant freedom. Partly it was the mythos — the clothes, the pose, the style, the talk, the image of Mike Fink and Davy Crockett with guitars in their hands, rippin' it up, tearin' it up. Partly it was the music itself with its promise of anarchy and self-expression, like a breath of pure fresh air to people in cultures sensed to be over-tidy and prepressed.

Take Ronny Weiser, for instance — a Jewish kid, born in Milan, raised here and there in Europe. Feeling alienated, feeling persecuted, feeling powerless and alone. Retiring to his room, with the American flag on the wall, putting on his Gene Vincent records and dreaming of freedom and possibility.

All through the Sixties and into the Seventies, collectors came from England and Europe and carted away from the United States all the rockabilly records they could find. They cleaned out the store. If you want a pretty accurate picture of what happened, you can imagine some Dutchman beating the hills of Tennessee looking for a farmer who once had his own small record label in the mid-Fifties, buying up his stock of records and his unissued tapes which had been sitting out in the hen house for the past fifteen years, brushing the chickenshit off his treasure, and rushing back to Europe chortling to himself. That's the way things have been.

The interest in Europe and England in rockabilly has grown geometrically during the Seventies. Specialty record shops have sprung up. Records whose origin and legitimacy were not plainly stated were issued. And rockabilly publications like NEW KOMMOTION and NOT FADE AWAY were started up. Performers like Charlie Feathers, Jack Scott and Carl Mann were brought out of retirement or obscurity and played again before English and European audiences. Warren Smith, one-time SUN rockabilly artist, even got the first standing ovation of his life from an English audience in '77. And English and European rockabilly performers began to appear, sometimes thin, sometimes off the mark, but sometimes amazingly good. Legitimate European record companies began to issue records. I have records from France, Germany, Belgium and Holland as well as from the United States and Canada. In particular, CHARLY RECORDS in England has concentrated on rockabilly and rock'n'roll material, both reissue and new.

America is way behind in catching up to rockabilly. Even so, there is activity. There are rockabillys playing here and there — like Sleepy LaBeef in residence in a truckstop in Massachusetts or Tex Rubinowitz with his fanatical audience in the Washington DC area. Records come out from one corner or another. RIPSAW RECORDS, for instance located just up the road from me in Easton, Pennsylvania. They record Tex Rubinowitz and Billy Hancock, keep their records in boxes in the front hallway at home, and sell a lot of copies of their singles in Norway.

Most interesting may be ROLLIN' ROCK RECORDS in Van Nuys, California. It's run by Ronny Weiser, grown up and come to America to make friends with Gene Vincent in his last days and be appalled at the lack of American interest in rockabilly. Ronny started by digging up old masters from the Fifties and reissuing them, but he soon found some young rockabilly performers still surviving from the Fifties like Ray Campi and Mac Curtis and goosed them into recording again. And now he puts out almost nothing but new material and has a stable of new young performers like Jimmie Lee Maslon and Johnny Legend. Rockin' Ronny has issued some fifty 45's and more than twenty rockabilly albums.

And something is happening now in the US. I'm finding it easier to find new records all the time, more and more are being issued, and the interest here, if behind Britain and Europe, is growing by leaps and bounds. Tex Rubinowitz's audience, for instance, is described as being a combination of aging hippies, truck drivers and New Wavers. That's a strange and powerful synthesis, and it may be a clue as to the kind of audience that the new rockabilly is going to attract.

I called Rockin' Ronny up on the phone the other night to ask his opinion. In his long, slow steady way, he's been working a long, long time to get rockabilly out in front of the public again.

"How much longer before rockabilly becomes visible?" I asked.

"Two or three more years", he said."We've got national distribution now. All that we are missing is support from the major record companies and support from the radio stations."

Two or three more years. That's a good guess. But I wouldn't make a bet that it will be that long. It's closer than that in England. In England, it may even be starting to happen right now. Buzz-buzz-a-diddle-it.

ALEXEI PANSHIN

INDEPENDENTS

As the recession in Anglo-American capitalism begins to bite, with a rabid fervour even the most fashionably apocalyptic harbingers of doom might find alarming, there's a grudging agreement whispering along and up the corridors of power within the corporate major record companies that the small label is indeed a Good Thing.

As the gross-out economics of massive-sales/chart oriented rock cross steeply rising costs of raw materials, services, borrowed money — everything in effect — on an overall graph which resembles the metabolic read-out of a terminally sick patient, so the realistic marginal cost exercises of the independents look healthier by the week.

As is screamingly necessary in many areas of rock commentary, however, one must be prepared to draw distinctions; between continents, regions and the labels themselves, which on closer examination reveal a surprising variety of aesthetic and business policies. Most importantly, the degree of genuine independence enjoyed by the non-majors is a matter of broad variation — a fact which is essential to consider in reassessing the blanket claims made for the indies' radical thrust and supposed subversion of the market.

It is a frequently repeated platitude that the United States limps a number of years — the figure quoted varies from two to ten — in both musical innovation and business practice in rock. One may take the element of musical chauvinism in this argument less seriously; take the singular failure of the new wave to figure in the American charts until it had mutated after a heavy dousing in FM sensibility.

Business-wise, though, Britain's microcosmic role is less fanciful; the US industry is bolstered by lower cost raw materials and easier credit, by the self-perpetuating massiveness of such a huge market, by having reaped large profits in the mid-seventies. It is being sheltered a little longer from the consequences of the mounting arcaneness of a generation of executives and, particularly, A&R men. Every indication is that its time will come.

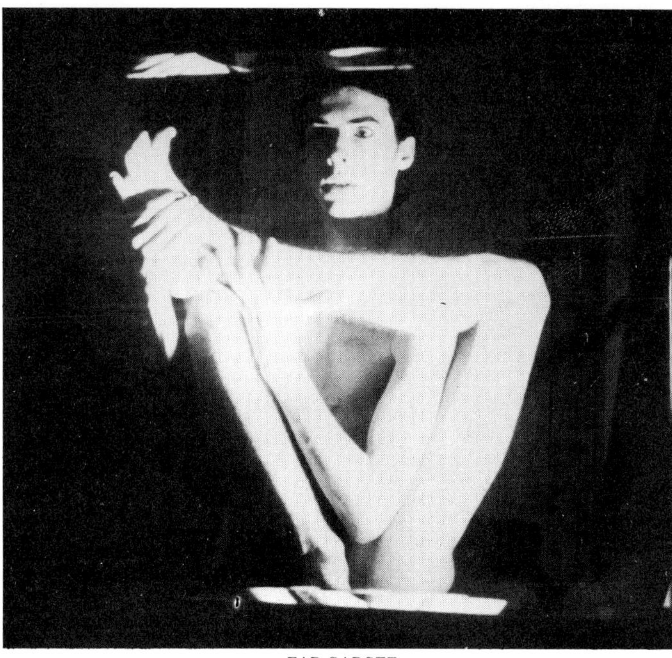

FAD GADGET

In the practical corollary to this decline, the growth of smaller, independent record labels, the US is at current count some two and a half years behind. It has no significant independent distribution service which might parallel the growth of ROUGH TRADE in Britain. Indeed, RT hope to reestablish the regional coverage destroyed by the price war of the mid-decade by repeating the pattern which they established in their home country.

Every account of the growth of independents in Britain cites a different epiphany as the authentic origin of the movement: the release of the Buzzcocks' 'Spiral Scratch' EP, the founding of STIFF RECORDS, The Desperate Bicycles' propagandist 'The Medium Is Tedium' EP. Or the point at which a punk/new wave record shop in London's traditionally freaky Notting Hill began to make contact with an informal network of like-minded shops around the country and began the unofficial distribution set-up which has enabled so many self-produced singles to penetrate the extremes of the British Isles.

There are other distributors, of course, as there were independent labels before punk — the generation of 'progressive' companies like ISLAND, CHRYSALIS, CHARISMA in the late sixties or — if you dig further and deeper — free jazz indies like INCUS. But there had never been labels and distributors specifically associated with the revulsion from the business's corporate excesses in the way that ROUGH TRADE and the labels with which it dealt were. From their viewpoint even STIFF looked suspiciously like little more than an effectively off-the-wall approach to marketing, a genial hype.

This missionary zeal, the rock press standing by as a vociferous acolyte, needs qualification, but is probably one of the profoundest differences between the independent sector in America and over the Atlantic. English labels trying to fix up distribution through, say JEM or BOMP, find their methods hopelessly oriented towards major business practices; the size of the distributor's percentage and the ninety-day delay on payout make the size and timing of cash-flow pretty hopeless for the very small-

MICK DOREY AND THE SIRENS

scale business that most fledgling labels are.

Hence, presumably, the relative success of a label like ZE. Floated by Michael Zilkha on a raft of family capital (Daddy owns the empire of Mothercare infant emporia), it has been able to survive a couple of years of dabbling with cult-bound New York staples such as James White/Chance before settling into its current roster of Puerto Rican disco and NY experimentalism. Even so, ZE found it necessary to licence through ISLAND (initially a verbal agreement on 10 12″ singles, including Cristina's 'Disco Clone'), ARISTA and finally ISLAND'S ANTILLES subsidiary, an unmistakeable acknowledgement of the tight monopoly of national distribution held by a handful of big companies.

Mythically renowned for the encouragement of individualistic business innovation, rock 'n' roll in the US has a tradition of independent entrepreneurism which stretches as far back as rock and roll itself, to Leonard Chess selling Muddy Waters' 'I Can't Be Satisfied' from the back of his car and further. Yet the country appears to have run short of such charismatic characters in comparison with Britain; the rather more pessimistic view from here is that the US simply doesn't have the necessary pool of radically-oriented bands.

British distributors point to a handful of labels over the continent — LUST/UNLUST, DANGERHOUSE, BOMP, HEARTHAN, 415, SYSTEMATIC, RALPH — but aver that the best stuff shipped over months ago; early Feelies, Pere Ubu and Devo. And since? BOMP in Los Angeles and 415 in San Francisco have both released regional compilation albums and little else of note; perhaps the recently-begun SLASH RECORDS in L.A. will be able to use their release of the debut album by X as the jumping-off point for an exposure of the city's prolific new wave.

THE FALL

Whilst taking full account of the considerable problems caused by the sheer size of the continent, the lack of a national weekly rock press and the predominant power of conservative radio programming, ROUGH TRADE intend to use their San Francisco shop as the basis for establishing direct contact with nuclei of independent activity, bypassing the wholesalers who have habitually supplied new wave imports by directly selling much of their English stock and releasing select items on their own label in the States. A compilation album and material by Joy Division, the Pop Group, A Certain Ratio and Pere Ubu (whose entire catalogue they now have) have started the ball rolling.

The eventual intention is to emulate and stimulate the kind of regional self-help and

THE POP GROUP

interdependence which is already rife in Britain, where there are several genuinely independent labels run by singular individuals in distinct and distinguished styles: Edinburgh's FAST PRODUCT (Bob Last), Manchester's FACTORY RECORDS (Tony Wilson), Liverpool's THE ZOO (Bill Drummond, Dave Balfe), Belfast's GOOD VIBRATIONS (Terri Hooley) and ROUGH TRADE (Geoff Travis).

Each has a marked musical identity; a half-hour's drive separates FACTORY's Mancunian gloom and dour humour from THE ZOO's blatantly and cheerfully commercial aspirations. ROUGH TRADE's own label filters bands through an ideological net which excludes sexism or racism and through an aesthetic one which sometimes appears to shun competence; the ZOO declare covert designs on the pop charts.

Currently, in spite of ROUGH TRADE's prominence as a distributor (they shifted a quarter of a million plus of the Specials' 'Gangsters', staggeringly) their inverted elitism as a label leaves the accolade of best British independent to Factory. As well as steadily directing bands in the direction of major-label deals — Orchestral Manoeuvres In The Dark to DINDISC, The Distractions to ISLAND — as the indies have always done, FACTORY have been able to use ROUGH TRADE's connections to establish a telling precedent. Joy Division, the Manchester band whose lead singer Ian Curtis tragically committed suicide earlier in 1980, have been selling sufficient numbers of their first album, 'Unknown Pleasures', to be able to survive financially without seeking a major label deal at all.

First under the wire; a departure which breaks a stranglehold on rock's eccentric economics that was previously thought ineluctable. In addition the downturn in sales has meant that the volume of singles necessary to a top thirty placing can now be sold on an independent label. Joy Division's 'Love Will Tear Us Apart' and both singles by the melodic reggae outfit UB40 on the Dudley-based GRADUATE label have all made the British top ten in the early summer of '80.

CRISTINA

As the independent sector in Britain has moved from being a practical necessity for bands who fail to elicit the majors' interest through a phase of very successful cult sales to making a direct assault on the once-impregnable charts, the majors themselves have been slowly taking some of the lessons of indie success to their hearts and reproducing some of the renegades' methods. Having learnt that some kinds of music can be marketed more effectively on this scale, there's been a tendency for larger labels to bud off pseudo-small ones: BACK DOOR from PHONOGRAM, PRE from CHARISMA, KOROVA from WEA, 4AD from BEGGARS BANQUET.

Sometimes the disguise is more complete, as in the case of the WEA-funded offshoot RADAR RECORDS which began in '78 with Elvis Costello on its books and gained an idealised status as *the* British independent. Only after a series of personal and financial upheavals in the summer of '79 was it made clear that WEA had funded RADAR themselves, retaining a casting vote which they used to dissolve the company at the end of the year.

Between the two extremes of thralldom and liberty the British record business has proliferated a host of variants on a theme, as the middle range of sales and economics — somewhere between 'My Geraniums Are Bulletproof' by the Deepfreeze Mice on MOLE EMBALMING RECORDS and 'The Wall' — becomes increasingly colonised from above and below. There are labels associated with bands; the Specials' constantly successful TWO-TONE RECORDS or Secret Affair's I-SPY, which bands use as buffers to maintain precious freedoms over release schedules, production, artwork and so forth. There are labels with a distinct political bias; the Pop Group/Slits Y or anarchist commune-dwellers Crass' own imprint. There are local labels, like OILY in Aberdeen; lunatic labels like RABID; labels based on magazines, shops or studios; many, many labels which conceal little more than the identity of one home-based musician. Yet even these are serious contenders; as I write Bill Nelson, the former BeBop DeLuxe guitar ace, is hovering around the thirty with his first single on his own COCTEAU label.

WAZMO NARIZ

This is serious business — in more senses than one. The independent record labels in Britain do not represent a common wave of radical onslaught on the hidebound majors, but their appropriateness to a new stratum of music, their financial realism, their refreshing lack of bullshit, their industry and humour are making them a very real part of the economics of record sales this side of the Pond; how long before the cold sweats break out in Burbank? STEVE TAYLOR

JAZZ/FUSION

1980 was the year in which, so it seemed, kids not old enough to remember the Beatles...or even the mod *revival*?...were trading in their space dust and taking to snorting smack. It was not, however, a year which saw any such tragi-comic scenarios for the jazz world.

If we track back a year or so, we find jazz getting a leg up and a hard on through the dirty money of disco. The alter-culture of chaser ropes and Steve Rubellism offered the music a lot of options that it was keen on taking up. There was straight, instant financial reward; there was a let-out from the old requisite of needing either a pretty face or a reputation; you didn't have to go gigging all year long. And yet musically, technically, there was a stable base for some hard creativity that the jazz-funk era had lacked. In fact, among the hard-core sophisticates, there was a genuine demand for anything that all but destroyed the small-town 4/4 bass line.

Cuts like 'I Thought It Was You' (the ultimate) and 'Turn The Music Up' and artists like Herbie ('Supermann') Mann were getting a rare slice of the action. Moreover, they were met more than halfway by other acts such as Toto, Bobby Caldwell, GQ and Instant Funk who carried much the same type of goods under a different banner.

Alas, this was a trend that has failed to spread into the eighties. OK, there have been some notable events such as the Crusaders plus 'Street Life' plus Randy Crawford bit in the summer and fall of '79. Equally, at the time when I was first approached by THE ROCK YEARBOOK, the MUSIC WEEK singles charts were quite liberally peppered with Jazz-esque hits: Narada Michael Walden's 'I Shoulda Loved Ya' and Rodney Franklin with 'The Groove', desperately

AL DI MEOLA

waiting behind the riff for something else to happen.

But getting down to crunchtacks, the fact is that while the wind has all but gone from disco sales, jazz of this kind has seemingly failed to explore and exploit the limits both in and beyond the field. The consumer may well see a battleground peppered with the dismantled spirits of veterans (Stanley Turrentine, Gary Bartz) and the smashed skulls of unproved youth (anyone you might have fancied), and decided that the firing range was just a lot of hot air. Meanwhile more fashions old and new — Heavy Metal, Two-tone — have created sufficient distractions anyway. The only PS here is that while working through the clutch of albums below, I found that lead pellets were getting into some strange places. Look at Ray Gomez, now.

If, for art's sake, we'd tracked back not one year but ten, then we'd have gotten something of another ballgame: the underground-gone-overground, but still with all its adventure and capriciousness spilling out in bands like Nucleus, Colosseum and If. Behind that, across the Atlantic, was Creed Taylor sugaring up Wes Montgomery for an audience who'd now be buying AOR (on floppy disc), and anyone with a head for heights went for Monk or Blakey anyway...

What sticks out a mile with hindsight, over the last decade, is the media's general refusal to look jazz in the ear, much less in the eye — to somehow shield the public as well as itself from that shrinkwrapped voodoo. The mighty irony is that a great many non-jazz musicians (and TV producers, and Fleet Street subs) have at least substantial respect for particular jazz performers. Yet the only real reflection has been the recent eruption of player and studio publications (the 'sound' cult as per Pat Metheny) such as MUSICIANS ONLY which have been able to talk nuts and bolts relatively free from the constrictions of fashion. Too often the hard-won opportunities in the daily and weekly British press, and the broadcast media, continue to be aborted with rigid, spiritless reporting. Meanwhile a writer for one of the leading pop weeklies was bleating at Joni Mitchell's Mingus album (admittedly weak on other counts) for having "too much jazz". It was hoped the aberration wouldn't be repeated.

The final twist in all this tale is that — if we take "jazz' as meaning music with an element of improvisation, or at least a sizeable kick — then there's more jazz if maybe less artistry in the horn break of The Beat's 'Mirror In The Bathroom' than a whole side of average Tappan Zee product. Life is both unjust and full of surprises.

So on many counts the last year or so hasn't been a wholly *ongoing* period. Even "consolidation" seems too good a word when so many opportunities are let slip by — though more of this shortly. Coming back from the disco to the armchair, the hip easy listening that was first giftwrapped by Creed Taylor and found an heir in Bob James, continues to sell adequately. It's also, thankfully, *just* starting to find a few things to say, notably in the Latin tinges of the Larry Rosen and Dave Grusin production team. Interestingly though it's a former Grusin protégé, Noel Pointer, who's finally beaten the whole fusion show at its own game, set and match.

At the same time, *pro tem*,

Chick Corea has backed off from the dry ice and strobe lights to play trenchant, individual music with largely acoustic instruments. Laudable as that can be, it points a finger at the ancient and otherwise unhonoured promise by fusion music to its critics, that fusion was always just an ambassador along the line to the real McCoy Tyner. Having got so far, clearly it's up to us, the audience, to start looking around.

One consolation is that the much saluted mergers and cutbacks among the majors havn't affected the small stream of jazz too much. Indeed the routing caused by independent labels like BEGGARS BANQUET and ROUGH TRADE has made things generally a lot easier for indies all down the line. In any case, in jazz once you're away from the heavy-duty money-spinners/eaters, it's always been a case of one-to-one enthusiasm, and labels like STEEPLECHASE, HORO and OWL have taken care of business basically by carving their own single niche. The invasion of COLUMBIA/CBS is but jam on top, no kidding.

Immediately, there's another surprise, and that's the very low level of crosstalk in the UK between new wave and new music over the last year. The best we managed was a rather untidy tour featuring the Slits, Creation Rebel and Don Cherry — rather, one felt, in that order. However, separate appearances by Old and New Dreams, Air and the like, away from the stuffy, righteous jazz establishment, have happily been sell-outs. The ska revival, Don Drummond, Tommy McCook and all those guys, might have sprung something more than a few Treasure Island compilations that got lost in the wash.

Pertinent and original British bands have been fairly few on the ground, the standout for me being former Greater London Arts Association winners Stinky Winkles, whose original lineup broke up in the spring of 1980, due in good part to lack of bookings.

On the European Continent, the crosstalk's generally been better, the resultant music much harder. This, I guess, is down in part to the continuing unspeakably terrible character of most Euro pop, and in part to the more sensible attitudes towards jazz, radical rock and about everything else.

JEAN-LUC PONTY

DEXTER GORDON

In the States, the Loft movement centring in on various major cities, has been slipping away for so many years now as to be quite self-adjusted to its own middle-age. That's not to say though that it's lost all trace of its *community* roots (music for people with no money and no time to stay up all night) or that it doesn't continue to foster some good music. What's far more worrying is the impenetrable varnish on top of the whole American business, with iniquitous segregation on the airwaves.

But against all this is the hard and inescapable power of the classic survivors. There should be no resentment for Ella Fitgerald when she can land 'The Incomparable Ella' ("as seen on TV") a pop chart placing. But that's only a kiss away from the wide, wide audience that, say, Dexter Gordon can pull, in both age, allegiance and experience. To a degree that's because he's now with COLUMBIA/CBS with the advantage of their distribution networks — but then they hardly do a heavy marketing number on his albums. Art Pepper records for GALAXY which is generally left well alone, but thanks to the grapevine he rips up a storm.

It's also worthwhile mentioning the huge volume of reissue material that continues to appear. Prime among these series I have to cite PRESTIGE, MILESTONE, BLUE NOTE and ATLANTIC (the "That's Jazz" silver-sleeve series) as great mansions of bop. But, interestingly, fusion jazz itself is now recycling its own short history, signally with the 'Best of' series featuring John McLaughlin, Eric Gale, etc. Gale's much-beloved 'De Rabbit' is now on a pedestal as one of the landmarks of the movement. There's also AFFINITY (ex-Byg) with its rerun of the infancy of the new music. Some may feel I'm a bit hard on the fusion side, lacing it rather too much with avant-gardists and octagenarians. In one light, that's very true, and it's meant I've omitted for lack of space names like Dave Sanborn, Jean-Luc Ponty and Al DiMeola that had as good a claim as any. I've also necessarily left out names from the other territories I've tracked, from the rock-jazz fringes such as Morrissey/Mullen and Annette Peacock, from the straight life such as the Heath Brothers, and from the new music cookpot with Air, Ameena Myers, James Blood Ulmer, etc.

The main thing I'm trying to underline, outside parading my own preferences, is the width of music that may lie beyond what you may pick up on an average weekend's radio, and the flexibility of many of the musicians involved therein. I do lean fairly heavily on new music (Chico Freeman, Cecil McBee) because I feel it illustrates exactly that flexibility, together with the musicians' own "voices", a very precious thing in jazz.

But then, the music can speak for itself. LINNET EVANS.

THIS WAS THE YEAR OF

BLONDIE

Deborah Harry grew up in Hawthorn, New Jersey. She was a majorette in high school and the prettiest girl in her class. After a brief stay in college she arrived in Manhattan in the late '60s. She drifted in and out of folk music, modelling, PLAYBOY bunnying, art school and table waiting at Max's Kansas City. By 1973 she was a third of the glam-trash girl group called The Stilletos who played multi-sexual hangouts like East 4th Street's Club 82, opening for bands like The New York Dolls. Blondie-the-Band was formed soon after, with guitarist/art student/boyfriend Chris Stein.

They played CBGB and other hot young punk hangouts. They weren't arty or profound like Television and Patti Smith though. They were a cartoon group, like the Ramones, and people liked them – especially people who had grown up on the previous decade's girl groups and pop songs – the music from which Blondie's seemed to have sprung. You might have thought them a passing fancy. But three albums, two record companies and several managers later, Blondie were a smash hit – topping the charts with 'Parallel Lines' and its disco/avant-pop single 'Heart of Glass'.

By 1980 Blondie-the-band were sitting pretty, preparing to record their fifth album, filming their second plug for Gloria Vanderbilt's clothes line, appearing in films and more. Deborah Harry had become a certified international star, profiled one page ahead of Norman Mailer in VOGUE. It was a long way from her days as a down-and-out junkie on the Bowery music fringes. From her penthouse apartment near New York's Central Park, Debbie gave this exclusive interview to THE ROCK YEARBOOK.

"When you know where you're going you know what to wear," Debbie sings in the commercial she wrote for Murjani International. The interview began when I wondered if Debbie now had to wear disguises in order to walk the streets.

"Sometimes I go out dressed as a bag lady. I smudge dirt all over my legs and everything, and wear these big clothes and pad up my chest so it looks like I have huge bosoms and I wear an old wig and disgusting clothes."

You've really done this?

"No."

So when you know where you're going, do you know what to wear?

"People are always immediately attracted by the blonde hair. I just wear a hat if I don't feel like being recognised. It's funny in New York. Paris too. Everyone's so blasé."

Do you ever revisit old haunts on the Bowery?

"I don't go to CBGB anymore. I never go. I go there very odd times...to see Nico. There's no nostalgia. Going past my old house on the Bowery near Prince Street makes me more nostalgic than CBGB."

Where will you be ten years from now?

"Gee...I don't know...on a rocket to the moon. (She laughs) In orbit!"

Is fame a dangerous drug?

"It's not what you think it's gonna be. That's one thing for sure. I think once you've been pampered by attentive fans, doted on, asked for autographs, been paid a lot of attention to and complimented, if it were just to stop suddenly it would really be a shock. But popularity comes and goes slowly.

"The first time I was asked for an autograph I was really plucked, shaking and nervous. I never turn anybody down unless they're expecting me to whip out a pen and paper. I really think there should be an autograph etiquette. When I ask people for autographs...and I do...I have my own autograph book. That's really a standard procedure."

What has surprised you in the last two years?

"I always wanted to be successful, appreciated, wanted in terms of the public and being a singer, an entertainer. I think that desire or need within them is what makes entertainers successful. But the whole process is not at all where I thought it would be. I honestly didn't think about it! I didn't think in terms of everyday living. I didn't think to myself in a calculated way that people would write about me.

"Everybody in the whole world has a story to tell...their emotions, their fortunes. That's why I decided to really put it on the line and tell people about myself and I'm a little disturbed by the sensationalistic approach I've been treated with (in the press). It seems almost senile. It hasn't improved. I think people have."

Tell me your most secret desire.

"Yeah...so everyone can read it?"

What would you most like to do?

"I'd like to entertain people, give them pleasure, relieve them from their problems. I feel privileged to be able to do that. Whatever man's primitive instincts are from being an animal – that fear and cautiousness – I'd like to help people and help myself overcome this. I think that music does this. I would like to be able to do it more."

What was the most discouraging moment you've had?

"There were probably 500 of those. There's been days when it's hardly been worth it.

"Finding out what the business was about after having been in it is a rude awakening. You have to find out what the business is about before you try to be an artist in it. It's really a struggle. Everyone says that. More than 50% of your energy goes into business at one point or another. That's where most artists fall down. They can't get their art to the public because they can't do any business. It's really a tragedy."

What motivation carries you through the bad days?

"To prove to myself that I could do it. To satisfy myself. In my bio (NB she means in her life, I think) I've had lots and lots of jobs. They didn't bring me the satisfaction I get from doing this. All the ambitions and experiences that led up to this have funnelled together and added to this for me."

But people say you ultimately want to be an actress.

"I am an actress, I always have been."

MICHAEL GROSS

RECORDINGS

BLONDIE (Private Stock/Chrysalis)
PLASTIC LETTERS (Chrysalis)
PARALLEL LINES (Chrysalis)
EAT TO THE BEAT (Chrysalis)

THIS WAS THE YEAR OF

THE CLASH

In February 1979, The Clash were two shows into their first visit to America – what they called their "Pearl Harbour Tour: Taking everybody by surprise".

In San Francisco, bass player Paul Simenon spoke to an interviewer about the image of The Clash. "We don't like to be pushed around. Too many times I've been pushed around at school and at work. But we think violence is really stupid; it's a waste of energy. Some kids who come to our concerts are real tough cunts and they really enjoy it. There's fuck-all else for them to do. But following us around the country and trying to get other bands together, they're doing something instead of just smashing things up. Breaking things up gets a bit boring after a while."

It's sentiments like that and the music that grows from them that best explains why, in 1980, The Clash became the first group from Britain's punk/new wave/whatever explosion of the late '70s to capture America's attention and in turn be captured by its energies.

Simenon formed The Clash in mid-1976 with a friend from Brixton, England, guitarist Mick Jones. They found singer Joe Strummer and another guitarist, Keith Levine (who quit the band almost immediately and is now a member of Public Image Ltd.). Drummerless, they still rehearsed each day in a warehouse they'd refurbished in London's Camden Town. They got a record contract with CBS, recorded an album, and hired a drummer, Topper Headon.

Later that year, The Clash joined the Sex Pistols on the ill-fated "Anarchy in the UK" tour that began the counter-reaction to and caused the success of what quickly became known as English "punk rock". The English commercial establishment rose up against the noise, banning punk songs and concerts, and the punks did their utmost to continue providing reasons for the controversy.

In May the Sex Pistols released 'God Save The Queen', and The Clash returned from their first headlining "White Riot" tour to play a show at London's Rainbow Theatre that ended in an audience riot, a sort of "coming-out party" for the new wave. NME wondered if it was nihilism. Lambeth Member of Parliament Marcus Lipton demanded that "if pop music is going to be used to destroy our established institutions, then it ought to be destroyed first".

The Clash "responded" by recording a tune produced by Lee "Scratch the Upsetter" Perry of Jamaica, 'Complete Control', and took off for a tour of Europe where they were hassled, attacked, threatened and reviled by officialdom from one end of the continent to the other. Back in the UK, the police were arresting The Clash every chance they got, on charges ranging from petty theft to pigeon murder. They released another single, 'White Man in Hammersmith Palais', and launched their "Clash Out on Parole" tour of England.

Meanwhile, in America, punk music was going nowhere fast. A visit to the States proved the undoing of the Sex Pistols. American CBS had yet to release 'The Clash'. But one American – Sandy Pearlman – producer of Blue Oyster Cult – heard clashing and liked it. He was hired to produce the next LP, their first in America, a No. 2 album in England, 'Give 'Em Enough Rope'. The song 'Tommy Gun' was their first British hit single. The album hardly scratched the surface of America. But their live appearances on the "Pearl Harbour Tour" were astounding to audiences, critics and music businessmen who'd written off, or done their level best to ignore the angry English who kept washing ashore. Playing only seven cities, selling out everywhere they went, The Clash served notice that they would be back. They'd also be reckoned with.

Back in England they worked on two projects: 'The Cost of Living' EP and 'Rude Boy', a film Topper Headon described as "about a 70% true story with film of actual gigs and incidents as they happened...the story of the group seen through the eyes of a bloke named Ray who we hang around with". The EP was released the day Margaret Thatcher was elected Prime Minister, and one song off it, their version of Bobby Fuller's 'I Fought the Law' got them their first significant US airplay. They played a Rock Against Racism benefit show in the Rainbow Theatre. This time their fans didn't riot; the seats had been removed, a bow to a longstanding Clash request of hall-owners.

Back in the studio with producer Guy Stevens, The Clash recorded a double album, then headed straight to America for another tour of America, this time of six weeks' duration. Back in England again, they put the finishing touches on their two-for-the-price-of-one LP, 'London Calling'.

Upon its release, 'London Calling' was justly hailed all around as a masterpiece. In the way critics often do, they compared it to records and historical moments of the past. The Clash were dubbed The New Rolling Stones, the album compared to 'Exile On Main Street'. Held up as evidence were the astonishing range of the two discs, the melodies, the hooks. All the things that assuredly make The Clash of 'London Calling' our finest extant rock ensemble.

Sure, they started off second to the Sex Pistols. Sure, they seemed to be following in the bad boy steps of the Stones. But the life of their music set them apart. And even more, their attitude brought them up, cream to the top of the bottle. Not even their record company could hold them back. In America, the first album wasn't released until after the second, and even then it was resequenced, with several singles added that are not of a piece with the rest of the album. But then that same record company did a bang-up job with 'London Calling', agreeing to sell it for less than they were used to, in a move that betrayed far more smarts than beneficience.

For what The Clash have proved...and what The Clash seem to stand for most of all...is that standing up may make you a target, but standing up also makes you strong. Anger *can* be power. Power *can* be put to good use, even if examples of that are hard to find.

The Clash are everything you ever wanted in a rock band. They're handsome. They're ugly. They're progressive. They're strong. You can sing along. You can shout along. You can believe because they do. You can look ahead, because they believe in today. MICHAEL GROSS

RECORDINGS

THE CLASH (CBS)
GIVE 'EM ENOUGH ROPE (Epic/CBS)
LONDON CALLING (Epic/CBS)

THIS WAS THE YEAR OF

GARY NUMAN

The 1976/7 punk/new wave explosion cleared away much dead wood. Suddenly, there was a vacuum at the centre of the pop world which established stars could no longer automatically expect to fill. And thus rock 'n' roll was returned not only to its roots, but also to the show-business traditions of the century, as the fabled 'overnight success', one of the enduring entertainment myths, became a genuine possibility again.

(There were admittedly other business factors, which precipitated this state of affairs — most notably, the overall decline in record sales, and the retail price-war which that, and the absence of resale price maintenance, encouraged.)

Although other new acts — The Police, The Pretenders — seemed to have taken their places in the higher echelons of rock-dom with both cool aplomb and breathtaking suddenness, in fact both had been building up their base following for some time — and members of both also had an experience of the business that could be measured in years rather than months.

Gary Numan (or Tubeway Army, as he was then) was the real overnight success. He literally had no groundswell of support, and his breakthrough took everyone (including, one suspects, his business advisers) by complete surprise. He was certainly unprepared personally. He had formulated a kind of success master-plan, but the possibility that 'Are 'Friends' Electric?' might get to No. 1 hadn't entered his calculations.

His early efforts as a leader of his own punk band (known initially as The Lasers) had been, by his own admission, entirely derivative. He adopted the musical and sartorial manners of the day to procure himself a recording contract. Once that had been realised, he exchanged his guitar for a synthesiser, and turned to introspective experimentation rather than self-promotion. Consequently, he had enjoyed no chart success of any description. Further, by the time that 'Replicas' was issued in April 1979, with the single following on May 4, he hadn't even played any live gigs for over a year.

There was simply nothing to which one could attribute Numan's sudden elevation other than the appeal of his single, his album and him. Promotion had certainly been minimal (there had been one appearance on *The Old Grey Whistle Test*); one MELODY MAKER writer ruefully confessed that Numan's career provided "an object-lesson in the unimportance of the press".

'Are 'Friends' Electric?' and 'Replicas' topped the singles and albums charts respectively in June 1979, a double-gold feat that he repeated as early as September with 'Cars' and 'The Pleasure Principle'. Two more Top 10 singles followed — 'Complex', another track from the latter album (on which all songs were restricted to one-word titles) later in 1979, and a new song, 'We Are Glass', early the following summer.

In years to come, Numan might have cause to regret that

it all happened so quickly — because, however precocious his musical talents, he was still very raw. When he started work on 'Replicas' he was still only 20, and yet the album was virtually all his own work. (In fact, the name-change between 'Replicas' and 'The Pleasure Principle' from Tubeway Army to Gary Numan wasn't the blindly egocentric step that it might have seemed; it was simply recognition of the fact that no 'band' as such existed.)

'Replicas' credited Numan with vocals, synthesisers and guitars. He had composed everything, and also produced the entire album. Of this assortment of chores, it was in the latter area (one in which, after all, experience is reckoned to be an inestimable advantage) where his proficiency was most startling. What was most remarkable about 'Are 'Friends' Electric?' was that it was an exceptionally powerful single, distinguished by a supremely confident production — the song just *sounded* perfect.

Ranged over an entire album, of course, Numan's talents seemed preternaturally assured. The overall sound then became monotonous and uninventive, and the hardly-original theme of human alienation in a technological environment provided insufficient lyrical substance. But, as reviewers were fond of pointing out, Numan took enduring SF themes, and the synthesised sounds of bands like Kraftwerk and the Human League, and swamped them with a pop music mentality — thus making it all accessible to a mass audience.

Certainly, a mass audience is what he won for himself. Suddenly his bleakly studied poses, like a youthful David Bowie in colourless, futuristic settings, became the most marketable of images. He became the most ubiquitous of male pin-ups.

By the time of the release of 'The Pleasure Principle', he had become one of that exclusive breed of performer who can afford to spurn the attentions of the media — he no longer needed to court their approval. It made good sense, though, in other respects — the mystique which he had constructed was clearly better preserved without publicity; further, he had been unhappily gauche when talking to reporters — disclosing, for example, his bizarre scheme to set up a commercially-viable operation, transporting war veterans back to the scenes of their battles (he expressed a fascination for all aspects of planes and flying). In any case, the account which he gave of himself probably hardly fitted the image which his mentors would have liked him to convey. He presented himself as a home-loving, middle-class lad, whose parents had always been exceptionally supportive — his mum acting as hairdresser, and his dad as roadie.

Still, it is strange; probably no major rock star of recent years has received less music press coverage.

It's as well that he didn't need to set aside days for press interviews, for his engagement diary was full anyway. Numan continued to play a dominant role in every aspect of his own career. He designed a complicated stage-show for his concert dates; it was a starkly-illuminated set with pillars and platforms. Great store was placed by lights and, inevitably, lasers. To complete the archetypal Numan setting of a world in which humans have been suppressed by machines, two pyramids danced together during the final number.

Naturally, the whole package could only be assembled in large concert halls, though by then Numan was hardly able to accommodate his growing following in smaller venues. It must, of course, be said that this was a costly operation, and also that he had had scant experience of performing live before any sort of audience. He was characteristically diffident about the whole undertaking. "I'll put on a show and see how it goes. If they don't like it, I'll stop doing live work again," he told Chris Bohn (MELODY MAKER, June 9, 1979).

The band he recruited for his stage shows comprised Paul Gardiner (bass), the only one who had been with him from the outset; Chris Payne and Billy Currie (synthesiser and keyboards); Russell Bell (guitar, synthesiser) and Ced Sharpley (drums). They toured the UK in September, and during the opening months of 1980 went through Europe, the US, Japan, Australia and New Zealand. In the event, the critics hardly went overboard, but most were prepared to admit that he had acquitted himself well in view of his inexperience.

The concert that had taken place at Hammersmith Odeon on September 28, 1979 was filmed, and subsequently became a video-cassette which went on sale in May 1980. This put Numan in the vanguard of that particular commercial development — a fact which could have surprised no-one except the staff of CHRYSALIS who had expected Blondie to be first in the field.

There was another, more oblique, manifestation of the burgeoning Numan cult. It was probably at least partly his unequivocal endorsement of Ultravox (at the time an unfashionable band) that enabled one of their number, John Foxx, to make some headway with a solo career.

And so, with the 1979/80 round completed, Numan arrived back at 'Go' to start all over again. A new album, 'Telekon', was scheduled for September release, with 'I Die, You Die', a single that he had already premiered on the *Kenny Everett Video Show*, preceding it. Another set of UK dates — the Gary Numan Teletour 80 — was announced, for which a more spectacular stage-show was promised.

Numan, though, had never committed himself to rock music, and he suggested that the tour, his second, could be his last. He said he'd like to work in video, or in films. Or there was always that plane enterprise... BOB WOFFINDEN

RECORDINGS

TUBEWAY ARMY (Atlantic/Beggars Banquet)
REPLICAS (Atlantic/Beggars Banquet)
THE PLEASURE PRINCIPLE (Atlantic/Beggars Banquet)
TELEKON (Atlantic/Beggars Banquet)

THIS WAS THE YEAR OF

TOM PETTY & THE HEARTBREAKERS

When Tom Petty got his first big pay cheque he went to a car lot. "I never had a car worth a shit in my life" he says. "So I went out to the lot and said I wanna hear all the radios." He found the best radio on the lot in a Silver Camaro. "I just paid him cash and took the car. The guy was standing there looking really dumbfounded. That was a giggle. I was broke the next day."

Need any more proof of TP's status as a genuine rock and roller?

Like in high school. He comes from the swamps. Gainesville, Florida. He grew up on The Beatles and Percy Sledge. He reminds you that Gainesville ain't like Miami. "Miami," he says, "that's just New York on the beach."

In high school he used to get beat up. Crackers would drawl "Ah'm-a gonna *kiyull* yooo."

"There's something about skinny blonde kids," Tom laughs. "That's what makes rock and rollers. You're not gonna get any chicks any other way."

He didn't like getting beat up, so he left. "This guy worrying about my hair touching my ears is gonna teach me something? I failed everything. Never did no homework." Once he was in a band, Mudcrutch, he was through with Florida. "We didn't cop to the barbeque...it's what drove us out. Florida. All them overalls and things."

In Los Angeles, he got a record deal for Mudcrutch, but it didn't work out. He tried solo recording. It didn't work out. He met The Heartbreakers – Mike Campbell, guitars; Stan Lynch, drums; Benmont Tench, piano; Ron Blair, bass. He recorded an album with them, named after the group, in the under-construction studios of SHELTER RECORDS. It came out. The critics marginally preferred another SHELTER act – the melodic Dwight Twilley Band. Neither group sold very well.

Fall 1976: SHELTER released a DJ-only album called 'Live Leg', recorded in Boston. It was the band's sixth gig. They were not pleased.

A couple of months later, things picked up. 'Breakdown' was released as a single and made the Top 40. They entered the studio to make a second album, writing the songs by day, recording them by night. 'You're Gonna Get It', which Tom describes as a "good headphones album", arrived. It confirmed a developing style.

"I don't have an attention span much longer than three minutes," he says. "I don't like any dead space. You can get all you want into three minutes if you use your head. Just don't put no bullshit on it. The word's on the street; everybody wants something new. They don't want their sisters' records...

"I can't sing lyrics I don't believe. I'd sound like an idiot. Nobody ever fools me with some shit they don't believe. And I have a slight aversion to people gettin' too cosmic on me."

"Music now," he said once on the radio, "is fresher, more immediate. It's over quicker." We're talking consistent vision here. That's not easy to find in this day and age.

Tom Petty and The Heartbreakers toured a lot then. "I dig bein' on the road. It's a good way of taking a clear cross-section of what's going on. A quick jaunt through 30 cities does wonders to your brain."

Then it all came to a halt. "I'd kinda like to do another record soon," Tom said in an interview with Stephen Demorest in 1978. That wasn't to be.

By mid-1979 he'd filed for Chapter XI bankruptcy – the right to work out a reorganization of his debts. SHELTER RECORDS had assigned its acts to ABC RECORDS, its distributor. ABC, in turn, sold its record company to MCA Records. Petty had a problem with SHELTER that now had to be taken up with MCA. He was also obligated to this new record company for six albums in five years. He was also said to owe them $600,000; money that would be automatically repaid if he stayed one of MCA's recording acts. MCA said "We have a valid binding contract that we're going to enforce."

A week later both MCA and SHELTER sued Petty for breach of contract, saying, in effect, "our lawyers are tougher than your lawyers. *Nyah, nyah.*"

They were sort of right. Tom had no money left to pay lawyers. His bankruptcy papers were filed and showed assets of $56,000 against debts of $575,000. He had nearly $25,000 in the bank, $113-worth of clothes, $7,000 invested in cars, $4,780 in equipment and $36 in cash. The actions against Petty by MCA and SHELTER were stayed. Petty, in effect, was saying to MCA and SHELTER that his losing a suit was meaningless as he had nothing to lose. Stalemate.

Out of the muck rose BACKSTREET RECORDS, a company run by 26-year-old Danny Bramson, his only recording artists 27-year-old Tom Petty and The Heartbreakers. His distributor? MCA, of course. Tom delivered 'Damn the Torpedoes' and his career was again going full speed ahead. He toured, giving shows that ran on some nuclear fuel, as the deal was being worked out.

The album was released and Petty shot to the top of the charts, the biggest success story of the last year. A lingering bad feeling remained. "I thought I was going to live with lawyers for years," Tom admitted on Robert Klein's radio show. 'Century City' shows a scar. The fact that Petty gives almost no interviews shows another. Public relations for the band consists of unreturned phone calls.

"I don't want no more than to be a working rock and roll band," Tom might justly conclude. He's said it before. "You don't have to get so fuckin' serious about it... My idea of rock and roll is you don't give a fuck about politics because you're listening to records, man. I don't have time for the news." MICHAEL GROSS

RECORDINGS

TOM PETTY AND THE HEARTBREAKERS (Shelter)
YOU'RE GONNA GET IT! (Shelter)
DAMN THE TORPEDOES (Backstreet/MCA)

THIS WAS THE YEAR OF

THE POLICE

It couldn't have happened more dramatically. At the beginning of August The Police, though they had been slowly building a reputation throughout 1979, were still little known on a national scale. By the end of September they were the hottest act in the country.

"The Police are an anachronism in many ways," Sting told NME's Paul Morley. "We've achieved overnight international riches and fame and success and that is a kind of Elvis Presley dream. It shouldn't happen in this day and age."

To assess how what shouldn't happen had actually happened, it might be best to recap: the début Police album, 'Outlandos d'Amour', had been recorded on a shoestring and released in September 1978, an event which only an alert few had noticed. A single, 'Roxanne', made some slight headway, although subsequent ones, 'Can't Stand Losing You', and 'So Lonely', failed to register. The band nevertheless determined to undertake a low-budget tour of the US – in the teeth of strong advice from A&M, their record company, who could see little point in playing gigs that weren't aimed to promote product. Not for the last time the band trusted their own instincts and went ahead. The tour was a success and, as import copies of Roxanne began to sell across the States, A&M were forced to rush-release 'Outlandos d'Amour'.

Both single and album climbed into the Top 30 there, and gradually there was a response at home. 'Roxanne' was reissued and climbed to the fringe of the Top 10, and then the second single, 'Can't Stand Losing You', finally made the impact its undoubted quality warranted. It entered the Top 5 in August.

Simultaneously, 'Quadrophenia' opened in London. It was a film in which Sting had an important part, portraying the charismatic mod-king, Ace Face. Outside commercials, he had had no previous acting experience; it was just, he explained, that he always seemed to pass auditions. (He had also taken a small part in 'The Great Rock 'n' Roll Swindle', though – to his eternal relief – his contribution had been excised at the editing stage.)

So The Police were in an enviable position. Over the period of the existence, they'd attracted a small band of followers (many, no doubt, recruited by Anne Nightingale who'd regularly featured the band's material on her Radio 1 Sunday afternoon request show); to these had now been added a host of recent converts, attracted to the band because of the hit single or the film or both. All that was needed to draw the two factions together was some new material.

Since 'Outlandos d'Amour' was almost a year old, new repertoire was indeed to hand. 'Message In A Bottle' was released in the middle of September, and wasted no time in reaching No.1. By the time the new album, 'Reggatta De

Blanc', had emulated this achievement, The Police were safely established as one of the country's top bands.

Rock music can offer few such felicitous tales. The Police were able to offer a product of exceptional quality at exactly the moment when commercial expectations were focused most sharply. Further, the band was an individual one and defied puritanical categorisation (new wave? old wave? street credibility? who cared?). It was because of this, as well as the personality of Sting, that they were able to attract and retain such a wide audience. Throughout the autumn, the careers of Sting the actor and Sting the Police-man were mutually supportive.

'Quadrophenia' itself was widely over-rated. Its re-creation of mid-60s adolescence and mod culture was very thin indeed; the second half was a particularly sorry mess, redeemed only by Sting. One regretted only that he was under-employed. Not that he saw it that way himself. He said of his role, "It was perfect – just long enough to create a big impression, and not long enough to blow it"; a strangely modest assessment from someone usually bristling with self-confidence.

Sting had an even smaller part in Chris Petit's 'Radio On'. He played a garage mechanic who lived in a caravan, cherishing memories of Eddie Cochran. Accompanying himself on guitar, he sang 'Three Steps To Heaven' (bootleg versions of which will presumably be fetching inflationary sums in the near future). A small part, then, but his appearance certainly helped to reduce the drag on a desperately dreary and pretentious film.

The second single from 'Reggatta De Blanc', 'Walking On The Moon', being somewhat repetitive, didn't quite have the classic structure of its predecessors (and it was accompanied by a video promotional film that was, in certain respects, very similar to *its* forerunner), but that's not to disparage a song that was nevertheless another fine composition. Certainly, it demonstrated how quickly The Police had evolved an immediately distinctive style of their own.

'Walking On The Moon' was released on November 23, and was No. 1 by the beginning of December. The band thus ended a year they had seen in as virtual unknowns as national heroes. They made a brief, highly successful, pre-Christmas UK tour, which took them from Leeds to Lewisham. This final concert was a charity show; money wouldn't buy you a ticket, but a toy for Dr. Barnado's homes would.

This scheme had been devised by London's Capital Radio (which had already employed it to good effect on previous occasions, with acts such as The Carpenters and Cliff Richard), but it dovetailed neatly with The Police's own line of thinking.

Even while the Stalinist wing of the New Wave was denouncing The Police on a variety of counts – their ages, their backgrounds in non-punk bands, their musical abilities, their success – the band themselves were pursuing their own course of non-alignment with traditional practices in the music business. Their rejection of the advice of their US parent company provided an early example of that.

Stewart Copeland and Sting both averred their abhorrence of the exploitative superstar syndrome, and accordingly worked hard to avoid similar traps. In this respect, they'd done their homework. As an undiscovered band, they had always lived within their means, refusing large advances, and were thus never placed in the position of having to compromise their philosophies just to square old debts. (The public, though, were given the opportunity to catch up on old product – 'So Lonely' and their very first single, 'Fall Out', were reissued, before all their 45's were combined in a Six Pack).

They also ensured that ticket prices were pegged to a reasonable maximum (£3 at their 1979 concerts). Equally, Sting declined to be distracted by flattering offers from film producers – of which there were many; Francis Ford Coppola was amongst those turned down. He was, however, tempted by a part in the James Bond movie, 'For Your Eyes Only'.

Like the Lewisham gig, the Police's solitary UK concerts in the first seven months of 1980 – at Newcastle and Milton Keynes – were charity shows. The latter event, christened 'Rockatta De Bowl', was the first major rock event in Britain's first major new town.

In fact, they'd gone to Milton Keynes the pretty way. The opening months of 1980 had been occupied by a world tour – a genuine world tour, one that had more in common with Phineas Fogg than the supercilious superstars who stopped off only at those places which were thought sufficiently rich in commercial potential.

Although they couldn't get a work permit to play in Taiwan, and couldn't find a suitable venue in Manila, The Police did play one date in Hong Kong (where the audience numbered 50; not bad – a year earlier they'd played to just four people in Syracuse, New York). Then, on March 21, they played Bangkok, before moving on to Bombay on March 26.

The idea of gigging in India was one that had tempted other groups, though none had been able – in old fart parlance – to get it together. Even with a hall holding 3,500, their concert there, a rare treat for West India, was a sell-out. They moved on to Athens on March 31, and gave the first-ever major outdoor concert there; it was also the first performance at all by a major rock act since the Rolling Stones had visited in 1967.

With the completion of this tour, the band took a holiday, and then directed their energies to their third album.

The Police? Well, the name's still an awful one, but at least they are pointing rock music in some interesting new directions. Bob Woffinden

RECORDINGS

OUTLANDOS D'AMOUR (A&M)
REGATTA DE BLANC (A&M)

THIS WAS THE YEAR OF

PRETENDERS

Suddenly, there were the Pretenders. They topped the charts soon after Christmas – the first group of the 1980's. 'I'm special', sang Chrissie Hynde, and she was. So was the song, 'Brass In Pocket'; Chrissie subsequently said she could have made one or two improvements in it, but to the public at large it was perfectly conceived and executed as it was. Certainly, its triumph neatly capped what could retrospectively be seen to have been a prudent and purposeful plan of campaign.

The group had apparently been dormant during the autumn. Other than some selected dates at the Marquee in London, they had played no gigs at all, and similarly had released no records.

Those who had followed the group's initially rapid progress understood why. The Pretenders had the confidence to take things at their own pace, and refuse to be dictated to by extraneous pressures. In fact, they finally made it when they did because, well, that was about the time they'd figured on making it.

The group was a foursome, consisting of vocalist-songwriter Chrissie Hynde, who had been born in Akron, Ohio, but who had made England her adopted home, and three English musicians from Hereford, a wholly different background: Pete Farndon (bass), James Honeyman Scott (guitar) and Martin Chambers (drums). They had only assembled in mid-1978, and began playing low-key gigs at the beginning of 1979. A debut single, a version of Ray Davies' 'Stop Your Sobbing', from the first Kinks' album, was issued in March. It was produced by Nick Lowe, to whom Chrissie had despatched some early demo tapes, and became a minor hit.

Even at this stage, however, the band seemed in danger of being suffocated by success, slight as it was. Well-enough aware themselves of their own inchoate stage of development, they tried to inhibit media interest, and resisted opportunities to attempt too much too soon. WEA, the parent organisation behind their record company, REAL, advised a rapid follow-up to 'Stop Your Sobbing' to capitalise on the favourable public reaction, but the group demurred. The second single, 'Kid', was eventually released in the summer, while the band was playing to audiences of varying sizes during a club tour of the UK. Like its predecessor, 'Kid' attained a modest chart placing; unlike 'Sobbing', it was an original composition, and thus gave more hint of the group's capabilities.

While the audiences became larger and more fervent, especially in London, and the music press ever more rapturous in its premature acclaim, the group persisted in their approach and astutely backed off from extravagant praise. They let it be known that they would prefer not to do cover stories; and Chrissie Hynde was punctilious in separating hard fact from fanciful speculation. "All we have had," she was fond of saying, "is a couple of minor hit singles".

Much as he had enthused about the band from the start, Nick Lowe had been unable to produce their album. It was nevertheless a measure of the professional respect already accorded the group that they were able to name their own man as replacement: Chris Thomas, well-known from his associations with Roxy Music and the Sex Pistols.

The recording turned out to be more time-consuming than had originally been anticipated – but the album itself transpired to be one of both unusual length and unusual quality.

'Brass In Pocket', the third single, was released just before Christmas, and 'The Pretenders' album followed in the New Year, on January 4th. A major UK tour, taking in 30 dates in a five-week period, was scheduled to begin on January 29th, and a US tour arranged to follow that.

Thus, by the time the UK tour got underway the band had a No.1 single and album. Now, they had truly arrived, and the critical acclamation could hardly be restrained – the more so since 'The Pretenders' actually is one of the finest debut albums in rock music history. Not that ecomiums were vouchsafed only by regular critics; Roger Daltrey averred that they were the best new band he'd heard since, well, The Who.

No-one could ever imply that the group had been marketed. All that had happened was that they had approached their own career with intuitive perspicacity, and been resolute in backing their own judgment. In doing so, they had probably formulated better marketing strategies than had hitherto existed.

The UK tour, with a major concert at Hammersmith Odeon, was an undoubted success, and by the time they debuted in the US the group were already high in the charts there as well. Despite this, the March/April tour went less smoothly than the UK one.

For a start, it was generally considered that the band – or, rather, their manager, Dave Hill – had made a major *faux pas* in choosing to make a stage entrance to the Ride Of The Valkyries – the section of Wagner's Ring cycle that had been so successfully used on the soundtrack of 'Apocalypse Now'. The choice was therefore both crassly unoriginal and unsuitably bombastic. The headline 'Pretentious Pretenders' (albeit an automatic stand-by for uninspired sub-editors) seemed hardly inappropriate.

Chrissie Hynde then encountered difficulties which had nothing to do with aesthetics. She was jailed overnight in Memphis, after allegedly causing an affray in a local club, and thereafter kicking out the window of a police car. She'd always been a wilful girl, but this behaviour seemed uncharacteristically ill-tempered. "Even Jerry Lee Lewis can't get away with that stuff when he comes to town," commented one of the club's officials.

It would take more than that to impede the Pretenders' progress, however. The band duly received the sometime accolade of appearing on the cover of ROLLING STONE; and, back in Britain, they further established their chart credentials with another Top 10 hit, 'Talk Of The Town'.

With that bout of sustained activity completed, the band reverted to their tactics of avoiding over-exposure, and withdrew to concentrate on completing their second album. It had been a decisive twelve months. In July 1979 they had had "a couple of minor hit singles"; by July 1980 they were safely established as one of the leading new groups, and already had an awful lot to live up to. BOB WOFFINDEN

RECORDINGS

THE PRETENDERS (Sire/Real)

THIS WAS THE YEAR OF

2-TONE

2-Tone was the realisation of the complete record industry dream. It wasn't just a successful record company, or a new style of music, or dress, or dance, or ideology. It was all of these put together; most importantly, it was a movement that set out to entertain.

Strange that the whole thing should originate in Coventry, which until then had been the most unfashionable of urban centres. Perhaps that was the significant point though – bands there felt uninhibited, and free to develop in their own ways, unaffected by the stifling demands of metropolitan fashion.

The Specials, who had once been known as the Coventry Automatics and a host of other names, were a multi-racial band whose music reflected the composition of their personnel, as much as the tastes of their founder, keyboard-player Jerry Dammers. Their music began, it was said, where rock'n'roll met reggae, where punk met ska; the resulting melange was lively, exuberant and highly danceable. That UK popular music and dancing should have enjoyed some kind of symbiotic relationship was something that had long been forgotten. The Specials refreshed our memories.

It was Dammers who masterminded the entire 2-Tone concept. His scheme waxed as The Specials' hopes of winning well-connected friends and influencing business people waned; even one apparent breakthrough when, at Joe Strummer's insistence, they had taken support spot on the 1978 Clash tour, had got them nowhere. So, if they couldn't bang down the front door, they'd have to sneak in the back...

The band pooled their financial reserves to make a single, 'Gangsters', a song Dammers had written when his disillusionment with the industry was at its most intense. Their resources didn't stretch to a B-side, so that was contributed by Neol Davies, another of the pool of local musicians, and attributed to The Selecter, a group which didn't actually exist at the time.

Dammers determined to release 'Gangsters' on The Specials' own 2-TONE label, and accordingly arranged a distribution deal with Rough Trade early in March 1979. An art college graduate, Dammers also designed the distinctive 2-TONE logo himself. The dapper black-and-white figure that was the label's trademark was to emerge as one of the most significant motifs in rock'n'roll history.

With this impetus, the band acquired a manager, Rick Rogers, who arranged a short tour of London clubs, so that the natives of the capital – and, of course, the press – could find out what they'd been missing. With the sudden excitement generated by these gigs, 'Gangsters' thus began to make headway in the charts and The Specials were suddenly surrounded by a stack of suitors. In the end, they plumped for CHRYSALIS, the company which seemed most able to guarantee the band its artistic freedom and the label its commercial independence.

The latter was important because by this time they had decided that the label was more than simply a means to achieving their own recording contract – they also wanted to help other bands. "2-Tone", they claimed, a trifle predictably perhaps, "is a label run by musicians instead of businessmen."

In the event, 'Gangsters' became a Top 5 hit, and Elvis Costello, who had been attracted to the band by their vivacious live performances, offered to produce their debut album.

The Specials tended to audition bands for their label by playing cassettes while on the road. They quickly agreed to a one-single deal with Madness, an all-white North London group; the paths of the two bands had never previously crossed, each had arrived at a similar musical standpoint by taking a different path. Whereas 'Gangsters' had merely included an acknowledgement to Prince Buster, Madness' 'The Prince' was a direct tribute. It duly became the second 2-Tone hit.

Even at this early stage, the magic had already worked. 2-Tone was the hottest sound in town (any town). 2-Tone was fresh, anarchic and irresistible, and – vouchsafed the music press, – 2-Tone was good for you. It was rather as though scientists had just revealed that jam doughnuts and cream cakes was the world's healthiest diet.

Meanwhile, Neol Davies had put together a fully-fledged group under The Selecter banner – one in which he was the only white member. After gaining experience gigging throughout the spring and summer, the band released the first single of their own at the end of September. Another hit.

ENGLISH BEAT/THE BEAT

SELECTER

MADNESS

The three bands then embarked on a nationwide tour throughout the autumn. Thirty-nine of the 40 dates took place in unseated venues (the exception was Manchester Apollo) and there was a top ticket-price of £2.50. The tour inevitably consolidated the burgeoning popularity of the whole movement, and helped to cement the chart success of the bands – both The Specials and Madness had debut albums released in October.

The tour also generated its own small piece of unfavourable publicity, with a fracas at the Hatfield Poly gig on October 27th. Most people there thought this a case of drunken Saturday night rowdyism given a spurious perspective by a press hungry for fresh news angles on the whole circus. In a way, the publicity was simply an inverted tribute to the potency of the movement.

And then, one November Thursday, all three bands appeared on the same edition of *Top Of The Pops*, all promoting their new, chart singles – 'A Message To You, Rudy' (The Specials), 'On My Radio' (The Selecter) and 'One Step Beyond' (Madness).

All bands benefit from such exposure, but the 2-Tone bands were always going to benefit more than most, since they were all so exciting visually. In Chas Smash, Madness had a resident dancer and wild man; for The Specials, Neville Staples supplemented Terry Hall's lead vocals with occasional toasting and energetic dancing, and The Selecter could put before the cameras not only a girl singer in a trilby (Pauline Black), but also a dreadlocked bass guitarist (Charley Anderson).

In fact, Madness were not strictly a 2-Tone band by this time, since they had left after their first single (quite without rancour) and signed to Stiff. They also left the 2-Tone tour half-way through (to fulfil previous commitments) and were replaced by Dexy's Midnight Runners – who in 1980 became yet another West Midlands band to use the 2-Tone connection to great effect.

With the departure of Madness, 2-Tone was left in the hands of The Specials and The Selecter, who were able to pursue their policy of blooding new bands by signing The Beat, a Birmingham band. Although in Dammers' more idealistic moments, he probably visualised 2-TONE as a British TAMLA-MOTOWN or STAX, it would be wrong to attribute to the label a common group identity, or a uniform sound. The Beat merely seemed to fulfil the two basic requirements of 2-Toners – they disseminated lively, danceable music, and they had bags of personality – largely thanks to Saxa, their 50-year-old Jamaican saxophonist, whose presence gave the group an age-range of over 30 years.

By the beginning of 1980, 2-Tone was buoyant indeed. The Beat's version of 'Tears Of A Clown' provided the sixth consecutive Top 10 single, and then The Specials' own live EP, 'Too Much Too Young' went to No.1 like a whirlwind, while the band itself was out of the country. Live EPs, the grey heads of the music industry, might have murmured to each other, just do not reach No.1 in the singles charts.

While another 2-Tone package tour was underway – this one featuring The Selecter, The Beat and The Bodysnatchers (the latest signing – an all-girl ska group), The Specials were gigging in America, and beginning to flag. They admitted that by the end of an arduous tour (supporting The Police on some dates, headlining on others) they were performing without enthusiasm.

Even though the chart success continued through the spring and the summer months, the 2-Tone story began to sour slightly, as success brought its own problems. The whole 2-Tone concept had become larger, more prestigious and powerful than any of them had ever anticipated. (There had at one point been rumours that Elvis Costello would sign to the label – although in the event he retained his association with WEA; even Desmond Dekker, a real name to conjure with, was submitting his tapes for consideration – although he followed Madness to Stiff.

They all saw their little label run by musicians becoming just like those large ones run by businessmen. They complained not that they were inundated with tapes (though they were), but rather that those tapes were tailored to fit what was thought to be the 2-Tone image, and not submitted in a spirit of creative independence – which is what they were looking for.

So had the outfit really become as starchy as the ones it was trying to provide an alternative to? One band, UB40, enjoyed substantial chart success after having been turned down by 2-TONE ("commercially unviable"), recording for the still-small independent, GRADUATE RECORDS of Dudley.

The Greater London Council then scuppered plans for the entire 2-Tone ensemble, past and present, to hold a free concert on Clapham Common to celebrate the first anniversary of the success of Gangsters.

The age of innocence truly seemed to have ended when The Selecter opted to leave the label, advising The Specials to wind it down as it was no longer capable of fulfilling its original objectives. The Specials affirmed their intentions of continuing, immediately filling the gap left by The Selecter's departure by signing a band called The Swinging Cats.

One way and another, it had been quite a year for 2-Tone.
BOB WOFFINDEN

RECORDINGS

MADNESS
One Step Beyond (Sire/Stiff)
THE SPECIALS
The Specials (Chrysalis/Two Tone)
SELECTER
Too Much Pressure (Chrysalis/Two Tone)
ENGLISH BEAT/THE BEAT
I Just Can't Stop It (Sire/Go Feet)

THE SPECIALS

THIS WAS THE YEAR OF

THE JAM

There can be few less likely places from which a supergroup might emerge than the London commuter suburb of Woking, but the Jam, a trio who first broke through during the wave of punk euphoria back in 1976/7, learned their trade playing to the massive indifference of the audiences attending working men's clubs in their home town. Based around the initially Pete Townshend-inspired songwriting of singer/guitarist Paul Weller, the group have achieved the enviable feat (unequalled by any of their original peers) of never missing the British chart with a single release – the score currently stands at ten hits out of ten, with March 1980's 'Going Underground', topping everything by entering the chart at number one, something which had not been accomplished since 1972.

A portion of the Jam's success is undoubtedly due to the close knit relationships between Weller, bass player Bruce Foxton and drummer Rick Buckler, who had known each other for several years before forming the group, and the camaraderie is further underlined by the fact that John Weller, Paul's ex-bricklayer father, has managed the group since they were unknowns. As well as the string of hit 45s, the Jam have released four LPs during their career, the most recent, 'Setting Sons', indicating that Weller, and to a lesser extent, Foxton, have outgrown their initial naiveté and are producing songs with themes of greater maturity than their early frantic thrashes.

At this point, the Jam are without doubt the most popular home produced group, although thus far, they have been unable to make much progress in America, where it is generally felt that their sound, particularly in the live situation, is too unsophisticated and raw for more than cult consumption. JT

RECORDINGS

IN THE CITY (Polydor)
THIS IS THE MODERN WORLD (Polydor)
ALL MOD CONS (Polydor)
SETTING SONS (Polydor)

THE ROCK ARISTOCRACY

BOB DYLAN

In August 1979 a rabbi travelled from Canada to Los Angeles to try to restore Bob Dylan to Judaism. Dylan, hardly surprisingly, sent him away. He was sticking with Jesus.

As usual, Dylan gave no interviews throughout the year, but reports filtered through from his camp tended to be unequivocal; he was indeed behaving in a generous, Christian fashion.

In any case, Dylan's recordings now left no room for doubt. Both 'Slow Train Coming' (August 1979) and 'Saved' (June 1980) were staunch affirmations of his newly-won Christian faith. The former album had been recorded with the assistance of two members of Dire Straits — Mark Knopfler and Pick Withers, while 'Saved' had been made with veteran session-players — Tim Drummond (bass), Spooner Oldham (keyboards), Fred Tackett (guitar) and Jim Keltner (drum). It was this band which backed Dylan on his live performances throughout the year.

He went out on the road in November. Having decided against a lengthy US tour, he instead played 14 consecutive dates in San Francisco. His act was limited to his new, religious material — even at this stage, many of the songs for 'Saved' had already been written. (This was a factor which ultimately facilitated the recording of the album — the songs had already been well-rehearsed in live performance).

Sections of the audience booed him, and demanded "rock 'n' roll". Unperturbed, Dylan persisted with his planned set, and concluded by expressing the hope that everyone had been uplifted.

His dates throughout the new year only confirmed this approach. In January he played 24 dates on the West Coast and in Southern states, and he undertook some Canadian gigs in April. Naturally, his audiences became more responsive as they came to realise what they could now expect of him. Certainly, two factors were crystal-clear. He had alienated many of his long-standing fans — but he had never shrunk from doing that on previous occasions (indeed, it had occasionally seemed a deliberate policy), and was hardly likely to do so now. Also apparent was the strength of his conversion. "I feel like I've been born again," he told his Montreal audience. "It took a lot for me to say that, because I've tried just about everything else."

The inner cover of 'Saved' contained a quote from Jeremiah — "Behold the days come, saith the Lord, that I will make a new covenant with the house of Israel and with the house of Judah" — that clearly reflected his own interests in Messianic Judaism, the point at which the Jewish faith interlinked with Christianity. BW

PETER GABRIEL

Vocalist/lyricist with Genesis from their inception in 1967 until he decided on a solo career in mid-1975, Peter Gabriel has subsequently employed a fairly low profile, only emerging from his presumed domestic solitude occasionally with an album and a handful of live appearances.

Before this year, Gabriel's solo records were eagerly snapped up by Genesis completists, although their number had tended to decrease significantly, as Gabriel moved further away from the safe blueprint of the group into less obviously predictable musical areas, working on his second LP with Robert Fripp as producer. The two year gap between that album and his latest (all three Gabriel LPs rejoice in the stunningly original title of 'Peter Gabriel', which can hardly improve their appeal to record retailers) saw a more lengthy hiatus than usual, when Gabriel's American record company, ATLANTIC, dubbed his third album "commercial suicide", and deleted the artist's name from their roster. The delay in organising a new US deal (his UK company, CHARISMA, insist on simultaneous worldwide release, apparently) slowed the album's arrival even more, which may have turned out to be an advantage — a single taken from it, 'Games Without Frontiers', became Gabriel's biggest hit single, and provided a perfect trailer for the LP, which finally topped the charts in Britain soon after release.

Quite what made the record so much more successful than its precursors is difficult to explain — certainly, it differed from earlier work in being recorded predominantly in Britain using more British musicians than previously (including Paul Weller of the Jam and Kate Bush), while several of its constituent songs were (probably quite unintentionally) rather commercial. The LP has also been recorded with lyics in German (a Japanese version is also planned), and conceivably, Gabriel has hit upon the kind of inspiration and pulse which have enabled David Bowie to remain ahead of the game for so many years. Whether or not Peter Gabriel is interested in being ahead, or even playing in the game, continues to be an enigma. JT

BILLY JOEL

Although Billy Joel has been making records since the late '60s (initially in unsuccessful bands like Hassles and Attila), it wasn't until the last two or three years that he achieved any commercial success. Interestingly, this has coincided, in Britain, at least, with a critical downgrading from cult hero to bland AOR performer, although Joel himself, remembering several hungry years, probably isn't too concerned about his critical fall from grace.

During the first half of the

1970s (undoubtedly rock music's most tedious and uninspiring, and least memorable period), Joel's LPs like 'Piano Man' and 'Streetlife Serenade', although hardly timeless classics, at least threatened that they had been made by a real person who wasn't surrounded by sun-bleached Californian beauties with coke spoons hanging round their necks, but were at least partially concerned with real life rather than cloud cuckoo land. The mood of the time was hardly sympathetic, however, and it wasn't until the release of 'The Stranger', at the end of 1977, that Billy Joel became a familiar sound on FM radio, as well as making some inroads into the British consciousness with hit singles like 'Just The Way You Are', 'Movin' Out' and 'My Life'. Of course, by this time British critics, at least, were prepared to damn Joel with faint praise, conveniently forgetting that he was one of the few lights during the dark years of time previous.

'The Stranger', it is claimed, was the biggest selling LP ever released by CBS, became platinum solely in the state of New York (an infrequent, if not unique occurrence), and transformed Joel from a second division contender to a fully fledged megastar. This status has prevailed ever since, through two more LPs, '52nd Street' and the latest 'Glass House' — at the start of the new decade, Joel, through sheer persistence and hard work, had reached the top of his profession. Even if you don't like him (and I strongly prefer his older work), it would be unjust to denigrate the man's recognition, although it may still be some years (if ever) before he can win similar acclaim in this country. JT

PINK FLOYD

Michael Watts it was who wrote in MELODY MAKER the week before the Floyd's week of concerts at Earls Court "they are unique among supergroups in that for 15 years they have steadily continued to get bigger, while (almost) totally ignoring the (almost) total hostility of the press". Certainly, Elvis Costello's almost total refusal to be interviewed during the last couple of years (presumably an attempt to echo the silence of his infinitely more famous namesake) pales into complete insignificance next to the example of the Pink Floyd, who have steadfastly turned down the opportunity

to speak to anyone from the music press who might know anything about them or be sufficiently interested to criticise them over most, if not all, of the last ten years.

Having commenced their activities in the second half of the '60s as an art school group from Cambridge who relocated in London, piloted by the over-psychedelicised mind of Syd Barrett, the Floyd were just one group among many who entertained their supporters at the semi-legendary UFO club, where tripping was considered almost obligatory. While their peers, like Tyrannosaurus Rex and the Crazy World of Arthur Brown, moved into different fields or oblivion, Syd, Roger Waters, Richard Wright and Nick Mason continued to provide a perfect soundtrack for mind expansion. However, by the time of the 1968 release of 'A Saucerful Of Secrets', Syd Barrett's mental condition had deteriorated to the point where the rest of the band found it impossible to work with him. Another Cambridge musician, guitarist Dave Gilmour, was recruited, since when the group's personnel has remained completely stable.

This has not led to the band becoming prolific — from 1972 to the end of the '70s, only four original albums were released, each of them selling mega-platinum, particularly in America. The longest gap occured between 1976 and December 1979, when the remarkable double LP, 'The Wall', was released, with a simultaneous extracted single, 'Another Brick In The Wall'. For several months, both single and album dominated the world's charts, while the new decade saw the group breaking a three year live performance silence with dates in Britain and America which sold out at some speed.

At this point, the Floyd appear, rather than as a democracy, to be a dictatorship under the direction of Roger Waters. Apparently, the idea of 'The Wall' came from Waters, who felt alienated from his audience to the point where it seemed as though an invisible brick wall had been erected between group and audience. This vision germinated to the point where the live shows during 1980 saw the building of a wall during each set which genuinely separated performers from punters.

The fact that there has been no adverse reaction to this extreme behaviour suggests that, in the minds of the fans, Pink Floyd can do no wrong, and even if it's five years until their next epic, their status will be in no way diminished. A very pleasant situation for a group to find themselves in... JT

BOB SEGER

It was a bittersweet year for Bob Seger. He reached a dizzy new plateau of popularity and simultaneously suffered the near-univerasal castigation of the critics.

Neither was undeserved.

As an apparently unyielding hard-rocker, he had been playing the circuit industriously since cutting his first record in 1965. No-one would have begrudged him his moment as 'Against The Wind', fuelled by the commercial momentum he had so painstakingly built up, rocketed unerringly to the No.1 position in the US album charts.

Hard analysis, however, produced one inescapable conclusion: it was an awful album. Even those of us who tend to be suckers for stupid songs with opening lines like, "A gypsy wind is blowing warm tonight..." registered the total absence of inspiration. It lacked musical fire and lyrical conviction, was bereft of originality and devoid of songs of genuine merit — in contrast to his previous albums, 'Night Moves' (1976) and 'Stranger In Town' (1978), which had been littered with them.

Seger had hitherto been recognised as one of the handfull of rock stars to have made it entirely on his own terms. 'Image' and 'marketing' were concepts which could never have applied to him — yet, here he was, composing to a commercially-proven formula. It was probably this paradox which bestirred the critics to reviews of especial truculence; and no doubt the fact that the potency of the formula was emphasised by the success of Against The Wind only reinforced their feelings.

The album had been made with the assistance, alternately, of Seger's long-serving backing group, the Silver Bullet Band and the Muscle Shoals Rhythm Section; various guest stars — three Eagles (Frey, Henley and Schmit), two Little Feat (Clayton and Payne) and Mac Rebennack also participated. It was difficult to say whether or not the Eagles' presence accounted for the fact that one track, 'Good For Me', bore similarities to 'Take It To The Limit'.

With 'Against The Wind' released on February 29, Seger naturally timed what was described as "an extensive and intensive US tour" to begin three weeks later, thereby ensuring that each could offer maximum promotional benefit to the other.

For the 1980 tour, Craig Frost, the ex-Grand Funk keyboard player, who had not contributed to the album, was added to the basic Silver Bullet Band of David

Teegarden (drums), Alto Reed (saxophones), Chris Campbell (bass) and Drew Abbott (lead guitar); there were also three back-up singers — Shaun Murphy, Kathy Lamb and Colleen Beaton.

Apart from the 'Against The Wind' tracks, one other new Seger recording appeared during the year; 'Nine Tonight' was débuted as the soundtrack of the John Travolta film, 'Urban Cowboy'. BW

THE YEAR'S CHARTS

United States record chart information

United Kingdom record chart information

WEEK ENDING SEPTEMBER 8 1979

US SINGLES

1 MY SHARONA
The Knack-Capitol
2 GOOD TIMES
Chic-Atlantic
3 AFTER THE LOVE HAS GONE
Earth, Wind & Fire-Arc
4 DON'T BRING ME DOWN
Electric Light Orchestra-Jet
5 THE DEVIL WENT DOWN
Charlie Daniels Band-Epic
6 LEAD ME ON
Maxine Nightingale-Windsong
7 SAD EYES
Robert John-EMI
8 MAIN EVENT/FIGHT
Barbra Streisand-Columbia
9 I'LL NEVER LOVE THIS WAY
Dionne Warwick-Arista
10 LONESOME LOSER
Little River Band-Capitol
11 MAMA CAN'T BUY YOU LOVE
Elton John-MCA
12 SAIL ON
Commodores-Motown
13 SUSPICIONS
Eddie Rabbitt-Elektra
14 LET'S GO
Cars-Elektra
15 GOODBYE STRANGER
Supertramp-A & M
16 RISE
Herb Alpert-A & M
17 HEAVEN MUST HAVE SENT
Bonnie Pointer-Motown
18 HOT SUMMER NIGHTS
Night-Planet
19 BAD CASE OF LOVING YOU
Robert Palmer-Island
20 DRIVERS SEAT
Sniff 'N' The Tears-Atlantic

US ALBUMS

1 GET THE KNACK
The Knack-Capitol
2 BREAKFAST IN AMERICA
Supertramp-A & M
3 CANDY-O
Cars-Elektra
4 I AM
Earth, Wind & Fire-Arc
5 MILLION MILE REFLECTION
Charlie Daniels Band-Epic
6 DISCOVERY
Electric Light Orchestra-Jet
7 RISQUE
Chic-Atlantic
8 RUST NEVER SLEEPS
Neil Young-Reprise
9 MIDNIGHT MAGIC
Commodores-Motown
10 IN THROUGH THE OUT DOOR
Led Zeppelin-Swan Song
11 LOW BUDGET
Kinks-Arista
12 REALITY WHAT A CONCEPT
Robin Williams-Casablanca
13 RICKIE LEE JONES
Rickie Lee Jones-Warner Bros.
14 FIRST UNDER THE WIRE
Little River Band-Capitol
15 THE BOSS
Diana Ross-Motown
16 BAD GIRLS
Donna Summer-Casablanca
17 BOMBS AWAY DREAM BABIES
John Stewart-RSO
18 DIONNE
Dionne Warwick-Arista
19 VOULEZ-VOUS
Abba-Epic
20 THE KIDS ARE ALRIGHT
The Who-MCA

UK SINGLES

1 WE DON'T TALK ANYMORE
Cliff Richard-EMI
2 CARS
Gary Numan-Beggars Banquet
3 BANG BANG
B.A. Robertson-Asylum
4 DON'T BRING ME DOWN
Electric Light Orchestra-Jet
5 STREET LIFE
Crusaders-MCA
6 ANGEL EYES
Roxy Music-Polydor
7 IF I SAID YOU HAD
Bellamy Bros.-Warner Bros.
8 JUST WHEN I NEEDED YOU
Randy Vanwarmer-Island
9 LOVE'S GOTTA HOLD ON ME
Dollar-Carrere
10 MONEY
Flying Lizards-Virgin
11 GANGSTERS
Specials-2 Tone
12 GOTTA GO HOME
Boney M-Atlantic/Hansa
13 OOH! WHAT A LIFE
Gibson Brothers-Island
14 DUCHESS
Stranglers-United Artists
15 AFTER THE LOVE HAS GONE
Earth, Wind & Fire-CBS
16 DON'T LIKE MONDAYS
Boomtown Rats-Ensign
17 LOST IN MUSIC
Sister Sledge-Atlantic
18 REGGAE FOR IT NOW
Bill Lovelady-Charisma
19 DUKE OF EARL
Darts-Magnet
20 IS SHE REALLY GOING OUT
Joe Jackson-A & M

UK ALBUMS

1 THE PLEASURE PRINCIPLE
Gary Numan-Beggars Banquet
2 IN THROUGH THE OUT DOOR
Led Zeppelin-Swansong
3 ROCK 'N' ROLL JUVENILE
Cliff Richard-EMI
4 DISCOVERY
Electric Light Orchestra-Jet
5 SLOW TRAIN COMING
Bob Dylan-CBS
6 STRING OF HITS
Shadows-EMI
7 I AM
Earth, Wind & Fire-CBS
8 PARALLEL LINES
Blondie-Chrysalis
9 THE BEST DISCO ALBUM
Various Artists-WEA
10 VOULEZ VOUS
Abba-Epic
11 REPLICAS
Tubeway Army-Beggars Banquet
12 BREAKFAST IN AMERICA
Surpertramp-A & M
13 JOIN HANDS
Siouxsie & The Banshees-Polydor
14 OUTLANDOS D'AMOUR
Police-A & M
15 STREET LIFE
Crusaders-MCA
16 NIGHT OWL
Gerry Rafferty-United Artists
17 MANIFESTO
Roxy Music-Polydor
18 MIDNIGHT MAGIC
Commodores-Motown
19 HIGHWAY TO HELL
AC/DC-Atlantic
20 MORNING DANCE
Spyro Gyra-Infinity

WEEK ENDING SEPTEMBER 15 1979

US SINGLES

1 MY SHARONA
The Knack-Capitol
2 AFTER THE LOVE HAS GONE
Earth, Wind & Fire-Arc
3 THE DEVIL WENT DOWN
Charlie Daniels Band-Epic
4 DON'T BRING ME DOWN
Electric Light Orchestra-Jet
5 LEAD ME ON
Maxine Nightingale-Windsong
6 SAD EYES
Robert John-EMI
7 LONESOME LOSER
Little River Band-Capitol
8 I'LL NEVER LOVE THIS WAY
Dionne Warwick-Arista
9 GOOD TIMES
Chic-Atlantic
10 SAIL ON
Commodores-Motown
11 MAIN EVENT/FIGHT
Barbra Streisand-Columbia
12 RISE
Herb Alpert-A & M
13 MAMA CAN'T BUY YOU LOVE
Elton John-MCA
14 LET'S GO
Cars-Elektra
15 GOODBYE STRANGER
Supertramp-A & M
16 HEAVEN MUST HAVE SENT
Bonnie Pointer-Motown
17 BAD CASE OF LOVING YOU
Robert Palmer-Island
18 DRIVERS SEAT
Sniff 'N' The Tears-Atlantic
19 POP MUZIK
M-Sire
20 BORN TO BE ALIVE
Patrick Hernandez-Columbia

US ALBUMS

1 IN THROUGH THE OUT DOOR
Led Zeppelin-Swansong
2 GET THE KNACK
The Knack-Capitol
3 CANDY-O
Cars-Elektra
4 BREAKFAST IN AMERICA
Supertramp-A & M
5 MILLION MILE REFLECTION
Charlie Daniels Band-Epic
6 RISQUE
Chic-Atlantic
7 I AM
Earth, Wind & Fire-Arc
8 MIDNIGHT MAGIC
Commodores-Motown
9 OFF THE WALL
Michael Jackson-Epic
10 REALITY WHAT A CONCEPT
Robin Williams-Casablanca
11 RUST NEVER SLEEPS
Neil Young-Reprise
12 FIRST UNDER THE WIRE
Little River Band-Capitol
13 DISCOVERY
Electric Light Orchestra-Jet
14 SLOW TRAIN COMING
Bob Dylan-Columbia
15 THE BOSS
Diana Ross-Motown
16 BAD GIRLS
Donna Summer-Casablanca
17 LOW BUDGET
Kinks-Arista
18 DIONNE
Dionne Warwick-Arista
19 STREET LIFE CRUSADERS
Crusaders-MCA
20 RICKIE LEE JONES
Rickie Lee Jones-Warner Bros.

UK SINGLES

1 CARS
Gary Numan-Beggars Banquet
2 WE DON'T TALK ANYMORE
Cliff Richard-EMI
3 DON'T BRING ME DOWN
Electric Light Orchestra-Jet
4 IF I SAID YOU HAD
Bellamy Bros.-Warner Bros.
5 LOVE'S GOTTA HOLD ON ME
Dollar-Carrere
6 STREET LIFE
Crusaders-MCA
7 BANG BANG
B.A. Robertson-Asylum
8 MESSAGE IN A BOTTLE
Police-A & M
9 JUST WHEN I NEEDED YOU
Randy Vanwarmer-Island
10 ANGEL EYES
Roxy Music-Polydor
11 STRUT YOUR FUNKY STUFF
Frantique-Philadelphia
12 REGGAE FOR IT NOW
Bill Lovelady-Charisma
13 GOTTA GO HOME
Boney M-Atlantic/Hansa
14 SAIL ON
Commodores-Motown
15 GONE GONE GONE
Johnny Mathis-CBS
16 CRUEL TO BE KIND
Nick Lowe-Radar
17 MONEY
Flying Lizards-Virgin
18 DUCHESS
Stranglers-United Artists
19 GANGSTERS
Specials-2 Tone
20 LOST IN MUSIC
Sister Sledge-Atlantic

UK ALBUMS

1 OCEANS OF FANTASY
Boney M-Atlantic/Hansa
2 THE PLEASURE PRINCIPLE
Gary Numan-Beggars Banquet
3 ROCK 'N' ROLL JUVENILE
Cliff Richard-EMI
4 DISCOVERY
Electric Light Orchestra-Jet
5 IN THROUGH THE OUT DOOR
Led Zeppelin-Swansong
6 STRING OF HITS
Shadows-EMI
7 SLOW TRAIN COMING
Bob Dylan-CBS
8 REVOLUTION BLUES
Sham 69-Polydor
9 I AM
Earth, Wind & Fire-CBS
10 THE BEST DISCO ALBUM
Various Artists-WEA
11 BREAKFAST IN AMERICA
Supertramp-A & M
12 VOULEZ VOUS
Abba-Epic
13 STREET LIFE
Crusaders-MCA
14 OUTLANDOS D'AMOUR
Police-A & M
15 PARALLEL LINES
Blondie-Chrysalis
16 REPLICAS
Tubeway Army-Beggars Banquet
17 NIGHT OWL
Gerry Rafferty-United Artists
18 JOIN HANDS
Siouxsie & The Banshees-Polydor
19 MANIFESTO
Roxy Music-Polydor
20 MIDNIGHT MAGIC
Commodores-Motown

WEEK ENDING SEPTEMBER 22 1979

US SINGLES

1	**MY SHARONA** *The Knack-Capitol*
2	**AFTER THE LOVE HAS GONE** *Earth, Wind & Fire-Arc*
3	**THE DEVIL WENT DOWN** *Charlie Daniels Band-Epic*
4	**RISE** *Herb Albert-A & M*
5	**LEAD ME ON** *Maxine Nightingale-Windsong*
6	**SAD EYES** *Robert John-EMI*
7	**LONESOME LOSER** *Little River Band-Capitol*
8	**I'LL NEVER LOVE** *Dionne Warwick-Arista*
9	**SAIL ON** *Commodores-Motown*
10	**DON'T BRING ME DOWN** *Electric Light Orchestra-Jet*
11	**GOOD TIMES** *Chic-Atlantic*
12	**DON'T STOP 'TIL YOU GET** *Michael Jackson-Epic*
13	**CRUEL TO BE KIND** *Nick Lowe-Columbia*
14	**HEAVEN MUST HAVE SENT** *Bonnie Pointer-Island*
15	**BAD CASE OF LOVING YOU** *Robert Palmer-Island*
16	**DRIVERS SEAT** *Sniff 'N' The Tears-Atlantic*
17	**POP MUZIK** *M-Sire*
18	**BORN TO BE ALIVE** *Patrick Hernandez-Columbia*
19	**MAIN EVENT/FIGHT** *Barbra Streisand-Columbia*
20	**I DO LOVE YOU** *G.Q.-Arista*

US ALBUMS

1	**IN THROUGH THE OUT DOOR** *Led Zeppelin-Swansong*
2	**GET THE KNACK** *The Knack-Capitol*
3	**SLOW TRAIN COMING** *Bob Dylan-Columbia*
4	**BREAKFAST IN AMERICA** *Supertramp-A & M*
5	**RISQUE** *Chic-Atlantic*
6	**OFF THE WALL** *Michael Jackson-Epic*
7	**MIDNIGHT MAGIC** *Commodores-Motown*
8	**I AM** *Earth, Wind & Fire-Arc*
9	**CANDY-O** *Cars-Elektra*
10	**REALITY WHAT A CONCEPT** *Robin Williams-Casablanca*
11	**RUST NEVER SLEEPS** *Neil Young-Reprise*
12	**FIRST UNDER THE WIRE** *Little River Band-Capitol*
13	**MILLION MILE REFLECTION** *Charlie Daniels Band-Capitol*
14	**DISCOVERY** *Electric Light Orchestra-Jet*
15	**THE BOSS** *Diana Ross-Motown*
16	**LOW BUDGET** *Kinks-Arista*
17	**DIONNE** *Dionne Warwick-Arista*
18	**STREET LIFE** *Crusaders-MCA*
19	**BAD GIRLS** *Donna Summer-Casablanca*
20	**RICKIE LEE JONES** *Rickie Lee Jones-Warner Bros.*

UK SINGLES

1	**MESSAGE IN A BOTTLE** *Police-A & M*
2	**CARS** *Gary Numan-Beggars Banquet*
3	**IF I SAID YOU HAD** *Bellamy Bros.-Warner Bros.*
4	**LOVE'S GOTTA HOLD ON ME** *Dollar-Carrere*
5	**DON'T BRING ME DOWN** *Electric Light Orchestra-Jet*
6	**WE DON'T TALK ANYMORE** *Cliff Richard-EMI*
7	**DREAMING** *Blondie-Chrysalis*
8	**SAIL ON** *Commodores-Motown*
9	**STREET LIFE** *Crusaders-MCA*
10	**STRUT YOUR FUNKY STUFF** *Frantique-Philadelphia*
11	**SINCE YOU BEEN GONE** *Rainbow-Polydor*
12	**WHATEVER YOU WANT** *Status Quo-Vertigo*
13	**TIME FOR ACTION** *Secret Affair-I-Spy*
14	**CRUEL TO BE KIND** *Nick Lowe-Radar*
15	**REGGAE FOR IT NOW** *Bill Lovelady-Charisma*
16	**DON'T STOP TILL YOU GET** *Michael Jackson-Epic*
17	**JUST WHEN I NEEDED YOU** *Randy Vanwarmer-Island*
18	**GONE GONE GONE** *Johnny Mathis-CBS*
19	**BANG BANG** *B.A. Robertson-Asylum*
20	**ANGEL EYES** *Roxy Music-Polydor*

UK ALBUMS

1	**THE PLEASURE PRINCIPLE** *Gary Numan-Beggars Banquet*
2	**OCEANS OF FANTASY** *Boney M-Atlantic/Hansa*
3	**ROCK 'N' ROLL JUVENILE** *Cliff Richard-EMI*
4	**STRING OF HITS** *Shadows-EMI*
5	**DISCOVERY** *Electric Light Orchestra-Jet*
6	**THE RAVEN** *Stranglers-United Artists*
7	**IN THROUGH THE OUT DOOR** *Led Zeppelin-Swansong*
8	**OUTLANDOS D'AMOUR** *Police-A & M*
9	**HERSHAM BOYS** *Sham 69-Polydor*
10	**SLOW TRAIN COMING** *Bob Dylan-CBS*
11	**UNLEASHED IN THE EAST** *Judas Priest-CBS*
12	**I AM** *Earth, Wind & Fire-CBS*
13	**PARALLEL LINES** *Blondie-Chrysalis*
14	**REPLICAS** *Tubeway Army-Beggars Banquet*
15	**MIDNIGHT MAGIC** *Commodores-Motown*
16	**NIGHT OWL** *Gerry Rafferty-United Artists*
17	**DOWN TO EARTH** *Rainbow-Polydor*
18	**STREET LIFE** *Crusaders-MCA*
19	**BREAKFAST IN AMERICA** *Supertramp-A & M*
20	**LAST THE WHOLE NIGHT** *James Last-Polydor*

WEEK ENDING SEPTEMBER 29 1979

US SINGLES

1	**MY SHARONA** *The Knack-Capitol*
2	**SAD EYES** *Robert John-EMI*
3	**RISE** *Herb Alpert-A&M*
4	**DON'T STOP 'TIL YOU GET** *Michael Jackson-Epic*
5	**AFTER THE LOVE HAS GONE** *Earth Wind And Fire-Arc*
6	**LONESOME LOSER** *Little River Band-Capitol*
7	**I'LL NEVER LOVE** *Dionne Warwick-Arista*
8	**SAIL ON** *Commodores-Motown*
9	**THE DEVIL WENT DOWN** *Charlie Daniels Band-Epic*
10	**DON'T BRING ME DOWN** *Electric Light Orchestra-Jet*
11	**POP MUZIK** *M-Sire*
12	**CRUEL TO BE KIND** *Nick Lowe-Columbia*
13	**HEAVEN MUST HAVE SENT** *Bonnie Pointer-Motown*
14	**BAD CASE OF LOVING YOU** *Robert Palmer-Island*
15	**DRIVERS SEAT** *Sniff 'N' The Tears-Atlantic*
16	**BORN TO BE ALIVE** *Patrick Hernandez-Columbia*
17	**LEAD ME ON** *Maxine Nightingale-Windsong*
18	**DIFFERENT WORLDS** *Maureen McGovern-Warner Bros*
19	**DIM ALL THE LIGHTS** *Donna Summer-Casablanca*
20	**I DO LOVE YOU** *G.Q.-Arista*

US ALBUMS

1	**IN THROUGH THE OUT DOOR** *Led Zeppelin-Swan Song*
2	**GET THE KNACK** *The Knack-Capitol*
3	**SLOW TRAIN COMING** *Bob Dylan-Columbia*
4	**BREAKFAST IN AMERICA** *Supertramp-A&M*
5	**RISQUE** *Chic-Atlantic*
6	**OFF THE WALL** *Michael Jackson-Epic*
7	**MIDNIGHT MAGIC** *Commodores-Motown*
8	**I AM** *Earth Wind And Fire-Arc*
9	**CANDY-0** *Cars-Elektra*
10	**FIRST UNDER THE WIRE** *Little River Band-Capitol*
11	**RUST NEVER SLEEPS** *Neil Young-Reprise*
12	**MILLION MILE REFLECTION** *Charlie Daniels Band-Epic*
13	**DISCOVERY** *Electric Light Orchestra-Jet*
14	**THE BOSS** *Diana Ross-Motown*
15	**REALITY WHAT A CONCEPT** *Robin Williams-Casablanca*
16	**DIONNE** *Dionne Warwick-Arista*
17	**LOW BUDGET** *Kinks-Arista*
18	**BAD GIRLS** *Donna Summer-Casablanca*
19	**HEAD GAMES** *Foreigner-Atlantic*
20	**SECRETS** *Robert Palmer-Island*

UK SINGLES

1	**MESSAGE IN A BOTTLE** *Police-A&M*
2	**CARS** *Gary Numan-Beggars Banquet*
3	**IF I SAID YOU HAD** *Bellamy Bros-Warner Bros*
4	**LOVE'S GOT A HOLD ON ME** *Dollar-Carrere*
5	**DON'T BRING ME DOWN** *Electric Light Orchestra-Jet*
6	**WE DON'T TALK ANYMORE** *Cliff Richard-EMI*
7	**DREAMING** *Blondie-Chrysalis*
8	**SAIL ON** *Commodores-Motown*
9	**STREET LIFE** *Crusaders-MCA*
10	**STRUT YOUR FUNKY STUFF** *Frantique-Phil Int*
11	**SINCE YOU'VE BEEN GONE** *Rainbow-Polydor*
12	**WHATEVER YOU WANT** *Status Quo-Vertigo*
13	**TIME FOR ACTION** *Secret Affair-I Spy*
14	**CRUEL TO BE KIND** *Nick Lowe-Radar*
15	**REGGAE FOR IT NOW** *Bill Lovelady-Charisma*
16	**DON'T STOP 'TIL YOU GET** *Michael Jackson-Epic*
17	**JUST WHEN I NEEDED YOU** *Randy Vanwarmer-Island*
18	**GONE GONE GONE** *Johnny Mathis-CBS*
19	**BANG BANG** *B.A. Robertson-Asylum*
20	**ANGEL EYES** *Roxy Music-E.G.*

UK ALBUMS

1	**THE PLEASURE PRINCIPLE** *Gary Numan-Beggars Banquet*
2	**OCEANS OF FANTASY** *Boney M-Atlantic*
3	**ROCK'N'ROLL JUVENILE** *Cliff Richard-EMI*
4	**STRING OF HITS** *Shadows-EMI*
5	**DISCOVERY** *Electric Light Orchestra-Jet*
6	**THE RAVEN** *Stranglers-United Artists*
7	**IN THROUGH THE OUT DOOR** *Led Zeppelin-Swan Song*
8	**OUTLANDOS D'AMOUR** *Police-A&M*
9	**HERSHAM BOYS** *Sham 69-Polydor*
10	**SLOW TRAIN COMING** *Bob Dylan-CBS*
11	**UNLEASHED IN THE EAST** *Judas Priest-CBS*
12	**I AM** *Earth Wind And Fire-CBS*
13	**PARALLEL LINES** *Blondie-Chrysalis*
14	**REPLICAS** *Tubeway Army-Beggars Banquet*
15	**MIDNIGHT MAGIC** *Commodores-Motown*
16	**NIGHT OWL** *Gerry Rafferty-United Artists*
17	**DOWN TO EARTH** *Rainbow-Polydor*
18	**STREET LIFE** *Crusaders-MCA*
19	**BREAKFAST IN AMERICA** *Supertramp-A&M*
20	**LAST THE WHOLE NIGHT** *James Last-Polydor*

WEEK ENDING OCTOBER 6 1979

US SINGLES

1 DON'T STOP 'TILL YOU GET
Michael Jackson-Epic

2 RISE
Herb Alpert-A&M

3 SAD EYES
Robert John-EMI

4 SAIL ON
Commodores-Motown

5 MY SHARONA
The Knack-Capitol

6 I'LL NEVER LOVE
Dionne Warwick-Arista

7 POP MUZIK
M-Sire

8 DIM ALL THE LIGHTS
Donna Summer-Casablanca

9 LONESOME LOSER
Little River Band-Capitol

10 AFTER THE LOVE HAS GONE
Earth, Wind & Fire-Arc

11 HEAVEN MUST HAVE
Bonnie Pointer-Motown

12 CRUEL TO BE KIND
Nick Lowe-Columbia

13 DON'T BRING ME DOWN
ELO-Jet

14 YOU DECORATED MY LIFE
Kenny Rogers-United Artists

15 HEARTACHE TONIGHT
Eagles-Asylum

16 BORN TO BE ALIVE
Patrick Hernandez-Columbia

17 SPOOKY
Atlanta Rhythm Section-Polydor

18 DIRTY WHITE BOY
Foreigner-Atlantic

19 THE BOSS
Diana Ross-Motown

20 LOVIN TOUCHIN SQUEEZIN
Journey-Columbia

US ALBUMS

1 IN THROUGH THE OUT DOOR
Led Zeppelin-Swan Song

2 GET THE KNACK
The Knack-Capitol

3 SLOW TRAIN COMING
Bob Dylan-Columbia

4 MIDNIGHT MAGIC
Commodores-Motown

5 OFF THE WALL
Michael Jackson-Epic

6 BREAKFAST IN AMERICA
Supertramp-A&M

7 RISQUE
Chic-Atlantic

8 HEAD GAMES
Foreigner-Atlantic

9 RUST NEVER SLEEPS
Neil Young-Reprise

10 FIRST UNDER THE WIRE
Little River Band-Capitol

11 I AM
Earth, Wind & Fire-Arc

12 CANDY-O
Cars-Elektra

13 DIONNE
Dionne Warwick-Arista

14 THE BOSS
Diana Ross-Motown

15 MILLION MILE REFLECTION
Charlie Daniels Band-Epic

16 EVE
The Alan Parsons Project-Arista

17 BAD GIRLS
Donna Summer-Casablanca

18 VOLCANO
Jimmy Buffett-MCA

19 SECRETS
Robert Palmer-Island

20 IDENTIFY YOURSELF
O'Jays-PIR

UK SINGLES

1 MESSAGE IN A BOTTLE
Police-A&M

2 VIDEO KILLED THE RADIO
Buggles-Island

3 DREAMING
Blondie-Chrysalis

4 DON'T STOP TILL YOU GET
Michael Jackson-Epic

5 WHATEVER YOU WANT
Status Quo-Vertigo

6 SINCE YOU BEEN GONE
Rainbow-Polydor

7 CARS
Gary Numan-Beggars Banquet

8 IF I SAID YOU HAD
Bellamy Bros.-Warner Bros.

9 ONE DAY AT A TIME
Lena Martell-Pye

10 LIVE ON STAGE
Kate Bush-EMI

11 EVERY DAY HURTS
Sad Cafe-RCA Victor

12 LOVE'S GOTTA HOLD ON ME
Dollar-Carrere

13 SAIL ON
Commodores-Motown

14 CRUEL TO BE KIND
Nick Lowe-Radar

15 YOU CAN DO IT
Al Hudson & The Soul Partners-MCA

16 CHOSEN FEW
Dooleys-GTO

17 STRUT YOUR FUNKY STUFF
Frantique-Philadelphia

18 QUEEN OF HEARTS
Dave Edmunds-Swansong

19 THE PRINCE
Madness-2 Tone

20 DON'T BRING ME DOWN
Electric Light Orchestra-Jet

UK ALBUMS

1 REGATTA DE BLANC
Police-A & M

2 EAT TO THE BEAT
Blondie-Chrysalis

3 THE PLEASURE PRINCIPLE
Gary Numan-Beggars Banquet

4 THE LONG RUN
Eagles-Asylum

5 OCENAS OF FANTASY
Boney M-Atlantic/Hansa

6 THE RAVEN
Stranglers-United Artists

7 DISCOVERY
Electric Light Orchestra-Jet

8 STRING OF HITS
Shadows-EMI

9 OUTLANDOS D' AMOUR
Police-A & M

10 OFF THE WALL
Michael Jackson-Epic

11 PARALLEL LINES
Blondie-Chrysalis

12 UNLEASHED IN THE EAST
Judas Priest-CBS

13 ROCK 'N' ROLL JUVENILE
Cliff Richards-EMI

14 BREAKFAST IN AMERICA
Supertramp-A & M

15 DOWN TO EARTH
Rainbow-Polydor

16 IN THROUGH THE OUT DOOR
Led Zeppelin-Swansong

17 REPLICAS
Tubeway Army-Beggars Banquet

18 I AM
Earth, Wind & Fire-CBS

19 GREAT HITS 1972-1978
10 c.c.-Mercury

20 VOULEZ VOUS
Abba-Epic

WEEK ENDING OCTOBER 13 1979

US SINGLES

1 DON'T STOP 'TILL YOU GET
Michael Jackson-Epic

2 RISE
Herb Alpert-A&M

3 SAD EYES
Robert John-EMI

4 SAIL ON
Commodores-Motown

5 MY SHARONA
The Knack-Capitol

6 I'LL NEVER LOVE
Dionne Warwick-Arista

7 POP MUZIK
M-Sire

8 DIM ALL THE LIGHTS
Donna Summer-Casablanca

9 LONESOME LOSER
Little River Band-Capitol

10 AFTER THE LOVE HAS GONE
Earth, Wind & Fire-Arc

11 HEAVEN MUST HAVE
Bonnie Pointer-Motown

12 CRUEL TO BE KIND
Nick Lowe l-Columbia

13 DON'T BRING ME DOWN
ELO-Jet

14 YOU DECORATED MY LIFE
Kenny Rogers-United Artists

15 HEARTACHE TONIGHT
Eagles-Asylum

16 BORN TO BE ALIVE
Patrick Hernandez-Columbia

17 SPOOKY
Atlanta Rhythm Section-Polydor

18 DIRTY WHITE BOY
Foreigner-Atlantic

19 THE BOSS
Diana Ross-Motown

20 LOVIN TOUCHIN SQUEEZIN
Journey-Columbia

US ALBUMS

1 IN THROUGH THE OUT DOOR
Led Zeppelin-Swan Song

2 GET THE KNACK
The Knack-Capitol

3 SLOW TRAIN COMING
Bob Dylan-Columbia

4 MIDNIGHT MAGIC
Commodores-Motown

5 OFF THE WALL
Michael Jackson-Epic

6 HEAD GAMES
Foreigner-Atlantic

7 BREAKFAST IN AMERICA
Supertramp-A&M

8 RISQUE
Chic-Atlantic

9 RUST NEVER SLEEPS
Neil Young-Reprise

10 FIRST UNDER THE WIRE
Little River Band-Capitol

11 DREAM POLICE
Cheap Trick-Epic

12 CANDY-O
Cars-Elektra

13 DIONNE
Dionne Warwick-Arista

14 EVE
The Alan Parsons Project-Arista

15 VOLCANO
Jimmy Buffett-MCA

16 BAD GIRLS
Donna Summer-Casablanca

17 I AM
Earth, Wind & Fire-Arc

18 IDENTIFY YOURSELF
O'Jays-PIR

19 MILLION MILE REFLECTION
Charlie Daniels Band-Epic

20 KENNY
Kenny Rogers-United Artists

UK SINGLES

1 MESSAGE IN A BOTTLE
Police-A&M

2 VIDEO KILLED THE RADIO
Buggles-Island

3 DREAMING
Blondie-Chrysalis

4 DON'T STOP 'TILL YOU GET
Michael Jackson-Epic

5 WHATEVER YOU WANT
Status Quo-Vertigo

6 SINCE YOU'VE BEEN GONE
Rainbow-Polydor

7 CARS
Gary Numan-Beggars Banquet

8 IF I SAID YOU HAD
Bellamy Bros.- Warner Bros.

9 ONE DAY AT A TIME
Lena Martell-Pye

10 KATE BUSH LIVE ON STAGE
Kate Bush-EMI

11 EVERYDAY HURTS
Sad Cafe-RCA

12 LOVE'S GOT A HOLD ON ME
Dollar-Carrere

13 SAIL ON
Commodores-Motown

14 CRUEL TO BE KIND
Nick Lowe-Radar

15 YOU CAN DO IT
Al Hudson-MCA

16 CHOSEN FEW
Dooleys-GTO

17 STRUT YOUR FUNKY STUFF
Frantique-Phil Int.

18 QUEEN OF HEARTS
Dave Edmunds-Swan Song

19 THE PRINCE
Madness-Two Tone

20 DON'T BRING ME DOWN
Electric Light Orchestra-Jet

UK ALBUMS

1 REGATTA DE BLANC
Police-A&M

2 EAT TO THE BEAT
Blondie-Chrysalis

3 THE PLEASURE PRINCIPLE
Gary Numan-Beggars Banquet

4 THE LONG RUN
Eagles-Asylum

5 OCEANS OF FANTASY
Boney M-Atlantic/Hansa

6 THE RAVEN
Stranglers-United Artists

7 DICOVERY
Electric Light Orchestra-Jet

8 STRING OF HITS
Shadows-EMI

9 OUTLANDOS D'AMOUR
Police-A&M

10 OFF THE WALL
Michael Jackson-Epic

11 PARALLEL LINES
Blondie-Chrysalis

12 UNLEASHED IN THE EAST
Judas Priest-CBS

13 ROCK 'N' ROLL JUVENILE
Cliff Richards-EMI

14 BREAKFAST IN AMERICA
Supertramp-A&M

15 DOWN TO EARTH
Rainbow-Polydor

16 IN THROUGH THE OUT DOOR
Led Zeppelin-Swan Song

17 REPLICAS
Tubeway Army-Beggars Banquet

18 I AM
Earth, Wind & Fire-CBS

19 GREATEST HITS 1972-1978
10 cc-Mercury

20 VOULEZ-VOUS
Abba-Epic

WEEK ENDING OCTOBER 20 1979

US SINGLES

1	**RISE** *Herb Alpert-A&M*
2	**DON'T STOP 'TIL YOU GET** *Michael Jackson-Epic*
3	**POP MUZIK** *M-Sire*
4	**SAIL ON** *Commodores-Motown*
5	**I'LL NEVER LOVE** *Dionne Warwick-Arista*
6	**DIM ALL THE LIGHTS** *Donna Summer-Casablanca*
7	**SAD EYES** *Robert John-EMI*
8	**MY SHARONA** *The Knack-Capitol*
9	**HEARTACHE TONIGHT** *Eagles-Asylum*
10	**STILL** *Commodores-Motown*
11	**HEAVEN MUST HAVE SENT** *Bonnie Pointer-Motown*
12	**YOU DECORATED MY LIFE** *Kenny Rogers-United Artists*
13	**LONESOME LOSER** *Little River Band-Capitol*
14	**DIRTY WHITE BOY** *Foreigner-Atlantic*
15	**TUSK** *Fleetwood Mac-Warner Bros*
16	**PLEASE DON'T GO** *KC & The Sunshine Band-TK*
17	**SPOOKY** *Atlanta Rhythm Section-Polydor*
18	**LOVIN TOUCHIN SQUEEZIN** *Journey-Columbia*
19	**GOOD GIRLS DON'T** *The Knack-Capitol*
20	**HOLD ON** *Ian Gomm-Stiff/Epic*

US ALBUMS

1	**IN THROUGH THE OUT DOOR** *Led Zeppelin-Swan Song*
2	**THE LONG RUN** *Eagles-Asylum*
3	**GET THE KNACK** *The Knack-Capitol*
4	**MIDNIGHT MAGIC** *Commodores-Motown*
5	**OFF THE WALL** *Michael Jackson-Epic*
6	**HEAD GAMES** *Foreigner-Atlantic*
7	**DREAM POLICE** *Cheap Tric-Epic*
8	**SLOW TRAIN COMING** *Bob Dylan-Columbia*
9	**BREAKFAST IN AMERICA** *Supertramp-A&M*
10	**CORNERSTONE** *Styx-A&M*
11	**RUST NEVER SLEEPS** *Neil Young & Crazy Horse-Reprise*
12	**DIONNE** *Dionne Warwick-Arista*
13	**EVE** *The Alan Parson Project-Arista*
14	**RISE** *Herb Alpert-A&M*
15	**VOLCANO** *Jimmy Buffett-MCA*
16	**IDENTIFY YOURSELF** *O'Jays-PIR*
17	**BAD GIRLS** *Donna Summer-Casablanca*
18	**KENNY** *Kenny Rogers-United Artists*
19	**RISQUE** *Chic-Atlantic*
20	**CANDY-O** *Cars-Elektra*

UK SINGLES

1	**VIDEO KILLED THE RADIO** *Buggles-Island*
2	**MESSAGE IN A BOTTLE** *Police-A&M*
3	**DON'T STOP TILL YOU GET** *Michael Jackson-Epic*
4	**DREAMING** *Blondie-Chrysalis*
5	**ONE DAY AT A TIME** *Lena Martell-Pye*
6	**EVERY DAY HURTS** *Sad Cafe-RCA*
7	**SINCE YOU'VE BEEN GONE** *Rainbow-Polydor*
8	**WHATEVER YOU WANT** *Status Quo-Vertigo*
9	**WHEN YOU'RE IN LOVE** *Dr Hook-Capitol*
10	**CHOSEN FEW** *Dooleys-GTO*
11	**QUEEN OF HEARTS** *Dave Edmunds-Swan Song*
12	**OK FRED** *Errol Dunkley-Scope*
13	**KATE BUSH LIVE ON STAGE** *Kate Bush-EMI*
14	**CARS** *Gary Numan-Beggars Banquet*
15	**YOU CAN DO IT** *Al Hudson and Partners-MCA*
16	**IF I SAID YOU HAD** *Bellamy Brothers-Warner Bros.*
17	**BACK OF MY HAND** *Jags-Island*
18	**TUSK** *Fleetwood Mac-Reprise*
19	**CRUEL TO BE KIND** *Nick Lowe-Radar*
20	**THE DEVIL WENT DOWN** *Charlie Daniels Band-Epic*

UK ALBUMS

1	**REGATTA DE BLANC** *Police-A&M*
2	**EAT TO THE BEAT** *Blondie-Chrysalis*
3	**WHATEVER YOU WANT** *Status Quo-Vertigo*
4	**THE LONG RUN** *Eagles-Asylum*
5	**OFF THE WALL** *Michael Jackson-Epic*
6	**THE PLEASURE PRINCIPLE** *Gary Numan-Beggars Banquet*
7	**OCEANS OF FANTASY** *Boney M-WEA*
8	**DISCOVERY** *Electric Light Orchestra-Jet*
9	**OUTLANDOS D'AMOUR** *Police-A&M*
10	**STRING OF HITS** *Shadows-EMI*
11	**DOWN TO EARTH** *Rainbow-Polydor*
12	**PARALLEL LINES** *Blondie-Chrysalis*
13	**IN THROUGH THE OUT DOOR** *Led Zeppelin-Swan Song*
14	**GREATEST HITS 1972-78** *10 CC-Mercury*
15	**THE RAVEN** *Stranglers-United Artists*
16	**THE CRACK** *Ruts-Virgin*
17	**I AM** *Earth Wind & Fire-CBS*
18	**BREAKFAST IN AMERICA** *Supertramp-A&M*
19	**MR UNIVERSE** *Gillian-Acrobat*
20	**SURVIVAL** *Bob Marley and The Wailers-Island*

WEEK ENDING OCTOBER 27 1979

US SINGLES

1	**RISE** *Herb Alpert-A&M*
2	**POP MUZIK** *M-Sire*
3	**DON'T STOP 'TIL YOU GET** *Michael Jackson-Epic*
4	**DIM ALL THE LIGHTS** *Donna Summer-Casablanca*
5	**I'LL NEVER LOVE** *Dionne Warwick-Arista*
6	**SAIL ON** *Commodores-Motown*
7	**HEARTACHE TONIGHT** *Eagles-Asylum*
8	**STILL** *Commodores-Motown*
9	**TUSK** *Fleetwood Mac-Warner Bros*
10	**YOU DECORATED MY LIFE** *Kenny Rogers-United Artists*
11	**SAD EYES** *Robert John-EMI*
12	**DIRTY WHITE BOY** *Foreigner-Atlantic*
13	**PLEASE DON'T GO** *KC & The Sunshine Band-TK*
14	**BABE** *Styx-A&M*
15	**GOOD GIRLS DON'T** *The Knack-Capitol*
16	**LOVIN TOUCHIN SQUEEZIN** *Journey-Columbia*
17	**COME TO ME** *France Joli-Prelude*
18	**HOLD ON** *Ian Gomm-Stiff/Epic*
19	**MY SHARONA** *The Knack-Capitol*
20	**SHIPS** *Barry Manilow-Arista*

US ALBUMS

1	**IN THROUGH THE OUT DOOR** *Led Zeppelin-Swan Song*
2	**THE LONG RUN** *Eagles-Asylum*
3	**MIDNIGHT MAGIC** *Commodores-Motown*
4	**CORNERSTONE** *Styx-A&M*
5	**HEAD GAMES** *Foreigner-Atlantic*
6	**DREAM POLICE** *Cheap Trick-Epic*
7	**GET THE KNACK** *The Knack-Capitol*
8	**RISE** *Herb Alpert-A&M*
9	**OFF THE WALL** *Michael Jackson-Epic*
10	**SLOW TRAIN COMING** *Bob Dylan-Columbia*
11	**BREAKFAST IN AMERICA** *Supertramp-A&M*
12	**RUST NEVER SLEEPS** *Neil Young and Crazy Horse-Reprise*
13	**EVE** *The Alan Parsons Project-Arista*
14	**VOLCANO** *Jimmy Buffet-MCA*
15	**KENNY** *Kenny Rogers-United Artists*
16	**IDENTIFY YOURSELF** *O'Jays-PIR*
17	**ONE VOICE** *Barry Manilow-Arista*
18	**CANDY-O** *Cars-Elektra*
19	**RISQUE** *Chic-Atlantic*
20	**HIGHWAY TO HELL** *AC/DC-Atlantic*

UK SINGLES

1	**ONE DAY AT A TIME** *Lena Martell-Pye*
2	**VIDEO KILLED THE RADIO** *Buggles-Island*
3	**WHEN YOU'RE IN LOVE** *Dr Hook-Capitol*
4	**DON'T STOP 'TIL YOU GET** *Michael Jackson-Epic*
5	**EVERY DAY HURTS** *Sad Cafe-RCA*
6	**GIMME GIMME GIMME** *Abba-Epic*
7	**CHOSEN FEW** *Dooleys-GTO*
8	**MESSAGE IN A BOTTLE** *Police-A&M*
9	**TUSK** *Fleetwood Mac-Reprise*
10	**DREAMING** *Blondie-Chrysalis*
11	**OK FRED** *Errol Dunkley-Scope*
12	**SINCE YOU'VE BEEN GONE** *Rainbow-Polydor*
13	**WHATEVER YOU WANT** *Status Quo-Vertigo*
14	**QUEEN OF HEARTS** *Dave Edmunds-Swan Song*
15	**THE DEVIL WENT DOWN** *Charlie Daniels Band-Epic*
16	**WITHOUT YOU NOW** *Viola Wills-Ariola*
17	**MAKING PLANS FOR NIGEL** *XTC-Virgin*
18	**MY FORBIDDEN LOVER** *Chic-Atlantic*
19	**YOU CAN DO IT** *Al Hudson and Partners-MCA*
20	**BACK OF MY HAND** *Jags-Island*

UK ALBUMS

1	**REGATTA DE BLANC** *Police-A&M*
2	**TUSK** *Fleetwood Mac-Warner Brothers*
3	**EAT TO THE BEAT** *Blondie-Chrysalis*
4	**WHATEVER YOU WANT** *Status Quo-Vertigo*
5	**THE LONG RUN** *Eagles-Asylum*
6	**OFF THE WALL** *Michael Jackson-Epic*
7	**OUTLANDOS D'AMOUR** *Police-A&M*
8	**LENA'S MUSIC ALBUM** *Lena Martell-Pye*
9	**DISCOVERY** *Electric Light Orchestra-Jet*
10	**THE PLEASURE PRINCIPLE** *Gary Numan-Beggars Banquet*
11	**MR UNIVERSE** *Gillan-Acrobat*
12	**BOMBER** *Motorhead-Bronze*
13	**OCEANS OF FANTASY** *Boney M-Atlantic*
14	**DOWN TO EARTH** *Rainbow-Polydor*
15	**STRING OF HITS** *Shadows-EMI*
16	**PARALLEL LINES** *Blondie-Chrysalis*
17	**I AM** *Earth Wind And Fire-CBS*
18	**ONE VOICE** *Barry Manilow-Arista*
19	**THE UNRECORDED** *Jasper Carrott-DJM*
20	**THE RAVEN** *Stranglers-United Artists*

WEEK ENDING NOVEMBER 3 1979

US SINGLES

1	**POP MUZIK** *M-Sire*
2	**HEARTACHE TONIGHT** *Eagles-Asylum*
3	**DIM ALL THE LIGHTS** *Donna Summer-Casablanca*
4	**RISE** *Herb Alpert-A&M*
5	**STILL** *Commodores-Motown*
6	**DON'T STOP 'TIL YOU GET** *Michael Jackson-Epic*
7	**BABE** *Styx-A&M*
8	**TUSK** *Fleetwood Mac-Warner Bros*
9	**YOU DECORATED MY LIFE** *Kenny Rogers-United Artists*
10	**NO MORE TEARS** *Streisand & Summer-Casablanca*
11	**PLEASE DON'T GO** *KC & The Sunshine Band-TK*
12	**DIRTY WHITE BOY** *Foreigner-Atlantic*
13	**I'LL NEVER LOVE THIS WAY** *Dionne Warwick-Arista*
14	**GOOD GIRLS DON'T** *The Knack-Capitol*
15	**SHIPS** *Barry Manilow-Arista*
16	**LOVIN TOUCHIN SQUEEZIN** *Journey-Columbia*
17	**COME TO ME** *France Joli-Prelude*
18	**HOLD ON** *Ian Gomm-Stiff/Epic*
19	**SAIL ON** *Commodores-Motown*
20	**I KNOW A HEARTACHE** *Jennifer Warnes-Arista*

US ALBUMS

1	**THE LONG RUN** *Eagles-Asylum*
2	**IN THROUGH THE OUT DOOR** *Led Zeppelin-Swan Song*
3	**MIDNIGHT MAGIC** *Commodores-Motown*
4	**CORNERSTONE** *Styx-A&M*
5	**HEAD GAMES** *Foreigner-Atlantic*
6	**DREAM POLICE** *Cheap Trick-Epic*
7	**TUSK** *Fleetwood Mac-Warner Bros*
8	**RISE** *Herb Alpert-A&M*
9	**OFF THE WALL** *Michael Jackson-Epic*
10	**GET THE KNACK** *The Knack-Capitol*
11	**SLOW TRAIN COMING** *Bob Dylan-Columbia*
12	**ONE VOICE** *Barry Manilow-Arista*
13	**KENNY** *Kenny Rogers-United Artists*
14	**BREAKFAST IN AMERICA** *Supertramp-A&M*
15	**RUST NEVER SLEEPS** *Neil Young And Crazy Horse-Reprise*
16	**EVE** *The Alan Parsons Project-Arista*
17	**CANDY-O** *Cars-Elektra*
18	**HIGHWAY TO HELL** *AC/DC-Atlantic*
19	**UNCLE JAM WANTS YOU** *Funkadelic-Warner Bros*
20	**DIONNE** *Dionne Warwick-Arista*

UK SINGLES

1	**ONE DAY AT A TIME** *Lena Martell-Pye*
2	**WHEN YOU'RE IN LOVE** *Dr Hook-Capitol*
3	**EVERY DAY HURTS** *Sad Cafe-RCA*
4	**GIMME GIMME GIMME** *Abba-Epic*
5	**VIDEO KILLED THE RADIO** *Buggles-Island*
6	**DON'T STOP TIL YOU GET** *Michael Jackson-Epic*
7	**CHOSEN FEW** *Dooleys-GTO*
8	**TUSK** *Fleetwood Mac-Reprise*
9	**WITHOUT YOU NOW** *Viola Wills-Ariola/Hansa*
10	**CRAZY LITTLE THING** *Queen-EMI*
11	**OK FRED** *Erroll Dunkley-Scope*
12	**MESSAGE IN A BOTTLE** *Police-A&M*
13	**DREAMING** *Blondie-Chrysalis*
14	**THE DEVIL WENT DOWN** *Charlie Daniels Band-Epic*
15	**MY FORBIDDEN LOVER** *Chic-Atlantic*
16	**STAR** *Earth Wind And Fire-CBS*
17	**QUEEN OF HEARTS** *Dave Edmunds-Swan Song*
18	**SINCE YOU'VE BEEN GONE** *Rainbow-Polydor*
19	**WHATEVER YOU WANT** *Status Quo-Vertigo*
20	**SHE'S IN LOVE WITH YOU** *Suzi Quatro-RAK*

UK ALBUMS

1	**REGATTA DE BLANC** *Police-A&M*
2	**TUSK** *Fleetwood Mac-Warner Brothers*
3	**EAT TO THE BEAT** *Blondie-Chrysalis*
4	**SPECIALS** *Specials-2 Tone*
5	**LENA'S MUSIC ALBUM** *Lena Martell-Pye*
6	**OFF THE WALL** *Michael Jackson-Epic*
7	**FINE ART OF SURFACING** *Boomtown Rats-Ensign*
8	**THE LONG RUN** *Eagles-Asylum*
9	**WHATEVER YOU WANT** *Status Quo-Vertigo*
10	**GREATEST HITS 1972-1978** *10 CC-Mercury*
11	**ROCK 'N' ROLLER DISCO** *Various-Ronco*
12	**BOMBER** *Motorhead-Bronze*
13	**I AM** *Earth Wind And Fire-CBS*
14	**PARALLEL LINES** *Blondie-Chrysalis*
15	**DISCOVERY** *Electric Light Orchestra-Jet*
16	**ONE STEP BEYOND** *Madness-Stiff*
17	**OUTLANDOS D'AMOUR** *Police-A&M*
18	**OCEANS OF FANTASY** *Boney M-Atlantic*
19	**STRING OF HITS** *Shadows-EMI*
20	**THE PLEASURE PRINCIPLE** *Gary Numan-Beggars Banquet*

WEEK ENDING NOVEMBER 10 1979

US SINGLES

1	**HEARTACHE TONIGHT** *Eagles-Asylum*
2	**DIM ALL THE LIGHTS** *Donna Summer-Casablanca*
3	**STILL** *Commodores-Motown*
4	**RISE** *Herb Alpert-A&M*
5	**POP MUZIK** *M-Sire*
6	**BABE** *Styx-A&M*
7	**NO MORE TEARS** *Streisand & Summer-Casablanca*
8	**TUSK** *Fleetwood Mac-Warner Bros.*
9	**YOU DECORATED MY LIFE** *Kenny Rogers-United Artists*
10	**PLEASE DON'T GO** *K.C. and the Sunshine Band-TK*
11	**GOOD GIRLS DON'T** *The Knack-Capitol*
12	**DON'T STOP TILL YOU GET** *Michael Jackson-Epic*
13	**SHIPS** *Barry Manilow-Arista*
14	**I'LL NEVER LOVE** *Dionne Warwick-Arista*
15	**DIRTY WHITE BOY** *Foreigner-Atlantic*
16	**COME TO ME** *France Joli-Atlantic*
17	**LOVIN TOUCHIN SQUEEZIN** *Journey-Columbia*
18	**BROKEN HEARTED ME** *Anne Murray-Capitol*
19	**I KNOWN A HEARTACHE** *Jennifer Warnes-Arista*
20	**THIS WON'T LAST** *Michael Johnson-EMI*

US ALBUMS

1	**THE LONG RUN** *Eagles-Asylum*
2	**IN THROUGH THE OUT DOOR** *Led Zeppelin-Swan Song*
3	**CORNERSTONE** *Styx-A&M*
4	**MIDNIGHT MAGIC** *Commodores-Motown*
5	**HEAD GAMES** *Foreigner-Atlantic*
6	**TUSK** *Fleetwood Mac-Warner Bros.*
7	**RISE** *Herb Alpert-A&M*
8	**ON THE ROAD** *Donna Summer-Casablanca*
9	**WET** *Barbara Streisand-Columbia*
10	**ONE VOICE** *Barry Manilow-Arista*
11	**KENNY** *Kenny Rogers-United Artist*
12	**OFF THE WALL** *Michael Jackson-Epic*
13	**GET THE KNACK** *The Knack-Capitol*
14	**BREAKFAST IN AMERICA** *Supertramp-A&M*
15	**DREAM POLICE** *Cheap Trick-Atlantic*
16	**SLOW TRAIN COMING** *Bob Dylan-Columbia*
17	**HIGHWAY TO HELL** *AC/DC-Atlantic*
18	**UNCLE JAM WANTS YOU** *Funkadelic-Warner Bros.*
19	**EVE** *Alan Parsons Project-Arista*
20	**DIONNE** *Dionne Warwick-Arista*

UK SINGLES

1	**ONE DAY AT A TIME** *Lena Martell-Pye*
2	**WHEN YOU'RE IN LOVE** *Dr Hook-Capitol*
3	**GIMME GIMME GIMME** *Abba-Epic*
4	**EVERY DAY HURTS** *Sad Cafe-RCA*
5	**CRAZY LITTLE THING** *Queen-EMI*
6	**TUSK** *Fleetwood Mac-Reprise*
7	**ETON RIFLES** *Jam-Polydor*
8	**WITHOUT YOU NOW** *Viola Wills-Ariola/Hansa*
9	**ON MY RADIO** *Selecter-2 Tone*
10	**STILL** *Commodores-Motown*
11	**SHE'S IN LOVE WITH YOU** *Suzi Quatro-RAK*
12	**VIDEO KILLED THE RADIO** *Buggles-Island*
13	**OK FRED** *Errol Dunkley-Scope*
14	**CHOSEN FEW** *Dooleys-GTO*
15	**THE SPARROW** *Ramblers-Decca*
16	**DON'T STOP TILL YOU GET** *Michael Jackson-Epic*
17	**MAKING PLANS FOR NIGEL** *XTC-Virgin*
18	**STAR** *Earth, Wind And Fire-CBS*
19	**MESSAGE TO YOU RUDY** *Specials/Rico-2Tone*
20	**MY FORBIDDEN LOVER** *Chic-Atlantic*

UK ALBUMS

1	**TUSK** *Fleetwood Mac-Warner Bros*
2	**REGATTA DE BLANC** *Police-A&M*
3	**ROCK 'N' ROLLER DISCO** *Various-Ronco*
4	**LENA'S MUSIC ALBUM** *Lena Martell-Pye*
5	**GREATEST HITS 1972-1978** *10 CC-Mercury*
6	**SPECIALS** *Specials-2 Tone*
7	**GREATEST HITS** *Rod Stewart-Riva*
8	**GREATEST HITS VOL 2** *Abba-Epic*
9	**FINE ART OF SURFACING** *Boomtown Rats-Ensign*
10	**SECRET LIFE OF PLANTS** *Stevie Wonder-Motown*
11	**OFF THE WALL** *Michael Jackson-Epic*
12	**EAT TO THE BEAT** *Blondie-Chrysalis*
13	**THE LONG RUN** *Eagles-Asylum*
14	**OUTLANDOS D'AMOUR** *Police-A&M*
15	**20 GOLDEN GREATS** *Mantovani-Warwick*
16	**ONE STEP BEYOND** *Madness-Stiff*
17	**I AM** *Earth Wind And Fire-CBS*
18	**WHATEVER YOU WANT** *Status Quo-Vertigo*
19	**STRING OF HITS** *Shadows-EMI*
20	**BOMBER** *Motorhead-Bronze*

WEEK ENDING NOVEMBER 17 1979

US SINGLES

1	**STILL** *Commodores-Motown*
2	**DIM ALL THE LIGHTS** *Donna Summer-Casablanca*
3	**NO MORE TEARS** *Streisand & Summer-Columbia/Casablanca*
4	**BABE** *Styx-A&M*
5	**HEARTACHE TONIGHT** *Eagles-Asylum*
6	**RISE** *Herb Alpert-A&M*
7	**YOU DECORATED MY LIFE** *Kenny Rogers-United Artist*
8	**TUSK** *Fleetwood Mac-Warner Bros.*
9	**PLEASE DON'T GO** *K.C. & THe Sunshine Band-TK*
10	**POP MUZIK** *M-Sire*
11	**GOOD GIRLS DON'T** *The Knack-Capitol*
12	**SHIPS** *Barry Manilow-Arista*
13	**DON'T STOP 'TILL YOU GET** *Michael Jackson-Epic*
14	**SEND ONE YOUR LOVE** *Stevie Wonder-Tamla*
15	**COME TO ME** *France Joli-Prelude*
16	**BROKEN HEARTED ME** *Anne Murray-Capitol*
17	**TAKE THE LONG WAY HOME** *Supertramp-A&M*
18	**YOU'RE ONLY LONELY** *J.D. Souther-Columbia*
19	**THIS NIGHT WON'T LAST** *Michael Jackson-EMI America*
20	**IF YOU REMEMBER ME** *Chris Thompson & Night-Planet*

US ALBUMS

1	**THE LONG RUN** *Eagles-Asylum*
2	**IN THROUGH THE OUT DOOR** *Led Zeppelin-Swan Song*
3	**CORNERSTONE** *Styx-A&M*
4	**TUSK** *Fleetwood Mac-Warner Bros.*
5	**ON THE RADIO** *Donna Summer-Casablanca*
6	**MIDNIGHT MAGIC** *Commodores-Motown*
7	**RISE** *Herb Alpert-A&M*
8	**WET** *Barbra Streisand-Columbia*
9	**ONE VOICE** *Barry Manilow-Arista*
10	**GREATEST** *Bee Gees-RSO*
11	**KENNY** *Kenny Rogers-United Artists*
12	**HEAD GAMES** *Foreigner-Atlantic*
13	**BREAKFAST IN AMERICA** *Supertramp-A&M*
14	**OFF THE WALL** *Michael Jackson-Epic*
15	**GET THE KNACK** *The Knack-Capitol*
16	**DREAM POLICE** *Cheap Trick-Epic*
17	**HIGHWAY TO HELL** *AC/DC-Atlantic*
18	**SLOW TRAIN COMING** *Bob Dylan-Columbia*
19	**EAT TO THE BEAT** *Blondie-Chrysalis*
20	**FLIRTIN' WITH DISASTER** *Molly Hatchet-Epic*

UK SINGLES

1	**WHEN YOU'RE IN LOVE** *Dr Hook-Capitol*
2	**ONE DAY AT A TIME** *Lena Martell-Pye*
3	**CRAZY LITTLE THING** *Queen-EMI*
4	**ETON RIFLES** *Jam-Polydor*
5	**STILL** *Commodores-Motown*
6	**GIMME GIMME GIMME** *Abba-Epic*
7	**EVERY DAY HURTS** *Sad Cafe-RCA*
8	**ON MY RADIO** *Selecter-2 Tone*
9	**TUSK** *Fleetwood Mac-Reprise*
10	**MESSAGE TO YOU RUDY** *Specials-2 Tone*
11	**SHE'S IN LOVE WITH YOU** *Suzi Quatro-RAK*
12	**WITHOUT YOU NOW** *Viola Wills-Ariola/Hansa*
13	**THE SPARROW** *Ramblers-Decca*
14	**NO MORE TEARS** *Summer/Streisand-Casablanca/CBS*
15	**KNOCKED IT OFF** *B.A. Robertson-Asylum*
16	**LADIES NIGHT** *Kool and the Gang-Mercury*
17	**RISE** *Herb Alpert-A&M*
18	**HE WAS BEAUTIFUL** *Iris Williams-Columbia*
19	**OK FRED** *Errol Dunkley-Scope*
20	**MAKING PLANS FOR NIGEL** *XTC-Virgin*

UK ALBUMS

1	**GREATEST HITS VOL. 2** *Abba-Epic*
2	**GREATEST HITS** *Rod Stewart-Riva*
3	**TUSK** *Fleetwood Mac-Warner-Bros.*
4	**REGATTA DE BLANC** *Police-A&M*
5	**ROCK 'N' ROLLER DISCO** *Various-Ronco*
6	**GREATEST HITS 1972-1978** *10 cc-Mercury*
7	**20 GOLDEN GREATS** *Diana Ross-Mercury*
8	**SECRET LIFE OF PLANTS** *Stevie Wonder-Motown*
9	**LENA'S MUSIC ALBUM** *Lena Martell-Pye*
10	**SPECIALS** *Specials-2 Tone*
11	**20 GOLDEN GREATS** *Mantovani-Warwick*
12	**OFF THE WALL** *Michael Jackson-Epic*
13	**STRING OF HITS** *Shadows-EMI*
14	**FINE ART OF SURFACING** *Boomtown Rats-Ensign*
15	**ONE STEP BEYOND** *Madness-Stiff*
16	**OUT OF THIS WORLD** *Moody Blues-Deram*
17	**EAT TO THE BEAT** *Blondie-Chrysalis*
18	**OUTLANDOS D'AMOUR** *Police-A&M*
19	**BEE GEES GREATEST HITS** *Bee Gees-RSO*
20	**I AM** *Earth, Wind And Fire-CBS*

WEEK ENDING NOVEMBER 24 1979

US SINGLES

1	**NO MORE TEARS** *Streisand & Summer-Columbia/Casablanca*
2	**BABE** *Styx-A&M*
3	**STILL** *Commodores-Motown*
4	**DIM ALL THE LIGHTS** *Donna Summer-Casablanca*
5	**HEARTACHE TONIGHT** *Eagles-Asylum*
6	**PLEASE DON'T GO** *K.C. And The Sunshine Band-TK*
7	**YOU DECORATED MY LIFE** *Kenny Rogers-United Artist*
8	**SEND ONE YOUR LOVE** *Stevie Wonder-Tamla*
9	**TUSK** *Fleetwood Mac-Warner Bros.*
10	**POP MUZIK** *M-Sire*
11	**SHIPS** *Barry Manilow-Arista*
12	**ESCAPE** *Rupert Holmes-MCA*
13	**YOU'RE ONLY LONELY** *J.D. Souther-Columbia*
14	**BROKEN HEARTED ME** *Anne Murray-Capitol*
15	**TAKE THE LONG WAY HOME** *Supertramp-A&M*
16	**RISE** *Herb Alpert A&M*
17	**LADIES NIGHT** *Kool & The Gang-De-Lite*
18	**IF YOU REMEMBER ME** *Chris Thompson & Night-Planet*
19	**DO THAT TO ME** *The Captain & Tennille-Casablanca*
20	**COOL CHANGE** *Little River Band-Capitol*

US ALBUMS

1	**THE LONG RUN** *Eagles-Asylum*
2	**CORNERSTONE** *Styx-A&M*
3	**IN THROUGH THE OUT DOOR** *Led Zeppelin-Swan Song*
4	**TUSK** *Fleetwood Mac-Warner-Bros.*
5	**ON THE RADIO** *Donna Summer-Casablanca*
6	**SECRET LIFE OF PLANTS** *Stevie Wonder-Motown*
7	**RISE** *Herb Alpert-A&M*
8	**WET** *Barbra Streisand-Columbia*
9	**ONE VOICE** *Barry Manilow-Arista*
10	**GREATEST** *Bee Gees-RSO*
11	**KENNY** *Kenny Rogers-United Artists*
12	**MIDNIGHT MAGIC** *Commodores-Motown*
13	**HEAD GAMES** *Foreigner-Atlantic*
14	**BREAKFAST IN AMERICA** *Supertramp-A&M*
15	**OFF THE WALL** *Michael Jackson-Epic*
16	**GET THE KNACK** *The Knack-Capitol*
17	**EAT TO THE BEAT** *Blondie-Chrysalis*
18	**DREAM POLICE** *Cheap Trick-Epic*
19	**LADIES NIGHT** *Kool And The Gang-De-Lite*
20	**FLIRTIN' WITH DISASTER** *Molly Hatchet-Epic*

UK SINGLES

1	**WHEN YOU'RE IN LOVE** *Dr Hook-Capitol*
2	**CRAZY LITTLE THING** *Queen-EMI*
3	**ETON RIFLES** *Jam-Polydor*
4	**STILL** *Commodores-Motown*
5	**ONE DAY AT A TIME** *Lena Martell-Pye*
6	**NO MORE TEARS** *Summer/Streisand-Casablanca/CBS*
7	**GIMME GIMME GIMME** *Abba-Epic*
8	**KNOCKED IT OFF** *B.A. Robertson-Asylum*
9	**LADIES NIGHT** *Kool and the Gang-Mercury*
10	**ONE STEP BEYOND** *Madness-Stiff*
11	**THE SPARROW** *Ramblers-Decca*
12	**MESSAGE TO YOU RUDY** *Specials-Rico/2 Tone*
13	**RISE** *Herb Alpert-A&M*
14	**SHE'S IN LOVE WITH YOU** *Suzi Quatro-Rak*
15	**COMPLEX** *Gary Numan-Beggars Banquet*
16	**ON MY RADIO** *Selecter-2 Tone*
17	**CONFUSION** *Electric Light Orchestra-Jet*
18	**QUE SERA MI VIDA** *Gibson Brothers-Island*
19	**WITHOUT YOU NOW** *Viola Wills-Ariola/Hansa*
20	**I DON'T WANT TO BE** *Dynasty-Solar*

UK ALBUMS

1	**GREATEST HITS VOL. 2** *Abba-Epic*
2	**20 GOLDEN GREATS** *Diana Ross-Mercury*
3	**GREATEST HITS** *Rod Stewart-Riva*
4	**SETTING SONS** *Jam-Polydor*
5	**REGATTA DE BLANC** *Police-A&M*
6	**TUSK** *Fleetwood Mac-Warner Bros.*
7	**ROCK 'N' ROLLER DISCO** *Various-Ronco*
8	**GREATEST HITS 1972-1978** *10cc-Mercury*
9	**20 GOLDEN GREATS** *Mantovani-Warwick*
10	**LENA'S MUSIC ALBUM** *Lena Martell-Pye*
11	**OFF THE WALL** *Michael Jackson-Epic*
12	**SPECIALS** *Specials-2 Tone*
13	**STRING OF HITS** *Shadows-EMI*
14	**ONE STEP BEYOND** *Madness-Stiff*
15	**OUT OF THIS WORLD** *Moody Blues-Deram*
16	**SECRET LIFE OF PLANTS** *Stevie Wonder-Motown*
17	**BEE GEE'S GREATEST HITS** *Bee Gees-RSO*
18	**OUTLANDOS D'AMOUR** *Police-A&M*
19	**ECHOES OF GOLD** *Adrian Brett-Warwick*
20	**SOMETIMES YOU WIN** *Dr Hook-Captitol*

WEEK ENDING DECEMBER 1 1979

US SINGLES

1	NO MORE TEARS *Streisand & Summer-Columbia/Casablanca*
2	BABE *Styx-A&M*
3	STILL *Commodores-Motown*
4	PLEASE DON'T GO *K.C. & The Sunshine Band*
5	HEARTACHE TONIGHT *Eagles-Asylum*
6	ESCAPE *Rupert Holmes-MCA*
7	SEND YOUR LOVE *Stevie Wonder-Tamla*
8	DIM ALL THE LIGHTS *Donna Summer-Casablanca*
9	SHIPS *Barry Manilow-Arista*
10	POP MUZIK *M-Sire*
11	YOU'RE ONLY LONELY *J.D. Souther-Columbia*
12	BROKEN HEARTED ME *Anne Murray-Capitol*
13	TAKE THE LONG WAY HOME *Supertramp-A&M*
14	DO THAT TO ME *The Captain & Tennille-Casablanca*
15	LADIES NIGHT *Kool & The Gang-De-Lite*
16	TUSK *Fleetwood Mac-Warner Bros.*
17	IF YOU REMEMBER ME *Chris Thompson & Night-Planet*
18	COOL CHANGE *Little River Band-Capitol*
19	YOU DECORATED MY LIFE *Kenny Rogers-United Artists*
20	WE DON'T TALK ANY MORE *Cliff Richard-EMI America*

US ALBUMS

1	THE LONG RUN *Eagles-Asylum*
2	ON THE RADIO *Donna Summer-Casablanca*
3	IN THROUGH THE OUT DOOR *Led Zeppelin-Swan Song*
4	TUSK *Fleetwood Mac-Warner Bros.*
5	SECRET LIFE OF PLANTS *Stevie Wonder-Motown*
6	RISE *Herb Alpert-A&M*
7	CORNERSTONE *Styx-A&M*
8	WET *Barbra Streisand-Columbia*
9	ONE VOICE *Barry Manilow-Arista*
10	GREATEST *Bee Gees-RSO*
11	OFF THE WALL *Michael Jackson-Epic*
12	MIDNIGHT MAGIC *Commodores-Motown*
13	KENNY *Kenny Rogers-United Artists*
14	BREAKFAST IN AMERICA *Supertramp-A&M*
15	LADIES NIGHT *Kool And The Gang-De-Lite*
16	DAMN THE TORPEDOES *Tom Petty-Backstreet*
17	EAT TO THE BEAT *Blondie-Chrysalis*
18	HEAD GAMES *Foreigner-Atlantic*
19	FLIRTIN' WITH DISASTER *Molly Hatchet-Epic*
20	DREAM POLICE *Cheap Trick-Epic*

UK SINGLES

1	WHEN YOU ARE IN LOVE *Dr Hook-Capitol*
2	CRAZY LITTLE THING *Queen-EMI*
3	NO MORE TEARS *Summer/Streisand-Casablanca/CBS*
4	STILL *Commodores-Motown*
5	WALKING ON THE MOON *Police-A&M*
6	COMPLEX *Gary Numan-Beggars Banquet*
7	ONE STEP BEYOND *Madness-Stiff*
8	CONFUSION *ELO-Jet*
9	ETON RIFLES *Jam-Polydor*
10	KNOCKED IT OFF *B.A. Robertson-Asylum*
11	LADIES NIGHT *Kool And The Gang-Mercury*
12	QUE SERA MI VIDA *Gibson Brothers-Island*
13	DIAMOND SMILES *Boomtown Rats-Ensign*
14	ROCK DON'T STOP *Isley Brothers-Epic*
15	THE SPARROW *Ramblers-Decca*
16	ONE DAY AT A TIME *Lena Martell-Pye*
17	A MESSAGE TO YOU RUDY *Specials-2 Tone*
18	ROCKABILLY REBEL *Matchbox-Magnet*
19	GIMME GIMME GIMME *Abba-Epic*
20	RISE *Herb Alpert-A&M*

UK ALBUMS

1	GREATEST HITS VOL 2 *Abba-Epic*
2	GREATEST HITS *Rod Stewart-Riva*
3	20 GOLDEN GREATS *Diana Ross-Mercury*
4	REGATTA DE BLANC *Police-A&M*
5	LOVE SONGS *Elvis Presley-K-Tel*
6	SETTING SONGS *Jam-Polydor*
7	ROCK 'N' ROLLER DISCO *Various-Ronco*
8	GREATEST HITS 1972-1978 *10cc-Mercury*
9	TUSK *Fleetwood Mac-Warner Bros.*
10	20 GOLDEN GREATS *Mantovani-Warwick*
11	LENA'S MUSIC ALBUM *Lena Martell-Pye*
12	OFF THE WALL *Michael Jackson-Epic*
13	STRING OF HITS *Shadows-EMI*
14	ELO'S GREATEST HITS *ELO-Jet*
15	ONE STEP BYOND *Madness-Stiff*
16	SPECIALS *Specials-Stiff*
17	OUT OF THIS WORLD *Moody Blues-Deram*
18	SOMETIMES YOU WIN *Dr Hook-Capitol*
19	CREPES AND DRAPES *Showaddywaddy-Arista*
20	EAT TO THE BEAT *Blondie-Chrysalis*

WEEK ENDING DECEMBER 8 1979

US SINGLES

1	BABE *Styx-A&M*
2	NO MORE TEARS *Streisand & Summer-Columbia/Casablanca*
3	STILL *Commodores-Motown*
4	PLEASE DON'T GO *K.C. & The Sunshine Band-TK*
5	ESCAPE *Rupert Holmes-MCA*
6	SEND ONE YOUR LOVE *Stevie Wonder-Tamla*
7	HEARTACHE TONIGHT *Eagles-Asylum*
8	YOU'RE ONLY LONELY *J.D. Souther-Columbia*
9	SHIPS *Barry Manilow-Arista*
10	DO THAT TO ME *The Captain & Tennille-Casablanca*
11	TAKE THE LONG WAY HOME *Supertramp-A&M*
12	BROKEN HEARTED ME *Anne Murray-Capitol*
13	LADIES NIGHT *Kool & The Gang-De-Lite*
14	POP MUZIK *M-Sire*
15	COOL CHANGE *Little River Band-Capitol*
16	HALF THE WAY *Crystal Gayle-Columbia*
17	WE DON'T TALK ANYMORE *Cliff Richard-EMI America*
18	HEAD GAMES *Foreigner-Atlantic*
19	DIM ALL THE LIGHTS *Donna Summer-Casablanca*
20	BETTER LOVE NEXT TIME *Dr. Hook-Capitol*

US ALBUMS

1	THE LONG RUN *Eagles-Asylum*
2	ON THE RADIO-ONE & TWO *Donna Summer-Casablanca*
3	CORNERSTONE *Styx-A&M*
4	SECRET LIFE OF PLANTS *Stevie Wonder-Tamla*
5	IN THROUGH THE OUT DOOR *Led Zeppelin-Swan Song*
6	GREATEST *Bee Gees-RSO*
7	WET *Barbara Streisand-Columbia*
8	TUSK *Fleetwood Mac-Warner Bros*
9	RISE *Herb Alpert-A&M*
10	DAMN THE TORPEDOES *Tom Petty & Heartbreakers-Backstreet*
11	OFF THE WALL *Michael Jackson-Epic*
12	MIDNIGHT MAGIC *Commodores-Motown*
13	ONE VOICE *Barry Manilow-Arista*
14	BREAKFAST IN AMERICA *Supertramp-A&M*
15	LADIES KNIGHT *Kool & The Gang-De-Lite*
16	HEAD GAMES *Foreigner-Atlantic*
17	EAT TO THE BEAT *Blondie-Chrysalis*
18	KENNY *Kenny Rogers-United Artists*
19	FLIRTIN' WITH DISASTER *Molly Hatchet-Epic*
20	MASTERJAM *Rufus & Chaka-MCA*

UK SINGLES

1	WALKING ON THE MOON *Police-A&M*
2	ANOTHER BRICK *Pink Floyd-Harvest*
3	NO MORE TEARS *Summer/Streisand-Casablanca*
4	WHEN YOU'RE IN LOVE *Dr Hook-Capitol*
5	QUE SERA MI VIDA *Gibson Brothers-Island*
6	I ONLY WANT TO BE *Tourists-Logo*
7	CRAZY LITTLE THING *Queen-EMI*
8	COMPLEX *Gary Numan-Beggars Banquet*
9	CONFUSION *Electric Light Orchestra-Jet*
10	ONE STEP BEYOND *Madness-Stiff*
11	STILL *Commodores-Motown*
12	RAPPER'S DELIGHT *Sugar Hill Gang-Sugar Hill*
13	ETON RIFLES *Jam-Polydor*
14	NIGHTS IN WHITE SATIN *Moody Blues-Dream*
15	DIAMOND SMILES *Boomtown Rats-Ensign*
16	UNION CITY BLUE *Blondie-Chrysalis*
17	IT'S A DISCO NIGHT *Isley Brothers-Epic*
18	LADIES NIGHT *Kool & The Gang-Mercury*
19	THE SPARROW *Ramblers-Decca*
20	KNOCKED IT OFF *B.A. Robertson-Asylum*

UK ALBUMS

1	GREATEST HITS *Rod Stewart-Riva*
2	GREATEST HITS VOL 2 *Abba-Epic*
3	THE WALL *Pink Floyd-Harvest*
4	20 GOLDEN GREATS *Diana Ross-Mercury*
5	REGATTA DE BLANC *Police-A&M*
6	LOVE SONGS *Elvis Presley-K Tel*
7	ELO'S GREATEST HITS *ELO-Jet*
8	CREPES AND DRAPES *Showaddywaddy-Arista*
9	ROCK'N'ROLLER DISCO *Various-Ronco*
10	LENA'S MUSIC ALBUM *Lena Martell-Pye*
11	SETTING SONS *Jam-Polydor*
12	NIGHT MOVES *Various-K Tel*
13	OFF THE WALL *Michael Jackson-Epic*
14	EAT TO THE BEAT *Blondie-Chrysalis*
15	TUSK *Fleetwood Mac-Warner Bros*
16	GREATEST HITS 1972-1978 *10CC-Mercury*
17	20 GOLDEN GREATS *Mantovani-Warwick*
18	METAL BOX *Public Image Ltd-Virgin*
19	ONE STEP BEYOND *Madness-Stiff*
20	SPECIALS *Specials-Chrysalis*

WEEK ENDING DECEMBER 15 1979

US SINGLES

1	BABE *Styx-A&M*
2	STILL *Commodores-Motown*
3	PLEASE DON'T GO *K.C. & The Sunshine Band-TK*
4	ESCAPE *Rupert Holmes-MCA*
5	SEND ONE YOUR LOVE *Stevie Wonder-Tamla*
6	NO MORE TEARS *Streisand/Summer-Columbia/Casablanca*
7	YOU'RE ONLY LONELY *J.D. Souther-Columbia*
8	DO THAT TO ME *The Captain & Tenille-Casablanca*
9	HEARTACHE TONIGHT *Eagles-Asylum*
10	TAKE THE LONG WAY HOME *Supertramp-A&M*
11	LADIES NIGHT *Kool & The Gang-De-Lite*
12	ROCK WITH YOU *Michael Jackson-Epic*
13	COOL CHANGE *Little River Band-Capitol*
14	WE DON'T TALK ANYMORE *Cliff Richard-EMI America*
15	HALF THE WAY *Crystal Gayle-Columbia*
16	HEAD GAMES *Foreigner-Atlantic*
17	SHIPS *Barry Manilow-Arista*
18	BETTER LOVE NEXT TIME *Dr. Hook-Capitol*
19	THE LONG RUN *Eagles-Asylum*
20	JANE *Jefferson Starship-Grunt*

US ALBUMS

1	THE LONG RUN *Eagles-Asylum*
2	ON THE RADIO *Donna Summer-Casablanca*
3	CORNERSTONE *Styx-A&M*
4	SECRET LIFE OF PLANTS *Stevie Wonder-Motown*
5	GREATEST *Bee Gees-RSO*
6	IN THROUGH THE OUT DOOR *Led Zeppelin-Swan Song*
7	WET *Barbara Streisand-Columbia*
8	TUSK *Fleetwood Mac-Warner Bros*
9	DAMN THE TORPEDOES *Tom Petty & Heartbreakers-Backstreet*
10	MIDNIGHT MAGIC *Commodores-Motown*
11	OFF THE WALL *Michael Jackson-Epic*
12	RISE *Herb Alpert-A&M*
13	LADIES NIGHT *Kool And The Gang-De-Lite*
14	HEAD GAMES *Foreigner-Atlantic*
15	MASTERJAM *Rufus And Chaka-MCA*
16	ONE VOICE *Barry Manilow-Arista*
17	FREEDOM AT POINT ZERO *Jefferson Starship-Grunt*
18	KEEP THE FIRE *Kenny Loggins-Columbia*
19	PHOENIX *Dan Fogelberg-Full Moon/Epic*
20	BREAKFAST IN AMERICA *Supertramp-A&M*

UK SINGLES

1	ANOTHER BRICK *Pink Floyd-Harvest*
2	WALKING ON THE MOON *Police-A&M*
3	RAPPERS DELIGHT *Sugarhill Gang-Sugar Hill*
4	I ONLY WANT TO BE *Tourists-Logo*
5	NO MORE TEARS *Summer/Streisand-Casablanca/CBS*
6	QUE SERA MI VIDA *Gibson Brothers-Island*
7	OFF THE WALL *Michael Jackson-Epic*
8	WHEN YOU'RE IN LOVE *Dr Hook-Capitol*
9	ONE STEP BEYOND *Madness-Stiff*
10	MY SIMPLE HEART *Three Degrees-Ariola*
11	CONFUSION *ELO-Jet*
12	CRAZY LITTLE THING *Queen-EMI*
13	UNION CITY BLUE *Blondie-Chrysalis*
14	NIGHTS IN WHITE SATIN *Moody Blues-Chrysalis*
15	COMPLEX *Gary Numan-Beggars Banquet*
16	DIAMOND SMILES *Boomtown Rats-Ensign*
17	STILL *Commodores-Motown*
18	LIVING ON AN ISLAND *Status Quo-Vertigo*
19	ROCKABILLY REBEL *Matchbox-Magnet*
20	WONDERFUL CHRISTMAS *Paul McCartney-Parlophone*

UK ALBUMS

1	GREATEST HITS *Rod Stewart-Riva*
2	GREATEST HITS VOL 2 *Abba-Epic*
3	THE WALL *Pink Floyd-Harvest*
4	REGGATTA DE BLANC *Police-A&M*
5	LOVE SONGS *Elvis Presley-K-Tel*
6	20 GOLDEN GREATS *Diana Ross-Mercury*
7	PEACE IN THE VALLEY *Various-Ronco*
8	CREPES AND DRAPES *Showaddywaddy-Arista*
9	ELO'S GREATEST HITS *ELO-Jet*
10	NIGHT MOVES *Various-K-Tel*
11	20 GREATEST HITS *Hot Chocolate-RAK*
12	SINGLES ALBUM *Kenny Rogers-United Artists*
13	LENA'S MUSIC ALBUM *Lena Martell-Pye*
14	ROCK'N'ROLLER DISCO *Various-Ronco*
15	OFF THE WALL *Michael Jackson-Epic*
16	TRANQUILITY *Mary O'Hara-Warwick*
17	EAT TO THE BEAT *Blondie-Chrysalis*
18	SETTING SONS *Jam-Polydor*
19	TUSK *Fleetwood Mac-Warner Bros*
20	ONE STEP BEYOND *Madness-Stiff*

WEEK ENDING DECEMBER 22 1979

US SINGLES

1	ESCAPE *Rupert Holmes-MCA*
2	PLEASE DON'T GO *K.C. & The Sunshine Band-TK*
3	BABE *Styx-A&M*
4	SEND ONE YOUR LOVE *Stevie Wonder-Tamla*
5	STILL *Commodores-Motown*
6	DO THAT TO ME *The Captain & Tennille-Casablanca*
7	YOU'RE ONLY LONELY *J.D. Souther-Columbia*
8	NO MORE TEARS *Streisand/Summer-Columbia/Casablanca*
9	LADIES NIGHT *Kool & The Gang-De-Lite*
10	TAKE THE LONG WAY HOME *Supertramp-A&M*
11	ROCK WITH YOU *Michael Jackson-Epic*
12	COOL CHANGE *Little River Band-Capitol*
13	WE DON'T TALK ANYMORE *Cliff Richard-EMI America*
14	HEAD GAMES *Foreigner-Atlantic*
15	CRUISIN' *Smokey Robinson*
16	BETTER LOVE NEXT TIME *Dr. Hook-Capitol*
17	THE LONG RUN *Eagles-Asylum*
18	JANE *Jefferson Starship-Grunt*
19	I WANT YOU TONIGHT *Pablo Cruise-A&M*
20	HEARTACHE TONIGHT *Eagles-Asylum*

US ALBUMS

1	THE LONG RUN *Eagles-Asylum*
2	ON THE RADIO *Donna Summer-Casablanca*
3	CORNERSTONE *Styx-A&M*
4	SECRET LIFE OF PLANTS *Stevie Wonder-Motown*
5	GREATEST HITS *Bee Gees-RSO*
6	IN THROUGH THE OUT DOOR *Led Zeppelin-Swan Song*
7	WET *Barbra Streisand-Columbia*
8	TUSK *Fleetwood Mac-Warner Bros*
9	DAMN THE TORPEDOES *Tom Petty & Heartbreakers-Backstreet*
10	MIDNIGHT MAGIC *Commodores-Motown*
11	OFF THE WALL *Michael Jackson-Epic*
12	RISE *Herb Alpert-A&M*
13	LADIES NIGHT *Kool And The Gang-De-Lite*
14	HEAD GAMES *Foreigner-Atlantic*
15	MASTERJAM *Rufus And Chaka-MCA*
16	ONCE VOICE *Barry Manilow-Arista*
17	FREEDOM AT POINT ZERO *Jefferson Starship-Grunt*
18	KEEP THE FIRE *Kenny Loggins-Columbia*
19	PHOENIX *Dan Fogelberg-Full Moon/Epic*
20	BREAKFAST IN AMERICA *Supertramp-A&M*

UK SINGLES

1	ANOTHER BRICK *Pink Floyd-Harvest*
2	I HAVE A DREAM *Abba-Epic*
3	WALKING ON THE MOON *Police-A&M*
4	DAY TRIP TO BANGOR *Fiddler's Dram-Dingles*
5	I ONLY WANT TO BE *Tourists-Logo*
6	RAPPER'S DELIGHT *Sugarhill Gang-Sugar Hill*
7	WONDERFUL CHRISTMAS *Paul McCartney-Parlophone*
8	QUE SERA MI VIDA *Gibson Brothers-Island*
9	MY SIMPLE HEART *Three Degrees-Ariola*
10	BRASS IN POCKET *Pretenders-Real*
11	NO MORE TEARS *Donna Summer-Casablanca/CBS*
12	OFF THE WALL *Michael Jackson-Epic*
13	JOHN I'M ONLY DANCING *David Bowie-RCA*
14	UNION CITY BLUE *Blondie-Chrysalis*
15	CONFUSION *Electric Light Orchestra-Jet*
16	LIVING ON AN ISLAND *Status Quo-Vertigo*
17	IS IT LOVE YOU'RE AFTER *Rose Royce-Whitfield*
18	NIGHTS IN WHITE SATIN *Moody Blues-Deram*
19	ONE STEP BEYOND *Madness-Stiff*
20	TEARS OF A CLOWN *The Beat-2 Tone*

UK ALBUMS

1	GREATEST HITS *Rod Stewart-Riva*
2	GREATEST HITS VOL 2 *Abba-Epic*
3	THE WALL *Pink Floyd-Harvest*
4	REGATTA DE BLANC *Police-A&M*
5	LOVE SONGS *Elvis Presley-K-Tel*
6	PEACE IN THE VALLEY *Various-Ronco*
7	HOTTEST HITS *Hot Chocolate-Rak*
8	20 GOLDEN GREATS *Diana Ross-Mercury*
9	LONDON CALLING *Clash-CBS*
10	ELO'S GREATEST HITS *ELO-Jet*
11	OFF THE WALL *Michael Jackson-Epic*
12	TRANQUILITY *Mary O'Hara-Warwick*
13	ALL ABOARD *Various-EMI*
14	NIGHT MOVES *Various-K-Tel*
15	SINGLES ALBUM *Kenny Rogers-United Artists*
16	CREPES AND DRAPES *Showaddywaddy-Arista*
17	EAT TO THE BEAT *Blondie-Chrysalis*
18	LENA'S MUSIC ALBUM *Lena Martell-Pye*
19	ROCK'N'ROLLER DISCO *Various-Ronco*
20	TUSK *Fleetwood Mac-Warner Brothers*

WEEK ENDING JANUARY 5 1980

US SINGLES

1	**PLEASE DON'T GO** *K.C. And The Sunshine Band-TK*
2	**ESCAPE** *Rupert Holmes-MCA*
3	**ROCK WITH YOU** *Michael Jackson-Epic*
4	**SEND ONE YOUR LOVE** *Stevie Wonder-Tamla*
5	**DO THAT TO ME** *The Captain & Tennille-Casablanca*
6	**BABE** *Styx-A&M*
7	**STILL** *Commodores-Motown*
8	**COWARD OF THE COUNTY** *Kenny Rogers-United Artists*
9	**LADIES NIGHT** *Kool & The Gang-De Lite*
10	**WE DON'T TALK ANYMORE** *Cliff Richard-EMI America*
11	**COOL CHANGE** *Little River Band-Capitol*
12	**CRUISIN'** *Smokey Robinson-Tamla*
13	**THE LONG RUN** *Eagles-Asylum*
14	**HEAD GAMES** *Foreigner-Atlantic*
15	**BETTER LOVE NEXT TIME** *Dr. Hook-Capitol*
16	**JANE** *Jefferson Starship-Grunt*
17	**I WANNA BE YOUR LOVER** *Prince-Warner Bros*
18	**THIS IS IT** *Kenny Loggins-Columbia*
19	**I WANT YOU TONIGHT** *Pablo Cruise-A&M*
20	**YOU'RE ONLY LONELY** *J.D. Souther-Columbia*

US ALBUMS

1	**ON THE RADIO** *Donna Summer-Casablanca*
2	**GREATEST** *Bee Gees-RSO*
3	**CORNERSTONE** *Styx-A&M*
4	**THE SECRET LIFE OF PLANTS** *Stevie Wonder-Motown*
5	**THE LONG RUN** *Eagles-Asylum*
6	**IN THROUGH THE DOOR** *Led Zeppelin-Swan Song*
7	**THE WALL** *Pink Floyd-Columbia*
8	**DAMN THE TORPEDOES** *Tom Petty & Heartbreakers-Backstreet*
9	**TUSK** *Fleetwood Mac-Warner Brothers*
10	**OFF THE WALL** *Michael Jackson-Epic*
11	**HEAD GAMES** *Foreigner-Atlantic*
12	**PHOENIX** *Dan Fogelberg-Full Moon-Epic*
13	**FREEDOM AT POINT ZERO** *Jefferson Starship-Grunt*
14	**MASTERJAM** *Rufus And Chaka-MCA*
15	**KENNY** *Kenny Rogers-United Artists*
16	**NIGHT IN THE RUTS** *Aerosmith-Columbia*
17	**KEEP THE FIRE** *Kenny Loggins-Columbia*
18	**WET** *Barbara Streisand-Columbia*
19	**MIDNIGHT MAGIC** *Commodores-Motown*
20	**LIVE RUST** *Neil Young & Crazy Horse-Warner Bros*

UK SINGLES

1	**ANOTHER BRICK** *Pink Floyd-Harvest*
2	**I HAVE A DREAM** *Abba-Epic*
3	**DAY TRIP TO BANGOR** *Fiddler's Dram-Dingles*
4	**I ONLY WANT TO BE** *Tourists-Logo*
5	**BRASS IN POCKET** *Pretenders-Real*
6	**WONDERFUL CHRISTMAS** *Paul McCartney-Parlophone*
7	**RAPPER'S DELIGHT** *Sugarhill Gang-Sugarhill*
8	**WALKING ON THE MOON** *Police-A&M*
9	**QUE SERA MI VIDA** *Gibson Brothers-Island*
10	**MY SIMPLE HEART** *Three Degrees-Ariola*
11	**OFF THE WALL** *Michael Jackson-Epic*
12	**JOHN I'M ONLY DANCING** *David Bowie-RCA*
13	**CHRISTMAS WITHOUT YOU** *Elvis Presley-RCA*
14	**NO MORE TEARS** *Summer/Streisand-Casablanca/CBS*
15	**IS IT LOVE YOU'RE AFTER** *Rose Royce-Whitfield*
16	**UNION CITY BLUE** *Blondie-Chrysalis*
17	**TEARS OF A CLOWN** *The Beat-2 Tone*
18	**LIVING ON AN ISLAND** *Status Quo-Vertigo*
19	**NIGHTS IN WHITE SATIN** *Moody Blues-Deram*
20	**PLEASE DON'T GO** *K.C. And The Sunshine Band*

UK ALBUMS

1	**GREATEST HITS** *Rod Stewart-Riva*
2	**GREATEST HITS VOL 2** *Abba-Epic*
3	**20 HOTTEST HITS** *Hot Chocolate-RAK*
4	**LOVE SONGS** *Elvis Presley-K-Tel*
5	**THE WALL** *Pink Floyd-Harvest*
6	**PEACE IN THE VALLEY** *Various-Ronco*
7	**REGATTA DE BLANC** *Police-A&M*
8	**20 GOLDEN GREATS** *Diana Ross-Motown*
9	**BEE GEES GREATEST HITS** *Bee Gees-RSO*
10	**ELO'S GREATEST HITS** *ELO-Jet*
11	**OFF THE WALL** *Michael Jackson-Jet*
12	**TRANQUILITY** *Mary O'Hara-Warwick*
13	**ALL ABOARD** *Various-EMI*
14	**NIGHT MOVES** *Various-K-Tel*
15	**EAT TO THE BEAT** *Blondie-Chrysalis*
16	**CREPES AND DRAPES** *Showaddywaddy-Arista*
17	**SINGLES ALBUM** *Kenny Rogers-United Artists*
18	**ONE STEP BEYOND** *Madness-Stiff*
19	**LENA'S MUSIC ALBUM** *Lena Martell-Pye*
20	**OUTLANDOS D'AMOUR** *Police-A&M*

WEEK ENDING JANUARY 12 1980

US SINGLES

1	**ESCAPE** *Rupert Holmes-MCA*
2	**ROCK WITH YOU** *Michael Jackson-Epic*
3	**DO THAT TO ME** *The Captain & Tennille-Casablanca*
4	**SEND ONE YOUR LOVE** *Stevie Wonder-Tamla*
5	**PLEASE DON'T GO** *K.C. And The Sunshine Band-TK*
6	**STILL** *Commodores-Motown*
7	**COWARD OF THE COUNTY** *Kenny Rogers-United Artists*
8	**LADIES NIGHT** *Kool & The Gang-De Lite*
9	**WE DON'T TALK ANYMORE** *Cliff Richard-EMI America*
10	**BABE** *Styx-A&M*
11	**COOL CHANGE** *Little River Band-Capitol*
12	**CRUISIN'** *Smokey Robinson-Tamla*
13	**THE LONG RUN** *Eagles-Asylum*
14	**BETTER LOVE NEXT TIME** *Dr. Hook-Capitol*
15	**JANE** *Jefferson Starship-Grunt*
16	**I WANNA BE YOUR LOVER** *Prince-Warner Bros*
17	**THIS IS IT** *Kenny Loggins-Columbia*
18	**HEAD GAMES** *Foreigner-Atlantic*
19	**DON'T DO ME LIKE THAT** *Tom Petty & Heartbreakers-Backstreet*
20	**SARA** *Fleetwood Mac-Warner Bros*

US ALBUMS

1	**GREATEST** *Bee Gees-RSO*
2	**ON THE RADIO** *Donna Summer-Casablanca*
3	**THE WALL** *Pink Floyd-Columbia*
4	**THE LONG RUN** *Eagles-Asylum*
5	**SECRET LIFE OF PLANTS** *Stevie Wonder-Motown*
6	**DAMN THE TORPEDOES** *Tom Petty & Heartbreakers-Backstreet*
7	**CORNERSTONE** *Styx-A&M*
8	**KENNY** *Kenny Rogers-United Artists*
9	**OFF THE WALL** *Michael Jackson-Epic*
10	**TUSK** *Fleetwood Mac-Warner Bros*
11	**IN THROUGH THE OUT DOOR** *Led Zeppelin-Swan Song*
12	**PHOENIX** *Dan Fogelberg-Full Moon*
13	**FREEDOM AT POINT ZERO** *Jefferson Starship-Grunt*
14	**HEAD GAMES** *Foreigner-Atlantic*
15	**MASTERJAM** *Rufus And Chaka-MCA*
16	**NIGHT IN THE RUTS** *Aerosmith-Columbia*
17	**WET** *Barbara Streisand-Columbia*
18	**MIDNIGHT MAGIC** *Commodores-Motown*
19	**KEEP THE FIRE** *Kenny Loggins-Columbia*
20	**LIVE RUST** *Neil Young & Crazy Horse-Warner Bros*

UK SINGLES

1	**ANOTHER BRICK** *Pink Floyd-Harvest*
2	**I HAVE A DREAM** *Abba-Epic*
3	**BRASS IN POCKET** *Pretenders-Real*
4	**DAY TRIP TO BANGOR** *Fiddler's Dram-Dingles*
5	**I ONLY WANT TO BE** *Tourists-Logo*
6	**TEARS OF A CLOWN** *The Beat-2 Tone*
7	**PLEASE DON'T GO** *K.C. And The Sunshine Band-TK*
8	**RAPPER'S DELIGHT** *Sugarhill Gang-Sugar Hill*
9	**WALKING ON THE MOON** *Police-A&M*
10	**MY SIMPLE HEART** *Three Degrees-Ariola*
11	**WITH YOU I'M BORN AGAIN** *Billy Preston/Syreeta-Motown*
12	**JOHN I'M ONLY DANCING** *David Bowie-RCA*
13	**IS IT LOVE YOU'RE AFTER** *Rose Royce-Whitfield*
14	**MY GIRL** *Madness-Stiff*
15	**LONDON CALLING** *Clash-CBS*
16	**QUE SERA MI VIDA** *Gibson Brothers-Island*
17	**LIVING ON AN ISLAND** *Status Quo-Vertigo*
18	**WONDERFUL CHRISTMAS** *Paul McCartney-Parlophone*
19	**BLUE PETER** *Mike Oldfield-Virgin*
20	**I'M IN THE MOOD** *Nolan Sisters-Epic*

UK ALBUMS

1	**GREATEST HITS VOL 2** *Abba-Epic*
2	**GREATEST HITS** *Rod Stewart-Riva*
3	**THE WALL** *Pink Floyd-Harvest*
4	**HOTTEST HITS** *Hot Chocolate-Rak*
5	**REGATTA DE BLANC** *Police-A&M*
6	**BEE GEE'S GREATEST HITS** *Bee Gees-RSO*
7	**EAT TO THE BEAT** *Blondie-Chrysalis*
8	**ELO'S GREATEST HITS** *ELO-Jet*
9	**LONDON CALLING** *Clash-CBS*
10	**ONE STEP BEYOND** *Madness-Stiff*
11	**OFF THE WALL** *Michael Jackson-Epic*
12	**LOVE SONGS** *Elvis Presley-K Tel*
13	**20 GOLDEN HITS** *Diana Ross-Motown*
14	**OUTLANDOS D'AMOUR** *Police-A&M*
15	**PARALLEL LINES** *Blondie-Chrysalis*
16	**CREPES AND DRAPES** *Showaddywaddy-Arista*
17	**PEACE IN THE VALLEY** *Various-Ronco*
18	**20 GREAT LOVE SONGS** *Slim Whitman-United Artists*
19	**TUSK** *Fleetwood Mac-Warner Bros*
20	**DISCOVERY** *ELO-Jet*

WEEK ENDING JANUARY 19 1980

	US SINGLES		US ALBUMS		UK SINGLES		UK ALBUMS
1	**ROCK WITH YOU** *Michael Jackson-Epic*	1	**THE WALL** *Pink Floyd-Columbia*	1	**BRASS IN POCKET** *Pretenders-Real*	1	**THE PRETENDERS** *The Pretenders-Real*
2	**DO THAT TO ME** *The Captain & Tennille-Casablanca*	2	**ON THE RADIO** *Donna Summer-Casablanca*	2	**WITH YOU I'M BORN AGAIN** *Billy Preston/Syreeta-Motown*	2	**GREATEST HITS VOL 2** *Abba-Epic*
3	**ESCAPE** *Rupert Holmes-MCA*	3	**THE LONG RUN** *Eagles-Asylum*	3	**PLEASE DON'T GO** *K.C. And The Sunshine Band-TK*	3	**REGATTA DE BLANC** *Police-A&M*
4	**COWARD OF THE COUNTY** *Kenny Rogers-United Artists*	4	**GREATEST** *Bee Gees-RSO*	4	**MY GIRL** *Madness-Stiff*	4	**THE WALL** *Pink Floyd-Harvest*
5	**SEND ONE YOUR LOVE** *Stevie Wonder-Tamla*	5	**DAMN THE TORPEDOES** *Tom Petty & Heartbreakers-MCA*	5	**ANOTHER BRICK** *Pink Floyd-Harvest*	5	**ONE STEP BEYOND** *Madness-Stiff*
6	**CRUISIN'** *Smokey Robinson-Tamla*	6	**SECRET LIFE OF PLANTS** *Stevie Wonder-Motown*	6	**I'M IN THE MOOD** *Nolans-Epic*	6	**GREATEST HITS** *Rod Stewart-Riva*
7	**WE DON'T TALK ANYMORE** *Cliff Richard-EMI America*	7	**KENNY** *Kenny Rogers-United Artists*	7	**I HAVE A DREAM** *Abba-Epic*	7	**BEE GEES GREATEST HITS** *Bee Gees-RSO*
8	**LADIES NIGHT** *Kool & The Gang-De Lita*	8	**OFF THE WALL** *Michael Jackson-Epic*	8	**TEARS OF A CLOWN** *Beat-2 Tone*	8	**VIDEO STARS** *Various-K Tel*
9	**PLEASE DON'T GO** *K.C. And The Sunshine Band-TK*	9	**CORNERSTONE** *Styx-A&M*	9	**DAY TRIP TO BANGOR** *Fiddler's Dram-Dingler*	9	**OFF THE WALL** *Michael Jackson-Epic*
10	**COOL CHANGE** *Little River Band-Capitol*	10	**TUSK** *Fleetwood Mac-Warner Bros*	10	**I ONLY WANT TO BE WITH YOU** *Tourists-Logo*	10	**20 HOTTEST HITS** *Hot Chocolate-Rak*
11	**THE LONG RUN** *Eagles-Asylum*	11	**PHOENIX** *Dan Fogelberg-Full Moon/Epic*	11	**LONDON CALLING** *Clash-CBS*	11	**SEMI DETACHED SUBURBAN** *Manfred Mann-Bronze*
12	**BETTER LOVE NEXT TIME** *Dr. Hook-Capitol*	12	**FREEDOM AT POINT ZERO** *Jefferson Starship-Grunt*	12	**GREEN ONIONS** *Booker T And The MG's-Atlantic*	12	**LONDON CALLING** *Clash-CBS*
13	**I WANNA BE YOUR LOVER** *Prince-Warner Bros*	13	**IN THROUGH THE OUT DOOR** *Led Zeppelin-Swan Song*	13	**IS IT LOVE YOU'RE AFTER** *Rose Royce-Whitfield*	13	**OUTLANDOS D'AMOUR** *Police-A&M*
14	**JANE** *Jefferson Starship-Grunt*	14	**NIGHT IN THE RUTS** *Aerosmith-Columbia*	14	**BETTER LOVE NEXT TIME** *Dr. Hook-Capitol*	14	**EAT TO THE BEAT** *Blondie-Chrysalis*
15	**SARA** *Fleetwood Mac-Warner Bros*	15	**MASTERJAM** *Rufus And Chaka-MCA*	15	**RAPPER'S DELIGHT** *Sugarhill Gang-Sugar Hill*	15	**PARALLEL LINES** *Blondie-Chrysalis*
16	**THIS IS IT** *Kenny Loggins-Columbia*	16	**HEAD GAMES** *Foreigner-Atlantic*	16	**MY SIMPLE HEART** *Three Degrees-Ariola*	16	**NO PLACE TO RUN** *UFO-Chrysalis*
17	**DON'T DO ME LIKE THAT** *Tom Petty & Heartbreakers-Backstreet*	17	**WET** *Barbara Streisand-Columbia*	17	**BABE** *Styx-A&M*	17	**20 GOLDEN GREATS** *Diana Ross-Motown*
18	**CRAZY LITTLE THING** *Queen-Elektra*	18	**MIDNIGHT MAGIC** *Commodores-Motown*	18	**JOHN I'M ONLY DANCING** *David Bowie-RCA*	18	**ELO'S GREATEST HITS** *Elo-Jet*
19	**WAIT FOR ME** *Darryl Hall & John Oates-RCA*	19	**LIVE RUST** *Neil Young & Crazy Horse-Warner*	19	**I WANNA HOLD YOUR HAND** *Dollar-Carrere*	19	**SPECIALS** *Specials-2 Tone*
20	**DON'T LET GO** *Isaac Hayes-Polydor*	20	**KEEP THE FIRE** *Kenny Young-Columbia*	20	**THE YANKEE DOLLAR** *Skids-Virgin*	20	**PEACE IN THE VALLEY** *Various-Ronco*

WEEK ENDING JANUARY 26 1980

	US SINGLES		US ALBUMS		UK SINGLES		UK ALBUMS
1	**ROCK WITH YOU** *Michael Jackson-Epic*	1	**THE WALL** *Pink Floyd-Columbia*	1	**BRASS IN POCKET** *The Pretenders-Real*	1	**PRETENDERS** *The Pretenders-Real*
2	**DO THAT TO ME** *The Captain & Tennille*	2	**THE LONG RUN** *Eagles-Asylum*	2	**WITH YOU I'M BORN AGAIN** *Billy Preston And Syreeta-Motown*	2	**REGATTA DE BLANC** *Police-A&M*
3	**COWARD OF THE COUNTY** *Kenny Rogers-United Artist*	3	**DAMN THE TORPEDOES** *Tom Petty & Heartbreakers-Backstreet*	3	**MY GIRL** *Madness-Stiff*	3	**ONE STEP BEYOND** *Madness-Stiff*
4	**ESCAPE** *Rupert Holmes-MCA*	4	**ON THE RADIO** *Donna Summer-Casablanca*	4	**I'M IN THE MOOD** *Nolans-Epic*	4	**GREATEST HITS VOL. 2** *Abba-Epic*
5	**CRUSIN'** *Smokey Robinson-Tamla*	5	**GREATEST HITS** *Bee Gees-RSO*	5	**PLEASE DON'T GO** *K.C. And The Sunshine Band-TK*	5	**VIDEO STARS** *Various-K-Tel*
6	**SEND ONE YOUR LOVE** *Stevie Wonder-Tamla*	6	**KENNY** *Kenny Rogers-United Artist*	6	**BABE** *Styx-A&M*	6	**BEE GEES GREATEST HITS** *Bee Gees-RSO*
7	**WE DON'T TALK ANYMORE** *Cliff Richard-EMI America*	7	**OFF THE WALL** *Michael Jackson-Epic*	7	**GREEN ONIONS** *Booker T And The MG's-Atlantic*	7	**THE WALL** *Pink Floyd-Harvest*
8	**CRAZY LTTLE THING** *Queen-Elektra*	8	**PHOENIX** *Dan Fogelberg-Full Moon/Epic*	8	**BETTER LOVE NEXT TIME** *Dr Hook-Capitol*	8	**GREATEST HITS** *Rod Stewart-Riva*
9	**THE LONG RUN** *Eagles-Asylum*	9	**CORNERSTONE** *Styx-A&M*	9	**I WANNA HOLD YOUR HAND** *Dollar-Carrere*	9	**SEMI DETACHED SUBURBAN** *Manfred Mann-Bronze*
10	**SARA** *Fleetwood Mac-Warner Bros*	10	**TUSK** *Fleetwood Mac-Warner Bros*	10	**ANOTHER BRICK** *Pink Floyd-Harvest*	10	**20 HOTTEST HITS** *Hot Chocolate-RAK*
11	**I WANNA BE YOUR LOVER** *Prince-Warner-Bros*	11	**FREEDOM AT POINT ZERO** *Jefferson Starship-Grunt*	11	**TEARS OF A CLOWN** *The Beat-2 Tone*	11	**NO PLACE TO RUN** *UFO-Chrysalis*
12	**BETTER LOVE NEXT TIME** *Dr Hook-Capitol*	12	**SECRET LIFE OF PLANTS** *Stevie Wonder-Motown*	12	**IT'S DIFFERENT FOR GIRLS** *Joe Jackson-A&M*	12	**OFF THE WALL** *Michael Jackson-Epic*
13	**LADIES NIGHT** *Kool & The Gang-De-Lite*	13	**IN THROUGH THE OUT DOOR** *Led Zeppelin-Swan Song*	13	**I HAVE A DREAM** *Abba-Epic*	13	**LONDON CALLING** *Clash-CBS*
14	**DON'T DO ME LIKE THAT** *Tom Petty & Heartbreakers-Backstreet*	14	**NIGHT IN THE RUTS** *Aerosmith-Columbia*	14	**LONDON CALLING** *Clash-CBS*	14	**PERMANENT WAVES** *Rush-Mercury*
15	**THIS IS IT** *Kenny Loggins-Columbia*	15	**MASTERJAM** *Rufus And Chaka-MCA*	15	**TOO MUCH TOO YOUNG** *Specials-2Tone*	15	**20 GOLDEN GREATS** *Diana Ross-Motown*
16	**YES, I'M READY** *Teri De Sario With K.C.-Casablanca*	16	**GOLD AND PLATINUM** *Lynyrd Skynyrd-MCA*	16	**SPIRITS HAVING FLOWN** *Bee Gees-RSO*	16	**OUTLANDOS D'AMOUR** *Police-A&M*
17	**DEJA VU** *Dionne Warwick-Arista*	17	**LIVE RUST** *Neil Young & Crazy Horse-Warner Bros*	17	**I HEAR YOU KNOW** *Jon And Vangelis-Polydor*	17	**SPECIALS** *Specials-2 Tone*
18	**WAIT FOR ME** *Daryl Hall & John Oates-RCA*	18	**WET** *Barbra Streisand-Columbia*	18	**WE GOT THE FUNK** *Positive Force-Sugar Hill*	18	**PARALLEL LINES** *Blondie-Chrysalis*
19	**DON'T LET GO** *Isaac Hayes-Polydor*	19	**SEPTEMBER MORN** *Neil Diamond-Columbia*	19	**IS IT LOVE YOU'RE AFTER** *Rose Royce-Whitfield*	19	**SEPTEMBER MORN** *Neil Diamond-CBS*
20	**PLEASE DON'T GO** *K.C. And The Sunshine Band-TK*	20	**RISE** *Herb Alpert-A&M*	20	**SPACER** *Sheile B Devotion-Carrere*	20	**ELO'S GREATEST HITS** *ELO-Jet*

WEEK ENDING FEBRUARY 2 1980

US SINGLES

1 **ROCK WITH YOU**
Michael Jackson-Epic
2 **DO THAT TO ME**
The Captain & Tennille-Casablance
3 **COWARD OF THE COUNTY**
Kenny Rogers-United Artist
4 **CRUISIN'**
Smokey Robinson-Tamla
5 **CRAZY LITTLE THING**
Queen-Elektra
6 **ESCAPE**
Rupert Holmes-MCA
7 **SARA**
Fleetwood Mac-Warner Bros
8 **THE LONG RUN**
Eagles-Asylum
9 **YES, I'M READY**
Teri De Sario with K.C.-Casablanca
10 **DON'T DO ME LIKE THAT**
Tom Petty & Heartbreakers-Backstreet
11 **I WANNA BE YOUR LOVER**
Prince-Warner Bros
12 **THIS IS IT**
Kenny Loggins-Columbia
13 **WE DON'T TALK ANYMORE**
Cliff Richard-EMI America
14 **SEND ONE YOUR LOVE**
Stevie Wonder-Tamla
15 **DEJA VU**
Dionne Warwick-Arista
16 **ON THE RADIO**
Donna Summer-Casablanca
17 **LONGER**
Dan Fogelberg-Full Moon/Epic
18 **DON'T LET GO**
Isaac Hayes-Poldyor
19 **ROMEO'S TUNE**
Steve Forbert-Nemperor
20 **DAYDREAM BELIEVER**
Anne Murray-Capitol

US ALBUMS

1 **THE WALL**
Pink Floyd-Columbia
2 **THE LONG RUN**
Eagles-Asylum
3 **DAMN THE TORPEDOES**
Tom Petty & Heartbreakers-Backstreet
4 **OFF THE WALL**
Michael Jackson-Epic
5 **KENNY**
Kenny Rogers-United Artist
6 **PHOENIX**
Dan Fogelberg-Full Moon
7 **ON THE RADIO**
Donna Summers-Casablanca
8 **TUSK**
Fleetwood Mac-Warner Bros.
9 **GREATEST HITS**
Bee Gees-RSO
10 **FREEDOM AT POINT ZERO**
Jefferson Starship-Grunt
11 **SECRET LIFE OF PLANTS**
Stevie Wonder-Motown
12 **CORNERSTONE**
Styx-A&M
13 **IN THROUGH THE OUT DOOR**
Led Zeppelin-Swan Song
14 **GOLD AND PLATINUM**
Lynyrd Skynyrd Band-MCA
15 **LIVE RUST**
Neil Young & Crazy Horse-Warner Bros
16 **THE ROSE**
Soundtrack-Atlantic
17 **SEPTEMBER MORN**
Neil Diamond-Columbia
18 **WET**
Barbra Streisand-Columbia
19 **RISE**
Herb Alpert-A&M
20 **NIGHT IN THE RUTS**
Aerosmith-Columbia

UK SINGLES

1 **TOO MUCH TOO YOUNG**
Specials-2 Tone
2 **BRASS IN POCKET**
Pretenders-Real
3 **MY GIRL**
Madness-Stiff
4 **I'M IN THE MOOD**
Nolans-Epic
5 **IT'S DIFFERENT FOR GIRLS**
Joe Jackson-A&M
6 **WITH YOU I'M BORN AGAIN**
Billy Preston/Syreeta-Motown
7 **BABE**
Styx-A&M
8 **PLEASE DON'T GO**
K.C. And The Sunshine Band-TK
9 **GREEN ONIONS**
Booker T And The MG's-Atlantic
10 **COWARD OF THE COUNTY**
Kenny Rogers-United Artist
11 **I WANNA HOLD YOUR HAND**
Dollar-Carrere
12 **7TEEN**
Regents-Rialto
13 **BETTER LOVE NEXT TIME**
Dr Hook-Capitol
14 **SOMEONE'S LOOKING**
Boomtown Rats-Ensign
15 **I HEAR YOU NOW**
Jon And Vangelis-Polydor
16 **LONDON CALLING**
Clash-CBS
17 **TEARS OF A CLOWN**
The Beat-2 Tone
18 **SPACER**
Sheila B. Devotion-Carrere
19 **JAZZ CARNIVAL**
Azymuth-Milestone
20 **LIVING BY NUMBERS**
New Music-GTO

UK ALBUMS

1 **PRETENDERS**
Pretenders-Real
2 **ONE STEP BEYOND**
Madness-Stiff
3 **PERMANENT WAVES**
Rush-Mercury
4 **REGATTA DE BLANC**
Police-A&M
5 **GREATEST HITS VOL 2**
Abba-Epic
6 **BEE GEES GREATEST HITS**
Bee Gees-RSO
7 **SHORT STORIES**
Jon And Vangelis-Polydor
8 **GOLDEN COLLECTION**
Charlie Pride-K Tel
9 **VIDEO STARS**
Various-K Tel
10 **THE WALL**
Pink Floyd-Harvest
11 **SPECIALS**
Specials-2 Tone
12 **OFF THE WALL**
Michael Jackson-Epic
13 **GREATEST HITS**
Rod Stewart-Riva
14 **SEMI DETACHED SUBURBAN**
Manfred Mann-Bronze
15 **20 HOTTEST HITS**
Hot Chocolate-Rak
16 **I'M THE MAN**
Joe Jackson-A&M
17 **PARALLEL LINES**
Blondie-Chrysalis
18 **NO PLACE TO RUN**
UFO-Chrysalis
19 **LONDON CALLING**
Clash-CBS
20 **OUTLANDOS D'AMOUR**
Police-A&M

WEEK ENDING FEBRUARY 9 1980

US SINGLES

1 **ROCK WITH YOU**
Michael Jackson-Epic
2 **DO THAT TO ME**
The Captain & Tennille-Casablanca
3 **COWARD OF THE COUNTY**
Kenny Rogers-United Artists
4 **CRUISIN'**
Smokey Robinson-Tamla
5 **CRAZY LITTLE THING**
Queen-Elektra
6 **YES I'M READY**
Teri De Sario With K.C.-Casablanca
7 **SARA**
Fleetwood Mac-Warner Bros
8 **THE LONG RUN**
Eagles-Asylum
9 **LONGER**
Dan Fogelberg-Full Moon/Epic
10 **DON'T DO ME LIKE THAT**
Tom Petty & Heartbreakers-Backstreet
11 **THIS IS IT**
Kenny Loggins-Columbia
12 **ESCAPE**
Rupert Holmes-MCA
13 **DESIRE**
Andy Gibb-RSO
14 **ON THE RADIO**
Donna Summer-Casablanca
15 **DEJA VU**
Dionne Warwick-Arista
16 **ROMEO'S TUNE**
Steve Forbert-Nemperor
17 **DAYDREAM BELIEVER**
Anne Murray-Capitol
18 **DON'T LET GO**
Isaac Hayes-Polydor
19 **AN AMERICAN DREAM**
The Dirt Band-United Artists
20 **I WANNA BE YOUR LOVER**
Prince-Warner Bros

US ALBUMS

1 **THE WALL**
Pink Floyd-Columbia
2 **DAMN THE TORPEDOES**
Tom Petty & Heartbreakers-Backstreet
3 **THE LONG RUN**
Eagles-Asylum
4 **OFF THE WALL**
Michael Jackson-Epic
5 **KENNY**
Kenny Rogers-United Artists
6 **PHOENIX**
Dan Fogelberg-Full Moon
7 **ON THE RADIO**
Donna Summer-Casablanca
8 **TUSK**
Fleetwood Mac-Warner Bros
9 **GREATEST HITS**
Bee Gees-RSO
10 **CORNERSTONE**
Styx-A&M
11 **FREEDOM AT POINT ZERO**
Jefferson Starship-Grunt
12 **GOLD AND PLATINUM**
Lynyrd Skynyrd Band-MCA
13 **THE ROSE**
Soundtrack-Atlantic
14 **SEPTEMBER MORN**
Neil Diamond-Columbia
15 **LIVE RUST**
Neil Young & Crazy Horse-Warner Bros
16 **SECRET LIFE OF PLANTS**
Stevie Wonder-Motown
17 **IN THROUGH THE OUT DOOR**
Led Zeppelin-Swan Song
18 **WET**
Barbra Streisand-Columbia
19 **NO NUKES**
Various Artists-Asylum
20 **MIDNIGHT MAGIC**
Commodores-Motown

UK SINGLES

1 **TOO MUCH TOO YOUNG**
Specials-2 Tone
2 **COWARD OF THE COUNTY**
Kenny Rogers-United Artist
3 **I'M IN THE MOOD**
Nolans-Epic
4 **MY GIRL**
Madness-Stiff
5 **IT'S DIFFERENT FOR GIRLS**
Joe Jackson-A&M
6 **BABE**
Styx-A&M
7 **BRASS IN POCKET**
Pretenders-Real
8 **SOMEONE'S LOOKING**
Boomtown Rats-Ensign
9 **WITH YOU I'M BORN AGAIN**
Billy Preston/Syreeta-Motown
10 **GREEN ONIONS**
Booker T And The MG's-Atlantic
11 **7TEEN**
Regents-Rialto
12 **I HEAR YOU NOW**
Jon And Vangelis-Polydor
13 **LIVING BY NUMBERS**
New Music-GTO
14 **PLEASE DON'T GO**
K.C. And The Sunshine Band-TK
15 **CAPTAIN BEAKY**
Keith Michel-Polydor
16 **I WANNA HOLD YOUR HAND**
Dollar-Carrere
17 **BETTER LOVE NEXT TIME**
Dr Hook-Capitol
18 **AND THE BEAT GOES ON**
Whispers-Solar
19 **SPACER**
Sheila B Devotion-Carrere
20 **SAVE ME**
Queen-EMI

UK ALBUMS

1 **PRETENDERS**
Pretenders-Real
2 **THE LAST DANCE**
Various-Motown
3 **ONE STEP BEYOND**
Madness-Stiff
4 **PERMANENT WAVES**
Rush-Mercury
5 **SHORT STORIES**
Jon And Vangelis-Polydor
6 **GOLDEN COLLECTION**
Charlie Pride-K-Tel
7 **REGATTA DE BLANC**
Police-A&M
8 **SPECIALS**
Specials-2 Tone
9 **OFF THE WALL**
Michael Jackson-Epic
10 **BEE GEE'S GREATEST HITS**
Bee Gees-RSO
11 **GREATEST HITS VOL 2**
Abba-Epic
12 **THE WALL**
Pink Floyd-Harvest
13 **I'M THE MAN**
Joe Jackson-A&M
14 **SEPTEMBER MORN**
Neil Diamond-CBS
15 **OUTLANDOS D'AMOUR**
Police-A&M
16 **GREATEST HITS**
Rod Stewart-Riva
17 **THE SUMMIT**
Various-K-Tel
18 **KENNY**
Kenny Rogers-United Artists
19 **FLEX**
Lene Lovich-Stiff
20 **SEMI DETACHED SUBURBAN**
Manfred Mann-Bronze

WEEK ENDING FEBRUARY 16 1980

US SINGLES

	Title	Artist-Label
1	DO THAT TO ME	The Captain & Tennille
2	CRAZY LITTLE THING	Queen-Elektra
3	COWARD OF THE COUNTY	Kenny Rogers-United Artists
4	CRUISN'	Smokey Robinson-Tamla
5	ROCK WITH YOU	Michael Jackson-Epic
6	YES, I'M READY	Teri De Sario With K.C.-Casablanca
7	SARA	Fleetwood Mac-Warner Bros
8	LONGER	Dan Fogelberg-Full Moon/Epic
9	ON THE RADIO	Donna Summer-Casablanca
10	DESIRE	Andy Gibb-RSO
11	THIS IS IT	Kenny Loggins-Columbia
12	DON'T DO ME LIKE THAT	Tom Petty & Heartbreakers-Backstreet
13	DAYDREAM BELIEVER	Anne Murray-Capitol
14	ROMEO'S TUNE	Steve Forbert-Nemperor
15	THE LONG RUN	Eagles-Asylum
16	AN AMERICAN DREAM	The Dirt Band-United Artist
17	WORKING MY WAY BACK	Spinners-Atlactic
18	ANOTHER BRICK	Pink Floyd-Columbia
19	SEPTEMBER MORN	Neil Diamond-Columbia
20	THE SECOND TIME AROUND	Shalamar-Solar

US ALBUMS

	Title	Artist-Label
1	THE WALL	Pink Floyd-Columbia
2	DAMN THE TORPEDOES	Tom Petty & Heartbreakers-Backstreet
3	OFF THE WALL	Michael Jackson-Epic
4	THE LONG RUN	Eagles-Asylum
5	PHOENIX	Dan Fogelberg-Full Moon
6	KENNY	Kenny Rogers-United Artist
7	ON THE RADIO	Donna Summers-Casablanca
8	TUSK	Fleetwood Mac-Warner Bros.
9	CORNERSTONE	Styx-A&M
10	SEMPTEMBER MORN	Neil Diamond-Columbia
11	FREEDOM AT POINT ZERO	Jefferson Starship-Grunt
12	GOLD AND PLATINUM	Lynyrd Skynyrd-MCA
13	THE ROSE	Soundtrack-Atlantic
14	GREATEST HITS	Bee Gees-RSO
15	PERMANENT WAVES	Rush-Mercury
16	THE WHISPERS	The Whispers-Solar
17	IN THROUGH THE OUT DOOR	Led Zeppelin-Swan Song
18	MIDNIGHT MAGIC	Commodores-Motown
19	NO NUKES	Various Artists-Asylum
20	WHERE THERE'S SMOKEY	Smokey Robinson-Motown

UK SINGLES

	Title	Artist-Label
1	COWARD OF THE COUNTY	Kenny Rogers-United Artist
2	TOO MUCH TOO YOUNG	Specials-2 Tone
3	I'M IN THE MOOD	Nolans-Epic
4	SOMEONE'S LOOKING	Boomtown Rats-Ensign
5	CAPTAIN BEAKY	Keith Michell-Polydor
6	AND THE BEAT GOES ON	Whispers-Solar
7	IT'S DIFFERENT FOR GIRLS	Joe Jackson-A&M
8	I HEAR YOU NOW	Jon And Vangelis-Polydor
9	BABE	Styx-A&M
10	MY GIRL	Madness-Stiff
11	SAVE ME	Queen-EMI
12	ROCK WITH YOU	Michael Jackson-Epic
13	CARRIE	Cliff Richard-EMI
14	LIVING BY NUMBERS	New Music-GTO
15	7-TEEN	Regents-Rialto
16	THREE MINUTE HERO	Selecter-2 Tone
17	I CAN'T STAND UP	Elvis Costello-F-Beat
18	SO GOOD TO BE BACK HOME	Tourists-Logo
19	BRASS IN PCOKET	Pretenders-Real
20	BABY I LOVE YOU	Ramones-Sire

UK ALBUMS

	Title	Artist-Label
1	THE LAST DANCE	Various-Motown
2	PRETENDERS	Pretenders-Real
3	ONE STEP BEYOND	Madness-Stiff
4	SHORT STORIES	Jon And Vangelis-Polydor
5	PERMANENT WAVES	Rush-Mercury
6	GOLDEN COLLECTION	Charley Pride-K-Tel
7	SPECIALS	Specials-2 Tone
8	REGATTA DE BLANC	Police-A&M
9	KENNY	Kenny Rogers-United Artists
10	OFF THE WALL	Michael Jackson-Epic
11	GREATEST HITS VOL 2	Abba-Epic
12	I'M THE MAN	Joe Jackson-A&M
13	THE WALL	Pink Floyd-Harvest
14	END OF THE CENTURY	Ramones-Sire
15	THE NOLAN SISTERS	The Nolan Sisters-Epic
16	BEE GEES' GREATEST HITS	Bee Gees-RSO
17	JUST FOR YOU	Des O'Connor-Warwick
18	METAMATIC	John Foxx-Metal Beat
19	LONDON CALLING	Clash-CBS
20	FLEX	Lene Lovich-Stiff

WEEK ENDING FEBRUARY 23 1980

US SINGLES

	Title	Artist-Label
1	CRAZY LITTLE THING	Queen-Elektra
2	DO THAT TO ME	The Captain & Tennille-Casablanca
3	YES I'M READY	Teri De Sario With K.C.-Casablanca
4	CRUISIN'	Smokey Robinson-Tamla
5	ROCK WITH YOU	Michael Jackson-Epic
6	LONGER	Dan Fogelberg-Full Moon/Epic
7	ON THE RADIO	Donna Summer-Casablanca
8	DESIRE	Andy Gibb-RSO
9	COWARD OF THE COUNTY	Kenny Rogers-United Artists
10	SARA	Fleetwood Mac-Warner Bros
11	ROMEO'S TUNE	Steve Forbert-Nemperor
12	DAYDREAM BELIEVER	Anne Murray-Capitol
13	WORKING MY WAY BACK	Spinners-Atlantic
14	AN AMERICAN DREAM	The Dirt Band-United Artists
15	ANOTHER BRICK	Pink Floyd-Columbia
16	THIS IS IT	Kenny Loggins-Columbia
17	THE SECOND TIME AROUND	Shalamar-Solar
18	SEPTEMBER MORN	Neil Diamond-Columbia
19	TOO HOT	Kool & The Gang-De-Lite
20	HOW DO I MAKE YOU	Linda Ronstadt-Asylum

US ALBUMS

	Title	Artist-Label
1	THE WALL	Pink Floyd-Columbia
2	DAMN THE TORPEDOES	Tom Petty & Heartbreakers-Backstreet
3	OFF THE WALL	Michael Jackson-Epic
4	PHOENIX	Dan Fogelberg Full Moon/Epic
5	THE LONG RUN	Eagles-Asylum
6	ON THE RADIO	Donna Summer-Casablanca
7	KENNY	Kenny Rogers-United Artists
8	PERMANENT WAVES	Rush-Mercury
9	CORNERSTONE	Styx-A&M
10	SEPTEMBER MORN	Neil Diamond-Columbia
11	FREEDOM AT POINT ZERO	Jefferson Starship-Grunt
12	THE ROSE	Soundtrack-Atlantic
13	THE WHISPERS	The Whispers-Solar
14	TUSK	Fleetwood Mac-Warner Bros
15	GOLD AND PLATINUM	Lynyrd Skynyrd-MCA
16	GREATEST HITS	Bee Gees-RSO
17	IN THROUGH THE OUT DOOR	Led Zeppelin-Swan Song
18	MIDNIGHT MAGIC	Commodores-Mowtown
19	WHERE THERE'S SMOKE	Smokey Robinson-Motown
20	KEEP THE FIRE	Kenny Loggins-Columbia

UK SINGLES

	Title	Artist-Label
1	COWARD OF THE COUNTY	Kenny Rogers-United Artists
2	AND THE BEAT GOES ON	Whispers-Solar
3	ATOMIC	Blondie-Chrysalis
4	TOO MUCH TOO YOUNG	Specials-2 Tone
5	CAPTAIN BEAKY	Keith Michell-Polydor
6	CARRIE	Cliff Richard-EMI
7	SOMEONE'S LOOKING	Boomtown Rats-Ensign
8	BABY I LOVE YOU	Ramones-Sire
9	I CAN'T STAND UP	Elvis Costello-F Beat
10	SO GOOD TO BE BACK HOME	Tourists-Logo
11	I'M IN THE MOOD	Nolans-Epic
12	ROCK WITH YOU	Michael Jackson-Epic
13	I HEAR YOU NOW	Jon And Vangelis-Polydor
14	TAKE THAT LOOK OFF	Marti Webb-Polydor
15	7TEEN	Regents-Rialto
16	RIDERS IN THE SKY	Shadows-EMI
17	BABE	Styx-A&M
18	THE PLASTIC AGE	Buggles-Island
19	IT'S DIFFERENT FOR GIRLS	Joe Jackson-A&M
20	SAVE	Queen-EMI

UK ALBUMS

	Title	Artist-Label
1	THE LAST DANCE	Various-Motown
2	GET HAPPY	Elvis Costello-F Beat
3	STRING OF HITS	Shadows-EMI
4	PRETENDERS	Pretenders-Real
5	TOO MUCH PRESSURE	Selecter-2 Tone
6	SHORT STORIES	Jon And Vangelis-Polydor
7	ONE STEP BEYOND	Madness-Stiff
8	TELL ME ON A SUNDAY	Marti Webb-Polydor
9	KENNY	Kenny Rogers-United Artists
10	SPECIALS	Specials-2 Tone
11	REGATTA DE BLANC	Police-A&M
12	OFF THE WALL	Michael Jackson-Epic
13	SMALLCREEP'S DAY	Mike Rutherford-Charisma
14	I'M THE MAN	Joe Jackson-EMI
15	GOLDEN COLLECTION	Charlie Pride-K-Tel
16	PERMANENT WAVES	Rush-Mercury
17	GREATEST HITS VOL 2	Abba-Epic
18	JUST FOR YOU	Des O'Connor-Warwick
19	THE NOLAN SISTERS	Nolans-Epic
20	THE WALL	Pink Floyd-Harvest

WEEK ENDING MARCH 1 1980

US SINGLES

	Title	Artist-Label
1	CRAZY LITTLE THING	*Queen-Elektra*
2	YES I'M READY	*Teri De Sario With K.C.-Casablanca*
3	DO THAT TO ME	*The Captain & Tennille-Casablanca*
4	LONGER	*Dan Fogelberg-Full Moon/Epic*
5	DESIRE	*Andy Gibb-RSO*
6	ON THE RADIO	*Donna Summer-Casablanca*
7	CRUISIN'	*Smokey Robinson-Motown*
8	ROCK WITH YOU	*Michael Jackson-Epic*
9	WORKING MY WAY BACK	*Spinners-Atlantic*
10	ANOTHER BRICK	*Pink Floyd-Columbia*
11	ROMEO'S TUNE	*Steve Forbert-Nemperor*
12	DAYDREAM BELIEVER	*Anne Murray-Capitol*
13	AN AMERICAN DREAM	*The Dirt Band-United Artist*
14	THE SECOND TIME AROUND	*Shalamar-Solar*
15	TOO HOT	*Kool And The Gang-De-Lite*
16	HIM	*Rupert Holmes-MCA*
17	SEPTEMBER MORN	*Neil Diamond-Columbia*
18	HOW DO I MAKE YOU	*Linda Ronstadt-Asylum*
19	REFUGEE	*Tom Petty & Heartbreakers-Backstreet*
20	WHEN I WANTED YOU	*Barry Manilow-Arista*

US ALBUMS

	Title	Artist-Label
1	THE WALL	*Pink Floyd-Columbia*
2	DAMN THE TORPEDOES	*Tom Petty & Heartbreakers-Backstreet*
3	OFF THE WALL	*Michael Jackson-Epic*
4	PHOENIX	*Dan Fogelberg-Full Moon/Epic*
5	PERMANENT WAVES	*Rush-Mercury*
6	ON THE RADIO	*Donna Summer-Casablanca*
7	THE LONG RUN	*Eagles-Asylum*
8	KENNY	*Kenny Rogers-United Artists*
9	THE WHISPERS	*The Whispers-Solar*
10	SEPTEMBER MORN	*Neil Diamond-Columbia*
11	FREEDOM AT POINT ZERO	*Jefferson Starship-Grunt*
12	THE ROSE	*Soundtrack-Atlantic*
13	CORNERSTONE	*Styx-A&M*
14	LADIES NIGHT	*Kool & The Gang-De-Lite*
15	GOLD AND PLATINUM	*Lynyrd Skynyrd-MCA*
16	IN THE HEAT OF THE NIGHT	*Pat Benatar-Chrysalis*
17	WHERE THERE'S SMOKE	*Smokey Robinson-Motown*
18	KEEP THE FIRE	*Kenny Loggins-Columbia*
19	TUSK	*Fleetwood Mac-Warner Bros*
20	JACKRABBIT SLIM	*Steve Forbert-Nemperor*

UK SINGLES

	Title	Artist-Label
1	ATOMIC	*Blondie-Chrysalis*
2	COWARD OF THE COUNTY	*Kenny Rogers-United Artists*
3	AND THE BEAT GOES ON	*Whispers-Solar*
4	CARRIE	*Cliff Richard-EMI*
5	I CAN'T STAND UP	*Elvis Costello-F-Beat*
6	TAKE THAT LOOK OFF	*Marti Webb-Polydor*
7	ROCK WITH YOU	*Michael Jackson-Epic*
8	SO GOOD TO BE BACK HOME	*Tourists-Logo*
9	TOGETHER WE ARE	*Fern Kinney-WEA*
10	CAPTAIN BEAKY	*Keith Michel-Polydor*
11	BABY I LOVE YOU	*Ramones-Sire*
12	RIDERS IN THE SKY	*Shadows-EMI*
13	TOO MUCH TOO YOUNG	*Specials-2 Tone*
14	SOMEONE'S LOOKING	*Boomtown Rats-Ensign*
15	I'M IN THE MOOD	*Nolan Sisters-Epic*
16	LIVING IN THE PLASTIC AGE	*Buggles-Island*
17	GAMES WITHOUT FRONTIERS	*Peter Gabriel-Charisma*
18	I HEAR YOU NOW	*Jon And Vangelis-Polydor*
19	SO LONELY	*Police-A&M*
20	HANDS OFF SHE'S MINE	*The Beat-Go Feet*

UK ALBUMS

	Title	Artist-Label
1	STRING OF HITS	*Shadows-EMI*
2	THE LAST DANCE	*Various-Motown*
3	GET HAPPY	*Elvis Costello-F Beat*
4	PRETENDERS	*Pretenders-Real*
5	TELL ME ON A SUNDAY	*Marti Webb-Polydor*
6	TOO MUCH PRESSURE	*Selecter-2 Tone*
7	KENNY	*Kenny Rogers-United Artists*
8	ONE STEP BEYOND	*Madness-Stiff*
9	OFF THE WALL	*Michael Jackson-Epic*
10	SHORT STORIES	*Jon And Vangelis-Polydor*
11	SPECIALS	*Specials-2 Tone*
12	REGETTA DE BLANC	*Police-A&M*
13	OUTLANDOS D'AMOUR	*Police-A&M*
14	SMALLCREEP'S DAY	*Mike Rutherford-Charisma*
15	GOLDEN COLLECTION	*Charley Pride-K-Tel*
16	METAL FOR MUTHAS	*Various-EMI*
17	EAT TO THE BEAT	*Blondie-Chrysalis*
18	THE WALL	*Pink Floyd-Harvest*
19	GREATEST HITS VOL 2	*Abba-Epic*
20	PERMANENT WAVES	*Rush-Mercury*

WEEK ENDING MARCH 8 1980

US SINGLES

	Title	Artist-Label
1	CRAZY LITTLE THING	*Queen-Elektra*
2	YES, I'M READY	*Teri De Sario & KC-Casablanca*
3	LONGER	*Dan Fogelberg-Full Moon/Epic*
4	DESIRE	*Andy Gibb-RSO*
5	ON THE RADIO	*Donner Summer-Casablanca*
6	ANOTHER BRICK	*Pink Floyd-Columbia*
7	DO THAT TO ME	*The Captain & Tennille-Casablanca*
8	WORKING MY WAY BACK	*Spinners-Atlantic*
9	HIM	*Rupert Holmes-MCA*
10	THE SECOND TIME AROUND	*Shalamar-Solar*
11	TOO HOT	*Kool & The Gang-De-Lite*
12	DAYDREAM BELIEVER	*Ann Murray-Capitol*
13	AN AMERICAN DREAM	*The Dirt Band-United Artists*
14	ROCK WITH YOU	*Michael Jackson-Epic*
15	CRUISIN	*Smokey Robinson-Motown*
16	HOW DO I MAKE YOU	*Linda Ronstadt-Asylum*
17	REFUGEE	*Tom Petty & Heartbreakers-Backstreet*
18	SEPTEMBER MORN	*Neil Diamond-Columbia*
19	SPECIAL LADY	*Ray, Goodman & Brown-Polydor*
20	WHEN I WANTED YOU	*Barry Manilow-Arista*

US ALBUMS

	Title	Artist-Label
1	THE WALL	*Pink Floyd-Columbia*
2	DAMN THE TORPEDOES	*Tom Petty & Heartbreakers-Backstreet*
3	PHOENIX	*Dan Fogelberg-Full Moon/Epic*
4	PERMANENT WAVES	*Rush-Mercury*
5	OFF THE WALL	*Michael Jackson-Epic*
6	ON THE RADIO	*Donna Summer-Casablanca*
7	THE LONG RUN	*Eagles-Asylum*
8	THE WHISPERS	*The Whispers-Solar*
9	KENNY	*Kenny Rogers-United Artists*
10	FUN AND GAMES	*Chuck Mangione-A&M*
11	SEPTEMBER MORN	*Neil Diamond-Columbia*
12	THE ROSE	*Soundtrack-Atlantic*
13	CORNERSTONE	*Styx-A&M*
14	LADIES NIGHT	*Kool & The Gang-De-Lite*
15	THE HEAT OF THE NIGHT	*Pat Benatar-Chrysalis*
16	KEEP THE FIRE	*Kenny Loggins-Columbia*
17	WHERE THERE'S SMOKE	*Smokey Robinson-Motown*
18	FREEDOM AT POINT ZERO	*Jefferson Starship-Grunt*
19	BEBE LE STRANGE	*Heart-Epic*
20	TUSK	*Fleetwood Mac-Warner Bros*

UK SINGLES

	Title	Artist-Label
1	ATOMIC	*Blondie-Chrysalis*
2	WE ARE BEAUTIFUL	*Fern Kinney-WEA*
3	TAKE THAT LOOK OFF	*Marti Webb-Polydor*
4	I CAN'T STAND UP	*Elvis Costello-F Beat*
5	AND THE BEAT GOES ON	*Whispers-Solar*
6	COWARD OF THE COUNTY	*Kenny Rogers-United Artists*
7	CARRIE	*Cliff Richard-EMI*
8	GAMES WITHOUT FRONTIERS	*Peter Gabriel-Charisma*
9	ROCK WITH YOU	*Michael Jackson-Epic*
10	ALL NIGHT LONG	*Rainbow-Polydor*
11	SO GOOD TO BE BACK HOME	*Tourists-Logo*
12	SO LONELY	*Police-A&M*
13	RIDERS IN THE SKY	*Shadows-EMI*
14	BABY I LOVE YOU	*Ramones-Sire*
15	AT THE EDGE	*Stiff Little Fingers-Chrysalis*
16	HANDS OFF SHE'S MINE	*The Beat-Go Feet*
17	CAPTAIN BEAKY	*Keith Michell-Polydor*
18	TURNING JAPANESE	*The Vapors-United Artists*
19	CUBA	*Gibson Brothers-Island*
20	THE PLASTIC AGE	*Buggles-Island*

UK ALBUMS

	Title	Artist-Label
1	STRING OF HITS	*Shadows-EMI*
2	GET HAPPY	*Elvis Costello-F Beat*
3	THE LAST DANCE	*Various-Motown*
4	GREATEST HITS	*Rose Royce-Whitfield*
5	TELL ME ON A SUNDAY	*Marti Webb-Polydor*
6	REGATTA DE BLANC	*Police-A&M*
7	OFF THE WALL	*Michael Jackson-Epic*
8	PRETENDERS	*Pretenders-Real*
9	KENNY	*Kenny Rogers-United Artists*
10	GREATEST HITS	*KC & The Sunshine Band-TK*
11	OUTLANDOS D'AMOUR	*Police-A&M*
12	ONE STEP BEYOND	*Madness-Stiff*
13	TOO MUCH PRESSURE	*Selecter-Two Tone*
14	EAT TO THE BEAT	*Blondie-Chrysalis*
15	GOLDEN COLLECTION	*Charley Pride-K-Tel*
16	SHORT STORIES	*Jon & Vangelis-Polydor*
17	SPECIALS	*Specials-Two Tone*
18	THE WALL	*Pink Floyd-Harvest*
19	SMALLCREEP'S DAY	*Mike Rutherford-Charisma*
20	PERMANENT WAVES	*Rush-Mercury*

WEEK ENDING MARCH 15 1980

US SINGLES

	Title	Artist-Label
1	CRAZY LITTLE THING	*Queen-Elektra*
2	LONGER	*Dan Fogelberg-Full Moon/Epic*
3	ANOTHER BRICK	*Pink Floyd-Columbia*
4	DESIRE	*Andy Gibb-RSO*
5	ON THE RADIO	*Donna Summer-Casablanca*
6	WORKING MY WAY BACK	*Spinners-Atlantic*
7	YES, I'M READY	*Teri De Sario with KC-Casablanca*
8	HIM	*Rupert Holmes-MCA*
9	THE SECOND TIME AROUND	*Shalamar-Solar*
10	TOO HOT	*Kool & The Gang-De-Lite*
11	HOW DO I MAKE YOU	*Linda Ronstadt-Asylum*
12	CALL ME	*Blondie-Chrysalis*
13	DO THAT TO ME	*The Captain & Tennille-Casablanca*
14	SPECIAL LADY	*Ray, Goodman & Brown-Polydor*
15	REFUGEE	*Tom Petty & Heartbreakers-Backstreet*
16	DAYDREAM BELIEVER	*Anne Murray-Capitol*
17	RIDE LIKE THE WIND	*Christopher Cross-Warner Bros.*
18	I CAN'T TELL YOU WHY	*Eagles-Asylum*
19	GIVE IT ALL YOU GOT	*Chuck Mangione-A&M*
20	OFF THE WALL	*Michael Jackson-Epic*

US ALBUMS

	Title	Artist-Label
1	THE WALL	*Pink Floyd-Columbia*
2	DAMN THE TORPEDOES	*Tom Petty & Heartbreakers-Backstreet*
3	PHOENIX	*Dan Fogelberg-Full Moon/Epic*
4	PERMANENT WAVES	*Rush-Mercury*
5	MAD LOVE	*Linda Ronstadt-Asylum*
6	BEBE LE STRANGE	*Heart-Epic*
7	THE WHISPERS	*The Whispers-Solar*
8	FUN AND GAMES	*Chuck Mangione-A&M*
9	KENNY	*Kenny Rogers-United Artists*
10	OFF THE WALL	*Michael Jackson-Epic*
11	THE LONG RUN	*Eagles-Asylum*
12	IN THE HEAT OF THE NIGHT	*Pat Benatar-Chrysalis*
13	LADIES NIGHT	*Kool & The Gang-De-Lite*
14	THE ROSE	*Soundtrack-Atlantic*
15	CORNERSTONE	*Styx-A&M*
16	KEEP THE FIRE	*Kenny Loggins-Columbia*
17	ON THE RADIO	*Donna Summer-Casablanca*
18	FREEDOM AT POINT ZERO	*Jefferson Starship-Grunt*
19	BUT THE LITTLE GIRLS	*The Knack-Capitol*
20	AGAINST THE WIND	*Bob Seger & Silver Bullet Band-Capitol*

UK SINGLES

	Title	Artist-Label
1	WE ARE BEAUTIFUL	*Fern Kinney-Warner Bros.*
2	ATOMIC	*Blondie-Chrysalis*
3	TAKE THAT LOOK OFF	*Marti Webb-Polydor*
4	GAMES WITHOUT FRONTIERS	*Peter Gabriel-Charisma*
5	ALL NIGHT LONG	*Rainbow-Polydor*
6	SO LONELY	*Police-A&M*
7	DO THAT TO ME	*The Captain & Tenille-Casablanca*
8	TURNING JAPANESE	*Vapors-United Artists*
9	HANDS OFF SHE'S MINE	*The Beat-Go Feet*
10	AND THE BEAT GOES ON	*The Whispers-Solar*
11	CARRIE	*Cliff Richard-EMI*
12	I CAN'T STAND UP	*Elvis Costello-F Beat*
13	ROCK WITH YOU	*Michael Jackson-Epic*
14	DANCE YOURSELF DIZZY	*Liquid Gold-Polo*
15	COWARD OF THE COUNTY	*Kenny Rogers-United Artists*
16	CUBA	*Gibson Brothers-Island*
17	RIDERS IN THE SKY	*Shadows-EMI*
18	AT THE EDGE	*Stiff Little Fingers-Chrysalis*
19	SO GOOD TO BE BACK HOME	*Tourists-Logo*
20	WORKING MY WAY BACK	*Detroit Spinners-Atlantic*

UK ALBUMS

	Title	Artist-Label
1	STRING OF HITS	*Shadows-EMI*
2	GET HAPPY	*Elvis Costello-F Beat*
3	GREATEST HITS	*Rose Royce-Whitfield*
4	TELL ME ON A SUNDAY	*Marti Webb-Polydor*
5	TEARS AND LAUGHTER	*Johnny Mathis-CBS*
6	REGATTA DE BLANC	*Police-A&M*
7	THE LAST DANCE	*Various-Motown*
8	OFF THE WALL	*Michael Jackson-Epic*
9	NOBODY'S HERO	*Stiff Little Fingers-Chrysalis*
10	PRETENDERS	*Pretenders-Real*
11	EAT TO THE BEAT	*Blondie-Chrysalis*
12	HEARTBREAKERS	*Matt Monro-EMI*
13	OUTLANDOS D'AMOUR	*Police-A&M*
14	ONE STEP BEYOND	*Madness-Stiff*
15	KENNY	*Kenny Rogers-United Artists*
16	GOLDEN COLLECTION	*Charley Pride-K-Tel*
17	SPECIALS	*Specials-Two Tone*
18	PYSCHEDELIC FURS	*Psychedelic Furs-CBS*
19	TOO MUCH PRESSURE	*Selecter-Two Tone*
20	GREATEST HITS	*KC & The Sunshine Band-TK*

WEEK ENDING MARCH 22 1980

US SINGLES

	Title	Artist-Label
1	ANOTHER BRICK	*Pink Floyd-Columbia*
2	LONGER	*Dan Fogelberg-Full Moon/Epic*
3	CRAZY LITTLE THING	*Queen-Elektra*
4	DESIRE	*Andy Gibb-RSO*
5	WORKING MY WAY BACK	*Spinners-Atlantic*
6	ON THE ROAD	*Donna Summer-Casablanca*
7	HIM	*Rupert Holmes-MCA*
8	THE SECOND TIME AROUND	*Shalamar-Solar*
9	TOO HOT	*Kool & The Gang-De-Lite*
10	HOW DO I MAKE YOU	*Linda Ronstadt-Asylum*
11	CALL ME	*Blondie-Chrysalis*
12	YES, I'M READY	*Teri De Sario with KC-Casablanca*
13	SPECIAL LADY	*Ray, Goodman and Brown-Polydor*
14	RIDE LIKE THE WIND	*Christopher Cross-Warner Bros.*
15	REFUGEE	*Tom Petty & Heartbreakers-Backstreet*
16	I CAN'T TELL YOU WHY	*Eagles-Asylum*
17	OFF THE WALL	*Michael Jackson-Epic*
18	GIVE IT ALL YOU GOT	*Chuck Mangione-Epic*
19	FIRE LAKE	*Bob Seger-Capitol*
20	THREE TIMES IN LOVE	*Tommy James-Millennium*

US ALBUMS

	Title	Artist-Label
1	THE WALL	*Pink Floyd-Columbia*
2	DAMN THE TORPEDOES	*Tom Petty & Heartbreakers-Backstreet*
3	MAD LOVE	*Linda Ronstadt-Asylum*
4	PERMANENT WAVES	*Rush-Mercury*
5	BEBE LE STRANGE	*Heart-Epic*
6	PHOENIX	*Dan Fogelberg-Full Moon/Epic*
7	THE WHISPERS	*The Whispers-Solar*
8	FUN AND GAMES	*Chuck Mangione-A&M*
9	AGAINST THE WIND	*Bob Seger & the Silver Bullet Band-Capitol*
10	OFF THE WALL	*Michael Jackson-Epic*
11	GLASS HOUSES	*Billy Joel-CBS*
12	THE HEAT OF THE NIGHT	*Pat Benatar-Chrysalis*
13	THE LONG RUN	*Eagles-Asylum*
14	LIGHT UP THE NIGHT	*Brothers Johnson-A&M*
15	KENNY	*Kenny Rogers-United Artists*
16	BUT THE LITTLE GIRLS	*The Knack-Capitol*
17	ON THE RADIO	*Donna Summer-Casablanca*
18	LADIES NIGHT	*Kool & The Gang-De-Lite*
19	THE ROSE	*Soundtrack-Atlantic*
20	RAY, GOODMAN AND BROWN	*Ray, Goodman and Brown-Polydor*

UK SINGLES

	Title	Artist-Label
1	GOING UNDERGROUND	*Jam-Polydor*
2	WE ARE BEAUTIFUL	*Fern Kinney-WEA*
3	TAKE THAT LOOK OFF	*Marti Webb-Polydor*
4	TURNING JAPANESE	*Vapors-United Artists*
5	DANCE YOURSELF DIZZY	*Liquid Gold-Polo*
6	GAMES WITHOUT FRONTIERS	*Peter Gabriel-Charisma*
7	ATOMIC	*Blondie-Chrysalis*
8	WORKING MY WAY BACK	*Detroit Spinners-Atlantic*
9	ALL NIGHT LONG	*Rainbow-Polydor*
10	DO THAT TO ME	*Captain and Tennille-Casablanca*
11	SO LONELY	*Police-A & M*
12	CUBA	*Gibson Brothers-Island*
13	HANDS OFF SHE'S MINE	*The Beat-Go Feet*
14	STOMP	*Brothers Johnson-A & M*
15	ECHO BEACH	*Martha & The Muffins-Dindisc*
16	SPIRIT OF RADIO	*Rush-Mercury*
17	AND THE BEAT GOES ON	*Whispers-Solar*
18	COWARD OF THE COUNTY	*Kenny Rogers-United Artists*
19	CARRIE	*Cliff Richard-EMI*
20	AT THE EDGE	*Stiff Little Fingers-Chrysalis*

UK ALBUMS

	Title	Artist-Label
1	TEARS AND LAUGHTER	*Johnny Mathis-CBS*
2	TELL ME ON A SUNDAY	*Marti Webb-Polydor*
3	STRING OF HITS	*Shadows-EMI*
4	GREATEST HITS	*Rose Royce-Whitfield*
5	HEARTBREAKERS	*Matt Monro-EMI*
6	GET HAPPY	*Elvis Costello-F Beat*
7	REGATTA DE BLANC	*Police-A&M*
8	NOBODY'S HERO	*Stiff Little Fingers-Chrysalis*
9	OUTLANDOS D'AMOUR	*Police-A&M*
10	THE LAST DANCE	*Various-Motown*
11	GLASS HOUSES	*Billy Joel-CBS*
12	THE SINGLES ALBUM	*Crystal Gayle-United Artists*
13	OFF THE WALL	*Michael Jackson-Epic*
14	12 GOLD BARS	*Status Quo-Vertigo*
15	DOWN TO EARTH	*Rainbow-Polydor*
16	EAT TO THE BEAT	*Blondie-Chrysalis*
17	PRETENDERS	*Pretenders-Real*
18	GOLDEN COLLECTION	*Charley Pride-K-Tel*
19	PSYCHEDELIC FURS	*Psychedelic Furs-CBS*
20	KENNY	*Kenny Rogers-United Artists*

WEEK ENDING MARCH 29 1980

US SINGLES

#	Title	Artist-Label
1	ANOTHER BRICK	Pink Floyd-Columbia
2	WORKING MY WAY BACK	Spinners-Atlantic
3	CRAZY LITTLE THING	Queen-Elektra
4	DESIRE	Andy Gibb-RSO
5	CALL ME	Blondie-Chrysalis
6	HIM	Rupert Holmes-MCA
7	TOO HOT	Kool & The Gang-De-Lite
8	THE SECOND TIME AROUND	Shalamar-Solar
9	RIDE LIKE THE WIND	Christopher Cross-Warner Bros.
10	HOW DO I MAKE YOU	Linda Ronstadt-Asylum
11	SPECIAL LADY	Ray, Goodman and Brown-Polydor
12	LONGER	Dan Fogelberg-Full Moon/Epic
13	I CAN'T TELL YOU WHY	Eagles-Asylum
14	OFF THE WALL	Michael Jackson-Epic
15	FIRE LAKE	Bob Seger-Capitol
16	ON THE RADIO	Donna Summer-Casablanca
17	WITH YOU I'M BORN AGAIN	Billy Preston and Syreeta-Motown
18	GIVE IT ALL YOU GOT	Chuck Mangione-A & M
19	THREE TIMES IN LOVE	Tommy James-Millennium
20	LOST IN LOVE	Air Supply-Arista

US ALBUMS

#	Title	Artist-Label
1	THE WALL	Pink Floyd-Columbia
2	AGAINST THE WIND	Bob Seger & Silver Bullet Band-Capitol
3	MAD LOVE	Linda Ronstadt-Asylum
4	DAMN THE TORPEDOES	Tom Petty & Heartbreakers-Backstreet
5	BEBE LE STRANGE	Heart-Epic
6	GLASS HOUSES	Billy Joel-CBS
7	THE WHISPERS	The Whispers-Solar
8	FUN AND GAMES	Chuck Mangione-A & M
9	PHOENIX	Dan Fogelberg-Full Moon/Epic
10	OFF THE WALL	Michael Jackson-Epic
11	PERMANENT WAVES	Rush-Mercury
12	LIGHT UP THE NIGHT	Brothers Johnson-A & M
13	THE LONG RUN	Eagles-Asylum
14	GET HAPPY	Elvis Costello-F Beat
15	BUT THE LITTLE GIRLS	The Knack-Capitol
16	AMERICAN GIGOLO	Soundtrack-Polydor
17	DEPARTURE	Journey-Columbia
18	THE HEAT OF THE NIGHT	Pat Benatar-Chrysalis
19	RAY, GOODMAN AND BROWN	Ray, Goodman and Brown-Polydor
20	ON THE RADIO	Donna Summer-Casablanca

UK SINGLES

#	Title	Artist-Label
1	GOING UNDERGROUND	Jam-Polydor
2	WE ARE BEAUTIFUL	Fern Kinney-WEA
3	TURNING JAPANESE	Vapors-United Artists
4	DANCE YOUSELF DIZZY	Liquid Gold-Polo
5	WORKING MY BACK TO YOU	Detroit Spinners-Atlantic
6	TAKE THAT LOOK OFF	Marti Webb-Polydor
7	ALL NIGHT LONG	Rainbow-Polydor
8	DO THAT TO ME	Captain and Tennille-Casablanca
9	GAMES WITHOUT FRONTIERS	Peter Gabriel-Charisma
10	ECHO BEACH	Martha & The Muffins-Dindisc
11	STOMP	Brothers Johnson-A & M
12	POISON IVY	The Lambrettas-Rocket
13	SPIRIT OF RADIO	Rush-Mercury
14	CUBA	Gibson Brothers-Island
15	HANDS OFF SHE'S MINE	The Beat-Go Feet
16	SO LONELY	Police-A & M
17	NAIL IN THE HEART	Squeeze-A & M
18	ATOMIC	Blondie-A & M
19	JANUARY FEBRUARY	Barbara Dickson-Epic
20	KING/FOOD FOR THOUGHT	UB40-Graduate

UK ALBUMS

#	Title	Artist-Label
1	TEARS AND LAUGHTER	Johnny Mathis-CBS
2	GREATEST HITS	Rose Royce-Whitfield
3	TELL ME ON A SUNDAY	Marti Webb-Polydor
4	TWELVE GOLD BARS	Status Quo-Vertigo
5	STRING OF HITS	Shadows-EMI
6	HEARTBREAKERS	Matt Monro-EMI
7	SINGLES ALBUM	Crystal Gayle-United Artists
8	REGATTA DE BLANC	Police-A & M
9	GLASS HOUSES	Billy Joel-CBS
10	NOBODY'S HERO	Stiff Little Fingers-Chrysalis
11	GET HAPPY	Elvis Costello-F Beat
12	LOUD AND CLEAR	Sammy Hagar-Capitol
13	OUTLANDOS D'AMOUR	Police-A & M
14	THE LAST DANCE	Various-Motown
15	ON THROUGH THE NIGHT	Def Leppard-Vertigo
16	OFF THE WALL	Michael Jackson-Epic
17	DOWN TO EARTH	Rainbow-Polydor
18	SPECIALS	Specials-Two Tone
19	EAT TO THE BEAT	Blondie-Chrysalis
20	STAR TRAKS	Various-K-Tel

WEEK ENDING APRIL 5 1980

US SINGLES

#	Title	Artist-Label
1	ANOTHER BRICK	Pink Floyd-Columbia
2	WORKING MY WAY BACK	Spinners-Atlantic
3	CALL ME	Blondie-Chrysalis
4	CRAZY LITTLE THING	Queen-Elektra
5	TOO HOT	Kool & The Gang-De Lite
6	HIM	Rupert Holmes-MCA
7	RIDE LIKE THE WIND	Christopher Cross-Warner Bros
8	SPECIAL LADY	Ray, Goodman & Brown-Polydor
9	DESIRE	Andy Gibb-RSO
10	HOW DO I MAKE YOU	Linda Ronstadt-Asylum
11	I CAN'T TELL YOU WHY	Eagles-Asylum
12	OFF THE WALL	Michael Jckson-Epic
13	FIRE LAKE	Bob Seger-Capitol
14	THE SECOND TIME AROUND	Shalamar-Solar
15	WITH YOU I'M BORN AGAIN	Billy Preston & Syreeta-Motown
16	LOST IN LOVE	Air Supply-Arista
17	YOU MAY BE RIGHT	Billy Joel-Columbia
18	SEXY EYES	Dr Hook-Capitol
19	THREE TIMES IN LOVE	Tommy James-Millennium
20	HOLD ON TO MY LOVE	Jimmy Ruffin-RSO

US ALBUMS

#	Title	Artist-Label
1	THE WALL	Pink Floyd-Columbia
2	AGAINST THE WIND	Bob Seger & Silver Bullet Band-Capitol
3	MAD LOVE	Linda Ronstadt-Asylum
4	GLASS HOUSES	Billy Joel-Columbia
5	DAMN THE TORPEDOES	Tom Petty & Heartbreakers-Backstreet
6	BEBE LE STRANGE	Heart-Epic
7	THE WHISPERS	The WHispers-Solar
8	FUN AND GAMES	Chuck Mangione-A&M
9	LIGHT UP THE NIGHT	Brothers Johnson-A&M
10	OFF THE WALL	Michael Jackson-Epic
11	PHOENIX	Dan Fogelberg-Full Moon/Epic
12	GET HAPPY	Elvis Costello-F Beat
13	DEPARTURE	Journey-Columbia
14	AMERICAN GIGOLO	Soundtrack-Polydor
15	PERMANENT WAVES	Rush-Mercury
16	THE LONG RUN	Eagles-Asylum
17	RAY, GOODMAN & BROWN	Ray, Goodman & Brown-Polydor
18	IN THE HEAT OF THE NIGHT	Pat Benatar-Chrysalis
19	LOVE STINKS	J Geils Band-EMI America
20	BAD LUCK STREAK	Warren Zevon-Asylum

UK SINGLES

#	Title	Artist-Label
1	GOING UNDERGROUND	Jam-Polydor
2	DANCE YOURSELF DIZZY	Liquid Gold-Polo
3	WORKING MY WAY BACK	Detroit Spinners-Atlantic
4	TURNING JAPANESE	Vapors-United Artists
5	WE ARE BEAUTIFUL	Fern Kinney-WEA
6	STOMP	Brothers Johnson-A & M
7	POISON IVY	Lambrettas-Rocket
8	TURN IT ON AGAIN	Genesis-Charisma
9	SEXY EYES	Dr Hook-Capitol
10	KING/FOOD FOR THOUGHT	UB40-Graduate
11	ECHO BEACH	Martha & The Muffins-Dindisc
12	JANUARY FEBRUARY	Barbara Dickson-Epic
13	ALL NIGHT LONG	Rainbow-Polydor
14	NIGHT BOAT TO CAIRO	Madness-Stiff
15	LIVING AFTER MIDNIGHT	Judas Priest-CBS
16	DO THAT TO ME	Captain and Tennille-Casablanca
17	MY WORLD	Secret Affair-I-Spy
18	NAIL IN MY HEART	Squeeze-A & M
19	DON'T PUSH IT	Leon Hayward-20th Century
20	HAPPY HOUSE	Siouxsie And The Banshees-Polydor

UK ALBUMS

#	Title	Artist-Label
1	DUKE	Genesis-Charisma
2	GREATEST HITS	Rose Royce-Whitfield
3	TWELVE GOLD BARS	Status Quo-Vertigo
4	TEARS AND LAUGHTER	Johnny Mathis-CBS
5	HEARTBREAKERS	Matt Monro-EMI
6	TELL ME ON A SUNDAY	Marti Webb-Polydor
7	STAR TRAKS	Various-K-Tel
8	THE SINGLES ALBUM	Crystal Gayle-United Artists
9	REGATTA DE BLANC	Police-A&M
10	STRING OF HITS	Shadows-EMI
11	GLASS HOUSES	Billy Joel-CBS
12	OUTLANDOS D'AMOUR	Police-A&M
13	FACADES	Sad Cafe-RCA
14	OFF THE WALL	Michael Jackson-Epic
15	ON THROUGH THE NIGHT	Def Leppard-Vertigo
16	LOUD AND CLEAR	Sammy Hagar-Capitol
17	DOWN TO EARTH	Rainbow-Polydor
18	NOBODY'S HEROES	Stiff Little Fingers-Chrysalis
19	SPECIALS	Specials-Two Tone
20	PRETENDERS	Pretenders-Real

WEEK ENDING APRIL 12 1980

US SINGLES

1	**ANOTHER BRICK** *Pink Floyd-Columbia*
2	**CALL ME** *Blondie-Chrysalis*
3	**WORKING MY WAY BACK** *Spinners-Atlantic*
4	**RIDE LIKE THE WIND** *Christopher Cross-Warner Bros*
5	**TOO HOT** *Kool & The Gang-De-Lite*
6	**SPECIAL LADY** *Ray, Goodman & Brown-Polydor*
7	**WITH YOU I'M BORN AGAIN** *Billy Preston & Syreeta-Motown*
8	**CRAZY LITTLE THING** *Queen-Elektra*
9	**I CAN'T TELL YOU WHY** *Eagles-Asylum*
10	**OFF THE WALL** *Michael Jackson-Epic*
11	**FIRE LAKE** *Bob Seger-Capitol*
12	**LOST IN LOVE** *Air Supply-Arista*
13	**HIM** *Rupert Holmes-MCA*
14	**YOU MAY BE RIGHT** *Billy Joel-Columbia*
15	**SEXY EYES** *Dr Hook-Capitol*
16	**THE SECOND TIME AROUND** *Shalamar-Solar*
17	**HOW DO I MAKE YOU** *Linda Ronstadt-Asylum*
18	**HOLD ON TO MY LOVE** *Jimmy Ruffin-RSO*
19	**AND THE BEAT GOES ON** *The Whispers-Solar*
20	**DESIRE** *Andy Gibb-RSO*

US ALBUMS

1	**THE WALL** *Pink Floyd-Columbia*
2	**AGAINST THE WIND** *Bob Seger & Silver Bullet Band-Capitol*
3	**MAD LOVE** *Linda Ronstadt-Asylum*
4	**GLASS HOUSES** *Billy Joel-Columbia*
5	**DAMN THE TORPEDOES** *Tom Petty & Heartbreakers-Backstreet*
6	**THE WHISPERS** *The Whispers-Solar*
7	**OFF THE WALL** *Michael Jackson-Epic*
8	**LIGHT UP THE NIGHT** *Brothers Johnson-A&M*
9	**AMERICAN GIGOLO** *Soundtrack-Polydor*
10	**DEPARTURE** *Journey-Columbia*
11	**GET HAPPY** *Elvis Costello-F Beat*
12	**BEBE LE STRANGE** *Heart-Epic*
13	**PHOENIX** *Dan Fogelberg-Full Moon/Epic*
14	**FUN AND GAMES** *Chuck Mangione-A&M*
15	**PERMANENT WAVES** *Rush-Mercury*
16	**THE LONG RUN** *Eagles-Asylum*
17	**RAY,GOODMAN & BROWN** *Ray,Goodman & Brown-Polydor*
18	**CHRISTOPHER CROSS** *Christopher Cross-Warner Bros*
19	**LOVE STINKS** *J. Geils Band-EMI America*
20	**PRETENDERS** *Pretenders-Sire*

UK SINGLES

1	**WORKING MY WAY BACK** *Detroit Spinners-Atlantic*
2	**DANCE YOURSELF DIZZY** *Liquid Gold-Polo*
3	**GOING UNDERGROUND** *Jam-Polydor*
4	**SEXY EYES** *Dr Hook-Capitol*
5	**KING/FOOD FOR THOUGHT** *UB40-Graduate*
6	**NIGHT BOAT TO CAIRO** *Madness-Stiff*
7	**TURNING JAPANESE** *Vapors-United Artists*
8	**POISON IVY** *Lambrettas-Rocket*
9	**STOMP** *Brothers Johnson-A&M*
10	**TURN IT ON AGAIN** *Genesis-Charisma*
11	**JANUARY FEBRUARY** *Barbara Dickson-Epic*
12	**LIVING AFTER MIDNIGHT** *Judas Priest-CBS*
13	**TALK OF THE TOWN** *Pretenders-Real*
14	**WE ARE BEAUTIFUL** *Fern Kinney-WEA*
15	**ECHO BEACH** *Martha & The Muffins-Dindisc*
16	**MY WORLD** *Secret Affair-I-Spy*
17	**HAPPY HOUSE** *Siouxie & The Banshees-Polydor*
18	**DON'T PUSH IT** *Leon Haywood-20th Century*
19	**SILVER DREAM MACHINE** *David Essex-Mercury*
20	**ALL NIGHT LONG** *Rainbow-Polydor*

UK ALBUMS

1	**DUKE** *Genesis-Charisma*
2	**GREATEST HITS** *Rose Royce-Whitfield*
3	**TWELVE GOLD BARS** *Status Quo-Vertigo*
4	**TEARS AND LAUGHTER** *Johnny Mathis-CBS*
5	**HEARTBREAKERS** *Matt Monro-EMI*
6	**STAR TRAKS** *Various-K-Tel*
7	**TELL ME ON A SUNDAY** *Marti Webb-Polydor*
8	**REGATTA DE BLANC** *Police-A&M*
9	**THE SINGLES ALBUM** *Crystal Gayle-United Artists*
10	**WHEELS OF STEEL** *Saxon-Carrere*
11	**STRING OF HITS** *Shadows-EMI*
12	**GLASS HOUSES** *Billy Joel-CBS*
13	**BARBARA DICKSON ALBUM** *Barbara Dickson-Epic*
14	**OUTLANDOS D'AMOUR** *Police-A&M*
15	**WOMEN & CHILDREN FIRST** *Van Halen-Warner Bros*
16	**PRETENDERS** *Pretenders-Real*
17	**FACADES** *Sad Cafe-RCA*
18	**THE MAGIC OF BONEY M** *Boney M-Atlantic-Hansa*
19	**DOWN TO EARTH** *Rainbow-Polydor*
20	**ON THROUGH THE NIGHT** *Def Leppard-Vertigo*

WEEK ENDING APRIL 19 1980

US SINGLES

1	**CALL ME** *Blondie-Chrysalis*
2	**ANOTHER BRICK** *Pink Floyd-Columbia*
3	**RIDE LIKE THE WIND** *Christopher Cross-Warner Bros*
4	**WITH YOU I'M BORN AGAIN** *Billy Preston & Syreeta-Motown*
5	**SPECIAL LADY** *Ray, Goodman & Brown-Polydor*
6	**LOST IN LOVE** *Air Supply-Arista*
7	**FIRE LAKE** *Bob Seger-Capitol*
8	**I CAN'T TELL YOU WHY** *Eagles-Asylum*
9	**WORKING MY WAY BACK** *Spinners-Atlantic*
10	**OFF THE WALL** *Michael Jackson-Epic*
11	**TOO HOT** *Kool And The Gang-De-Lite*
12	**YOU MAY BE RIGHT** *Billy Joel-Columbia*
13	**SEXY EYES** *Dr Hook-Capitol*
14	**HOLD ON TO MY LOVE** *Jimmy Ruffin-RSO*
15	**CRAZY LITTLE THING** *Queen-Elektra*
16	**DON'T FALL IN LOVE** *Kenny Rogers/Kim Carnes-United Artists*
17	**PILOT OF THE AIRWAYS** *Charlie Dore-Island*
18	**HOW DO I MAKE YOU** *Linda Ronstadt-Asylum*
19	**AND THE BEAT GOES ON** *The Whispers-Solar*
20	**I PLEDGE MY LOVE** *Peaches And Herb-Polydor*

US ALBUMS

1	**THE WALL** *Pink Floyd-Columbia*
2	**AGAINST THE WIND** *Bob Seger/Silver Bullet Band-Capitol*
3	**GLASS HOUSES** *Billy Joel-Columbia*
4	**MAD LOVE** *Linda Ronstadt-Asylum*
5	**OFF THE WALL** *Michael Jackson-Epic*
6	**THE WHISPERS** *The Whispers-Solar*
7	**LIGHT UP THE NIGHT** *The Brothers Johnson-A&M*
8	**AMERICAN GIGOLO** *Soundtrack-Polydor*
9	**DEPARTURE** *Journey-Columbia*
10	**DAMN THE TORPEDOES** *Tom Petty & Heartbreakers-Backstreet*
11	**GET HAPPY** *Elvis Costello-Columbia*
12	**BEBE LE STRANGE** *Heart-Epic*
13	**PHOENIX** *Dan Fogelberg-Full Moon/Epic*
14	**CHRISTOPHER CROSS** *Christopher Cross-Warner Bros*
15	**THE LONG RUN** *Eagles-Asylum*
16	**PERMANENT WAVES** *Rush-Mercury*
17	**PRETENDERS** *Pretenders-Sire*
18	**LOVE STINKS** *J. Geils Band-EMI*
19	**FUN AND GAMES** *Chuck Mangione-A&M*
20	**GO ALL THE WAY** *Isley Brothers-T-Neck*

UK SINGLES

1	**WORKING MY WAY BACK** *Detroit Spinners-Atlantic*
2	**CALL ME** *Blondie-Chrysalis*
3	**DANCE YOURSELF DIZZY** *Liquid Gold-Polo*
4	**KING/FOOD FOR THOUGHT** *UB40-Graduate*
5	**SEXY EYES** *Dr Hook-Capitol*
6	**GOING UNDERGROUND** *Jam-Polydor*
7	**NIGHT BOAT TO CAIRO EP** *Madness-Stiff*
8	**TALK OF THE TOWN** *Pretenders-Real*
9	**SILVER DREAM MACHINE** *David Essex-Mercury*
10	**POISON IVY** *Lambrettas-Rocket*
11	**JANUARY FEBRUARY** *Barbara Dickson-Epic*
12	**GENO** *Dexy's Midnight Runners-Parlophone*
13	**TURN IT ON AGAIN** *Genesis-Charisma*
14	**DON'T PUSH IT** *Leon Haywood-20th Century*
15	**STOMP** *Brothers Johnson-A&M*
16	**LIVING AFTER MIDNIGHT** *Judas Priest-CBS*
17	**TURNING JAPANESE** *Vapors-United Artists*
18	**MY WORLD** *Secret Affair-I-Spy*
19	**KOOL IN THE KAFTAN** *BA Robertson-Asylum*
20	**HAPPY HOUSE** *Siouxie & The Banshees-Polydor*

UK ALBUMS

1	**GREATEST HITS** *Rose Royce-Whitfield*
2	**DUKE** *Genesis-Charisma*
3	**TWELVE GOLD BARS** *Status Quo-Vertigo*
4	**BRITISH STEEL** *Judas Priest-CBS*
5	**WHEELS OF STEEL** *Saxon-Carrere*
6	**THE MAGIC OF BONEY M** *Boney M-Atlantic*
7	**BARBARA DICKSON ALBUM** *Barbara Dickson-Epic*
8	**FACADES** *Sad Cafe-Epic*
9	**TEARS AND LAUGHTER** *Johnny Mathis-CBS*
10	**REGATTA DE BLANC** *Police-A&M*
11	**HEARTBREAKERS** *Matt Monro-EMI*
12	**STAR TRACKS** *Various-K-Tel*
13	**COUNTRY NUMBER ONE** *Don Gibson-Warwick*
14	**PRETENDERS** *Pretenders-Real*
15	**TELL ME ON A SUNDAY** *Marti Webb-Polydor*
16	**OUTLANDOS D'AMOUR** *Police-A&M*
17	**ONE STEP BEYOND** *Madness-Stiff*
18	**GLASS HOUSES** *Billy Joel-CBS*
19	**BRAND NEW AGE** *UK Subs-Gem*
20	**THE SINGLES ALBUM** *Bobby Vee-United Artists*

WEEK ENDING APRIL 26 1980

US SINGLES

1 **CALL ME**
Blondie-Chrysalis
2 **RIDE LIKE THE WIND**
Christopher Cross-Warner Bros
3 **ANOTHER BRICK**
Pink Floyd-Columbia
4 **WITH YOU I'M BORN AGAIN**
Billy Preston & Syreeta-Motown
5 **SPECIAL LADY**
Ray, Goodman & Brown-Polydor
6 **LOST IN LOVE**
Air Supply-Arista
7 **FIRE LAKE**
Bob Seger-Capitol
8 **I CAN'T TELL YOU WHY**
Eagles-Asylum
9 **YOU MAY BE RIGHT**
Billy Joel-Columbia
10 **SEXY EYES**
Dr Hook-Capitol
11 **WORKING MY WAY BACK**
Spinners-Atlantic
12 **HOLD ON TO MY LOVE**
Jimmy Ruffin-RSO
13 **DON'T FALL IN LOVE**
Kenny Rogers/Kim Carnes-United Artists
14 **TOO HOT**
Kool And The Gang-De-Lite
15 **PILOT OF THE AIRWAYS**
Charlie Dore-Island
16 **OFF THE WALL**
Michael Jackson-Epic
17 **BIGGEST PART OF ME**
Ambrosia-Warner Bros
18 **HURT SO BAD**
Linda Ronstadt-Asylum
19 **I PLEDGE MY LOVE**
Peaches And Herb-Polydor
20 **I THINK ABOUT ME**
Fleetwood Mac-Warner Bros

US ALBUMS

1 **THE WALL**
Pink Floyd-Columbia
2 **AGAINST THE WIND**
Bob Seger & Silver Bullet Band-Capitol
3 **GLASS HOUSES**
Billy Joel-Columbia
4 **MAD LOVE**
Linda Ronstadt-Asylum
5 **OFF THE WALL**
Michael Jackson-Epic
6 **LIGHT UP THE NIGHT**
The Brothers Johnson-A&M
7 **AMERICAN GIGOLO**
Soundtrack-Polydor
8 **DEPARTURE**
Journey-Columbia
9 **THE WHISPERS**
The Whispers-Solar
10 **WOMEN & CHILDREN FIRST**
Van Halen-Warner Bros
11 **CHRISTOPHER CROSS**
Christopher Cross-Warner Bros
12 **DAMN THE TORPEDOES**
Tom Petty & Heartbreakers-Backstreet
13 **GO ALL THE WAY**
Isley Brothers-T-Neck
14 **PRETENDERS**
Pretenders-Sire
15 **THE LONG RUN**
Eagles-Asylum
16 **PHOENIX**
Dan Fogelberg-Full Moon
17 **BEBE LE STRANGE**
Heart-Epic
18 **LOVE STINKS**
J. Geils Band-EMI
19 **GET HAPPY**
Elvis Costello-Columbia
20 **CATCHING THE SUN**
Spyro-Gyra-MCA

UK SINGLES

1 **CALL ME**
Blondie-Chrysalis
2 **GENO**
Dexy's Midnight Runners-Parlophone
3 **WORKING MY WAY BACK**
Detroit Spinners-Atlantic
4 **KING/FOOD FOR THOUGHT**
UB 40-Graduate
5 **SEXY EYES**
Dr Hook-Capitol
6 **SILVER DREAM MACHINE**
David Essex-Mercury
7 **COMING UP**
Paul McCartney-Parlophone
8 **DANCE YOURSELF DIZZY**
Liquid Gold-Polo
9 **TALK OF THE TOWN**
Pretenders-Real
10 **NIGHT BOAT TO CAIRO**
Madness-Stiff
11 **TOCCATA**
Sky-Ariola
12 **DON'T PUSH IT**
Leon Haywood-20th Century
13 **JANUARY FEBRUARY**
Barbara Dickson-Epic
14 **MY OH MY**
Sad Cafe-RCA
15 **POISON IVY**
Lambrettas-Rocket
16 **TURN IT ON AGAIN**
Genesis-Charisma
17 **KOOL IN THE KAFTAN**
B.A. Robertson-Asylum
18 **LIVING AFTER MIDNIGHT**
Judas Priest-CBS
19 **MY WORLD**
Secret Affair-I-Spy
20 **GOING UNDERGROUND**
Jam-Polydor

UK ALBUMS

1 **GREATEST HITS**
Rose Royce-Whitfield
2 **DUKE**
Genesis-Charisma
3 **TWELVE GOLD BARS**
Status Quo-Vertigo
4 **IRON MAIDEN**
Iron Maiden-EMI
5 **THE SINGLES ALBUM**
Bobby Vee-United Artists
6 **HYPNOTISED**
Undertones-Sire
7 **SKY 2**
Sky-Ariola
8 **BRITISH STEEL**
Judas Priest-CBS
9 **GREATEST HITS**
Suzi Quatro-RAK
10 **THE MAGIC OF BONEY M**
Boney M-Atlantic
11 **BARBARA DICKSON ALBUM**
Barbara Dickson-Epic
12 **WHEELS OF STEEL**
Saxon-Carrere
13 **FACADES**
Sad Cafe-RCA
14 **BY REQUEST**
Lena Martell-Ronco
15 **PRETENDERS**
Pretenders-Real
16 **COUNTRY NUMBER ONE**
Don Gibson-Warwick
17 **REGATTA DE BLANC**
Police-A&M
18 **BRAND NEW AGE**
UK Subs-Gem
19 **SNAKES AND LADDERS**
Gerry Rafferty-United Artists
20 **HEARTBREAKERS**
Matt Monro-EMI

WEEK ENDING MAY 3 1980

US SINGLES

1 **CALL ME**
Blondie-Chrysalis
2 **RIDE LIKE THE WIND**
Christopher Cross-Warner Bros
3 **LOST IN LOVE**
Air Supply-Arista
4 **WITH YOU I'M BORN AGAIN**
Billy Preston And Syreeta-Motown
5 **ANOTHER BRICK**
Pink Floyd-Columbia
6 **FIRE LAKE**
Bob Seger-Capitol
7 **YOU MAY BE RIGHT**
Billy Joel-Columbia
8 **I CAN'T TELL YOU WHY**
Eagles-Asylum
9 **SEXY EYES**
Dr Hook-Capitol
10 **HOLD ON TO MY LOVE**
Jimmy Ruffin-RSO
11 **DON'T FALL IN LOVE**
Kenny Rogers/Kim Carnes-United Artist
12 **SPECIAL LADY**
Ray Goodman And Brown-Polydor
13 **PILOT OF THE AIRWAVES**
Charlie Dore-Island
14 **BIGGEST PART OF ME**
Ambrosia-Warner Bros
15 **HURT SO BAD**
Linda Ronstadt-Asylum
16 **WORKING MY WAY BACK**
Spinners-Atlantic
17 **I CAN'T HELP IT**
Andy Gibb And Olivia Newton-John-RSO
18 **CARS**
Gary Numan-Atco
19 **BREAKDOWN DEAD AHEAD**
Boz Scaggs-Columbia
20 **THINK ABOUT ME**
Fleetwodd Mac-Warner Bros

US ALBUMS

1 **AGAINST THE WIND**
Bob Seger & Silver Bullet-Capitol
2 **THE WALL**
Pink Floyd-Columbia
3 **GLASS HOUSES**
Billy Joel-Columbia
4 **MAD LOVE**
Linda Ronstadt-Asylum
5 **LIGHT UP THE NIGHT**
The Brothers Johnson-A&M
6 **OFF THE WALL**
Michael Jackson-Epic
7 **AMERICAN GIGOLO**
Soundtrack-Polydor
8 **DEPARTURE**
Journey-Columbia
9 **WOMEN AND CHILDREN FIRST**
Van Halen-Warner Bros
10 **CHRISTOPHER CROSS**
Christopher Cross-Warner Bros
11 **THE WHISPERS**
The Whispers-Solar
12 **GO ALL THE WAY**
Isley Brothers-T-Neck
13 **PRETENDERS**
Pretenders-Sire
14 **DAMN THE TORPEDOES**
Tom Petty & Heartbreakers-Backstreet
15 **THE LONG RUN**
Eagles-Asylum
16 **PHOENIX**
Dan Fogelberg-Full Moon
17 **MIDDLE MAN**
Boz Scaggs-Columbia
18 **GIDEON**
Kenny Rogers-United Artists
19 **CATCHING THE SUN**
Spyro Gyra-MCA
20 **WARM THOUGHTS**
Smokey Robinson-Tamla

UK SINGLES

1 **GENO**
Dexy's Midnight Runners-Parlophone
2 **COMING UP**
Paul McCartney-Parlophone
3 **CALL ME**
Blondie-Chrysalis
4 **SILVER DREAM MACHINE**
David Essex-Mercury
5 **TOCCATA**
Sky-Ariola
6 **KING/FOOD FOR THOUGHT**
UB40-Graduate
7 **WORKING MY WAY BACK**
Detroit Spinners-Atlantic
8 **SEXY EYES**
Dr Hook-Capitol
9 **TALK OF THE TOWN**
Pretenders-Real
10 **CHECK OUT THE GROOVE**
Bobby Thurston-Epic
11 **MY PERFECT COUSIN**
Undertones-Sire
12 **DON'T PUSH IT**
Leon Haywood-20th Century
13 **THE GROOVE**
Rodney Franklin-CBS
14 **NIGHT BOAT TO CAIRO**
Madness-Stiff
15 **WHAT'S ANOTHER YEAR**
Johnny Logan-Epic
16 **MY OH MY**
Sad Cafe-RCA
17 **DANCE YOURSELF DIZZY**
Liquid Gold-Polo
18 **JANUARY FEBRUARY**
Barbara Dickson-Epic
19 **I SHOULDA LOVED YA**
Narada Michael Walden-Atlantic
20 **WHEELS OF STEEL**
Saxon-Carrere

UK ALBUMS

1 **SKY 2**
Sky-Ariola
2 **GREATEST HITS**
Rose Royce-Whitfield
3 **THE MAGIC OF BONEY M**
Boney M-Atlantic
4 **DUKE**
Genesis-Charisma
5 **GREATEST HITS**
Suzi Quatro-RAK
6 **TWELVE GOLD BARS**
Status Quo-Vertigo
7 **THE SINGLES ALBUM**
Bobby Vee-United Artists
8 **HYPNOTISED**
Undertones-Sire
9 **HEAVEN AND HELL**
Black Sabbath-Vertigo
10 **IRON MAIDEN**
Iron Maiden-EMI
11 **BARBARA DICKSON ALBUM**
Barbara Dickson-Epic
12 **BY REQUEST**
Lena Martell-Ronco
13 **WHEELS OF STEEL**
Saxon-Carrere
14 **EMPTY GLASS**
Peter Townshend-Atco
15 **SNAKES AND LADDERS**
Gerry Rafferty-United Artists
16 **PRETENDERS**
Pretenders-Real
17 **BRITISH STEEL**
Judas Priest-CBS
18 **REGATTA DE BLANC**
Police-A&M
19 **SOMETIMES YOU WIN**
Dr Hook-Capitol
20 **ONE STEP BEYOND**
Madness-Stiff

WEEK ENDING MAY 10 1980

US SINGLES

1 CALL ME
Blondie-Chrysalis
2 RIDE LIKE THE WIND
Christopher Cross-Warner Bros
3 LOST IN LOVE
Air Supply-Arista
4 WITH YOU I'M BORN AGAIN
Billy Preston And Syreeta-Motown
5 ANOTHER BRICK
Pink Floyd-Columbia
6 FIRE LAKE
Bob Seger-Capitol
7 YOU MAY BE RIGHT
Billy Joel-Columbia
8 SEXY EYES
Dr Hook-Capitol
9 DON'T FALL IN LOVE
Kenny Rogers/Kim Carnes-United Artists
10 HOLD ON TO MY LOVE
Jimmy Ruffin-RSO
11 BIGGEST PART OF ME
Ambrosia-Warner Bros
12 HURT SO BAD
Linda Ronstadt-Asylum
13 PILOT OF THE AIRWAVES
Charlie Dore-Island
14 I CAN'T HELP IT
Andy Gibb And Olivia Newton-John-RSO
15 CARS
Gary Numan-Atco
16 I CAN'T TELL YOU WHY
Eagles-Asylum
17 BREAKDOWN DEAD AHEAD
Boz Scaggs-Columbia
18 STOMP
The Brothers Johnson-A&M
19 FUNKY TWON
Lipps Inc.-Casablanca
20 BRASS IN POCKET
Pretenders-Sire

US ALBUMS

1 AGAINST THE WIND
Bob Seger & Silver Bullet Band-Capitol
2 THE WALL
Pink Floyd-Columbia
3 GLASS HOUSES
Billy Joel-Columbia
4 MAD LOVE
Linda Ronstadt-Asylum
5 LIGHT UP THE NIGHT
The Brothers Johnson-A&M
6 OFF THE WALL
Michael Jackson-Epic
7 AMERICAN GIGOLO
Soundtrack-Polydor
8 WOMEN AND CHILDREN FIRST
Van Halen-Warner Bros
9 CHRISTOPHER CROSS
Christopher Cross-Warner Bros
10 DEPARTURE
Journey-Columbia
11 GO ALL THE WAY
Isley Brothers-T-Neck
12 PRETENDERS
Pretenders-Sire
13 THE WHISPERS
The Whispers-Solar
14 DAMN THE TORPEDOES
Tom Petty & Heartbreakers-Backstreet
15 MIDDLE MAN
Boz Scaggs-Columbia
16 GIDEON
Kenny Rogers-United Artists
17 WARM THOUGHTS
Smokey Robinson-Tamla
18 PHOENIX
Dan Fogelberg-Full Moon
19 MOUTH TO MOUTH
Lipps Inc.-Casablanca
20 THE PLEASURE PRINCIPLE
Gary Numan-Atco

UK SINGLES

1 GENO
Dexy's Midnight Runners-Parlophone
2 WHAT'S ANOTHER YEAR
Johnny Logan-Epic
3 COMING UP
Paul McCartney-Parlophone
4 CALL ME
Blondie-Chrysalis
5 SILVER DREAM MACHINE
David Essex-Mercury
6 TOCCATA
Sky-Ariola
7 THE GROOVE
Rodney Franklin-CBS
8 GOLDEN YEARS LIVE EP
Motorhead-Bronze
9 NO DOUBT ABOUT IT
Hot Chocolate-RAK
10 MY PERFECT COUSIN
Undertones-Sire
11 I SHOULDA LOVED YA
Narada Michael Walden-Atlantic
12 CHECK OUT THE GROOVE
Bobby Thurston-Epic
13 KING/FOOD FOR THOUGHT
UB40-Graduate
14 HOLD ONTO MY LOVE
Jimmy Ruffin-RSO
15 DON'T MAKE WAVES
Nolans-Epic
16 SEXY EYES
Dr Hook-Capitol
17 MIRROR IN THE BATHROOM
The Beat-Go Feet
18 WORKING MY WAY BACK
Detroit Spinners-Atlantic
19 DON'T PUSH IT
Leon Haywood-20th Century
20 WHEELS OF STEEL
Saxon-Carrere

UK ALBUMS

1 SKY 2
Sky-Ariola
2 THE MAGIC OF BONEY M
Boney M-Atlantic
3 GREATEST HITS
Rose Royce-Whitfiled
4 GREATEST HITS
Suzi Quatro-RAK
5 DUKE
Genesis-Charisma
6 TWELVE GOLD BARS
Status Quo-Vertigo
7 THE SINGLES ALBUM
Bobby Vee-United Artists
8 HYPNOTISED
Undertones-Sire
9 BY REQUEST
Lena Martell-Ronco
10 HEAVEN AND HELL
Black Sabbath-Vertigo
11 EMPTY GLASS
Pete Townshend-Atco
12 BARBARA DICKSON ALBUM
Barbara Dickson-Epic
13 WHEELS OF STEEL
Saxon-Carrere
14 SOMETIMES YOU WIN
Dr Hook-Capitol
15 CHAMPAGNE AND ROSES
Various Artists-Polystar
16 IRON MAIDEN
Iron Maiden-EMI
17 GOLDEN MELODIES
National Brass Band-K-Tel
18 REGATTA DE BLANC
Police-A&M
19 SNAKES AND LADDERS
Gerry Rafferty-United Artists
20 17 SECONDS
Cure-Fiction

WEEK ENDING MAY 17 1980

US SINGLES

1 CALL ME
Blondie-Chrysalis
2 RIDE LIKE THE WIND
Christopher Cross-Warner Bros
3 LOST IN LOVE
Air Supply-Arista
4 FUNKYTOWN
Lipps Inc.-Casablanca
5 WITH YOU I'M BORN AGAIN
Billy Preston And Syreeta-Motown
6 SEXY EYES
Dr Hook-Capitol
7 YOU MAY BE RIGHT
Billy Joel-Columbia
8 DON'T FALL IN LOVE
Kenny Rogers/Kim Carnes-United Artists
9 ANOTHER BRICK
Pink Floyd-Columbia
10 BIGGEST PART OF ME
Ambrosia-Warner Bros
11 HURT SO BAD
Linda Ronstadt-Asylum
12 CARS
Gary Numan-Atco
13 I CAN'T HELP IT
Andy Gibb And Olivia Newton-John-RSO
14 PILOT OF THE AIRWAVES
Charlie Dore-Island
15 BREAKDOWN DEAD AHEAD
Bob Scaggs-Columbia
16 STOMP
The Brothers Johnson-A&M
17 BRASS IN POCKET
Pretenders-Sire
18 AGAINST THE WIND
Bob Seger & Silver Bullet Band-Capitol
19 COMING UP
Paul McCartney-Columbia
20 THE ROSE
Bette Midler-Atlantic

US ALBUMS

1 AGAINST THE WIND
Bob Seger & Silver Bullet Band-Capitol
2 THE WALL
Pink Floyd-Columbia
3 GLASS HOUSES
Billy Joel-Columbia
4 MAD LOVE
Linda Ronstadt-Asylum
5 JUST ONE NIGHT
Eric Clapton-RSO
6 WOMEN AND CHILDREN FIRST
Van Halen-Warner Bros
7 CHRISTOPHER CROSS
Christopher Cross-Warner Bros
8 GO ALL THE WAY
Isley Brothers-T-Neck
9 OFF THE WALL
Michael Jackson-Epic
10 LIGHT UP THE NIGHT
The Brothers Johnson-A&M
11 PRETENDERS
Pretenders-Sire
12 MOUTH TO MOUTH
Lipps Inc.-Casablanca
13 MIDDLE MAN
Bob Scaggs-Columbia
14 GIDEON
Kenny Rogers-United Artists
15 WARM THOUGHTS
Smokey Robinson-Motown
16 AMERICAN GIGOLO
Soundtrack-Polydor
17 PHOENIX
Dan Fogelberg-Full Moon
18 THE PLEASURE PRINCIPLE
Gary Numan-Atco
19 DEPARTURE
Journey-Columbia
20 CRASH AND BURN
Pat Travers Band-Polydor

UK SINGLES

1 WHAT'S ANOTHER YEAR
Johnny Logan-Epic
2 GENO
Dexy's Midnight Runners-Parlophone
3 COMING UP
Paul McCartney-Parlophone
4 MIRROR IN THE BATHROOM
The Beat-Go Feet
5 SHE'S OUT OF MY LIFE
Michael Jackson-Epic
6 NO DOUBT ABOUT IT
Hot Chocolate-Rak
7 HOLD ON TO MY LOVE
Jimmy Ruffin-RSO
8 I SHOULDA LOVED YA
Narada Michael Walden-Atlantic
9 MY PERFECT COUSIN
Undertones-Sire
10 SILVER DREAM MACHINE
David Essex-Mercury
11 THE GROOVE
Rodney Franklin-CBS
12 GOLDEN YEARS EP
Motorhead-Bronze
13 DON'T MAKE WAVES
Nolans-Epic
14 CALL ME
Blondie-Chrysalis
15 TOCCATA
Sky-Ariola
16 CHECK OUT THE GROOVE
Bobby Thurston-Epic
17 LET'S GO ROUND AGAIN
Average White Band-RCA
18 OVER YOU
Roxy Music-Polydor
19 BREATHING
Kate Bush-EMI
20 FOOL FOR YOUR LOVING
Whitesnake-United Artists

UK ALBUMS

1 THE MAGIC OF BONEY M
Boney M-Atlantic
2 SKY 2
Sky-Ariola
3 JUST ONE NIGHT
Eric Clapton-RSO
4 GREATEST HITS
Rose Royce-Whitfield
5 DUKE
Genesis-Charisma
6 GREATEST HITS
Suzi Quatro-Rak
7 TWELVE GOOD BARS
Status Quo-Vertigo
8 SPORTS CAR
Judie Tzuke-Rocket
9 HEAVEN AND HELL
Black Sabbath-Vertigo
10 HYPNOTISED
Undertones-Sire
11 OFF THE WALL
Michael Jackson-Epic
12 THE SINGLES ALBUM
Bobby Vee-United Artists
13 EMPTY GLASS
Peter Townshend-Atco
14 BARBARA DICKSON ALBUM
Barbara Dickson-Epic
15 GOLDEN MELODIES
National Brass Band-K-Tel
16 REGATTA DE BLANC
Police-A&M
17 IRON MAIDEN
Iron Maiden-EMI
18 BY REQUEST
Lena Martell-Ronco
19 PRETENDERS
Pretenders-Sire
20 WHEELS OF STEEL
Saxon-Carrere

WEEK ENDING MAY 24 1980

US SINGLES

1	**CALL ME** *Blondie-Chrysalis*
2	**FUNKY TOWN** *Lipps Inc.-Casablanca*
3	**LOST IN LOVE** *Air Supply-Arista*
4	**DON'T FALL IN LOVE** *Kenny Roberts/Kim Carnes-United Artists*
5	**SEXY EYES** *Dr Hook-Capitol*
6	**BIGGEST PART OF ME** *Ambrosia-Warner Bros*
7	**STOMP** *The Brothers Johnson-A&M*
8	**HURT SO BAD** *Linda Ronstadt-Asylum*
9	**RIDE LIKE THE WIND** *Christopher Cross-Warner Bros*
10	**CARS** *Gary Numan-Atco*
11	**AGAINST THE WIND** *Bob Seger & Silver Bullet Band-Capitol*
12	**I CAN'T HELP IT** *Andy Gibb And Olivia Newton-John-RSO*
13	**THE ROSE** *Bette Midler-Atlantic*
14	**COMING UP** *Paul MacCartney-Columbia*
15	**BREAKDOWN DEAD AHEAD** *Boz Scaggs-Columbia*
16	**BRASS IN POCKET** *Pretenders-Sire*
17	**ANOTHER BRICK** *Pink Floyd-Columbia*
18	**STEAL AWAY** *Robbie Dupree-Elektra*
19	**SHE'S OUT OF MY LIFE** *Michael Jackson-Epic*
20	**LITTLE JEANNIE** *Elton John-MCA*

US ALBUMS

1	**AGAINST THE WIND** *Bob Seger & Silver Bullet Band-Capitol*
2	**GLASS HOUSES** *Billy Joel-Columbia*
3	**THE WALL** *Pink Floyd-Columbia*
4	**MAD LOVE** *Linda Ronstadt-Asylum*
5	**JUST ONE NIGHT** *Eric Clapton-RSO*
6	**WOMEN AND CHILDREN FIRST** *Van Halen-Warner Bros*
7	**CHRISTOPHER CROSS** *Christopher Cross-Warner Bros*
8	**GO ALL THE WAY** *Isley Brothers-T-Neck*
9	**OFF THE WALL** *Michael Jackson-Epic*
10	**PRETENDERS** *Pretenders-Sire*
11	**MOUTH TO MOUTH** *Lipps Inc.-Casablanca*
12	**MIDDLE MAN** *Boz Scaggs-Columbia*
13	**GIDEON** *Kenny Rogers-United Artists*
14	**WARM THOUGHTS** *Smokey Robinson-Motown*
15	**LIGHT UP THE NIGHT** *The Brothers Johnson-A&M*
16	**THE PLEASURE PRINCIPLE** *Gary Numan-Atco*
17	**AMERICAN GIGOLO** *Soundtrack-Polydor*
18	**DEPARTURE** *Journey-Columbia*
19	**LET'S GET SERIOUS** *Jermaine Jackson-Motown*
20	**EMPTY GLASS** *Pete Townshend-Atco*

UK SINGLES

1	**WHAT'S ANOTHER YEAR** *Johnny Logan-Epic*
2	**NO DOUBT ABOUT IT** *Hot Chocolate-Rak*
3	**SHE'S OUT OF MY LIFE** *Michael Jackson-Epic*
4	**MIRROR IN THE BATHROOM** *The Beat-Go Feet*
5	**GENO** *Dexy's Midnight Runners-Parlophone*
6	**THEME FROM MASH** *The Mash-CBS*
7	**OVER YOU** *Roxy Music-Polydor*
8	**HOLD ON TO MY LOVE** *Jimmy Ruffin-RSO*
9	**I SHOULDA LOVED YA** *Narada Michael Walden-Atlantic*
10	**WE ARE GLASS** *Gary Numan-Beggars Banquet*
11	**COMING UP** *Paul McCartney-Parlophone*
12	**DON'T MAKE WAVES** *Nolans-Epic*
13	**FOOL FOR YOUR LOVING** *Whitesnake-United Artists*
14	**THE GROOVE** *Rodney Franklin-CBS*
15	**SILVER DREAM MACHINE** *David Essex-Mercury*
16	**BREATHING** *Kate Bush-EMI*
17	**LET'S GO ROUND AGAIN** *Average White Band-RCA*
18	**RAT RACE/RUDE BOYS** *Specials-2 Tone*
19	**YOU GAVE ME LOVE** *Crown Heights Affair-Mercury*
20	**GOLDEN YEARS EP** *Motorhead-Bronze*

UK ALBUMS

1	**THE MAGIC OF BONEY M** *Boney M-Atlantic*
2	**SKY 2** *Sky-Ariola*
3	**JUST ONE NIGHT** *Eric Clapton-RSO*
4	**GREATEST HITS** *Rose Royce-Whitfield*
5	**DUKE** *Genesis-Charisma*
6	**OFF THE WALL** *Michael Jackson-Epic*
7	**SPORTS CAR** *Judie Tzuke-Rocket*
8	**TWELVE GOLD BARS** *Status Quo-Vertigo*
9	**ONE STEP BEYOND** *Madness-Stiff*
10	**HEAVEN AND HELL** *Black Sabbath-Vertigo*
11	**HYPNOTISED** *Undertones-Sire*
12	**GREATEST HITS** *Suzi Quatro-Rak*
13	**THE SINGLES ALBUM** *Bobby Vee-United Artists*
14	**ME MYSELF I** *Joan Armatrading-A&M*
15	**REGATTA DE BLANC** *Police-A&M*
16	**PRETENDERS** *Pretenders-Real*
17	**GOOD MORNING AMERICA** *Various-K-Tel*
18	**MAGIC REGGAE** *Various-K-Tel*
19	**WHEELS OF STEEL** *Saxon-Carrere*
20	**17 SECONDS** *Cure-Fiction*

WEEK ENDING MAY 31 1980

US SINGLES

1	**FUNKY TOWN** *Lipps Inc-Casablanca*
2	**CALL ME** *Blondie-Chrysalis*
3	**COMING UP** *Paul McCartney-Columbia*
4	**DON'T FALL IN LOVE** *Rogers/Carnes-United Artists*
5	**SEXY EYES** *Dr Hook-Capitol*
6	**BIGGEST PART OF ME** *Ambrosia-Warner Bros*
7	**STOMP** *The Brothers Johnson-A&M*
8	**HURT SO BAD** *Linda Ronstadt-Asylum*
9	**AGAINST THE WIND** *Bob Seger & Silver Bullet Band-Capitol*
10	**CARS** *Gary Numan-Atco*
11	**THE ROSE** *Bette Midler-Atlantic*
12	**I CAN'T HELP IT** *Andy Gibb And Olivia Newton-John-RSO*
13	**LITTLE JEANNIE** *Elton John-MCA*
14	**BRASS IN POCKET** *Pretenders-Sire*
15	**BREAKDOWN DEAD AHEAD** *Boz Scaggs-Columbia*
16	**STEAL AWAY** *Robbie Dupree-Elektra*
17	**SHE'S OUT OF MY LIFE** *Michael Jackson-Epic*
18	**LOST IN LOVE** *Air Supply-Arista*
19	**CUPID** *Spinners-Atlantic*
20	**LET'S GET SERIOUS** *Jermaine Jackson-Motown*

US ALBUMS

1	**AGAINST THE WIND** *Bob Seger & Silver Bullet Band-Capitol*
2	**GLASS HOUSES** *Billy Joel-Columbia*
3	**THE WALL** *Pink Floyd-Columbia*
4	**JUST ONE NIGHT** *Eric Clapton-RSO*
5	**MOUTH TO MOUTH** *Lipps Inc-Casablanca*
6	**WOMEN AND CHILDREN FIRST** *Van Halen-Warner Bros*
7	**CHRISTOPHER CROSS** *Christopher Cross-Warner Bros*
8	**GO ALL THE WAY** *Isley Brothers-T-Neck*
9	**MAD LOVE** *Linda Ronstadt-Asylum*
10	**PRETENDERS** *Pretenders-Sire*
11	**MIDDLE MAN** *Boz Scaggs-Columbia*
12	**GIDEON** *Kenny Rogers-United Artists*
13	**OFF THE WALL** *Michael Jackson-Epic*
14	**WARM THOUGHTS** *Smokey Robinson-Motown*
15	**LIGHT UP THE NIGHT** *The Brothers Johnson-A&M*
16	**THE PLEASURE PRINCIPLE** *Gary Numan-Atco*
17	**EMPTY GLASS** *Pete Townshend-Atco*
18	**LET'S GET SERIOUS** *Jermaine Jackson-Motown*
19	**DUKE** *Genesis-Atlantic*
20	**THE EMPIRE STRIKES BACK** *Soundtrack-RSO*

UK SINGLES

1	**THEME FROM MASH** *The Mash-CBS*
2	**NO DOUBT ABOUT IT** *Hot Chocolate-RAK*
3	**WHAT'S ANOTHER YEAR** *Johnny Logan-Epic*
4	**SHE'S OUT OF MY LIFE** *Michael Jackson-Epic*
5	**WE ARE GLASS** *Gary Numan-Beggars Banquet*
6	**OVER YOU** *Roxy Music-Polydor*
7	**MIRROR IN THE BATHROOM** *The Beat-Go Feet*
8	**RAT RACE** *Specials-2 Tone*
9	**FUNKY TOWN** *Lipps Inc.-Casablanca*
10	**GENO** *Dexy's Midnight Runners-Parlophone*
11	**HOLD ON TO MY LOVE** *Jimmy Ruffin-RSO*
12	**LET'S GO ROUND AGAIN** *Average White Band-RCA*
13	**CRYING** *Don McLean-EMI*
14	**FOOL FOR YOUR LOVING** *Whitesnake-United Artists*
15	**DON'T MAKE WAVES** *Nolans-Epic*
16	**I SHOULDA LOVED YA** *Narada Michael Walden-Atlantic*
17	**YOU GAVE ME LOVE** *Crown Heights Affair-Mercury*
18	**MIDNITE DYNAMOS** *Matchbox-Magnet*
19	**YOU'LL ALWAYS FIND ME** *Jona Lewie-Stiff*
20	**D-A-A-ANCE** *The Lambrettas-Rocket*

UK ALBUMS

1	**McCARTNEY II** *Paul McCartney-Parlophone*
2	**THE MAGIC OF BONEY M** *Boney M-Atlantic*
3	**JUST CAN'T STOP** *The Beat-Go Feet*
4	**SKY 2** *Sky-Ariola*
5	**ME MYSELF I** *Joan Armatrading-A&M*
6	**OFF THE WALL** *Michael Jackson-Epic*
7	**FLESH AND BLOOD** *Roxy Music-Polydor*
8	**JUST ONE NIGHT** *Eric Clapton-RSO*
9	**GREATEST HITS** *Rose Royce-Whitfield*
10	**CHAMPAGNE AND ROSES** *Various-Polystar*
11	**DUKE** *Genesis-Charisma*
12	**TWELVE GOLD BARS** *Status Quo-Vertigo*
13	**SPORTS CAR** *Judie Tzuke-Rocket*
14	**HEAVEN AND HELL** *Black Sabbath-Vertigo*
15	**TELL ME ON A SUNDAY** *Marti Webb-Polydor*
16	**TRAVELOGUE** *Human League-Virgin*
17	**GREATEST HITS** *Suzi Quatro-RAK*
18	**ONE STEP BEYOND** *Madness-Stiff*
19	**MAGIC REGGAE** *Various-K-Tel*
20	**REGATTA DE BLANC** *Police-A&M*

WEEK ENDING JUNE 7 1980

US SINGLES

1	FUNKY TOWN *Lipps Inc-Casablanca*
2	COMING UP *Paul McCartney-Columbia*
3	DON'T FALL IN LOVE *Rogers/Carnes-United Artists*
4	CALL ME *Blondie-Chrysalis*
5	THE ROSE *Bette Midler-Atlantic*
6	AGAINST THE WIND *Bob Seger & Silver Bullet Band-Capitol*
7	HURT SO BAD *Linda Ronstadt-Asylum*
8	CARS *Gary Numan-Atco*
9	LITTLE JEANNIE *Elton John-MCA*
10	STILL ROCK AND ROLL *Billy Joel-Columbia*
11	SHE'S OUT OF MY LIFE *Michael Jackson-Epic*
12	STEAL AWAY *Robbie Dupree-Elektra*
13	BRASS IN POCKET *Pretenders-Sire*
14	CUPID *Spinners-Atlantic*
15	SEXY EYES *Dr Hook-Capitol*
16	STOMP *The Brothers Johnson-A&M*
17	LET'S GET SERIOUS *Jermaine Jackson-Motown*
18	LOST IN LOVE *Air Supply-Arista*
19	LET ME LOVE YOU TONIGHT *Pure Prairie League-Casablanca*
20	WONDERING WHERE *Bruce Cockburn-Millenium*

US ALBUMS

1	AGAINST THE WIND *Bob Seger & Silver Bullet Band-Capitol*
2	GLASS HOUSES *Billy Joel-Columbia*
3	THE WALL *Pink Floyd-Columbia*
4	JUST ONE NIGHT *Eric Clapton-RSO*
5	MOUTH TO MOUTH *Lipps Inc.-Casablanca*
6	WOMEN AND CHILDREN FIRST *Val Halen-Warner Bros*
7	CHRISTOPHER CROSS *Christopher Cross-Warner Bros*
8	GO ALL THE WAY *Isley Brothers-T-Neck*
9	PRETENDERS *Pretenders-Sire*
10	MIDDLE MAN *Boz Scaggs-Columbia*
11	MAD LOVE *Linda Ronstadt-Asylum*
12	GIDEON *Kenny Rogers-United Artists*
13	OFF THE WALL *Michael Jackson-Epic*
14	EMPTY GLASS *Pete Townshend-Atco*
15	LET'S GET SERIOUS *Jermaine Jackson-Motown*
16	DUKE *Genesis-Atlantic*
17	THE EMPIRE STRIKES BACK *Soundtrack-RSO*
18	LIGHT UP THE NIGHT *The Brothers Johnson-A&M*
19	SWEET SENSATION *Stephanie Mills-20th Century*
20	THE PLEASURE PRINCIPLE *Gary Numan-Atco*

UK SINGLES

1	THEME FROM MASH *The Mash-CBS*
2	NO DOUBT ABOUT IT *Hot Chocolate-RAK*
3	FUNKY TOWN *Lipps Inc-Casablanca*
4	CRYING *Don McLean-EMI*
5	RAT RACE *Specials-2 Tone*
6	OVER YOU *Roxy Music-Polydor*
7	WE ARE GLASS *Gary Numan-Beggars-Banquet*
8	SHE'S OUT OF MY LIFE *Michael Jackson-Epic*
9	LET'S GET SERIOUS *Jermaine Jackson-Motown*
10	WHAT'S ANOTHER YEAR *Johnny Logan-Epic*
11	MIRROR IN THE BATHROOM *The Beat-Go Feet*
12	YOU GAVE ME LOVE *Crown Heights Affair-Mercury*
13	LET'S GO ROUND AGAIN *Average White Band-RCA*
14	BACK TOGETHER AGAIN *Roberta Flack/Donny Hathaway-Atlantic*
15	HOLD ON TO MY LOVE *Jimmy Ruffin-RSO*
16	MIDNITE DYNAMOS *Matchbox-Magnet*
17	GENO *Dexy's Midnight Runners-Parlophone*
18	FOOL FOR YOUR LOVING *Whitesnake-United Artists*
19	YOU'LL ALWAYS FIND ME *Jona Lewie-Stiff*
20	JUST CAN'T GIVE YOU UP *Mystic Merlin-Capitol*

UK ALBUMS

1	McCARTNEY II *Paul McCartney-Parlophone*
2	FLESH AND BLOOD *Roxy Music-Polydor*
3	PETER GABRIEL *Peter Gabriel-Charisma*
4	I JUST CAN'T STOP *Beat-Go Feet*
5	ME MYSELF I *Joan Armatrading-A&M*
6	SKY 2 *Sky-Ariola*
7	THE MAGIC OF BONEY M *Boney M-Atlantic*
8	OFF THE WALL *Michael Jackson-Epic*
9	READY AN' WILLING *Whitesnake-United Artists*
10	CHAMPAGNE AND ROSES *Various-Polystar*
11	DUKE *Genesis-Charisma*
12	GREATEST HITS *Rose Royce-Whitfield*
13	JUST ONE NIGHT *Eric Clapton-RSO*
14	21 AT 33 *Elton John-Rocket*
15	GOOD MORNING AMERICA *Various-K-Tel*
16	TWELVE GOLD BARS *Status Quo-Vertigo*
17	SOMETIMES WHEN WE TOUCH *Cleo Laine And James Galway-RCA*
18	ONE STEP BEYOND *Madness-Stiff*
19	HAPPY DAYS *Various-K-Tel*
20	REGATTA DE BLANC *Police A&M*

WEEK ENDING JUNE 14 1980

US SINGLES

1	FUNKY TOWN *Lipps Inc-Casablanca*
2	COMING UP *Paul McCartney-Columbia*
3	BIGGEST PART OF ME *Ambrosia-Warner Bros*
4	THE ROSE *Bette Midler-Atlantic*
5	AGAINST THE WIND *Bob Seger & Silver Bullet Band-Capitol*
6	CALL ME *Blondie-Chrysalis*
7	STILL ROCK AND ROLL *Billy Joel-Columbia*
8	LITTLE JEANNIE *Elton John-MCA*
9	CARS *Gary Numan-Atco*
10	STEAL AWAY *Robbie Dupree-Elektra*
11	SHE'S OUT OF MY LIFE *Michael Jackson-Epic*
12	DON'T FALL IN LOVE *Rogers/Carnes-United Artists*
13	CUPID *Spinners-Atlantic*
14	LET'S GET SERIOUS *Jermain Jackson-Motown*
15	HURT SO BAD *Linda Ronstadt-Asylum*
16	BRASS IN POCKET *Pretenders-Sire*
17	STOMP *The Brothers Johnson-A&M*
18	LET ME LOVE YOU TONIGHT *Pure Prairie League-Casablanca*
19	SEXY EYES *Dr Hook-Capitol*
20	LOST IN LOVE *Air Supply-Arista*

US ALBUMS

1	GLASS HOUSE *Billy Joel-Columbia*
2	AGAINST THE WIND *Bob Seger & Silver Bullet-Capitol*
3	JUST ONE NIGHT *Eric Clapton-RSO*
4	THE WALL *Pink Floyd-Columbia*
5	MOUTH TO MOUTH *Lipps Inc-Casablanca*
6	WOMEN AND CHILDREN FIRST *Van Halen-Warner Bros*
7	CHRISTOPHER CROSS *Christopher Cross-Warner Bros*
8	MIDDLE MAN *Boz Scaggs-Columbia*
9	PRETENDERS *Pretenders-Sire*
10	THE EMPIRE STRIKES BACK *Soundtrack-RSO*
11	EMPTY GLASS *Pete Townshend-Atco*
12	OFF THE WALL *Michael Jackson-Epic*
13	LET'S GET SERIOUS *Jermaine Jackson-Motown*
14	MAD LOVE *Linda Ronstadt-Asylum*
15	DUKE *Genesis-Atlantic*
16	McCARTNEY II *Paul McCartney-Columbia*
17	SWEET SENSATION *Stephanie Mills-20th Century*
18	GO ALL THE WAY *Isley Brothers-T Neck*
19	SCREAM DREAM *Ted Nugent-Epic*
20	TRILOGY *Frank Sinatra-Reprise*

UK SINGLES

1	THEME FROM MASH *The Mash-CBS*
2	CRYING *Don McLean-EMI*
3	FUNKY TOWN *Lipps Inc-Casablanca*
4	NO DOUBT ABOUT IT *Hot Chocolate-RAK*
5	OVER YOU *Roxy Music-Polydor*
6	BACK TOGETHER AGAIN *Roberta Flack/Donny Hathaway-Atlantic*
7	RAT RACE *Specials-2 Tone*
8	LET'S GET SERIOUS *Jermaine Jackson-Motown*
9	WE ARE GLASS *Gary Numan-Beggars Banquet*
10	YOU GAVE ME LOVE *Crown Heights Affair-Mercury*
11	SHE'S OUT OF MY LIFE *Michael Jackson-Epic*
12	D-A-A-ANCE *Lambrettas-Epic*
13	LET'S GO ROUND AGAIN *Average White Band-RCA*
14	MESSAGES *Orchestral Manoeuvres-Dindisc*
15	MIDNITE DYNAMOS *Matchbox-Magnet*
16	YOU'LL ALWAYS FIND ME *Jona Lewie-Stiff*
17	BEHIND THE GROOVE *Teena Marie-Motown*
18	BREAKING THE LAW *Judas Priest-CBS*
19	EVERYBODY'S GOT TO LEARN *Korgis-Rialto*
20	I'M ALIVE *Electric Light Orchestra-Jet*

UK ALBUMS

1	PETER GABRIEL *Peter Gabriel-Charisma*
2	FLESH AND BLOOD *Roxy Music-Polydor*
3	McCARTNEY II *Paul McCartney-Parlophone*
4	JUST CAN'T STOP *The Beat-Go Feet*
5	ME MYSELF I *Joan Armatrading-A&M*
6	READY AND WILLING *Whitesnake-United Artists*
7	CHAMPAGNE AND ROSES *Various-Polystar*
8	SKY 2 *Sky-Ariola*
9	OFF THE WALL *Michael Jackson-Epic*
10	THE MAGIC OF BONEY M *Boney M-Atlantic*
11	THE UP ESCALATOR *Grahma Parker & Rumour-Stiff*
12	21 AT 33 *Elton John-Rocket*
13	THEMES FOR DREAMS *Pierre Belmonde-K Tel*
14	JUST ONE NIGHT *Eric Clapton-RSO*
15	DUKE *Genesis-Charisma*
16	ROCK AND ROLL SWINDLE *Original Soundtrack-Virgin*
17	GREATEST HITS *Rose Royce-Whitfield*
18	REGATTA DE BLANC *Police-A&M*
19	MAGIC REGGAE *Various-K Tel*
20	SOMETIMES WHEN WE TOUCH *Cleo Laine/James Galway-RCA*

WEEK ENDING JUNE 21 1980

US SINGLES

1 FUNKY TOWN
Lipps Inc-Casablanca
2 COMING UP
Paul McCartney-Columbia
3 BIGGEST PART OF ME
Ambrosia-Warner Bros
4 THE ROSE
Bette Midler-Atlantic
5 AGAINST THE WIND
Bob Seger & Silver Bullet-Capitol
6 STILL ROCK AND ROLL
Billy Joel-Columbia
7 LITTLE JEANNIE
Elton John-MCA
8 STEAL AWAY
Robbie Dupree-Elektra
9 CARS
Gary Numan-Atco
10 SHE'S OUT OF MY LIFE
Michael Jackson-Epic
11 CUPID
Spinners-Atlantic
12 CALL ME
Blondie-Chrysalis
13 LET'S GET SERIOUS
Jermaine Jackson-Motown
14 DON'T FALL IN LOVE
Kenny Rogers/Kim Carnes-United Artists
15 LET ME LOVE YOU TONIGHT
Pure Prairie League-Casablanca
16 SHINING STAR
Manhattan-Columbia
17 BRASS IN POCKET
Pretenders-Sire
18 STOMP
The Brothers Jackson-A&M
19 HURT SO BAD
Linda Ronstadt-Asylum
20 TIRED OF TOEING THE LINE
Rocky Burnette-EMI

US ALBUMS

1 GLASS HOUSES
Billy Joel-Columbia
2 JUST ONE NIGHT
Eric Clapton-RSO
3 McCARTNEY II
Paul McCartney-Columbia
4 AGAINST THE WIND
Bob Seger & Silver Bullet-Capitol
5 MOUTH TO MOUTH
Lipps Inc-Casablanca
6 THE WALL
Pink FLoyd-Columbia
7 THE EMPIRE STRIKES BACK
Soundtrack-RSO
8 MIDDLE MAN
Boz Scaggs-Columbia
9 WOMEN AND CHILDREN FIRST
Van Halen-Warner Bros
10 EMPTY GLASS
Pete Townshend-Atco
11 OFF THE WALL
Michael Jackson-Epic
12 LET'S GET SERIOUS
Jermaine Jackson-Motown
13 CHRISTOPHER CROSS
Christopher Cross-Warner Bros
14 PRETENDERS
Pretenders-Sire
15 DUKE
Genesis-Atlantic
16 SWEET SENSATION
Stephanie Mills-20th Century
17 SCREAM DREAM
Ted Nugent-Epic
18 MAD LOVE
Linda Ronstadt-Asylum
19 GO ALL THE WAY
Isley Brothers-T Neck
20 TRILOGY
Frank Sinatra-Surprise

UK SINGLES

1 CRYING
Don McLean-EMI
2 THEME FROM MASH
The Mash-CBS
3 FUNKY TOWN
Lipps Inc-Casablanca
4 BACK TOGETHER AGAIN
Roberta Flack/Donny Hathaway-Atlantic
5 NO DOUBT ABOUT IT
Hot Chocolate-Rak
6 EVERYBODYS GOT TO LEARN
Korgis-Rialto
7 BEHIND THE GROOVE
Teena Marie-Motown
8 LET'S GET SERIOUS
Jermaine Jackson-Motown
9 OVER YOU
Roxy Music-Polydor
10 YOU GAVE ME LOVE
Crown Heights Affair-Mercury
11 RAT RACE
Specials-2 Tone
12 BREAKING THE LAW
Judas Priest-CBS
13 MESSAGES
Orchestral Manoeuvres-Dindisc
14 MIDNITE DYNAMOS
Matchbox-Magnet
15 D-A-A—ANCE
Lambrettas-Rocket
16 SUBSTITUTE
Liquid Gold-Polo
17 SIX PACK
Police-A&M
18 PLAY THE GAME
Queen-EMI
19 WE ARE GLASS
Gary Numan-Beggars Banquet
20 I'M ALIVE
Electric Light Orchestra-Jet

UK ALBUMS

1 PETER GABRIEL
Peter Gabriel-Charisma
2 FLESH AND BLOOD
Roxy Music-Polydor
3 HOTWAX
Various-K Tel
4 McCARTNEY II
Paul McCartney-Parlophone
5 ME MYSELF I
Joan Armatrading-A&M
6 JUST CAN'T STOP
The Beat-Go Feet
7 READY AND WILLING
Whitesnake-United Artists
8 SKY II
Sky-Ariola
9 MAGIC REGGAE
Various-K Tel
10 CHAMPAGNE AND ROSES
Various-Polystar
11 THE PHOTOS
Photos-CBS
12 OFF THE WALL
Michael Jackson-Epic
13 THE MAGIC OF BONEY M
Boney M-Atlantic
14 SHINE
Average White Band-RCA
15 SOMETIMES WHEN WE TOUCH
Cleo Lane & James Galway-RCA
16 DEFECTOR
Steve Hackett-Charisma
17 REGATTA DE BLANC
Police-A&M
18 GREATEST HITS
Rose Royce-Whitfield
19 THE UP ESCALATOR
Graham Parker & The Rumour-Stiff
20 THEMES FOR DREAMS
Pierre Belmonde-K Tel

WEEK ENDING JUNE 28 1980

US SINGLES

1 COMING UP
Paul McCartney
2 FUNKY TOWN
Lipps Inc-Casablanca
3 THE ROSE
Bette Midler-Atlantic
4 STILL ROCK AND ROLL
Billy Joel-Columbia
5 AGAINST THE WIND
Bob Seger & Silver Bullet-Capitol
6 LITTLE JEANNIE
Elton John-MCA
7 STEAL AWAY
Robbie Dupree-Elektra
8 BIGGEST PART OF ME
Ambrosia-Warner Bros
9 CUPID
Spinners-Atlantic
10 SHE'S OUT OF MY LIFE
Michael Jackson-Epic
11 LET'S GET SERIOUS
Jermaine Jackson-Motown
12 LET ME LOVE TONIGHT
Pure Prairie League-Casablanca
13 SHINING STAR
Manhattan-Columbia
14 CARS
Gary Numan-Atco
15 CALL ME
Blondie-Chrysalis
16 MAGIC
Olivia Newton John-MCA
17 ONE FINE DAY
Carole King-Capitol
18 TIRED OF TOEING THE LINE
Rocky Burnette-EMI America
19 SHOULD'VE NEVER LET YOU
Neil Sedaka & Dara Sedaka-Elektra
20 DON'T FALL IN LOVE
Kenny Rogers/Kim Carnes-United Artists

US ALBUMS

1 GLASS HOUSES
Billy Joel-Columbia
2 JUST ONE NIGHT
Eric Clapton-RSO
3 McCARTNEY II
Paul McCartney-Columbia
4 AGAINST THE WIND
Bob Seger & Silver Bullet-Capitol
5 MOUTH TO MOUTH
Lipps Inc-Casablanca
6 THE EMPIRE STRIKES BACK
Soundtrack-RSO
7 THE WALL
Pink Floyd-Columbia
8 LET'S GET SERIOUS
Jermaine Jackson-Motown
9 EMPTY GLASS
Pete Townshend-Atco
10 MIDDLE MAN
Boz Scaggs-Columbia
11 WOMEN CHILDREN FIRST
Van Halen-Warner Bros
12 CHRISTOPHER CROSS
Christopher Cross-Warner Bros
13 DUKE
Genesis-Atlantic
14 HEROES
Commodore-Motown
15 SCREAM DREAM
Ted Nugent-Epic
16 SWEET SENSATION
Stephanie Mills-20th Century
17 OFF THE WALL
Michael Jackson-Epic
18 TRILOGY
Frank Sinatra-Reprise
19 21 AT 33
Elton John-MCA
20 THE ROSE
Soundtrack-Atlantic

UK SINGLES

1 CRYING
Don McLean-EMI
2 FUNKY TOWN
Lipps Inc-Casablanca
3 BACK TOGETHER AGAIN
Roberta Flack/Donny Hathaway-Atlantic
4 THEME FROM MASH
The Mash-CBS
5 EVERYBODYS GOT TO LEARN
Korgis-Rialto
6 BEHIND THE GROOVE
Teena Marie-Motown
7 TWO PINTS OF LAGER
Splodgenessabounds-Deram
8 SUBSTITUTE
Liquid Gold-Polo
9 LET'S GET SERIOUS
Jermaine Jackson-Motown
10 RAT RACE
Specials-2 Tone
11 JUMP TO THE BEAT
Stacy Lattisaw-Atlantic
12 YOU GAVE ME LOVE
Crown Heights Affair-Mercury
13 MESSAGES
Orchestral Manoeuvres-Dindisc
14 XANADU
Olivia Newton John/ELO-Jet
15 NO DOUBT ABOUT IT
Hot Chocolate-Rak
16 PLAY THE GAME
Queen-EMI
17 OVER YOU
Roxy Music-Polydor
18 BREAKING THE LAW
Judas Priest-CBS
19 MY WAY OF THINKING
UB40-Graduate
20 WATERFALLS
Paul McCartney-Parlophone

UK ALBUMS

1 FLESH AND BLOOD
Roxy Music-Polydor
2 PETER GABRIEL
Peter Gabriel-Charisma
3 HOT WAX
Various-K Tel
4 PHOTOS
Photos-CBS
5 SAVED
Bob Dylan-CBS
6 McCARTNEY II
Paul McCartney-Parlophone
7 ME MYSELF I
Joan Armatrading-A&M
8 JUST CAN'T STOP
The Beat-Go Feet
9 DEFECTOR
Steve Hackett-Charisma
10 SKY
Sky-Ariola
11 OFF THE WALL
Michael Jackson-Epic
12 MAGIC REGGAE
Various-K Tel
13 READY AND WILLING
Whitesnake-United Artists
14 UPRISING
Bob Marley-Island
15 THE MAGIC OF BONEY M
Boney M-Atlantic/Hansa
16 DUKE
Genesis-Charisma
17 REGATTA DE BLANC
Police-A&M
18 SHINE
Average White Band-RCA
19 THE UP ESCALATOR
Graham Parker-Stiff
20 SOMETIMES WHEN WE TOUCH
Cleo Laine/James Galway-RCA

WEEK ENDING JULY 5 1980

US SINGLES

	Title	Artist-Label
1	COMING UP	Paul McCartney & Wings-Columbia
2	FUNKY TOWN	Lipps Inc.-Casablanca
3	THE ROSE	Bette Midler-Atlantic
4	STILL ROCK AND ROLL	Billy Joel-Columbia
5	LITTLE JEANNIE	Elton John-MCA
6	AGAINST THE WIND	Bob Seger & Silver Bullet-Capitol
7	STEAL AWAY	Robbie Dupree-Elektra
8	CUPID	Spinners-Atlantic
9	BIGGEST PART OF ME	Ambrosia-Warner Bros.
10	LET'S GET SERIOUS	Jermaine Jackson-Motown
11	LET ME LOVE YOU TONIGHT	Pure Prairie League-Casablanca
12	SHINING STAR	Manhattans-Columbia
13	SHE'S OUT OF MY LIFE	Michael Jackson-Epic
14	MAGIC	Olivia Newton-John-MCA
15	TIRED OF TOEIN' THE LINE	Rocky Burnette-EMI America
16	ONE FINE DAY	Carole King-Capitol
17	CARS	Gary Numan-Atco
18	I'M ALIVE	Electric Light Orchestra-MCA
19	SHOULD'VE NEVER LET YOU	Neil & Dara Sedaka-Elektra
20	IN AMERICA	The Charlie Daniels Band-Epic

US ALBUMS

	Title	Artist-Label
1	GLASS HOUSES	Billy Joel-Columbia
2	JUST ONE NIGHT	Eric Clapton-RSO
3	McCARTNEY II	Paul McCartney-Columbia
4	AGAINST THE WIND	Bob Seger & Silver Bullet-Capitol
5	THE EMPIRE STRIKES BACK	Soundtrack-RSO
6	EMPTY GLASS	Pete Townshend-Atco
7	LET'S GET SERIOUS	Jermaine Jackson-Motown
8	HEROES	Commodores-Motown
9	MOUTH TO MOUTH	Lipps Inc.-Casablanca
10	THE WALL	Pink Floyd-Columbia
11	URBAN COWBOY	Soundtrack-Asylum
12	DUKE	Genesis-Atlantic
13	SCREAM DREAM	Ted Nugent-Epic
14	DIANA	Diana Ross-Motown
15	MIDDLE MAN	Boz Scaggs-Columbia
16	OFF THE WALL	Michael Jackson-Epic
17	TRILOGY	Frank Sinatra-Reprise
18	21 AT 33	Elton John-MCA
19	THE ROSE	Soundtrack-Atlantic
20	WOMEN CHILDREN FIRST	Van Halen-Warner Bros.

UK SINGLES

	Title	Artist-Label
1	CRYING	Don McLean-EMI
2	FUNKY TOWN	Lipps Inc-Casablanca
3	XANADU	Newton-John/Electric Light Orchestra-Jet
4	BACK TOGETHER AGAIN	Roberta Flack/Donny Hathaway-Atlantic
5	EVERYBODY'S GOT TO LEARN	Korgis-Rialto
6	JUMP TO THE BEAT	Stacy Lattisaw-Atlantic
7	TWO PINTS OF LAGER	Splodgenessabounds-Deram
8	MY WAY OF THINKING	UB40-Graduate
9	TO BE OR NOT TO BE	B.A. Robertson-Asylum
10	BEHIND THE GROOVE	Teena Marie-Motown
11	WATERFALLS	Paul McCartney-Parlophone
12	USE IT UP	Odyssey-RCA
13	SUBSTITUTE	Liquid Gold-Polo
14	PLAY THE GAME	Queen-EMI
15	THEME FROM MASH	The Mash-CBS
16	CUPID	Detroit Spinners-Atlantic
17	MIDNITE DYNAMOES	Matchbox-Magnet
18	LET'S GET SERIOUS	Jermaine Jackson-Motown
19	747(STRANGERS IN THE NIGHT)	Saxon-Carrere
20	MESSAGES	Orchestral Manoeuvres-Dindisc

UK ALBUMS

	Title	Artist-Label
1	EMOTIONAL RESCUE	Rolling Stones-Rolling Stones
2	FLESH AND BLOOD	Roxy Music-Polydor
3	SAVED	Bob Dylan-CBS
4	HOT WAX	Various-K Tel
5	PETER GABRIEL	Peter Gabriel-Charisma
6	McCARTNEY II	Paul McCartney-Parlophone
7	SKY 2	Sky-Ariola
8	ME MYSELF I	Joan Armatrading-A&M
9	THE PHOTOS	The Photos-CBS
10	UPRISING	Bob Marley-Island
11	JUST CAN'T STOP	The Beat-Go Feet
12	OFF THE WALL	Michael Jackson-Epic
13	DUKE	Genesis-Charisma
14	MAGIC REGGAE	Various-K Tel
15	REGATTA DE BLANC	Police-A&M
16	READY AND WILLLING	Whitesnake-United Artists
17	SHINE	Average White Band-RCA
18	DEFECTOR	Steve Hackett-Charisma
19	CHAIN LIGHTING	Don McLean-EMI
20	LIVE AT LAST	Black Sabbath-NEMS

WEEK ENDING JULY 12 1980

US SINGLES

	Title	Artist-Label
1	COMING UP	Paul McCartney-Columbia
2	STILL ROCK AND ROLL	Billy Joel-Columbia
3	THE ROSE	Bette Midler-Atlantic
4	LITTLE JEANNIE	Elton John-MCA
5	CUPID	Spinners-Atlantic
6	STEAL AWAY	Robbie Dupree-Elektra
7	FUNKY TOWN	Lipps Inc.-Casablanca
8	MAGIC	Olivia Newton-John-MCA
9	LET'S GET SERIOUS	Jermaine Jackson-Motown
10	LET ME LOVE YOU TONIGHT	Pure Prairie League-Casablanca
11	SHINING STAR	Manhattans-Columbia
12	AGAINST THE WIND	Bob Seger & Silver Bullet-Capitol
13	TIRED OF TOEIN' THE LINE	Rocky Burnette-EMI-America
14	ONE FINE DAY	Carole King-Capitol
15	IN AMERICA	The Charlie Daniels Band-Epic
16	I'M ALIVE	Electric Light Orchestra-MCA
17	MORE LOVE	Kim Carnes-EMI-America
18	BIGGEST PART OF ME	Ambrosia-Warner Bros.
19	TAKE YOUR TIME	SOS Band-Tabu
20	GIMME SOME LOVIN'	Blues Brothers-Atlantic

US ALBUMS

	Title	Artist-Label
1	GLASS HOUSES	Billy Joel-Columbia
2	JUST ONE NIGHT	Eric Clapton-RSO
3	McCARTNEY II	Paul McCartney-Columbia
4	THE EMPIRE STRIKES BACK	Soundtrack-RSO
5	EMPTY GLASS	Pete Townshend-Atco
6	LET'S GET SERIOUS	Jermaine Jackson-Motown
7	HEROES	Commodores-Motown
8	AGAINST THE WIND	Bob Seger & Silver Bullet-Capitol
9	URBAN COWBOY	Soundtrack-Asylum
10	MOUTH TO MOUTH	Lipps Inc.-Casablanca
11	DUKE	Genesis-Atlantic
12	DIANA	Diana Ross-Motown
13	SCREAM DREAM	Ted Nugent-Epic
14	21 AT 33	Elton John-MCA
15	THE ROSE	Soundtrack-Atlantic
16	THE WALL	Pink Floyd-Columbia
17	TRILOGY	Frank Sinatra-Reprise
18	OFF THE WALL	Michael Jackson-Epic
19	THE BLUES BROTHERS	Soundtrack-Atlantic
20	MIDDLE MAN	Boz Scaggs-Columbia

UK SINGLES

	Title	Artist-Label
1	XANADU	Olivia Newton-John, ELO-Jet
2	USE IT UP	Odyssey-RCA
3	JUMP TO THE BEAT	Stacy Lattisaw-Atlantic
4	CRYING	Don McLean-EMI
5	CUPID	Detroit Spinners-Atlantic
6	FUNKY TOWN	Lipps Inc.-Casablanca
7	MY WAY OF THINKING	UB40-Graduate
8	EVERYBODY'S GOT TO LEARN	Korgis-Rialto
9	COULD YOU BE LOVED	Bob Marley & The Wailers-Island
10	TWO PINTS OF LAGER	Splodgenessabounds-Dream
11	WATERFALLS	Paul McCartney-Parlophone
12	TO BE OR NOT TO BE	B A Robertson-Asylum
13	BACK TOGETHER AGAIN	Roberta Flack/Donny Hathaway-Atlantic
14	747	Saxon-Carrere
15	BEHIND THE GROOVE	Teena Marie-Motown
16	BABOOSHKA	Kate Bush-EMI
17	PLAY THE GAME	Queen-EMI
18	LOVE WILL TEAR US APART	Joy Division-Factory
19	SUBSTITUTE	Liquid Gold-Polo
20	EMOTIONAL RESCUE	Rolling Stones-Rolling Stones

UK ALBUMS

	Title	Artist-Label
1	EMOTIONAL RESCUE	Rolling Stones-Rolling Stones
2	THE GAME	Queen-EMI
3	FLESH AND BLOOD	Roxy Music-Polydor
4	PETER GABRIEL	Peter Gabriel-Charisma
5	LIVE AT LAST	Black Sabbath-Nems
6	UPRISING	Bob Marley-Island
7	ME MYSELF I	Joan Armatrading-A&M
8	SAVED	Bob Dylan-CBS
9	McCARTNEY II	Paul McCartney-Parlophone
10	SKY 2	Sky-Ariola
11	THE PHOTOS	The Photos-CBS
12	HOT WAX	Various-K Tel
13	JUST CAN'T STOP	The Beat-Go Feet
14	OFF THE WALL	Michael Jackson-Epic
15	READY AND WILLING	Whitesnake-United Artists
16	DUKE	Genesis-Charisma
17	SOUNDS SENSATIONAL	Bert Kaempfert-Polydor
18	KING OF THE ROAD	Boxcar Willie-Warwick
19	SHINE	Average White Band-RCA
20	CHAIN LIGHTNING	Don McLean-EMI

WEEK ENDING JULY 19 1980

US SINGLES

1 **STILL ROCK AND ROLL** *Billy Joel-Columbia*
2 **COMING UP** *Paul McCartney & Wings-Columbia*
3 **LITTLE JEANNIE** *Elton John-MCA*
4 **CUPID** *Spinners-Atlantic*
5 **SHINING STAR** *Manhattans-Columbia*
6 **STEAL AWAY** *Robbie Dupree-Elektra*
7 **MAGIC** *Olivia Newton-John-MCA*
8 **THE ROSE** *Bette Midler-Atlantic*
9 **LET'S GET SERIOUS** *Jermaine Jackson-Motown*
10 **LET ME LOVE YOU TONIGHT** *Pure Prairie League-Casablanca*
11 **TAKE YOUR TIME** *SOS Band-Tabu*
12 **TIRED OF TOEIN' THE LINE** *Rocky Burnett-EMI-America*
13 **ONE FINE DAY** *Carole King-Capital*
14 **IN AMERICA** *The Charlie Daniels Band-Epic*
15 **MORE LOVE** *Kim Carnes-EMI-America*
16 **I'M ALIVE** *Electric Light Orchestra-MCA*
17 **EMOTIONAL RESCUE** *The Rolling Stones-Rolling Stones*
18 **LOVE THE WORLD AWAY** *Kenny Rogers-United Artists*
19 **GIMME SOME LOVIN'** *Blues Brothers-Atlantic*
20 **FUNKY TOWN** *Lipps Inc.-Casablanca*

US ALBUMS

1 **GLASS HOUSES** *Billy Joel-Columbia*
2 **JUST ONE NIGHT** *Eric Clapton-RSO*
3 **McCARTNEY II** *Paul McCartney-Columbia*
4 **THE EMPIRE STRIKES BACK** *Soundtrack-RSO*
5 **EMPTY GLASS** *Pete Townshend-Atco*
6 **LET'S GET SERIOUS** *Jermaine Jackson-Motown*
7 **HEROES** *Commodores-Motown*
8 **EMOTIONAL RESCUE** *The Rolling Stones-Rolling Stones*
9 **URBAN COWBOY** *Soundtrack-Asylum*
10 **HOLD OUT** *Jackson Browne-Asylum*
11 **DUKE** *Genesis-Atlantic*
12 **DIANA** *Diana Ross-Motown*
13 **21 AT 33** *Elton John-MCA*
14 **THE ROSE** *Soundtrack-Atlantic*
15 **AGAINST THE WIND** *Bob Seger & Silver Bullet-Capitol*
16 **THE WALL** *Pink Floyd-Columbia*
17 **THE BLUES BROTHERS** *Soundtrack-Atlantic*
18 **OFF THE WALL** *Michael Jackson-Epic*
19 **ONE FOR THE ROAD** *The Kinks-Arista*
20 **THE GAME** *Queen-Elektra*

UK SINGLES

1 **XANADU** *Olivia Newton John, ELO-Jet*
2 **USE IT UP** *Odyssey-RCA*
3 **JUMP TO THE BEAT** *Stacy Lattisaw-Atlantic*
4 **CUPID** *Detroit Spinners-Atlantic*
5 **COULD YOU BE LOVED** *Bob Marley & The Wailers-Island*
6 **MY WAY OF THINKING** *UB40-Graduate*
7 **BABOOSHKA** *Kata Bush-EMI*
8 **CRYING** *Don McLean-EMI*
9 **WATERFALLS** *Paul McCartney-Parlophone*
10 **MORE THAN I CAN SAY** *Leo Sayer-Chrysalis*
11 **TO BE OR NOT TO BE** *B A Robertson-Asylum*
12 **FUNKY TOWN** *Lipps Inc.-Casablanca*
13 **747** *Saxon-Carrere*
14 **EVERYBODY'S GOT TO LEARN** *Korgis-Rialto*
15 **TWO PINTS OF LAGER** *Splodgenessabounds-Deram*
16 **LET'S HANG ON** *Darts-Magnet*
17 **LOVE WILL TEAR US APART** *Joy Division-Factory*
18 **BACK TOGETHER AGAIN** *Roberta Flack/Donny Hathaway-Atlantic*
19 **EMOTIONAL RESCUE** *Rolling Stones-Rolling Stones*
20 **THERE THERE MY DEAR** *Dexy's Midnight Runners, Parlophone*

UK ALBUMS

1 **THE GAME** *Queen-EMI*
2 **THE EMOTIONAL RESCUE** *Rolling Stones-Rolling Stones*
3 **DEEPEST PURPLE** *Deep Purple-Harvest*
4 **FLESH AND BLOOD** *Roxy Music-Polydor*
5 **KING OF THE ROAD** *Boxcar Willie-Warwick*
6 **UPRISING** *Bob Marley-Island*
7 **XANADU** *Soundtrack-Jet*
8 **LIVE AT LAST** *Black Sabbath-Nems*
9 **ME MYSELF I** *Joan Armatrading-A&M*
10 **McCARTNEY II** *Paul McCartney-Parlophone*
11 **OFF THE WALL** *Michael Jackson-Epic*
12 **CULTOSAURUS ERECTUS** *Blue Oyster Cult-CBS*
13 **SKY 2** *Sky-Ariola*
14 **VIENNA** *Ultravox-Chrysalis*
15 **HOT WAX** *Various-K-Tel*
16 **PETER GABRIEL** *Peter Gabriel-Charisma*
17 **READY AND WILLING** *Whitesnake-United Artists*
18 **I JUST CAN'T STOP IT** *The Beat-Go Feat*
19 **REGATTA DE BLANC** *Police-A&M*
20 **SAVED** *Bob Dylan-CBS*

WEEK ENDING JULY 26 1980

US SINGLES

1 **STILL ROCK AND ROLL** *Billy Joel-Columbia*
2 **MAGIC** *Olivia Newton-John-MCA*
3 **LITTLE JEANNIE** *Elton John-MCA*
4 **CUPID** *Spinners-Atlantic*
5 **SHINING STAR** *Manhattans-Columbia*
6 **COMING UP** *Paul McCartney & Wings-Columbia*
7 **STEAL AWAY** *Robbie Dupree-Elektra*
8 **TIRED OF TOEIN THE LINE** *Rocky Burnette-EMI America*
9 **TAKE YOUR TIME** *SOS Band-Tabu*
10 **THE ROSE** *Bette Midler-Atlantic*
11 **EMOTIONAL RESUCE** *The Rolling Stones-Rolling Stones*
12 **ONE FINE DAY** *Carole King-Capitol*
13 **IN AMERICA** *The Charlie Daniels Band-Epic*
14 **MORE LOVE** *Kim Carnes-EMI America*
15 **LET ME LOVE YOU TONIGHT** *Pure Prairie League-Casablanca*
16 **LOVE THE WORLD AWAY** *Kenny Rogers-United Artists*
17 **SAILING** *Christopher Cross-Warner Bros*
18 **GIMME SOME LOVIN'** *Blues Brothers-Atlantic*
19 **ALL NIGHT LONG** *Joe Walsh-Asylum*
20 **EMPIRE STRIKES BACK** *Meco-RSO*

US ALBUMS

1 **EMOTIONAL RESCUE** *The Rolling Stones-Rolling Stones*
2 **JUST ONE NIGHT** *Eric Clapton-RSO*
3 **GLASS HOUSES** *Billy Joel-Columbia*
4 **THE EMPIRE STRIKES BACK** *Soundtrack-RSO*
5 **EMPTY GLASS** *Pete Townshend-Atco*
6 **LET'S GET SERIOUS** *Jermaine Jackson-Motown*
7 **HEROES** *Commodores-Motown*
8 **URBAN COWBOY** *Soundtrack-Asylum*
9 **HOLD OUT** *Jackson Browne-Asylum*
10 **McCARTNEY 11** *Paul McCartney-Columbia*
11 **DIANA** *Diana Ross-Motown*
12 **AGAINST THE WIND** *Bob Seger & Silver Bullet Band-Capitol*
13 **21 AT 33** *Elton John-MCA*
14 **THE ROSE** *Soundtrack-Atlantic*
15 **THE BLUES BROTHERS** *Soundtrack-Atlantic*
16 **THE GAME** *Queen-Elektra*
17 **DUKE** *Genesis-Atlantic*
18 **ONE FOR THE ROAD** *The Kinks-Arista*
19 **OFF THE WALL** *Michael Jackson-Epic*
20 **FAME** *Soundtrack-RSO*

UK SINGLES

1 **USE IT UP** *Odyssey-RCA*
2 **XANADU** *Olivia Newton John/ELO-Jet*
3 **MORE THAN I CAN SAY** *Leo Sayer-Chrysalis*
4 **JUMP TO THE BEAT** *Stacy Lattisaw-Atlantic*
5 **COULD YOU BE LOVED** *Bob Marley-Island*
6 **CUPID** *Detroit Spinners-Atlantic*
7 **BABOOSHKA** *Kate Bush-EMI*
8 **UPSIDE DOWN** *Diana Ross-Motown*
9 **EMOTIONAL RESCUE** *Rolling Stones-Rolling Stones*
10 **MY WAY OF THINKING** *UB40-Graduate*
11 **LET'S HANG ON** *Darts-Magnet*
12 **THERE THERE MY DEAR** *Dexy's Midnight Runners-Parlophone*
13 **LOVE WILL TEAR US APART** *Joy Division-Factory*
14 **A LOVERS HOLIDAY** *Change-WEA*
15 **747** *Saxon-Carrere*
16 **WATERFALLS** *Paul McCartney-Parlophone*
17 **THEME FROM INVADERS** *Yellow Magic Orchestra-A&M*
18 **CRYING** *Don McLean-EMI*
19 **OOPS UPSIDE YOUR HEAD** *Gap Band-Mercury*
20 **WEDNESDAY WEEK** *Undertones-Sire*

UK ALBUMS

1 **THE GAME** *Queen-EMI*
2 **EMOTIONAL RESCUE** *Rolling Stones-Rolling Stones*
3 **XANADU** *Original Soundtrack-Jet*
4 **DEEPEST PURPLE** *Deep Purple-Harvest*
5 **FLESH AND BLOOD** *Roxy Music-Polydor*
6 **THE YOUNG SOUL REBELS** *Dexy's Midnight Runners-Parlophone*
7 **GIVE ME THE NIGHT** *George Benson-Warner Bros*
8 **UPRISING** *Bob Marley-Island*
9 **OFF THE WALL** *Michael Jackson-Epic*
10 **ME MYSELF I** *Joan Armatrading-A&M*
11 **CLOSER** *Joy Division-Factory*
12 **CULTOSAURUS ERECTUS** *Blue Oyster Cult-CBS*
13 **McCARTNEY 11** *Paul McCartney-Parlophone*
14 **LIVE AT LAST** *Black Sabbath-NEMS*
15 **KING OF THE ROAD** *Boxcar Willie-Warwick*
16 **MAGIC REGGAE** *Various-K-Tel*
17 **MANILOW MAGIC** *Barry Manilow-Arista*
18 **SKY 2** *Sky-Ariola*
19 **PETER GABRIEL** *Peter Gabriel-Charisma*
20 **VIENNA** *Ultravox-Chrysalis*

WEEK ENDING AUGUST 2 1980

US SINGLES

1 MAGIC
Olivia Newton-John-MCA

2 STILL ROCK AND ROLL
Billy Joel-Columbia

3 LITTLE JEANIE
Elton John-MCA

4 CUPID
Spinners-Atlantic

5 SHINING STAR
Manhattan-Columbia

6 TAKE YOUR TIME
SOS Band

7 COMING UP
Paul McCartney & Wings-Columbia

8 TIRED OF TOEIN THE LINE
Rocky Burnette-EMI America

9 EMOTIONAL RESCUE
Rolling Stones-Rolling Stones

10 SAILING
Christopher Cross-Warner Bros

11 IN AMERICA
The Charlie Daniels Band-Epic

12 ONE FINE DAY
Carole King-Capitol

13 MORE LOVE
Kim Carnes-EMI America

14 LOVE THE WORLD AWAY
Kenny Rogers-United Artists

15 STEAL AWAY
Robbie Dupree-Elektra

16 THE ROSE
Bette Midler-Atlantic

17 MISUNDERSTANDING
Genesis-Atlantic

18 GIMME SOME LOVIN'
Blues Brothers-Atlantic

19 ALL NIGHT LONG
Joe Walsh-Asylum

20 EMPIRE STRIKES BACK
Meco-RSO

US ALBUMS

1 EMOTIONAL RESCUE
Rolling Stones-Rolling Stones

2 GLASS HOUSES
Billy Joel-Columbia

3 HOLD OUT
Jackson Browne-Asylum

4 THE EMPIRE STRIKES BACK
Soundtrack-RSO

5 URBAN COWBOY
Soundtrack-Asylum

6 THE GAME
Queen-Elektra

7 EMPTY GLASS
Pete Townshend-Atco

8 HEROES
Commodores-Motown

9 DIANA
Diana Ross-Motown

10 McCARTNEY 11
Paul McCartney-Columbia

11 AGAINST THE WIND
Bob Seger & Silver Bullet Band-Capitol

12 JUST ONE NIGHT
Eric Clapton-RSO

13 THE SOS BAND
SOS-Tabu

14 THE BLUES BROTHERS
Soundtrack-Atlantic

15 FAME
Soundtrack-RSO

16 DUKE
Genesis-Atlantic

17 ONE FOR THE ROAD
The Kinks-Arista

18 LET'S GET SERIOUS
Jermaine Jackson-Motown

19 CHRISTOPHER CROSS
Christopher Cross-Warner Bros

20 OFF THE WALL
Michael Jackson-Epic

UK SINGLES

1 USE IT UP
Odyssey-RCA

2 MORE THAN I CAN SAY
Leo Sayer-Chrysalis

3 UPSIDE DOWN
Diana Ross-Motown

4 XANADU
Olivia Newton-John/ELO-Jet

5 BABOOSHKA
Kate Bush-EMI

6 COULD YOU BE LOVED
Bob Marley & The Wailers-Island

7 THERE THERE MY DEAR
Dexy's Midnight Runners-Parlophone

8 JUMP TO THE BEAT
Stacy Lattisaw-Atlantic

9 WINNER TAKES IT ALL
Abba-Epic

10 CUPID
Detroit Spinners-Atlantic

11 WEDNESDAY WEEK
Undertones-Sire

12 EMOTIONAL RESCUE
Rolling Stones-Rolling Stones

13 LET'S HANG ON
Darts-Magnet

14 MY WAY OF THINKING
UB40-Graduate

15 LIP UP FATTY
Bad Manners-Magnet

16 LOVE WILL TEAR US APART
Joy Division-Factory

17 A LOVERS HOLIDAY
Change-WEA

18 OOPS UPSIDE YOUR HEAD
Gap Band-Mercury

19 THEME FROM THE INVADERS
Yellow Magic Orchestra-A&M

20 9 TO 5
Sheena Easton-EMI

UK ALBUMS

1 DEEPEST PURPLE
Deep Purple-Harvest

2 XANADU
Soundtrack-Jet

3 EMOTIONAL RESCUE
Rolling Stones-Rolling Stones

4 FLESH AND BLOOD
Roxy Music-Polydor

5 THE GAME
Queen-EMI

6 CLOSER
Joy Division-Factory

7 GIVE ME THE NIGHT
George Benson-Warner Bros

8 THE YOUNG SOUL REBELS
Dexy's Midnight Runners-Parlophone

9 OFF THE WALL
Michael Jackson-Epic

10 UPRISING
Bob Marley-Island

11 SKY
Sky-Ariola

12 ME MYSELF I
Joan Armatrading-A&M

13 McCARTNEY 11
Paul McCartney-Parlophone

14 VIENNA
Ultravox-Chrysalis

15 PETER GABRIEL
Peter Gabriel-Charisma

16 ANOTHER STRING OF HITS
Shadows-EMI

17 CROCODILES
Echo & The Bunnymen-Korova

18 MANILOW MAGIC
Barry Manilow-Arista

19 MAGIC REGGAE
Various-K-Tel

20 ALL FOR YOU
Johnny Mathis-CBS

WEEK ENDING AUGUST 9 1980

US SINGLES

1 MAGIC
Olivia Newton-John-MCA

2 STILL ROCK AND ROLL
Billy Joel-Columbia

3 LITTLE JEANNIE
Elton John-MCA

4 TAKE YOUR TIME
SOS Band-Tabu

5 SAILING
Christopher Cross-Warner Bros.

6 SHINING STAR
Manhattans-Columbia

7 EMOTIONAL RESCUE
The Rolling Stones-Rolling Stones

8 CUPID
Spinners-Atlantic

9 COMING UP
Paul McCartney & Wings-Columbia

10 UPSIDE DOWN
Diana Ross-Motown

11 IN AMERICA
The Charlie Daniels Band-Epic

12 MORE LOVE
Kim Carnes-EMI-America

13 TIRED OF TOEIN' THE LINE
Rocky Burnette-EMI-America

14 LOVE THE WORLD AWAY
Kenny Rogers-United Artists

15 MISUNDERSTANDING
Genesis-Atlantic

16 ONE FINE DAY
Carole King-Capitol

17 FAME
Irene Cara-RSO

18 THE EMPIRE STRIKES BACK
Meco-RSO

19 LET MY LOVE OPEN
Pete Townshend-Atco

20 INTO THE NIGHT
Benny Mardones-Polydor

US ALBUMS

1 EMOTIONAL RESCUE
The Rolling Stones-Rolling Stones

2 HOLD OUT
Jackson Browne-Asylum

3 GLASS HOUSES
Billy Joel-Columbia

4 URBAN COWBOY
Soundtrack-Asylum

5 THE GAME
Queen-Elektra

6 DIANA
Diana Ross-Motown

7 EMPTY GLASS
Pete Townshend-Atco

8 THE EMPIRE STRIKES BACK
Soundtrack-RSO

9 CHRISTOPHER CROSS
Christopher Cross-Warner Bros.

10 AGAINST THE WIND
Bob Seger & Silver Bullet-Capitol

11 FAME
Soundtrack-RSO

12 SOS
The SOS Band-Tabu

13 THE BLUES BROTHERS
Soundtrack-Atlantic

14 JUST ONE NIGHT
Eric Clapton-RSO

15 DUKE
Genesis-Atlantic

16 ONE FOR THE ROAD
The Kinks-Arista

17 HEROES
Commodores-Motown

18 McCARTNEY II
Paul McCartney-Columbia

19 ANYTIME, ANYPLACE
Rossington Collins Band-MCA

20 OFF THE WALL
Michael Jackson-Epic

UK SINGLES

1 WINNER TAKES IT ALL
Abba-Epic

2 UPSIDE DOWN
Diana Ross-Motown

3 USE IT UP WEAR IT OUT
Odyssey-RCA

4 MORE THAN I CAN SAY
Leo Sayer-Chrysalis

5 9 TO 5
Sheena Easton-EMI

6 BABOOSHKA
Kate Bush-EMI

7 OOPS UPSIDE YOUR HEAD
Gap Band-Mercury

8 COULD YOU BE LOVED
Bob Marley & The Wailers-Island

9 OH YEAH
Roxy Music-Polydor

10 GIVE ME THE NIGHT
George Benson-Warner Bros.

11 THERE THERE MY DEAR
Dexy's Midnight Runners-Parlophone

12 WEDNESDAY WEEK
Undertones-Sire

13 XANADU
Olivia Newton-John/ELO-Jet

14 MARIANA
Gibson Brothers-Island

15 LIP UP FATTY
Bad Manners-Magnet

16 FUNKIN' FOR JAMAICA
Tom Browne-Arista

17 JUMP TO THE BEAT
Stacy Lattisaw-Atlantic

18 LET'S HANG ON
Darts-Magnet

19 EMOTIONAL RESCUE
Rolling Stones-Rolling Stones

20 CUPID
Detroit Spinners-Atlantic

UK ALBUMS

1 BACK IN BLACK
AC/DC-Atlantic

2 DEEPEST PURPLE
Deep Purple-Harvest

3 XANADU
Soundtrack-Jet

4 FLESH AND BLOOD
Roxy Music-Polydor

5 EMOTIONAL RESCUE
Rolling Stones-Rolling Stones

6 THE YOUNG SOUL REBELS
Dexy's Midnight Runners-Parlophone

7 GIVE ME THE NIGHT
George Benson-Warner Bros.

8 CLOSER
Joy Division-Factory

9 OFF THE WALL
Michael Jackson-Epic

10 SKY 2
Sky-Ariola

11 THE GAME
Queen-EMI

12 UPRISING
Bob Marley-Island

13 McCARTNEY II
Paul McCartney-Parlophone

14 DIANA
Diana Ross-Motown

15 LIVE 1979
Hawkwind-Bronze

16 REGATTA DE BLANC
Police-A&M

17 ANOTHER STRING OF HITS
Shadows-EMI

18 MAGIC REGGAE
Various-K-Tel

19 MANILOW MAGIC
Barry Manilow-Arista

20 VIENNA
Ultravox-Chrysalis

TECHNICAL PROFILE

BOB GELDOF

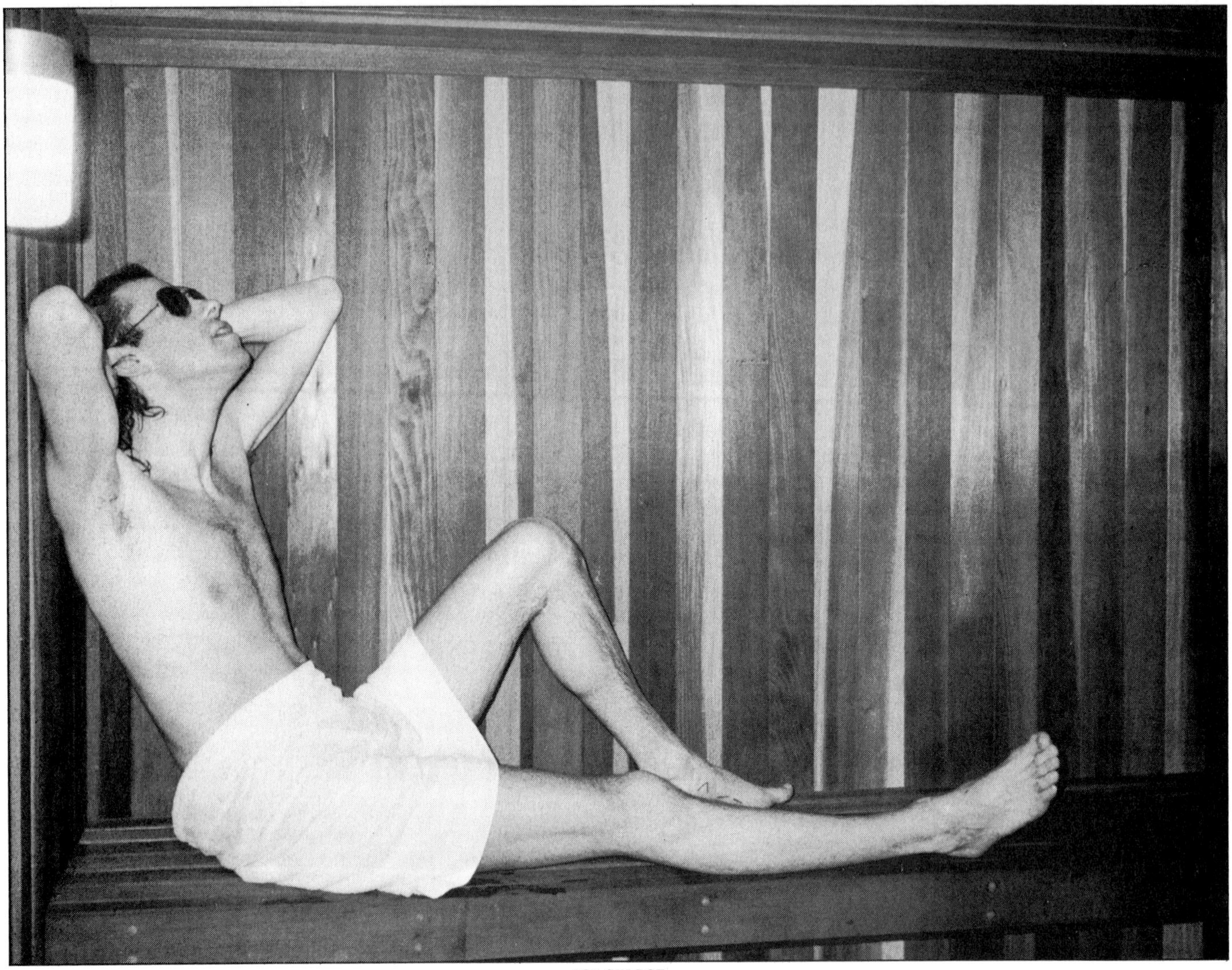

BOB GELDOF

Chief Rat Bob Geldof possesses a hi-fi system which he bought during 1979. "I'd never owned a hi-fi before this one — what I used before was a radiogram which wasn't even stereo, and I decided that when I got some money, I'd invest in something decent. Initially, I put aside £400, but then I met this guy who was setting up his own business, and he offered to get me something reasonably priced, but of good quality. Eventually, it cost me about £500, but I'm very happy with it — my Kef speakers sound like studio monitors as far as quality goes, although they're obviously not so powerful, and they're better than most other people's that I've heard. The thing I like about my set up, apart from the sound, is that it's very compact, and can be moved around easily, which'll be an advantage when it's time to find somewhere else to live".

Most of Bob's equipment is made by TECHNICS — his amplifier is an SU-7300, his FM/AM tuner an FT-7300, his turntable an SL-230 and his cassette deck a 616. Apart from that, he uses a pair of KEF 104aB speakers, plus a TEAC A/33405 four track reel to reel tape machine, while for less formal use, Bob has a SONY Soundabout portable cassette player (this machine has no loudspeaker, but emits its output via headphones — Bob's particular model has capacity for two headsets.) He also carries a Sony mini-cassette recorder around with him "for snatches of songs and things like that which may occur to me when I'm travelling". As far as his record collection goes, Bob claims to maintain a limited library of around 400 LPs, 200 singles, and 200 cassettes, and says that he is constantly turfing out records which he no longer listens to. This quantity of recorded material, however, does not seem to include what he termed "about six thousand Boomtown Rats records"!

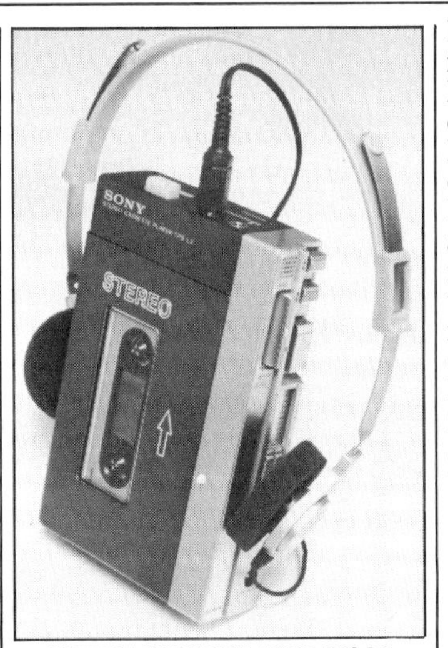

SONY CASSETTE PLAYER TPS-L2

MAJOR ALBUMS

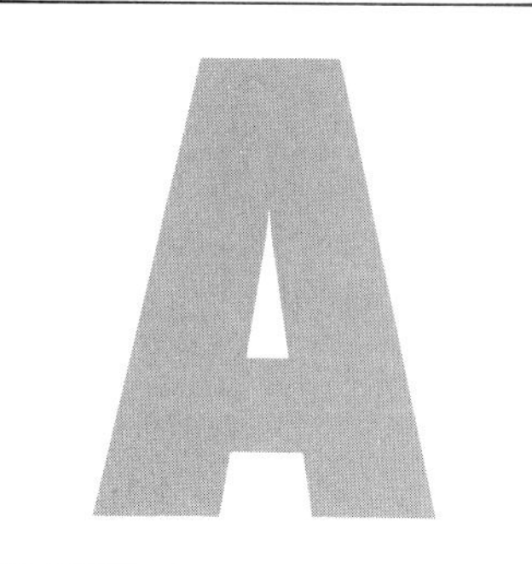

THE A'S
The A's *(Arista)*
Easy listening power pop from America. AB-F

ABBA
Greatest Hits, Volume 2
(Atlantic/Epic)
The sound of money making money from the perfect pop singles machine. DN

AC/DC
Back in Black *(Atlantic)*
Deep Purple imitators still on the golden trail after losing lead singer. Their new acquisition, Brian Johnson (ex-Geordie), is a clone of the late Bon Scott voice-wise. Let's just hope they treat him more carefully. The mixture as before. AB-F

ANDY ADAMS
One of the Boys *(DJM)*
One of the Billy Joel imitators, more like it. AB-F

BRYAN ADAMS
Bryan Adams *(A&M)*
Cynical rock, carefully calculated to appeal to mass-audiences by Canadian singer. The public wasn't fooled.

GAYLE ADAMS
Gayle Adams *(Epic)*
Disco from the team behind the success of Bobby Thurston. AB-F

ADC BAND
Renaissance (*Cotillion*)
Mass production job in both respects. AB-F

AEROSMITH
Night In The Ruts
(Columbia/CBS)
This album isn't nearly as bad as it could have been considering that guitarist/co-writer Joe Perry was starting to work with his own Joe Perry project during the recording. He saved his best tunes for himself, was mixed down into oblivion, and didn't play at all on several cuts. There's never been so much filler on an Aerosmith album before and the tracks with the most bite are the Yardbirds' 'Think About It' and the down-in-the-alley blues 'Reefer Head Woman'. DN

AFTER THE FIRE
Laser Love *(CBS)*
Derivative pomp rock from the league of the doomed and the also-ran. AB-F

AIR
Air Lore *(Arista/Novus)*
One of the best avant-garde jazz groups tackle classic themes by Scott Joplin and Jelly Roll Morton in a surprisingly listenable manner. DN

JANE AIRE AND THE BELVEDERES
Jane Aire and the Belvederes
(Virgin)
Promising singer revealed by the Akron sampler falls somewhat flat on her face on this first album produced by Akron potentate Liam Sternberg. His unsympathetic production and workmanlike choice of material never allow Jane Aire to take full flight. Try again, please. AB-F

JAN AKKERMAN
3 *(Atlantic)*
Light jazz guitar excursion from Focus specialist. AB-F

DUANE ALLMAN
The Best of Duane Allman
(Capricorn)
Yet another repackage of the late guitarist's limited output. A must, of course, but the tracks are all availale in various other vinyl formats elsewhere. AB-F

HERB ALPERT
Rise *(A&M)*
The cash registers of the world have already delivered their verdict so another review isn't going to change the course of things. AB-F

HERB ALPERT
Beyond *(A&M)*
It would be cheap thrills to pillory Herb Alpert for jumping — great latecomer at that — on the disco bandwagon with 'Rise' and similar delights of ten-ton mash. Probably it's more prudent to recognise that as a *musician* he's been semi-permanently enshrined by a relatively middle-aged audience into a Tijuana timewarp. Opportunites like 'Rise' can only arise when the two streams can meet halfway.

'Beyond' admittedly tends to carry some of the evils over, with cuts like 'The Continental' with its token percussion break only emphasising the number of times the rather dismissive, tight-lipped trumpet has rolled out the same old lick. But taken as a whole the album is rather fresher and more varied, betraying I guess Alpert's bettered sense of acclimatisation. It's also a far more consciously produced album, digitally recorded, and using a gallon of electronic goodies coming to a head in the title track — whose rather fine percussion/keyboard underlay is yet again half-killed by the tacky tune on top. But takes like 'Interlude' and 'Keep It Goin' conversely work out on muscular acoustic frameworks.

Credibility stakes may yet be won. LE

MARK ANDREW AND THE GENTS
Big Boy *(A&M)*
Nice sound from oddly-coiffed Mark Andrews. Solid pop with Farfisa tin organ sound to the front and a dollop of rock 'n' roll. Worth watching out for in the bargain bins. AB-F

ANGEL CITY
Face to Face *(Epic)*
Die-hard Australian rockers compilation for American ears. "Heavy metal to punk to power pop and back across the International Date Line again." (CREEM) AB-F

ANGELIC UPSTARTS
We Gotta Get Out of this Place *(Warners)*
Crude but surprisingly effective and catchy punk survivors whose style is evolving beyond the restrictive straitjacket of the genre. Strong North-East of England feeling characterized by the title track which used to be an Eric Burdon and the Animals cry of the heart. AB-F

ANY TROUBLE
Any Trouble *(Stiff)*
Heavily-hyped (in the UK) Costello pub rock clones. Catchy tunes and familiar delivery. Might all well have sounded so much better a few years ago, but the (pleasantish) formula has now become a bit of a bore. This has been a harsh review. They deserve better, but I just can't raise the necessary enthusiasm for Clive Gregson's songs. Oh, yes, there's also a touch of the Graham Parker's in there. Sorry, the lads at Stiff. MJ

JOAN ARMATRADING
Me, Myself, I *(A&M)*
Surprisingly strong new platter from Joan Armatrading. Produced with genuine punch by Richard Gottehrer, could even be her best. What more can we say? AB-F

JOAN ARMATRADING
Steppin' Out *(A&M)*
Live recording that catches Armatrading on her best behaviour. AB-F

BILLY BOY ARNOLD
Checkin' It Out *(Red Lightnin')*
That rarity, a blues LP recorded in England that is none the poorer for it; indeed, perhaps better off, since T.S. McPhee's red-eyed guitar parts, with the air of '60s extravagance, nudge Arnold into an assertiveness his records have sometimes lacked. Chicago band blues in the great tradition, short, sharp and direct, with Arnold's best singing and harp-playing yet. TR

ARROGANCE
Suddenly *(Warner Brothers)*
Good solid mainstream rock in silly new wave drag. DN

ART ENSEMBLE OF CHICAGO
Full Force *(ECM)*
The ceding of the Art Ensemble's work — part of it at least — to Manfred Eicher's ECM label has provided both a glinting foil to that company's image of delicate soggy liberalism, and also, arguably, given the band itsef the smallest push towards useful temperance in their presentation. It's also, signally, at last allowed the five-man, fifty-instrument outfit to swim and be seen practically in the mainstream, at a period when their music is once more trenchantly bounding forwards.

AEC's tag line has long been 'Great Black Music, Ancient to the Future': hence the superbly disciplined 'Charlie M' redolent in its soft, scooping horn lines not only of its namesake, but the almost timeless harmony and spirit of 'Black & Tan Fantasy'. A more 'traditional' free-jazz free-fall, engineered by Joseph Jarman — a very crazy guy — illuminates the pitted, witty landscape of Don Moye drums on 'Old Time Southside Dance'. On the title track, what one takes for a moment as bursting collective improvisation, has all the material qualities but subject to immense material discipline.

The one anomaly here is the comparative submission of Lester Bowie, such a prominent figure on stage. But overall, 'Full Force' is a varied, pertinent, humourful and vastly enjoyable album which should flavour the decade. LE

ASLEEP AT THE WHEEL
Served 'Live' *(Capitol*
Texas rock and pedal steel waltzes with no studio trickery. AB-F

THE ASSOCIATES
The Affectionate Punch *(Fiction)*
Strongly effective début album by British duo of Billy Mackenzie and Alan Rankine, often reminiscent in its romantic, operatic bleakness of the David Bowie of 'Station to Station'. Not a bad influence to labour under. Sparse instrumentation and lush vocals work surprisingly well and make their LP a memorable one. The Associates: a name to look out for. MJ

ATHLETICO SPIZZ 80
Do A Runner *(A&M)*
Somewhat lacklustre album from emerging new wave-with-a-touch-of-humour band whose earlier, independently released singles were a sheer delight. MJ

THE ATTRACTIONS
Mad About The Wrong Boy *(F-Beat)*
Run-of-the-mill pub rock by Elvis Costello backing outfit set loose for a harmless sabbatical. AB-F

AVERAGE WHITE BAND
Shine *(RCA)*
Tired funksters move into disco territory with all horns firing. One year, at least, too late. AB-F

AXE
Living on the Edge *(MCA)*
Heavy cliché hard rock. AB-F

HOYT AXTON
A Rusty Old Halo *(Youngblood)*
Outlaw rock from the clichéd pages of old western movies. Pleasant but all rather dishonest. AB-F

KEVIN AYERS
That's What You Get Babe *(Harvest)*
A disappointment from old deep-smooth-voice. An erratic artist at his best, this new album has no memorable songs and soon fades from the memory. Can do (and has done) better. MJ

ROY AYERS & WAYNE HENDERSON
Prime Time *(Polydor)*
It's a real irony that Roy Ayers, who mixed up one of the master potions of fusion in the last decade — and landed more flak than sales — has become such a wasted asset on the last few outings: pitched by funk and fondness into barren route marches. Wayne Henderson, on the other foot, has had fingers in all kinds of pies, though often with more craft than art.

'Prime Time' has mixed assets. The funk bunk has its way at times, including a blind and spongy treatment of the previously ennervating 'It Ain't Your Sign'. Ayers' occasional capacity for something really mad and raunchy is here bypassed, but what is projected is his taste and love for a good tasty timeless ballad. 'Thank You Thank You' demonstrates his quite unsung genius with group vocals, with himself one of the very few really worthwhile instrumentalists turned singers. 'Weekend Love', samba flavoured, knits up an embarrassingly irresistable snake rhythm, a humble tune, refreshingly extended if still hidebound solos from both leaders, and a smart, smart little lyric.

Roy Ayers' work (yes, it's certainly *his* album) is still awash with triteness, but with imperative disco soaking away fast maybe he can now find a firmer, more honest perch. LE

AZYMUTH
Light as a Feather *(Milestone)*
With the plethora of Latin infusions into virtually every area of popular music over the last ten years, Azymuth have been one of a very rare breed — a Latin American band who have actually struck home in their own right.
An easy option could be to condemn as directionless what is a generally successful and appealing attempt to cast a stylistic net as wide as the band can reach. OK, there's a pervasion of big, soft West Coast thinking (itself of course half-moulded by the Hispanic input — witness Flora Purim and Opa). José Roberto Bertrami's keyboard mixes and Mamao's synth, always for whatever reason a prime feature of the Brazilian

school, consistently guide the outfit through a span of styles and functions. These range from sheer, razor-crisp easy listening ('Partido Alto') and cheeky, hurlaway jingles ('Young Embrace') round to a moderately tedious extended version of the song that broke the band to the DJs, 'Jazz Carnival'. While both Azymuth and album have their limits, it certainly leaves me wondering what other goodies lie hidden for no more sin than being other than all-American boys. LE

THE BABYS
Union Jacks *(Chrysalis)*
Since expanding into a quintet on their previous album 'Head First', the Babys have toughened up their sound and started having regular AM hits. This album contains two — 'Back On My Feet Again' and 'Midnight Rendezvous'. But they are still basically a light pop singles version of Bad Company and Foreigner — it's not for nothing that their publishing company is called Paperwaite Music. DN

BAD MANNERS
Ska 'n' B *(Magnet)*
Surprisingly varied album including competent re-workings of oldies, novelty numbers and even a 'big band' track amongst the original songs. The album title is a perfect description of their kind of fun music. VH

MOE BANDY & JOE STAMPLEY
Just Good Ol' Boys *(Columbia/CBS)*
Singalongacountry. AB-F

BARCLAY JAMES HARVEST
Eyes of the Universe *(Polydor)*
Inflated pretentions by anonymous British retards. AB-F

PETE BARDENS
Heart to Heart *(Arista)*
Bardens is no man to rest on his laurels and left Camel to pursue a solo career (not the first time he's attempted this, either). Pleasant, jazzy, quietly insubstantial album. AB-F

BOBBY BARE
Down and Dirty *(Columbia/CBS)*
Country pop cross-over from seasoned old trooper. MJ

BAREFOOT JERRY
Watchin' TV *(Criminal)*
First out on Monument back in 1974, enjoyable country rock reissue. AB-F

JESSE BARISH
Mercury Shoes *(RCA)*
Amiable, bland wimp rock produced by Marty Balin. AB-F

CLAUDE BARTHELEMY
Jaune et Encore *(Cobalt)*
An album of a certain symbolic as well as actual importance here, 'Jaune et Encore' ('Yellow and Again') picks up both on the more open attitude that most of the continent of Europe has had towards jazz and improvised music, and equally on the studied innovations of maturing new wave pop.

Barthelemy is a young and modestly documented guitarist behind whose occasionally defiant art-style lies long familiarity with Django ('Hullo Police'), bepop masters ('Sonny') and the cutting edges of rock ('Banlieue'). He retains a gentle lead as much as is reasonably possible in music that never lodges in one groove any longer than is necessary to hit the appropriate emotional pitch, witness the tangled run-up to the cinematic chordal warmth of 'L'Air de Rien'.

Prime among partners in crime here are drummer Alain Breton with his tightly-moulded drumming nicely soured by outgoing opportunism, the icy keyboard work of of Mico Nissim, and the grunting, nudging contrabasse of Henri Texier, beautifully plaited in with Barthelemy's own electric bass on 'Chimere'. A bold, joyous and long-term album that nevertheless catches the spirit of a singular time and place. LE

COUNT BASIE & HIS ORCHESTRA
On the Road *(Pablo Today)*
If you've gotten into that game of counting who's left now that Mingus is gone, then William Basie — *the* Count — will likely be numero uno on the list. Certainly for Joe Public, his is the ultimate big band, nurturing a whole generation of radio orchestras in the UK. So much so, that the version of 'In a Mellow Tone' inluded herein reads entirely like a copy itself.

For 'On the Road', aside from being Pablo's first digital recording, is a moderately varied but firmly conventional gig. The distinction lies in that quality of complete big-bandism with cracking pace (Mickey Roker) and ripping horns winning in their bulky brassiness every time. When Pete Minger or Bootie Wood get a solo in, it's with the band at his heels and the crowd at his trouser cuffs, made with adulation. A literally lone exception is bass player John Clayton breaking and raking up time on 'John the III'. Guitarist Freddie Green remains, of course, perched behind the sound barrier, emerging for a quick lick on 'Basie' along with the leader's own highly condensed piano.

It's tempting to slate at once a performance like this, too much controlled by bonhomie and too little by bon mots. But, be honest, if it's hard enough in this business to stay a legend, it's almost harder to stay alive. LE

MIKE BATT AND FRIENDS
Tarot Suite *(Epic)*
Friends number: London Symphony Orchestra (no less), Mel Collins, Rory Gallagher, Jim Cregan, Tony McPhee, Roger Chapman, Chris Spedding, Ray Cooper, Colin Blunstone, etc... They should be ashamed. MJ

BATTLEFIELD
Stand Easy *(Topic)*
One of the boldest and most exciting folk releases for a long time: Scots traditional music played with uplifting passion, using bagpipes with synthesizer, topped off by a delicate lady singer. Occasionally indulgent, sometimes crowded and muddled, but still innovative and vital. As a début album for this line-up it's superb. CI

THE BEACH BOYS
Girls on the Beach *(Capitol)*
Usual summer re-release of Beach Boys summer hits of six or seven centuries ago. Nice ditties, of course, but who the hell hasn't got these songs in his vinyl collection in one combination or another. Flogging a surfing horse. AB-F

THE BEACH BOYS
Keepin' The Summer Alive *(Caribou/CBS)*
This album shows distressingly few signs of life. Some cuts like 'When Girls Get Together' and Chuck Berry's 'School Day' sound like outtakes dredged up from the vault. Clearly there'll never be another 'Pet Sounds'. DN

KIM BEACON
Ravenna *(Rialto)*
Fledging singer-songwriters should never cover John Lennon songs. Few can get away with it; Kim Beacon doesn't. The rest of this self-penned material is pleasant but doesn't make any mountains move. MJ

RICHARD T. BEAR
Bear *(RCA)*
All of the most bombastic qualities of Bruce Springsteen and Bob Seger rolled into one...if you can stand it. DN

THE BEAT
I Just Can't Stop It *(Sire/Go Feet)*
Like fellow ex-Two Toners, The Selecter, The Beat pole vaulted to national notoriety with few preliminaries, and in similar consequence may have hurried into their début album a little prematurely.

Not that it's remotely unworthy. In fact, the first

side is nothing short of spiffing. Charging in with 'Mirror In The Bathroom' and 'Hands Off...She's Mine', their third and second hit singles respectively, it whisks through 'Two Swords' and 'Twist and Crawl' (the perfect examples of how commitment and sheer fun share an infectious co-existence in the Beat's scheme of things) and out again with an animated version of Prince Buster's 'Rough Rider' and the deceptively zappy 'Click Click' in one breathless, exhilarating rush.

Perhaps it's just in comparison with such highly charged excellence that the second side seems to fall a little flat. More likely, however, is that the band simply didn't have enough top flight numbers to last them through a complete album. Certainly 'Noise In The World' is nothing wonderful, and their adaptation of 'Can't Get Used To Losing You' is uncomfortably closer to nightclubs than youth clubs.

Nevertheless, sharing the general "ska" bands' philosophy of providing thinking persons' dance music, The Beat have done as much as any to give popular music back its smile, its conscience and its sense of proportion. And 'I Just Can't Stop It' is good stuff indeed, with the promise of even better to come. PK

BEATLES
Rarities *(Capitol/Parlophone)*
Corporations have no memory. They are not alive, but rather skeletons fleshed out by transitory groups of living things. In the case of record companies, there are employees — migrant workers — and the indentured servants known as "acts" or "artists" and only rarely treated as such. A new group of lettuce pickers at Capitol Records have finally seen fit to release the "butcher block" cover of 'Yesterday and Today', on the inside of this shrink-wrapped package, and it alone is almost worth the price of admission. You certainly don't want this collection of off-takes and Outer Mongolian versions of world-wide hits unless you are a late blooming Beatles fanatic, a collector who needs one of everything or a rock critic who gets his copy free. Then again, my 45 of 'You Know My Name (Look Up the Number)' *was* getting a little worn... MG

JEFF BECK
There and Back *(Epic)*
Beck's always amazing guitar work swings closer to the rock side of the jazz-rock spectrum than it has in years. An essential purchase, especially for those who have written off Beck's recent records as "elevator music". DN

CAPTAIN BEEFHEART AND THE MAGIC BAND
Shiny Beast (Bat Chain Puller) *(Virgin)*
Released in the UK at long last (it appeared Stateside with Warners some years ago), the divine Captain's latest instalment in a fertile career of musical charmed lunacy. Although he remains as unpredictable as ever, there are claims for 'Shiny Beast' as his best ever (since 'Trout Mast Replica'?). Indispensable. MJ

BEE GEES
Greatest Hits *(RSO)*
If you haven't been near a radio in the last three years, here are all the hits — the boogies, the ballads, no filler, plenty of falsettos. If you have been near a radio, you're already sick of this stuff. DN

BELLAMY BROTHERS
You Can Get Crazy *(Warners)*
Featuring the hit single 'If I Said You Had a Beautiful Body'. Infectious sound of saccharin rock. AB-F

PETER BELLAMY
Both Sides Then *(Topic)*
Traditional, austere folk singing in the best traditions of the genre. For the converted only, but it's class anyway. AB-F

PAT BENATAR
In the Heat of the Night *(Chrysalis)*
She might be stiff on stage compared to Debbie the Harry or competing upcomer Ellen Foley, but

PAT BENATAR

under the guiding hand of Mike Chapman her first album is full of fire and hooks and silly lyrics (for which, in most cases, she only has herself to blame). She'll go far. MJ

GEORGE BENSON
Give Me the Night *(Warners)*
Produced by Quincy Jones, another classy outing from this stylish jazz-soul guitarist and singer. Title song has charted. MJ

BIG YOUTH
Everyday Skank *(Trojan)*
Another Trojan collection of oldies; this was specially compiled, and the difference shows. The music begins with sides cut for Gussie Clarke, Joe Gibbs and Keith Hudson: the supporting rhythms are excellent throughout. Youth strings together his lighthearted catchphrases, rarely indulging in anything thought-provoking. On side two, the tone of the music changes abruptly with the seven tracks Youth produced himself; allowing himself his full head of steam, he opts for much denser rhythms, and his toasts are appropriately weightier. This is Big Youth The Preacher, making the music he'd been wanting to make for other producers, but hadn't been able to because his rasta beliefs were unacceptable. Youth was the first to popularise this style of toasting, and still does it better than the rest. NK

BLACK SABBATH
Heaven and Hell
(Warners/Vertigo)
Heavy metal ancients emerge from the grave of time, now that the genre is triumphant and roaming the lands again. All sounds very familiar. AB-F

BLACK SABBATH
Live At Last *(Nems)*
We thought these kamikaze classic Sabbath tracks had been forgotten! Still as obnoxious and powerful. AB-F

BLACK UHURU
Sinsemilla *(Island)*
First notch reggae. AB-F

DEBBIE HARRY

BLACKBEARD
I Wah Dub *(More Cut)*
Workmanlike reggae effort by ace producer Dennis Bovell under pseudonym. Maybe he didn't even like it himself... AB-F

BLACKFOOT
Tomcattin' *(Atco)*
Earth rock for those in the know. AB-F

RAN BLAKE
Film Noir *(Arista)*
Sloughing off the old worthiness of Third Stream ("with voices", you know?), Ran Blake has proved a fine freestyler in the new developments department.

Basically, this is an album of Great Movie Themes. Basically again, such concept albums are just cheap, shiny luggage where the artist can stuff his chainstore shirts and socks for the duration. In reality, the bag here is a far more loaded one, movie *essences* reinterpreted and redeployed on a completely off-the-wall, one-to-one basis. Very furtive and murderous movies too, like 'Doktor Mabuse' and 'Le Boucher'.

Only two tracks stay as solo pieces, but Blake's own playing tends to command both form and content throughout. His tricks and techniques are vast, chosen with dedicated ease to fit each situation; other instruments take on support roles in the burgeoning portraits. Typical is 'Streetcar Named Desire', a wayward, vacillating piece where a bruised piano vamp is the support system for a vagrant alto and tense, percussive guitar figures. These alternate with twisting, brittle phrases under railroad drums to produce a strong sense of narrative and an appropriate one of destiny. An inspired and inspiring album. LE

C.I. BLAST
I Wanna Get Down
(Cotillion)
R & R (and gospel) ditties. AB-F

BLONDIE
Eat to the Beat *(Chrysalis)*
Joyous celebration of all the virtues of modern pop. It might be formula stuff, but Debbie Harry and the Boys sure are adept at injecting new life and soul into the fray. Almost every track a frothy winner and potential hit single (most of them were). AB-F

BLOOD SWEAT AND TEARS
Nuclear Blues *(MCA)*
Fossil jazz rock. Worth mentioning is the fact that B S & T now no longer sport any musician from the original line-up. It shows. AB-F

THE BLUES BAND
The Official Blues Band Bootleg Album *(Arista)*
Boring old blues in the immaculate tradition of yesteryear. Surprisingly commercially successful album by bunch of ageing musicians, most from the first Manfred Mann school of hits generation: Paul Jones is vocalist and makes a come-back from the legions of the living dead. All very professional but oh so uninspiring. MJ

BLUE OYSTER CULT
Cultosaurus Erectus
(Columbia/CBS)
The heavy metal thunder lizard wakes from its sleep of the past few years and roars again. Mike Moorcock wrote one of the lyrics. DN

BLUE STEEL
No More Lonely Nights
(Infinity)
Heavy roaring rock of US origin. AB-F

THE BLUES BROTHERS
The Blues Brothers
(Atlantic)
Soundtrack of the demolition derby, car wrecking extravaganza film. Pristine renderings of rhythm and blues classics by the zany duo and their more-than-experienced band (Steve Cropper, Duck Dunne, Matt Murphy et al). Contributions from Ray Charles, Aretha Franklin, Cab Calloway and James Brown spice up the proceedings. Makes sense even if you haven't seen the film. MJ

ARTHUR BLYTHE
In the Tradition
(Columbia/CBS)
A pro almost since High School, it's only lately that altoist Black Arthur Blythe has become at all widely known, signally through

gigging with Gil Evans. 'The Grip' (India Navigation), almost a début waxing, was a significant envoy in the overloaded ocean of new/loft music, while 'Lenox Avenue Breakdown' showed (among other things) exactly how you can multiply your audience without dividing your allegiances.

With 'In the Tradition' Blythe naturalises another aspect of his own/his music's capabilities, with a catalogue of handpicked pre- and post-war classics — 'Jitterbug Waltz', 'Caravan', 'Naima' — each saluting a genre genius. One is conscious of the weight of Ellington and Coltrane being carried on those shoulders, but our hero is never prim or plaintive: his neatness and tension are plus factors, and his wayward, bluesy boldness a trademark. Fred Hopkins and Steve McCall, otherwise two-thirds of Air, push the rhythm in appropriate directions, but partner in crime is the oft-forgot pianist Stanley Cowell whose percussive gambits convert even 'In A Sentimental Mood' into a spinechiller.

Prematurely, this has to be one of the albums of the decade — and not only for Black Arthur. LE

ANGELA BOFILL
Angel of the Night
(GRP/Arista)
Angela Bofill mixes enough street smarts into her slick pop/jazz style to avoid slipping into the sugar swamps inhabited by nonentities like Al Jarreau, despite a somewhat cluttered production by CRP label owners Dave Grusin and Larry Rosen. DN

THE BOGEY BOYS
Jimmy Did It *(Chrysalis)*
Good-time unasssuming rock by new Irish band. Feeds the boogie feet but not the brains. MJ

BONEY M
Oceans of Fantasy *(Atlantic)*
Sargassos of schlock. Manufactured disco stars on the (fast) way out. MJ

KARLA BONOFF
Restless Nights
(Columbia/CBS)
Criminally-overlooked singer and songwriter, Karla Bonoff lives in the shadows of La Ronstadt, for whom she has provided so many good songs. This is her second album, a long time coming and worth every minute of the wait. Every song a gem. A masterpiece of restrained emotions and melodies. Go and buy it this very moment, this is no Ronstadt-clone, this is the real thing. MJ

BOB GELDOF

BOOMTOWN RATS
The Fine Art of Surfacing
(Columbia/Ensign)
Will Stiff Little Fingers and the Undertones sound this stiff once they get successful? I hope not! The Rats continue to make great singles, but with the exception of 'Tonic for the Troops', not great albums. DN

BOSS BROS.
Stalling for Time *(Mercury)*
Unnecessary rock: a new genre? AB-F

TERENCE BOYLAN
Suzy *(Asylum)*
Schizophrenic album which betrays a patchy production history. Boylan is still a master of the non-wimpish bittersweet love song and ballad, but the album also has intriguing snatches of a possible gutsier new style. AB-F

BOYS OF THE LOUGH
Regrouped *(Topic)*
English folk at its most pristine. AB-F

THE BRAINS
The Brains *(Mercury)*
British producer Steve

Lillywhite's first American production job. "Undiluted emotionalism" (TROUSER PRESS). AB-F

BRAND X
Do They Hurt? *(Passport/Charisma)*
All down to the forces of destiny, outfits like National Health and Nova have largely been and gone. Brand X, however, goes on for ever: the one token, monumental, static, elastic, British jazz-rock band.

In the glorious past, Messrs. Lumley, Collins and the hallmarking Morris Pert held sway. Now, apart from the genuinely arresting Hipgnosis artwork, it's the songs and sounds of John Goodsall and Percy Jones running the show. Even the nippy keyboard forays on 'Noddy Goes to Sweden' are traumatic echoes of the bass's clucking nerve centre.

But after faintly inglorious recent precedents such as 'Masques', which withers by comparison, 'Hurt' lets some real blood run down the channels in harder, riper melodies, textured chord cladding and a Pledge-sheened mahogony production. The mashing, meshing heroics of 'Voiderama', Hendrix changes on 'Cambodia' and funny vocals plus HM riff (pinched methinks from Manfred Mann's 'Buddha') on 'Act of Will' make for some real rock anthems. If you live by categories, the ambivalence is amazing. But then again, considering that rock itself down at pub and college level has broadened so much, and that so much UK jazz remains hidebound and forelock-tugging, it's a fairly imperative corner to be driven into. LE

BRASS CONSTRUCTION
Brass Construction 5 *(UA)*
Heavy disco onslaught with strings and brass galore called on for reinforcements. You shall dance...or else. AB-F

PAUL BRETT
Romantic Guitar *(K-Tel)*
The title says it all. Hoary chestnuts given the once-over treatment. For masochists only. AB-F

THE BRIDES OF FUNKENSTEIN
Never Buy Texas from a Cowboy *(Atlantic)*
George Clinton, manipulator extraordinaire, single-handedly creates a new genre: 'Funktry and Western'. Raises a smile or two. AB-F

THE BRITISH LIONS
Trouble with Women *(Cherry Red)*
Defunct band composed of survivors from Mott the Hoople and Medicine Head see their second album finally unleashed upon the world after a gap of three years. Not world shattering but always interesting: John Fiddler has one of the more moving voices in the business. MJ

BROKEN HOME
Broken Home *(WEA)*
Moody riffing in a minor vein. AB-F

DAVID BOMBERG
You Should See the Rest of the Band *(Fantasy)*
Bromberg's vocal cords will never match his guitar chords. DN

HERMAN BROOD AND HIS WILD ROMANCE
Go Nutz *(Ariola)*
Brood, an ex-junkie indecently proud of the fact, is big in Holland. Let it stay that way and let's keep his music, all plagiarisms and heavy dubious influences, out of our clean English-speaking countries. Patriotism apart, the man is a bore and his music is no better. MJ

GARY BROOKER
No More Fear of Flying *(Chrysalis)*
Procul Harum singer emerges with solo effort. The voice is as gripping as ever but his deliberate effort to distance himself from the symphonic rock strictures of the group doesn't always suit him and the choice of material lets him down at times. Enjoyable in small doses. AB-F

ELKIE BROOKS
Live and Learn *(A&M)*
Once good blues singer goes soft and joins the dinner-dance set. MJ

THE BROUGHTONS
Parlez-vous English? *(EMI)*
Old hippies never die. They just keep on recording. AB-F

DENNIS BROWN
Joseph's Coat of Many Colours *(Laser)*
One hit reggae artist goes for second album. Fodder. AB-F

DUNCAN BROWNE
Duncan Browne *(Sire/Logo)*
British folkie who hit last year with 'Wild Places' offers a tame follow-up full of super-overproduced slush. DN

JACKSON BROWNE
Hold Out *(Asylum)*
Disappointing offering from Jackson Browne after a long wait. Well crafted and produced but lacks the usual sparkle of sensitivity and care. Browne seems to have run out of misery, and sadly enough, a reasonable form of happiness doesn't appear to suit his inspiration. David Lindley helps out as usual but it could have been so much better. Certainly not 'Son of the Pretender', more like a distant cousin. MJ

TOM BROWNE
Love Approach *(Arista)*
Second disco album with tinges of jazz peering through the beat. AB-F

BILL BRUFORD
The Bruford Tapes *(Polydor)*
Live radio broadcast with limited release. Competent but uninspired jazz rock. AB-F

BILL BRUFORD
Gradually Going Tornado *(Polydor/EG)*
Metronomically-precise fusion rock from King Crimson drummer Bill Bruford with a band of stalwart experienced Anglo-US musicians. The technique is always impeccable, the sound quasi-perfect, but a distinct lack of soul is also on sorry display. AB-F

HAROLD BUDD/BRIAN ENO
Plateaux of mirror *(EG)*
Crystalline doodlings by masters of the genre. Ambient music the way the Lord (and Eno) decreed. MJ

BUDDY ODOR
Buddy Odor is a Gas *(Ariola)*
Possibly the worst title of the year. Gruppo Sportivo remnants try to be too funny and spoil their whole pitch. They could have been contenders, though. AB-F

JIMMY BUFFETT
Volcano *(MCA)*
Laid-back island, laid back snore rock. AB-F

BUGGLES
The Age of Plastic *(Island)*
Plastic techno-pop by plastic people for plastic people. The only problem with Buggles is that they know they are clever. Light weight divertimento. MJ

CINDY BULLENS
Steal The Night *(Casablanca)*
This album begins with the lines "I'm a full tilt rocker and I'm just sixteen". That's two lies in just thirty seconds and its downhill from there. DN

THE LEGENDARY HANK C BURNETTE
Hot Licks and Fancy Tricks *(Sonet)*
The legendary Hank C. Burnette is a rockabilly rock 'n' roller and he may be a genius. This record, on clear yellow vinyl, is a mixture of originals and standards like 'That's All Right' and 'Boppin' the Blues' — altogether six deep-voiced vocal tracks and eight electric-and-electronic instrumentals. Hank is really a Swede named Högberg. He plays all instruments, produces, arranges, engineers and mixes himself. I have a mental image of Hank C. growing up in the Land of the Midnight Sun with his reindeer, his rockabilly records, and his private recording studio. The only objection to this record is that it's a bit too smooth, a bit too much one man alone in a studio. Hank needs to get out and bop with the boys. But the tribute here to Elvis 'The King of Rock 'n' Roll' is really fine, and who could dislike a man who's out "standin' on the corner lookin' for a hippie broad"? Go Hank, go! AP

ROCKY BURNETTE
The Son of Rock and Roll *(EMI America)*
It's the age-old rock 'n' roll Cinderella story. A year ago, Rocky Burnette, son of original era rockabilly and later teen-star Johnny Burnette, was starving and penniless. Now here he is with his first album. Its first track, 'Tired of Toein' the Line', has been a summer hit. But I don't know why it couldn't throw off six more before this is published: 'Baby tonight', 'You're So Easy to Love', even 'Clowns from Outer Space'. This record is one attempt to get back to rock 'n' roll that succeeds. The title of the album is not just a reference to the Johnny Burnette connection. It's a subtle boast. But the boast is justified. Burnette-and-company's original songs cover the bases of rock 'n' roll from boogie to ballad, from rockabilly to McCartney. The arrangements are as tight as disco, the production is brilliant, there is riff on riff to hook into your head, hot eight-bar instrumental breaks, and Burnette's splendid rock 'n' roll singing. For my money, this is not just an incredible debut album — it's the record of the year. AP

THE BUZZARDS
Jellied Eels to Record Deals *(Chrysalis)*
East of London band previously known as the Leighton Buzzards. Amusing vignettes which might require subtitles in the USA. AB-F

BUZZCOCKS
A Different Kind of Tension *(IRS/UA)*
Great pop toons with manic depressive lyrics as only Pete Shelley can write them. Fascinating but uneven. MJ

BUZZCOCKS
Singles Goin' Steady *(IRS)*
All the menacing British singles by the Buzzcocks all grouped into one awesome package that clearly shows the strength and imagination of a band still deserving of more consideration. AB-F

ZIGGY BYFIELD AND THE BLACKHEART BAND
Running *(PVK)*
Ziggy tries to be Rod Stewart with balls and fails. Run. AB-F

THE BYRDS
The Byrds Play Dylan *(Columbia/CBS)*
A shoddy compilation that spans the Byrds' career from 1965 to 1970 without giving much of an idea what they were about. Although it includes four chart items including the No1 hit 'Mr. Tambourine Man' which began the "folk-rock" era and their last top forty hit 'My Back Pages' from April 1967, most of this set is old LP tracks drawing heavily on their later, poorer efforts. DN

D. L. BYRON
This Day And Age *(Arista)*
Byron is a spunky, engaging rocker who makes a few too many Springsteen moves for his own good on this debut, but it figures, since producer Jimmy Iovine has done the Boss' studio engineering since 1975. A bundle of good raw material. DN

ZIGGY BYFIELD

CABARET VOLTAIRE
Mix Up *(Rough Trade)*
Impenetrable, murky, confused aural curtain of random sounds by British exponents of high pretension. AB-F

CABARET VOLTAIRE
Live at the YMCA *(Rough Trade)*
Sons of Stockhausen ride again and bore audience's pants off. Some people get away with murder in the name of art. AB-F

JOHN CALE
Sabotage Live *(Spy)*
The original eccentric of art rock strikes again with this deceptively approachable live album on small independent label. Mercenaries and WW3 figure in prominent place in Cale's new pantheon. An album that disturbs and enchants. MJ

RANDY CALIFORNIA
Kapt. Kopter and the (Fabulous) Twirly Birds *(CBS)*
Timely re-issue of Spirit mainman solo effort. A minor classic now very much dated but still greatly enjoyable if you're willing to make a few concessions to the fashionable sounds of yesteryear and Hendrixy look-alikes. AB-F

CAMEL
I Can See Your House From Here *(Decca)*
Without Peter Bardens, Camel succumb to pomp and theatricality. A sorry sight. Lousy cover. AB-F

JIM CAPALDI
The Sweet Smell of Success *(Carrere)*
Ex-Traffic drummer keeps churning out solo albums to no avail. He's now reduced to plundering (and destroying) Traffic hits he wrote with Stevie Winwood (where are you now that we need you?). A bad initiative altogether. AB-F

CAPITAL LETTERS
Headline News *(Greensleeves)*
Reggae from the people who haven't sold out to the syndrum syndrome. AB-F

CAPTAIN AND TENNILLE
Make Your Move *(Casablanca)*
Sweet nothings. AB-F

KIM CARNES
Romance Dance *(EMI/UA)*
Lovely lady with Rod Stewart-like voice deserves all her success (made possible by a somewhat soppy duet on a Kenny Rogers single hit), but this is a hasty collection of motley songs. Has done better. AB-F

JIM CARROLL
A Catholic Boy *(Rolling Stones)*
"I'm here to give you my heart and you want some fashion show", Jim Carroll sings in his debut as the perfect second act for Rolling Stones Records. Carroll's the only true contender to rise from the subway hideaways of urban poetry since Lou Reed. He cuts no corners, but his edges are sharp. Some of his songs are double-edged bladeloads of heroin propaganda. Others will give you shivers without making the insides of your elbows twitch. You may recognize Patti Smith as the character he calls "Crow". Then there's 'When The City Drops (Into The Night)', a dense tour-de-force that includes these lines: 'It's when my woman pawns her voice...so she can make her old excuses sound new...because when the city drops into the night, before the darkness there's one moment of light." Sure, Carroll's disc has some flaws, but that's the price paid for riding the razor's edge and coming back to tell the tale. MG

THE CARS
Candy-O *(Elektra)*
Disappointing second album from Rick Ocasek's boys. Power pop with too much confidence and not enough hooks. AB-F

CARLENE CARTER
Two Sides to Every Woman *(Warners)*
Uneventful second album by long-legged Carlene. Lack of strong material. Probably a minor lapse as she's capable of so much better. MJ

CARLENE CARTER
Musical Shapes *(F-Beat)*
Great sleeve solo (photo by our mate Chalkie Davies). Great lady. Great album. Mrs. Nick Lowe (and daughter-in-law of Johnny Cash — what a pedigree) turns up trumps in this, her third LP. Recorded with Rockpile and featuring a dynamite tearjerker country ballad with, of all hard-boiled people, Dave Edmunds and a great rendering of the evergreen 'Ring of Fire' which even Blondie can't touch. Carlene Carter, the lady who puts the C...T back into country. PS: she can also rock. AB-F

LYNDA CARTER
Lynda Carter *(Epic)*
Wonderwoman sings. Lynda Carter can't sing. But, oh those eyes... AB-F

JOHNNY CASH
Silver *(Columbia/CBS)*
There's a point where radical and conservative meet, and I think Johnny Cash has found it in 'Silver', an album celebrating twenty-five years as a singer. As always, the record is anchored by the Tennessee Two — Marshall Grant on bass and W.S. Holland on drums — who have been with Cash throughout his career. And the songs on the album include oldies like 'Cocaine Blues' and 'Ghost Riders in the Sky'. That's as conservative as you could like. On the other hand, this record is a radical new country album. It's produced by Emmylou Harris' husband, Brian Ahern. There's no string slush, no filler. Instead, Cash is arranged as never before, simply but tastefully, with modern sound quality and every track made as though it counted. I think the secret of Cash's contradictory images — Big Bad John, the country radical, the original Daddy Outlaw; and Preacher John, the conservative frock coated early American — is that this is a man looking for the essence of his native land. On 'Silver' he finds it. Who knows what he'll be by the time he records *Gold*? I think he will contain multitudes. AP

ROSANNE CASH
Right or Wrong *(Columbia/Ariola)*
Out in California, there's a new country music emerging, more pure and more simple than the Nashville product, less sentimental and with a contemporary bite that Nashville music doesn't have. This record is a state of the art example, but it's also something more than that — the debut of an astonishing talent. That Rosanne Cash's father is Johnny Cash may have opened doors at Columbia. That her husband is Rodney Crowell — sometime musician in Emmylou Harris' band and one of New Country's finest talents — certainly helped this album. Crowell produced this record, wrote four of its best songs, sings some backup and occasionally sits in with a guitar.(Oh, the duet album that Crowell and Cash will surely do!). But set her father and husband aside and call this young woman Rosanne Smith and she would still be a truly unusual talent. Rosanne Cash has a strong, sweet and expressive voice and she sings from within the material as very few can or do. She's a singer I expect to be listening to for a long time. AP

CASINO MUSIC
Jungle Love *(Ze)*
French band produced by Chris Stein of Blondie. Not too convincing, I fear. A disappointing Ze offering. Well, they can't all be perfect. MJ

SHAUN CASSIDY
Live *(Warner Brothers)*
Dead on arrival — but at least all the hits are laid out in one place. DN

FELIX CAVALIERE
Castles In The Air *(Epic)*
Cavaliere tries hard but somehow doesn't summon up the firey Italian soul of his 60's group the Rascals, as his slowed down, funked up remake for 'People Got To Free' shows. This is a bit more respectable than fellow ex-Rascals Dino Danelli and Gene Cornish who made total fools of themselves with Fotomaker, but nothing to make you want to jump and shout. DN

GENE CHANDLER
'80 *(20th Century)*
Dance music at its best. MJ

MARSHALL CHAPMAN
Marshall *(Epic)*
A lady with determination and grit making an uneasy transition from country to rock. Gravel-voiced and packing a mean punch, she is well on her way to achieving her aims. Marshall Chapman: a name to watch for. AB-F

MICHAEL CHAPMAN
Fully Qualified Survivor *(Criminal)*
Reissue of one of Chapman's best albums, from the days back when he was still a great original and hadn't fallen into a damaging rut. Investigate. AB-F

MICHAEL CHAPMAN
Looking for Eleven *(Criminal)*
Once upon a time, Michael Chapman was an electric folkie with a very distinctive style of mumbling vocals and jangling guitar. His originality, as he shifts from label to label, has faded fast over the years and 'Looking for Eleven' is just more of the same as before. File under *Pleasantly dated* but also utterly innocuous. An 11 minute four-part mostly instrumental piece 'Spain' doesn't help the proceeds along one iota. Ex-members of Lindisfarne provide the backing. MJ

CHEAP TRICK
Cheap Trick *(Epic)*
Produced by Jack Douglas, Cheap Trick's first album is released in the UK years too late. Lovely songs and feeling; some say they haven't improved on it in the years that followed. AB-F

CHEAP TRICK
Dream Police *(Columbia/Epic)*
Foot-tapping rockers by masters of the genre, straddling with insolent ease the borderline between pop and heavy metal, without ever indulging in the excesses of either genre. MJ

CHIC
Risque *(Atlantic)*
More from the house of elegant hits. Gives disco a good name. AB-F

CHIC
Chic's Greatest Hits *(Atlantic)*
Disco haute-couture. AB-F

CHIC
Street People *(Atlantic)*
Surprisingly listless album

from the Nile Rodgers and Bernard Edwards axis. Maybe they've been producing too many hits for others (Sheila B. Devotion, Diana Ross) and had no good hooks left for their own flagship. Polished, but forgettable this time round, I fear. MJ

CHICAGO
Street Player *(Columbia/CBS)*
They shoot tired horses, don't they? AB-F

CHICAGO
Chicago *(Columbia/CBS)*
Number 14. AB-F

THE CHIEFTAINS
Boil the Breakfast Early *(Columbia/CBS)*
Irish folk champions champion on and make it all sound so effortlessly easy. AB-F

CHILD
Total Recall *(Ariola)*
Teeny-bop chartbusters. MJ

DESMOND CHILD AND ROUGE
Runners in the Night *(Capitol)*
Splendid collection of emotive panoramas produced in the grand old Spector style by Richard Landis. Desmond Child and his three female cohorts share lead vocal credits and interweave subtle harmonies throughout their fiery tales of boulevard love and New York summer nights. A discovery. AB-F

ALEX CHILTON
Like Flies on Sherbet *(Aura)*
Sad effort by once great (Big Star) Alex Chilton. Should never have been released. AB-F

CHIPMUNKS
Chipmunk Punk *(Excelsior)*
Perversely enjoyable. Those good old moptops dust away the spider webs and go new wave modern. Go, go, go... MJ

CHROME
Red Exposure *(Beggars Banquet)*
Dense electronic wash of sound by American duo consisting of Damon Edge (who also produced) and Helios Creed. Experimental but not always sufficiently accessible. Great music to type by, though. Or, for that matter, for whatever purpose you require unaggressive but slightly hypnotic background music as opposed to muzak. AB-F

ERIC CLAPTON
Just One Night *(RSO)*
Eric at the Budokan. Double live set with all the familiar classics and semi-classics, but Clapton and his band are so mellifluously laidback that there is no fire or life in there to tickle the muscles of your heart or the muscles of your guts. Tired. AB-F

STANLEY CLARKE
Rocks, Pebbles & Sand *(Epic)*
Avoiding phrases like getting your pebbles off...those among us who were drawn to the wry wistful side of Stanley Clarke in 'School Days' may not find much ado this time. That's due not only to the common law of individual musician subjugated to common cause, but the cause itself. Getting away from the watery bumptiousness of 'Modern Man' and 'I Wanna Play For You', Clarke had headed straight for pile-driving, primary coloured metal. Asphalting drums (Simon Phillips) and lightning-conductor guitar (Charles Johnson) render items like 'Danger Street' rather closer to Aerosmith than Bessie Smith, with the distinctive bass (electric rather than alembic) coming up for air now and then.

Let's be fair, of it's kind it's very good music, and what wrecks the album's overdrive are the alternatives: Stan's mangled warblings on the straggling slowie 'You/Me Together', and a factory-floor funker, 'We Supply', co-owned by Louis Johnson and, interestingly, the choice for a first take-off single. One case where variety doesn't pay. LE

THE CLASH
London Calling *(Epic/CBS)*
It's taken me a long time to get to like the Clash and, with this, Guy Stevens-produced third (double) album, I can at last see what the majority of other critics see in them. Commitment and energy and a revolutionary sense of values abound on 'London Calling'. If music could influence political events, then this is the music that might do it. MJ

JIMMY CLIFF
I Am The Living *(Atlantic/WEA)*
A Jamaican singer (with an enviable hit-strewn past) who does not dabble in rasta folklore and is, as a result, somewhat out of fashion. Tom Scott and Deniece Williams help out, but the band is bland. Better see Cliff live. AB-F

BRUCE COCKBURN
Dancing in the Dragon's Jaws *(Millenium/RCA)*
Canadian folkie goes his own sweet way (he's been around some ten years now) and scores fluke hit. Why not? He thoroughly deserves it. More of the same on the album. AB-F

COCKNEY REJECTS
Greatest Hits Vol I *(Zonophone)*
Gives even punk a bad name. Could you believe it. Brainless chanting and instrument bashing. Some call it music. AB-F

LEONARD COHEN
Recent Songs *(Columbia/CBS)*
A strong return to form by poet Leonard Cohen after the walking disaster of his last, Phil Spector-manipulated album. More of the same, but that's what people want from Lennie the smile. Intriguing choice of instrumentation and hypnotic dirges of lost love, despair and impotence from the master himself. MJ

ALBERT COLLINS
Frostbite *(Alligator/Sonet)*
Collins puts on as powerful a show as anyone in contemporary blues, and his records lose little of it. If not quite as triumphantly excellent as 'Ice Pickin' (ALLIGATOR/SONET) (1978) — perhaps because it's not very different in conception — Frostbite is an album of unremittingly fine, involving music, extremely well-recorded. The horn arrangements are done with discretion and genuinely embrace the playing of the six-piece nuclear band. Collins himself is an irresistible guitarist, rarely plays a boring phrase, and uses special effects with real skill in the narrative piece 'Snowed In'. The programme is mostly slow blues and faster shuffle numbers, and Collins is equally commanding in both. TR

JUDY COLLINS
Running for my Life *(Elektra)*
Desperately mundane album by great singer of yesteryear now sadly going through the motions. A tragic loss. MJ

PAUL COLLINS' BEAT
Paul Collins' Beat *(Columbia/CBS)*
Polished first division power pop as only American bands can do it. AB-F

COMMODORES
Heroes *(Motown)*
Almost experimental LP from the Commodores which tackles varied genres with equal success: jazz, ballad, soul, gospel 'Jesus is Love', funk and social comment. MJ

JEFF CONAWAY
Jeff Conaway *(Columbia)*
Ex-Springsteen manager Mike Appel's new protégé. Pale imitation of the real thing. AB-F

THE CONTORTIONS
Buy the Contortions *(Ze)*
Avant-garde jazz with tenuous disco back beat by James White/Chance, darling of the New York low-life intelligentsia. Overrated pap. AB-F

RY COODER
The Long Riders — Original Soundtrack *(Warner)*
Suitably bucolic and melancholy soundtrack for Walter Hill's splendidly stylized western movie. Ry Cooder pursues his ethno-musicological roots through a tasty modern amalgam and recreation of the West at the end of the last century, with shades of hillbilly, bluegrass, kaleidoscope, Texas ballads and Little Feat in its Lowell George heyday. A plethora of musicians join him with gusto, including Milt Holland, John Dickinson, David Lindley, Bill Bryson, Jim Keltner and George Bohannon. A soundtrack that stands up on its own with no hesitation. MJ

ALICE COOPER
Flush the Fashion *(Warners)*
Alice Cooper's past theatrical excesses have often obscured the fact of his continuous excellence in the pantheon of clean, no frills American rock 'n' roll. This is another example, tinged this time around, with new wave and

JOHN COOPER CLARKE

electropop influences, of quality rock. And what else can you ask of the man? MJ

JOHN COOPER CLARKE
Ou Est la Maison de Fromage? *(Rabid)*
Early recordings by the Mancunian poet. One for the archives. AB-F

JOHN COOPER CLARKE
Snap, Crackle (&) Bop *(Epic)*
Northern British so-called punk poet almost begins to sing his idiosyncratic texts to the accompaniment of music by Martin Hannet (ubiquitous producer) and Steve Hopkins alias the Invisible Girls. Long 'Beasley Street' impresses, like an English 'Desolate Row'. AB-F

CHICK COREA
Tap Step *(Warner Bros.)*
CHICK COREA
Delphi I *(Polydor)*
Refreshingly — imperatively — having had his jump-suited fling with RTF, Chick Corea has avoided hanging round with the disco flashers and returned to base. On stage he's been working with his temperamental opposite, Gary Burton, while on record he keeps himself and his followers well exercised with two different but generally effective and articulate albums.

'Tap Step' you may view as a selective, polished retrospective; or more simply as flavoursome dogs' breakfast. Latin roots have a dastardly jolly romp in 'Samba LA' (Purim, Moreira, Laudir Oliviera), reappearing in refined, sheltered form in 'The Slide'. Gayle Moran heads 'The Embrace', earnest and bloodless. Both 'Magic Carpet' and the title number are fine showcases for Corea's wisdom with all types of keyboard — and both lead and infill — rolling across Bunny Brunel's burrowing, fretless bass and the acidic, spilling drums of Tom Brechtlein. Certain placid jazz rock ghosts are in the air, but the spirits of 'Tap Step' are futuristic too.

'Delphi I' is a solo piano performance, recorded at the Scientologists' Delphian School. If you cast aside Corea's overt enrapturement with this movement, the first half — 'Alma Mater for Delphi' — remains very special. A run of linked improvisations, including some familiar stylistic decor, it's variously exploratory, reflective, celebrational, occasionally self-critical, and strikingly naked in this guarded world. The second set, subtitled 'Stride Time', is all skipping, raggy workouts straight from the hip of Art Tatum. Imperative class. And magic. LE

CHICK COREA & HERBIE HANCOCK
Corea/Hancock *(Polydor)*
Second album taken from a 1978 concert by the two fusion whizzkids. Jazz piano playing for the converted. AB-F

LARRY CORYELL
Return *(Vanguard)*
Despite having been virtually the umbilical chord to fusion music in the latter 60s, Larry Coryell is curiously tagged more with the company he keeps (*with* Steve Khan, *with* Stephane Grappelli) than remembered for the man or the music.

'Return' does not find the circle coming round again to emphasise his capacity as writer and as leader, in context of an electric-ish small group but with a far greater balance and serenity than the overtaxed Eleventh House.

Apart from percussionist Ray Mantilla, sidesmen here are three of the many sons of Dave Brubeck — drummer Dan, bassman Chris and keyboarder Darius. On his self-penned title track, Darius shows himself as a generous, sculptural soloist with a knack for a wayward yet highly palatable melody: keep an ear open here. Featherlight bass and a throwaway hook line on 'Sweet Shuffle' tellingly extend outwards under the wacky guitar breeze that indeed recalls House pyrotechnics. Even 'Cisco at the Disco' with the cheapest of all rhythm tricks shows that the axe blade is kept very clean; elsewhere his textured, measured side is much on show.

Individually, almost all of Coryell's prolific output can feel physically slight if intellectually capable; collectively that impression is only reinforced. But take 'Return' as you find it. LE

ELVIS COSTELLO AND THE ATTRACTIONS
Get Happy *(F.Beat)*
Never one to tread the well-trodden path, Costello's fourth long player sees him making several long strides away from the angry young man stance which served him so nobly on the previous three.

The whole sound of the music has become denser, less superficially poppy, less slickly arranged. And, despite flashes of the old aggressions on 'Beaten To The Punch' and incisive facade-stripping on 'The Imposter', the predominant themes of this ironically titled collection are bittersweet reflections on times gone by, and views of disintegrating scenes and relationships in a changing world.

Behind the maestro, Messrs. Naive, Thomas and Thomas are so soulfully superb as ever. Naive's keyboards, especially, are crucial in giving shape and form to the many moods of the songs.

Amongst the embarrassment of riches offered by the twenty (!) tracks on 'Get Happy', special mention should be made of the rending regret of 'Motel Matches', the cocky strut of 'Man Called Uncle', the rare spidery guitar solo crawling briskly across 'Five Gears In Reverse', and the exquisite delicacy and wordplay of 'New Amsterdam'.

Nearly every song is a highlight, though. And the fact that Costello, who has been a major songwriter from the moment he surfaced back in '76, clearly has much more to offer cannot be applauded too loudly. PK

JAYNE COUNTY
Rock 'n' Roll Resurrection *(Safari)*
Derivative punkitude by the thing that called itself Wayne County before a certain sex-change operation. She sure doesn't look or sing or speak like a lady to me. AB-F

COWBOYS INTERNATIONAL
The Original Sin *(Virgin)*
Overlooked album by British band led by Ken Lockie. Mean melodies and harmonies with a touch of the David Bowie inflections and vistas. Worth digging out from that deletion bin. AB-F

KEVIN COYNE
Bursting Bubbles *(Virgin)*
The social conscience of British music with another LP. More of the worthy same. Unfortunately will not reach beyond his devoted small circle of admirers. MJ

THE CRAMPS
Songs The Lord Taught Us *(IRS/Illegal)*
Produced by legendary Alex Chilton this is an album with a marked difference. Some call it voodoo rockabilly, but whatever slot you might want to classify the Cramps in, you can't deny their originality and not give them full marks for trying. Harking back to the prehistoric beat of primal rock 'n' roll their crypt and gore scenari beat the night away with the stealth of an overfed vampire. Others call it punkabilly, well why not? The energy initially re-energised by punk permeates their every chord, even despite the fact they have no bass player. One for your must list, I fear. AB-F

CRASS
Stations of the Crass *(Crass)*
Anarchist rock. For true blooded anarchists only. MJ

RANDY CRAWFORD
Now We May Begin *(Warner Bros.)*
If Randy Crawford is primarily remembered by British audiences for her sign-off comment after appearing at London's Hammersmith Odeon with the Crusaders last year, "Thank you for having me", she is also remembered with affection and awe. Having been condemned to batter a thousand times through 'Street Life', she glides and slices fresh and clean through this second-debut album like the veteran she almost is.

Joe, Stix and Wilton themselves have trumped almost every other similar hand (the emergent Angela Bofill comes to mind) with a collection that drifts remarkably into instant classics. You are vaguely aware of something trotting around the soft-disco/hipeasy-listening circuit, with standard-issue arrangements playing the games in subtly positive fashion. More important, the voice at the helm is made of sturdy stuff, staunch and tasty or cool and cloudy but very rarely stylised. Prime feature however is the calibre of the songs themselves, penned interestingly mainly by Sample and Will Jennings. 'My heart is not as young as it used to be', 'Last night at Danceland' and the title cut stick in the mind like the

CRETONES

taste of green onions or visions of Wolfman Jack. More here surely than meets the ear. LE

THE CRETONES
Thin Red Line *(Planet)*
Band leader/guitarist/ songwriter/singer Mark Goldenberg is the man who put punk in Linda Ronstadt on 'Mad Love'. Her versions of his songs come off tougher than Goldenberg's own treatments here. Punk for pencilneck geeks. DN

CHRISTINA
Christina *(Ze)*
Challenging camp. Conceptual disco. Decadent chic. And the lady has great legs. AB-F

CHRISTOPHER CROSS
Christopher Cross *(Warner Bros.)*
Texas M.O.R. rocker who topped the charts with his debut single 'Ride Like The Wind'. Nothing else on the album matches it. DN

THE CROOKS
Just Released *(Blueprint)*
Jam clones in the world-weary third (or is it fourth or fifth) instalment of the mod revival. Boringly predictable. AB-F

RODNEY CROWELL
But What Will the Neighbors Think *(Warner Bros.)*
Rodney Crowell is an original songwriter and a fine singer. In my neck of the woods, his excellent first album, 'Ain't Living Long Like This', got categorized as California New Country and placed in the country bins. People have been dipping into it and pulling out plums to cover since it was released. Crowell's new record, 'But What Will the Neighbors Think' is a step farther out. It's hard to call it country. Its muscial referents stretch too wide – to blues, to rock 'n' roll and to rock. Around here, the song 'Here Come the Eighties' has gotten rock station airplay and Crowell's new album is turning up in rock music bins. That's not inappropriate – the rock music audience may take to Crowell. But I hear the record not as rock, but as totally radical country music, an attempt to dramatically widen musical parameters. This is New Country carried to a new degree. I think Crowell will be listened to and followed – he's about to graduate from "influence" to "motive force". You're sure to be hearing Crowell's music in the future. Why piss around? Go straight to the real thing now. AP

JIMMY CROWLEY & STOKERS LODGE
Camp House Ballads *(Mulligan)*
In The Boys of Fair Hill (1977) Jimmy Crowley introduced himself as an eccentric 20th-century reincarnation of the old street-singing balladmonger, hymning the pursuits and characters of his native Cork with a style and accent as solidly believable as a pint of porter. Camp House Ballads extends him farther and gives an equal part to the group Stokers Lodge, who are sensitive and innovative by turns, whether backing Crowley or playing instrumental medleys. Few singers can move as deftly as Crowley from lament to lovesong to lampoon. TR

PABLO CRUISE
Part Of The Game *(A&M)*
R&B tinged MOR rock hewing closely to the formula of their 1978 hit album 'Worlds Away'. DN

THE CRUSADERS
Rhapsody and Blues *(MCA)*
The last couple of Crusaders albums have, despite the general acclamation, for me been slow to grow to maturity. It wasn't just a case of go/no-go signals on the instant appeal graph, but more a feeling that the band's slowbone Southern rolling with all the tried-and-tested trappings, was now walking a thin line between hallmark and formula. Nothing seemed to recapture the full, basking sunshine of 'Free as the Wind.'

Same again here, if slightly less so. The options presented by the charting of 'Street Life' have (judiciously) been given a wide berth: the vocal cut this time is 'Soul Shadows', running as a tidy and undramatic arrangement on the selfsame changes. Bill Withers, surprisingly, is a dull and unwholesome frontman, and the whole thing's far too long. The title track is a rather bad marriage between tripping funk and synth and strings. Far better is the plainer background to 'Last Call' with the smoky, choky Wilton Felder gradually rounding up the dimensions in his long horn solo, and the calculating piano of Joe Sample spilling out of the framework of 'Sweet Gentle Love'.

'Rhapsody and Blues' is an entirely adequate album, but I still feel the Crusaders are beat after all that hullabaloo. LE

CULTURE
Baldhead Bridge *(Laser)*
Early recording sessions by the splendid reggae group responsible for Two Sevens Clash. Gospel overtones. MJ

CULTURE
International Herb *(Virgin)*
Quality reggae fom popular trio. AB-F

CHERIE AND MARIE CURRIE
Messin' With The Boys *(Capitol)*
Ex-Runaway jailbait queen Cherie Currie heads upmarket, aided by identical twin/co-lead singer Marie and Jai Winding's expensive and slick LA production which includes most of Toto. Top tracks are the single 'Since You've Been Gone', 'This Time' (by Billy Bizeau, who wrote the Runaways' 'Queens Of Noise'), and the Raspberries' 'Overnight Sensation (Hit Record)' which sounds as if some of the original backing tracks were recycled. DN

THE CURE
Boys Don't Cry *(PVC)*
US-only release of compilation Cure early tracks and singles. Sometimes Buzzcocks-like ('Jumping Someone Else's Train') these older songs are not yet characteristic of the eerily evocative sound of the Cure's 'Seventeen Seconds' period, but nevertheless remains striking forceful. 'Killing An Arab', perhaps the first rock song directly inspired by Albert Camus, is as sparse and chilling as ever, while 'Another Day' and

'Grinding Halt' are both an object lesson in the dynamics of sound and a bleak urban tale of woe. An indispensable album by a band who are going to be very big indeed. MJ

THE CURE
Seventeen Seconds *(Fiction)*
A slightly unfocused production is the only drawback to this, the Cure's second album and first with their present line-up. Intense and evocative music highlighting haunting, distant vocals. The Cure, like Joy Division, are adept at weaving aural mood tapestries and are now poised to cross the dividing line between cult status and large-scale success. Robert Smith's ever-jangling guitar and half-reticent vocals figure prominently but the Cure's greatest asset must surely be their long rambling instrumentals shaping up shifting walls of blurred, rainy-day landscapes well captured by the album's cover art. Charted in the UK, proving that there is till hope for some — sometimes. MJ

SONNY CURTIS
Sonny Curtis *(Elektra)*
Revamped versions of old chestnuts by Cricket vocalist. AB-F

HOLGER CZUKAY
Movies *(EMI)*
Fascinating musical collages by ex-Can musician. But there's nothing German about these songs, or it might be better to call them short films. Oriental dirges, musical cut-ups, cacophony rock, a whole spectrum of sound, always compulsive listening. There's even a long disco-like track! Goes to show that experimental music can also be fun. MJ

DALEK I
Compass *(Back Door)*
Wallpaper electronic muzak. Amateurish. AB-F

ROGER DALTREY
McVicar *(Polydor)*
Sorry outing by Who vocalist saddled with portentous Jeff Wayne production for McVicar film soundtrack. A dubious film anyway. AB-F

THE DAMNED
Machine Gun Etiquette *(Chiswick)*
Punk survivors, punk losers. AB-F

THE CHARLIE DANIELS BAND
Million Miles Reflections *(Epic)*
Volunteer Jam VI *(Epic)*
Full Moon *(Epic)*
The fickle finger of fate has decreed that Charlie Daniel's time has come. One hit 'The Devil Came from Georgia', is all it took after years of toil and unrewarding session work. The fact that the music he's playing now is the same as a decade ago makes little difference. Jolly good time fiddling in a country vein. 'Volunteer Jam VI' is a live momento of a summer picnic with Ted Nugent and Crystal Gayle amongst the guests on parade, and Daniels hosting the proceedings. MJ

PHIL DANIELS AND THE CROSS
Phil Daniels and the Cross *(RCA)*
Actor (Qudrophrenia, Breaking Glass) tries his hand at singing. Here today, gone tomorrow. AB-F

CHRIS DARROW
A Southern California Drive *(Wild Bunch)*
Tasty collection of songs by old-timer Darrow on new Italian label of all places. For all San Francisco sound freaks. MJ

PHILLIP D'ARROW
Sub Zero *(Polydor)*
Mr. "Burn The Disco Down" with an LP that doesn't generate much heat. DN

DARTS
Darts *(Polydor)*
British master doo-woppers compilation (of three first albums) for the US market. Fun if derivative. AB-F

DAVE DAVIES
AFL1-3603 *(RCA)*
Some good songs, more emotionally direct than brother Ray's, but dragged down by excessive overdubbing with Dave playing almost every instrument. DN

MILES DAVIS
Circle in the Round *(Columbia/CBS)*
Record company raid the vaults for worthy unreleased material as Davis is presently a stranger to the studios. Double album covering all his major periods and associations. Indispensible for the jazz fan; never uninteresting for the rock fan. MJ

ELTON DEAN QUINTET
Boundaries *(Japo)*
Four of the five musicians here will be familiar to fans of the now-suspended Ogun school as the limbs and backbone of a dozen outfits — Ark, Ninesense, EDQ etc. The fifth, bassist Marcio Mattos, is but a step away from the marginally more radical camps of London Musician's Collective and similar.

Deprived of the pictorial cultural crutches of so much American free jazz, British and European work such as this has to live even more by its wits. Pride has to be the bitter momentum of the two horns, Dean's saxello and alto with their swooping, glaring phrasing, and the slightly-hidden cavernous declamations of cornettist Marc Charig. Keith Tippett — a major British talent if there is one — provides new colouring with marimba on 'Out of Bounds' while profiting from the limitations in emphasis of that instrument. Mattos' contributions are solid and mobile as truck wheels, with lovely, sandy filmic bowed work on occasions like 'Fast News', and ironically it's the drumming of Louis Moholo, so bright and nervy in Ninesense, that's the awkward, fussy customer here. Despite this niggle, 'Boundaries' is a generally successful session, with a warmth and substantiality that too often, in the cause of either Art or Fight, seems to evade this mode of music. LE

DEEP PURPLE
Deepest Purple *(EMI)*
Repackaging. I wonder why? AB-F

DEF LEPPARD
On Through the Night *(Mercury/Vertigo)*
After the late 70s orgies of disco, punk, and "skinny tie" new wave, the first great trend of the early 1980's is the rebirth of heavy metal rock, thanks to hot young outfits like Van Halen and Def Leppard. A few pseudo-cosmic profundities intrude here and there but the DefLeps make all the right noises to go with them. DN

DESMOND DEKKER
Black and Dekker *(Stiff)*
Pleasant new offering by ska and bluebeat pioneer who serves up his old successes (and some new material) with star-studded backing. Cashing in on the 2-Tone phenomenon. Unconvincing really, but the man deserves a gentle break. MJ

JOHN DENVER & THE MUPPETS
A Christmas Together *(RCA)*
...And I thought Miss Piggy had better taste in men! Seriously, if you must buy Christmas records, stick with:
1) Huey 'Piano' Smith & The Clowns' 'Twas The Night Before Christmas' (ACE),
2) 'A Christmas Gift For You' (PHILLES — Phil Spector's masterwork),
3) 'Rhythm & Blues Christmas' (UNITED ARTISTS). All other Christmas records are guaranteed to bring on terminal diabetic attacks. DN

LIZZY MERCIER DESCLOUX
Press Color *(Ze)*
Erratic but compelling disco warblings with ze strong French accent. Worth a detour (as is anything on Ze these days). AB-F

DETROIT SPINNERS
Dancin' and Lovin' *(Atlantic)*
It almost feels like the Detroit Spinners monthly album...Smoothly fashioned disco by soul immigrants. AB-F

DETROIT SPINNERS
Love Tripping *(Atlantic)*
Produced by Michael Zager, includes the hit 'Working My Way Back To You'. Professional outing by veterans of the genre. AB-F

DEXYS MIDNIGHT RUNNERS

DEVO
Freedon of Choice *(Warners/Virgin)*
Akron's best third attempt at mass domination of the world's youth. A great improvement on their last assault, but still unconvincing in parts. Nevertheless still miles superior to a good 90% of today's releases. A manic metal beat introduced, I suspect, by Robert Margouleff, he of Tonto's old Head Band, upgrades the backdrop and allows the wild Akron boys to discourse zanily away. Great tunes you can even dance to, and surely you never expected that of Devo, did you? 'Girl for You' should have been a hit single but wasn't. Pity. AB-F

SHEILA B. DEVOTION
King of the World *(Carrere)*
Once upon a time, Sheila was a long-limbed pop songstress in France, a mindless exponent of yé-yé. Then, the kindly wizards of the Chic Organization came along (no doubt tempted by the treasures offered to them by the kindly sages of the record company) and provided her with hit and hit beyond the French-speaking desolation. Sheila never did understand the words she was singing, but that didn't matter, because the sound was just great. Ah, what money won't do! AB-F

DEXY's MIDNIGHT RUNNERS
Searching for the Young Soul Rebels *(Parlophone)*
Birmingham soul revivalists succeed in following derivative hit single 'Geno' with strong album with varied material, if somewhat confused lyrics. Kevin Rowlands has good, emotional voice and the brass section revamps Stax riffs with aplomb. Still a lack of unity, despite clean Pete Wingfield production. Early pretenders for the big time, Dexy's woolly-hatted bunch have put in a vigorous sprint round the first bend. MJ

NEIL DIAMOND
September Morn *(Columbia/CBS)*
Once upon a time Diamond was an ingenious rock/pop songwriter and interpreter of his own lyrics. But those were different times. Today he seems incapable of writing a coherent song – the best original on the album is his fifteen year old 'I'm A Believer' – and completely fails to get to grips with old foot stompers like 'Stagger Lee' and 'Dancing In The Street'. DN

THE DICKIES
Dawn of the Dickies *(A&M)*
Caricature rock in the eternal American mode. AB-F

BARBARA DICKSON
The Barbara Dickson Album *(Epic)*
Middle of the road warbler. AB-F

THE DIRT BAND
An American Dream *(UA)*
It's a long mean march down this here recording road. During the course of their prolific journeys, the Dirt Band have lost their Nitty Gritty and moved closer to bland laid-back Californian mellow AOR rock. Their brilliance still shines through but the results are dissapointing. AB-f

DIRTY LOOKS
Dirty Looks *(Epic/Stiff)*
Trio with teen rock ambitions. Strange signing to Stiff, but who knows? AB-F

DR BUZZARD'S ORIGINAL SAVANNAH BAND
James Monroe H.S. Presents Dr. Buzzards's Original Savannah Band Goes to Washington *(Elektra)*
Listen to while drinking a glass of bourbon. MJ

DR FEELGOOD
Let It Roll *(UA)*
The usual pub rhythm and blues. Nice, but didn't their last albums sound similar? Band in a rut. AB-F

DR STRUT
Struttin' *(Motown)*
Much of the fuss surrounding Dr Strut and their eponymous debut LP was down to their being Motown's first jazz signing (and white).

This one, the follow up, shows a commendable firming of intent. Broadly, they're in a straight raunchy-funk bag, no strings, no girlies, but probably a lotta liquor. It's a drift that can still be very closed and full ('Flip City') and drummer Claude Pepper commits the frequent sin of being too much rock-bound and hence *needing* the aid of a percussionist to keep up appearances.

However on its better side, Strut's music is loose and forceful. Saxophonist David Woodford appreciates decorations, but cheerfully shows his gunning, greasy side. Guitarist Tim Weston cuts up some strong solos including leading a heady, Allmans-type 'Acufunkture'. Production is always intent, sometimes imaginative, and the hunky, spacey 'Blue Lodge' carries some exquisite details of arrangements.

The dead wood presumably doesn't grow as fast as the live, and with suitable pruning, plus maybe more promotion of that country-energy side, Dr Strut should prescribe well for the eighties. LE

THE DOLL
Listen to the Silence *(Beggars Banquet)*
One (small) hit wonders in the Blondie mould. AB-F

DOLL BY DOLL
Gypsy Blood *(Automatic)*
Sober, ambitious wall of gloom and despair rock from haunting British group. AB-F

CHARLIE DORE
Where to Now *(Island)*
British country singer with strong cross-over potential. Lightweight but cleverly catchy (songs about deejays and radio have an easier access to the airwaves...). MJ

DUFFO
The Disappearing Boy *(PVK)*
Should have done a disappearing act instead of beng released. MJ

GEORGE DUKE
A Brazilian Love Affair *(Epic)*
Recorded in Brazil with respected Brazilian musicians this album, although pleasant, is slightly disappointing. Some fine individual performances but the whole adds up to smooth, but bland, MOR jazz/funk. VH

THE DUKES
The Dukes *(Warners)*
Run-of-the-mill rock from a band that never got beyond the starting block following Jimmy McCulloch's untimely death shortly before the album's release. AB-F

ROBBIE DUPREE
Robbie Dupree *(Elektra)*
Doobie Brothers clone music with extra magic hit ingredient. MJ

BOB DYLAN
Saved *(Columbia/CBS)*
One of the most joyless gospel albums ever. DN

THE EAGLES
The Long Run *(Asylum)*
Uneven, at times schizophrenic megabucks offering by the Eagles. Unfailingly cool and tasteful, but each individual track too often reflects the personality of its composer with Joe Walsh emerging with highest honours. What was once an 'Eagles' sound' is now oddly fragmented and the magic of yesterday's hits is no longer present in the mix. Other highpoint is a contribution by Bob Seger. However, as good music goes, it'll have to do

until the Eagles regain their sense of urgency and stop just coasting along. But, I doubt they will. Money speaks. AB-F

ECHO AND THE BUNNYMEN
Crocodiles *(Korova)*
Young British band with unusual Doors-like sound. First album is patchy but shows great promise. MJ

DAVE EDMUNDS & LOVE SCULPTURE
Singles A's and B's *(Harvest)*
Classic memories. AB-F

WALTER EGAN
The Last Stroll
(Columbia/CBS)
First-class California rock with a deceptively hard edge, despite Egan's archetypal laidback subject matter: love, girls, car rides, Tuesday Weld images, sun-drenched beaches and other 'Motel Broken Hearts'. Clean and crisp production by Earle Mankey. A protege of the Buckingham-Nicks Fleetwood Mac axis, Walter Egan, ever-youthful on the cover as a blond and younger Jack Nicholson, grin and all, dispenses with his well-known superstar friends' assistance this time around, but surpringly enrols ex-Man Welsh guitar wizard Deke Leonard, whose absence from the music scene over the past years had been mourned by many. 'Baby let's run away' full of quirky time signatures and the driving 'Waiting for the rain' are possibly the more outstanding tracks, but the overall standards are high. Consummate pop. MJ

FRANKIE ELDORADO
Frankie Eldorado *(Epic)*
Bubblegum in the 1980's! MJ

ELECTRIC LIGHT ORCHESTRA
Greatest Hits *(Jet)*
Combined with the earlier UA compilation 'Olè ELO' this is all the ELO you'll need until their next 'Greatest Hits' package comes along. DN

ELEVATORS
Front Line *(Arista)*
This year's clones in last year's Car clothes. DN

YVONNE ELLIMAN
Yvonne *(RSO)*
You can't get much more boring than this. DN

KEN ELLIOTT
Body Music *(RCA)*
Synthesised disco from Seventh Wave survivor. He should have drowned. AB-F

ELVIS, SCOTTY AND BILL
The First Year *(Virgin)*
Tracks from the vaults. Elvis Presley's early days in the business: five previously unreleased tracks padded out by contemporary interviews and miscellaneous bumph (and booklet). A must for fans and collectors of Presleyana. A bit of a dead loss for non-Presleyites, I fear. MJ

JOE ELY

JOE ELY
Live Shots *(MCA)*
A souvenir of a highly successful tour of Europe by modern American country singer this has only been released in England. The sound is not what it should be, but the songs are all future classics. AB-F

EMERSON LAKE & PALMER
In Concert *(Atlantic)*
The last desperate thrashings-out of a now-dead dinosaur. DN

ESSENTIAL LOGIC
Beat Rhythm News *(Rough Trade)*
Saxophone led band new wave avant-gardist in fine fettle. Grating but bouncy enough for a quick soft shoe shuffle. MJ

DAVID ESSEX
Hot Love *(Mercury)*
Hot? You must be joking. Tepid, at the most. AB-F

ETHEL THE FROG
Ethel the Frog *(EMI)*
Standard issue heavy metal but with a name like that, you can't help laughing, can you? AB-F

GIL EVANS
Little Wing *(Circle)*
Plainly a godfather of fusion ('Sketches of Spain'), Gil Evans' more rationed latterday activities have still found him signally on the frontiers. The pop option and electric instrumentation have been blended into more orthodox arrangement forms: thus, a new classic in Hendrix' 'Little Wing'.

Leaving aside any political stormclouds around this recording — live, but quite muggy in sound quality, incidentally, — herein is not Evans at his best. In arrangement, the tracks are low on colour and contrast, and the 9-strong band feel close to exhaustion. A particular casualty is Jackie McLean's 'Dr. Jackyll' with Gerry Niewood, Lew Soloff all busy going nowhere. Best by far is George Adams hammering and sickleing through 'The Meaning of the Blues' over chiming rustling brass scoring, almost a single instrument in itself. 'Litte Wing' simply, dynamically fails just to justify 26 minutes, with an irrelevant Ron Crowder drum solo.

But even given it wasn't all right on the night, this is a rare testimony to one of the frankly undersung forces of the era. LE

FCC (FUNKY COMMUNICATION COMMITTEE)
Baby I Want You *(Free Flight/RCA)*
Muscle Shoals assembly-line white boy funk, produced by Clayton Ivey and Terry Woodford, who have been responsible for such recent non-events as Hot and Roy Orbison's "comeback" effort 'Laminar Flow'. DN

FABULOUS POODLES
Think Pink *(Epic/Blueprint)*
Barking up the wrong tree. DN

THE FABULOUS THUNDERBYRDS
The Fabulous Thunderbyrds *(Takoma/Chrysalis)*
What's The Word *(Takoma/Chrysalis)*
Texas bar band hooked into international spotlight by a recording contract and the influential support of Rockpile. Distinctive, solid R&B played and sung with heart and authority. Leaders in their field. PF

FAIRPORT CONVENTION
Farewell Farewell *(Simons)*
An inauspicious final album from the first and very nearly the last folk-rock band of them all. Their contribution has been so mammoth over the years, this is a woefully inadaequate epitaph, though erraticism always was one of their characteristic traits. A live recording from their farewell tour seemingly catching all their worst moments — the titles include some of their most momentous works from 'Mr. Lacey' to 'Meet On The Ledge' to 'Walk Awhile' to 'Sir Patrick Spens' to 'John Lee'. If 'Meet On The Ledge' sounds wrong without Richard Thompson, then 'Matty Groves' is catastrophic without Sandy Denny. CI

MARIANNE FAITHFUL
Broken English *(Island)*
Femme fatale of rock's satanic heyday makes striking comeback. Her voice has gone down several octaves and bears the weight of the ages as she tackles a selection of fine contemporary material with style and venom. Enticing late-night listening; perversely sexy. MJ

THE FEELIES
Crazy Rhythm *(Stiff)*
More New Jersey scions (pace Springsteen!). Idiosyncratic. percussive new-wave rock with a maniac energy that belies the group's deceptive superwimp image. 'Moscow nights' might not have a particularly Russian melody line, but the tune keeps on lingering insistently as does 'Fa-Ce-La' and other jolly ditties. AB-F

SUZANNE FELLINI
Suzanne Fellini *(Casablanca)*
Late one night, switching back and forth across the radio dial looking for something that wasn't just the same old rock thing, I stumbled across Suzanne Fellini's first album and

stayed to listen. It was the right time and setting to hear this brash, tough, but also romantic album. What kind of stretch is it that can reach from the punkishness of "You die your hair blue and red...you're a bad influence" and "That one, look at that one, he's a double take" to the haunted yearning of 'The First Kiss' and 'Give Me the Light'? What I think is that Fellini and her gang of co-writers and collaborators are trying to get from a New Wave stance to a new rock'n'roll for the Eighties. There are occasional overtunes of Deborah Harry and Linda Ronstadt, but all-in-all Fellini is fresh and original. Since that first runthrough of the album, I haven't heard a note of it on the radio. No matter, I own the record now. And I can tell you that Fellini *is* something new and you *will* be hearing from her. AP

KAREL FIALKA
Still Life *(Blueprint)*
Synthesizer-rock but with a pleasant melodic and percussive feel as Fialka's medium-size hit 'The eyes have it' denotes in all its chirpy (quirky?) splendour. Unfortunately none of the other songs on the album are anywhere as good as it and quickly slide from one ear to another towards aural oblivion. Reasonably nice cover (if a trifle sexist). AB-F

FIDDLER'S DRAM
Fiddlers Dram *(Dingles)*
Novelty folk tunes, including the British surprise hit of the year 'Day Trip to Bangor'. MJ

FRINGERPRINTZ

FINGERPRINTZ
Distiguishing Marks *(Virgin)*
Utterly perfect pop, every track a gem. No pomp and circumstance and ambition here, just carefully crafted and tuned nuggets of danceable sound. Investigate for yourself. MJ

FIREFALL
Undertow *(Atlantic)*
More synthetic country-rock from this pathetic collection of Eagles clones. DN

FISCHER Z
Going Deaf For a Living *(UA)*
Good English, unpretentious rock. AB-F

MATTHEW FISHER
Matthew Fisher
(A&M/Vertigo)
Ex-Procul Harum organist established his characteristic sound of keyboard-based breathy pop with galloping string arrangements on his first and best solo LP 'Journey's End' way back in 1973. A couple of others have emerged since but like his latest effort they were little more than reruns. Obviously Fisher didn't learn much from producing Roderick Falconer's incredible "New Nation". DN

FLEETWOOD MAC
Tusk *(Warners)*
Forget the millions of dollars this double set has reputedly cost and just sit back and enjoy it. In fact, 'Tusk' is refreshingly adventurous coming from a band and a previous somewhat successful album that could well have justified a repeat offering of 'more of the same'. With Stevie Nicks in a subdued mood this time around, it's Lindsey Buckingham's guitar-playing and songwriting which now occupy the centre stage and easily steal the show (as usual Christine McVie's contributions are splendid but suffer from a lack of modesty). After the traumas of 'Rumours', there might well be less evident naked feelings in evidence, but this is mature music by master musicians and it would be foolish to overlook Fleetwood Mac's vital contribution to todays music scene because of the exaggerated importance of their commercial success. MJ

FLYING LIZARDS
The Flying Lizards *(Virgin)*
Many wondered whether the quirky electronic sounds of the Lizards could be spread over a whole album without becoming samey, but in fact

they managed the trick here with ease. The fidgety keyboard and percussion trademarks are widely present, but that devastatingly deadpan female lead voice is used both with economy and surprising variety. The strongest cuts are those which appeared as singles: their debut effort 'Summertime Blues', with cardboardbox drumming; the smash 'Money' in a considerably extended version; and 'TV' with its twinkling organ riff redolent of those one-time hits by Johnny And The Hurricanes. BL

FM
Surveillance *(Arista/Passport)*
An interesting technical exercise by this Canadian studio trio. Cameron Hawkins makes his synthesizer sound like a guitar — which is sort of like teaching a dog to walk on three legs. Their version of Yardbirds/Jeff Beck classic 'Shapes Of Things' must have Keith Relf rolling over in his grave. DN

DAN FOGELBERG
Phoenix *(Epic/Full Moon)*
L.A. folkie indulges in the usual navel-staring and belly-scratching but rocks enough to stay this side of respectable. Perfect US FM radio fodder right down to the obligatory anti-nuclear song. DN

ELLEN FOLEY
Night Out *(Cleveland International/Epic)*
Goggle-eyed Ellen Foley used to sing with Meatloaf on his mini-operas of teenage angst. Here, on her first album, she retains the wide-screen bravura orchestral sound (ably woven by Mick Ronson,

ELLEN FOLEY

whose guitar work is also sheer delight) and goes straight for the jugular. An unerring taste for the right material (Philip Ranbow, Jagger-Richards, Ronson, Hunter) and one of the most powerful voices in the business make this first album a small masterpiece and I stand in awe of such a small lady with big talent. Let's wish she doesn't stumble at the next hurdle. We need performers like Ellen Foley who refuse to accept that there are limits to taste and bragadoccio. AB-F

KIM FOWLEY
Snake Document Masquerade *(Island)*
Fowley sees himself as the missing link between Orson Welles and Chuck Berry. In fact, he's the Sgt. Bilko of rock'n'roll and he's found yet another label willing to take a chance on his idiosyncratic ejaculations. His considerable talents do not lie in his singing — but this was obviously designed for those people who get a perverse pleasure from listening to really unspeakable albums. PF

JOHN FOXX

THE FOOLS
Sold Out *(EMI)*
Accessible dance tunes by electric group. MJ

STEVE FORBERT
Jackrabbit Slim
(Nemperor/Epic)
Messy production and indifferent songs spoil the enjoyment of young Steve Forbert's second album, even though it provided him with a useful hit single with 'Romeo's Song'. Lacks the naivety and truth of his first outing. Will improve with time, will Forbert, I remain confident. AB-F

JOHN FOXX
Metamatic *(Metalbeat)*
Numan-like electronic panoramas by the man who gave Numan his original inspiration. Bleak, soul-less vistas often reminiscent of J.G. Ballard. Relentless monotony turned into a virtue. MJ

RODNEY FRANKLIN
You'll Never Know
(Columbia/CBS)
'The Groove', being one of *the* get-hit singles of 1980 was, unsurprisingly, the first that the average punter heard of Rodney Franklin. That's despite his several previous albums and worthy touring mileage under his belt; but again, that's jazzbiz.

'The Groove' is a neat enough little stepper, with a distinct sense — like so many of those 1950's instrumental one-offs — that something else might be happening soon. Indeed it is; the commercial devilishness of that track and to a lesser extent 'You'll Never Know' are matched fairly and squarely by the spaciousness and finesse of 'Felix Leo' and 'God Bless the Blues'. Franklin keeps his own playing rather under wraps here, but on the solo cut 'Journey' he roams the range of Tatum, Garner, Peterson and Phineas Newborn emerging well-read if not yet self-styled.

With aides like the purring bass clarinet of Ray Pizzi and the electric lightness of drummer Randy Merrit, Franklin's best arrangements are richly economical, filled with sweat-breaking shades and pauses. Definitely more here than meets the groove. LE

CHICO FREEMAN QUARTET
No Time Left *(Black Saint)*
Chico Freeman is clearly one of the strongest hands to emerge in this fresh wave of new music, and like many of his peers has already been extensively recorded (with 'Kings of Mali' a stepping stone). The quartet here, his favourite working outfit, was the one with which he successfully toured Europe in 1979.

It's well-measured, cool-talking but substantial session, with a relaxing sense of discipline and a marked emphasis on sound texture and modulation. In this respect, Freeman's certainly the mentor with his love of spiky, grassy patterns, the full, ballooning quality of his bottom tenor and clarinet range, and his extraordinary ability to twist and flex his sound quality as he holds his longer notes — a knack more unsually found on the synthesizer.

Powerful too is drummer Don Moye, crisp, agile, loquacious, qualities that light up the whole show. Bassist Rick Rozie too often trails in the wake of this, witness his enframed solo on the title track. Jay Hoggard on vibes halfways takes over the bass 'role' with nodding clusters of notes before spanning into sheets of glowing texture. A really satisfying album, very rootsy, very clear. LE

JANIE FRICKE
From the Heart
(Columbia/CBS)
Another twanging lady of country produced by the Billy Sherill assembly line. AB-F

ROBERT FRIPP
God Save the Queen/Under Heavy Manners *(Polydor/EG)*
Or, two records for the price of one. Side a features Frippertronics and side b catchy songs (with David Byrne collaborating). For all the clever talk by Fripp about his 'drive to 1981', this is just a badly-balanced album with little hints of his past genius and guitar wizardry. MJ

EDGAR FROESE
Stuntman *(Virgin)*
Surprisingly pleasant solo outing by Tangerine Dream frontman. So much more melodic than many of the latest band efforts, 'Stuntman' is a breath of fresh air without the usual portentiousness of German electronics sturm and drang. AB-F

JOHNNY G.
G-Beat *(Beggars Banquet)*
Blues with a difference from a most individual performer and artist. Exemplary production job by Ed Hollis who knows exactly when not to interfere. A record which improves with every listening. And there's not many of those around. MJ

BB GABOR
BB Gabor *(Blueprint)*
Like so many first albums by newcomers, this initial effort by Canadian guitarist BB Gabor starts off on a pleasant enough note but rather than get better, only fades away

as every passing tune blends into a forgetable wallpaper background and an hour or two after the initial listening you just don't remember any of the melodies. One strong novelty piece 'Moscow Drug Club' stands out but is quite unrepresentative of the album as a whole. The rest of the time BB Gabor is inoffensive, gently melodic but could also be a dozen other singers (who didn't make the grade). AB-F

PETER GABRIEL
Peter Gabriel (III)
(Mercury/Charisma)
Splendid third album from the unpredictable Gabriel. At times moving and compassionate ('Biko'), at times witty and cynical ('Games without Frontiers'), often biting and angry, Peter Gabriel weaves a magic touch around his diverse songs and subjects like a magician. Able production by Steve Lillywhite enhances the material without ever becoming too flashy. One of my albums of the year. AB-F

SERGE GAINSBOURG
Enregistrement Public au Theatre Le Palace *(Philips)*
Double live souvenir of the French tour which Gainsbourg made to follow-up his grand reggae platter 'Aux Armes Et Caetara' which featured his controversial reggae version of French national hymn 'La Marseillaise'. Using the 'creme de la creme' of Kingston musicians to back him (Sly Dunbar, Robbie Shakespeare, Mao Chung and others) Gainsbourg wins his bet by managing to gallicize reggae with his delightfully salty lyrics. Over two albums, the initial impact is slightly diluted but an interesting momento nevertheless. MJ

GANG OF FOUR
Entertainment *(Warners/EMI)*
British minimalist debut album in strong socio-political mood is a bit of an enigma. Supremely intelligent and provocative lyrics blend in with immaculately well-played music but somehow the end result doesn't bowl me over as if one or another dimension is missing. A difficult recording by a difficult band but worth spending more time on than the usual dance platter. AB-F

LEIF GARRETT
Same Goes For You *(Scotti Brothers)*
Dave Marsh once tried to give Shaun Cassidy some credibility (and ended up destroying his own) by calling weenybopper idol Leif "an odius Shaun Cassidy clone" in ROLLING STONE. Garrett must have taken it to heart and tried to toughen up his image with this album, although his version of "Kicks" will never replace Paul Revere & The Raiders. DN

GARRISON AND VAN DYKE
Garrison and Van Dyke
(ATCO)
Dutch mellow rock. MJ

DAVID GATES
Falling in Love Again
(Elektra)
Gates began his musical career as an Oklahoma rockabilly alongside Leon Russell in the late 50s, became a top LA session player and arranger in the 60s, and led Bread, the most successful soft-rock group of the early 70s, making a couple of earlier solo LP's after the groups demise in 1973. Needless to say, this album is well-played and arranged, and totally insipid. DN

LARRY GATLIN
Straight ahead
(Columbia/CBS)
Cowboy sings the blues (with strings). AB-F

J GEILS BAND
Love Stinks *(EMI/UA)*
The title track is the best thing this Boston band has ever released for AM radio consumption. But their first couple albums are still their best, more integrated work. Peter Wolf is still the fastest mouth in the West. The cover art is sensational. If it's true they've changed their name to Juke Joint Jimmy and his House Party Rockers, there may be hope yet for bluesy, urban rock and roll. MG

GENESIS
Duke *(Charisma)*
As an English gentleman of the old school, one's finer sentiments are naturally aroused by the sight of three chaps struggling on in doughty fashion against all the odds, refusing to give up despite the loss of two chums in fairly quick succession.

But really, sympathy and forbearance are severely tested by offerings as awesomely turgid and tedious as this.

The harsh truth is that Genesis lost their essential dramatic feel when Peter Gabriel bowed out. And as his influence has faded into the dim and distant past, so they have become

increasingly less dynamic in every sense.

The hit single, 'Turn It On Again', is moderately snappy, and certainly the other tunes composed by the group are much stronger than their individual efforts. Which isn't actually saying much, when those efforts are as flabby as Banks 'Heathaze'.

But the whole album, both musically and in the lyrically handling of its "concept" theme of bewildered loss and alienation, reeks of a paucity of inspiration and even sheer lethargy.

Yet the fact remains that Genesis continue to be one of the most popular bands in the universe. And the ghastly thought occurs that a few years from now there may be just one of them left, still making increasingly dull records, which *still* turn into various kinds of precious metal. The mind boggles and quakes. PK

GENTLE GIANT
Civilian *(Columbia/Chrysalis)*
A progressive band who give progressive music a tainted name. Not their first offence, either. MJ

LOWELL GEORGE
Thanks, I'll Eat It Here
(Warner Brothers)
Lowell's swan song was his best performance since the halcyon days of Little Feat's 'Sailin' Shoes' and 'Dixie Chicken'. What a way to go! DN

G-FORCE
G-Force *(Jet)*
First album from Gary Moore's new band. Rack fodder. AB-F

GIANTS
Giants *(MCA)*
Midgets. DN

ANDY GIBB
After Dark *(RSO)*
The littlest Gibb both in years and talent. Without his brothers, he's nothing. Pure pop for the pram and pushchair set. DN

GILLAN
Glory Road *(Virgin)*
Deep Purple vocalist of yesteryear re-emerges yet again with the mixture as before. Not as offensive as many heavy metal bands kicking their heels on the rock circuit these days, but still somewhat lacking in originality. Solid musicanship and production are sole redeeming features. MJ

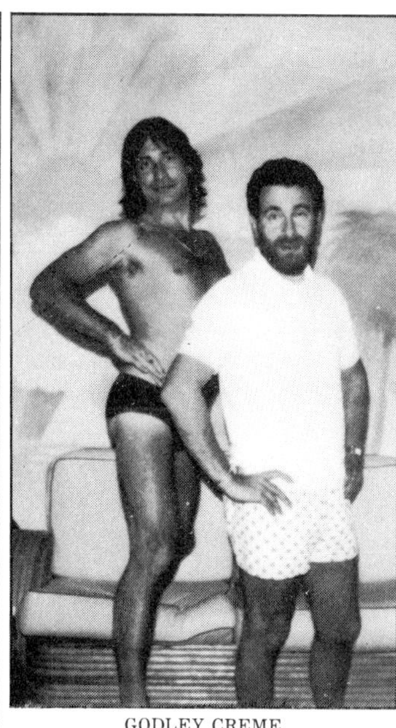

GODLEY CREME

MICKEY GILLEY
That's All That Matters To Me *(Epic)*
Country-rock pianist and singer who owns the 'Urban Cowboy' movie set "Gilley's" offers his usual sort of recent country-pop album, too heavy on the strings and ballads without Gilley's own piano work. Decidely less rocking than his cousin Jerry Lee Lewis' last few albums. DN

GORDON GILTRAP
Performance *(K-Tel)*
Guitar virtuoso serenades the middle-class audiences. MJ

GIRL
Sheer Greed *(Jet)*
Heavy metal division 2. class of 1980. Must try harder. MJ

GIRLSCHOOL
Demolition *(Bronze)*
Debut heavy metal album. Sounds much the same as usual. Difference this time around is that it's an all lady group. Well, why not? It's an equal opportunity world and if that's what they want to do for a living... AB-F

PHILIP GLASS
Dance no. 1 & 3 *(Tomato)*
Pure enchantment, even if this is no dance music in the rock tradition. AB-F

PATRICK GLEESON
Rainbow Delta *(Passport)*
Synthesizer doodles school of Tangerine Dream. Unfortunately Mr. Gleeson does not succeed in transcending boredom the way the German inventors of the genre sometimes do. Electronic muzak at its uninspiring best. MJ

GODLEY CREME
Freeze Frame *(Polydor)*
All the cleverness that has now deserted 10CC can be found with Godley and Creme now that they have disposed of their gargantuan 'Consequences' project and reverted to short, whitty vignettes of every day life. AB-F

RON GOEDERT
Breaking All the Rules
(Polydor)
Rule one: if you can't sing, don't record. MJ

ANDREW GOLD
Whirlwind *(Asylum)*
Linda Ronstadt ex-musical director's new solo outing where we witness our hero trying to metamorphose his previous incarnation as laid-back West Coast saccharin-voiced boring old fart into a harder rocking power pop modern-style persona. It doesn't work. Full stop. AB-F

RAY GOMEZ
Volume *(Columbia/CBS)*
Jazz fusion guitarist breaks away from group and goes solo with cohort of friends giving a helping hand: Narada Michael Walden, Randy Brecker and David Sancious. Guts and fire and a blistering over-the-top version of 'Summer in the City' make this a good album, so much more superior to the average funker rocking it away in search of a big bucks. AB-F

IAN GOMM
Gomm With The Wind
(Albion)
A reissue of Gomm's 'Summer Holiday' release of 1978, brought about by a combination of the Albion label's switch of distributors, and the US success of the single 'Hold On', which gets plenteous airplay and good reviews each time it's re-re-repromoted here, but has so far always failed to make the magical transition from dealers shelves to record decks which is what the game is really all about. The one-time Brinsley Schwartz vocalist, whose forte is satisfying pure pop rythms and melodies — with which the album is choc-a-bloc — really does need to score on that hit singles level before enough people who might be interested in his albums are likely to bother listening to them. BL

PHILIP GOODHAND-TAIT
Good Old Phil's *(Gundog)*
Pleasant rockaboogie by ex-Elton John soundalike. MJ

DEXTER GORDON
Great Encounters
(Columbia/CBS7
Contentiously, quite a few saxmen of Dexter Gordon's generation — Stanley Turrentine, Yusef Lateef — have chosen (or been chosen to) put in at least a token appearance on the electric/fusion arena. Others, too numerous to mention, have simply grown old in clubland. Dex however is an artist who's cut loose from both options. By dint of both his unmistakable style with its quite langorous, embracing quality and its wry, shuddering finials around the hard-bop imperatives, and his pure, six feet persona, he feels like both godfather and brother to half the disco generation.

This LP draws on several sessions with the tenorist and usual crew of George Cables, Rufus Reid and Eddie Gladden at the centre and healthy historicism as the main theme. Side One co-stars another hard bopper of recent renaissance, Johnny Griffen; their gunning out on the old Gene Ammons/Sonny Stitt battlefield 'Blues Up and Down' is kicks indeed. Side Two includes a couple of exchanges with the roots outrage of vocalist Eddie Jefferson, tragically killed shortly after: skidding and hustling through 'Paper Moon' like a dodgem driver with fellow guest Curtis Fuller and Woody Shaw looking on somewhat more soberly. For any newcomer to this neck of the woods, 'Encounters' makes a fine introduction. LE

ROBERT GORDON
Bad Boy *(RCA)*
Familiar rock unsophisticate doing what he does best: unsophisticated rock. AB-F

GRAHAM GOULDMAN
Animalympics *(Mercury)*
10 CC man goes solo soundtracking to the rescue of hopeless film and loses 90 % of his identity and talent: 1 CC? MJ

GRADUATE
Acting My Age *(Precision)*
First album by new band on new major sub-label. Indifferent power pop. AB-F

EDDIE GRANT
Love in Exile *(Ice)*
A touch of soul (with strings), a zest of cocktail lounge reggae and a pinch of Santana-like South American guitar solos and percussion do not a good record make. Full of good intentions, Eddie Grant seems to suffer from a belief in his own infallibility, but is unfortunately just one more small-league contender trying for the big stakes. MJ

THE GRATEFUL DEAD
Go To Heaven *(Arista)*
Despite death, drugs, debts and debilitation, the Grateful Dead have remained remarkably stable these past 15 years. Formerly psychedelic standard bearers, they are now an establishment band, playing mature, coffee table AOR. Strangely, this album found itself higher in the US charts than any of their heyday epics — which must say something about the current state of the American rock market. PF

PETER GREEN
Little Dreamer *(PVK)*
The second of Peter Green's comeback albums, and it doesn't possess the same curiosity value as its predecessor. A reasonable cover version of Albert King's 'Born Under A Bad Sign', plus a series of generally undistinguished originals, lyrics courtesy one of Pete's brothers, of which 'Walkin' The Road'(a turntable hit) is probably the best. The man's desire to emphasise his Jewish heritage does little to enhance his work, especially vocally, and perhaps a modicum of quality control in song selection might enhance future Green LPs, if, indeed, the comeback continues. JT

DAVE GREENSLADE
The Pentateuch *(EMI)*
Pomp-synthesizer rock at its most overblown and redundant. Combined with fantasy illustrated book by Patrick Woodroffe which suffers from same mistakes but is, at least, pleasant to look at. MJ

ROB GRILL
Uprooted *(Mercury)*
No wonder it took Fleetwood Mac so long to finish 'Tusk' — they spent so much time helping out various friends like Walter Egan, Turley Richards, and Rob Grill in the studio. Grill's 'Rock Sugar' features John McVie, Mick Fleetwood, and Lindsey Buckingham and was a deserved hit. But when his Mac buddies weren't around, Grill amused himself by trying, not too successfully, to sound like Bad Company. DN

GROWLING TIGER
Knockdown Calypsos
(Rounder)
This album features a semi-retired calypso singer recorded recently in New York with various expatriate Caribbean musicians. The calypso is of a kind that's hardly been heard since the Second War, and this is the hard stuff which would have surrounded Eric Gale, Billy Cobham and half of the unheralded musicians in New York in their youth. What calypso and its stepson salsa lack publically they make up in private.

Working within the formalised, minor-key structure of the music, Tiger is a hypnotic toaster/singer, his gentle tones sliding from ritualised chorus to bunchy, cutting declamation and back. Striking too are the soloists who cut loose on occasion from the ordained arrangements, notably the sharp, snakelike clarinet lines of Mauricio Smith and the throaty, driving violin of Chombo Silva — both overtly characteristic of the whole wave of that low-down, dirty music. Among other musicians, the name Candido will be well enough known for his work with Gillespie, Parker, Ellington, Mingus and Nina Simone.

In the neon lights of today, an album such as this could feel long-winded and parochial. But it definitely fills a gap however small in the jigsaw puzzle of jazz. LE

GRUPPO SPORTIVO
Mistakes *(Sire)*
Dutch jokesters set free amongst the icons. Mucho breakage. MJ

ADRIAN GURVITZ
Il Assasino *(Jet)*
Schizophrenic solo offering by ex-Gun man. Lacks any distinct personality and tries to cover too many musical genres. Brother Paul also helps out, keeping the mess in the family. AB-F

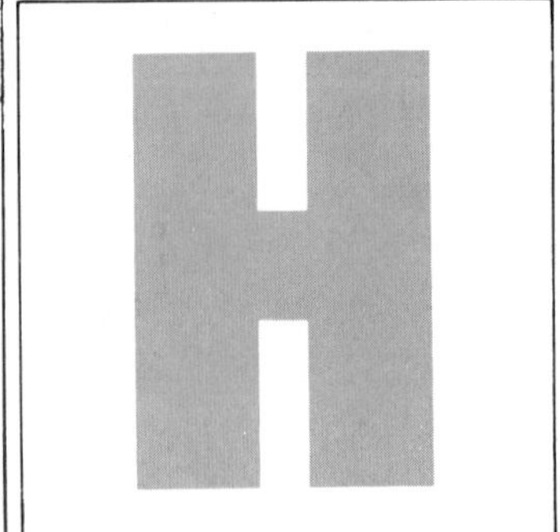

STEVE HACKETT
Defector *(Charisma)*
Genesis guitar deserter. Big in suburbia. AB-F

NINA HAGEN BAND
Unbehagen *(CBS)*
Initially a marketing man's dream (an East Berliner who was expelled to the West (!) due to her subversive activities, briefly the fiancee of Euro ex-junky superstar Herman Brood, friend of Ari of the Slits, trained in opera singing, patronised by John Peel), Nina Hagen to these ears at least, has one major disadvantage — listening to her records is about as pleasant as living in a septic tank. Her Germanic version of Lene Lovich (another celebrated friend)'s 'Lucky Number' (or 'Wir Leben Noch') is only listenable because the melody is faintly familiar, while "African Reggae" contains little Jamaican influence (or African, for that matter), but does include the full gamut of her gimmickry — yodelling, operatic screaming and lyrics in several languages. Which brings us to the only barrier being broken down here — the lyric sheet is auf Deutsch, en Francais and in English, and the most amusing thing about the package is reading the (not used) English words, and marvelling about such poetry as 'Hermann's balls turn blue/he says to himself:/shit, that's all I needed, ow-owww' (from 'Hermann Hiess Er') or the somewhat bestial sentiments expressed in 'Bow-Wow' — I'm your doggie/bite cha in the leg/and in the balls/bite like a bastard/chop chop/piss all over ya/shit on ya too/piss a load/wherever I can/crap in your bed/and lick you off". Nina seems to have a thing about balls, of which this is a load. JT

BILL HALEY AND THE COMETS
Everyone Can Rock & Roll
(Sonet)
The former rock'n'roll titan, now 55, gets it on with second string Muscle Shoals session men. The results are not exactly redolent of past glories. PF

NINA HAGEN

DARYL HALL
Secret Songs *(RCA)*
The famous tapes RCA wouldn't release. Hall (of & Oates) goes on the solo trip with Bob Fripp at the producing console. Pleasant, but certainly never worth all the fuss that was kicked about. Unlike Hall's usual fare of goods, but nevertheless melodic and reasonably commercial and two years too late. AB-F

DARYL HALL & JOHN OATES
X-Static *(RCA)*
Hall and Oates take few chances with their successful formula on 'X-Static'. Me, I'm waiting for the next Daryl Hall solo album. DN

DIRK HAMILTON
Thug of Love *(Elektra)*
Much underrated American singer with soft jazz and folk background tinged with soul influence, often reminiscent of Van Morrison (particularly so in 'I Will Acquiesce') steadily keeps on building an 'ouvre'. Unspectacular but always tasteful and consistent, Dirk Hamilton deserves more attention for his rambling tunes and carefully-crafted lyrics; variations on traditional love cum men-and-women themes granted, but original variations nevertheless. Garth Hudson of the much regretted Band puts in a guest appearance on accordion and synthesizer, while Don Evans takes the main credit for his fluid lead electric guitar. AB-F

PETER HAMMILL
PH 7 *(Polydor/Charisma)*
Black Box *(S-Type)*
Anguished primal scream rock from idiosyncratic loner. Since the break-up of Van der Graf Generators, Hammill keeps on charting a harrowing path through personal hell that verges on the embarrassing, but never fails to compel. MJ

BUTCH HANCOCK
The Winds Dominion *(Rainlight)*
Barren but forceful double album by little-known American singer in the tradition of Woody Guthrie and the early Dylan. A pure version of the American dream and country unsullied by time and fashion. MJ

HERBIE HANCOCK
Monster *(Columbia/CBS)*
More than once, Herbie Hancock has turned *JAZZ* into *CASH* (in not more than six moves). 'I Thought It Was You' was plain opportunism, but once its impact had ridden out in tandem with the Chick Corea accoustic bit, any customer who's not totally occupied with building fallout shelters in his backyard, surely, really hoped for something above 'Monster'. It's a bitterly accurate title for an album showing infantile regression to the artistic level of TV commercials with haggard old rhythms, minimal solos, low-level kicks etc. There's not even dancefloor compulsion to excuse it. The final tragedy is the opportunities that are missed, such as the attractive, Arabic piano phrase which is used as the cosmetic filler on 'Saturday Night' instead of the spiritual muscle.

Adding insult to injury are fairly shocking lyrics (mouthed by session singers rather than the Vocoder) whose facile tack borders variously on mysogeny or misery. "Went down to a disco/ couldn't believe my eyes/ the woman was so beuatiful/ but she was in disguise.." is hardly the worst. Commercial maybe, lazy for cert. I hope our hero is conserving his energy for a better cause. LE

STEVE HARLEY
The Candidate *(EMI)*
Archaic waxing from a man who saw it all slip through his fingers. PF

ROY HARPER
The Unknown Soldier *(Harvest)*
Another sensitive album by troubled troubadour Roy Harper. Pink Floyd staff and Kate Bush help out. Literate and worthy, but, as usual, likely to fall on deaf ears. Harper cultivates his idiosyncrasies and is probably quite happy to release the occasional album, in the knowledge he will never be a major name. An admirable man who deserves to be called an artist. AB-F

EMMYLOU HARRIS
Roses in the Snow *(Warners)*
Emmylou the beautiful moves one step nearer to bluegrass. A vast improvement on her Xmas mistake, but still nowhere near her earlier standards. Still, always pleasing and immaculately played. MJ

DAN HARTMAN
Relight my Fire *(Blue Sky)*
American middle of the road tasteful, forgettable, boring, unnecessary toons. AB-F

HATFIELD AND THE NORTH
Afters *(Virgin)*
A labour of love by Al Clark who put together this compilation of snippets, new and old tracks by idionsyncratic (and long since gone) Hatfield and the North. Strong on nostalgia but always pleasant if not earth shattering. Nice to see a compilation by a band who didn't make it (and in fact never had a chance — though they deserved it by sheer dint of integrity) and not the, usual, other way around. Historical artifact, but nowhere near as dusty as you might expect. AB-F

RONNIE HAWKINS
The Hawk *(United Artists)*
Canadas' only halfway decent fifties rocker swaggers but suffers in eighties studio perfection. Music for middle-aged habitues of sawdust bars or their fantasy counterparts. PF

HAWKWIND
Live '79 *(Bronze)*
Psychedelia rides again with a necessary injection of diluted (bastard?) heavy metal in this live offering from the Hawklords on yet another label. Legends never die.. MJ

JUSTIN HAYWARD
Night Flight *(Decca)*
Moody Blues goes all moody and gooey, ably assisted by arranger Jeff Wayne, well-known for his undelicate touch in many other areas. AB-F

THE HEADBOYS
The Headboys *(RSO)*
...on second thought, maybe you can be more boring than Yvonne Elliman. DN

HEART
Bebe Le Strange *(Epic/Portrait)*
This album, vaguely autobiographical, rocks harder than the rest of their catalog. Lead guitarist Roger Fisher is gone and although up to five guitars (through the magic of overdubbing) are used on some cuts, they never kick into overdrive. DN

JIMI HENDRIX
Nine To The Universe *(Polydor)*
The sound of the ground beneath the barrel being scraped. Hendrix was a guitarist in a million, there's no doubt about that, but tripe like this, directionless jamming which sounds as though all participants were bored/out of their heads, does little justice to his memory. Familiar Hendrix associates like Mitchell, Cox and Miles are present, plus a couple of others, the best known of which is Larry Young (an erstwhile Jack Bruce sideman). An idea of the standard of the material can be gleaned from titles like 'Jimi/Jimmy Jam' and 'Drone Blues' — memorable tunes are conspicuous by their absence. Alan Douglas, the man responsible for 'saving' a substantial number of unreleased Hendrix performances, takes the credit/blame for this travesty — the only blessing is that, according to the sleeve note, some of these jams were originally up to thirty minutes in length. Vinyl necrophilia lives! Can that be right? JT

HEROES
Border Raiders *(Polydor)*
Power pop clones. MJ

JOHN HIATT
Two-bit Monsters *(MCA)*
Costello-clone with guts and clean American style. AB-F

JIMMY HIBBERT
Heavy Duty *(Logo)*
Solo album from ex-Alberto Jimmy Hibbert doesn't quite shake off the comedy overtones of his earlier band. Tries hard, though. MJ

STEVE HILLAGE
Open *(Virgin)*
Last hippy in town tunes his wondrous guitar to the rhythm of disco one year too late and alienates ever-faithful audience. MJ

MARCIA HINES
Ooh Child *(Logo)*
I understand this songlady is big in Australia. Ah, colonials... AB-F

HUMAN LEAGUE

JAY HOGGARD
Days Like These *(Arista)*
As noted elsewhere, GRP is one of the sharpest developments in fusion music; there's string and sealing wax behind that gatefold packaging. That's leastways the case with Jay Hoggard a 24 year old New York freelancer who (despite having majored in ethno-musicology) spans the whole, strange, burnished, untraditioned world of vibraphone with telling ease on this, his debut headliner.

Currently, Hoggard's forte is plainly as a hard-cutting frontline man, witness his workout on Grusin's throwaway 'West End Dancer' with some of the chilly, swearing sadness of Gary Burton but an ambition and exhilaration of his own. Unlike Burton, Hoggard also comes up as no mean writer with half the album to his credit. Among these is 'Samba Pa Negre', a forgiveably showy hustler with cuica trappings (Nana Vasconcelos and a vaguely unsteady 'Kalima's Garden Song' doing time for the romantic side.

Hoggard's technique is indisputable; his poise as an ensemble player is still in the cask. But, given the context, Grusin and Rosen offer the vibes player all the support and all the space he needs, with commanding keyboard backup too. No more to say. LE

THE HOLLYWOOD BRATS
The Hollywood Brats *(Cherry Red)*
Recorded in 1973, this album shows no sign of age and should have been released long before (it was...in Norway!), Energetic new wave led by Andrew Matheson and Casiono Steel. A discovery. MJ

RUPERT HOLMES
Partners in Crime *(MCA)*
O.K. if you like to drink "Pina Colada", otherwise unlistenable. DN

CISSY HOUSTON
Step Aside for a Lady *(EMI)*
Soul and gospel lady goes disco. Unconvincing and a waste of talent. MJ

STEVE HOWE
The Steve Howe Album *(Atlantic)*
Outside the bombastic excesses of Yes, Steve Howe is a master guitarist and his album is surprisingly modest and enjoyable. The too-little-seen Claire Hamill provides some delightful vocals, while Howe's virtuosity on a selection of guitars never degenerates into gratuitousness. AB-F

HOWLIN' WOLF
Heart Like Railroad Steel *(Blues Ball)*
Can't Put Me Out *(Blues Ball)*
From Early 'Till Late *(Blue Night)*
A subterranean threesome of unissued and alternative takes spanning most of Wolf's recording career, but chiefly from the '50s. Unlike many LPs of this description, these are continously interesting, often exciting, and occasionally revelatory. The earliest sides, made before Wolf left the South, have the outstanding guitarist Willie Johnson, who puts adventure into the most ordinary of blues, and many of these rock like the devil. The more arranged Chicago sides, from the late '50s and '60s, often sacrificed the tearaway spirit of their predecessors for what can be taken as an exploration of sheer vocal sound, and are full of the moaning, growling and bellowing that have bewitched a generation of rock singers. Side 2 of 'Can't Put Me Down', in particular, rejoices in that combination of the light-footed and the elephantine that characterised both Wolf and his music. No lost masterpeices, but for discarded material an uncommonly high rating. TR

HUMAN LEAGUE
Travelogue *(Virgin)*
Seductive second album by synthesizer band with a strong touch of both humour and humanity. Evocative vistas and surprisingly varied moods and subjects make this one a definite winner, although my favourite track is the old 'Being Boiled' with its compulsive 'Listen to the Voice of Buddah' hook. Gives electronics a very good name, indeed. MJ

HUMBLE PIE
On to Victory *(Atlantic/Jet)*
Misfiring comeback for Stevie Marriot's old band (now, of course, minus Peter Frampton who no longer needs the money). A bad idea. AB-F

IAN HUNTER
Shades of Ian Hunter *(Columbia/CBS)*
Basically a double set of the best of Mott the Hoople and Hunter. Already part of the rock history and a more than worthwhile re-issue. MJ

IAN HUNTER
Welcome to the Club *(Chrysalis)*
Old trooper on the live circuit over three sides with one side of new studio material. Tonic. AB-F

ROBERT HUNTER
Jack of Roses *(Dark Star)*
Third album for little-known Grateful Dead lyricist. Lovely deep voice and powerful acoustic versions of Grateful Dead classics, including a complete 'Terrapin Station'. Not everyone will like this, but a good acoustic set is still beyond compare. Nice sleeve, in the usual Dead tradition. AB-F

MISSISSIPPI JOHN HURT
Monday Morning Blues *(Flyright)*
The delicate music of Mississippi John Hurt, which always sounds as if made for a few friends in a front parlour, utterly confounds conventional notions of the blues, and is all the more to be treasured. Much more than a bluesman, Hurt was a voice of the older generation that the blues inadvertently almost drowned out of hearing — the songsters of the Old South. The songs and tunes of this album, recorded for the Library of Congress in 1963, were done by Hurt on other occasions — there is nothing particularly distinctive about this collection as such. Nevertheless, it has the confiding charm of the man, and unlike most of the other records he made it is readily available. Above all it demonstrates his extraordinary ability to transform simple little songs into moments of poignant grace. TR

PHYLLIS HYMAN
You Know How to Love Me *(Arista)*
Multi-talented jazz soul songstress pens great effort. AB-F

INTERVIEW
Snakes and Lovers *(Virgin)*
Competent but anonymous. PF

IRONHORSE
Everything is Grey *(Scotti)*
Randy Bachman (of Bachman Turner Overdrive fame) repeats the old succesful formula. MJ

IRON MAIDEN
Iron Maiden *(EMI)*
Comic-strip heavy metal. Come back Led Zeppelin, all is forgiven! AB-F

JABULA
Jabula Happiness *(Jabula)*
Of the small knot of African musicians in the UK, Sebothane (Julian) Bahula and his friends in Jabula have one of the longest histories and certainly the strongest business heads. Ironically their real maturity has come in their two years based on the Continent.

As easily as American jazz could spill into the townships of Southern Africa, the resulting hybrid roots thereof are still very close to the surface with jagged or bobbing rhythms, a loquacious bass line (Mogotsi (Ernest) Mothle) and chanting, leaping melodies. The recruitment of Vicky Busiswe Mhlongo has given an indisputably African voice to the frontline — check her on 'Siakala'. But there's also been a very conscious effort to widen the net: if the funk of 'Thandi' is an ugly compromise, the trap drums of Graham Morgan on the heady, hunky 'Our Fathers' shows the bridge can be gapped. The shrill, chipping guitar playing of Madumetja (Lucky) Ranku is a superb straddle between rhythm and electrifying lead — 'Let Us Be Free' — while ripping reed playing from Ken Eley and Dudu Pukwana is liberation again.

Odd names pop up now and again: Letta Mbulu, Fela Kuti: and fade quietly or are brutally driven off. If the real Afro-jazz fusion will stand up...this could be it. LE

JOE JACKSON
I'm The Man *(A&M)*
A second LP from Jackson and his three cohorts which appears to show minimal progression on his breakthrough debut. Although a couple of minor hit 45s (It's Different For Girls' and the title track) are included, nothing here reaches the outstanding qualities of 'Is She Really Going Out With Him?', and the continuing absence of a lead instrument to effectively provide the necessary contrast to Joe's Costelloesque vocals remains irritating, except, apparently, to other reviewers. While it would be difficult to deny that JJ has at least one dynamite album in him, thus far he has failed to produce it, and probably his subsequent forays into white reggae suggest that he himself is searching for a different runway for his platinum ambitions. JT

MILLIE JACKSON
For Men Only *(Polydor)*
Rude lady of soul in typical brash outing. AB-F

MILLIE JACKSON
Live and Uncensored *(Polydor)*
Live at the Roxy raunchy funk compilation by the self-confessed dirty lady of soul. AB-F

RAY JACKSON
In the Night *(Mercury)*
Ex-Lindisfarne goes the solo route. Some live in hope. And cows will fly. AB-F

PAUL WELLER/THE JAM

JAM
Setting Sons *(Polydor)*
The Jam's fourth album, recorded after the Mod trend which they had helped create with their sharp sartorial visual style and their frequent echoes of the early Who, had burst wide open into a visible cultural trend which looked like replacing the punk lifestyle. And ironically, in this light, it contains the least overt references (in either musical style or song matter) to the Mod/Who theme of any of their releases to date. However, it is their most tightly-produced album yet, and their most lyrically conceptual, centering on an anti-military theme of protest. The single 'The Eaton Rifles' is the stand-out cut, but exemplifies the band's stacatto bursts of social conscience. BL

BOB JAMES & EARL KLUGH
One on One *(Columbia/CBS)*
In an arena dominated by Arp and Fender, presenting an all-acoustic artist isn't easy — though there's undoubtedly money in the after-hours bit.

In his own Tappan Zee shop, Bob James has curiously often failed to find the flair of CTI days: 'Lucky 7' was unplayably dire. And Klugh's Blue Note collections have generally succeeded, like certain brands of coffee granules, by virtue of being extra mild. It's some relief to find in this tie-in both parties benefitting from the experience.

For the first time, Klugh gains some sense of persona: his fawning fragility has mellowed and sharpened alike. Rubbing shoulders with Gary King on the puckered 'Love Lips' he's able to marshall this own rhythm and counter-waves. James makes no attempt at upstaging (once he was a wide boy who played for ESP...) but it is the notable commanding force on the bittersweet Winding River. To catch the pair swapping eights here is as gratifying as hearing it rest so securely in the hands of Ron Carter. Sweetenings are devastatingly discreet, strings often replaced by flutes. The main regret is that it all didn't happen sooner. LE

FREDDIE JAMES
Get Up and Boogie *(Warner)*
When I was a little bitty boy, my mother warned me to beware of any album bearing the word 'boogie'...particulary when it's the work of a 14-year old. MJ

RICK JAMES
Fire it Up *(Motown)*
So called punk funk? MJ

TOMMY JAMES
Three Times In Love *(Millennium/RCA)*
It's hard to believe that Tommy James (nee Tommy Jackson) started his musical career almost twenty years ago and is only 32 now. Unfortunately the punk-bubblegum sound of such early hits as 'Hanky Panky' and 'Mony Mony' and the pop-progressive style of Crystal Blue Persuasion' and 'Crimson and Clover' have been replaced by mid-tempo ballads given a slick, bland production on this "comeback" effort. But James' instinct for a hit sound is still working; 'You Got Me' and the title cut both made the US top 20. DN

KEITH JARRETT
Nude Ants *(EMI)*
However you rate him artistically, it's undeniable that Keith Jarrett has been one of the huge, calling voices of the seventies — and that's with a musical bent that runs right against the grain of most 'popular' jazz artists.

Jarrett has always honoured freedom: the right to choose. (In this case it runs from warm, wayward bop on the title track, the rough blues/rock hangover on 'innocence' to limpid Debussy/Bill Evans impressionism with 'Sunshine Song', all vaguely Arabic and saffron-stained). But he's also been an intensely disciplined performer, working either solo or with a small, snug unit of proven calibre — here, the European brotherhood of Jan Garbarek, Palle Denielson and the vivid Jon Christensen.

Being taken from a Village Vanguard gig may explain why 'Nude Ants' is a more robust and public show than their previous encounters such as 'My Song'. The four players are knitted together crucially — a real quartet — yet can alter course with the grace of birds in flight. 'Processional' is a fiercely descriptive piece with tight, bitter, sighing piano over a swelling cortege rhythm; 'Chant of the Soil' all green harmonies over a pulsy heavy, half-samba rhythm. No energy crisis here. LE

JEFFERSON STARSHIP
Freedom At Point Zero *(Grunt)*
With personality kids Martin Balin and Grace Slick having bailed out, the Starship is flying pretty much on automatic pilot. DN

THE JAGS
Evening Standards *(Island)*
An Elvis Costello xerox band who have the ability to make headway if they can develop a style of their own quickly enough. PF

JUDAS PRIEST

JAPAN
Quiet Life *(Ariola)*
A touch of the Roxy Music's, a zest of heavy metal, a pinch of fashion and chic images, stir thoroughly and you're suddenly big in Japan. MJ

GARLAND JEFFREYS
American Boy and Girl *(A&M)*
Evangelical effort by uneven singer who has always promised much but never quite managed to deliver the goods. The mixture as before. Frustrating. MJ

JETHRO TULL
Stormwatch *(Chrysalis)*
And they plod on and on. MJ

JOAN JETT
Joan Jett *(Ariola)*
Runaways solo girl on macho trip. Flaccid. MJ

JO JO ZEP AND THE FALCONS
Takin' the Wraps Off *(Rockburgh)*
Sweaty bar-room stomping music on this double album by one of the more interesting Australian bands. AB-F

JO JO ZEP AND THE FALCONS
Screaming Targets *(Columbia/WEA)*
Australian rockers work the midnight shift to bring out yet another album this year. Pete Solley produces their version of the Melbourne wall of sound. Spectacular. AB-F

BILLY JOEL
Glass Houses *(CBS)*
Fresh-faced pop with a touch of class in the lyric and a boot in the belly, though Joel's beginning to sound a bit contrived. A couple of maudling ballads don't help, and the rockers somehow don't sound as if he quite means it. Sounds like he's being dictated to by AOR success rather than the other way about, though the wry Randy Newmanesque 'It's All Rock 'n Roll To Me' compensates for much. CI

DAVID JOHANSEN
In Style *(Blue Sky)*
Grandiose and mannered outing by ex-Doll and darling of the New York set. Once you get used to the Springsteen-opera windscreen pathos, it becomes surprisingly good (see Editors' Hobbyhorses section). MJ

ELTON JOHN
Lady Samantha *(DJM)*
Old (some moderately rare) tracks by Reg Dwight now packaged for the budget market. Melodies still hold up well but the cover is the pits. AB-F

ELTON JOHN
21 at 33 *(MCA/Rocket)*
Elton in a better format than his last, slightly dismal efforts. Bernie Taupin returns part-time on lyrics while Tom Robinson and Judie Tzuke are also called on as reinforcements. Strong songs tastefully done and produced. Careful mixture of mournful ballads and third gear rockers. No innovation or great risks taken; all in all a very professional job. MJ

ELTON JOHN
Victim of Love *(MCA/Rocket)*
Elton's 20th album. A disco disaster better worth forgetting about, and fast. MJ

JOHNNY AND THE JAILBIRDS
Out on Bail *(Charly)*
Johnny and the Jailbirds is a new British group that plays Eddie Cochran-style urban rockabilly. Rockabilly is the source for the three-piece drums, and clean spare hot electric lead guitar — and for the general style. Much of the original-era material covered is rockabilly — like a version of Elvis' Sun session number, 'Just Because', that follows the original but swings just a little bit more. But the Jailbirds add backup harmonies to Johnny Red's lead vocals that extend the groups's range as far afield as 'Zoom Zoom' by the Collegians. The six covers are not at all obvious and are well done, but I'm most impressed by the eight original songs. For once — with the exception of the first song, 'Oklahoma Baby', sung as though they weren't quite sure what or where Oklahoma is — a British revival band offers new material that can stand up in feel, in bite, and in power to the songs they resurrect from the Fifties. I believed the toughness of 'Rockin' Boy Blue', and I loved the unexpected harmonies and the sharp timing of 'Hang On Baby'. If rockabilly rock 'n' roll can break out into the international big time, Johnny and the Jailbirds may just be the group to do it. AP

JIMMY JOHNSON BAND
Johnson's Whacks *(Delmark)*
A Chicago bluesman, but not quite in any of the standard moulds. Johnson is a flexible, penetrating singer and an elegant guitarist, but how he most distinguishes himself here is in his material — witty and interesting original blues compositions, with hardly a formula of language or scene-setting to be detected. The country number 'Drivin' Nails in My Coffin' fits into the programme successfully too. One of the least hackneyed records to come out of Chicago for ages. TR

LINTON KWESI JOHNSON
Bass Culture *(Island)*
Black London poet sets strongly political poems to music. The two never quite mix but the result is still impressive, even though the US listener might require sub-titles. AB-F

ROBERT JOHNSON
The Memphis Demos *(Ensign)*
Solid guitar-bashing blues-rock. If these are indeed demos, they are certainly well-produced but, on the other hand, there was really

little point in releasing them: surely Robert Johnson (despite his marginal Stones connection) has not yet attained bootleg-type cult status. Forgettable. AB-F

FRANCE JOLI
France Joli *(Ariola)*
Workmanlike Canadian disco attempt by pretty lady. AB-F

JOHN & VANGELIS
Short Stories *(Polydor)*
So this is what Jon Anderson ditched Yes to do? Amiable melodies with more than a sprinkling of sugar. Commercial. Not my cup of tea. MJ

GEORGE JONES
My Very Special Guests *(Polydor)*
Country singer ventures into the twentieth century. Meets country chums and the occasional modern songster like Elvis Costello. AB-F

GEORGE JONES AND JOHNNY PAYCHECK
Double Trouble *(Epic)*
George Jones keeps on mining duet possibilities, this time with so-called outlaw lungs Johnny Paycheck. Classic rock tunes well done but lacking any genuine excitement. AB-F

GRACE JONES
Warm Leatherette *(Island)*
Iconoclastic sophisticated lady of the cafe society set tortures well-known songs by the Pretenders ('Private Life'), Roxy Music('Love is the Drug') or Tom Petty ('Breakdown') and almost gets away with murder. It's chic to admire this demolition act, but it no more is art (or rock 'n' roll) than action painting is. Awfully pretentious. AB-F

NIC JONES
Penguin Eggs *(Topic)*
Jones in towering form, applying highly contemporary, rock-orientated rhythm and sense of phrasing to the barest of instrumentation. He's overly obsessed with songs about the sea (he says it's 'cos he used to be a lifeguard) but otherwise it works brilliantly and this is even better than the superb 'Noah's Ark Trap' album. Jones is now one of the few uncompromising folk acts who look capable of achieving cross-over success (whatever that means). CI

JOURNEY
Departure *(CBS)*
Highly professional pomp and circumstance rock designed to make lots and lots of money. Okay, so I'm jealous. MJ

JOY DIVISION
Closer *(Factory)*
Released in England a few weeks following the unfortunate suicide of lead singer Ian Curtis, 'Closer' is a perfect epitaph for a band that had the power to change the face of modern music. At times vindictive, at others dirge-like, the sound of Joy Division in this, their ultimate recording with the origianl line-up, is a perfect soundtrack for our trouble times. The rest is silence. AB-F

JUDAS PRIEST
British Steel *(Columbia/CBS)*
Undisputed kings of the British heavy metal scene with fifth CBS album. Powerful stuff this, but does anyone remember when the group were into a much different (and quieter) brand of inconsequential pop music? MJ

JUDAS PRIEST
Unleashed in the East *(Columbia/CBS)*
Another live Budokan set. This time around, it's the Britsh heavy leather rockers who make the obligatory pilgrimage to the shrine of the caught in concert recordings. MJ

THE JUKE JUMPERS WITH JIM COLGROVE
Border Radio *(Amazing)*
In these times of rising record prices and changing audiences, the door has become opened once again to independent record labels with special product to offer. Here is the first release on Amazing Records ("If it's a hit it's Amazing") out of Fort Worth, Texas. The Juke Jumpers are two electric guitarists who've been around, a sax player, and a young rhythm section, and they play late nite Texas roadhouse music. It's a mix of styles — "blues, jump, jazz, rockabilly, soul and good old rock 'n' roll". I found it in a rockabilly bin in New York City, maybe because it had no other obvious place to go. Four originals, eight covers. I especially liked 'I'm a Little Mixed Up', Robert Johnson's classic blues, 'Me and the Devil', and leader Jim Colegroves's 'The Jump' — but this is all good stuff. On T-Bone Walker's 'You Don't Love Me', guitarist Sumter Bruton says, "All right, reedman, play it like ya own it", and these boys do. This is state-of-the-art music you don't get to hear, except from over the border, wherever your border is. AP

JUNIOR WALKER
Backstreet Boogie *(Whitfield)*
Goodtime boogie disc. AB-F

KC & THE SUNSHINE BAND
Greatest Hits *(TK)*
The rise, decline, and fall of the avatars of the Miami disco sound. DN

BETSY KASKE
Last Night in Town *(Mountain Railroad)*
Gutsy-looking lady goes middle of the road. A touch of blues, a touch of soul, a touch of bland conformity. AB-F

KAYAK
Periscope Life *(Mercury)*
Can't even remember it now. Couldn't have been that good... AB-F

GRACE KENNEDY
Desire *(DJM)*
Left me cold. But the lady has her fans. AB-F

KENNY AND THE CASUALS
Garage Kings *(Mark)*
Good time by old-time survivors. MJ

KLARK KENT
Klark Kent *(Kryptone/A&M)*
Workmanlike toons and ditties by Policeman Stewart Copeland on a sabbatical. Self-indulgent and unmemorable. MJ

GREG KHIN BAND
Glass House Rock *(Beserkley)*
Kihn is improving as a songwriter all the time and the band rocks hard. This is just a bit too clean and healthy for me. DN

BEN E. KING
Music Trance *(Atlantic)*
Ben E. King, once of the legendary drifters, returns to the Atlantic family fold with versatile album which shows how well he understands all the strands of today's music fashions and uses them to his own advantage. Welcome back, Ben. AB-F

CAROLE KING
Pearls *(Capitol)*
The old lady is sure desperate for a comeback to the limelight of fame and platinum sales. These are all new recordings of the classic songs she wrote all those years ago (let's be kind and not count them) with Gerry Goffin. 'Goin Back', 'The Locomotion', 'One Fine Day' etc... The songs are still as good but the new production that surrounds them (and Carole King even dabbled here) does nothing for them and, in some embarrassing cases, in fact obliterates all the past glory. But maybe all you nostalgiacs out there might disagree. Worth a listen before you buy. AB-F

THE KINGBEES
The Kingbees *(RSO)*
The Kingbees are an example of the new developing rock 'n' roll as presently practiced on the west coast of the US. On the face of it, this group is an ungainly mix of elements. Their lineup is pure power-trio — guitar, bass and drums — and their sound owes something to heavy metal clang. Their presentation is New Wave — they've got short hair — and their music has a well-cultivated punk abrasiveness. But, along with the eight original numbers on this album, they cover two rockabilly songs from the Fifties, including a strong version of Buddy Holly's Nashville session number, 'Ting-a-Ling'. And just to prove they've got licks as well as pure power, they do convincing rock 'n' roll-jazz solos on 'Everybody's Gone'. And what binds all this variousness together is the central intent — to get back to rock 'n' roll again. They sing: "Lonely hearts love rock

'n' roll/Broken hearts love rock 'n' roll/Cheatin' hearts love rock 'n' roll/Sweethearts love rock 'n' roll". And: "I'll never leave this rock 'n' roll". Right on. AP

THE KINKS
Low Budget *(Arista)*
Remembering that for nearly ten years these men made music as uplifting, innovative and beautifully observed as anything else pop history can offer, this is a desperately sad record.

Few vestiges of that past remain. 'Low Budget' is a ragbag of crude, often depressing sentiments, executed with all the exquisite finesse of hippos rutting. It's ham-fisted baseball stadium rock, sometimes downright plagiaristic ('Catch Me Now I'm Falling' pinches the 'Honky Tonk Women' riff quite shamelessly) and consistently joyless.

Only '(I Wish I Could Fly Like) Superman' shows any trace of the delicate self-mocking wit which Davies pulls off like nobody else. As for the other songs, titles like 'Pressure ' and 'Misery' pretty well sum up their drift, and their insights into life 1980 style are not worth the vinyl they're immortalised on.

Rudely displanted from his natural environment, left to stand hopelessly out of context, a hollow mockery of his former glory, of further interest only to Americans too ignorant to know better, Ray Davies is the London Bridge of rock. For 'Low Budget', please read 'Cheap and Nasty'. PK

THE KINKS
One For The Road *(Arista)*
Double live recording of assorted gigs by the Kinks in America and ....Switzerland. All the good old songs we've heard time and time again in anthologies, compilations and live platters already. Nice but not really necessary. AB-F

FERN KINNEY
Groove Me *(WEA)*
One hit groove popster spreads thin talent even thinner. AB-F

KISS
Unmasked *(Mercury)*
Derivative but well done rock by slick purveyors of chic trash. MJ

KLAATU
Endangered Species *(Capitol)*
Hold the front page! Beatle-clones seen approaching. MJ

EARL KLUGH
Dream Come True *(UA)*
Funk jazz for the initiate who has all the main competitors and wishes to investigate the second division and also-rans. MJ

THE KNACK
...But The Little Girls Understand *(Capitol)*
If you liked the first Knack album (and millions did) you'll like this one 'cause it sounds just like it. If you didn't, this won't change your opinion. DN

GLADYS KNIGHT AND THE PIPS
About Love *(Columbia/CBS)*
Their first album in over a year. The fans will like it and you can move your backside to the beat, but the magic isn't there any longer, is it?. AB-F

KORGIS
Dumb Waiters *(Rialto)*
Indifferent album to follow-up a few minor hit singles. Disposable power pop. Lovely cover, though. AB-F

DANNY KORTCHMAR
Innuendo *(Asylum)*
LA's top studio guitarist, master of that laid-back cocaine beat, takes his place in the punk-pop parade with every hair carefully out of place. Jody Reynold's death-rock ballad 'Endless Sleep' is his idea of roots-rock. DN

LEO KOTTKE
Live in Europe *(Chrysalis)*
Amiable if a trifle bland momento of the American acoustic guitarist on stage. It sounds much the same as in the studio, anyway, apart from the scattered applause. MJ

SONJA KRISTINA
Sonja Kristina *(Chopper)*
Solo outing by lady from Curved Air who returns to the scene after long absence. Produced by Nigel Gray of Police fame but the material is not really up to standard. AB-F

KRIS KRISTOFFERSON
Shake Hands with the Devil *(Monument)*
A minor return to form by Kris after a score of dullish albums, this is still nowhere near the magnetic qualities of his first two or three albums. But at least we can see he's still got it in him. Kristofferson imitating Kristofferson is still superior to anyone else doing it. AB-F

KROKUS
Metal Rendez-Vous *(Ariola)*
Heavy metal invades Switzerland. And there I was thinking neutral countries were safe ... MJ

LEAH KUNKEL
I Run With Trouble *(Columbia)*
This California pop-folkie wouldn't recognize trouble if it bit her on the ass ... and on the New York City subway car shown on the cover she'd be taking her chances. DN

VALERIE LAGRANGE
Valerie Lagrange *(Virgin)*
Rock music always sounds wrong in French. Furthermore, when the lyrics are as clumsy as ex-starlet Lagrange's, the results are enough to make you blush. Good backing, solid voice with reggae influences, but oh the words... MJ

THE LAMBRETTAS
Beat Boys In The Jet Age *(Rocket)*
Mod Rock. In fact it's the sort of beat music you could tap your feet to and shake your extremities to quite some years ago. Pleasant but not really necessary, but then isn't that often the case for all of rock 'n' roll. AB-F

ROBIN LANE & THE CHARTBUSTERS
Robin Lane & The Chartbusters *(Warner Brothers)*
In which Californian folkie Robin Lane moves to Boston and discovers that you don't stand a chance if you don't play fast. With the aid of a couple of ex-Modern Lovers (Asa Brebner and Leroy Radcliffe on guitars and vocals) and a rough and ready rhythm section, she comes up with one great song ('When Things Go Wrong') and an album that's clean, snappy, and ultimately disposable. Buy the single instead. DN

RONNIE LANE
See Me *(Gem)*
Everybody worth talking to in the music business has a great deal of respect and affection for Ronnie Lane. This, his first album after four years hibernation, is a typically unassuming pastoral affair. PF

CLIVE LANGER & THE BOXES
Splash *(F-Beat)*
F-Beat's first dud. Langer might well have produced Madness and shown a magic touch, but this Deaf School alumni doesn't cut it on his own. His version of the Small Faces 'Half As Nice' is a walking disaster area. Try again, son. AB-F

LARAAJI
Day of Radiance — Ambient 3 *(EG)*
Hypnotic guitar improvisations produced and processed by the peripatetic Brian Eno. Clever, compelling effects; all part of the master plan, no doubt. MJ

NEIL LARSEN
High Gear *(Horizon)*
For me, Neil Larsen has been a happy example of an artist who's been able to stay in touch with convention, stay in touch with his convictions, stay plain, and stay alive. Curiously for a white boy from Florida, a largeish slice of his life went as house musician and writer for Philly International. His debut album 'Jungle Fever' — far more asphalt than Tarzan — was an assertively relevant yet individual project, and 'High Gear' unashamedly reiterates that formula.

Larsen's writing is terse yet rich, with incandescent melodies underpinned by the smiling sadness of his own keyboard line or the Allmanesque compulsion of Buzzy Feiten's guitar. It's deceptively schematized music: the lapping, snapping pulse that scored unexpectedly in some of the more searching discos also launches some of the most cunning solos of Michael Recker's studio career. Where there are sweetenings, they're very discreet, and Tommy LiPuma's production is a cheer. On acoustic piano or electric organ, Larsen is very much a band man: the relatively naked 'Rio Este' finds him lacking the clarity of the kelim weaving of 'Night Letter'. But once heard, ne'er forgetten — naked truth, that — and a big wish would be to hear him guesting on more sessions. LE

NICOLETTE LARSON
In The Nick Of Time
(Warners)
LA country/folkie and Neil Young associate Larson sounds rather lost among Ted Templeman's Sturm und Drang grandiose pop production, even double-tracked. DN

THE LAST
L.A. Explosion *(Bomp)*
Obscure to the point of darkness. AB-F

STACY LATTISAW
Let Me Be Your Angel
(Cotillion)
Almost sounds like the Jackson Five in their heyday, but the girl is white and well under the legal age. Mega huge hit single. Might well prove to be a flash in the pan or the biggest thing that has hit the charts and dance floor since Travolta began shaving. The future will tell. This is what is called hedging your bets... AB-F

LAURIE AND THE SIGHS
Laurie and the Sighs
(Atlantic)
It's hard to believe there are Pat Benatar clones already. DN.

SUSSMAN LAURENCE
Hail to the Modern Hero
(Bigger Than Life)
Eclectic pop rock by American group that tries to sound like an English group trying to sound like an American group, yes, you know the type. Minor fun. AB-F

RONNIE LAWS
Every Generation *(Blue Note)*
Ronnie Laws, kid brother to Hubert and Eloise, cut his LA teeth with such as EW&F (briefly), Hugh Masekela and Ujima. When he went solo, it was with the uneasy distinction of having in 'Pressure Sensitive' the biggest-selling debut album in the history of Blue Note. In many ways, he's never since rekindled the raw earnestness of tracks like 'Almost There': no more anthems here.

What does emerge in this, his first self-produced effort, is a more balanced set, crisper, high-stepping and more pictorial than its precedents. Laws' dry, tense reed-playing, not always the loveliest, gets stronger more resounding backdrops, like the moody 'Thoughts and Memories' and the slugalong cuica-backed 'As One'.

Something quite wierd in this mass-media age, too, is the sudden reminders of Ronnie's Texas roots. More than occasionally you catch a whiff of big, booming blues and distinctive sour changes, all homing in on 'Never Get Back to Houston'.

Laws is a likeable guy, but a lot is demanded of the listener to get anything much out. Whether he really has the persona to survive a change of idiom or fashion, remains to be seen. LE

LAZY RACER
Formula II *(A&M)*
Fleetwood Mac copycats. MJ

AMANDA LEAR
Diamonds for Breakfast
(Ariola)
Her second album held promises but Amanda Lear reverts here to mindless, gruff voiced glitter disco with a zest of intellectual (European?) pretentions. Painful. MJ

ALVIN LEE/TEN YEARS LATER
Ride On *(Polydor)*
I thought the punk detergent was supposed to have flushed this sort of shit out of the system. PF

JO LEMAIRE AND FLOUZE
Jo Lemaire and Flouze
(Rocket)
Blood and guts from Belgium. AB-F

GRAHAM LEWIS AND BRUCE GILBERT
Dome *(Rough Trade)*
Survivors from experimental band Wire go it alone. Dense, abstract electronic jungle music for late night brainstorming. MJ

HUEY LEWIS AND THE NEWS
Huey Lewis and the News
(Chrysalis)
Bad news. Faceless obscurities whose main claim to fame is to have assisted on tracks by Dave Edmunds and Elvis Costello, give San Francisco new wave a bad name. Indifferent tunes and lousy sleeve. Takes a whole two minutes to forget the complete album. AB-F

JERRY LEE LEWIS
When Two Worlds Collide
(Elektra)
Perennial rock and roller as fresh and profane as ever. Just a slight tilt towards country, but then he's done much worse in the past. Refreshingly unexperimental. AB-F

WEBSTER LEWIS
8 for the 80's *(Epic)*
Like Ran Blake and indeed many others, Webster Lewis' background is academia, third streaming and education; he's also a well-worked session player. '8 for the 80's' is as formula-bound as you'll probably care to meet in the decade, a real bit of wake of the flood, riding prettily in the grooves cut by others before.

Having said this, it's an album which in its handclaps and horn runs, its clarinets and whey-voiced session singers, has an intangibly awful panache at points. 'Give Me Some Emotion', also a single outtake, is pure EW&F clone with shunting vocal choruses and man-sized chops of brass. Signally more distinctive is 'The Love You Gave to Me', bubbling along on a little piano/brass knot, sliding into an appropriately urbane keyboard workout in the centre. 'Go For It' goes for the authentic horny riff bit, nice dry butt-waving bridge sections, and Herbie H. centre stage if you but knew it. 'Heavenly' which follows is one of those ubiquitous disasters, a ballad that can't ball, while Lewis' solo piano slot that winds up the show, 'Mild Wind' is a half-caste pop-boogie, more fun than profundity.

Fortunately, that's not the end of the 80's. LE

GORDON LIGHTFOOT
Dream Street Rose *(Warners)*
One no longer expects any surprises from a Gordon Lightfoot album. This one is par for the course, utterly pleasant and for the die-hard fans. MJ

LINDISFARNE
The News *(Mercury)*
Predictably jolly singalongs from the Tyneside quintet, immaculately played and about as relevant to rock music in 1980 as Mantovani (RIP). A must for the young executive with a music centre. JT

LION
Running All Night *(A&M)*
Hyperbole rock with few redeeming features. AB-F

LONNIE LISTON SMITH
Love is the Answer
(Columbia(CBS)
Mid-decade Lonnie Liston Smith (who's not, natch, confusable with TK organ grinder Lonnie Smith) seemed poised to be one of the new, real fusion powers. The shimmering, shivering Brazilian slant of 'Cosmic Echoes', the hallmark flute and voices, love and peace, didn't survive. Love was not entirely the answer and LLS slid back into disaffected orthodoxy.

As so often, the disco flip offered both instant fame and less tangible inputs. 'Answer' perhaps for the first time catches at an equilibrium in between. Presentation is warm and crystalline, with rich melodies leading into forgiveable vocal hooks. Title crack is a plainly seductive rolling, twitchy ballad built on well-aired Cosmic changes. The same theme translates into lazy, bassy pastels for the instrumental 'The Enchantress'; a gospel-strobe reworking of 'Give Peace a Chance' has a Doors-type organ hunting all the chances it can get. While the gravitational pull of the industry hypermarkets is all-apparent, the lilting, burnished Lonnie Liston Smith sound is reasserting itself, none the worse for the experience. LE

LONNIE LISTON SMITH
A Song for the Children *(Columbia/CBS)*
Jazz, cool funk keyboards. AB-F

LITTLE BO BITCH
Little Bo Bitch *(Cobra)*
Bargain bin fodder. AB-F

LITTLE FEAT
Down On The Farm *(Warner Brothers)*
The last, if not best Little Feat album. Even if Lowell George hadn't died, this was his last album with the band as he had quit to go solo. Recognition came too late to Litle Feat as one of the best bands of the 70's. DN

LITTLE RIVER BAND
Backstage Pass *(Capitol)*
You'll have as much fun backstage with this comfortably middle-aged Australian band as you will at a funeral. This album proves that they're just as boring live as they are in the studio. Perfect FM radio fodder. DN

LIVE WIRE
Pick it Up *(A&M)*
Pleasant power pop with a suspicious touch of the Dire Straits. MJ

LIVE WIRE
No Fright *(A&M)*
Amiable guitar-sounding British group's second album. Not much more to say. MJ

KERRY LIVGREN
Seeds of Change *(Kirshner)*
A chip off the old Kansas block. AB-F

IAN LLOYD
Goose Bumps *(Scotti)*
Ex-vocalist for Stories, Lloyd has lost none of the raspy characteristics in his unique voice but is still in dire need of better songs. Uneven but interesting album. MJ

RICHARD LLOYD
Alchemy *(Elektra)*
Initial solo by the lesser known of Television's two lead guitarists (Tom Verlaine, also in this year's solo stakes is the other, of course). There are still echoes of the earlier group and Lloyd fails to convince of his ability to survive outside the confines of a group, but when it's good (every guitar break-out) it really is quite stunning. Needs better material, but still a wonderful musician. AB-F

PROFESSOR LONGHAIR

LOCKSMITH
Unlock the Funk *(Arista)*
Jazz disco to dance the night away while the strobe lights flash on and off and on. AB-F

KENNY LOGGINS
Keep The Fire *(Columbia/CBS)*
On his own Kenny Loggins moves from the breezy pop of his Loggins & Messina days into the classy jazz/R&B turf inhabited by Steely Dan and the Doobie Brothers (whose lead singer Michael McDonald co-wrote and sang duet on this LP's big hit 'This Is It'). DN

THE LONELY BOYS
The Lonely Boys *(Harvest)*
See Little Bo Bitch (between the UK and USA, sleeves often change but seldom band's names. Apparently the UK name tag was, here, deemed unacceptable for chaste Yankee ears...). MJ

PROFESSOR LONGHAIR
Crawfish Fiesta *(Alligator/Sonet)*
Atlantic millionaire Jerry Wexler describes him as a "seminal force, the grand master", while Allen Toussaint calls him "the Bach of rock". A respectable finale for the New Orleans pioneer, who died a couple of months after these sessions. PF

JACQUES LOUSSIER
Pulsion *(Columbia/CBS)*
Having ditched his side-kick (some obscure German session kid by the name of Bach), Jacques Loussier now unveils his own compositions which veer towards rock and Keith Jarrett-land. Unconvincing. MJ

LENE LOVICH
Flex *(Stiff)*
The goddess of the glottal stop and mistress of monkey talk with another amusing collection. Check out her version of the Four Seasons' 'The Night'. DN

LIQUID GOLD
Liquid Gold *(Polo)*
Two hit singles and now the album. For the fans. AB-F

LYDIA LUNCH
Queen of Siam *(Ze)*
Surprisingly musical offering from ex-Teenage Jesus & the Jerks vocalist-of-sorts Lydia Lunch. Eclectic, from primal screech rock to jazz cocktail lounge mooching, 'Queen of Siam' never ceases to surprise, what with the shifting moods and giddy melodies and nightmares. Conquer your prejudices and investigate this one. It'll be around for a long time. AB-F

PHILIP LYNOTT
Solo in Soho *(Vertigo)*
Thin Lizzy mainman goes solo. However the end result sounds very like another, good quality, sensitive, schizophrenic Thin Lizzy album. Very romantic, my dears and Mark Knopfler of Dire Straits helps out. Some very strong songs and some more dubious, maudlin choices. But, overall, a good LP. MJ

LYNYRD SKYNYRD
Gold & Platinum *(MCA)*
Lynyrd Skynyrd had all the muscle often incorrectly attributed to other southern rock bands. Their plane crash flame-out sounded the end of the great era of southern rock. Though the Rossington-Collins band goes on, it is here that listeners can find a basic course in modern Confederate music. 'Free Bird', 'What's Your Name', 'Sweet Home Alabama', 'Give Me Back My Bullets' and three-and-a-half sides more of bourbon-soaked rock music better than almost anything made in Los Angeles in the last ten years. The only way to mourn the loss of Ronnie Van Zandt would be to play these two records all the way through at top volume while polishing off a bottle of your favourite spirit, then carousing through town singing these songs out of the window of a car with a broken radio. When you get out of jail you'll have a memory worth keeping. And who the fuck are the Rolling Stones anyway? MG

M
New York, Paris, London, Munich *(Sire/MCA)*
Robin Scott's M burst upon the scene with the infectiously catching 'Pop Musik' and this is the album follow-on. The heights of the single are never matched but the whole platter is an interesting attempt at promoting a specifically intelligent form of disco. Ambitious and maybe that little bit above the average dance music consumer's head (or feet). MJ

MX 80 SOUND
Out of the Tunnel *(Ralph)*
Raw, tense heavy metal punk in the American mode. Noteworthy. AB-F

CECIL McBEE
Alternate Spaces *(India Navigation)*
With his bop-pop schooling (Charles Lloyd, Alice Coltrane), bass player Cecil Mcbee is well placed for the softer, more consciously "produced" albums that have lately been emerging from India Navigation. 'Alternate Spaces' has its wayward moments — not least in the title track, all dispossessed military drums and burrowing melody lines. But generally it's a good indication of the growing sense of roundness and presentability within this phase of new music.

It's also a very good showcase for one man's compositions knitted to six men's musicianship. Setting vary widely, yet nothing's transparent or clichéd, witness the brooding, querulous quality inside the Latino 'Come Sunrise'. McBee is also a strongly coloured soloist with taut, twitchy, horn-like bowed playing a standout on 'Consequence'. Pianist Don Pullen's staunch impressionism is kept in harness, but his sloping percussive phrasing is frequently an essential anchorage to wandering toplines. Tenorist Chico Freeman, with the mellowness of an applestore, adds quintessential texture. If you rate this as a compromise, it's certainly invigorating. LE

PAUL McCARTNEY
McCartney 11
(Columbia/Parlophone)
Produced, engineered, composed and sung by young Paul, a solo effort worthy of respect. This youngster will go far, he has a knack for catchy melodies and a nice voice. Paul McCartney: a name to look out for. AB-F

ROGER McGUINN & CHRIS HILLMAN
City *(Capitol)*
It's fascinating to see how previous generations' heroes are settling into middle age in their various different ways. McGuinn and Hillman seem to have become a cabaret act for people who admired the Byrds through the last half of the sixties, when they were one of the most imaginative and innovative groups in America. This album is somewhat mediocre, but one can't dismiss their past magnificence, even as they slip towards the lounges of Las Vegas to become a living jukebox and fly forever as The Byrds. (Strangely, the Byrds' sound has come creeping back stronger than ever this year, with groups like Roxy Music, Wah Heat and Robin Lane and The Chartbusters nodding in their direction). PF

IAN MACLAGAN
Troublemaker *(Mercury)*
Gently forgettable ditties by ex-Faces man joined here by famous friends to no avail. MJ

MADNESS
One Step Beyond *(Stiff)*
It's always been a truism in the wunnerful world of pop that if you come up with a new dance or a new look, or preferably both simultaneously, then you've got it made.

So from the moment that Madness first graced Top of the Pops with those silly suits and pork pie hats, that nutter dancing as if lobotomised and wired direct into a rhythm box, and a back beat that drilled right through to your foot bones, it was obvious that they were going to be very big indeed.

Of course, the look, the sound, in fact the whole deal was pretty well lifted from various Caribbean gentlemen of the 60s (most now probably impoverished or incarcerated), and merely spiced up with a little East End humour and music hall style.

But then Madness wouldn't claim to be great innovators, or indeed trenchant social commentators. Good Time Music is the name of their fun and games.

Here, on the album of the show, you get all the hit singles and numerous other pieces of catchy nonsense (including the Madness treatment of 'Swan Lake' no less). Listened to cold it actually wears thin pretty rapidly, but for a jolly get-together with a few schoolmates, nothing could be nicer. Mad they may be... stupid they ain't. PK

MAGAZINE
The Correct Use of Soap
(Virgin)
Howard DeVoto and band's third album as they keep on deliberately fitting in nowhere and never quite making it. Honest new wave rock with a dearth of hit riffs, hooks or memorable loony tunes. 'Song From Under The Floorboards' should have been a hit and an unrecognizable Sly & The Family Stone cover wasn't and sticks out like a sore thumb. Intellectual pretences keep all the fun away. MJ

HOWARD DEVOTO/MAGAZINE

MAGNUM
Marauder *(Jet)*
A live momento of a band in the lighter category of heavy metal, tempered by the presence of flute and keyboards. Recorded at the Marquee and produced by ex-Ten Years After Leo Lyons. AB-F

MELISSA MANCHESTER
Melissa *(Arista)*
Lightweight pop singer/songwriter drowning in a sea of syrup. DN

NAN MANCINI & JDB
It's A Man's World *(Windsong)*
Formerly known as Johnny's Dance Band, this is yet another entry in the 1980 'power pop band fronted by tough chick' sweepstakes. Nan Mancini certainly looks tough enough to take on the whole JDB even if she doesn't sing so hot...what do you expect from a band on John Denver's record label? DN

CHUCK MANGIONE
Fun & Games *(A&M)*
Just before his final big breakout with 'Main Squeeze' and 'Feels So Good', Chuck Mangione's timetable was dominated by his TV credits, slots like 'CBS Skiing', 'ABC's Wild World of Sports' and the like. Maybe this explains how quite a bit of his music (including the opening track herein, commissioned by ABC for the 1980 Winter Olympics, 'Give It All You Got') shows dedicated mastery of the gentle art of foot-tapping while waiting for some other dude's big number to come up.

Such appraisal apart, in 'Fun & Games', Mangione has gotten to his smoothest, most settled location to date — no offence made and a welcome contrast to the brashness and oversell of 'Hollywood Bowl'. Even with added brass, 'Pina Colada' is a brisk, well-oiled turnaround on a Fania-type theme, with Grant Geissman's guitar snipping through like there was no tomorrow. The breezy ballad 'You're The Best There Is' and the smilingly eccentric title track are good genre pieces: hand-hot flugelhorn, nipping around the main theme, followed by a distinguished amount of solo space and a happy ensemble ending. For once, you can honestly applaud Mangione's fabulously wide following: a very superior wallpaper. LE

THE MANHATTAN TRANSFER
Extensions *(Atlantic)*
Man. Transfer shift uneasily from close harmonies in the retro. mood to a more jazzy

feel (even covering Weather Report Joe Zawinul material). Almost futuristic feel with synthesizers and a galaxy of top ranking session men helping out. A transitional, patchy album. Watch out for the next one. AB-F

BARRY MANILOW
One Voice *(Arista)*
Housewives fave Manilow croons as soullessly and successfully as ever. But think about this: Ian Hunter made more money from Manilow's cover of 'Ships', which came through as a huge hit single, than from his entire career with Mott The Hoople and as a solo artist. DN

MANU DIBANGO
Gone Clear *(Island)*
Although produced by ace reggae man Geoffrey Chung, this new album by Manu Dibango is nowhere near his now classic 'Soul Makossa'. A hotch-potch of influences and styles which seldom coalesce into a satisfactory whole. MJ

BENNY MARDONES
Never Run Never Hide
(Polydor)
Nifty pop. AB-F

STUART MARGOLIN
And The Angel Sings
(Warner)
This review is a public service. Stuart Margolin is an actor, a fuzz-faced Texan who plays a con-man named 'Angel' on James Garner's tv show, The Rockford Files, hence the album title. In short, a funny-cute second banana with secret musical ambitions and a minimal musical talent has been handed one of those now-and-then opportunities to put out a record album. It's just the sort of record you can confidently expect to turn up in the cut-out bins in a year or two. And it will be a damn shame. Stuart Margolin may have minimal talent, but he's got taste, timing, spirit and lots of love for what he's doing, and that makes this off-the-wall collection of the varieties of Texas music a special record. Margolin covers all the bases, from jazz-flavoured rock'n'roll through boogie and blues to country and swing, and eight of the twelve cuts are his own songs. He's got top musicians playing including Byron Berline, Sonny Terry, Jim Messina and Jim Horn. This record is highly unlikely to be the popular thing, but it's the real thing, strange be the ways of the Lord. AP

FRANK MARINO & MAHAGONY RUSH
What's Next *(Columbia/CBS)*
What's next from this Canadian power trio is probably more of the same Hendrix riffs the band has been rehashing for years. Meanwhile it's business as usual, with mangled versions of Doors' Roadhouse Blues and Bo Diddley's Mona along with 'original' material. DN

BOB MARLEY AND THE WAILERS
The Birth of a Legend *(CBS)*
Prehistoric tracks for reggae historians and rip-off prone tourists in rastaland. AB-F

BOB MARLEY AND THE WAILERS
Survival *(Island)*
Soul Revolution Part 11
(Maroon)
'Survival' in many ways welcomed Marley back to the reggae fold; the cover depicted his abiding obsessions: on the front, the various African flags, on the back, Haile Selassie perched behind a machine gun. If these emblems have outlived their usefulness, at least the music has its strengths, although the best tracks, 'Ambush' and 'One Drop', sounded better as Tuff Gong singles than submerged as album tracks. 'Soul Revolution' takes us back to 1969-71, when the Wailers were working with Lee Perry and producing what still stands as their best music. This is a slightly different version of the UK album 'African Herbsman' and has the original cover design, wittier and more to the point than its English counterpart. There is unity and imagination on 'Soul Revolution' which only occasionally shows on the later work — perhaps Marley would do better to make singles like 'Ambush' for a while, and forget trying to put together whole albums at a time. NK

BOB MARLEY AND THE WAILERS
Uprising *(Island)*
Reggae for those who say they don't like reggae. There's something about Marley's sound that makes him more appealing to simple-minded Europeans' ears than all his more didactic fellow Jamaican performers, although it must be said that his lyrics in no way sell-out from the usual themes of freedom from oppression, Ethiopia and other assorted rastafarian credos. Sometimes compared to a black Dylan, Marley is even, in French magazines, called a Black Jesus... Uprising is a treat for the ears, at times mellow and soothing, at others vindictive and full of contained rage. Probably his best album in a very long time. AB-F

MARTHA AND THE MUFFINS

MARTHA AND THE MUFFINS
Metro Music *(Dindisc)*
Perky art rock from new Canadian band who had to come all the way to England to make it. At times not dissimilar to the US B52's, the Muffins tread an uneasy path between pop and a mild form of would-be avant garde. The sound is reasonably novel, but too much of their material sounds alike. 'Echo Beach' was a hit single in England, but follow-up 'Saigon', musically meatier but less catchy, wasn't. MJ

MOON MARTIN
Escape from Domination
(Capitol)
Moon Martin, out of Oklahoma by way of LA, wears glasses and a British Invasion salad bowl haircut — as though strange thoughts of Buddy Holly and the Beatles were dancing in the back of his head. He might make it, too. He's got all the tools. On the strength

BOB MARLEY

MATCHBOX

of the music delivered in his first two albums — 'Shots From A Cold Nightmare' and 'Escape From Domination' - Moon Martin should already be the hottest thing in America. But there are impediments. One is those misleadingly paranoid album titles and covers. Another block is an almost brutal ambivalence about women. 'I think somebody should/Stick it to you good' is a too-typical lyric. If you can get past those barriers, Martin is a tremendous talent. He plays a tough, sweet, hot brand of rock'n'roll. He's got an original and identifiable sound. He writes one song after another destined to become a standard. 'Hot Nite in Dallas', 'Cadillac Walk' and 'Bad Case of Lovin' You' all came off his first album. There are at least as many hits waiting in the new record. And this time, at least, it's Martin's own version of 'Rolene' that has gotten airplay. But Moon Martin hasn't really yet been heard. Maybe the next album will do it. AP

CAROLYNE MAS
Carolyne Mas *(Mercury)*
Weak initial album by one of the strongly-fancied bunch of hot US ladies in the Springsteen street-wise mold. MJ

DAVE MASON
Old Crest on a New Wave *(Columbia/CBS)*
Bland pap. Why do musicians who have nothing left in them keep on churning the stuff out. Dave Mason was once in fact quite good, but that was so many unnecessary albums ago that few of us even remember the day. This is no better or worse than his last few forgettable offerings and features a feeble attempt at 'funkiness'. The (bad) cover comes in various colours with the US release; probably the only thing people might remember of this album in the not-so-distant future. MJ

MATCHBOX
Rockabilly Rebel/Matchbox *(Sire/Magnet)*
As Ricky Nelson was to original era rockabilly, so may Matchbox be to the rockabilly revival. This album has so far produced two hits in England, the original song 'Rockabilly Rebel', written by lead guitarist Steve Bloomfield, and the even stronger 'Buzz Buzz A Diddle It'. But how well you like this record depends on the attitude you take toward it. To a rockabilly purist, it isn't wild and raw and off the wall enough to be a realio-trulio rockabilly. But if you think of this album as rock'n'roll, covering a range from rockabilly to skiffle, this is a neat young group. Six originals, six covers — including a note-for-note copy of Buddy Holly's 'Tell Me How'. The cover material is stronger than the original stuff — but it's all good fun. This group is a comer. And come to think of it, Ricky Nelson did get it on once or twice. AP

JOHNNY MATHIS
All For You *(Columbia/CBS)*
An album of new songs by Johnny Mathis... AB-F

IAN MATTHEWS
Siamese Friends *(Rockburgh)*
Dullish outing by the usually more interesting Ian Matthews. Cover versions are superior to his own songs, this time around. MJ

IAN MATTHEWS
Discreet Repeat *(Rockburgh)*
Double album featuring a well-selected assortment of Ian Matthews' material spanning the last nine years. If you've missed some (or most) of this the first time around, don't let it happen again: Ian Matthews is a superlatively underrated singer and interpreter whose time may yet come, though I sometimes do have nagging doubts. AB-F

IAN MATTHEWS
Spot of Interference *(Rockburgh)*
Possibly spurred by his previously generally accepted soft (wimpish?) image, Ian Matthews rocks out with a semblance of style this time around and, by God and Chuck Berry, it doesn't suit him one bit. Good, melodic songs are mercifully bashed into the ground with a flurry of hi-hat drumming and Matthews' soft, evocative voice, always his best asset, is mercilessly drowned in the din. 'For The Lonely Hunter' typifies the disaster area, an already-recorded beautiful song now hammered in oblivion with little subtlety. File under 'grave mistakes' (see Dylan's 'Saved' for other similar lunacies). AB-F

MATUMBI
Point of View *(EMI)*
Run of the mill reggae. MJ

MAX DEMIAN
The Call of the Wild *(RCA)*
Plodding heavy metal. AB-F

THE MEKONS
The Quality of Mercy is not Strnen *(Virgin)*
Dole queue rock by self-confessed bad musicians. Intriguing first time around, but the novelty soon wears off. AB-F

THE MEMBERS
1980 — The Choice Is Yours *(Virgin)*
Well, 1980 wasn't their year: The Members were dropped by their record label soon after the release of this, their second album. As a band, they had been overtaken by the Two Tone ska phenomenon and their brand of white reggae dance tunes never quite caught on. A pity as there are interesting things on the album, including an almost Shadows-like instrumental 'The Ayatollah Harmony'. A strangely schizophrenic album. But always listenable. AB-F

MENTAL AS ANYTHING
Mental As Anything *(Virgin)*
Australian band with good songs, but also lacking that vital spark that might assist them into higher bound-for-glory gear. Literate songs and good melodies. At least, not a waste of precious vinyl. MJ

AL DI MEOLA
Splendido Hotel *(Columbia/CBS)*
Return to Forever jazz fusion virtuoso guitarist makes one or two compromises to necessary commercial requirements and comes up trumps. Delicate, danceable, good-humoured. Pity about the syndrums, though. Double platter with a few friends helping out, including Chick Corea, Jan Hammer, Steve Gadd and Mingo Lewis. MJ

MERTON PARKAS
Face In The Crowd *(Beggars Banquet)*
The twilight of mod. Label-mate Numan made it with synthorock; Merton Parkas faded into obscurity. One fad per year is enough. AB-F

JIMMY MESSINA
Oasis *(Columbia/CBS)*
Dull dull dull — and far overshadowed commercially and musically by his former partner Kenny Loggins' 'Keep The Fire'. DN

THE METEORS
Teenage Heart
(PVC/Passport)
Dutch punk survivors now insinuating their way into the field of mainstream rock. MJ

PAT METHENY GROUP
American Garage *(ECM)*
Pat Metheny is undoubtedly fuelled by not only his cutting, relentless playing but also his utterly dedicated and incandescent 'sound'. Behind this there is of course sound writing, profound showmanship, and a strong backup squad, notably in keyboard player Lyle Mays.

Bravely and fortunately, Metheny hasn't rested on his Rotosounds for 'American Garage'. Not much garage is evident, but there's a great deal of general mingling and deciphering leading to generally less extroverted results. The 13 minutes of 'The Epic' is a disappointment, with superficial brilliance over a flighty plot; 'The Heartland' explores shifts of colour to better purpose, with some gripping deep synth and piano fusions. If there's a winner, it's 'The Search', with the long piano prelude over tranquil/nervous rhythm providing a fine springboard for chiming guitar chops. One simply hopes that the fuel doesn't run dry for this garage. LE

BETTE MIDLER
Thighs and Whisper *(Atlantic)*
Second-rate album by first-rate live performer but perfunctory recording artist. AB-F

BETTE MIDLER
The Rose *(Atlantic)*
Soundtrack for the film. Bette Midler sings the blues (with thanks to Otis Redding and Janis Joplin). AB-F

FRANKIE MILLER
Easy Money *(Chrysalis)*
Boring good time music from another of that bunch of eternal losers with sterling hopes and professionalism but no real originality. AB-F

MINGUS DYNASTY
Chair In The Sky *(Elektra)*
As so often, there was that niggling feeling back in January '79 that the man was being more honoured in his death than his lifetime. In this case, it's needless to mutter about the spirit living on: of course it does. And Charles Mingus carried no passengers in his enterprises: certainly in later years almost all his musicians were mature, independent men of proven calibre. That in itself is reason enough for the loosely-built Mingus Dynasty collective which, under the direction of widow Susan Graham has been a huge box-office pull in the interim years.

Much of the material on this, their debut waxing, came from Mingus' collaboration with Joni Mitchell: the version here of 'Dry Cleaner From Des Moines', shouting bop pitched away by Jimmy Knepper's galloping trombone, is curiously not so far from her own extraordinary rendering. The title track rides on staunch, earthy lyricism underlined by Don Pullen's cut-loose tailpiece. 'My Jelly Roll Soul' is overtly 'in the tradition', wild scampering of the vaudeville era with a reformed Jimmy Owens turning out a Bubber Miley salute. Even that danger zone of 'Pork Pie Hat' has not time to drown in its own tears thanks to Joe Farrell's leaping-salmon opening and the watching fire of drummer Danny Richmond. LE

MINK DE VILLE
Le Chat Bleu *(Capitol)*
Long-delayed (and only released in America after Capitol had witnessed its European success) this third album by Willy and his shady doo-wop gang was recorded in Paris. The much vaunted string arrangements don't impress me one iota, but all the rest is fine: switch-blade rock mini-sagas and operatic emoting. Urban rock with Southern blood on the boil. Dandy ass-shaking tunes, from the pen of a master. MJ

SUGAR MINOTT
Black Roots *(Island)*
Whatever it takes to win the affection of the fickle youth market, Sugar certainly has it. Some of the necessary ingredients are easily identified: an apparently unending flow of new music, songs that divide themselves evenly between affection ('Two Time Loser') and oppression ('Hard Time Pressure'), unaffected vocal style, straightforward musical approach — the final ingredient is probably the inescapable feeling that Sugar is one of the youth himself, not at all set apart. This album is the best of his self-produced efforts, proving that he knows how to put together first-rate modern reggae without falling prey to too many passing trends — listen to the way the old-fashioned melodica combines with the modish drumming on 'Mankind'. There's a distinct feeling that Sugar's lyrics are a bit hack, but he's not alone there; in every other department he does the business, and does it well. NK

MI-SEX
Computer Games *(Epic/CBS)*
The title cut was a great single. The rest of the album sounds like this Australian outfit was eating integrated circuit silicon chips while they were playing. DN

MOEBIUS
Moebius *(Moonwind)*
Purposefully eclectic electronic cocktail from Germany. Strictly minor league stuff. AB-F

MOEBIUS & PLANK
Rastakraut Pasta *(Sky)*
Eminence grise producer Connie Plank makes his first vinyl appearance here with Moebius (ex-Cluster). Dense electronic wash with strong percussive backdrop (rasta-reggae inspired?). Repetitive. AB-F

PIERRE MOERLEN'S GONG
Live *(Arista)*
First there was banana and tea pot Daevid Allen, then mercurial mystic guitar wizard Steve Hillage. These days, Gong no longer resembles the group it once was, either in appearance or sound. This live souvenir of the latest incarnation of the band is really for fans or completists. MJ

EDDIE MONEY
Playing For Keeps *(Columbia)*
Tasteful, semi-heavy rock on this album by Bill Graham protégé Eddie Money. Great, slightly hoarse voice in the Bob Seger-Rod Stewart tradition. Duet with Valerie Carter on one track; lilting melodies and dancing music. Eddie Money might not be getting a lot of press these days, but he remains unerringly tasteful and likeable. His career could well parallel that of Bob Seger and see mega-fame coming his way in another five years. He can't remain a secret eternally. AB-F

THE MONKEES
Monkeemania *(Arista)*
It's all here in this double set: the glory and the naïveity, the fun and the waste. Come back, Monkees, all is forgiven. MJ

THE MONOCHROME SET

THE MONOCHROME SET
The Strange Boutique
(Dindisc)
Multicoloured début by British art rockers supreme. Surprisingly diverse sound with echoes of both The Doors and Spanish guitar extravaganzas. Delightful and witty guitar by Lester Square. Tomorrow's cabaret music? AB-F

A. MORE
Flying Doesn't Help *(Quango)*
A. More hides the shifting persona of ex-Slapp Happy Anthony Moore. This album is an authentically original piece of work, sometimes reminiscent of early Velvet Underground or the mercurial John Cale at his most idiosyncratic. However, there is much humour in evidence, even when More/Moore tackles more unusual themes like... necrophilia. A must for every record collection that extends beyond the limited realm of traditional rock and requires a taste for the bizarre. MJ

GIORGIO MORODER
E=MC2 *(Oasis)*
Interesting electronic doodles by the king of disco. AB-F

VAN MORRISON
Into The Music
(Warners/Mercury)
For anybody else, this would be a great album; coming from Van Morrison it feels unfinished and unsatisfying. The man has got us used to higher standards. Always mellow and pleasant, with a disturbing reliance on born-again religious lyrics. Oh, Dylan, is it contagious? AB-F

MOTELS
Motels *(Capitol)*
Highly original and distinctive first album by LA group with throaty vocalist Martha Davis. Quirky time signatures and memorable songs ('Celia', 'Rubber Bullets') make this an outstanding début despite a frightfully dubious cover. MJ

THE MOTELS
Careful *(Capitol)*
One of these days, and it won't be long, there'll be a steel cage death wrestling match in Madison Square Garden with all the 'tough chick' singers. The Motels' Martha Davis won't come out on top. DN

I don't agree. I like it. It might not be the future of rock'n'roll, but it'll do in the meantime. AB-F

THE MOTORS
Tenement Steps *(Virgin)*
Produced by Jimmy Iovine as if Phil Spector had never existed, this album gives a new meaning to the expression 'wall of sound'. Immaculately-crafted rock which inexplicably flopped in the market-place both in England and America. Ah, those punters have no taste. Seriously though, every track is strong and distinctive and the cover's good. It must be because Garvey and McMasters are rather ugly. Well, musicians can't all look like Leif Garrett or stay eternally young like McCartney (who's sold his soul to the devil of beat, as we all know). If it's already in the bargain racks, pick it up, you won't regret it. MJ

THE MOTORS

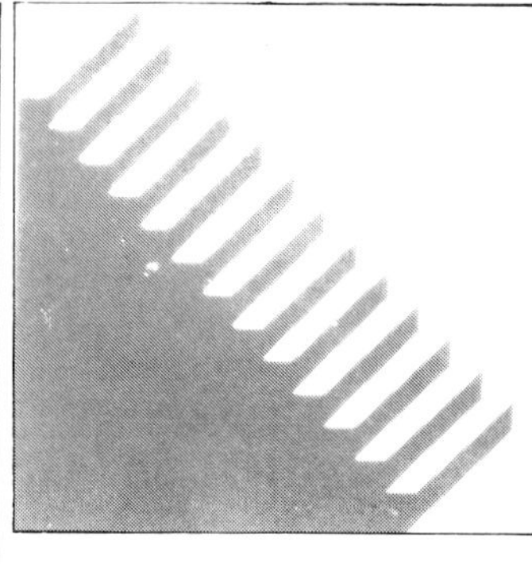

THE MOVIES
India *(Gem)*
Workmanlike, mild pop rock. AB-F

GEOFF MULDAUR
Blues Boy *(Flying Fish)*
Geoff 'Mole' Muldaur was born to be musically out of step. When he was five, his older brother would hit him up-side the head if he failed to identify Bix Beiderbecke solos. With training like that, it's not surprising that he grew up to have one of the great extended invisible recording careers. The Mole has made music with the Jim Kweskin Jug Band, with his (onetime) wife Maria, with Paul Butterfield's Better Days, and most recently as a solo artist doing strange, not-quite-satisfying versions of Thirties' and Forties' material. But somehow he's never been the stuff that major label record careers are made out of, and he never quite ever managed to live up to the promise of his first solo country blues album, 'Sleepy Man Blues', laid down way back in '63. Now, after taking time out to augment his natural funkiness with formal musical training, Muldaur is back with a record covering the spectrum of city blues on Chicago's small but righteous Flying Fish label – and it's his best record yet. The right music at last in the right place, seven covers and three originals. If you want to hear a Mole moan, this is it. AP

ANNE MURRAY
Somebody's Waiting *(Capitol)*
The usual bland MOR, including the obligatory lame Beatles' cover – in this case 'I'm Happy Just To Dance With You'. DN

DAVID MURRAY
Sweet Lovely *(Black Saint)*
The ultimate young lion of new music, David Murray has had as much flak as he had praise, and rumours abound of big-star behaviour, blowing advances and not showing for gigs. True, he's chronicled up to the hilt by the relevant media, and worryingly over-recorded by a hundred indie labels all hoping for a quick buck (reggae artist Barrington Levy is one parallel that comes to mind). Strange thing is, he's often at his clearest where least seen, either solo or in some big, crazy showband.

'Sweet Lovely' is a somewhat introspective album that speaks volumes for Murray's admiration for Albert Ayler. His more locquacious attacks show remarkable technique and similarly notable control: witness the squiggling, spinning passage with its unexpected blues cries in the centre of 'Hope/Scope', or the sense of measured ambition that runs through the floating opening to 'The Hill'. There's often however a curious sense of the tenor player being carried by his more experienced companions, Fred Hopkins (with some striking voice-like bowed bass work) and the genial, inexhaustible Steve McCall on drums. But once the rumpus has cooled off, David Murray should be a good name to watch again for the eighties. LE

999
The Biggest Prize in Sport
(Polydor)
After punk, rock purgatory? MJ

WAZMO NARIZ
Things Aren't Right *(Illegal)*
The Waz and his Wazband come off as a midwestern version of the Talking Heads on songs like the almost hit 'Checking Out The Checkout Girl' and 'The Mind Is Willing But The Flesh Is Weak'. Good in small doses but excessive listening may make you as much of a wimp as the Waz himself. DN

GRAHAM NASH
Earth and Sky *(Capitol)*
Graham Nash still lives in the 1960s and writes fey, pleasant songs with a dash of protest and environmentalism here and there. He's good at what he does and should be judged accordingly. MJ

NAZARETH
Malice in Wonderland
(A&M/Mountain)
The melodic side of heavy metal, but far from Nazareth's best. Somewhat shop-soiled even in the original shrinkwrap. AB-F

WILLIE NELSON
Willie Nelson sings Kristofferson *(Columbia/CBS)*
Willie Nelson destroys good songs by Kris Kristofferson. AB-F

MICHAEL NESMITH
Infinite Rider on the Big Dogma *(Pacific Arts)*
Year after year, Nesmith is carving himself a comfortable niche as one of the true originals of the rock scene. This new album is as quirkily enjoyable as usual and, as usual, didn't sell. Shame on you all. MJ

NEW MUZIK
From A to B *(GTO)*
Surprisingly catchy and varied set from synthesizer popsters. Class production by Tony Mansfield provides glossy attractive veneer. Hummable and hard to get out of your head once you've lived with the album for a few days. Overcome your prejudices and give it a listening. AB-F

RANDY NEWMAN
Born Again *(Warners)*
Accomplished short stories from Mr Newman. Maybe not as abrasive as in the past, but always worth consideration. The ultimate iconoclast in rock this time takes on Kiss, ELO, Wall Street and human nature. David against Goliath. A victory on points. MJ

WILLIE NILE
Willie Nile *(Arista)*
Diminutive singer-songwriter is new big white hope out of Greenwich Village. Unfortunately Steve Forbert got his songs onto vinyl first. And the similarities are evident. Though, I am told by a lady in the know that Forbert is the one who got the inspiration from Nile. Great talent in evidence nevertheless. Driving songs of love, New York and New Jersey and no, it ain't this year's Springsteen. Nile has a strong style and will go far. A man to watch. Strongly tipped. AB-F

NITTY GRITTY DIRT BAND
Gold From Dirt *(UA)*
Representative sampler of this underrated country band's past production. Should have appeal well outside the country market. MJ

IAN NORTH
Neo *(Aura)*
Good, original songs but no voice worth its salt spoils this new British singer's chances. AB-F

TED NUGENT & FRIENDS

TED NUGENT
Scream Dream *(Epic)*
Jock-strap rock: smelly, sweaty, loud and odorous. MJ

GARY NUMAN
The Pleasure Principle
(Atco/Beggars Banquet)
Gary Numan, the sultan of the synthesizer, the man who put Beggar's Banquet Records on the map, would probably give his eyeteeth for John Foxx's style, while Foxx would yank out his own in return for Numan's level of success. 'Cars' was one of the biggest hits of the year but nothing else on the album matches it. DN

GARY NUMAN

BILLY OCEAN
City Limit *(GTO)*
Gentle. AB-F

MARTIN O'CONNOR
The Connachtman's Rambles
(Mulligan)
O'Connor is one of the most extraordinarily skilled Irish musicians of his generation, and this, his first record, sets new standards in the playing of the accordion and melodeon. His technical command and audacity invest his repertoire — all traditional — with breakneck excitement. Here, rather than in more overt attempts at 'fusion', is a genuine synthesis of popular and traditional musical sensibilities: O'Connor is not only as impressive as many a rock guitarist (say) but impressive in much the same way. This is a record to revive the spirits of anyone dissatisfied with the present state of traditional music. TR

OCTOBER CHERRIES
Baking Hot *(Baal)*
Unswallowable. AB-F

OFF BROADWAY
On *(Atlantic)*
Plucked from the Ken Adamany school of junior Cheap Tricks, this midwestern band utilizes Cheap Tricks' producer, engineer, studio, and keyboard player in a futile effort to summon up some of the Tricks' endearing qualities. DN

DANNY O'KEEFE
Danny O'Keefe *(Criminal)*
Reissue of Arif Mardin produced first O'Keefe album. A minor classic of the early '70s. A bit dated now. O'Keefe never did improve on this one. MJ

OLD AND NEW DREAMS
Old and New Dreams *(ECM)*
It's one of history's small ironies that the four members of this band who were variously launching or launched by the Free Jazz of 20 years ago, have in the interim individually and together performed with rather more dignity and momentum than their erstwhile figurehead Ornette Coleman. Long freed from the demands of vanguarding, Don Cherry, Dewey Redman, Ed Blackwell and Charlie Haden have onstage been reworking their freedom from the ground upwards in the richer but more complacent late seventies.

On record, an earlier eponymous album for Black Saint showed a gritty, spontaneous approach. Living right up to ECM expectations, this one goes the other way with a carefully sculpted, serenely projected opus that many veteran punters will find annoyingly urbane. Cherry's contributions in particular are conspicuous in their righteousness, similarly Blackwell's tightlipped workout on a Ghanese traditional theme, 'Togo'.

In relieving contrast are 'New Guinea' where Redman cuts well loose over a vampy rhythm, followed by the manna of a piano notion from Cherry, and a new version of Haden's 'Song for the Whales' where the liberty to play as one wishes has been channelled into very specific and emotionally compelling use. Perhaps by definition, a limited vision of a quintessential outfit. LE

MIKE OLDFIELD
Platinum *(Virgin)*
Tubular Bells potentate seeks new inspiration and graduates late in the day to shorter length compositions. An haphazard collection which flirts with both greatness and disaster (the vocal tracks sung by Wendy Roberts). Also a touch of the electronic discos to keep the doctor and your dancing shoes happy. A transitional album which marks a possible new phase in (still) young Oldfield's career. The next one should be very interesting indeed. MJ

MIKE OLDFIELD

MIKE OLDFIELD
Airborn *(Virgin)*
US compilation of a combination of past Oldfield tracks generally successful in the UK. Yet another attempt to break him in the difficult American market where his brand of wistful tunes and one-man symphonic excesses have never really caught on. AB-F

ONE WAY FEATURING AL HUDSON
One Way Featuring Al Hudson
(MCA)
One Way used to be known as Al Hudson and the Soul Partners, under which name they clocked up a quick run of disco hits on both sides of the

O.M.D.

THE ORCHIDS

Atlantic culminating in the ultra-infectious hustler 'You Can Do It', perhaps the epitome of Hudson's understated vocal style and the band's strong support. Most of the album doesn't quite hit the magic buzz of that track, but is certainly a superior disco/funk set in a part of the market where singles normally say it all and therefore usually have it all their own way. BL

THE ONLY ONES
Baby's Got a Gun *(Epic/CBS)*
Produced by Colin Thurston, the Only Ones third album is a vast improvement on its predecessors and, once more, shows how different a band they are from all the other after-punk survivors still in existence. Art rock? Power pop? Difficult to see where to classify Peter Perrett's cohorts. Nice duo with Pauline Murray, ex-Penetration, on one song which is, however, untypical of the album which, elsewhere, simmers with menace. AB-F

THE ONLY ONES
Special View *(Epic)*
Digest of Only Ones' first two British albums packaged aseptically for US audience. AB-F

ORCHESTRAL MANOEUVRES IN THE DARK
Orchestral Manoeuvres in the Dark *(Dindisc)*
Factory records group signs to fledgling major and takes off in grand style. Romantic electronics at its best. 'Electricity' and 'Messages' typify their endearing and emotional style. Gives monochrome rock both colours and a good reputation. AB-F

ORCHIDS
Orchids *(MCA)*
More Los Angeles dogmeat brought to you by Kim Fowley, the man behind the Runaways, Venus & The Razorblades, Hollywood Stars, etc. Fowley makes the best disposable records in rock. DN

ORIGINAL MIRRORS

ORIGINAL MIRRORS
Original Mirrors
(Arista/Mercury)
Great quality, unpretentious solid rock with melodies, superlative instrumental breaks and a genuine sense of style. Original Mirrors are a young British outfit who deserve more attention, lost as they have been in the awesome avalanche of punk and new wave product. Their second album will be very important indeed. AB-F

ORIGINAL SOUNDTRACK
Silver Dream Racer *(Mercury)*
David Essex sings songs from David Essex film. I suppose there's no one else he trusts with the (dubious) job. AB-F

ORION
Reborn *(Sun/Charly)*
Sunrise *(Sun)*
If God had wanted us to hear more Presley, he wouldn't have killed him off. MJ

JOHN OTWAY AND WILD WILLY BARRETT
Way Bar *(Polydor)*
The wild pair regroup after a lover's tiff and their come-back platter is the usual idiosyncratic but endearing mixture as before. Love it or hate it; it all depends how seriously you are willing to take them. I've got a slight soft spot for the dear old loonies so I enjoyed it, although I had to put my critical faculties in hibernation from time to time. MJ

OUTLAWS
In The Eye Of The Storm
(Arista)
Lowest common denominator Southern boogie...and y'know it's gotten pretty low when they feel compelled to tackle Elvis Costello's 'Miracle Man' in a stab at relevance. DN

OZARK MOUNTAIN DAREDEVILS
Ozark Mountain Daredevils
(Columbia/CBS)
First one on a new label for the Ozarks. Pleasant but bland country sounds. AB-F

P.M.
1 P.M. *(Ariola)*
Five-piece school of blood and thunder band led by Carl Palmer after the drawn-out end of ELP. Unremarkable debut. AB-F

GRAHAM PARKER
The Up Escalator
(Arista/Stiff)
There's even Springsteen himself helping out on one track with background vocals and Jimmy Iovine producing. So why do I find the final result unsatisfactory (as have been all of Parker's previous efforts, apart from, maybe, 'Squeezing out the Sparks'). Good singer, with emotional rocking voice, good material, solid live act (with the Rumour), Parker has everything going but I now seriously suspect he's never going to make it to the top. Why? He lacks star quality. Easy to enjoy and unpretentious, though and that's the way his records should be taken. Sorry, Graham. MJ

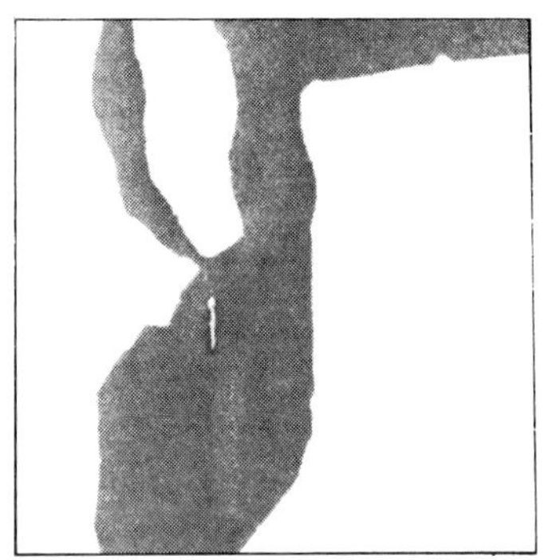

GRAHAM PARKER & THE RUMOUR
The Best of Graham Parker & the Rumour *(Vertigo)*
Compilation released to coincide with Parker's switch to a different label. A good selection showing him at his past best and highlighting his perplexing inability to score beyond a small circle of passionate devotees. AB-F

ALAN PARSONS PROJECT
Eve *(Arista)*
Another brick from the concept album factory. Just what the public wants (or does it?). MJ

MR. PARTRIDGE
Take Away (The Lure of Salvage) *(Virgin)*
Andy Partridge, XTC virtuoso, goes solo the different way. An opaque experimental album consisting partly of revamped XTC tracks, now unrecognizable sometimes under the cloak and dagger of dub techniques. Well done and imaginative, but never quite connects with the pleasure centres. Good effort, must try again says big teacher in the sky. AB-F

THE PASSIONS
Michael & Miranda *(Fiction)*
Tepid semi-minimalist punkoid art rock. Sounds as black and bleak and white as the colourless sleeve art. Maybe this was intentional. For a lesson in how to master the art of this particular growing genre, refer to Young Marble Giants' album offering. MJ

TOM PAXTON
Up and Up *(Evolution)*
Old folkie keeps on roaming up that dusty road with guitar on shoulder and a weary song between his parched lips. He wears a cap on his wise old head to hide the fact he's gone bald... MJ

JOHNNY PAYCHECK
Everybody's got a Family...Meet Mine *(Epic)*
Production by the eponymous (obligatory) Billy Sherrill. This time around it ain't a country lady but a country macho outlaw. Sounds almost the same to me. Cliches abound in the Nashville disaster area. AB-F

ANNETTE PEACOCK
The Perfect Release *(Tomato/Aura)*
Never-ageing lady of the avant-garde jazz scene of many moons ago comes up trumps with a totally personal, unclassifiable new album. Often confused feminist/cosmic school of life lyrics, but transcendent vocals spanning many octaves on quirky jazz/disco/rock tinged recitatives and songs. Yes, what a voice. AB-F

PEARL HARBOR AND THE EXPLOSIONS
Pearl Harbor and the Explosions *(Warners)*
Great white hopes of the West Coast new wave explosion fall flat on their faces with this low-profile, gutless first album. Dull is the word and the group broke up soon afterwards. MJ

ART PEPPER
'Straight Life' *(Galaxy)*
With the bonafide revival of the fortunes and popularity of Art Pepper, it's good to find his newest recordings retaining the values of his landmark 'Living Legend' session. 'Straight Life' it may be, but not without its compensations: a dextrous, measured, athletic, relaxed performer in tune with himself, his horn, his (top-flight) sidesmen and his audience.

Of the five tracks, 'September Song' is the one most closely endorsing the textbook image of the disciple of Konitz and the Blues. Consequently, a taste of Paul Desmond has to colour the opening of an extended 'Nature Boy', the determined, questioning quality of which is carried over by a fine dialogue between Red Mitchell (bass and Tommy Flanagan (piano). Flanagan, frankly, gets the best bite from a revamped 'Surf Ride' and underpins the flock again on 'Make a List', an emancipation of the usual token Latin rut with a veritably chattering Pepper showing superb command of speed and temperature. It's drummer Billy Higgins however who holds a spiritual calm through his superbly marshalled freneticism on the title track, whose breakneck pace sometimes causes even its creator to skid.

Art Pepper is in the happy position of being an all-rounder with a voice of his own. More important, he's a joy to listen to — certainly in this instance. LE

PERE UBU
New Picnic Time *(Chrysalis)*
Hardly country music, more like bulldozer romances and hard-hat urban melodies put through a mangler. Takes time to get into but ultimately rewarding. MJ

JOE PERRY PROJECT

JOE PERRY PROJECT
Let The Music Do The Talking *(Columbia/CBS)*
Perry post-Aerosmith sounds rejuvenated by his hot young band. The only problem with this very respectable debut effort is that Perry's a better guitarist than singer. The best cuts are the ones that feature Ralph Morman on lead or duet vocals like 'Life At A Glance' and the bitterly autobiographical 'Conflict Of Interest'. DN

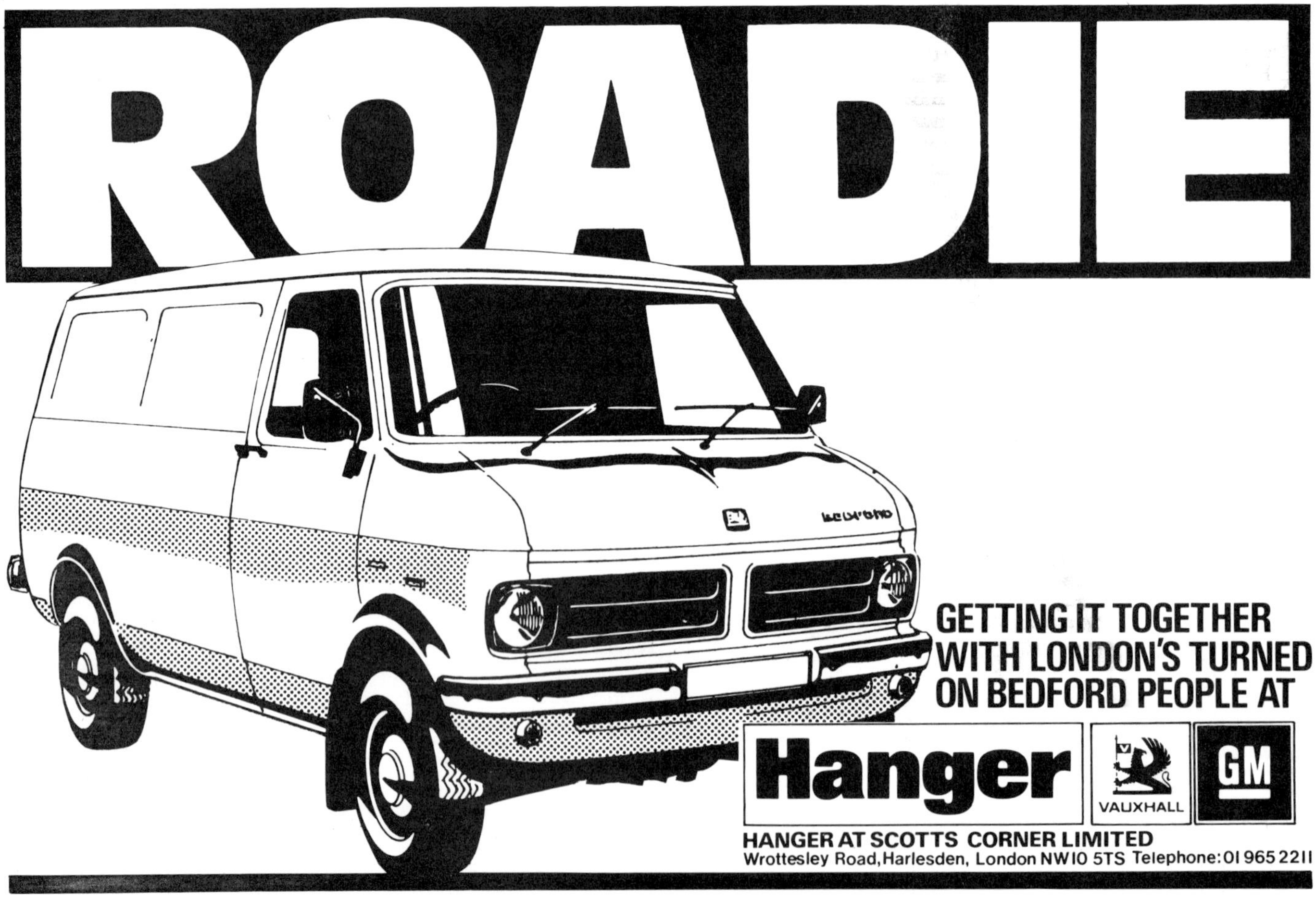

TOM PETTY & THE HEARTBREAKERS
Damn The Torpedoes *(MCA)*
Petty's most successful album ever in the USA, while raising only moderate sales in Britain. The reason for this presumably lies in the road down which he has taken himself since heralding a part of the new wave of American rock a few years ago — to a raunchy but always-under-control style with strong production values, stopping short of the aggression of heavy metal, and pretty well hermetically sealed from the angry thrash of punk. All of which makes for A-1 radio fare in the States and consequent sales success, whilst adding up to a minority commodity for the UK market. The controlled power and Springsteenesque production of cuts like 'Refugee', however, defends Petty's rock credibility effortlessly. BL

PHILLIPS/McLEOD
Phillips/McLeod *(Polydor)*
Glib bargain bin material. AB-F

WENDY WU/THE PHOTOS

THE PHOTOS *(Epic)*
British Blondie-clone; singer Wendy Wu has long dark hair and that's not the only difference, unfortunately. The songs are all polished, articulate pop but always lack the necessary sparkle of originality. Indifferent production (with obstrusive strings thrashing about in the background on several tracks) by Roger Bechirian and Wendy Wu's inexpressive flat voice make the whole thing rather boring. No, I didn't enjoy it! (British release also includes a free additional album 'The Blackmail Tapes' allegedly the band's early demos; for masochists only, who wish to hear punkoid destruction jobs of already dubious standards like 'The lady is a tramp' or revered personal classics like the Beatles' 'I saw her standing there'). MJ

RICHARD PINHAS
Iceland *(Pulse/Polydor)*
French synth wizard in slightly more accessible and romantic mood. Repays the attention. MJ

PINK FLOYD
The Wall *(Columbia/Harvest)*
Roger Waters' magnum opus. Towering, if often confused, masterpiece of gargantuan proportion and ambition. 'Another Brick in the Wall' is mesmerizing and is already becoming a misread hymn for school children (my six-year old daughter who has yet to really suffer from the British educational system happily sings along to the chorus at the finale of her school disco!). Even if you dislike the music and what the Floyd represent in contemporary rock, a must for your collection. MJ

PINK MILITARY
Do Animals Believe in God *(Eric's)*
Liverpool group unlike any other. Vocalist Jane veers between primal scream techniques and soft melodies on this schizophrenic album which embodies many of the contradictions of the art school approach to new wave rock but is always interesting even when it doesn't reach its lofty, appointed targets. MJ

PLAIN SAILING
Dangerous Times *(Chrysalis)*
AOR fodder. MJ

PLANXTY
After The Break *(Tara)*
The finest folk band that ever breathed justify their reunion by sounding (almost) as fresh as on their first classic album in 1973. Irish music at its most exhilerating, with the band's characteristic blend and empathy reassuringly intact, and Liam O'Flynn again proving himself the young master of the uilleann pipes. Fine vocal performances from Christy Moore and Andy Irvine and a couple of surprise tracks, notably a furious-paced Rumanian dance tune, 'Smeceno Horo'. CI

PLAYER'S ASSOCIATION
We Got the Groove *(Vanguard)*
So What? AB-F

POCO
Under the Gun *(MCA)*
Produced by Mike Flicker, yet another generally pleasant album from Poco. The new line-up's second effort, in fact, 'Under the Gun' sees the group veer away from its usual country harmonies and tones and rock harder. Professional and hard to criticize but as always missing that extra vital ingredient that could make it great. MJ

BONNIE POINTER
2 *(Motown)*
Quality soul in the grand old tradition. AB-F

STING/THE POLICE

NOEL POINTER
Feel It *(UA)*
For an artist who guested as a schoolkid with a hundred symphony orchestras (don't they all?) and promptly got caught on the blandstand, Noel Pointer is coming through remarkably well.

'Feel It' is his third LP, and the first in which he has a substantial hand in production and arrangement, partnered by Paul Riser. Other things apart, his very playing seems neater, more relaxed and (dare I say?) pointed than in the Dave Grusin days — check out the skydiving centrepiece of 'For You' or the vivid romanticism of 'Niteroi'. There's some standout playing from other members of the crew inside the impeccably polished exterior, notably Michael Boddicker's synth work making earth tremors across 'Captain Jarvis' and sniping like rifle fire on the title number. As a foil for all this, Riser has cooked up some pretty rippy string arrangements, giving tacky, purposeful colouring to the tasks in hand: even the Jones Girls, chipping away on the statutory vocal hooks, are quite forgiveable. For Noel Pointer, the buck shouldn't stop here. LE

THE POLICE
Regatta de Blanc *(A&M)*
Out of the ruins of punk comes the perfect sound of the late 70's and early 80's. Police have one of the most distinctive sounds around, having blended the raw energy of the (younger) new wave with a subtle zest of jazz inflections and white reggae beat. Every track a winner and a radio must. Still, nine months after its initial release, every song still sounds as fresh and original. (see Groups of the Year section). MJ

THE POP
Go! *(Arista)*
This is one of the few power pop groups who aren't shameless textbook copyists. Unfortunately after this was made, lead guitarist Tim McGovern quit to join the dreadful Motels. DN

IGGY POP
Soldier *(Arista)*
Erratic and shambolic set of songs by the Ig who seems to spend too long in the recording studios these days. The 'genius' image so well nurtured by the past years of vinyl silence is getting tarnished pretty fast by his over-production. Great band behind him: Glen Matlock, Ivan Kral, Barry Andrews and Steve New, does little to deter from the light weight material on show. Could Iggy's comeback be solely attributable to Bowie's assistance? AB-F

THE POP GROUP
How Much Longer *(Rough Trade)*
Ambitious attempt at solving's society's errors. Naive wishful thinking. MJ

COZY POWELL
Over the Top *(Ariola)*
Never trust a drummer with a solo album or his own band. This album proves the rule and is no exception to a long line of failures. AB-F

ROGER POWELL
Air Pocket *(Bearsville)*
Solo promenade by Todd Rundgren's Utopia sidekick. Todd, why didn't you keep the door closed? Synthesizer show-off gala. MJ

THE PRETENDERS
The Pretenders *(Sire/Real)*
Greatly expected and is in fact even better than we ever thought it could be. What is almost the point of a retrospective review now that the album has conquered every heart and soul. Chrissie Hynde's songs reach straight for the funny bone and give it a twist that is unforgettable. The band provide imaginative support (apart from one minor 'Space Invader' instrumental) and this must surely be one of the major albums of the year (see other sections of the Rock Yearbook). AB-F

ALAN PRICE
Rising Sun *(Jet)*
Uninspired revival of 'House of the Rising Sun' and dire ballads. Deliberately unfashionable, Alan Price is also very much short of inspiration these days. MJ

PRINCE
Prince *(Warners)*
Rhythms to dance to on a Saturday night, but with distinct lack of fever. AB-F

JOHN PRINE
Pink Cadillac *(Asylum)*
These ten songs — rockabilly, rock and country — are the result of five months in Memphis with the production team of Knox and Jerry Phillips, with two cuts produced by Father Sam Phillips himself. John Prine is a classic case of alienation — a good old country boy uprooted and raised in Chicago. He's never quite appeared to know who he is and where he belongs. This record, however, seems to be his attempt to get back to basics. It's the album he might have made if he'd been left to grow up in the wilds of Kentucky. He's not fooling around about it, either. 'Pink Cadillac' is not sweet and good-humoured, not laid-back, not funky-folky or funny-cute. It's rough as a cob. In spite of the rockabilly influence — including a blistering performance of 'Baby Let's Play House' and a 'No Name Girl' performed with Billy Lee Riley — the style here isn't really rockabilly. Call the album gut rock. I think Prine reaches deeper into his true self than he ever has before on this album. If he's up to it — and can stand the pain of retraining his audience — it's a direction worth continuing to pursue. AP

PRISM
Armageddon *(Capitol)*
Schlock rock. AB-F

PRIVATE LIGHTNING
Private Lightning *(A&M)*
Heavy but subtle, this US sextet's first album figures in good placing amongst the many unfortunately overlooked albums of the year. Featuring electric violin, Private Lightning are at times reminiscent of a younger, post-modern Jefferson Airplane without the meaningful lyrics. Worth keeping an eye open for. Might go far if given a chance. MJ

THE PSYCHEDELIC FURS
The Psychedelic Furs *(CBS)*
Panoramic production by Steve Lillywhite for new British band in strong European mould. Not so much a throwback to psychedelia but a more contemporary attempt to grasp reality through repeated layers of sound that deliberately owe nothing to art or pomp rock. Does not always succeed, but always interesting. MJ

JOHN LYDON/P.I.L.

PUBLIC IMAGE LIMITED
Metal Box *(Virgin)*
Second Edition *(Island/Virgin)*
A challenge to the orthodoxy of rock by Johnny Rotten-now-John Lydon's new band. Keith Levine is an amazingly deft and economical guitarist and his musical panoramas underpin Lydon's vocals-recitations with eerie accuracy and bleakness of feeling. Not so much rock but a possible new art form born of anger and reaction to the facileness of much of today's music. Menacing and ironical, Public Image Limited are the group of the year. 1984, that is. AB-F

Q-TIPS
Q-Tips *(Chrysalis)*
Deep production by Bob Sergeant for British soul revivalists first album. Amiable reworking of many standards, unerring professionalism but, as too often, no spark of genuine life or originality. MJ

QUARTZ
Deleted *(Jet)*
Birmingham heavy metal bunch whose first album, then simply titled Quartz appeared in 1977 and is now re-issued to take advantage of the winds of change and boogie woogie sweeping across rock consumer's wallet's. Production chores by Tommy Iommi of Black Sabbath reputation. AB-F

QUEEN
The Game *(Elektra/EMI)*
Pomp rock at its most flatulent. No, sirree, there ain't no justice in this world when you see how well this rubbish sells. AB-F

TREVOR RABIN
Face to Face *(Chrysalis)*
South African heavy metal rocker with one slight problem: he belongs in the light-weight category of guitar riffers. A major disadvantage. MJ

GERRY RAFFERTY
Snakes & Ladders *(United Artists)*
It's tentative, but there are definite signs that Rafferty is seriously attempting to break

out of the cosy cocoon of AOR steadily engulfing him after (or as a result of) the success of 'Baker Street'. Rafferty's inhibited by the lushness of his own voice, but here he opens up a bit with producer Hugh Murphy apparently consciously wary of smothering him. The material is a huge improvement after the disappointment of 'Night Owl', and 'The Royal Mile' is the perfect Rafferty track. CI

RAGGS
Nutz and Buttz *(Bigger Than Life)*
Nondescript compromise between pop and country. No good in either category. MJ

THE RAINCOATS
The Raincoats *(Rough Trade)*
Or the virtues of amateurism. British feminist combo battle on in their own sweet way. Ragged at the edges, but pleasantly personal debut. Great reworking of Ray Davies' 'Lola'! MJ

BONNIE RAITT
The Glow *(Warners)*
Nice lady who also plays a mean guitar. Unadvised attempt at increasing her audience leads her to neglect her blues forte for Ronstadt territory. Pleasant but very Californian and forgettable. AB-F

PHILIP RAMBOW
Shooting Gallery *(EMI)*
Philip Rambow has been around and never obtained the recognition his pedigree warrants. 'The Winkies' were very much a seminal band, years before the New Wave came and went. He was on the famous CBGB compilation and his songs have been covered more recently by Ellen Foley. At long last, this is his first album and it fulfills all the years of promise. Eclectic, hummable, dance music with hooks and riffs galore. MJ

RAMONES
End Of The Century *(Sire)*
If this album hadn't been a success, the Ramones would have been Sire bossman Seymour Stein's personal slaves for the rest of their lives to pay off Phil Spector's production fee. Keep up the good work, bros! DN

KENNY RANKIN
After the Roses *(Atlantic)*
A romantic mess. AB-F

GENYA RAVAN
...And I Mean It! *(20th Century)*
Genya might be singing 'I Won't Sleep on The Wet Spot No More' but after her long string of flops as a singer and producer she sounds desperate enough here to eat the whole sheet on national TV if it would help move copies of this turkey. DN

RAY, GOODMAN AND BROWN
Ray, Goodman and Brown *(Mercury)*
During the 70's, Ray, Goodman and Brown were the Moments, and made several conquests of the pre-disco black music market with exquisitely harmonised soul ballads and uptempo dancers like 'Love On A Two-Way Street', 'Dolly My Love', and 'Girls'. Back on the scene via a different record company and under their own collective monikers, they have re-emerged with those magic harmonies fully intact, and applied them to an albumsworth of sweetly flowing delights, exemplified by 'Special Lady', a top-drawer ballad which slept its way to eventually becoming a huge American single hit. The best two-on-a-couch black music since the heyday of the Chi-Lites. BL

RAYDIO
Two Places at the Same Time *(Arista)*
The band led, produced, written for and generally svengali'd by ever-smiling ace guitarist Ray Parker Jr., Parker's selling point is strong, chugging disco/funk-based music, but whipped into something special by slick and subtle production touches. Their big hit single 'Jack and Jill' in 1978 set the style with its zippy vocal blend and strong melody (another Parker forte), and much of this album aspires to the same standard, particularly the title track and the disco winner 'For Those Who Like To Groove'. BL

CHRIS REA
Tennis *(Columbia/Magnet)*
The kind of instantly disposable record you won't remember one song from ten minutes after you throw it away. DN

THE RECORDS

THE RECORDS
Crashes *(Virgin)*
One of my best albums of the year (and no, I haven't accepted a bribe by the publishers' cousins down the road!). A wealth of tuneful, catchy melodies by a band now reinforced by Jude Cole who used to play guitar with Moon Martin. Taste rock at its most immaculate with splendid harmonies galore. Okay, so the lyrics don't match up to Hegel or John Fowles, but all you have to do is close you eyes and sway softly along. And it's got a rocking bite to it, too, when required. Come on, go and make up your own mind. Rush out and buy it. Supa-dupa-great. AB-F

RED RIDER
Don't Fight It *(Capitol)*
12-string guitar rock in the Byrds/Tom Petty mode. AB-F

THE REDS
The Reds *(A&M)*
Clean, clinical US power pop. Liked the free tee-shirt, though. AB-F

LOU REED
Growing Up in Public *(Arista)*
Greeted by a majority of critics on both sides of the pond as a small triumph for Reed, I keep on finding this album wanting. The confessional lyrics are fine, barbed, pungent, witty but it's the music which doesn't stand up to Reed's past masterpieces. The sharing of credits with ex-Rhinoceros taskmaster Michael Fonfara might be the reason. No, not a major Lou Reed effort. Some critics must have short memories, or else I'm getting old. AB-F

VINI REILLY
The Return of the Durutti Column *(Factory)*
Produced by the ever-present Martin Hannett, a fascinating collage of sounds by reclusive Manchester guitarist Vini Reilly. Almost 'Tubular Bells' without the bells and less melodic strength. An invaluable little record. First pressing came in a highly original but somewhat impractical (and dangerous) sandpaper sleeve. Electronic music at its most impressive and exemplary. MJ

RENE & ANGELA
Rene & Angela *(Capitol)*
Vocal duo do the disco and do the 'Hotel California'. Oops, pardon me while I guffaw. AB-F

TIM RENWICK
Tim Renwick *(CBS)*
Ex-Quiver and Sutherland Brothers guitarist goes the solo way. Instrumental breaks are the more forceful aspect of this album, while lyrics range from trite to unoriginal. MJ

REO SPEEDWAGON
A Decade of Rock And Roll 1970 To 1980 *(Epic)*
A textbook example of a not particularly original or inspired rock band that built a substantial following on a midwest base through relentless touring and sheer sweat. Of course, success is 90% perspiration and 10% inspiration and this music is predictably sweaty. What's more interesting is how little their concept and sound has changed in the 1971 – 1979 period covered here — this "Decade" business is just a marketing concept. DN

ALDA RESERVE
Love Goes On *(Sire)*
New York rock of the clever variety. Produced by Marshall Chess. AB-F

THE RESIDENTS
Eskimo *(Ralph)*
The wind howled through the white, frozen wastelands. Bozo thought "So this is what life is all about" and sighed sadly while the sky switched confusedly from white to grey to white again. Odd noises filled the air and he unplugged one ear better to catch the floating sounds now permeating the Christmas-like landscape. The Eskimo laughed. MJ

MARTIN REV
Solo *(Lust/Unlust)*
The other side of Suicide. AB-F

RHYTHM DEVILS
Play River Music *(Passport)*
Left-over soundtrack for 'Apocalypse Now' by assortment of Grateful Dead and other percussion specialists. Eerie jungle and river music that catches the feeling of the film in a disturbing sort of way. MJ

CLIFF RICHARD
We Don't Talk Anymore *(EMI)*
The only man to ever sell his soul to Jesus instead of the Devil in exchange for eternal youth. This LP is high class M.O.R. rock and about as good as it gets. DN

JONATHAN RICHMAN AND THE MODERN LOVERS
Back in Your Life *(Beserkley)*
Well, Jonathan Richman has definitely gone too far this time. You always thought he would, didn't you? He's such a strange bird — geekish uncertain voice with a half-octave range, off-the-wall lyrics varying between sentimentality and cynicism, minimalist rock 'n' roll music. But scratch a cynic and you find a romantic — and now our Jonathan has decided to come out of the closet. He lets it all hang out on this record. All is much the same as before, except that the cynicism is gone. The truth is that Jonathan Richman actually *believes* in discredited stuff like respect, affection, patience, faith and true love, and he's finally willing to come out and say so. It makes for his purest and most expressive record, a mix of covers like an instrumental version of Billy Swan's 'Lover Please' and the old 'Buzz buzz buzz goes the bumble bee, tweedle-ee-deedle-ee-dee go the birds' (remember that one?), and his own funny-dumb songs. If you know better, this record isn't for you. But Jonathan Richman thinks it's a matter of decision, and he's finally made his. I've made mine too. I *love* this record. AP

TERRY RILEY
Shri Camel *(CBS)*
Long, hypnotizing improvisations by withered old experimentalist. OK, so it ain't rock, but we like it. So, there. AB-F

RIOT
Narita *(Capitol)*
Heavy metal for the uncultured masses. AB-F

THE RIVITS
Multiplay *(Antilles/Island)*
New band full of promise and versatility comprises Jess Roden, ex-Bronco and J R Band, and Pete Wood ex-Sutherland Bros. and Quiver. Tasteful licks. Should grow on you after several listenings. MJ

B.A. ROBERTSON
Initial Success *(Asylum)*
Rare British signing to the more usually West Coast orientated Asylum label. B.A. Robertson is also quite unexpectedly British and, unlike Ian Dury who also trades heavily on his idiosyncrasies, should remain forever terra incognita for American audiences. Despite four UK hit singles all lifted from this one album, Robertson's witty, clever 'short-story' songs never quite transcend their jolly novelty value and 'Initial Success' only succeeds in disappointing. Robertson is such a protean and articulate entertainer one wishes he could make it big in the wide, wonderful world of popular music (as they say in the fairy tale), but the odds are heavily stacked against him, I fear: intelligence and a canny sense of perspective on fashions in rock are just bad currency these days. AB-F

THE ROCHES
The Roches *(Warner Brothers)*
Coy, giggly charm from three wacky New Jersey sisters who get compared a lot to the McGarrigles. The barest possible production by Robert Fripp brings out their underlying humour and bizarre view of life's quirks, but frivolity is balanced by occasional bouts of lyrical profundity and stunning harmonies. No other group could possibly think of opening an album with a singing press release 'We'. CI

THE ROCKETS
No Ballads *(RSO)*
Patchy southern boogie. One of the few RSO bands which isn't making a fortune... AB-F

ROCKIN' DOPSIE & HIS CAJUN TWISTERS
Hold On *(Rounder/Sonet)*
Saturday night party dance music blending across ethnic musical genres with consummate ease. AB-F

JESS RODEN
Stonechaser *(Island)*
Limp album from singer who has seen better times. MJ

HANS-JOACHIM ROEDELIUS
Selbstportrait *(Sky)*
Spare and often enigmatic synthesizer hypnotism lesson soundtrack by German specialist. MJ

KENNY ROGERS
Gideon *(UA)*
Ambitious country concept album which almost pulls it off. Kenny Rogers has one of the best gruff voices in the trade, even if he is not always served by the best of material. Surprisingly good. AB-F

ROLLING STONES
Emotional Rescue *(Rolling Stones)*
Although this two-years-in-the-making album lacks the pleasing stylistic diversity of 'Some Girls', this album ranks as the Stones' 'Sticky Fingers' for the 80's. DN

SONNY ROLLINS
Don't Ask *(Milestone)*
Here's a prime example of an established player who's translated himself easily — properly — into more modern modes from his stamping-ground of hard bop. Indeed, keeping the solid, swinging roots alive has been half the winning of the battle: Rollins is a voice that just can't be swamped. In the sixties, when the New Thing was in the ascendent, he was hanging out with Don Cherry and Billy Higgins: and whatever he's done, it's never been with strings.

'Don't Ask' generally bears this out. While it has its dull spots, tracks such as the opening 'Harlem Boys' find Rollins walking boldly across a tight but vibrant soft-funk landscape, coloured up by Bill Summers' percussion. 'Tai-Chi' plays the oriental game with freshness and grace, lyricon now spinning the lead line and (the ascendent) Mark Soskin's flowery piano line much in evidence. 'The File' is a duo with Larry Coryell on acoustic guitar. Coryell is well used to running the planes and edges of tacky rhythm round an essential harmonic base, and for Rollins himself it halfway brings out a new man — lighter, drier, with more forays into flattened notes and gambles on the timing. A well-balanced and happy affair. LE

THE ROMANTICS
The Romantics
(Nemperor/Epic)
Motor city band playing a tight, energetic brand of Anglo/Mersey power pop. Their red leather suits are as retrograde as their music. Top tracks are 'Little White Lies', 'Tell It To Carrie', and the Kinks' 'She's Got Everything'. MG

RONIN
Ronin *(Mercury)*
Ronin are a bunch of ace US sessionmen, well-known for their expert backing of people like Linda Ronstadt, Warren Zevon, J.D. Souther or Nicolette Larson and many other West Coast luminaries. However, Waddy Wachtel, Dan Dugmore, Stanley Seldon and Rick Marotta never coalesce as a band in their own right and the resultant album stands utterly limp. It's polished, professional but lacks life, originality and bite; mainstream rock with little to say which never captures the genuine talent of the musicians involved, so well displayed elsewhere in their backing capacity. Nice textured cover design torpedoed by the ugly faces

THE RECORD LABEL YOU CAN'T PUT A LABEL ON.

STEVE HACKETT
Defector
CDS 4018

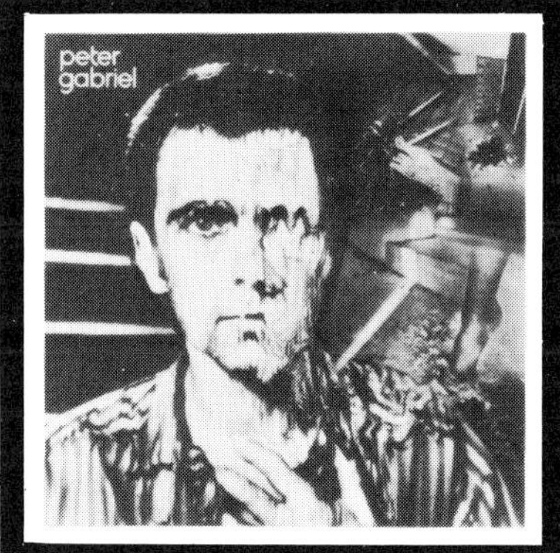

PETER GABRIEL
CDS 4019

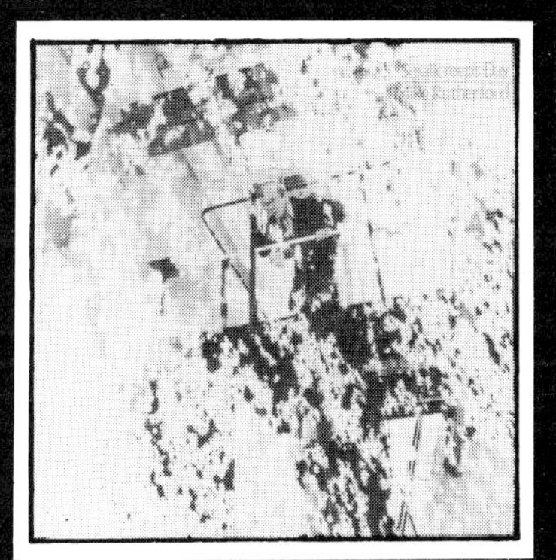

MIKE RUTHERFORD
Smallcreep's Day
CAS 1149

MONTY PYTHON
Monty Python's Contractual Obligation Album **CAS 1152**

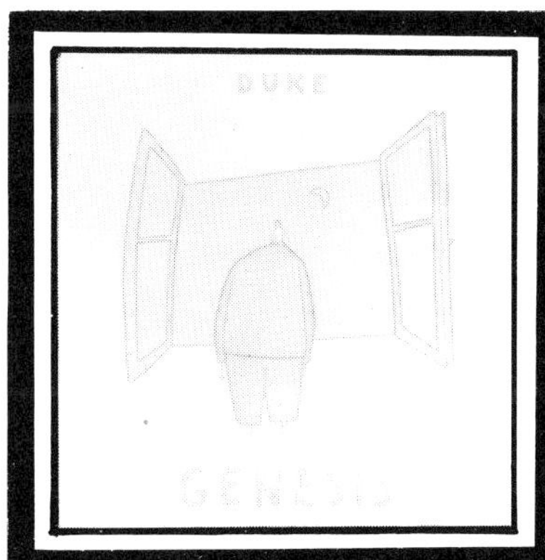

GENESIS
Duke
CBR 101

HAWKWIND
Repeat Performance
BG 2

Marketed by Charisma Records.

of the band's members. Peter Asher must have completed his production chores whilst sleepwalking. AB-F

ROOT BOY SLIM AND THE SEX CHANGE BAND WITH THE ROOTETTES
Zoom *(Illegal/IRS)*
Pleasantly offensive ditties for those who think good taste is something you can eat with relish and tomato ketchup. Music for guiltless philistines. MJ

DIANA ROSS
Diana *(Motown)*
Produced by the Chic organisation, possibly the very best of Diana Ross' solo outings. Apart from a few icky ballads which the Motown moguls must have imposed, Edwards and Rogers have accomplished a miracle while still sticking very closely to their usual formula. Percussive strings, quirky disco beats, it's all there but, this time around, it's Ross' voice to the fore and she does the material credit. Chock a block with potential (and actual) hits. Investigate, even if, like me, you previously were rather weary of later years Motown. MJ

LEON ROSSELSON & ROY BAILEY
If I Knew Who The Enemy Was... *(Acorn)*
Rosselson must be the most radical songwriter in Britain today, and he gets no mellower as he gets older. The tender voiced Bailey is an admirable foil, but this Martin Carthy produced work is too bitty and inconsistent to be ranked with their best. Untempered left-wing vitriol can be wearing as well as refreshing. 'On Her Silver Julilee', a merciless attack on the monarchy, would have landed Rosselson in the Tower a few years ago.

ROSSINGTON-COLLINS BAND
Anytime Anyplace Anywhere *(MCA)*
Strong bluesy feel for the return of Lynyrd Skynyrd in another guise with gutsy new lady singer Dale Krantz. Quality, fiery rock. MJ

MICHAEL ROTHER
Katzenmuzik *(Sky)*
Romantic electronic swirls by Michael Rother, ex-Neu. The beauty of much of pomp rock without their pretentions. A delight for the ears and the soul. AB-F

ROXY MUSIC
Flesh + Blood *(Atco/EG)*
'Manifesto' was an encouraging comeback last year but this album sounds distressingly like Roxy's swan song. Paul Thompson isn't around at all, Andy Mackay and Phil Manzanera contribute little, and the whole affair sounds like a Bryan Ferry solo album, including ludicrous cover versions of 'Eight Miles High' and 'The Midnight Hour'. DN

NEIL PEART/RUSH

RUSH
Permanent Wave *(Mercury)*
And permanent clichés... AB-F

PATRICE RUSHEN
Pizzazz *(Elektra)*
In her Prestige days, the then very youthful Patrice was a mere cult figure. Now released from that establishment, the Elektra set-up has allowed her to cut loose and some. The 'Patrice' album presented not only the player/writer but a keen and purposeful all-rounder behind some delightful and arresting songs.

After all the revelations, 'Pizzazz' is an album that stands back and takes stock. The centrepiece is a set of solidly constructed, worthy dance songs at medium to brisk tempos. Bass and keyboard clusters are gathered up to give a feeling more of dropping weight than of funk, and the big release is always the sublime and glassy whoa-whoa vocals at which Rushen seems to be getting neater than ever.

'Haven't You Heard' is the one that everyone's heard, typical if not the best with a bright steely weave of high-tensioned rhythm, a blo-wave piano break and a fishy hook line. Ballad-time tension comes up in 'Givin It Up Is Givin Up', but anyone who had the hots for the coaxing, tearing qualities of 'Changes (In Your Life)' will leave here still unsatisfied.

'Pizzazz' is a fairly specialised album: as so often, season according to taste. But no way, never, just a pretty face. LE

THE RUTS

RUSSIA
Russia *(Warners)*
Alas, this is no Soviet rock, just another limp Zeppelin avatar. AB-F

MIKE RUTHERFORD
Smallcreep's Day *(Passport/Charisma)*
Imitation Genesis by ex-Genesis member for Genesis fans. MJ

THE RUTS
The Crack *(Virgin)*
Post punk homecoming of one of the few predominantly punk groups to have emerged with more maturity and thoughtfulness from the pogo days of yonder. Reggae cross-over tunes and fiercely political lyrics blend with surprising ease and the whole album cultivates a menacing feel of subdued violence, permeating every chord. Ambitious, doesn't always reach its (high-placed) targets but all the more commendable for it. AB-F

DOUG SAHM
Hell of a Spell *(Takoma/Chrysalis)*
San Antonio blues record by much underrated musician out of the public eye. MJ

SCORPIONS

LEO SAYER

SANTANA
Marathon *(Columbia/CBS)*
Indefatigable band still in search of yesterday's magic but, in the meantime, today's slightly tired melodies will do, for want of anything better in the genre. MJ

SCORPIONS
Animal Magnetism *(Mercury/Harvest)*
Cock Rock. MJ

GIL SCOTT-HERON AND BRIAN JACKSON
1980 *(Arista)*
Political funk. Cool. AB-F

SCREEN IDOLS
Premiere *(Cobra)*
Survivors from lower division name bands item up for yet another doomed attempt at the big time. Born to fail. AB-F

SUE SAAD AND THE NEXT
Sue Saad and the Next *(Planet)*
First, they cloned Blondie and got Pat Benatar. Then, they cloned Pat Benatar and got Sue Saad. Clones of clones? Sad. MJ

SAMSON
Head On *(Gem)*
British heavy metal rocker's first album. Predictable (aren't they all in the heavy metal leather brigade) but, all in all, tuneful and won't harm your digestion. S & M overtones on sleeve. Could it be a new upcoming fashion? AB-F

SAXON
Wheels of Steel *(Carrere)*
Unsophisticated straight to the guts brand of British heavy metal. AB-F

LEO SAYER
Here *(Warner Brothers/Chrysalis)*
It's hard to believe that Leo Sayer was once considered provocative and was commercially successful. This album was negligible both musically and commercially. DN

LEO SAYER
Living in a fantasy *(Chrysalis)*
Consummate showman's new album. Now prisoner of middle-class audience and lost to rock. MJ

BOZ SCAGGS
Middleman *(Columbia/CBS)*
Scaggs' upper-crust R & B style is on the rebound after the disastrous 'Down Two Then Left'. This is still a long way from the sublime 'Silk Degrees' but this album's rockers 'Breakdown Dead Again' and 'You Got Some Imagination' suggest that he could do it again. DN

TOM SCOTT
Street Beat *(Columbia/CBS)*
Quite suddenly, Tom Scott has become one of the prime culprits behind fusion jazz, with a run of top-selling headline albums attracting the detractors of the music as much as the fans. Curiously still an eminence grise (despite touring with the CBS Allstars et al), Scott's background has included, significantly, Don Ellis, movie scores, Joni Mitchell and the LA Express. He's also exceptionally widely worked as a session player with less statutory credits including Wings, the Carpenters and Les Dudek.

Naturally, the neatly-sloganed 'Street Beat' scarcely shows all: but it does show dedication of funk-rock coupled with life from the neck upwards. Capping all is a Fillmore-wide meaty production that would do credit to any metal band, witness the verve with which the title track launches his collection.

Melodies are plain, bold, riffy, memorable and instrumental: 'Give Me Your Love leans on stylised girly choruses but that's exceptional. Scott himself is no longer goaded by electronic gimmicks. He plays a quite conventional melody line, breaking it up with devilishly subtle timing adjustments, while cohorts like trumpeter Chuck Findley can still get the grip for the odd solo launch. Interplay with Neil Larsen (keyboards) on 'We Can Fly' is ace.

For the disbeliever 'Street Beat' is essentially safe as milk; but it's also an album that knows a deal about lactic acid. LE

TONY SCUITO
Island Nights *(Epic)*
A Paul McCartney clone. DN

SEARCHERS
The Searchers *(Sire)*
First released during the latter half of 1979, then reserviced during the spring of 1980 with some track adjustments (making a collector's item of the future out of the original pressing, no doubt), this album marks a notable return in artistic terms for the mid-60s superstars. Coincidentally it

appears at a time when their influence, long ignored or at least underrated by critics and historians, has been fully acknowledged as being seminal to the Byrds, the Critters and much of the rest of the teen folk-rock boom in the States, and thus by implication to later generations of that West Coast rock stream like the Eagles. Ironic, too, that the Searchers of 1979/80 show, as well as echoes of their own roots, a whole lot of feedback from that same Byrds/Eagle school. In fact, this album is probably far too American/AOR for the average British ears of today, which is why it has hardly sold as befits its stature — though the single 'Hearts In Her Eyes' clocked a bit of UK airplay with its flowing pure pop harmonies. Nobody should mind anachronisms who make such fine music, though. BL

SECRET AFFAIR
Glory Boys *(Sire/I Spy)*
The epitome of the mod revival. Ian Page, leader of Secret Affair, vies for mouth of the year award but his music is anything but derivative. Revivals come and go. AB-F

NEIL SEDAKA
In The Pocket *(Polydor)*
Mushy ballads. Duet with his daughter almost becomes an embarrassment, as it's so difficult to distinguish the female voice. MJ

BOB SEGER
Against The Wind *(Capitol)*
This is not one of the great Bob Seger albums. There's none of the emotional intensity of 'Night Moves' or 'Feel Like A Number' or the sheer joy in rocking out of 'Live Bullet'. Here Seger doesn't move past a canter until the second side is half over and by then the throbbing needle is already thrusting towards liftoff. DN

THE SELECTER
Too Much Pressure *(2Tone)*
The second string of the 2 Tone operation, the Selecter were probably rushed into making this, their debut LP, and sometimes it shows. Five of the thirteen tracks are also available on singles, including "Three Minute Hero" and "Missing Words", but once the initial chequer board completism hoopla was over, this didn't seem like a record to play for pleasure. Within its limits (the group newly formed, the record made in a hurry), it is however a highly promising effort, and lead singer Pauline Black's uncompromising manipulation of the media has given the band a focal point which should ensure that their next effort will be more considered and less uneven. JT

THE SEX PISTOLS

THE SEX PISTOLS
Flogging A Dead Horse *(Virgin)*
Virtually most of the Pistols tracks in a different order. The title says it all and the front and back cover artwork are on a par with the whole spirit of the enterprise. MJ

THE SHAGGS
Philosophy Of The World *(Rounder)*
And so ends the world of music as we know it...*The worst sound of the year*; it's so bad some critics might well begin to like it and will rhapsodize about the virtues of minimalism. Aaargh... MJ

SHAKIN' STEVENS
Take One *(Epic)*
Rockabilly survivor at the top of his form. Never innovative but always enjoyable and unpretentious. Backing by big name session gentleman numbering Albert Lee, Geraint Watkins and ubiquitous pedal steel wizard of twang B.J. Cole. AB-F

SHAKIN' STREET
Shaking' Street *(Columbia/CBS)*
French heavy metal rockers noticed by critics mainly because of the Sandy Pearlman production job and the presence of Ross the Boss, ex Dictators guitarist. Lead singer Fabienne Shine has noticeable upfront assets which unfortunately don't include her voice or, at times, ridiculous strong accent which sounds just wrong singing in English. The music is an unspectacular din, anyway. Forget it. MJ

SHAM 69
The Game *(Polydor)*
Hersham Boys *(Polydor)*
Tired sloganeering from Jimmy Pursey's outfit. How they could ever have reached popular heights in England with their distinctly unsubtle football-terrace chants and ultra-naive social commentaries has always eluded me. Anyway, they're almost forgotten already. MJ

ELLEN SHIPLEY
Ellen Shipley *(New York International)*
Streetwise lady in the traditional NY mold. Not as good as Foley but better than Mas. The usual Springsteen influence, but if you don't feel in too acutely critical mood, you'll probably enjoy this in a moderate way. AB-F

SHIRTS
Street Shine *(Capitol/Harvest)*
Annie Golden's film involvement with 'Hair' must have interfered with their first lukewarm album. However, 'Street Shine' redeems the balance and delivers the goods one had always expected from the band. An invigorating platter. MJ

THE SHIRTS
Inner Sleeve *(Capitol)*
Though always pleasant, the Shirts third album sees them blocked in an uneasy zone between first and second division rock band status. Lightweight material and Annie Golden's sometimes fey mannerisms appear to be holding them back, but I fear they have already reached their pinnacle. MJ

THE SHOES
Present Tense *(Elektra)*
Produced at the Manor, this is absolutely perfect pop. If the Beatles had recorded an aprocryphal album, this would be it. Awesomely good. AB-F

SHOOTING STAR
Shooting Star *(Virgin)*
US signing to British label display workmanlike knowledge of soft centre heavy metal macho dynamics. Pedestrian production job by Gus Dudgeon just about enhances run of the mill riffs and the usual trite genre lyrics. Shooting Star are not going to change the world. AB-F

SILICON TEENS
Music For Parties *(Sire/Mute)*
And if ever an album title was appropriate, this is it! Delightful synthesizer cover versions of affectionate old classics. A labour of love and painstaking modern recreation that sucessfully manages never to be condescending or cheap. Features 'Memphis, Tennessee', 'Yesterday Man', 'Doo-Wah-Diddy-Diddy', 'You Really Got Me', 'Do You Love Me?', 'Let's Dance', 'Oh Boy', 'Sweet Little Sixteen', 'Just Like Eddie', 'Judy In Disguise' and a few brilliant self-penned instrumentals. No party should begin without this record on the turntable. The perfect antidote to things like Gary Numan who give the synthesizer a bad name. AB-F

CARLY SIMON
Come Upstairs *(Warners)*
A change of label sees Carly Simon's return to the front ranks of US lady vocalists after several years and albums in the easy listening doldrums. Symphathetic production by Mike Mainieri helps, but the truth of the matter is that Carly is back in aggressive form, enticing, erotic and touching. One of her best albums. MJ

FRANK SINATRA
Trilogy *(Reprise)*
Frank Sinatra in the Rock Year Book? Lavishly packaged triple album set on the concept of Past, Present and Future. The first two albums are devoted to predictable but smooth Sinatra standards but the third LP goes over the top and beyond in the search for the lost chord and cosmic significance to the meaning of life, the sex of the angles and other arcane minor questions. As portentous as the Moody Blues, but sounds better coming from Ol' Blue Eyes himself. Worth a listen or two. AB-F

SIOUXSIE AND THE BANSHEES
Kaleidoscope *(Polydor)*
Often cryptic album, this third effort by Siouxsie and her now-depleted Banshees, suffers from lack of immediacy and obvious hooks, but is still as hypnotic and compulsive as ever. An act apart. MJ

SISTER SLEDGE
Love Somebody Today *(Cotillion/Atlantic)*
Polished, and still shining brightly, off the Chic Organisation masterful assembly line for disco success. If we must have disco, then this is by far the best way of digesting it. Seductive shuffling in an uptempo mood. AB-F

SKAFISH

SKAFISH
Skafish *(Illegal)*
The latest in a long line of American eccentrics, Skafish is not just a solo clown but also a band, with worthy musical credentials and a very distinctive sound used to good effect on quirky songs ideal for the amateur practicing psychiatrist. AB-F

PETER SKELLERN
Astaire *(Mercury)*
Strongly regional British singer tackles the songs of Fred Astaire and combines with brass and backing. Curiosity. MJ

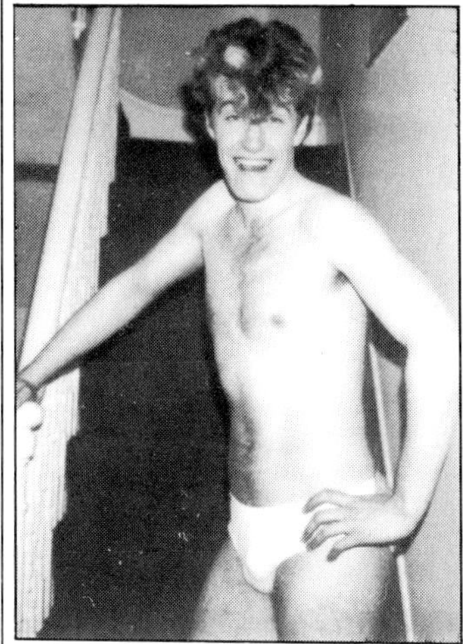
RICHARD JOBSON/THE SKIDS

SKIDS
Days In Europe *(Virgin)*
Bill Nelson of Be Bop de Luxe fame tries his hand as producer on this much improved effort by Scottish punk band in transit between street credibility thumping and art (as exemplified by lead singer Richard Jobson's obscure would-be intellectual lyrics). Big in England. Haven't crossed many borders yet. AB-F

SKY
Sky 2 *(Ariola)*
Impeccably hollow pomp classical rock by its foremost contemporary exponents. MJ

SLAUGHTER
Bite Back *(DJM)*
Formerly Slaughter and the Dogs which I suppose explains the title. Ah, the imagination of musicians and record company executives. Ah, the lack of inspiration of this reviewer who can't find a suitable pun or witty repartee for this assembly-line album of this punk/heavy metal/rock/you name it we can imitate it group. MJ

SLAVE
Just A Touch Of Love *(Cotillion)*
Pop/funk with hot guitar licks and frantic percussion. Assembly-line thrills. AB-F

SLEEPY LA BEEF
Downhome Rockabilly *(Charly/Sun)*
One way or another, Sleepy LaBeef has been surviving and playing rockabilly for twenty-five years, but it is only since rockabilly has developed an international audience that his recording career has started to show movement. This bass-voiced man mountain knows a million of them, and here are fifteen standards, including 'Honky Tonk Hardwood Floor', 'Red Hot', and 'Mystery Train'. Sleepy doesn't yip, moan or holler, and maybe it's his slow-footedness that has kept him alive all these years when so many of his contemporaries have crashed out. But Sleepy does have authority. He's solid, even, if he isn't exciting, and this album easily tops his 'Beefy Rockabilly' of a couple of years ago. Nonetheless, the record I'm looking forward to is the one that Sleepy recorded in England last year. My hope is that those English boys were able to light that fire under him that play-it-by-the-numbers Nashville cats no longer remember how to do. AP

GRACE SLICK
Dreams *(RCA)*
Grandiose, pompous, orchestral, Grace Slick has never been famous for temperance and discretion. This new solo album has all the faults and qualities of her past work. Confusing, sometimes doggone brilliant, a record that still takes some getting into, but is, in the long run, quite rewarding. The lady is far from being washed up, as some think she is. MJ

SLITS

SLITS
Cut *(Antilles/Island)*
Minimalist punk rock by agressively feminist and (often) badly discordant lady amateurs. The energy and the commitment sure is there, but I'm not sure the necessary talent is. AB-F

SLY STONE
Ten Years Too Soon *(Epic)*
Or the art of opportunist meddling. Seven old Sly tracks are operated upon by philistines and given the disco treatment. Avoid. AB-F

SNIFF

SLY AND THE FAMILIY STONE
Back On The Right Track *(Warners)*
Well, not quite the right track yet. Sly has still a lot of way to go before he regains his ascendancy in black music. Tries hard and has seen much worse days. MJ

THE SMALL FACES
Ogden's Nut Gone Flake *(Immediate/Virgin)*
Reissue of the classic Small Faces album in its original round package. Side one is still a treasure hoard of virtually classic pop songs while side two has dated somewhat and lumbers under the weight of too much whimsy. MJ

SMOKEY ROBINSON
Warm Thoughts *(Tamla)*
With the Miracles, Smokey Robinson was one of the great writers and singers of 60s soul. His solo recordings of the 70s were very much mixed bags, but 'Warm Thoughts' sound more relaxed and assured than anything since 'A Quiet Storm'. DN

SNAKEFINGER
Chewing Hides The Sound *(Ralph/Virgin)*
Residents accomplice covers Kraftwerk (!) and scales new heights of enjoyable absurdity. Love it. What else can I say? MJ

SNIFF 'N' THE TEARS
The Game's Up *(Atlantic/Chiswick)*
Now that Dire Straits are slowing down in the home straight, could a band like Sniff 'n' the Tears take up the mantle? Lead singer (and cover illustrator Paul Roberts) has a very distinctive, plaintive voice and crafty easy-listening, strong melodies. Lacks the winner punch but will do better in the USA than in England. AB-F

THE SOFT BOYS
Underwater Moonlight *(Armageddon)*
Interesting sixties rock for the eighties. MJ

SORROWS
Teenage Heartbreak *(Pavillion/CBS)*
The Sorrows evolved from an earlier New York Merseybeat revival band called the Popes. This album is clean, slick, bland, and predictable. DN

J.D. SOUTHER
You're Only Lonely *(Columbia/CBS)*
Second solo outing by Ronstadt cohort since the break-up of the much vaunted Souther-Hillman-Furay Band. The usual galaxy of mellow, laid back, snoozing West Coast mafia session players and dull, though always melodic songs about love, broken hearts, love, love and love. AB-F

SOUTHSIDE JOHNNY AND THE ASBURY JUKES
The Jukes *(Mercury)*
Big brass white-eyed rhythm and blues from sterling exponents of the genre. Lacks drive and good songs this time around with Springsteen sidekick Miami Steve no longer at the producing helm or contributing material. Disappointing. MJ

SPARKS
Terminal Jive *(Virgin)*
Produced by Giorgio Moroder, this is almost the perfect disco album. Cartoon pop with the tap your feet dance beat. Even if it goes in one ear and out of the other, you can't fail to enjoy it. A commercial flop of some note, it also highlights the Mael Brothers' dilemma of now being 'Rock 'n' Roll people in a disco world'. Tasty. MJ

BILLIE JOE SPEARS
Standing Tall *(Liberty-United)*
Easy-listening country tales of woe. AB-F

THE SPECIALS
The Specials *(Chrysalis/Two Tone)*
The triumph of Two Tone (see Groups of the Year). Ska reigns supreme. AB-F

SPHERICAL OBJECTS
Elliptical Optimism *(Object Music)*
Garage psychedelia from Manchester. Caught in the time-warp with that experimental blues again.. MJ

SPIDER
Spider *(Dreamland)*
Mike Chapman's label early offering: teen rock and tacky at that. AB-F

SPLIT ENZ
True Colours *(A&M)*
Antipodean band now go for straight approach, having ditched earlier staged craziness. A vast improvement. Snappy, modern pop. AB-F

THE SPORTS
Don't Throw Stones *(Arista/Sire)*
The Sports ask the age-old musical question 'Who Listens To The Radio?' Not I, as long as they play dull stuff like this. DN

SPYROGYRA
Spyrogyra *(Infinity)*
Gossamer-light fusion jazz for sunny days. AB-F

SPYROGYRA
Catching The Sun *(MCA)*
The fast run of success that Spyrogyra have enjoyed, explained as usual by the quip of giving the public what they want, leaves the blame as much with Western society today as it does with Spyro yesterday or tomorrow. Despite the monkey dancing of Geraldo Velez, onstage they've remained miraculously solemn and monstrously dull for too long. On record, begrudgingly you must admit there's an odd bit of magic there. Prime among these is Jay Beckenstein's startling, changeling alto cutting apart the title track where the bubble-packed monosodium glutemate rhythm doens't matter no more. There's also a good-bad-but-not-evil joke in the form of 'Laser Material', put together like a cheesecake version of the Brothers Johnson's 'Blam'. Guest trumpeter Randy Brecker gets a goodish look in here, and the marimba of David Samuels always comes in as a welcome light.

To date, Spyrogyra have been a tight, tidy light entertainment module just west of disco and south of AOR, here on 'Catching the Sun', the anomalies suggest they may be either stretching out or falling apart: no real clues either way. Better grit next time. LE

SQUEEZE
Argybargy *(A&M)*
Squeeze's supreme effort on record remains their first, John Cale produced album. Since then they've become much lighter textured (and more successful commercially) although the band still rocks out live. Madcap keyboardist Jools Holland's influence on the group's sound has steadily decreased, to their detriment. DN

BILLY SQUIER
The Tale of the Tape *(Capitol)*
Hard rock from US newcomer with teeny bopper appeal looks. Solid sound. MJ

STAPLES SINGERS
Brand New Day *(Stax)*
Mixed bag piece of catalogue exploitation. Surely, the artists don't approve. AB-F

STARSHOOTER
Chez les autres *(Pathe Marconi)*
French Rock is a problem; sometimes it's even an embarrassment. They have the writers, the film-makers, the pretty women and the intelligence, so why (Gainsbourg and the other assorted electronic wizards excepted) are their rock musicians so uninspiring? To be fair, Starshooter belong to the upper league of modern French groups, alongside the likes of Telephone, Shakin' Street, Trust, Edith Nylon and Marquis de Sade, the lyrics (in French) are reasonably witty and the musicianship is more than competent; so why oh why is it all so forgettable? Tasty cover package by Kiki Picasso, of the Bazooka art group, though. AB-F

STATUS QUO
Whatever You Want *(Vertigo)*
Head banging rock from the experts. MJ

STEPASIDE
Sit Down and Relapse *(Gale)*
Mainstream rock Irish band with lack of identity. AB-F

JOHN STEWART
Dream Babies Go Hollywood *(RSO)*
The deep-toned American troubadour, after almost two decades of trying via the Kingston Trio and then a long line of critically-acclaimed nowhere-bound solo albums, finally made it in America in 1979 via the top 5 single 'Gold' and its parent album 'Bombs Away Dream Babies'. This follow-up album as the title suggests, is very much a part two of the previous package, a collection of robust ballads and dramatic uptempo numbers with Stewart's vocals counterpointed by a superstar choir and quite the smoothest, richest production job he has ever had (he did it himself). Some of us may pine for the earthier days of 'The Lonesome Picker Rides Again' etc., but nobody would surely begrudge the man his hard-won commercial success. BL

THE ROY SUNDHOLM BAND

ROD STEWART
Greatest Hits *(Warner Brothers/Riva)*
How can you review Rod Stewart without reviewing his lifestyle? You can call him the best rock singer extant. You can be informative and note that 'D'Ya Think I'm Sexy' (included herein) has now outsold 'Maggie May'. You can quibble with success and say that Rod's work on 'Footloose and Fancy Free' and 'Blondes Have More Fun" is decidedly inferior to 'Atlantic Crossing' and 'A Night On The Town'. You can nod towards Tom Dowd who revitalized Rod's sagging solo fortunes by producing those four albums, anthologized here. Then you return to lifestyle — Britt, Alana, even Bebe— and the stiff little rooster of Holmby Hills will dance away, limper than before, but no doubt still proud. D'ya think he's happy? Does he still have what it takes? Does it take more than that wonderful voice? As long as you've got the tools, you can build something. Even if they're not "Greatest" hits. MG

STIFF LITTLE FINGERS
Nobody's Heroes *(Chrysalis)*
In the transition from independent label to major, Stiff Little Fingers have lost none of their fire and aggression. The more respectable side of the drawn-out aftermath of punk. Watch out for singer and guitarist Jake Burns. MJ

ROB STONER
Patriotic Duty *(MCA)*
Dylan sideman and mainstay of the lamented and much underrated Alpha Band goes solo and comes up with a surprisingly strong album of modern rockabilly. Will delight both the purists and many bystanders. MJ

STREETBAND
Dilemma *(Logo)*
Paul Young leads polished pop band better known for their quirky but amusing novelty hit 'Toast'. AB-F

BARBRA STREISAND
Wet *(Columbia/CBS)*
A concept album of sorts that sounds like it was left in the hot tub too long. Enough money was spent on the duet single with Donna Summer 'No More Tears (Enough Is Enough)' to run five independent labels for a year. DN

STYX
Cornerstone *(A&M)*
The worst kind of corporate progressive rock, and understandably very commercially successful. DN

SUGARHILL GANG
Sugarhill Gang *(Sugarhill)*
Includes a 15 minute version of 'Rapper's Delight'. AB-F

SUICIDE
Alan Vega/Martin Rev *(Ze)*
Produced by Rick Ocasek of Cars, Suicide now almost sounds commercial and far from the deliberately arty excesses of their stark first album. Electronic experimentation often verging on the repetitive but always compulsive listening. Takes a time to get into but handsomely repays the necessary effort. MJ

SUICIDE ROMEO
Pictures *(Ze)*
Not one of Ze's strongest offerings, this French band is never unpleasant but always strictly derivative. MJ

DONNA SUMMER
On The Radio *(Casablanca)*
A greatest hits collection in which Miss Summer proves that for the chosen few there is life after disco. One hopes so, simply because a voice of Summer's quality should not be lost with the passing of a trend. Contained herein are all the songs you ever thought might make disco palatable, themselves forming a sort of mini-history of the rise and fall of the genre. 'Love to Love You Baby' is the 16-minute-long orgasm that first catapulted Summer to fame. But it's the later material — 'Last Dance', 'Bad Girls' and the terrific 'On The Radio' that show off Miss Summer's singing to the fullest and lead you to believe that after producer Peter Bellotte and his Munich Machine are long gone, Donna will still be around and making music. Two discs, including a ludicrous poster. *The* Donna Summer LP for disco-haters. MG

SUMNER
Sumner *(Asylum)*
A criminally overlooked album by a new group who seem to have had no publicity whatsoever. Great voice and songs, viola from Novi (of Chunky, Ernie and...). Maybe good melodies are no longer in fashion. The sort of record I'd pawn the whole history of punk for. Rush out and get yourself a copy. Fast, even though stocks are probably massively high... AB-F

ROY SUNDHOLM
The Chinese Method *(Polydor/Ensign)*
And unknown performers keep on coming and coming. Yet another first-rate debut from unexpected quarters. British singer Roy Sundholm has the right knack for winning melodies and his album is chock-a-block with strong, quirky songs. Where next? MJ

SURVIVOR
Survivor *(Scotti Brothers)*
Dead on arrival. DN

SWEET
Waters Edge *(Polydor)*
Old popsters never grow old, they just improve with age. Just like the Searchers,

Sweet are now putting out interesting and thoughtful pop music. Swallow your prejudices. AB-F

RACHEL SWEET
Protect The Innocent *(Stiff)*
Maybe I'm debauched, but I'd much rather watch Rachel Sweet and Cherie Currie in a nude wrestling match than listen to either of them sing. DN

SWITCH
Reaching For Tomorrow *(Motown)*
Varied melodies and multi-instrumental work-out by new, promising Motown signing, produced by Jermaine and Hazel Jackson. Detroit's next generation hit machine? MJ

SYLVAIN SYLVAIN
Sylvain Sylvain *(RCA)*
Rock'n'roll has returned to the streets of the city. Sylvain Sylvain, the curly-topped kid with the French movie star name who used to provide the doo-wah touches for the New York Dolls, has pushed on in his first solo album to write and play pure post-New Wave rock'n'roll. It seems that everybody who's trying to get-back-and-go-beyond has his own understanding of rock'n'roll. Sylvain Sylvain's rock'n'roll is not freaky, not good-timey, not angry. No, his is the rock'n'roll of loneliness, pimples and teenage alienation. Pure New York City. Its true spirit comes out in '14th Street Beat' with its subway noises and in the one instrumental number, 'Tonight', which is rooftop jazz. There are nine original cuts and one adaptation — a radically rewritten version of Clarence 'Frogman' Henry's 'Ain't Got No Home'. My only objection to this record is the 15 minute sides. Otherwise, I'm very impressed. If you want to hear contemporary New York rock'n'roll, try this record. AP

SYLVESTER
Living Proof *(Fantasy)*
Double offering in the USA and single album in the UK. Mixes live and studio material. Quality soul; a fact often forgotten because of the strong visual elements in Sylvester's act and personality. Make up your own mind. AB-F

SYREETA
For Love *(Motown)*
Ex Wonder-woman (sorry, couldn't help that one...) makes good with tasty selection of moving tunes, including several duets with Billy Preston. AB-F

3-D
3-D *(Polydor)*
Yet another band with no personality, just influences. Produced by Ken Scott (Bowie, Devo) which can't have helped. MJ

10CC
Greatest Hits *(Polydor)*
Not quite the 'best' of 10CC since many of their (early) B-sides and album tracks were just as strong and well-crafted as the hits, but a decent compact collection spanning the range from 'Donna' (1972) and 'Rubber Bullets' (1973) to 'Good Morning Judge' (1977) and 'Dreadlock Holiday'(1978). Some of the purest, most exhilarating pop music ever. DN

10CC
Look Hear? *(Polydor/Mercury)*
Stewart and Gouldman behave in a democratic manner and delegate part of the songwriting to their lesser cohorts. Unfortunately, as we all know, democracy never really works, whether in music or elsewhere, and the result is an uninspired 10CC album. No obvious hit songs and a slight sense of weary déja-vu dominates the proceedings. All rather pretty though. AB-F

20/20
20/20 *(Epic/Portrait)*
Almost perfect American rock with a veneer of electronics. Rounded songs and melodies impeccably sung and produced (by Earle Mankey). Made little impact; not to worry, 20/20 will breakthrough in a big way, sooner or later. AB-F

JUNE TABOR & MARTIN SIMPSON
A Cut Above *(Topic)*
Folk's femme fatale joins youthful guitar wizard in a brave experiment combining traditional songs with futuristic arrangements. Heavy going at times and some of the ideas are desperately misguided (there's a six-minute French song 'Le Roi Renaud') but at a time of fear about musical development with folk music, it must be enthusiastically applauded. June sings starkly but atmospherically, and ex-Soft Machine violinist Ric Sanders weighs in with some marvellously evocative and haunting playing. CI

TALKING HEADS

TALKING HEADS
Fear of Music *(Sire)*
Voted by several of the British music papers as the album of 1979, 'Fear of Music' proves that intelligent music can still find its way to the right public. Produced by Eno, Talking Head's third album is the epitome of art rock at its best. David Byrne's high-pitched manic voice and obsessions battle it out with one of the most solid rhythm sections in the business. Don't read this, listen to the album instead. Sometimes, words are insufficient. AB-F

TANGERINE DREAM
Tangram *(Virgin)*
More of the usual electronic-symphonic-astral doodles from the mob from Berlin. Soothing but unadventurous music by a group in need of new inspiration. The cover by Monique Froese is a mess. MJ

TANGERINE DREAM

TANTRUM
Rather Be Rockin' *(Ovation)*
Interesting Chicago band with three female vocalists. Very FM, very poised and tasty. More, please. MJ

THE TAPES
Party *(Passport)*
Talking Head clones, already! AB-F

BERNIE TAUPIN
He Who Rides The Tiger *(Asylum)*
He who writes the words for Elton John and Alice Cooper makes a few almost convincing rock'n'roll moves on 'Blitz Baby' and 'Monkey On My Back (The Last Run)' but continues to mix overblown metaphors with occasional acute observations. The music (by ex-Buckingham's lead singer Dennis Tufano) is nowhere near as well-crafted as the classic Taupin-John collaborations. DN

CECIL TAYLOR
Live in the Black Forest *(MPS)*
Few can have ignored Cecil Taylor. Even now, hollowed out by hindsight and softened by new waves, Taylor remains one of the, variously, most hallowed and most vilified of all creative musicians. Certainly he's one of the most assertively articulate.

Of a somewhat patchy recording run in recent years, 'Black Forest' has to date been generally reckoned one of the pianist's finest dates. It's a sextet affair, but not to the exclusion of his quite different qualities as a solo artist. In a lone passage in 'The Eel Pot', his statements are more aerated, the notes more individual, and he toys with a half-raggy blues line before trotting away Bartokwards. In group context he's a far more driving, demanding figure, his famous cluster techniques running whole carpets under altoist Jimmy Lyons towards the opening of 'Sperichill on Calling'.

More prominent generally in the unit are drummer Ron Jackson, whose thrusting, wafting figures echo Taylor's moods, and violinist Ramsey Ameen, a voluble and percussive player who achieves honourable failure status in his duet later on 'Sperichill'. The roll-call winds up with trumpeter Raphe Malik and bass player Sirone. Not without its struggles or mishaps, 'Black Forest' is a fun album, and Cecil Taylor's playing still ranks among the great independents. LE

THE TAZMANIAN DEVILS
The Tazmanian Devils
(Warners)
No, not Australian rockers as one might suspect from the band's moniker, but pure American corn rock. Perversely enjoyable. AB-F

BRAM TCHAIKOVSKY
Pressure *(Polydor)*
The Russians Are Coming
(Radar)
Separate titles for separate countries. The USA is somewhat sensitive to mentions of Russkies? but they do exist, you know... Quality rock from experienced band. Could make it big. MJ

THE TEARDROPS
Final Vinyl *(Illuminated)*
Enterprising new Manchester band featuring ex-Buzzcock Steve Garvey. Worth looking out for, as its small label might militate against easy access. AB-F

RICHARD TEE
Natural Ingredients
(Columbia/CBS)
Well-known funker with second album. Plays it safe with a whole galaxy of prime-time session fellow funkers: Steve Gadd, Tom Scott, Ralph McDonald, Randy Brecker et al. MJ

TELEX
Neurovision *(Sire)*
European synthesizer band still living off their early one-off single 'St Tropez'. Dispensable. AB-F

TEMPTATIONS
Power *(Motown)*
The Temptations return to Motown after four years in the corporate wilderness. A celebratory album that shows how good Motown can sound when it is really good. MJ

TERRY AND THE PIRATES
Too Close For Comfort *(Wild Bunch)*
Legendary San Francisco bar band at last recorded for posterity by curious Italian West-Coast biased label. Terry is Terry Dolan and His Pirates include Quicksilver Messenger Service alumni John Cipollina, Nicky Hopkins and others. Nothing earth shattering here, but a lot to enjoy at leisure. Just another good time band. AB-F

MARTY THAU
Presents 2x5 *(Criminal)*
Compilation of recent 'new wave' New York bands produced by Jimmy Destri, on a sabbatical from Blondie. The general standard is high but as with so many compilations, none of the bands are really given enough of a chance to display their individuality (despite being allocated two tracks each). So, a deferred judgement for Fleshtones, Student Teachers (both slightly ahead of the pack) and Bloodless Pharoahs, Revelons and Comateens. AB-F

BARBARA THOMPSON'S PARAPHERNALIA
Wilde Tales *(MCA)*
Two specials for Barbara Thompson: she's among the very few British jazz players to be signed to (and promoted by) a major label, and she's among the few women instrumentalists to be successful (successfully sanctioned, at least) in this business. The front row is usually awash with ogling youth.

In 'Wilde Tales', studio work for the first time achieves some of the zest and verve of a live date - and that's a direct result of the narrative form of the Oscar Wilde story 'The Selfish Giant' which occupies the first side. With Jon Hiseman exquisitely sketching in the main figures, there's a welter of standard goodies like time-switches and harmonic warmth, and a few extras like pure fun. It also offers a base for Colin Dudman's conspicuously liberated keyboards and Dill Katz' similarly inclined fretless bass. Thompson herself, often reserved yet always exact, here comes across as that vital jot more physical and tacky, notably on tenor. After such momentum, the four conversational tracks with the exception of 'Late Again', back off gloomily towards the realms of stylised overfabrication.

Still, that's a powerful album that cuts a swathe right through the selfsame domestic/modern jazz field wherein Paraphernalia was first seeded. LE

RICHARD & LINDA THOMPSON
Sunnyvista *(Chrysalis)*
Title track uses clumsy holiday camp imagery, which is also reflected in the appalling sleeve design, and the album never really lives it down. Thompson's songs are less stinging than his devotees have come to expect, though Linda turns in an epic vocal display, and the barbed 'Sisters' must rank amongst their best work. Elsewhere they just don't sound as if they mean it, and drift into pleasant anonymity. CI

THROBBING GRISTLE
20 Jazz Funk Greats
(Industrial)
Parodic title conceals sonic landscape of urban bleakness. Experimental electronics at its most severe. Uneasy access. AB-F

THROBBING GRISTLE
Heathen Hearth *(Industrial)*
Throbbing Gristle improvise live. Much the same as their studio efforts. Difficult to take in one go. AB-F

BOBBY THURSTON
You Got What It Takes
(Prelude/Epic)
Consummate soul pop. MJ

STEVE TIBBETTS
Yr *(Frammis)*
Guitarist at ease in all genres: acoustic, electric, percussive. Interesting home-made recording. AB-F

TONIO K.
Amerika *(Arista)*
Crazy man plays crazy music with all his heart. AB-F

TOTO
Hydra *(Columbia/CBS)*
Faceless corporate rock by musicians who appear on at least half the records made in LA today. 'All Us Boys' at least generates a vicarious excitement but the rest of this album proves that you can count money and play at the same time. DN

TOUCH
Touch *(Atco/Ariola)*
New hard rocking band who look and sound exactly the same as last week's new hard rocking band. AB-F

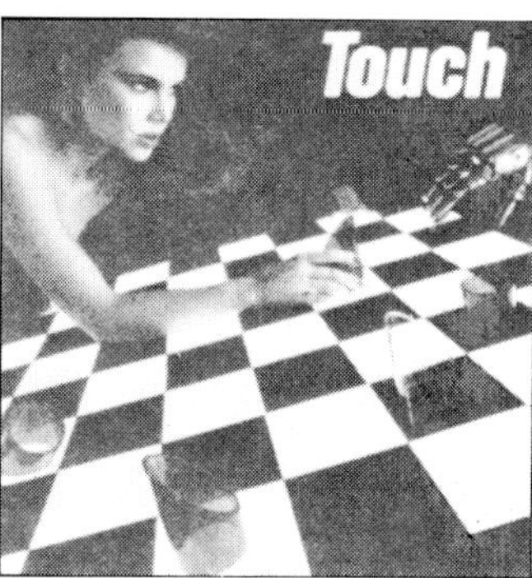

TOUCH
Touch *(Atlantic)*
Vocal quartet striving for first division harmonics. There's only one problem, they have no music to speak of, to harmonize with. MJ

THE TOURISTS
Reality Effect *(Epic/Logo)*
Power pop in the 1967 mode. Lotsa hits. Lotsa fun. Lotsa emptiness. MJ

JOHN TOWNLEY
Townley *(Capitol)*
Zzzzzzzzzzzz. DN

PETE TOWNSHEND
Empty Glass *(Atlantic)*
Thoughtfully considered and crafted first genuine solo attempt by the Who's

intellectual fuhrer. Strong, often pointed, songs, which all benefit greatly by being performed by other musicians than the Who, therefore avoiding predictable musical cliches. Often a heartfelt cry for the heart, this is Townshend at his most aggressively articulate and challenging. Great rock but also great intelligence at play here. Sometimes, I think Townshend is too good for his audience who will only see hard driving, stomping, frenetic rock songs here without delving one step beyond. Worthy beyond all expectations. Great guitar work (and cover) of course. AB-F

TOY
Bad Night *(Logo)*
Belgian Rock with English lyrics. MJ

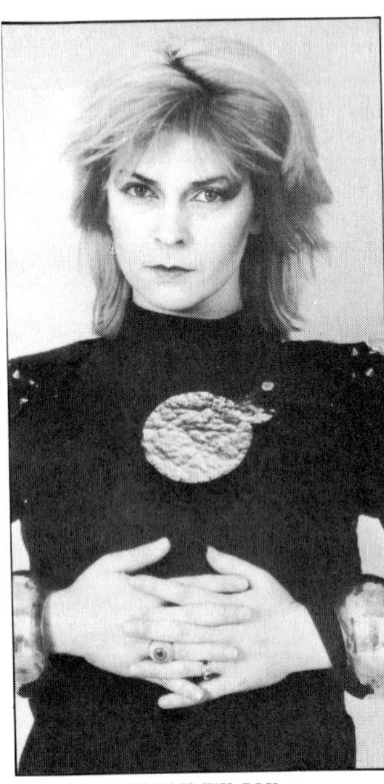

TOYAH WILCOX

TOYAH
Sheep Farming In Barnet
(Safari)
This album, predating by a couple of months the first official Toyah album release 'The Blue Meaning', was actually a German-originated compilation which Safari made available over her to capitalise upon the sales of a 'Bird In Flight' single and the six-track 'Sheep Farming in Barnet' AP (meaning 'alternative play' - halfway 'twixt a single and an album). As such it's sort of potted history-of-Toyah-so-far, and thus a good purchase for those who only caught up on the intense style of new-wave theatre purveyed by Ms Wilcox and cohorts via their memorable showcasing within an episode of the 'Shoestring' TV series. Most of the 'Sheep Farming' AP came from that show, and it's all usefully reprised here, together with the strong ex-single cut 'Victim Of The Riddle'. BL

TOYAH
The Blue Meaning *(Safari)*
Histrionic vignettes by singing actress, full of her own self-importance. Strong cult appeal in England but won't cross the waters. MJ

THE TRAMPS
Mixin' It Up *(Atlantic)*
Rock'n'roll and disco are here to stay, let's mix it up, let's put it together, sings black vocal group. Hmmm... AB-F

PAT TRAVERS BAND
Crash and Burn *(Polydor)*
Hairy-chested rock in all its menacing awesomeness. MJ

TRIUMPH
Progressions Of Power *(RCA)*
Progression? Not on your life, bah, just that good old heavy metal crash and thump. Not a lick of originality but fast and loud for sure. DN

TROOPER
Hot Shots *(MCA)*
Compilation of Trooper's (who?) biggest non-hits. AB-F

ROBIN TROWER
Victims of the Fury
(Chrysalis)
Fine professional effort by Dewar and Trower, but they don't seem to be capable of getting lift-off from their early '70s time-warp. AB-F

TANYA TUCKER
Tear Me Apart *(MCA)*
Tanya Tucker is everything Rachel Sweet tries to be but never will - a world class country singer who's a natural rock'n'roller. Mike Chapman's production casts Tanya as Blondie for rednecks. Let's bop, cats! DN

TOMMY TUTONE
Tommy Tutone
(Columbia/CBS)
Neither Cars-style electro-pop or skabeat, so don't be fooled by the packaging. Another mainstream power pop model. DN

TUXEDO MOON
Halfmute *(Ralph)*
Masterful blend of all the disparate poles of electronic music: Eno, Kraftwerk, label-fellowmen The Residents. Digital rock is here at last. AB-F

McCOY TYNER
Passion Dance *(Milestone)*
By some almost supernatural feat of physics and chemistry, McCoy Tyner's recordings (if not always his live work) have an unrelenting identity and cohesion that never palls - and has never invited imitators. More exotic and sumptuous surroundings like 'Fly With the Wind', and the tempered public setting of the Milestone Jazzstars, have only led back to the realisation of what a highly sumptuous yet private stylist he is in himself.

Two tracks on 'Passion Dance' - as so often, a live date - are in the company of Ron Carter and Tony Williams, whose own rich restraint adds no more than a little protective wrapping. The remaining three are solo lights. As ever, the warhorse left hand and glistening, scree-running right are no mere stylish diversions but agents of (let's admit it) the pianist's roving, epic and untrussed vision. But his steering through the connived dissonances of Coltrane's 'Moment's Notice', or his knowing celebrations on the title track are also heirs to the cloudy, probing moods of albums like 'Trident'.

The format is unlikely to change; but for McCoy Tyner, the story is sure to continue - hopefully with the same grace and purpose as in this chapter. LE

JUDIE TZUKE
Racing Car *(Rocket)*
British songbird's second album after a surprising UK single chart success was taken off her first effort. An idiosyncratic, lilting strong voice blends well with tasteful material, hopeless lyrics and a decided knack for catchy melodies full of unexpected quirks. Judie Tzuke visibly enjoys a challenge and succeeds here by putting a harder bite into her music than we earlier suspected from her fey appearance and prominent front teeth. Commendable and half-way there. Where? Well, that might be Judie Tzuke's next problem: to map out a specific direction for her undeniable assets. AB-F

UFO
No Place to Run *(Chrysalis)*
Heavy metal produced by George Martin. Surely a touch of class. Raunchy, mean and hard-hitting no mercy rock. AB-F

UK
Night After Night *(Polydor)*
Rigorous jazz/rock fusion minor improvisations. MJ

UK SUBS
Brand New Age *(Gem)*
Prehistoric punk, 1978 variety. Mindless. AB-F

ULTRAVOX
Three Into One *(Island)*
Compilation best of three albums released by Island now that band have resurfaced elsewhere. Ultravox were always an underrated group when featuring John Foxx and this album shows why. However the compilation is somewhat lopsided and the order of the tracks could have been better arranged. AB-F

ULTRAVOX
Vienna *(Chrysalis)*
Old glitter-synthesizer rockers gain new lease of life with addition of man of all rock seasons Midge Ure. Surprisingly catchy and good with sterling 'Sleepwalk' hit single scoring. Connie Plank produced this LP—should establish them right at the top of the hill, where they should have been long since the Foxx days. First-class album which keeps on improving aurally on every play. Still full of unsuspecting treasures, I suspect (and look forward to). MJ

THE UNDERTONES
The Undertones *(Sire)*
Ambitious Irish group try to break away from the main body of punk and make some progress towards individuality. Idiosyncratic subject matter and good songs support rasping voice of singer Feargal Sharkey. AB-F

THE UNDERTONES
Hypnotised *(Sire)*
A massive step forward for this Irish band. Strongly articulate and witty songs about Ireland, growing up and Britain's social system wrapped around perfect three-minute tunes that would have done the Beatles pride. Puts the Undertones into the First Division. AB-F

URBAN VERBS
Urban Verbs *(Warners)*
Vigorous debut by new art rock US band featuring brother of Talking Head Chris Frantz, Roddy. Urban subject matter with calculated injection of drama and dynamics. A good buy. MJ

URIAH HEEP
Conquest *(Bronze)*
Uriah Heep soldier on down the mean road that is rock'n'roll. This time around they blood their new vocalist John Sloman and drummer Chris Slade (ex Manfred Mann!). The same as before. The same as the next one. AB-F

U ROY AND DENNIS ALCAPONE
Version Galore Vol 2 *(Trojan)*
One of a rash of reissues from Trojan, with the original cover (girl wearing Marks and Sparks knickers - it makes a change from the sham primitivism which afflicts most reggae sleeves). The seventeen albums reissued simultaneously made a pretty random ragbag, but that's because Trojan only put out those albums for which they still had sleeves. This one was definitely worth the effort: U Roy's old work (the material here dates from 1970/71) is generally well-known, but most of these tracks are less than familiar, and include one of the very few records he produced himself, 'Love I Bring'. ('Musical Pleasure', credited to U Roy, is actually U Roy's first recording). It's Dennis Alcapone who emerges as the star though; Alcapone was U Roy's main rival in the early days of toasting, but is pretty much a forgotten man now. His selection here shows how enthusiastic he was, with his glide into falsetto and his babbling nonsense: 'Now come in to my musical school, where I teach you to use your tool, now don't be late, come on in and be my musical classmate'. You'll notice the absence of politico-philosophical sermons: the early toasters fed directly off the backing track, and didn't bother with serious talk of the sort Big Youth and U Roy later indulged in. Their approach isn't necessarily superior, but when rasta jargon has drained reggae of just about all of its lyrical vitality, it's at least fun to listen to this gibberish. NK

UTOPIA
Adventures In Utopia *(Bearsville)*
The Todd Rundgren album for the non-fanatic fan. His last several albums have been maddening. At last Utopia achieves that kinetic hook-laden pop sound that made 'Something/Anything' such a joy. DN

ULTRAVOX

DAVE VALENTIN
The Hawk *(GRP)*
To date, flautist Valentin hasn't been hyperactive in public: beyond working as a house musician for GRP, most of his recordings have been with close outsiders like Lee Ritenour. Notwithstanding, 'Legends' his debut under his own name, created a fair stir and gleaned appropriate downbeat honours.

Valentin is a remarkably mature and commanding player, closer to Jeremy Steig in both toughness and curiosity, than to many mentors of the idiom like Herbie Mann. His basic agility is developed into long, strong exciting workouts, witness the old McCartney/Lennon 'Blackbird'. He swims and swings with credit out of Steely Dan's 'Do It Again' an otherwise burdensome treatment where the well-worn funk whimper of Marcus Miller's bass seems quite misplaced.

Latin trappings flurry in very naturally on occasion, while the self-penned title track, a knowingly cheerful demonstration model built on a fluxing brass line uses a striking oriental-type theme, with again mucho solo space for both flute and piano. Can't resist the platitude that the eighties should see a lot more of this guy. LE

VAN HALEN
Women & Children First *(Warner Brothers)*
More brain bending heavy metal thunder from the band that was almost singlehanded responsible or launching the rebirth of heavy metal in the late 70s.

RANDY VANWARMER
Terraform *(Bearsville)*
Wimp rock strikes again. AB-F

RANDY VANWARMER
Warmer *(Bearsville)*
Wimp rock par excellence. AB-F

THE VAPOURS

VAPORS
New Clear Days *(UA)*
One hit wonders with 'Turning Japanese' try to repeat the formula. No go. AB-F

VARIOUS
American Gigolo *(Polydor)*
Sterling soundtrack for the Paul Schrader film featuring Blondie's infectious Moroder-produced 'Call Me'. The album has the usual number of soundtrack album fillers but also has many good moments. MJ

VARIOUS
Apocalypse Now *(Warners)*
Not just The Doors, Wagner and Flash Cadillac but also dialogue from the film. A genuine soundtrack of a rather impressive film. AB-F

VARIOUS
Avon Calling *(Heartbeat)*
New wave punk regional compilation from Bristol area of all places. AB-F

VARIOUS
The Bitch *(Warwick)*
Disco film soundtrack featuring the likes of Gloria Gaynor, Three Degrees, Real Thing, Blondie, etc... AB-F

VARIOUS
Bowling Balls from Hell *(Clone)*
Despite the redundant title, rewarding compilation of new wave bands from Ohio. Some will break through; listen to them here first. AB-F

VARIOUS (& HAZEL O'CONNOR)
Breaking Glass *(A&M)*
Much-hyped rock film soundtrack. Redundant and dishonest music. MJ

VARIOUS
Bronco Billy *(Elektra)*
Country and western workmanlike soundtrack for amiable Clint Eastwood film. MJ

VARIOUS
Can't Stop The Music *(Mercury)*
Film soundtrack. On the screen, it's downright embarrassing to watch; on vinyl, you can listen to it without harming your grey cells. Disco to dance to if your feet are really itching. Courtesy of Village People, Ritchie Family and other non-entities. AB-F

THE RITCHIE FAMILY

VARIOUS
Catch This Beat *(Island)*
The Rock Steady years 1966-1968 is the subtitle, proving that the grandparents of ska were active a long time ago now. AB-F

VARIOUS
Cha Cha *(Ariola)*
Soundtrack for rock film not seen in UK or US, featuring Herman Brood, Lene Lovich, Nina Hagen and various dutch groups. MJ

VARIOUS
Cruising *(Lorimar)*
Excellent soundtrack for very dubious film. Mink de Ville in top street chic gear, John Hiatt, the Germs and the Cripples all offer hard-bitten rock to while the heavy night away. AB-F

VARIOUS
Fame *(RSO)*
Soundtrack of the film. Mild middle of the road fare which wouldn't mind passing itself off as rock. But we're not fooled, are we? AB-F

VARIOUS
First Offenders *(Criminal)*
Patchy compilation of new wave bands from Canterbury. None seem to spin sufficiently tall musical tales at first hearing. AB-F

VARIOUS
Front Line 3 *(Virgin)*
Reggae Sampler. MJ

SID VICIOUS

VARIOUS
The Great Rock'n'Roll Swindle *(Virgin)*
Now that the film has finally seen the light of day, the soundtrack makes another appearance in the shops, but, this time around, as a single album. Features the Sex Pistols, of course, but also the loony Tenpole Tudor and others. Makes so much more sense now one has seen the film. MJ

VARIOUS
Hicks From The Sticks *(Rockburgh)*
Compilation (by Des Moines) of unknown bands whose main virtue seems to be to reside in Yorkshire. Some are good, some are bad and some are unmentionable. The law of averages, in fact. Noteworthy is Wah! Heat's early vinyl appearance here. AB-F

VARIOUS
Hybrid Kids *(Cherry Red)*
For various, read Morgan Fisher, who also produced. The oddity of the year. Subtitled 'A collection of classic mutants', this consists of hilarious and apposite renderings of well known pieces by apocryphal bands. A laugh a track. No good record collection should be without it; it puts the fun back into rock'n'roll at a time when too many people are taking things too seriously. MJ

VARIOUS
The Immediate Story *(Virgin)*
Seventeen assorted, well-annotated museum pieces for £3.99. Where else would Rod Stewart and Fleetwood Mac rub shoulders with Nico and Sam Cooke? Interesting. PF

ALEX LIFESON/RUSH

VARIOUS
Killer Watts *(Epic)*
Compilation of Yank heavy metal wall of sound destructo rockers (and the odd Pommie): Nugent, Molly Hatchet, Blue Oyster Cult, Aerosmith, Mahogany Rush...What's the word? Oh yes, subtlety... AB-F

VARIOUS
Logical Steps *(Future Earth)*
Doncaster compilation. And they keep on coming. AB-F

VARIOUS
The London R & B Sessions *(Albion)*
Live at the London Hope and Anchor a number of bands and worthy performers do their thing for the Rhythm and Blues revival. Features the Blues Band, Lew Lewis and the Pirates. Derivative but enjoyable. MJ

VARIOUS
Metal for Muthas *(EMI)*
Heavy metal manifesto. Earplugs recommended. MJ

VARIOUS
Metal for Muthas Vol 11 *(EMI)*
More macho music men on the ladder to Valhalla. AB-F

VARIOUS
More American Graffitti *(MCA)*
More jolly songs from the vaults of the revered rocking past on this film sountrack. Not as good as the first time around. MJ

VARIOUS
No Nukes *(Asylum)*
A lavishly packaged double set full of more bullshit and jive than a nuclear industry press kit. About a side and a half out of the four are worth hearing. The performers who rise above their surroundings are Bonnie Raitt (always wonderful), The Doobie Brothers (strong, but predictable), Jackson Browne (his duet with Springsteen on 'Stay'), Bruce hisself and Tom Petty (whose 'Cry To Me' is the best cut on the album). Though not exactly Luddites these musicians still get pretty strident. Yet this record won't change anyone's mind about nuclear energy. In fact, these Pied Pipers of modernity are only barely entertaining. It's all so smug and serious - except for that ludicrous word 'nukes' that sounds like toys, and small cars from Italy, or a new candy. They make it sound cute - not dangerous. Don't buy this album out of liberal guilt. Instead spend the money on a couple of books about nuclear power. You'll feel better instead of cheated, and you may learn enough to make up your own mind. Those who preach to the already converted don't make good records. MG

VARIOUS
Precious Metal *(MCA)*
Not quite the usual heavy metal compilation, this MCA anthology deftly combines acknowledged classics such as Steppenwolf's 'Born to be Wild', big names past and present like Lynyrd Skynyrd, Wishbone Ash, Gillan and Budgie with newcomer outfits like The Tygers of Pantang. Imaginative programing. MJ

VARIOUS
Roadie *(Warners)*
Varied film soundtrack with a curious Blondie treatment of 'Ring of Fire', Alice Cooper, Pat Benatar, Sue Saad, Jerry Lee Lewis, Hank Williams Jnr, Cheap Trick, Joe Ely, Asleep at the Wheel, and many other different acts. Reasonably good tracks on the whole, but a bit short on length at 4 sides totalling under fifteen minutes on average each. AB-F

VARIOUS
Rock'n'Roll High School *(Sire)*
Ramones and other shriekers on soundtrack of iconoclastic film. MJ

VARIOUS
Rockabilly Vol.3 *(CBS)*
The past few years, rockabilly compilation albums have been issued for all the major American labels of the fifties. By reaching down into its subsidiary labels, Epic and Okeh, this Columbia volume maintains the high standard of what has easily been the most distinguished series of these reissue records. This one may even be the best of the lot. As in the first two volumes, Vol.3 is anchored by the solid work of the Collins Kids, Sid King and the Five Strings, and Ronnie Self, but truth to tell, there isn't a clinker among these twenty tracks. A wide spectrum of music is represented here. Retroactively, it seems, rockabilly is swallowing up all the different strains of music that went into its making. I particularly like 'That's All She Wrote' by the Skee Brothers and 'It's a Great Big Day' by Derrell Felts. And I outright love 'Boogie Blues' by Earl Peterson, 'Michigan's Singing Cowboy'. By my book, there's no way that this neo-Jimmie Rodgers tune can be called rockabilly, but I don't care. I just shut up and listen. Yum. AP

VARIOUS
Rockers *(Island)*
Film soundtrack with a hoard of highly-rated reggae artists. MJ

VARIOUS
The Shape of Finns To Come *(Cherry Red)*
Compilation of Finnish new wave. Could be any country's, in fact. Bland. AB-F

VARIOUS
Sharp Cuts *(Planet)*
Uneven compilation by all-new to vinyl bands. AB-F

VARIOUS
Southend Rock *(Sonet)*
Seaside resort which has already spawned many British R & B stalwarts goes in for the new talent compilation game. Kursaal Flyers and Mickey Jupp, both already established in a small way, are the only performers to convince. MJ

VARIOUS
Subterranean Modern *(Ralph)*
Zany Ralph compilation with all your loony favourites: Residents, MX80, Tuxedo Moon, Snakefinger. Bop that night away to the Martian beat. AB-F

VARIOUS
Xanadu *(MCA/Jet)*
And the Lord said: Let the Various encompass Olivia Newton-John, Electric Light Orchestra, Cliff Richard, Gene Kelly, the Tubes. Seven minutes into it (film? soundtrack? media event?) I fell asleep. Will go down a bomb in Kingston upon Thames and Schenectady. AB-F

OLIVIA NEWTON-JOHN

NANA VASCONCELOS
Saudades *(ECM)*
Although it's on ECM, it ain't really jazz. South American percussion fiesta; much more varied than can be expected. MJ

SARAH VAUGHAN
Duke Ellington Song Book, Vol.1 *(Pablo Today)*
Though Sarah Vaughan can be 'Sassy' and play straight into the Pimms Number Six glasses of clubland, that doesn't hide the fact that she remains both a great and original jazz singer, and a thoroughbred performer with the capacity to handle anything, anywhere.
Her most recent recording association, with Pablo, has produced results in line with her stature: the 'How Long...' album worked through a splendid choice of material, a skin-tight house quartet and a dimensional sense of time, space and drama to achieve monumental status.
'Ellington' pales -surprisingly so - by contrast. One problem is that not all Duke's material is mainline vocal fodder, and items like 'In A Mellow Tone' feel uneasy with the spotlight constantly on the mike. Similarly the big-band arrangements used for some tracks are arrogant and inflexible, quite un-Ellington. In these situations, as per 'In A Sentimental Mood', the singer's brassy command veers towards the maudlin and theatrical. Even the small-band settings drift towards the fussy and lacklustre side, and you hang on moments of release like the entry of burnished, lilting Zoot Sims in a wheedling 'All Too Soon'.
But these are relative criticisms. She's insurpassable. LE

TOM VERLAINE
Tom Verlaine *(Elektra)*
Solo outing following the demise of Television sounds just like what the third Television album would have sounded. Quicksilver quitar solos, painful voice and patchy would-be obscure lyrics. But when it's good, it's fantastic. Verlaine must surely be one of today's guitar heroes. If only he could find a group with a good singer. MJ

SID VICIOUS
Sid Sings *(Virgin)*
Sorry sweep-up by Virgin of bad quality tapes featuring the late punk. It sold; and that's no credit to the public either. Even the cover and packaging is in dubious taste. AB-F

VILLAGE PEOPLE
Live and Sleazy, Can't Stop The Music *(Casablanca)*
These guys have gotten more mileage out of one joke than anybody since George Burns. The 'Live' album is a surprisingly poor sound quality rehashing of such disco favourites as 'Macho Man, 'YMCA', 'In The Navy' and 'Fire Island'. For the 'Sleazy' studio album ex-lead singer/lyricist Victor Willis hands over the mike to his replacement Ray Simpson (brother of Valerie Simpson of Ashford & Simpson). Too bad they couldn't get Valerie to throw a few songs into the deal. They desperately need them as shown by their latest effort, the soundtrack album 'Can't Stop the Music', which reprises 'YMCA' yet again. Although the film devotes much footage to displaying arrogant male meat, the music is flabby, flaccid gristle. DN

VIOLINSKI
Stop Cloning About *(Jet)*
Silly title. Silly music which takes itself seriously. AB-F

ROGER VOUDOURIS
A Guy Like Me *(Warner Brothers)*
You and what army? DN

VOYAGER
Act of Love *(RCA/Mountain)*
Redundant Rock. MJ

LOUDON WAINWRIGHT 111
Alive One *(Radar)*
The king of folk/rock jokers caught on stage. Worth a chuckle or two. AB-F

NARADA MICHAEL WALDEN:
The Dance of Life *(Atlantic)*
Time was when Sri Chinmoy was outtastyle and 'The Garden of Lovelight', all red roses and yellow moonlight, aching love and mincing peace to all men, was something you wouldn't play frisbee with. Now, all that lovebiz is a harmless bygone, like authentic skinheads (UK readers only), and Narada and many more have turned it into the commercially fortuitous dance of life.
Walden is a drummer, pianist, singer, writer, and was a passerby for Mahavishnu, Jeff Beck's 'Wired', Tommy Bolin and Weather Report before going alone in '76. He still allows the message to transcend the medium. He's an excellent player to the rules of disco, viz 'I Shoulda Loved Ya' and 'Tonight I'm Alright', thrusting cooky rhythms and zippy takeaway decor on top. But, albeit remotely, he's still creating music for the head. It's annoying to find slower cuts like 'Carry On' simply downmoted versions of that formula and mundane by comparison. Old and new dreams finally fuse in the instrumental title cut, with Corrado Rustici handling the necessarily spectacular guitar part. Not a genius; often a wide boy. LE

PHILLIP WALKER
Someday You'll Have These Blues *(Alligator/Sonet)*
Twenty-five years of experience lie behind this remarkable album. Walker has worked and recorded with fellow Louisianan Clifton Chenier, with the R&B pioneer Rosco Gordon, and with countless other musicians all over the Southwest and the West

Coast. He's now one of the foremost Texas-style blues guitarists, a touch mellower than Albert Collins, and a gripping singer, reminiscent of Ray Charles at his peak, and almost equally versatile. The LP, first issued on JOLIET in 1977, mixes blues, soul numbers both classic and new, and gospel songs. Everything works; Walker is entirely convincing, and the mystery of his modest repute deepens. Buttressed alike by the blues tradition and the best qualities of soul music, Walker stands firm on a middle ground where neither is traduced. TR

STEVE WALSH
Schemer-Dreamer *(Kirshner)*
Kansas' lead singer's solo effort — about one sixth as listenable as any given Kansas album. DN

WAR
The Music Band 2 *(MCA)*
A lot less streetwise than they used to be and consequently a lot less fun. DN

GROVER WASHINGTON, JR
Skylarkin *(Motown)*
In the face of his publicised rift with the big blue M, Grover Washington arrived at 'Skylarkin' to honour his contractual obligations with Motown. The rub is that the Rosebud Studios whipround ends up as a superior being to the album made just a few months earlier for newie Elektra, 'Paradise'.

The problem is broadly this: a relatively inexperienced and reticent artist was offered a lucky break when the star (Hank Crawford) had gotten lost on the subway. Once right inside of the music machine, whatever self-confidence or vision our hero may have had, it was dragged from beneath his feet and some. On release, it's a long process of rehabilitation.

It would be wrong to demand too much grit or emotion in Washington's playing. His forte is clearly in his light, singing qualities. As a writer, he works lineally, towards "tunes". Put the two together, and rather than do honest battle with the dynamics of the band, too often he's shredding up and jettisoning a good melody by doing dirty battle with its volume: look at 'Open Your Mind'. But then look again at the open-textured section of 'Easy Loving You', the hip pulse of 'Snake Eyes' for where the paths of righteousness may lead. Look out also for exceptionally neat work from Richard Tee. LE

WEATHER REPORT
8.30 *(Columbia/CBS)*
Without a blue note of doubt, Weather Report are the ultimate in pop jazz rock: securing great intellectual minds amongst their following as well as punters hot from the Commodores/EW&F arena.

A live album, especially after so many studio deals, is always one way round the greatest hits stand, and so be it here, with inclusions like 'Black Market', 'Teen Town' and, natch, 'Birdland'. But no way is it a retrospective: one vivid message is that Report's music is an ongoing situation, and nothing stays sacred for too long. In fact, about half the tracks would be virtually unknown to the more casual client.

Technically its Zawinul's gig as much as anyone's. Frequently he provides both line artwork and infill colour: and at times, as with 'Brown Street' it's impossible to credit that the playing comes from one head at one time. A niggle remains in the shownanship — Pastorius and 'Slang' being but the most overt example — which as with the live act seems rather to outstay its welcome. But winner takes all, and in the fullness of time it's that extreme sense of life and aliveness — not really from the audience, not much from the sound quality, and mostly from the kick inside — that keeps this one a winner. LE

MARTI WEBB
Tell me on a Sunday *(Polydor)*
The undoubted middle of the road success of the year. Andrew Lloyd Webber supplies the music but, this time around with new lyricist Don Black the magic touch propels the relatively unknown Marti Webb to mega-buck stardom. A tale of witty woe of a young British lady and her sorry sentimental life Stateside, melodies and hooks galore. You'll hate the whole concept but find yourself singing the songs against your own will. Catching. Catchy. AB-F

PETA WEBB & ALISON MCMORLAND
Peta Webb & Alison McMorland *(Topic)*
Superficially a dour specialist album of unaccompanied female treatments of traditional folk ballads: but in reality a beautifully warm and varied selection. The harmonies are loose and spontaneous and Webb re-affirms herself as the finest female folk singer in the land (though few seem to know it!) After a while you don't even notice it's unaccompanied, and 'Jogging Up To Claudy' is a gem. CI

MAX WEBSTER
Magnetic Air *(Capitol)*
Canadian more-melodic-than-usual heavy metal. That touch of schizophrenia does help and make the package more aurally attractive. AB-F

WEE GEE
Hold on (To Your Dreams) *(Cotillion)*
No frills quality black soul. MJ

BOB WELCH
The Other One *(Capitol)*
MOR rock. The only reason for keeping any Bob Welch album is if you have a copy of the 'French Kiss' picture disc, one of the few picdiscs to retain any collector value due to limited circulation. DN

DAVID WERNER
David Werner *(Epic)*
Quiet, modern urban rock by an overlooked singer who's been around for some time now but has to achieve the critical recognition he deserves. Has taken a leaf from punk and new wave. AB-F

MIKE WESTBROOK
Mama Chicago *(RCA)*
After some while working on an almost private level with the cunningly-titled Brass Band, Mike Westbrook has been enjoying an explosion of popularity in the continent with some exciting projects to boot. So much so, that onstage 'Mama Chicago' can already feel a little outmoded.

An amalgamation of narrative, fantasy, public power and private picture, loosely based on images of Mafia-run Windy City, 1929, its judicious scoring often generates orchestral weight and colour from just a handful of players. At the same time there's plenty of individual cut and thrust, notable from the lithe and licking alto of Chris Hunter and the dextrous authority of trombonist Malcolm Griffiths. Vocal quality too comes close to the genuine onstage article, spearheaded by Phil Minton's hammer-drill improvisation on the terminal-zone vision 'Concrete'. Lyrics throughout — mainly from Kate Westbrook and Mike Kustow — are splendid, capping the perfect tension overall between bright entertainment and stormy, studied melancholy. A really fine collection. LE

THE WHISPERS
The Whispers *(Solar)*
Soul harmony act with spit and polish and one hit under their belt. The rest of the album is unremarkable filler material. Oh, yes, in case you don't remember it, the hit in question was 'And the Beat Goes On'. AB-F

JAMES WHITE AND THE BLACKS
Off White *(Ze)*
New Yawk punk jazz hybrid. Surprisingly effective. AB-F

WHITESNAKE
Love Hunter *(UA)*
Genital rock not known for its subtlety. MJ

WHITESNAKE
Ready and Willing *(UA)*
Deep purple offshoot and, needless to say, imitators. MJ

SLIM WHITMAN
Till We Meet Again *(UA)*
Prehistoric ballads by Cro-Magnon balladeer. For the geriatric swingers. AB-F

WILD HORSES
Wild Horses *(EMI)*
Jimmy Bain and Brian Robertson, alumni of past name bands team up and give birth to a mouse with mountain-like ambitions. MJ

WILSON GALE AND CO.
Gift Wrapped *(Jet)*
Dull ELO offshoot with little new on offer. AB-F

EDGAR WINTER
The Edgar Winter Album *(Blue Sky)*
Boogie blues, competent variety. MJ

JOHNNY WINTER
Raisin' Cain *(Blue Sky)*
Good standard albino blues by a master of the form. MJ

WIRE
154 *(Warners/Harvest)*
The farthest reaches of electronic rock and experimentation by now-defunct British group. Rigorous, ice-cold and uneasy alliance of theories and sounds. AB-F

WISHBONE ASH
Just Testing *(MCA)*
Tired retread of familiar chords and sounds by famous band with little to say. Wishbone Ash are in dire need of a blood transfusion. They were once great and amazed us with what could be done with a dual lead guitar line-up. MJ

JAH WOBBLE
Betrayal *(Virgin)*
Bass player for Public Image Limited pens quirky, eccentric album which grows on you if you allow that sort of thing. The man can't sing, some might even say he can't really play, but the mixture is engaging fun. Try it. AB-F

BRUCE WOOLLEY & THE CAMERA CLUB
English Garden *(Columbia/Epic)*
Woolley rocks more convincingly than his co-authorship of Buggles' 'Video Killed The Radio Star' bubble-pop hit would lead you to expect. DN

STEVIE WONDER
Stevie Wonder's Journey Through The Secret Life Of Plants *(Tamla)*
What sounds unbearably precious and pretentious on record sounded great when Stevie got it together for a rare live gig in New York. 'Scuse me while I go replay 'Superstition' and 'I Was Made To Love Her'. DN

WRECKLESS ERIC
Big Smash! *(Stiff)*
A double album, the first of which is devoted to new idiosyncratic, drunken Wreckless Eric songs and the second reminding us of past hits which weren't but should have been if the vulgar public at large had a better understanding of what makes British eccentric musicians run. Endearing and unique musical madness. AB-F

WRECKLESS ERIC
The Whole Wide World *(Stiff)*
Compilation of best singles and carefully selected album tracks to introduce the fantabulously often drunk Wreckless Eric to an unsuspecting US public. Of course, we've known him for some years over here in Blighty and can still pretend to be all very blasé... wonder what they made of him? MJ

WRECKLESS ERIC

TAMMY WYNETTE
Only Lonely Sometimes *(Epic)*
More tearjerkers immaculately produced by old hand Billy Sherrill. MJ

X
Los Angeles *(Slash)*
If this the latest in new wave punk extraordinaire from LA, then all we can say is that LA is years behind London, where we got through the wham bam punch fuck society can't sing but I can scream phase an eternity ago. A sorry platter, indeed. AB-F

XTC
Drums and Wires *(Virgin)*
Catchy art rock fraught with ambitions and not always hitting its targets. Production by Steve Lillywhite brings out the best in XTC who keep on improving with every album as they tighten up and multi-layer their infectious hooks. Worthy of note are 'Making Plans for Nigel' and 'Life Begins at the Hop'. The way XTC are going, the next album must surely be a monster. MJ

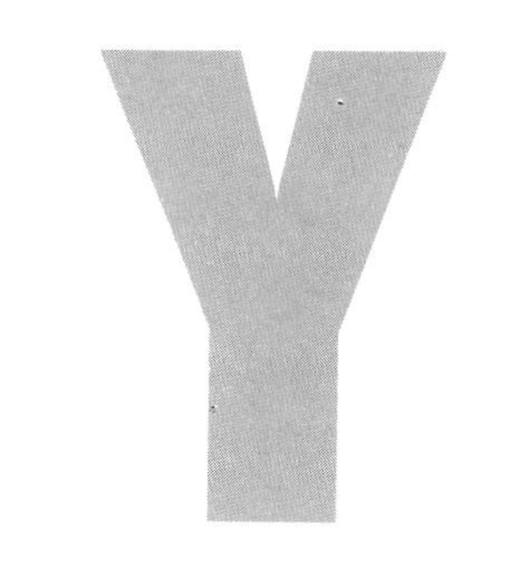

YELLOW MAGIC ORCHESTRA
Solid State Survivor *(A&M)*
Japanese electronic rock. It ain't as easy as putting transistors together, fellows. Marks for trying but come back next year. AB-F

YELLOW MAGIC ORCHESTRA
XOO Multiples *(A&M)*
The more they try to blend European electronic influences with Japanese know-how, the more the cracks show. AB-F

NEIL YOUNG AND CRAZY HORSE
Live Rust *(Warners)*
Double live set from the one man who valiantly resists all passing fashions and miraculously ends up on top of the pile. Older and newer Neil Young classics given a hard edge of steel, fire and rust. A perfect anthology. MJ

FRANK ZAPPA
Joe's Garage Act I, Acts II & III *(Zappa Records/CBS)*
Zappa's live concerts are usually amusing and he always has good musicians in his band(s), but he hasn't made a really solid album in over five years. In his liner notes for this "rock opera", Zappa observes "Joe's Garage is a stupid story about how the government is going to try to do away with music". There ought to be a law against albums *this* boring. Obviously Phonogram, distributor of these LP's on the Zappa label, thought so too; his most recent effort as of this writing, the non-LP single 'I Don't Wanna Get Drafted' is independently distributed. DN

WARREN ZEVON
Bad Streak In Dancing School *(Asylum)*
Patchy but always fascinating offering of Raymond Chandler-like LA tackiness and hard-boiled cynicism by the only west coast musician without a terminal suntan. Guns, violence and fetching idiosyncrasies abound. When Zevon is good he's dynamite, when off form (or drunk) he's only a part-time genius. Buy. MJ

WARREN ZEVON
Wanted Dead or Alive *(Pickwick)*
Old youthful Zevon tracks which he thought had been forgotten. Moral: never trust a record company. Stop blushing, Warren. AB-F

ZZ TOP
Deguello *(Warners)*
Deep-fried hot-ass boogie. MJ

THE SINGLES SCENE
US

There's one thing you can say for sure about the last twelve months' singles; as usual, since about 1964, the most interesting action wasn't at the top of the charts.

The action there was predictable – like it's been for ten years. The best new singles hardly ever rose to visibility. And I'm not talking about the BJ's gay version of 'My Boyfriend's Back', available only from a small New Jersey firm. I'm talking about Elvis Costello, Talking Heads, Ramones and Neil Young – the best talent there is in the record releasing universe. Sure, 'I, Zimbra,' 'Accidents Will Happen' and 'My, My, Hey Hey' (or whatever it's called) made the charts, but their entry was in each instance an accident, and they never rose to true Top Ten visibility.

The audience is too diverse for that. None of these artists has a popular enough voice to reach that far. And those of us who ponder rock and roll are getting a little old for 45-buying. More likely, the singles buyers of the Eighties are the children of the rock crit estab. And what relation does a 32-year-old with a mouth full of diaper pins have to the Top 40?

Granted that, it remains notable that the Brothers Gibb had considerably less visibility on the charts this year than any other recent one. And disco, except in the rarest instances of greatness, was finally reconfined to the dance market.*

Superstars still reigned at the turn of the decade. The Eagles, Billy Joel, Michael Jackson, Donna Summer, Paul McCartney, Queen and Pink Floyd all had no trouble reaching No.1 positions. New superstars were created as were songs that cut through genres and the rest of the aural atmosphere like hot knives through butter: 'Call Me', 'Funkytown', 'My Sharona' and 'Ring My Bell' among them. Blondie should be able to do it again. The Knack seem to have lost theirs. Lipps, Inc. hardly exists and Anita Ward, confined on TK Records, seems to have little chance of becoming more than another faceless disco voice. Sort of like Donna Summer...

DONNA SUMMER

Donna was at the top of the charts in summer 1979 with two singles from her 'Bad Girls' album, the title track and the rocking 'Hot Stuff'. Anita Ward was nipping at Donna's heels. Sister Sledge chimed in with 'We Are Family' (and The Pittsburgh Pirates helped). Rex Smith and Cheap Trick, white kids with **16**-Magazine appeal, bubbled to the top of the charts, but only hit the tops spots in isolated markets. Rex had 'You Take My Breath Away'. At this writing he's performing in Joseph Papp's Central Park production of 'Pirates of Penzance'. The Trick were still working off their 'Live at Budokan' album with 'I Want You To Want Me'. The middle of the country was well represented by Kenny Rogers with 'She Believes in Me' and Doctor Hook's 'When You're In Love With A Beautiful Woman'.

Suddenly, at the start of August, The Knack rocketed up the charts with 'My Sharona', a song which made new wave music viable commercially and led to the resurgence of rock dancing around the country. It was actually played at Studio 54 and Xenon in New York, and the dancefloor population would swell each time it came on. John Stewart's hit, 'Gold' didn't get that kind of attention. In fact, I don't even remember it.

In the same way that kids with teen appeal are likely to sell a couple of singles here and there, so is Barbra Streisand of Brooklyn. Her theme song for a rotten film about boxing, 'The Main Event' charted in August, and we'd be hearing more from her quite soon.

Chic were represented in the lofty aerie of hitdom in August by'Good Times'. Earth, Wind and Fire weighed in with 'After The Love Has Gone'. And Charlie Daniels took the first steps toward becoming a 1980-version message-song singer with 'The Devil Went Down To Georgia'.

The children (yes, you) went back to school in September and 'My Sharona', that infectious little ditty produced by Commander Mike Chapman went to school with them. 'Sharona' had the year's best picture sleeve, starring Sharona herself in all her post-pubescent glory. But Robert John was waiting in the wings. 'Sad Eyes' looked out from the top of the charts 'til well into October.

Under it, MOR rock reigned once The Knack were finally knuked. ELO was there, and the mellow Little River Band and 'Sail On' by the Commodores. Dionne Warwick even revisited the top of the charts with 'I'll Never Love This Way Again'.

*dance market: a rock business euphemism for blacks and gays.

Though the song's success was a tribute to Clive Davis' promotional talents, what it told us was that the great ship Radio had hit a time warp and we were all back in September 1962, waiting for The Beatles.

Thence came Michael Jackson, potentially the Smokey Robinson of the '80s, thus no disproof of the 1962 theory. Disco is Motown. Rex Smith is Fabian. And Barbra Streisand can't burp without making the charts.

'Don't Stop 'til You Get Enough' was/is a wonderful song. Compare it to the tune that beat it to No.1 and you'll see what I mean. Introducing Herb Alpert's 'Rise'.

Like any good theory, this 1962 bit is about to die. For along came M with 'Pop Musik', not something you'll listen to a lot in years to come, but the best novelty track of the year, a terrific laugh even on its tenth trip around a turntable, and a lovely synthetic pop piece.

Surrounding it on the radio were a batch of new superstar tracks, released in time to sell their respective LPs through the holidays. Donna Summer was back with the ballad 'Dim All the Lights', a lush slice of romanticism. Styx crossed the river with something called 'Babe'. The Eagles had the hot 'Heartache Tonight'. Kenny Rogers (yawn) was back with 'You Decorated My Life', a tune about two gay interior decorators in Cobble Hill. (Note to libel lawyers: That's not really what the song's about).

CAPTAIN & TENNILLE

LINDA RONSTADT

And, whataya know! Barbra Streisand was back, Donna Summer at her side, with a song that appeared on both their current albums (to market we will go...), 'No More Tears (Enough is Enough)', a song that was partially rewritten to fit the imagistic boundaries of La Streisand's concept album 'Wet'.

Welcome to December 1979. What earthshaking news have the pop charts got for social historians of tomorrow, bent on discovering clues to the reasons for the demise of a once-great civilization? 'Please Don't Go' by KC and The Sunshine Band. 'Escape (The Pina Colada Song)' by Rupert Holmes. 'Ladies Night' by Kool and The Gang. And Styx, Donna, Barbra and Kenny. And then in the last week of 1979, The Captain and Tennille crawled from the video jungle with the most useless and cruel message ever written to greet a new decade: 'Do That To Me One More Time'.

Things could only improve, though 'The Pina Colada Song' did have its partisans. Entering the new year, the charts saw this interesting action: J.D. Souther's mournful 'You're Only Lonely' dropped from No.7 to No.20 in one week. Streisand, Summer, Styx and Supertramp ('Take The Long Way Home') were dropping along with it. Michael Jackson's joyful 'Rock With You' was rising, as was a track from Stevie Wonder's 'Secret Life of Plants'. The Nitty Gritty Dirt Band were getting an able assist from Linda Ronstadt that helped push their 'An American Dream' from No.59 to No.33 in a week.

Fleetwood Mac's hit off 'Tusk' was the second single from it, Steve Nicks' 'Sara'. 'Cruisin' by Smokey Robinson entered the Top 5 as Stevie Wonder dropped out. KC and Kool were fading fast. Andy Gibb entered the charts with 'Desire', Donna Summer was coming back strong with 'On The Radio' off the similarly titled Hits compilation set. Doctor Hook and Cliff Richard had been bubbling near the chart's top with 'Better Love Next Time' and 'We Don't Talk Anymore' respectively, but neither broke through to nationwide acceptance. Kenny Rogers' 'Coward For The Country' was about the most popular song there was in America as February 1980 began.

But energy was stirring. Both Tom Petty and the Heartbreakers and Pink Floyd were charging up the charts. Floyd had the pounding 'Another Brick in The Wall' and Petty was standing out with 'Refugee'. Queen were nearing No.1 with the atypical 'Crazy Little Thing Called Love'. Even in success you could tell Queen were a band near the end of its road.

Queen and Floyd slugged it

MICHAEL JACKSON

out for the No.1 spot all through February and March. A regular battle of the dinosaurs. But these dinosaurs deserved credit for reaching out to a whole new generation of audience. 'Refugee' reached its highest point in mid-March, No.15. The Eagles tried 'The Long Run' and 'I Can't Tell You Why' and received modest success with each. Michael Jackson was rising with 'Off The Wall', his album's title track, and Jimmy Ruffin represented the Bee Gees with a song penned by Robin Gibb, 'Hold On To My Love'.

Steve Forbert, an energetic young folk performer with gobs of promise came and went with 'Romeo's Tune', one of the strongest tracks off his more generally disappointing second album. And the first single off Linda Ronstadt's formula-breaking 'Mad Love' album, 'How Do I Make You', peaked at No.10 on the charts late in March.

Fleetwood Mac's 'Think About Me' began to rise late that month, too, but its performance overall was a disappointment. 'Call Me' by Blondie was the surprise hit of the season, a cross-over of sorts, produced by Giorgio Moroder of Euro-disco fame. Once again, modern *soul* was ascendant. Kool and the Gang were back with 'Too Hot', the Spinners were on the charts too. White pop was adequately represented in April by Christopher Cross' 'Ride Like The Wind', and the reappearance of Linda Ronstadt, with the beautiful 'Hurt So Bad', entering the charts mid-April at No.46. Boz Scaggs came on the charts with 'Breakdown Dead Ahead' a week later, and Fleetwood Mac's 'Think About Me' peaked a week after that at No.20. 'The Biggest Part of Me' by Ambrosia began a two-month climb and Ray, Goodman and Brown's innocuous 'Special Lady' began a comfortable occupancy of a Top 5 niche.

RUPERT HOLMES AND M

TOM PETTY

Queen had occupied the No.1 spot for four weeks. Then Pink Floyd took it over for four. Now Blondie ascended for a six week stay at the top of the pops. During that tenure, "New Wave" made the charts in various other guises as well. Robbie Dupree, a sort of outlaw country star, came on with 'Steal Away', not a new wave song by any means, but still a good sign. By Mid-May, 'Hurt So Bad' had peaked at No.8 for a three-week stay before dropping, and that same week, Lipps Inc. rose from No.19 to No.4 with their hot, fabulous disco exception, 'Funkytown'.

More interesting, though, were the chart appearances by The Pretenders and The Clash that month. Suddenly the album market had gotten more exciting than it had been in years. But how would these same acts fare in the singles market? 'Train In Vain' peaked at No.23 in the last week in May, and by the first week in June, The Pretenders had been stopped too, at No.14 with 'Brass in Pocket'. Though neither of these chart performances were glowing successes in context, it was important to note that no British 'New Wave' act had thus far done so well as these two promising groups. For the rest of the year the superstars took over again. Billy Joel had hit after hit off 'Glass Houses'. Paul McCartney's 'Coming Up' ditty-bopped its way to No.1, after kissing 'Funkytown's' bottom for several weeks. 'Call Me' began a slow drop, Bob Segar rose with 'Against The Wind', Kenny Rogers came back like a bad cold.

As the summer dog days began the charts were back to 1962. ELO was up there. So was Bette Midler. And God Damn! There came Elton John! Clearly consumers who, a few weeks before had been buying Strummer and Hynde were now lost in the commercial cotton candy of the pop charts again. It was all too sweet for words. The most exciting songs on the horizon were by performers who'd been around over a dozen years: The Rolling Stones' Curtis Mayfield tribute, 'Emotional Rescue' and Pete Townshend's touching, artful 'Let My Love Open The Door'.

And those of us who'd stopped buying singles a long time ago were *still* sitting around, waiting for The Beatles.

MICHAEL GROSS

BETTE MIDLER

The decades (so superfluous to everything but our superstitions — but superstitions maketh the man) changed on a creepy singles chart: Donna Summer shedding her credibility (but not for me) on the altar of 'No More Tears', she and Streisand such strange sleepovers in the big soft king-size bed of showbiz. But then everyone has turned out to be odd bedfellows; the turn of the year chart saw Gary Numan, Queen, the Two-Tone gaggle, B. A. Robertson, Pink Floyd, the merry olde Rats, the useless Tourists, Herb Alpert, Abba, Pretenders, Paul McCartney, Blondie, Dr Hook, pathetic Mike 'Old Hat' Oldfield, the UK Subs murdering 'She's Not There'. Yes, a bunch of mindless beach bums, interested only in their own tan but willing to share the same sun. They all lay together so easily — the Pretenders and Paulie, Alpert and Android Numan — because they always saw the same crock, they just quarrelled over the rainbow. And why not! You've got to have *something* in the bank, Frank. Only the Jam and the Clash didn't agree — they were as attractively angry as ever with 'Eton Rifles' and 'London Calling' — but their stale scorn was simply absorbed into the cauldron as that essential bit of spice, the squeeze of lemon that sets your teeth so delicately on edge — so necessary! We don't want to get bland and blase around here; shake us up, please, please.

Undoubedly the worst thing to happen to popular music since, say, Pink Floyd formed was the occupation of the Number One single position by Pink Floyd during this country's crossover into the Eighties. Superstitious or not, there's something really sickening about going into something new when something so old and dead is doing so well (ironic, too, that punk — SO important — was caught in the middle — the middle of anything being just where it shoudn't be — the start of something or the end, yes — it wasn't for nothing

ABBA

that the adolescent Rotten embellished a Pink Floyd T-shirt with the sacred, scathing 'I HATE' — Pink Floyd represent everything that is sloppy and inferior about this country); 'Another Brick In The Wall' really was another nail in my heart (a beautiful, under-rated single by the ugly, over-rated Squeeze) — imagine people buying like sheep a record telling them not to let themselves be rounded up by collies.

The way spineless libertarians flocked to the pap as being "anti-establishment" was great fun to see; the incredible brainlessness of liking anything "anti-establishment," no matter how hack! Talking of hacks, the NEW MUSICAL EXPRESS in a moment of sublime shallow stupidity (it wasn't irony or sarcasm; the NME hasn't had a sense of humour for, oh, a good two years now) called it "the most anti-establishment Number One since 'God Save The Queen' ". As if "anti-establishment" was synonymous with "glamour" or "rebellion" or "excitement"! Just the opposite! Keith Joseph, God knows, is as out of touch and unperceptive as Pink Floyd themselves — but he has more looks, money and shock value than all the acts in the chart put together.

This has been a year of jokes; 'The Sparrow', 'Daytrip To Bangor', at Christmas a brace of 'rapping' singles, the eternal B. A. Robertson — Robertson's shoddy, clodhopping career has basically been as a (public, perky) Dury placebo. No sooner had singles-buyers come to love the Bow Bells chiming, rhyming side of Ian Dury than Chas Jankel, the tunesmith, departed, leaving Dury wallowing in an unlucrative sea of tuneless neurosis; Robertson stepped smartly in with 'Bang Bang', 'Knocked It Off', 'Kool In A Kaftan' and 'To Be Or Not To Be' (his performing career has been entirely erected in the course of just twelve months, although it seems he's been boring us forever) and the singles-buyers never knew the difference (indeed, the only difference between them is that Dury is pretentious). A royal pain though the singing Robertson is, as a writer he provided the singles market with one of the years most dynamic/atmospheric moments; the shades-of-Gene Tierney-as-Laura, *film noir* 'Carrie', transmitted through the unlikely medium of Cliff Richard. That's why the medium is a mess!

A year of one-offs; singles-buyers raising the feeble hopes of simple rock folk and then ignoring them the morning after. Pathetic little examples of the syndrome were The Ramones with 'Baby I Love You', The Tourists and 'I Only Want To Be With You', the Lambrettas 'Poison Ivy' (when in doubt of your own talents, tout the tried and tested — a formula which has also given old fools like Don McLean, Leo Sayer and Rod Stewart hit singles this year), The Vapors 'Turning Japanese', the Regents '7 Teen', Martha and The Muffins 'Echo Beach', Rickie Lee Jones (that girlish, gilt-free Springsteen substitute) 'Chuck E's In Love', The Knack (one-track, slack and hack) and 'My Sharona', Janet Kay's pedigree in poignancy 'Silly Games', Marti Webb's soapy operatic 'Take That Look Off Your Face', Barbara Dicksons's 'January February' (the song and the singer surely the last word in homeliness), Fern Kinney's 'Together We Are Beautiful', Iris Williams' 'He Was Beautiful', Rupert Holmes loathsomely popular 'Escape' — the last five artistes illustrating the recent eerie desire for entertainers who resemble one's least favourite aunt or uncle, the last also illustrating the readiness of British singles-buyers to purchase anything by anyone with a paunch, a penis and an American passport (see Dr Hook, Don McLean, Kenny Rogers, Herb Alpert.)

Why all these one-offs were hits no one but Gallup could know. Why others — razor sharp songs with clever words, pretty tunes, dynamic ideas, songs like Snips desperate '9 O'Clock', The Quick's exotic 'Sharks Are Cool, Jets Are Hot', Karel Fialka's sinful synthetic beauty 'The Eyes Have It', The Modettes shocking, sweet 'White Mice' — weren't is probably because they were too rich and good for public taste, too luscious in thought and deed, the tunes too pretty, the words too clever, the ideas too dynamic, the whole too desperate, exotic, synthetic and sweet. There are few things more unpopular these days than someone who gets everthing right.

Disco has smelt increasingly fishy over the last twelve months, but the mouths that sing it have never looked better. It's the only corny glamour magnet left in entertainment, like films were in the Fifties, fashion in the Sixties, white rock in the Seventies. All the best girls only have ears for it; the charming, declining, charismatic Donna Summer, so pseudo-slick in 'Sunset People', so embarrassingly miscast in 'Bad Girls', so perfect in the beautiful 'On The Radio'; the super-white, super-sly Deborah Harry of 'Atomic' — sole Blondie English mega-hit of the past year, the pop 'Union City Blue' and the rock 'Call Me' doing relatively badly (remember, though, that Blondie's commercial worst is practically everyone else's commercial best) due to complacent promotion and the simple fact that they weren't disco; the valiant, inarticulate old Trojan warhorse Sheila B. Devotion, slipping into the disco citadel via the Chic Organisation and maybe the year's most ecstatic three minutes — 'Spacer'; the 13-year-old king-maker Stacey Lattislaw, whose beautiful hope-against-hope voice transforms 'Jump To The Beat'.

Disco men, though, have had barely — bar the melodramatic, hypnotic 'Just Can't Give You Up' by Mystic Merlin, and the heartwrenching optimistic ennui of The Whisperers 'And The Beat Goes On' (*'You did me wrong, but I've been through stormy weather'* — a perfect balm for those raised and betrayed by Punk) — a saving face; anonymous session men padding out our airwaves and their wallets with the pioneering in black dance music of the rotten malaise that struck white rock decades ago — making music about music, as in 'Music Is My First Love (And It Shall Be My Last)' and 'Rock And Roll (I Gave You All The Best Years Of My Life)'

THE BEAT

The year has been blighted by disco singles called things like 'Behind The Groove'. 'Check Out The Groove', 'We've Got The Groove', 'We've Got The Funk', 'Music Makes You Feel Like Dancing', 'Music', 'Stomp', 'Jazz Carnival', 'Rock With You' (the one blot in Michael Jackson's platinum-bound copybook), and, God forgive them, the monstrously-named 'It's A Disco Night' by the Isley Brothers.

Previously perfect disco careers have declined with the past twelve months, too; the most missable (though dramatic) career decline has been that of The Bee Gees, 'Spirits Having Flown' being their only recent, hardly decent, hit. With their lack of looks, voices and sex appeal, they're hardly the kind of people you miss. Unlike the flamboyant, sickening Boney M, whose demise has been the only subtle thing they've ever done — and their minor hits of the past year, 'Gotta Go Home', and 'My Friend Jack' have been amazingly restrained and tasteful.

Edwards and Rogers a.k.a. the Chic Organization are well established as deevy, dynamic deities in the weak minds of the wishful; but of course they are mortals, and their talent is as finite as yours and mine (well, *yours*). The Chic hits of this year — 'My Feet Keep Dancing', 'Good Times', 'Rebels Are We' — are extremely plain fare, only the soft 'My Forbidden Lover' coming close to such previous works as 'I Want Your Love' and their mindless de Mille dancing opera. One must admire Edwards and Rogers, though, for being the only disco band not to wear sequinned spacesuits, and for knocking them out so quickly. While hardly in the black-hack-and-a-half class of Marley (who has written 'Could You Be Loved' at least two score times before), Chic certainly beat Barbara Cartland hands down when it comes to being prolific. Of course, there is the point that *all* of her output is trash, and only half of Chic's is — the cloying, annoying 'Upside Down' for Diana Ross, their recent Chic product, the embarrassingly feeble recent flops for Sister Sledge, 'Easy Street' and 'Reach Your Peak'. Talking about Sister Sledge, this is a good time to talk about the exceptions to Chic's tacky output — the first two Sister Sledge singles of the past twelve months were gorgeous, as near to perfection as puppets get — 'Lost In Music' (a minor hit) and 'Got To Love Somebody' (not a hit at all, but equally ravishing) — and as for 'Spacer' — what a silk purse Chic made out of a Frog ignoramus.

DAVE EDMUNDS

Disco torch classic of the year was Randy Crawford and The Crusaders' 'Street Life', a gem that Gershwin wouldn't have disowned. Disco joke of year were the Village People; at the end of 1979 they released a single called 'Ready For The Eighties', which was a spectacular failure. If ever there was anyone who wasn't ready for the Eighties, it was the Village People!

This has been a year of rebound, people madly trying to convince themselves that at long last this is love. People supressed punk, which was so young and strong and true, then rushed to hug it when it began throwing up sweet nothings like the Boomtown Rats; determined not to make that mistake again, the radio, papers, T.V. have rushed through the past twelve month sniffling out signs of ska, Two-Tone, Moderne, the new soul, all of which, incredibly, have only been with us for a year. Even poor Joe Jackson (responsible for one of the years most epic moments with 'It's Different For Girls' and one of the years most pathetic moments with 'The Harder They Come') was joyfully pounced upon and touted as a practitioner of "Spiv Rock", whatever *that* is.

The Two Tone bands dress beautifully, the blacks involved all look like Andrew Young when he was Martin Luther King's great black hope; the whites in the Two Tone Bands have coasted rather on the blacks, although Jerry Dammers is a great businessman and a charismatically decent sort, although a blonde in The Bodysnatchers is beautiful, although Madness can be so pure prole music hall

THE JAM

entertaining. The real appeal of the ska movement has been the well-dressed, non-liberal racial mix; at last a meeting of black and white that didn't wear Afros and dungarees!

But the product is another matter; the cold black plastic overrules the warm black and white. The ska bands combined – The Specials, Selecter, Madness, The Beat, The Bodysnatchers – have had over twenty hits in the past twelve months, ranging from the horrifically hack ('Missing Words', 'Ratrace') to the passable ('Gangsters', 'On My Radio') to the lonely excellence of 'My Girl'. All there is to Two Tone is that which meets the eye – the suits, the integration.

Dave Edmunds is a fright and 'Girls Talk' was a hit but 'Queen Of Hearts' was exquisite. It was a year of plenty of nothing for the Buzzcocks with only one minor hit in 'Harmony In My Head'. Roxy Music and Abba both shared a song title – 'Angel Eyes' – and a similar way of falling apart; after the blood-letting the anaemia – the model, the marriage, the couch, the career, 'Over You', 'I Have A Dream', 'Oh Yeah', 'Gimme Gimme Gimme'...

This has been a bad year for the new, 'good' Elvis Costello – the mad menacing midget stance swapped for that of a thoughtful courting jester. 'I Can't Stand Up' only making the charts on the strength of the video, 'High Fidelity' and the lush 'New Amsterdam' being commercial failures. The Jam, on the other hand, have become *more* intense and successful, building up through the innocuous 'When You Are Young' through the apopthemagmatic 'Eton Rifles' to the apoplectic 'Going Underground' (apocalyptic is a word maimed by misuse. In white rock there seem to be 45 apocalypses per minute) – fire and brimstone in loafers.

'Beat The Clock' was a hit for Sparks but 'Number One Song In Heaven', 'When I'm With You' and 'Young Girls' weren't; a shame, because Ron Mael is an interesting example of how sick in the head a person can get if they grow up in California not blonde, not tanned, not brainless. The Sex Pistol's – 'C'Mon Everybody', 'I'm Not Your Stepping Stone' – haunted every twist and turn of white rock singles like a Greek Chorus, making most music seem like a bad joke. The Electric Light Orchestra, I fear, will, like poverty, always be with us and 'Xanadu' is simply the latest proof; they are the only band I can look into infinity and never see asunder.

The Police have consolidated the success of everybore's fave rave punky wave record ('Roxanne' – Keith Richard, Ted Nugent, Hank Marvin, Bill Wyman, all make a point of loving it and congratulate themselves for genuinely liking and understanding the dread "punk") with this year's 'Can't Stand Losing You' (the only foot they've ever put right), 'Message In A Bottle' 'Walking On The Moon' and (the final insult, the straw drowners grasp at) 'So Lonely'. Sting; a gaudy bawd of our time. At first glance neat, sweet and rest petite, at second stare a peroxide pain, Sting has rapidly developed into a big-head housing a small brain, who in every damn song adopts the same old persona – "Look at me, I'm so beautiful and yes, I'm sensitive, too sensitive for my own good, I've been hurt – but could YOU be the one who'll make me believe again?" Sting's so acceptable and empty and such an accessory to an easy life; he reminds me of nothing so much as Erica Jong. Will there be such a fuss – film parts, hurt hearts – about Sting this time next year? Don't bet money, honey.

Lightweight Kate Bush surprised me with 'Babooshka', the best account of a bad marriage since *Anna Karenina*. Eddie Howell's soppy 'Hatcheck Girl' charmed me and reminded me of a delicate little F. Scott Fitz short story, *Jacob's Ladder*. Many thanks to Dexy's Midnight Runners for 'Geno' and 'There, There, My Dear', which gave me the best good old-fashioned cheap laugh I've had this year. Yes, Dexy's (what a great fast name for such a band of po-faced Bunters), there are few things so facile and inane as making singles about what a junkyard the world is. If you're worried, if you want to change anything, make madly commercial records and put the MONEY into things you believe in – *that's* the only way you change anything, not with insignificant little singles.

The past year has seen the Pop Group whining about everyone being prostitutes, The Slits whining about the white uptight, Joy Division having a non-specific whine – the nerve of these people, in a year when 'Under The Boardwalk', 'Behind A Painted Smile' and 'Dock Of The Bay' were re-released! *That's* about as far as a single ought to go – the nerve of putting your own dowdy little neurosis on the market with *these* great singles! It's a fact; blacks can complain and sound great, whites who complain just make you want to shoot them.

Serious white music causes nothing but unhappiness; why don't you kill yourself if you're so sad? (The Pop Group don't know but Ian

KATE BUSH

"Laughing Boy" Curtis understood.) Have you seen pictures of the bare bones of the old Alexandra Palace after it was burned out? That's what the notion of music as anything more than entertainment is.

Home truth of the year; Ian Curtis practising what he preaches. Memo to all the serious white bands who've released singles in the past twelve months; get some guts about you. Buck up or fuck off. JULIE BURCHILL

ROCK FILMS

ALL THAT JAZZ
Bob Fosse

An extravagant, beautiful and intelligently crafted gem of a movie. Bob Fosse is the only great musical director of our time, an aging, self-destructive wunderkind, filled with primal passions and nervous neuroses. 'All That Jazz,' promoted as a veiled autobiography, is french pastry for the eyes, a dazzling, beautiful show. Roy Scheider is remarkable as choreographer Joe Gideon. He reminds you of what Richard Farina once said about Bob Dylan: "He doesn't burn the candle at both ends. He takes a blowtorch to the middle." Marred only by a soupcon of self-indulgence, 'All That Jazz', despite not winning the Oscar, was the best American movie, and the best musical of the past year. MG

APOCALYPSE NOW
Francis Coppola

Featuring sounds by The Doors, The Rolling Stones and Flash Cadillac; now competing hard with Kubrick's '2001, A Space Odyssey' for the supreme title of all-time rock head movie (downer division). Nevertheless a major film whose main fault is probably to tackle a subject of the 60s and 70s in the style (to be) of the 1980s, i.e. a film ahead of its time. Vietnam, war, Marlon Brando's studied mannerisms, modern man's emotional psyche (inspired by Conrad), explosives galore and hardware, a potent and unforgettable cocktail for all the senses. AB-F & MG

THE BLUES BROTHERS

THE BLUES BROTHERS

THE BITCH
Gerry O'Hara

Sequel to the horrendous 'The Stud', these new adventures of Joan Collins almost seem to be an afterthought marketing device for the launch of the disco soundtrack. Rubbish of course. AB-F

THE BLUES BROTHERS
John Landis

One of the biggest film budgets ever, and when you see the mayhem and destruction, mostly involving buildings and a car or two, you begin to understand where the money all went. Dan Aykroyd and John Belushi play the comically villainous Blues Brothers who, after Elwood's sojourn in jail, try to get their old band together again to raise money for an orphanage. "On a mission from the Lord" is the password throughout their comic-strip-like misadventures around Chicago and provides us with prize sequences involving Ray Charles, James Brown, Aretha Franklin and Cab Calloway. Aykroyd and Belushi are perfect as the Blues Bros. but their singing seldom convinces if you close your eyes to their antics. However, when the film is good, it's very good indeed and it would be churlish to discriminate against such a pleasant comedy and reverent homage to soul music. AB-F

BREAKING GLASS
Brian Gibson

Oh no, not yet another 'rags to riches and down again' story! This time around, the supposed originality of the project was to make the sad heroine (let me unashamedly give the ending away: she ends up in an asylum after the traditional melodramatic nervous breakdown) a punkette singer extraordinaire manipulated by young intense and forceful manager (gently) and record company sharks (nasty meanies all, you can tell by the way their eyes move so shiftily). Possibly during the course of the film's production, someone must have noticed that punk was on its way out, so poor old Hazel O'Connor's role metamorphosed into a Bowie-glitter-electronic Numan persona of the female gender (a Numanette?). Well-filmed but so utterly predictable, 'Breaking Glass' might well make a lot of money for its backers, but it would be a pity. And if you believe the caricatural picture it shows of the rock world and assorted record companies, don't. AB-F

CAN'T STOP THE MUSIC
Nancy Walker

The first all-singing, all-dancing, all-gay TV show to reach the silver screen. Alan Carr, the man who brought you 'Grease', 'Survive!' and 'Tommy', has built 'Broadway Melody 1980' as a vehicle for the Village People. As to them: the Indian is a real charmer, the leatherman does a terrific rendition of 'Danny Boy', and they all take part in breathtaking production numbers built around their hit, 'YMCA' and a pseudo-advertisement for milk shakes. One reviewer made sure to note that "Valerie Perrine plays a woman." Paul Sand is death-defying as a record exec hooked on his telephone. The most damning thing you can say about this bachelor party is that the second most credible performance is turned in by Bruce "Wheaties" Jenner. The message: Homosexuality is wholesome. MG

CARNY
Robert Kaylor

Robbie Robertson, Gary Busey and Jody Foster star in a film about rock touring and friendship masquerading as a film about lust in the carnival. The sexiest American film of 1980. All three characters start on the boil and get hotter, as Foster, a runaway, falls for Busey, the carnival's Bozo (the man who goads people on the midway into throwing balls at a target and knocking him in a tank of water), moves into the trailer he shares with Robertson (the carnival's expediter and bag man),

CAN'T STOP THE MUSIC

almost breaks up their friendship, tries to become a stripper, causes a minor riot when she suddenly gets cold feet on the runway and then gains the respect of all concerned. Producer/star Robertson has made the first film to adequately capture the hardships, joys and dependencies of life on the road. Too gritty to be popular. This may be a film for the schools, books and late night circuits. MG

COAL MINER'S DAUGHTER
Michael Apted
Sissy Spacek does her own singing in this Hollywood version of country artist Loretta Lynn's life. Excellent acting by Tommy Lee Jones and The Band's drummer, Levon Helm, but the story drags. DM

DISCO FEVER
Hubert Frank
German soft-core sex comedy with occasional disco video inserts featuring Boney M and lesser dance floor luminaries. AB-F

ELVIS
John Carpenter
Creditable impersonations of Elvis and Priscilla by Kurt Russell and Season Hubley in this sober, factual telefilm released into cinemas in Britain. Carpenter is of course better known for his horror/suspense movies, but nevertheless emerges with full honours from this exercise in style. By the way, Shelley Winters plays Presley's mum... AB-F

FAME
Alan Parker
Well, there is music in there somewhere, I suppose. Unexciting middle of the road sounds as would-be actors, singers and dancers of dubious calibre go about their way to the top of the ladder with predictable results and misadventures. Long. Very long. AB-F

FANTASTICA
Gilles Carle
French-Canadian musical extravaganza which opened the 1980 Cannes film festival. Music by the very much underrated Lewis Furey, voice, body and nudity by the delectable Carole Laure (better remembered for her chocolate bath in Dusan Makavejev's 'Sweet Movie'). Fey and embarrassing for all concerned. AB-F

THE GREAT ROCK 'N' ROLL SWINDLE
Julien Temple
Long-awaited with a mixture of fear and anticipation, the Sex Pistols movie is a surprising success. Part documentary, part animated cartoon (irrepressably funny sequences, these), part fiction à la Chandler-private-eye, part historical and part tongue in cheek exposé of the record and entertainment industry, 'The Great Rock 'n' Roll Swindle' is, in all its profane diversity, more than just a rock movie. Always irreverent, often vulgar but a constant joy to watch, Temple's film almost takes a perverse pleasure in threading together the various strands of the notorious Pistols' story and the avatars of the film's own patchy production. A gleeful iconoclastic mock comedy by a new director who might soon be on every producer's shopping list, albeit for possibly all the wrong reasons. AB-F

HONEYSUCKLE ROSE
Jerry Schatzberg
Country singer with seven-year itch neglects wife (Dyan Cannon) and son for wayward lady guitarist (Amy Irving), broods, sings and finally gets back on the right, virtuous path. As sickening and coy as the worst country music, the movie's reason for being is a tailor-made vehicle for Willie Nelson's first screen starring role. AB-F

MONTY PYTHON'S LIFE OF BRIAN
Terry Jones
Was Jesus an apocryphal rock 'n' roller? Partly produced by George Harrison, an obscure ancient, who was rewarded with a walk-on part. AB-F

NO NUKES
Julian Schlossberg, Danny Goldberg, Anthony Portenza
Unlike the record of the same name, this is a touching and convincing tribute to the energy and commitment of Musicians United for Safe Energy. It makes the simplest and most compelling points about power with skill and humour and sends you out of the theatre thinking. Musical highlights include James Taylor and Carly Simon's 'Mockingbird', Jackson Browne's 'After the Deluge', Bonnie Raitt's 'Runaway', Bruce Springsteen's 'The River' and 'Quarter to Three' and the Doobie Brothers and friends doing 'Taking It To The Streets'. Other things to notice: the sexy screen images of Simon, Taylor, Browne, Raitt and especially Springsteen. An excellent concert film. MG

QUADROPHENIA
Franc Roddam
An exotic rendering of an alien culture. To an American audience this is an explanation of the English rage and anomie that led to and formed around a certain, well-loved group of rock bands. A gritty film with the ring of truth and yet a disquieting sense of not revealing the whole picture. On the more visceral level of a music movie built around a pre-existing rock score, 'Quadrophenia' is a huge success — exciting, sometimes painful, a brutally clear visualization of Townshend's major work sparked by several outstanding performances. To the English the film has been more problematic, as it strikes close-to-home, sometimes glancing off the bulls eye. Regardless, its power is undeniable. A solid 8½ on a 1-10 scale. MG

RADIO ON
Chris Petit
Alternative magazine film critic becomes film director and finds it impossible to

ROADIE

THE ROSE

banish all forms of didacticism. A rock movie by virtue of its intensely modern soundtrack and a cameo performance by Sting of Police, 'Radio On' is bleak, boring and much too ambitious; worse, it has nothing to say and says it badly. Apart from its splendid black and white photography, 'Radio On's' major quality is to function as the perfect litmus test for detecting pseuds, phonies and would-be intellectuals. Sounds by Bowie, Lene Lovich, the Rumour, Kraftwerk, Ian Dury, Wreckless Eric, Devo and Robert Fripp and an affectionate Eddie Cochran cryptical homage. AB-F

ROADIE
Alan Rudolph
A nice idea: Meatloaf as a miracle roadie capable of solving any equipment or mechanical problem (even when there is no power ...). This touch of Lil' Abner and Candide in the world of rock features Roy Orbison, Blondie and Alice Cooper and a few good jokes. But the film never really gels as it should, and it soon becomes obvious that the director (responsible for the never uninteresting 'Welcome to Los Angeles' and 'Remember My Name') lacks any genuine sympathy for his subject. Warning: very few of the tracks on the double album of the film are in fact featured therein. AB-F

ROCK AND ROLL HIGH SCHOOL
Allan Arkush
A showcase for the remarkable Ramones, 'Rock and Roll High School' was planned as a B-movie quickie for the Drive-In circuit and accidently became one of rock's classic flicks. Where else can you hear Brownsville Station's 'Smoking in the Boys Room', see Joey Ramone seduce PJ Soles with a song, and then get to watch the students actually burn down their school! 'Leave it to Beaver' grows up, twisted from seeing too many John Waters films. Wonderful, just wonderful. MG

ROCKERS
Theodoros Bafaloukos
Engaging Jamaican Robin Hood yarn set in Kingston's reggae studios backyards. Many of the cast provide the music: Gregory Isaacs, the late Jacob Miller, Burning Spear, Big Youth, Dillinger, the Mighty Diamonds, Robbie Shakespeare, Prince Hammer etc.... Oddly enough, an American production. AB-F

ROLLER BOOGIE
Mark Lester
The title says it all, or does it? See at your own peril. AB-F

THE ROSE
Mark Rydell
The hackneyed 'up and up then down and even further down' storyline which film scriptwriters searching for inspiration always fall back on somehow, but 'The Rose' nevertheless survives all its stereotypes thanks to Bette Midler. Although never quite believable as a Janis Joplin singer on the skids, her histrionic performance makes for compulsive viewing and helps the movie to transcend its base material. I still remain unconvinced as to whether Bette Midler could really cut it as a rock singer (not that she should want to now, with Hollywood at her stockinged feet), but she has a fair stab at it and inhabits her role with fury and compassion. The usual clichés about the road, rock 'n' roll managers and the business abound, and, thanks to Midler, I almost found myself believing them wholesale. AB-F

RUDE BOY
Jack Hazan, David Mingay
A blend of reality and fiction centered around The Clash, 'Rude Boy' succeeds in pinpointing much of what is wrong in contemporary England today and is more a political statement than a rock movie. Racial demonstrations, political propaganda and the decided lack of articulacy of the musicians involved as well as the 'Rude Boy' of the title, a young lout who serves as roadie for the band, unfortunately make the message somewhat too one-sided for comfort. Ironically enough, The Clash, one of the supposedly most politically-motivated bands around these days have since repudiated the film. A strident but ineffective cry of protest. AB-F

SUMMER NIGHT FEVER
Siggi Gotz
Continental beach-party movie, would you believe it? AB-F

TO RUSSIA ... WITH ELTON
Dick Clement, Ian La Frenais
Reg Dwight aka Elton John performs in Moscow and Leningrad in the spring of 1979. A documentary. It might be on film but it sure ain't cinema. AB-F

URBAN COWBOY
James Bridges
John Travolta as modern cowboy and an electrifying new female discovery: Debra Winger, make 'Urban Cowboy' a must to see. Travolta still isn't too good an actor, but physical presence and naivety (or is he really acting?) are all that is really required of him in this tale of Texas night-club rituals centred around a hypnotic mechanical bronco. Delving deep into the psyche of country and western music, the film also features Bonnie Raitt, Charlie Daniels and Mickey Gilley (in whose club a majority of the action occurs) but once again the double soundtrack album is mercilessly padded out by songs not featured in the film (even indirectly, as on a car radio), so don't go to the cinema expecting Bob Seger, Joe Walsh or the Eagles ... well worth seeing. AB-F

THE WANDERERS
Philip Kaufman
Only partly successful gang movie, with exemplary compilation soundtrack: Four Seasons, Lee Dorsey, the Shirelles, Chantays, Smokey Robinson and the Miracles, the Surfaris, Ben E. King, the Isley Brothers, Dylan, Dion and many others. AB-F

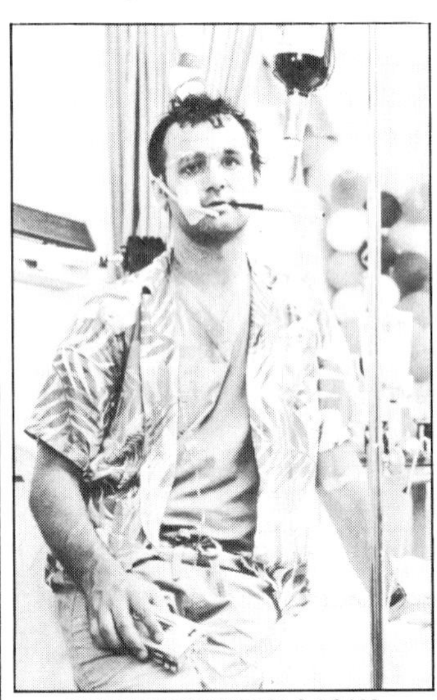
WHERE THE BUFFALO ROAM

WHERE THE BUFFALO ROAM
Art Linson
Bill Murray portrays the prince of "Gonzo" journalism and he alone is responsible for what little life there is in this movie. Peter Boyle roams aimlessly over the celluloid in the role of Karl 'Buffalo' Lazlo and the plot is not visible to the naked eye. However, there are a few comedic moments that make the whole thing worthwhile. DM

ROCK BOOKS

NOVOVISION *(Les Humanoides Associés)*
Philippe Adrien
A novel that lives, breathes and thinks rock. Utterly fascinating but, unfortunately, almost impossible to translate from its mutated, synthetically colloquialized French. See what I mean? AB-F

LE ROCK AU FEMININ *(Albin Michel)*
Marjorie Alessandrini
In French, the women of rock, from early days to now. The author, a respected music journalist, leaves no stone unturned but never allows herself sufficient space for an in-depth report or analysis. Very complete, accurate, up-to-date but superficial study of a worthwhile subject. AB-F

PUNK NOVEL *(Macmillan)*
Bad Al
A distressing piece of shit that barely stands up to its own masquerade of exploitation. You Brits will be pleased to hear it opens with an attack on unions, and goes on to be so silly it loses its own race toward blatant offensiveness. Bad Al describes himself as having "missed the boat". 'Nuf said. MG

BLONDIE *(Fireside/Delilah/Omnibus)*
Lester Bangs
Mick Rock's cover photo is worth the price of entry, and so is Lester Bangs' book. Clearly written in the wink of an eye, it is redeemed by not swallowing its subject's hook, line and sinker. Delilah (self-congratulation) make the best books on rock that have ever burned up B Dalton, and *Blondie*'s the best one yet. Profusely illustrated, and more necessary to the fan than the disco single of 'Heart of Glass'. MG

MODS! *(Eel Pie Publishing)*
Richard Barnes
A fascinating and comprehensive photographic record of the Carnabetian army, that mutual admiration society which spread itself across the front pages between 1963 and 1965. Conformity within the group was the name of the game: the correct clothes, hairstyles, drugs, transport, music and behaviour. Narcissistic bigots who did little but pose. What became of them all? "They're probably in garages, second-hand car outfits and scrapyards" mused seminal mod Peter Meaden, one of the handful to die before he got old. Incidentally, the book must have been an invaluable reference for those involved in the comical "mod revival". PF

L'AGE D'OR DU ROCK 'N' ROLL *(Ramsay)*
Jacques Barsamian & Francois Jouffa
Exemplary study (in French) of the long-gone golden days of rock 'n' roll. The text is maddeningly accurate and exhaustive, while the iconography is plentiful, often surprising and fascinating. AB-F

THE STORY OF MOTOWN *(Grove Press)*
Peter Benjaminson
Solid, well-illustrated survey of the history of the famous Detroit label. For once, the author doesn't rely too heavily on press releases and does a good job in putting the Motown phenomenon in the right perspective. AB-F

BACK STREET RUNNER *(Michael Joseph)*
Paul Breeze
A sequel to the author's hard hitting 'While My Guitar Gently Weeps' (1979). And, yet again, Paul Breeze eschews the well-worn 'rags to riches' rock novel pattern for a gut-wrenching naturalistic ambience set in the working class North of England where character development and social commentary are as important as the authentically sketched musical background. After the earlier book's pattern of revenge, this one is in the chase thriller mode, and would make a great movie. AB-F

THE BASKETBALL DIARIES *(Bantam)*
Jim Carroll
A spike in the mainline of the American Dream. Carroll (whose first LP, *Catholic Boy*, recently made him the only other act on Rolling Stones Records), wrote these Diaries between 1963 and 1966 while living in Manhattan. In both consciousness of his world and ability to communicate facts and feelings about it, he is the first "new" writer in years worthy of inclusion in the line leading from the Beats and Burroughs through the Velvet Underground, past CBGB and into the dark tunnel of the future. Carroll is a writer for anyone who's ever bought a record, listened with pleasure to an electric instrument, made love on tar beach, felt the needle's sweet sting or known someone who's died. Judge Carroll by his work and not by the voices raised in his interest, and you'll discover what they call a Voice in Literature 305. And that's just where he'll end up if enough of you buy the book to keep it in print. MG

KEITH RICHARD *(Futura)*
Barbara Charone
Rock 'n' roll and the Stones' bad boy semi-official biography. Haven't we heard it all before? AB-F

STARART *(Starart Productions)*
Debbie Chesher (ed.)
Young Canadian girl pesters big-name stars to allow the publication of their paintings, illustrations and sketches. Succeeds and publishes the book herself at horrendous cost to fledgling publisher and prospective buyer alike. Joni Mitchell, John Mayall, Cat Stevens, Klaus Voormann, Ron Wood and Commander Cody participate. More than music, the enjoyment of visual art is highly subjective so we shall refrain from pointing out which of the amateur artists should rather stick to music (or should give up music for painting ...) Would make a great book, with different cover design and more accessible paperback format. AB-F

DEATH OF A LADY'S MAN *(Deutsch)*
Leonard Cohen
A rock book? Well, maybe not. But after all, Cohen is still an important recording artist and this, his latest collection of poems/prose is as beautiful and utterly fascinating as his best songs. AB-F

THE ROCK PRIMER *(Penguin)*
John Collis (ed.)
Or how to learn all about rock in 10 easy lessons. The critics who make up the teaching ranks are all good, but 'The Rock Primer' can never quite decide whether it should be a reference book or an educational tome. As with

so many books of this kind, is more noticeable for its many glaring omissions. AB-F

DEATH OF A REBEL
(Doubleday/Anchor)
Marc Eliot
Touching, lengthy biography of folk-singer and activist Phil Ochs whose relentless bouts with manic depression mirrored the collective insanity of an American decade gone crazy. Long considered second only to Dylan, Ochs committed suicide, shortly after a marriage break-up, a writing block and losing his voice. More than the life of a doomed musician, this is also a compulsive portrait of a human being whose luck just didn't extend far enough. Depressing reading, but a piece of history nonetheless. AB-F

THE ILLUSTRATED HISTORY OF THE ROCK ALBUM COVER *(Octopus)*
Angie Errigo & Steve Leaning
Murkily printed coffee-table book offering yet another variation on the album cover theme. The Hipgnosis/Dean volume of years back ('The Album Cover Album') was the first, and still is the best. AB-F

THE ROCK SOURCE BOOK
(Doubleday)
P. Fornatale and others
If you want to pin down the 1873 songs which rhyme 'moon' with 'june' and other trivia. Admire the sheer amount of needless work put into the project, but, apart from that, avoid at all costs. AB-F

ROCK FAMILY TREES
(Quick Fox/Omnibus)
Pete Frame
Subtitled "The development and history of rock bands including...." Though Frame's device gets a little more involuted than one always wants, it also makes rock music seem more organic and human than the rock music business allows it to be. Frame pictorializes in time and space the history of entities as diverse as Gene Vincent and the Blue Caps, Clapton/Yardbirds/Traffic/-

Mayall/ad infinitum, San Francisco, Fairport, CSN&Y, Crimson and Roxy and all of the new wave. Tiny factual errors are the only negative. MG

MARY FRAMPTON'S BOOK OF ROCK RECIPES
(Doubleday)
If you really want to know that Ringo likes fish and chips and what Alvin Lee prefers in the realm of gastronomy. Recipes apart, embarrassingly chummy and elitist text of the "when Eric, Patti, Peter and I were in the Bahamas ..." type. Enough to give you a severe indigestion. AB-F

THE MUSIC GOES ROUND AND ROUND *(Quartet)*
Peter Gammond + Raymond Horricks
Subtitled 'A cool look at the record industry' this collection of essays is of no interest whatsoever. If you are genuinely interested in the in's and out's of the biz, then any of the trade magazines will be more informative (even if they seldom give away any real secrets). AB-F

JAMBEAUX *(Harcourt, Brace, Jovanovich)*
Laurence Gonzales
This is simply the best novel about rock and roll ever written, and that is the reason you've probably never heard of it. You see, conventional wisdom in the US (less so the UK) book business is that books about rock don't sell. Not even the one you're reading, which will have a smaller initial printing in America than in England. The group Jambeaux, even without the promotion it benefits from as a superstar band, would sell much better. You can tell by its members, especially singer Page and bass player Link, two Vietnam veterans (don't be put off — it all fits). The dialogue bites like the '66 Stones. Everything's real but the music. Let's face it, there ain't nothing like the real thing. And *Jambeaux* is realler'n it's ever gotten. MG

BOB DYLAN, AN ILLUSTRATED HISTORY
(Ace)
Michael Gross
Paperback-format version of Michael Gross' 1978 larger-size volume; contains a necessary update on Dylan's career since. The book enjoyed great critical success on the occasion of its original publication. AB-F

LOST HIGHWAY *(Godine)*
Peter Guralnick
Subtitled 'Journeys & Arrivals of American Musicians', Peter Guralnick's engrossing study of the emergence of rockabilly focuses on the lives and careers (through first person narratives) of pioneers such as Ernest Tubb, Charlie Feathers, Waylon Jennings, Presley, Rufus Thomas, Sleepy LaBeef, Hank Snow, Merle Haggard, Howlin' Wolf, Bobbie Bland, etc. Irreproachable scholarship, research and feeling for his subject make Guralnick's book an exemplary genre study, which few future writers are likely to surpass. A word should be said about the remarkable design,

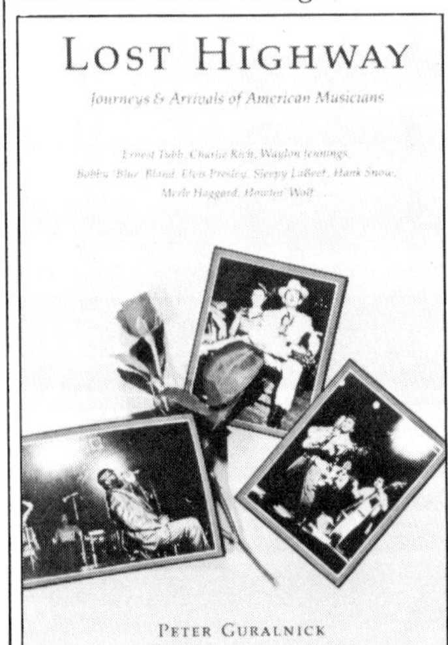

setting and printing of the book by small Boston publishers David R. Godine. A labour of love by all involved; highly recommended. AB-F

ELVIS *(Bantam)*
Betty Harper
A well-intentioned but culturally sordid little marketing idea. Betty Harper is a Tennessee artist who apparently draws little else but portrait after portrait of Elvis ... his lips, his eyes, and who knows what else that they didn't include in the book! He's portrayed in every way but stoned. Has this book disappeared from the market yet? It deserves an early and merciful departure. MG

SUBCULTURE: THE MEANING OF STYLE
(Methuen)
Dick Hebdige
Weighty, well-meaning dollop of sociology. You've been warned! AB-F

TRIPLE PLATINUM *(Dell)*
Stephen Holden
Slick paperback thriller with a studied background of corporate record companies, music, cocaine and sex. Could have been written by anybody, in fact wasn't (Holden is generally a good music writer), supremely unnecessary but an easy, entertaining read all the same. AB-F

ELVIS, THE FINAL YEARS
(St. Martin's Press)
Jerry Hopkins
By the author of the already best-selling definitive Elvis biography, an update which only warranted one or two chapters at least but is here stretched beyond human endurance (and interest) to the size of a full book. Trivia. AB-F

NO ONE HERE GETS OUT ALIVE *(Warner Books)*
Jerry Hopkins & Daniel Sugerman
The long-awaited biography of Jim Morrison, singer with The Doors, is a major disappointment. The haphazard feel of the book betrays conflicting interests by the two authors and one

suspects that Sugerman's gushing sycophancy and sensationalistic tendencies got the better of a possibly duller, more academic, accurate and serious draft by Hopkins. The book comes years too late anyway to shed a revelatory light on the Morrison phenomena. Bet you they'll film this book. I wonder who will play Morrison? Please, not Travolta! A-BF

DENNY LAINE'S GUITAR BOOK *(Whizzard Press)*
Denny Laine
How to play acoustic guitar made simple by Wings' Denny Laine. Gentle educational project severely let down by appalling design work. AB-F

ONLY ROCK 'N' ROLL *(New Manchester Review)*
Ray Lowry
The best of Ray Lowry's rock cartoons from the pages of New Musical Express and elsewhere. His trenchant wit and talent for debunking the pretentions of the rock fauna are seen here at their best and enhance Lowry's status as a foremost satirist of the music scene. AB-F

STRANDED, ROCK AND ROLL FOR A DESERT ISLAND *(Knopf)*
Greil Marcus (ed.)
Shares my 'Best Rock Book of the Year' award with Pete Frame's Book Of Family Trees. Twenty leading rock critics, forced to choose, pick the one album they would take to a desert island. This classic and contrived theme delivers twenty passionate declarations of allegiance — at once definitive essays and fan's statements — that articulate perfectly the excitement, vitality, diversity and paradox that have always characterised rock 'n' roll.

And who do the critics, (numbering Dave Marsh, Simon Frith, Lester Bangs, Ellen Willis, John Rockwell, Langdon Winner, Jim Miller, Nick Tosches, Jay Cocks, Robert Christgau, Ed Ward and 9 others) pick: many well-worn classics — Stones, Van Morrison, Neil Young, Kinks, Jackson Browne, Velvet Underground, Springsteen, Beefheart — as well as more obscure albums by the likes of the Ronettes, the '5' Royales, Huey Smith, Thomas Dorsey, the New York Dolls, Little Willie John, etc....

There's even an hilariously articulate fantasy favourite ('Onan's Greatest Hits'), dedicated to the solitary pleasures imposed by life on a desert island; this one courtesy of David Marsh.

A superb book, worth a full essay in its own right. AB-F

BORN TO RUN — THE BRUCE SPRINGSTEEN STORY
(Delilah/Doubleday/Dolphin)
Dave Marsh
The best Boss product of 1979. The only Boss product of '79 too. Beautifully designed cover, less well-designed interior, many great photos and a fawning, turgid text take your hand and walk you down the boardwalks of Asbury Park, thence around the world. MG

THE ROLLING STONE RECORD GUIDE *(Random House/Rolling Stone/Virgin Books)*
Editors, Dave Marsh and John Swenson
Another of those mistake-prone, comprehensive and professorial rock encyclopedias with none of the life of Lillian Roxon's. This time, the youth marketers at *Rolling Stone*, by way of the rock critic establishment, tell you what records are and are not worth buying and offer some opinions as to why. My question, exactly: Why? Anyone who buys a record because a critic says to deserves whatever he gets. Journalist's jobs are to sell papers, not records, and most of the writers in this tome are journalists. Hey, don't take my word for it. Go drop $8.95 to find out you have no taste *or sense*. Then use the book to raise one of your speakers and see how many times you run to check what it says. MG

A VIEW FROM A BROAD *(Simon & Schuster; Angus & Robertson)*
Bette Midler
Midler by Bette herself. The writing is as sparkling as her talk-show repartee as she gives us the lowdown on her world tour. Compliments to the gag writers or could it be the lady herself?

As she engagingly puts it at the end of this lavishly-illustrated tome:

"You know, I wanted so to leave you with the memory of the good beneath the gaudy, the saint beneath the paint, the pure little soul that lurks beneath this lurid exterior ... but then again I figured: Fuck 'em if they can't take a joke!" AB-F

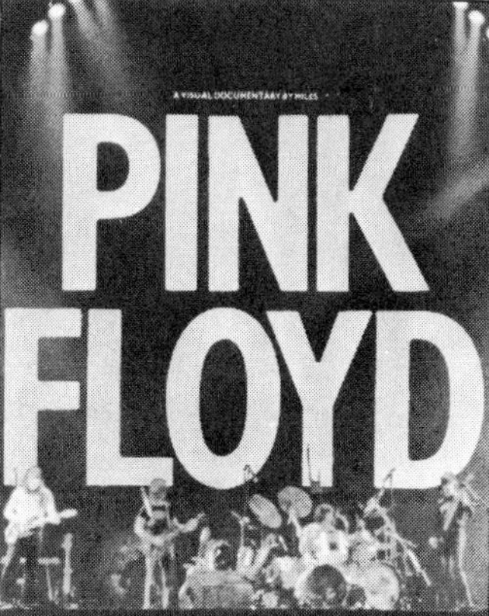

PINK FLOYD, A VISUAL DOCUMENTARY *(Omnibus Press)*
Miles
A lavish, large-format record of the Pink Floyd's career in text, photos and memorabilia of all sorts. Nothing is missing, although the years since 1975 are not really covered in depth. An excellent example of how to treat a rock band bookwise; I can't fault it but a nagging thought lurks and remains telling me that it's all rather unexciting (and I like the group) ... AB-F

THE GREAT ROCK 'N' ROLL SWINDLE *(Virgin Books)*
Michael Moorcock
Inspired by the Sex Pistols' film it says on the front page of this curious novel published as a broadsheet (a first?) At times you wonder if there is any connection at all with the film, so tenuous are the links in this rock 'n' roll coda to Moorcock's Cornelius series. The ultimate rock novel? Well it's witty, non-linear, profane and compulsive reading. Another successful attempt by the grown-up hippies at Virgin at subverting the late spirit of punk. AB-F

MOUSE AND KELLEY
(Paper Tiger)
Impeccable all-colour art-book devoted to the work of Alton Kelley and Stanley Mouse. The epitome of psychedelic artistry, once closely associated with the Grateful Dead and the whole San Francisco musical renaissance. The book comes years too late, the style is now out of fashion but I still would heartily recommend it to anyone interested in the interface between music and the visual arts. What about a Rick Griffin book, now? AB-F

GLORY *(Pocket)*
David Nemeroff
Yet another would-be blockbuster about the sound and the fury of the rock world. You've read it all before; you'll read it all again. Good enough for a plane or train journey. P.S. The novel is supposed to be about Aretha Franklin. AB-F

THE GREAT TROUSER MYSTERY *(Stiff/Wyndham)*
Graham Parker
Written in 1972/3 (and universally rejected by publishers at the time) when he was pumping gas, this bizarre slab of psychedelic s-f parody/lunacy is considerably more spaced than Parker's disciplined music. Featuring equally zonked comic strip illustrations by Willy Smax, it has been described by the author as "great bedtime reading for the bozos who go and watch Rush or Genesis". It got well hammered by the critics, who apparently fail to realise that books are for people, not egg-heads. PF

THE POLICE RELEASED
(Big O)
110 photographs (50 in full colour) of the rock group of the day. Of course, they are all rather photogenic and the rabid fans will lap up this nicely printed volume; but the flimsy text (excerpts of past interviews) and inadequate discography easily reveal the big bucks rip-off nature of the enterprise. AB-F

DAVID REDFERN'S JAZZ ALBUM *(Eel Pie)*
Lots of quality photos of jazz musicians, not many pages but a lot of money asked. I'd like to meet somebody who has actually bought this book. AB-F

ROCK & FOLK INTERVIEWS *(Les Humanoides Associés)*
For those who read French, an anthology of the best (or more interesting) interviews to have appeared in recent years in the leading French monthly rock magazine, Rock & Folk. French interviewers are always so much more irreverent and disrespectful than their UK or US counterparts that the ensuing conversations often manage to be utterly spellbinding and revelatory. A fascinating read. AB-F

GRACE SLICK, THE BIOGRAPHY *(Doubleday)*
Barbara Rowes
Like in any authorized biography, the worst wrinkles must have been ironed out. However, it all reads reasonably true and provides some interesting glimpses into Slick's involvement with Jefferson Airplane/Starship. When off the bottle, Grace Slick is articulate and argumentative but I would still have preferred a scurriless unauthorized bio. AB-F

UP AND DOWN WITH THE ROLLING STONES *(Morrow)*
Tony Sanchez
All the dirt and nothing but the dirt about those awful Stones – sensationalist treatment with a holier-than-thou attitude about the whole problem of drugs in rock circles. Oh yes, there's a fair dollop of sex, too. It's sold thousands already, so what difference will another bad review really make? AB-F

THE SID VICIOUS FAMILY ALBUM *(Virgin Books)*
Lots of photos of the late punk rocker as he was before he became Sid Vicious in earnest in this mercenary scrapbook for the fans. Sid as a baby, toddler, teenager, truant and Bowie-lookalike. Of some historical interest, if you feel in need of documentation. AB-F

AQUARIAN ODYSSEY *(Liveright; Phin)*
Don Snyder
A photographic trip into the sixties which reminds us of all that was most embarrassing about those mixed-up years: nude hippies galore in fields full of flowers, the sartorial ineptitude, etc.... I'd rather forget. AB-F

BAREFOOT IN BABYLON *(Viking)*
Robert Stephen Spitz
A massive 500+ pages book on the creation of the 1969 Woodstock music festival. Weighty, detailed and, no doubt, the final authority on the subject, Spitz's volume makes for easy reading but does come a bit late in the day. AB-F

THE HARDER THEY COME *(Grove Press)*
Michael Thedwell
This is the novel on which the Jimmy Cliff film would have been based had the novel actually preceded the film. In other words it is fatter, more of a story, more accurate, lacking a soundtrack and worth an equal exertion of time and interest. Ivan, *rhygin*, a really Johnny Too Bad, rises from the hills and valleys of inner Jamaica to become a legendary man. MG

THE GREAT SHARK HUNT *(Rolling Stone Press/Summit/Picador)*
Hunter S. Thompson
Gonzo far there's nowhere to turn, run or hide. Thompson, the Mencken of our age, is a truth teller with nothing but contempt for his audience's prejudices, here offering pages and pages of pleasure. Some pages have aged, some matured. In all, the writer is revealed as one of the great perceivers and revealers of our time, in a class with Joan Didion, Tom Wolfe and Woody Allen. This immense book has its ups and downs but contains more than enough satisfaction for anyone first reading Thompson and a fine shelf book for those who've read him since *Hell's Angels* and *Fear and Loathing*. The Doctor's greatest achievement is his political reportage. Though this may not be the gospel truth, it is the truth about America in the '70s. MG

ELVIS: WE LOVE YOU TENDER *(Delacorte)*
M. Torgoff and others
Another brick in the wall of Presleyana. Was never keen on the man, myself. AB-F

KATE BUSH: PRINCESS OF SUBURBIA *(Target Books)*
Fred & Judy Vermorel
Glossy, large-format, but thin potted biography of Kate Bush, full of innuendo, gossip and very few facts. A rather crude effort best left on the shelves. AB-F

ELVIS '56: IN THE BEGINNING *(Macmillan/Cassell)*
Alfred Wertheimer
Containing the best ever photographs of the man, this marvellous book is essential reading for any fan of the real Elvis – before he was closeted, fattened up and sanitized for mass consumption. Precise at work, lascivious at play, Presley is displayed at the peak of his influence, grooving as he breaks nationally, creating rock 'n' roll for the waiting world. As Ian Dury was heard to remark: "If you had the Sun sessions and the early RCAs and this book you'd be alright." PF

DYLAN – WHAT HAPPENED? *(and/entwhistle)*
Paul Williams
What happened? Nothing this serious. MG

HONKY TONKIN' – A GUIDE TO AMERICAN MUSIC *(Travelaid Publishing)*
Richard Wootton
The definitive guide for transAmerican explorers or a fascinating reference work for stuck-at-home dreamers. Full details of worthwhile clubs, record shops, radio stations, publications and points of interest in all major US cities. Compiled with the assistance of local connoisseurs, this is the revised third edition. PF

ROCK STARS IN THEIR UNDERPANTS *(Virgin Books)*
Paula Yates
Arguably, the most unexpected rock book of the year! Model and gossip columnist Paula Yates has used her charm and guile to convince various musicians on both sides of the Atlantic to reveal unknown facets of their personality. It could have been as pointless and boring as Yoko Ono's film on backsides but the whole enterprise has a winning charm all of its own partly due to the author's self-deflating wit and the right spirit of fun in which the photographs were taken. So, if you wish to see more of

Blondie, Ted Nugent, McCartney, the Pretenders, the Boomtown Rats, Sparks, Bowie, Zappa and many others, this is your book. Ideal joke gift. AB-F

CONTEMPORARY MUSIC ALMANAC 1980/81 *(Schirmer Books)*
Ronald Zalkind
Not dissimilar to the present project, but certainly lacks a touch of visual splendour. Far be it for us to criticize, but the whole feeling is somewhat dull and lifeless and one wonders to which of the public the book is catering: the music business or the fans. Many inaccuracies in the listings, but a lot of information nonetheless (although some of it is quite irrelevant). AB-F

EXCLUSIVE!

LOWELL GEORGE: FROM THE GHETTOES OF HOLLYWOOD

LOWELL GEORGE AND MICHAEL GROSS

Lowell George's death in a hotel room in Washington, D.C. on June 29, 1979 can be viewed in many ways: as another in a long string of tragic and probably drug-related musical flameouts, as the final chapter in the decade-long career of America's finest rock band, Little Feat, or, saddest of all, as the end, just at the start, of a solo career filled with promise and a life that had hardly begun.

Lowell was in the midst of his first solo tour. It had begun auspiciously. His New York City performances just a few days before his death were among the most exciting ever seen at the Bottom Line. 'Thanks, I'll Eat it Here', his only solo recording, was generally viewed as a masterpiece. Even after his death, Lowell George's influence continues to be felt in most every area of popular music.

It had always been that way, since 1969, when Lowell, Bill Payne, ex-Fraternity of Man drummer Richard Hayward and Mothers of Invention bassist Roy Estrada formed a band named after Lowell's dainty shoe size (by Jimmy Carl Black, the Indian of the group Lowell and Roy had both served time in – The Mothers).

Little Feat's first album was released in 1971 and captured, like The Band's first disc, a sense of the whole history of American music in songs like 'Truck Stop Girl' and 'Willin''. Early in 1972 came 'Sailin' Shoes,' Estrada's departure to join Captain Beefheart and Lowell's first venture into record production with Bonnie Raitt, the GTO's and Tret Fure. Many thought the Feat would stop moving, but 'Dixie Chicken' was compelling proof otherwise. Kenny Gradney (bass), Paul Barrere (guitar/vocals) and Sam Clayton (congas) joined up and the band's stage sound turned even the hardasses of the rock press into raving Little Feat fanatics. Tracks like the Allen Toussaint-penned 'On Your Way Down' showed off Lowell's front-man talents and the band's impeccable ensemble sound.

'Feats Don't Fail Me', released in 1974, brought Little Feat to commercial prominence. Just after its release, the band toured Europe as part of the Warner Brothers Music Show, and went down a smash. It was during the interval between that disc and the next, 1975's 'The Last Record Album' that the interview below was recorded. It was also at this time that Little Feat reached the pinnacle of its success, a success confirmed by 'Time Loves A Hero' and 1978's live double set 'Waiting For Columbus'. But through these three albums, Lowell George ceased to play the prominent frontman role in the band, stopped producing their records and began to consider a solo career. The tensions of Little Feat's decade on the brink of stardom and the need of each of its members to express themselves were the likeliest causes for the band's breakup. 'Down On The Farm', their last album, released after Lowell's death, was a fitting final shot. Payne joined Linda Ronstadt's tour band, Barrere and Gradney began performing with Nicolette Larson, Sam Clayton formed his own group. "There was just no future for Little Feat without Lowell," Bill Payne said, "no reason to continue."

It was November 13, 1975. Lowell was eating breakfast in the St. Moritz Hotel on Central Park South in New York. He and his band were preparing for a sold-out concert at the largest venue they'd yet played in New York. The following interview has never been published before. MICHAEL GROSS

On Frank Zappa:
I was in the group (The Mothers of Invention) in '68.... He tried to get some records on the COLUMBIA MASTERWORKS series. They weren't going for it. They said "You're not a major composer."

On the story of Little Feat:
Where is my bio? I guess that it was about 1970, '69 when the band got started. Bill Payne arrived at my house one afternoon and said he wanted to meet Frank Zappa.

I had played in The Mothers so I said sure, let's go over and meet Frank. I took him over to Frank's house and Frank didn't have time to hear him play so he didn't get into the band and the Little Feat story started right at that point.

Ritchie Hayward joined then and we went searching for a bass player and went through fifteen folks. They could play but nobody fit in. Then Roy Estrada quit The Mothers and joined us. We rambled through the ghettoes of Hollywood for about a year before we were signed and made that first record. (We played) the circuit. You could call them the psychedelic dungeons. Much worse than the Starwood. Much worse. Lower than that.

A couple of producers fell by the wayside and then I said "I'm taking over" and got ebullient and insouciant at the same time which made it a little pressing for the rest of the band. But it turned out nice because the last album we did, 'The Last Record Album', in terms of production I think I did a relatively good job. It was expensive, but I'm proud of it. It was an absolute bear. Ritchie fell off his motorcycle and that cost us a month. It took six months to finish....

On Little Feat's high and low points:
Let me think of a few great ones. Oh, I know! Elmer (Valentine) coming up to meet the other night at the Roxy in LA saying, "Work for me! Work for me!" Where seven years ago he was saying "Get out of here, you play too loud!"

We appeared on the TV show *The FBI.* Because we were associated with Warner Brothers Records they said, we need a group, and we happened to be in the building and they said "You!" It was a show with John Davidson. We never saw him. They hired Hollywood hippies. They gave these kids serapes and wigs and there was supposed to be a Love-In. John Davidson was being kidnapped and that was the whole content of this FBI show. That was a real highpoint, I have to say. That was about 1970. It was funny — I mean to appear on *The FBI.* I got some mail from it. It's on the air everywhere, along with the *Star Trek* reruns, which is okay, and *The Hollywood Squares.*

On the first Little Feat breakup:
It broke up once. Before 'Feats Don't Fail Me'. I went out and started playing with The Meters in New Orleans for Robert Palmer's album. And I saw the same kind of strife going on within that group that's happening to us. And I said "Oops! They're great musicians. The Meters are really fantastic." So that planted the seed of concern that maybe I'd made a mistake.

It was only about four weeks or so since the band had broken up. And I called everybody up and said, "You're hired." Eventually what we decided was we broke up for more money. Which wasn't much.

You get out and see a lot of other musicians and players and you discover that everybody's the same. I discovered that my band is, the players are, very good. There is a lot of potential. And it's turned out that way, so I will continue with them.

(Palmer's second solo album) 'Pressure Drop' was a lot of fun. They hired me as a guitar player. I kept saying "Oh I shouldn't play this one. There are enough musicians up there." I would make suggestions and play producer. Which was nice. I suggested the title tune. I said it would be great for political reasons, being that it's Island Records involved *and* a good song. And Robert is a good singer. It's nice to work with someone who's really adept at getting in a studio and almost doing every track with a live vocal. Just patching up a couple spots.

On being shown a New Musical Express article on Little Feat:
Oh God! The electrician over there writes those!

On George's studio technique:
The way I work in a studio in terms of production is that I usually just let it happen. Waste a little time and sort of stand around and hem and haw and then say "Oh, let's go to work." And when the music eventually gets recorded, it's done on a very spontaneous level. And the complexity is then intensified by some overdoses, not as many as before, but a few. And in that regard it is spontaneous, it's not formulated or manufactured. I'm really trying not to manufacture it. I hate the thought of, well, let's aim for the 12-14 year old category and come up with something.

On the prime demographic:
As the group progresses it seems to get further and further away somehow. I don't know? If we hit it, hooray! Maybe. Who knows?

On Little Feat's structure:
I am taking a lower profile mostly because the rest of the players in the band, like Paul has written some great songs. I like him a whole lot. And Bill Payne is insouciant and ebullient also and he's got to get his way. I think that's also very important for a group. For the people within a group to feel comfortable with what they play. And get an opportunity to play it.

It has been a problem in that I felt that I was taking centre stage, even though I still am, but I shouldn't be all the time. I thought that it should be distributed amongst the group. The effort onstage should be split amongst the people playing ... The attention can be drawn to other people within the group at any given point depending on the material. Which, I think, is essential for this group ... We're

LITTLE FEAT

LITTLE FEAT

looking for that middle ground.

On the rock and roll lifestyle and attendant attrition:
The lifestyle creeps up on you. There is not much you can do about it. I ran into, what's his name, Bogota Bob. I had never met him before but he cornered me. I don't know him, really. It was great. He was trying to sell me all sorts of bizarre medications. He cornered me at an Allman Brothers concert where a dancing bear was the opening act. Who is this guy? Get me out of here.

We try to portray a friendliness, also a sort of aloofness that most people don't get. We'll get to a gig and be cornered by all sorts of bizarre, unusual people just before we're supposed to play. The band has given the impression of a 24-hour party and I can't make it. I'm sorry, all bets are off. (Laughs) The sleep aspect of it! This plane flight yesterday. I could not get to sleep til ... God! It was 8 o'clock this morning.

On Mandrax and other medictions:
Speaking of mandies, where is he? No, never mind. I'm sorry. I shouldn't even bring that up. I'll get bad rapped.

On the Warner Brothers' Road Show that made Little Feat stars in Europe; beginning with its result:
We're just about to re-sign with WARNER BROTHERS at a much more reasonable deal. Much more fitting the supposed rock and roll success that we have gathered for ourselves. That's kind of a weight off my shoulders because I was kind of concerned about the structure of the group in that regard. We've also got plans to build a studio.

We still cannot get arrested in Los Angeles. We're still an opening act or we can play like the Fox Venice Theatre. But we play there so rarely that it really becomes an event. We played two shows at the Fox Venice and the second show was ... I mean ... Led Zeppelin came to see us and Ringo and the Hager Brothers from "Hee Haw". Oh, God! It went on! Illuminaries at every turn. I was shocked that they would come to a funky little theatre to see us play. We had a great time too. I would much prefer to do that kind of thing.

What happened in England was we got that same kind of audience. A fanatic audience that kind of stacked the deck against the Beach Boys.... The Doobie Brothers! Boy am I in trouble this morning! But the audience was stacked which created that whole series of events. I don't know if it was planned. I don't think it was.

If we find out from the archives that it was planned I would be a little disappointed. And I would much rather be on a show where there are two artists and it's homogeneous.

On the resultant burst of promotion for Little Feat:
The money that changes hands to change your mind. The Conception Perforation had a bit about the record business and that's a direct lift from their record. But it's true. Springsteen, you know. Before anybody responsible

should try to get that kind of media going, they better have product. It's just pure marketing sense. But it's interesting how record companies are spending so much money. I don't know why. It's time for a new star.

On working with Cher:
I was working with Cher on 'Rock and Roll Doctor', that she had on her album. I was singing the melody in her ear while she was singing it. And she said "Why don't you sing it to us?" And I said "Oh, no. I wouldn't want to be Tammy Wynette and George Jones." And she said "or Sonny and Cher." *Oops!* The girl's on. She's very quick, but a little lazy at this point in terms of records. She looks tall, but isn't. Racquel Welch is also very short. What was that film? *She*? She was huge, spitting nails, nine feet tall. My God! But there you go, it's the media again. Then when you finally run into someone!

On the munchkins in "The Wizard of Oz":
The story goes that the munchkins were between scenes, between takes. They were all off fucking. People would have to go round them up, because they were all off fucking. They had never seen that many other midgets before and they were really getting it on. It fried me out to hear that. I don't know if you need to print all that.

On Art and other things:
Gary Burden in Los Angeles had an opening at a gallery on La Cienaga. He got out of his car, struck a flare, threw it in the street and pulled a sheet over himself. He says "Drop a wire in the water," water he's in, "and watch me fry". But he's great. A very mild and soft spoken man. It's like sliding down a six foot razor blade. Remember that one? We had another where you take a glass of water and a paper napkin and put it over the top of the glass. You put a coin in the midde and burn holes around it. The person who dropped the coin in the water had to drink what was in there. Oh, it was horrible. That was a really swell one too. I mean, self-abuse, you know? It's amazing.

English groups come here and play music loud, too loud. American groups go to the other extreme. More self-abuse. Many American groups play too loud for that matter. It just boggles my mind.

I remember just out of college playing surf music. You have to play surf music very loud, because otherwise you can't get the cheesey, cheesey guitar tone. The boinka-boinka sound.

On Kim Fowley:
He's insane. He's a major contact. He also knows Rodney Bingenheimer. He's got the scoop on everybody. He's very funny. I've known him for ... God ... it's sort of peripheral ... I've known him ... it's difficult to know the guy ... he keeps jumping out of cars going, "Hey, young lady, hey, lady!"

On stage presence:
I don't know if you've heard about Vito and Sue Franklin. They were some freakers and dancers that travelled some gigs with Frank Zappa. They were just great. Vito was great with the crowd. He would talk. He would make announcements. He was a ballet teacher and an art teacher. Had a little studio in the ghettoes of Hollywood. Ladies from the Valley would come over the hills for his art classes. He would be teaching pudgy dowagers. "Plie'. Plie'." He was magnificent at crowd control. He ... would ... talk ... very ... slowly ... every ... word ... was ... heard. When I got onstage I never think of doing anything like that. It just escapes me. All I want is to get on with what I should be doing. MICHAEL GROSS

EXCLUSIVE!

NATTY DREAD IT INA ZIMBABWE

At midnight on April 17, 1980, the Union Jack was lowered in the Rufaro Stadium, Salisbury, Rhodesia. Two minutes later the new Zimbabwe flag was raised in its place. Thus 90 years of white dominance had come to an end. Rhodesia had become independent Zimbabwe.

The struggle had started as soon as the first white settlers occupied Mashonaland, in the north of the country, in 1890. Three years later the whites had defeated the Ndebele tribe and taken to Matabeleland, in the south-west. The Shona and Ndebele tribes revolted against white rule in 1896 — an uprising known as Chimurenga — but their resistance was destroyed by the British the following year.

Until 1965 Rhodesia was an autonomous British colony. Then, on November 11, the right-wing Rhodesian Front party made a Unilateral Declaration of Independence. Led by Ian Smith, a wealthy landowner and self-proclaimed war hero, the RF had made the move to preserve white minority rule. Against a backdrop of UN sanctions and fruitless negotiations with the British, the RF adopted a policy of petty apartheid, excluding Africans not only from power but also from the mainstream of Rhodesian society.

In 1971 the newly-elected Conservative Government in Britain proposed terms for a settlement which would have effectively denied African majority rule until the end of the century. Ian Smith accepted the terms. The following year the Pearce Commission canvassed African opinion about the settlement terms. The result was an overwhelming rejection by the black population, an outcome which staggered both the British

Government and Ian Smith, who had previously noted: "My Africans are the happiest in the world". Later that same year modern Chimurenga, the guerrilla war, started with attacks on white farms in north-east Rhodesia.

By the late-Seventies Smith and his Rhodesian Front government were under siege. Although the Rhodesian armed forces were winning skirmishes against the guerrilla armies of ZIPRA and ZANLA — now united as the Patriotic Front — their ability to win the war was open to question. The South Africans, who had initially supported UDI, were now joined with the governments of Zambia, the United States, Mozambique and Britain in demanding a settlement. Supplies for the Rhodesian Army were running short, white emigration from the country was reaching epidemic proportions; the Patriotic Front had the *will* to win.

Smith attempted an internal settlement, with Bishop Abel Muzorewa installed as the first black Prime Minister of Zimbabwe Rhodesia on June 1, 1979. Few, however, doubted that the Rhodesian Front was still in control of the country. Joshua Nkomo and Robert Mugabe, the joint leaders of the Patriotic Front, vowed to destroy the internal settlement. Chimurenga continued.

The following year, after talks at Lancaster House in London, Smith and Muzorewa were forced to call new elections. ZANU and ZAPU, the political factions controlling the ZANLA and ZIPRA guerrilla armies, were now allowed to take part in the election although the Rhodesian Special Branch were still assuring the country's white population that Muzorewa was certain to win.

The election was won, overwhelmingly, by Robert Mugabe and ZANU. Joshua Nkomo became Minister for Home Affairs in the new Government. On Independence Night Ian Smith found himself unable to postpone a speaking engagement in South Africa. Independent Zimbabwe came of age.

Two immediate impressions of Zimbabwe are offered from the windows of the Boeing 747 as we land at Salisbury Airport. A Spitfire revs its engine, preparing for take-off. It is owned by one of the major sanctions-breakers who regularly used the airport for his black market runs into Angola and Mozambique — when they were Portuguese colonies — and of course South Africa. Today, however, the Spitfire seemed loaded with bathos, a Canute fighting against the inevitable.

Then, as we prepare to disembark, we notice a line of officials standing on the tarmac, a ribbon of people leading to the airport lounge. As we descend the steps of the aircraft we realise this is the entire cabinet of the new Zimbabwe Government minus only Comrade Robert Gabriel Mugabe who, ahead of us, has accompanied Prince Charles into Salisbury. We start with Joshua Nkomo and work our way down the line, exchanging fraternal greetings with Zimbabwe's revolutionary comrades.

It is early afternoon on Wednesday, April 16. The southern African winter is about to begin, with a cooling wind in the air. The airport, unused to so much business after fifteen years of international isolation, is in some confusion although the British South African Police, as they are still unfortunately named, stand by and watch with bemused smiles. It has been a long journey, starting for Bob Marley and the Wailers back in Jamaica the previous Sunday.

The first contact between the new Zimbabwe Government and Bob Marley had come in March. It was, simply, an invitation for Bob Marley to attend the country's Independence Celebrations.

During the years of Chimurenga Bob Marley's music had been adopted by the guerrilla forces of the Patriotic Front; indeed, there were stories of ZANLA troops playing Marley cassettes in the bush. Certainly, Marley's music has a potency and a commitment which goes far beyond simple entertainment. He now enjoys a special place in Third World culture; an artist who directly identifies with the black African struggle. Thus he was the only outside artist asked to participate in Zimbabwe's Independence Celebrations.

In the weeks following the initial invitation the idea grew that, maybe, Bob Marley and the Wailers could actually perform at the Celebrations. The Zimbabwe Government put negotiations in the hands of Jobs Kadengu and Gordon Muchanyuka, two African businessmen with heavy ZANU credentials.

The weekend before the Independence Ceremony Muchanyuka flew to Kingston, Jamaica, for discussions with Marley. By the Sunday it was agreed that Bob Marley and the Wailers would be an official part of the Independence Ceremony.

By midday, April 17, downtown Salisbury is transformed into one enormous freebie. The trucks park at the road junctions, making traffic conditions even more impossible; the official LONG LIVE COMRADE MUGABE paper sun-hats are distributed to the grasping crowds, clutching expectantly to the sides of the lorries.

Uptown Salisbury, at the Monomatapa Hotel, the world's press congregate. The BBC's Ian Smith (who once had the misfortune to sign off one of his 9 O'Clock News reports from Rhodesia with "This is Ian Smith from Wankey, Rhodesia") stands in the restaurant, displaying his ornate Robert Mugabe shirt. At the beginning of the year no Africans were allowed past the door of this hotel unless accompanied by a collar and tie. Now the white Rhodesians, as they still insist they are, merely bitch about the 'inevitable decline' in standards since Mugabe came to power.

At the Rufaro Stadium, ten minutes drive from the centre of town, Zimbabwe Television is finding its best camera positions while the seating arrangements for the world's dignitaries are decided. To one side of the stadium a construction crew complete work on a massive stage. This is for Bob Marley and the Wailers. Now, 'massive', of course, is a relative word. It's the kind of stage accepted as par for the course at most European rock festivals. In Zimbabwe, it's one of the greatest construction jobs ever seen. And it's been built in something like six hours.

Bob Marley and the Wailers, plus cooks and children, departed from Jamaica for London on the Sunday evening.

By the time the band had arrived, a chartered Boeing 707 was on its way from London to Salisbury with 21 tons of equipment; a full 35-thousand watt p.a. It was one of the most extraordinary logistics operations. Mick Cater, from Alec Leslie Entertainments, flew down with the equipment and then set himself the problem of building a stage in time for the Independence Celebrations.

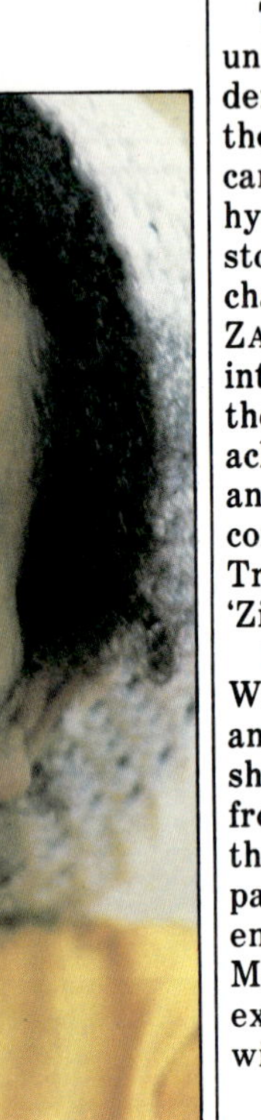

By Wednesday, when the 12-strong road crew had arrived in Zimbabwe, he had six hours in which to construct the stage and find sufficient power for the p.a. By the time the Independence Ceremony had started, the stage was ready.

We find Bob Marley and the Wailers at Joby's Place, a downtown nightclub in the black area of Salisbury. They had spent the previous night with the guerrillas in a small motel outside of town: all hotel space in Salisbury had long since been taken by the Government for official guests and, of course, by the media.

At 8.30 pm we leave for the Rufaro Stadium, working our way backstage. The Ceremony has already started, with eager young black and white schoolkids going through gymnastics routines. At 10 pm Bob Marley and the Wailers are introduced.

It's a poignant moment; Bob Marley takes a celebratory stance at front of stage, calling out *Viva Zimbabwe!* and each time eliciting a greater response from the audience. It is a moment pregnant with possibilities. Rastafari in our father's land. A realisation of the inherent unity in black culture, as emotional for the audience as it is for the band. Homecoming.

We stand by the mixing desk, located halfway down the side of the stadium, watching black Africa respond to Bob Marley and the Wailers. The people have left their seats in the grandstands, finding room to dance and, well, simply *express* themselves. It is, indeed, an extraordinary night. Even though the majority of the audience speak Shona – Salisbury is situated in Mashonaland – and the cries of Jah Rastafari find no response (indeed, the Haile Selassie backdrop behind the band mystifies at least one person) this is a night of some great significance and enjoyment, undiminished by the police action some ten minutes into the set when the acrid stench of teargas wafts across stage.

The police, worried by a unit of ZANLA troops demanding to be allowed into the stadium, set off a teargas cannister. The audience run hysterically, while the band stop playing. A moment of chaos resolved when the ZANLA guerrillas are allowed into the stadium. They run to the side of the stage, acknowledging Bob Marley and the Wailers. The show continues with 'War/No More Trouble' and, of course, 'Zimbabwe'.

Bob Marley and the Wailers are on stage for half an hour. It's one of the shortest sets we've ever seen from the band but, of course, they are not in Zimbabwe as part of some commercial enterprise. Tonight Bob Marley and the Wailers have expressed a potent solidarity with the Zimbabwe struggle:

Natty dread it ina Zimbabwe
Set it up ina Zimbabwe
Mash it up ina Zimbabwe
Africans a liberate Zimbabwe

No more internal power
struggle
We come together, to
overcome
The little trouble
Soon We will find out
Who is the real revolutionary

Brother you're right, you're
right
You're right, you're right
you're so right

ROB PARTRIDGE

Lyrics by kind permission of
RONDOR MUSIC

The ROCK YEARBOOK sent out a detailed questionnaire to a multitude of critics, musicians and music world denizens. The general concensus of opinion gleaned from the forms we were sent back can be found in the pages of this book, viz. The Groups of the Year, the album sleeves, the Underrated section etc. Rather than repeat some of the more familiar names and sights of the year, we thought it would be infinitely more interesting to peek at random at our kind contributors' more arcane, unusual and idiosyncratic choices.

BEST & WORST AWARDS

LINDA LEWIS IN SILK UNDIES

DEXY'S MIDNIGHT RUNNERS

RICK PARFITT/STATUS QUO

PHIL WAY/UFO

Michael Gross
Best Sleeve: 'Nocturna'
Musical Publication: Jam (Japanese)
Rock Journalist: Pete Townshend
Worst Sleeve: 'Go to Heaven' Grateful Dead
Publicity Gimmick: Bob Dylan finds Jesus
Best Fashion: Silk Undies

GRATEFUL DEAD

Maxim Jakubowski
Best Albums: 'Escape from Domination' Moon Martin/'Closer' Joy Division
Male Singer: Hilly Michaels
Best Concert: Robert Hunter & the Roches, both at London Venue
Least Pleasant Trend: Return of Heavy Metal
Most Overrated and Pretentious Groups: Clash & Dexy's Midnight Runners

ANNIE LENNOX/TOURISTS

Anonymous London-based contributor
Publicity Gimmick: Al Clark
Most Interesting Musical Development: Women lead singers
Worst Rip-Off: Sex Pistols re-packaging
Best Fashion: Black and white
Brightest Hope: Rock against Thatcher

BLONDIE

Barry Simpson
Favorite Albums: 'Hegel'
Worst Albums: 'American Gigolo', 'Eat to the Beat'
Musical Publication: still waiting for a decent one
Radio Show: Who listens to the radio?
Publicity Gimmick: Tommy Tutone's glove compartment

DREW MOSELEY

Drew Moseley
Best Albums: 'Suzy' Terence Boylan/'Christopher Cross'
Worst albums: 'The Flying Lizards
Female Singer: Irene Coco
Most Overlooked Artists: Elliott Murphy, Dane Donohue & Sarah Kernochan
Least Pleasant Trend: Inflation
Best Fashion: Mini-skirts

THE FLYING LIZARDS

THE SELECTER

Michael Zwerin
Male Singer: Sugar Blue
Musical Development: Ska/Punk marriage
Hero of the Year: Robert Wyatt
Best Fashion: Dreadlocks and ganja

DAVID JOHANSEN

Kate Simon
Best Songwriter: David Johansen
Relatively New Group: David Johansen
Male Singer: David Johansen
Most Overlooked Artist: David Johansen
Hero of the Year: The Pope

DEVO

David Britton
Best Albums: 'Eskimo' The Residents/'Buy' The Contortions
Worst Sleeve: Anything to do with pictures of Costello and Queen
Hero of the Year: Devo, for resilience in the face of critical incomprehension

Linnet Evans
Worst Singles: Too many to chronicle
Best Concert: Pass! (Doctor's orders — gone deaf for a living)
Most Interesting Musical Development: Boney M
Least Pleasant Trend: Space Invaders
Best Fashion: Bo Derek hair

BONEY M

David Wingrove
Worst Singles: anything by Madness, Nick Lowe and Wreckless Eric
Male Singer: Peter Hamill
Least Pleasant Trend: Dylan's salvation trail
Worst Rip-Off: Two-Tone music

WRECKLESS ERIC

JAH WOBBLE

Kris Needs
Best Albums: 'Suicide'/'Bass Culture' L.K. Johnson/'Betrayal' Jah Wobble
Heroine of the Year: Mariannne Faithfull
Least Pleasant Trend: mod

AL CLARK

Al Clark
Best Album: 'Drums and Wires' XTC — predictably
Favorite Singles: 'New Amsterdam' Elvis Costello/'I Can't Help Myself' Flowers
Worst Albums: I no longer have, nor remember, my least favorite albums. All record companies were dreary and unimaginative
The Least Pleasant Trend: Random intimidation at gigs

XTC

Mark Williams
Best Singles: 'A Song from Under the Floorboards' Magazine/'Real Fun' Tenpole Tudor.
Worst Singles: Anything by B.A. Robertson.
Best Sleeve: 'Los Angeles' X
Male Singer: David Werner
Year's Best Fashion: Professional acid casualities

B.A. ROBERTSON

MAGAZINE

QUEEN

Colin Irwin
Worst Singles: 'Wonderful Christmas Time' Paul McCartney/'Save Me' Queen
Worst Sleeves: 'Look Hear' 10 CC
Songwriter: Eric Bogle
Publicity Gimmick: No such thing as a good publicity gimmick
Best Fashion: Slit skirts and huge conglomerates going broke

LEMMY & PHIL/MOTORHEAD

Philippe Manoeuvre
Favorite Albums: the next Talking Heads
Worst Single: some French lunatic nobody knows out there
Worst Sleeve: 'Emotional Rescue' The Rolling Stones
Female Singer: Lio
Publicity Gimmick: Jagger growing a beard without realising how ridiculous he looks now
Most Interesting Musical Development: Joy Division's singer committing suicide
Hero of the Year: Sid, where are you?
Brightest Hope: Motorhead to record live LP in Afghanistan

SID VICIOUS

David Martin
Best Albums: 'Red Exposure' Chrome/'Tuxedo Moon'
Worst Album: Young Marble Giants
Worst Singles: Any singles by famous sportsmen
Male Singer: Philip Oakey (Human League)
Female Singer: Karen Carpenter & Pauline Murray
Best Fashion: Monochrome clothing

KAREN & RICHARD CARPENTER

PAULINE MURRAY

PHIL OAKEY/HUMAN LEAGUE

MONOCHROME SET

Andy Murray
Best Albums: 'Bad Streak in Dancing School' Warren Zevon
Worst Albums: 'Strange Boutique' Monochrome Set/'Songs the Lord Taught Us' The Cramps
Musical Development: Ambient drum-sounds and lease-tape deals
Best Fashion: Psychedelia

EDITORS' HOBBY-HORSES

TERRY ALLEN

Terry Allen is a true enigma. Which in musical layman's terms means that very little is known about him. So let's cut the crap (and other assorted adjectives and expletives) and stick to the essential: Terry Allen should be much better known, and not by half.

His 'New Delhi Freight Train' song was recorded in 1977 by the other critics' fave rave, Little Feat, on their 'Time Loves A Hero' album. His other claim to underrated fame is to have unleashed two of his own albums on an unsuspecting world.

'Juarez', a wide-screen intimist movie in words and sounds, appeared in 1975 on LANDFALL (63 West Ontario Street, Chicago, Ill.), a small independent label.

This was followed, in 1978 by a double-set, 'Lubbock (on everything)' on FATE RECORDS (same address as LANDFALL).

Both (or all three if you feel pedantic) are masterpieces.

Bobbie Bare has also, reputedly, covered some of Allen's songs.

So, tell us more, you say.

Terry Allen sings country, with a zest of hillbilly and a touch of rockabilly.

Terry Allen's songs are complete short stories in their own right (and 'Juarez' is a full-length novel of love and passions, with etched-out characters, immediacy, plot, drama and pathos).

Terry Allen writes of women, losers and booze, small Texas and Mexican towns and bars, highways and factories, wolfmen, Lubbock broads, farmers and singers and sailors and deserters. His world contains a thousand and one vignettes that ring true to life in all its myriad minor dramas and upsets. In Terry Allen's songs, you can smell the sweat of reality and the pain that love and loss often inflict.

He also pens a mean Texas waltz (with accordion, and all).

Terry Allen is a compassionate observer of other's foibles, a wit and the best unknown songwriter and singer in America (or elsewhere) today and his fans (count me in!) wouldn't quite mind keeping him a secret, a closely-guarded treasure, but then it wouldn't be fair, would it?

If you don't like country, Mr. Allen will probably change your mind. If you think you know what country music is, he will open up wide new horizons.

Terry Allen: he won't be unknown much longer (or there's no justice in this mean ol' world). MJ

CAPTAIN BEEFHEART

The main continuity running through Captain Beefheart's musical career is that he has been so consistently ahead of his time. As John Peel, the astute British disc-jockey has said: "Echoes of what he was doing eight years ago are just emerging in today's bands".

Don Van Vliet aka Captain Beefheart is generally accepted as a genuinely original musician. However, there are certain stylistic influences that can be discerned in his music. Rural blues can be seen to have inspired his use of slide guitar to provide a sound texture over which another guitar could play a more conventional line. Avant-garde jazz musicians have affected his rhythmic approach and saxophone playing. Nevertheless, Beefheart's surreal personality, his extraordinary vocal style, which spans several octaves, and his highly idiosyncratic lyrics represent a unique persona and an inspired talent that has yet to reach a sufficiently large mass audience.

Captain Beefheart's past has sadly been punctuated by a variety of contractual and management problems. These have tended to break up his creative output into several definable stages.

The first period extended from 1964 to 1969. 'The Mirror Man' was the first occasion Captain Beefheart & The Magic Band were recorded for posterity. This took palce live one night in LA in 1965, although the record was not finally released until 1971. As a result, the first opportunity for the world at large to sample the mad world of Van Vliet came with the release of 'Safe As Milk', a striking studio album featuring the then unknown Ry Cooder. 'Strictly Personal', in 1968, demonstrated a move towards greater improvisation.

Phase two, the more publicised period of the Captain's career, arose out of his association with Frank Zappa. This relationship ultimately dissolved in acrimony but gave rise to some of Beefheart's most unforgettable records. Most notable is the classic double set 'Trout Mask Replica'. Magic Band member Zoot Horn Rollo remembers the recording sessions: "We went into the studio, and Mr. Zappa said it had to be done in a hurry. So we did a couple of songs, and he fell asleep. When he woke up four and a half hours later, we had just about finished a whole album." However other accounts would have us believe that it was a very expensive production and that members of the band were supposed to have starved afterwards. This contradiction is typical of the myth-building that characterised this period, which perpetuated Beefheart's cult-figure status. The subsequent 'Lick My Decals Off' was partly in a similar vein although slightly schizophrenic in nature. Following this, Zappa and the Captain fell out.

His next two LPs, 'Spotlight Kid' and 'Clear Spot', saw a gradual movement towards a more melodic and accessible approach. During 1974, Beefheart released two efforts, 'Unconditionally Guaranteed' and 'Bluejeans and Moonbeams', featuring a substantially revised Magic Band not yet quite at ease with the Captain's wild flights of fancy. Beefheart appeared for a time to have lost his fire and some of his originality.

A period of silence followed as a result of yet another shift in management with contractual problems which delayed the release in the UK of his splendid, rejuvenated 'Shiny Beast (Bat Chain Puller)'.

The summer of 1980 saw Beefheart active again and his album 'Doc At The Radar Satation' is a remarkable synthesis of his past and future music, at once marvellously accessible while retaining all his humourous and quirky touches and the discordant experimentation with sound which has long been his forte.

Captain Beefheart: a man for all seasons. MJ (with thanks to the Virgin Press Archives)

DESMOND CHILD & ROUGE

One of the greater tragedies in the music industry this last year was the dissolution of the New York-based band, Desmond Child and Rouge. Comprised of four extremely talented vocalists, singer/songwriter Desmond Child and singers Maria Vidal, Myriam Valle and Diana Grasselli, the group was praised by critics for its new and uncategorizable sound. Unfortunately, the sound of the eighties – new wave – drowned them out. Their record company had no idea how they should be marketed, and tried to sell their first album as a disco record, causing a good deal of confusion during the bands's first tour. Maria remembers: "We'd have interviews set up for us on the disco radio stations, because Capitol had released 'Our Love Is Insane' as the single, and so everyone who listened to those stations showed up at our gigs, and the audience we should have reached thought we were a disco group."

Desmond Child and Rouge began in New York in 1975 when Desmond and Maria moved up from Florida to study at New York University. Diana flew up to join them and they met Myriam at school. For awhile, the four of them all lived in a tiny apartment on 81st Street, working as cashiers and waitresses during the day and singing all night long. Since the only instrument available to them was an old upright piano, they devised intricate vocal arrangements to fill out the sound, and the lush harmonies eventually became their trademark.

In three years they built up a following, and signed a two record deal with CAPITOL in 1978, which resulted in 'Desmond Child and Rouge' and 'Runners in the Night'. Unfortunately, their second album received very little publicity and was released on the same day that two other major albums were released. It didn't stand a chance.

"We were so disillusioned at that point", Maria recalls, "that we just didn't have the heart to write. When our contract was up with Capitol, they told us that they wanted to hear some new songs, they wanted to go on and make some more records, but we felt like the sound record was still unfinished. No one heard these songs, really, and we couldn't write more until something happened. Our managerial contract was up soon, our CAPITOL contract was up, and we found ourselves with no contracts and almost no reason to be together anymore. We'd grown kind of separately. Desmond had grown to a point where he wanted to do certain kinds of songs and only those kind of songs. The ideas that everyone had weren't really jiving and making one strong thing, it was more like our ideas were fighting against each other.

"From the inception none of us had really developed as single artists, certain parts of our artistry. We made something really great together, but that almost negated the other things that were great about the individuals. It wasn't coming from our hearts the way it used to and if it's not inspired then the business side of it isn't worth anything. Now we're growing in different ways, like Desmond is getting his songs covered by other artists and developing a more introspective kind of writing that doesn't lend itself to the vocal acrobatics and layered effect that was our trademark."

For the moment, Desmond Child and Rouge are gone, but there is hope for the future. All four members are busy writing now, where before it was only Desmond, and they have remained each other's closest friends. They're all looking forward to coming together again in a few years time to make a third album – and with any luck, the next time around they'll receive the recognition they deserve. DM

DAVID JOHANSEN

David Johansen makes people think back and that's much of the reason why he's in this "Underrated" section instead of the "Act of the Year" section where all us initiates know he belongs. He's the kind of rock artist you either understand, or you don't and the past works both for and against that understanding. It's awful hard to write a lead about David without mentioning the New York Dolls, and that's the problem in a nutshell.

ROLLING STONE calls him an "ex-Doll". CRAWDADDY calls him "living Doll" and THE NEW YORK TIMES calls him "A chip off the old Dolls". Every one of them preaches to the already converted and we all know how far that's bound to get you. Fact is, most people hated the Dolls and that's why they aren't around anymore. And those of us who loved them (the 5000 or so who bought their second album 'Too Much Too Soon') know better than to talk about them in a crowd of Americans.

The Dolls took one step over the line of outrage in the year Richard Nixon was re-elected by a landslide. David was their singer-songwriter. He'd come to Manhattan on the ferry from Staten Island, a good home, and a family he's still in touch with. He'd formed a couple of bar bands — garage groups called Fast Eddie and the Electric Japs and The Vagabond Missionaries. Then he met some guys who dressed as weird as he did, rehearsed with them in a bicycle shop, took up a residency at a club called The Mercer Arts Centre, and, playing R&B-based pop songs way too loud, became the great white hopes of Manhattan's music scene.

Two albums. One in '73 produced by Todd Rundgren. One in 1974 produced by Shadow Morton. Hysterical Songs. Anarchic arrangements. Drugs. Women. Nights in Max's Kansas City just before Mickey Ruskin sold the joint and moved downtown. A coterie of fans who were downright vicious in their love for this band that crossed the best and worst of anyone who'd ever mattered. The title of 'Too Much Too Soon' sadly summed things up.

So very few people got to see the Dolls. They never had the opportunity to relate to David's braggadocio, his pout, Johnny Thunder's speed-inspired guitar slices, Syl Sylvain's pre-pubie backup vocals. But still there was an effect. As David told Jim Farber, "We did succeed in lowering the standards of the industry ... we were more like Fidel Castro coming to the Hotel Theresa than the Monkees coming to your town".

In their last futile gasp, they were managed by Malcolm McLaren, who took the formula and delivered the Sex Pistols. Meantime, David dropped from sight. His wife left him to marry the singer in Aerosmith. Like so many of 1980's success stories, he spent the Seventies a victim of the music business, tied up and kept from recording by pieces of paper co-signed by people who thought they owned a piece of his soul.

The people who kept David from making music went on to produce BEATLEMANIA and make a fortune. David went on to produce two classic solo albums that rose from the rubble of the Dolls like a New York University gym is rising from the rubble of the Broadway Central Hotel (another hulking beast that died of its own weight), home of the Mercer Arts Center, a basement that deserves a plaque commemorating its days as the birthplace of forgotten legend.

The proof of David's cause is in the grooves. 'Lonely Tenement', 'Donna', 'Cool Metro' and 'Frenchette' from the first solo album. 'Melody', 'Flamingo Road', and the majestic 'Swaheto Woman' on the second, 'In Style'. As the release of Johansen's third solo disc approaches, Johansen is still fighting the same fight he fought with the boys in the Dolls. Is this something new, or just another retread of the past? Is Johansen's English-tinged Motown sound misunderstood by a world that understands him (wrongly and only) as the very first punk! Is the world ready, yet, for a true believing, soul singing white city boy?

"I remember when you sang a cruel and simple song", he croons in 'Donna'."You filled the room with bedlam and we all sang along." Ya hadda be there then. David Johansen will be again. MG

RICHARD PINHAS

Despite a handful of albums to his credit, Richard Pinhas is still the invisible man of European electronic music. Based in Paris, he suffers from the blanket of indifference that usually surrounds French musicians, a negative attitude that somehow never affected Pinhas' German equivalents like Roedelius, Klaus Schulze or Edgar Froese to the same extent.

A 28-year old ex-lecturer in philosophy at the Paris Sorbonne, Richard Pinhas formed Heldon in 1974, releasing a first LP 'Electronic Guerilla' on his own DISJUNCTA label. Strongly influenced by Fripp and Eno, the album marks the growing disenchantment with the growing tendency towards muzak of his teutonic counterparts and flirts with violence and political rage with an added veneer of science-fiction (Richard is a close friend of US writer Norman Spinrad who sings through a vocoder on the still to be released 'East/West' album). 'Allez Teia' and the double offering 'It's Always Rock 'n' Roll' followed in quick succession, establishing Heldon's unique cyclical sound, almost electronic punk, as one prophetic critic put it.

Following album no. 4 'Agneta Nilsson' (dedicated to his Swedish wife), Pinhas sold DISJUNCTA and joined the COBRA label, while finalizing Heldon's staff around himself, Didier Batard and Francois Auger. Between 1976 and 1978, he released 'Rêve Sans Conséquence Spéciale', 'Rhizosphères' (his first solo LP), 'Interface' and 'Chronolyse' (another solo outing inspired by the Michel Jeury novel — now published in the USA by Macmillan, and the SF works of Philip K. Dick and Frank Herbert). All these 'metal age' albums see Pinhas mastering yet more electronic hardware as his haunting music straddles the paper thin borderline between electronic and industrial music; troubled mood music for the robot minds. Patrick Gauthier then joined the group on bass, adding a percussive element to the overall sound and bringing Heldon and Pinhas one dimension nearer to rock.

In 1979, by now on the well-known experimental EGG label (Conny Schnitzler, Popol Vuh, Ose, etc...), Heldon released 'Standby', their major commercial success to date, with Klaus Blasquiz (ex-Magma) on occasional vocals; a long electronic lament reminiscent of King Crimson at their most forceful.

'Iceland' on POLYDOR in France, Germany and Japan, PULSE in the UK and JEM in the USA, appeared in late 1979 and is the solo album that captures Pinhas' art at its most illusive and seductive. Full of lengthy melodic synthesizer meditations on landscape and time, the music nevertheless reveals great warmth and syncopation. You can almost dance to parts of it...

Pinhas and the group have garnered much critical acclaim in Europe and Japan but seldom perform live (although Richard did, at short notice, open for Devo on their summer 1980 European tour) and, in his more depressive moment, Pinhas confesses to becoming increasingly dissatisfied with the restrictive structures of the rock business in France and is now seeking a more international audience by spreading his activities to English-speaking countries, where his numerous past albums regularly appear in the upper echelons of the import charts. 1981 could be the year his name becomes more of a household name. MJ

GAUTIER PINHAS AUGER (HELDON)

FADS 'N' FASHION

When you think you're in — you're out

About fifteen yards away from me the fine grey grit is still settling into the pitch of a freshly covered store-room roof, aided in no small measure by the 92-degree Californian sun. Six months ago this same roof was littered with broken furniture, several empty wine bottles and dozens of crushed beer cans ... there had been a wake of sorts, although the participants probably didn't realise it at the time, and the roof wasn't expecting it either (you know how roofs are).

What was going on was a photo session for NEW WEST magazine, a glossy fortnightly that fulfills roughly the same function as TIME OUT does in London, but minus the middle-class guilt. NEW WEST had finally caught on to the punk scene here in Los Angeles, only a year after rather hipper media like L.A. WEEKLY and L.A. READER had penned their own absolutely *definitive* pieces on the subject, but fully three years after the spikey topped underground had gotten cranked up into its full methedrine roar.

Now it has not escaped the attention of the puritan outside world that Beverly Hills and environs are hardly known for their willingness to embrace social malcontents and, predictably enough, NEW WEST chose to emasculate any threatening elements it perceived in this highly anachronistic phenomenon by treating the whole thing as fashion. Worse, they conned some of the prime movers and shakers to pose for what the prime movers and shakers supposed to be a sort of "identify the villains" picture-spread, an idea which definitely appealed to their sense of the terminally absurd. What appeared instead was a visual shopping list for young realtors and music business secretaries who felt they might be left out of this sudden swing to breadline sartoria if they didn't hit the thrift shops, but soon. Oh how cute — plastic tennis shoes and hand-me-down Sears trousers, ideal for the play-as-you-work lifestyle these punkers seem to enjoy. The whole schtick betrayed the glaring overstatement it so obviously was, along with a jokey "innocents-abroad-in-the-punk-netherworld" cover feature that completely invalidated any serious or even interesting aspects the So. Cal. new wave might have to offer.

But the roof party outside SLASH's offices (SLASH magazine being the interdependent catalyst of all this craziness) was pretty wild, although no-one could've predicted that the NEW WEST piece that it augured would ironically sound some kind of death knell: The new wave in Los Angeles, vilified and sneered at by yankee music business and British rock papers alike, had finally permeated the milk-fed consciousness of the smart press, and six months later these protagonists of whatever anarchy or cultural doublethink it was that brought the unlikely spectre of pogo-power to tinsel-town-on-sea, the writers and the bandleaders and the artists and the scenemakers, they're gone from their posts. The offices of SLASH magazine are sad and empty, and the landlord's re-covered the roof.

The abiding lesson to be learnt from all that — if it isn't by now obvious — is that when the establishment rubber-stamps any self-generated cultural innovation with the word "chic", then it's time to move on. Or as Dead Kennedy's singer Jello Biafra puts it: "Bands when they get bigger, writers when they get more popular, leaders when they get more powerful ... either they flake out, they slowly go nuts ... or they get more and more paranoid. If there's going to be a revolution in this country, it damn well better be run by people who are mentally prepared for the pressure." And every movement you can think of that's relied on musicians or anyone under thirty for its momentum has floundered for just such a lack of backbone, relegated to fad or fashion in the rosy glow of retrospect.

It was no coincidence that we all sighed knowingly when those dreadful "punk" and "mod" fashion features started appearing in the SUN and the DAILY MIRROR ... usually with tits akimbo for the truck-driving and deskbound punks and mods who of course read the SUN and the MIRROR. And thus "fad" and "fashion" became schizophrenic candidates for uneasy definition. Is it a fad when the clothing ads start appearing in the back of SOUNDS and NME and a fashion editress in a Top Shop jump suit starts planning her 2-Tone colour spread for HONEY? Or is it fashion when the broken bottles are getting ground into the shag-pile of a rudely intervened Laurel Canyon party and here's Trudi in a grimy, lacerated ballet tutu, Dr. Martens and make-up that looks like it's been slept in for a week screaming loudly about heroin etiquette, so that Saturday next a small squad of her disciples are dripping their Coors over identikit outfits at the Masque Club, by which time Trudi has moved on to jungle-issue battle fatigues, pink streaks and matching glitter gumboots?

Well the latter behavioural mode has altogether more class, *n'est ce pas,* and classy acts are what fashion is and what fads try and follow. The former should interest and even inspire, the latter are predictable as the next Suzi Quatro single. It's also true that fashions in music invariably become fads when the big bucks get behind them, but precisely because those self-appointed bankers have little or no empathy with the fashion in the first place, they're incapable of avoiding the stylistic gaffs that expose the frailty of something that's essentially ephemeral ... and the customers move on.

Rock 'n' roll fashion used to be inextricably bound up with art schools, but since punk lowered the age at which it was considered essential to drop out of the system to fifteen, colleges lost their clout. Indeed everyone knows that nowadays, in London at least, fashion begins at Blitz. Tuesday night at this Covent Garden teenage camp — well some of its habitues must be under twenty, the rest just mainline Peter Pan-stick — is when a collective, if somewhat nervous sartorial outrage clings to its Pils and g-and-t's. Blitz is where Bridget Riley got revisited and a whole new industry in ex-WRAC raincoat retailing got started. PVC was big at Blitz fully seven months before young mums in Canning Town could be seen wheeling their way to Tesco's on a Saturday morning in a pair of Britannia vinyl jeans. And if you can't get to Blitz, any Human League concert brings 'em out in public: At the Lyceum concert last year, there were a trio of young things with these huge, rigid bouffants with papier-maché dolls faces pinned into them ... and hair lacquer shares took a brief upswing. Now that is fashion that is just too bizarre for most people to entertain and is thus spared the cheap dilution of faddism.

The Sex Pistols were probably the last actual rock 'n' roll musicians to originate a fad out of a fashion they themselves created, and none of the fads of the past twelve months were in fact the product of any teen icon or weird-arse musician. Madness and the Specials may've got a lot of kids into dog-hair suits and sent a whole new generation rummaging around for tab collar shirts, but up in the North and the Midlands where sixties soul never died, time-warp tailoring was not so much an anachronism, more a way of life.

The gratuitously self-conscious black 'n' white garb of the 2-Toners, however well intentioned as rather gauche sociological point, was just so much re-hashed op-art. If you're under 21 of course, you probably won't remember op-art and for that very reason it's likely that in ten years time someone will revive punk rock, pick-up on bondage tartan and the kids who're still left sniffing glue in the Music Machine's sickly

smelling corridors will smile wistfully to themselves ... for however quickly fads and fashions change, there are always little pockets of resistance left behind.

Like Status Quo fans who, metaphorically speaking, never got out of their denim flares (in themselves the spiritual successors to loon pants) and the Black Sabbath faithful who are buffing up the studded wristbands they bought in '71, it's a fair bet that committed spikey-tops will live to see the day when Nick Cash and 999 spearhead a pogo-revival in the mid-eighties and bathtub sulphate will launch a renewed attack on the nation's mucous membranes.

But for the moment we find a plethora of mini-fads reflecting the general uncertainty of the times and the general confusion of a record industry wallowing around helplessly in the absence of one major trend it can milk relentlessly for the next two or three years. The fashion ads in the music papers enjoin chamois leather fringed jackets with pegged slacks, leather biker jackets and Clash SS-style armbands. Some say it's healthier that so many disparate little batallions exist, but divide and conquer is not a philosophy the record companies or the clothing manufacturers are happiest with.

Probably the only fad to have successfully spread its tentacles beyond the capricious metropolis this year (apart from Space Invaders, more's the pity), was the bald barnet, boots, braces and beer gut of the nouveau skinhead. These determined belligerents admittedly nicked their modes from various antecedents (e.g. '60's skins, mods and Guy the Gorilla) but the end product is notable for its widespread adoption if not its stylish eccentricity. The real test of a fad, see, is when you walk into a ballroom in Grimsby in your red Beatle boots, black drain-pipes, bondage shirts and mauve Tonik jacket (i.e. thoroughly bi-partisan and playing it safe) and feel hideously threatened by the sheer consolidation of a particular type of raiment. This is, of course, even truer in the case of the shaven headed masses (even though a lot of them are girls) where a fundamental aspect of "the look" is facial menace, an affectation compounded by an utter willingness to apply boot to groin.

Indeed it could be said that violence in itself is now a fashion to be reckoned with. There's been more aggro at gigs in the past year than during any other 12 month period in recollection and the most disturbing/screwball trend is the propensity of the fairer sex to throw punches at each other. More and more fights are breaking out between girls and since the limitations of their hair-do's obviate traditional methods of feminine combat, they thump and kick just like their male peers who stand round in an ungentlemanly manner and laugh.

(If you're looking for a serious explanation of this, and indeed *any* of the aforegoing, listen to Dr. Robert Langel, director of the $23-million Magsat (Magnetic Field Satellite) Programme which is monitoring the earth's crust from Greenbelt, Maryland. Langel's findings confirm dark rumours about the imminent reversal of the earth's magnetic poles. Any ship's pilot will tell you that the earth's magnetic field (i.e. polar north) is getting weaker and more erratic by the year, and Langel believes, like many other scientists, that the polar field diminishing is the prelude to a pole reversal and that recent volcanic activity and extreme climatic behaviour (e.g. the prolonged heatwave in America, Britain's cold, wet summer) are clear symptoms of what's happening. "Reversal of the earth's main field creates an evolutionary pressure," says Dr. Langel, "and certain animals are unable to adapt." Remember Babylon ...?)

In America itself, where

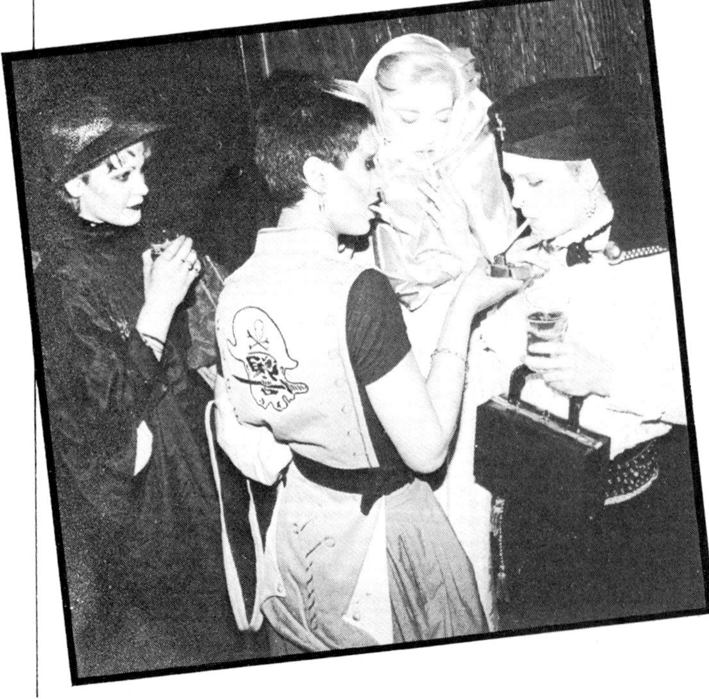

natural disasters are commonplace and the size of the country is such that should a plague of potato beetles or an earthquake render a particular area uninhabitable, Mr. and Mrs. Joe Public can always uproot themselves to Ekalaka, Montana and start all over again, fashion is far more eclectic, deeply rooted and fads are almost unheard of. The REO Speedwagons of this world thunder endlessly around the mid-west playing to thousands of straggly haired good 'ole boys n'girls at a shot, but in the coastal media meccas reaction to the turbulent economy and impending pole reversal is the same old mayhem we're seeing on this little island of ours.

New York can turn out a decent showing of just about any quasi-ethnic fashion grouping you care to think of when the appropriate band hops over from England. Irving Plaza, the Mudd Club, Hurrah, Danceteria or whichever teen-inclined nighterie is hot that month will boast a full compliment of 2-toners, punks, rockers or flat-out crazies to order, providing someone smart is handling the guest list. Self-conscious in the extreme, these kids spend their bucks at Trash & Vaudeville, a truly wonderful supermarket of just about every style going down in England at any one time. There's no coyness about the segue from vinyl jeans to op-art to heavy metal t-shirts to campus casuals at Trash & Vaudeville, and if you're irrevocably locked into the Woodstock era, you can go upstairs and rummage around a whole 'nother store full of crushed velvet, lace and granny prints. The staff all look like chameleon groupies or ex-members of the N.Y. Dolls and spend hours ignoring you whilst they discuss which roadie gave their best friend the clap and who's dealing the best coke. And the final thing that's outrageous about T & V is, of course, the prices, English imports notwithstanding, $70 for a pair of Shelley's brothel creepers is a bit strong.

But anglophiles in America are willing to pay through the nose for what is still considered the smartest country to copy, just as they're willing to huddle anxiously outside the Roxy or Hurrah and wait for some surly doorman to adjudge them suitably groovy for entrance to their overpriced bar and disco. Somewhere down the line the frontier spirit went AWOL, and this despite the fact that the latest pose adopted wholesale by American gig-goers, at least some of the ladies, is the Chrissie Hynde biker-girl image, all swagger, sneer and take no shit.

Taking absolutely *no* shit are the Southern Californian beach people, the extremist faction of the L.A. punk movement which though lacking in leaders, shows no signs of dissipating at street level. I should get personal here and say that I'm entirely tired of the fifth form hacks of the UK rock papers dismissing Los Angeles' new music as re-fried British pogo fodder from the cosy security of their IPC offices thousands of miles away. You've got to spend some time in the city to understand how much more brutal it is to be at the lower end of the pecking order in a city that's built its reputation on the accessibility of dreams and the promotion of affluence; nowhere is a sense of dispossession dealt out more cruelly, or casually, than in LA. The kids who live on the beaches beg, steal and take casual jobs to subsist and their bands are the most unremittingly loud and nasty you could wish for. Urinals, Black Flag, Circle Jerks and Fear are banned from playing in most LA clubs for the violence they seem to generate and the slam-dancing that scares punters used to the relatively delicate gyrations of the pogo. So they play places like the Fleetwood at Huntingdon Beach and "the church", which is a de-consecrated home for various bands and their hangers-on in Hermosa Beach. Lest you're in any doubt that America can breed violence as aimless and relentless as Britain, go to a Circle Jerks gig which could best be described as a mass fight with musical accompaniment. Or, if you're hard up, wait for Penelope Spheeris' film 'The Decline (Of Western Civilisation)' which is a convincing and thoroughly entertaining documentary of alien life on the West Coast.

The beach people, and to a lesser extent mainstream LA new-wavers, dress only in what's practical; jeans, t-shirts and grubby sneakers. Tatoos are favoured, so are S & M wristbands and chains, and it's considered sharp *not* to have a tan. Short hair isn't the prerequisite it used to be, so the only thing to differentiate the punks from the surfers is that tan ... and the speed of motor reactions driven variously by grass or speed (the latter being four times the price it is in England and therefore a status drug).

Back on Sunset Strip the spandex and Gucci loafer set still turn up to see John Hiatt or the Orchids go through their leaden paces, believing as they do that *they're* the smart young moderns setting the trends. That self-conscious assumption by a bunch of naive shit-suckers precisely confirms the perfidy of rock 'n' roll fashion; just as soon as you think you're in — you're out. MARK WILLIAMS

PRODUCERS OF THE YEAR

PETER ASHER

Over the years, Peter Asher has managed to become one of the best known producers in America, especially for his work with such talented writers as James Taylor, Bonnie Raitt, J.D. Souther and Linda Ronstadt. Perhaps as a result of having spent time on the performing side of the music industry — as half of a gold record scoring duo known as Peter and Gordon — Asher seems to have a sharp sense of what it takes to make a record sound just right.

In 1968, at the age of 24, Asher was invited to take charge of the Beatles' newly formed record company. His first move was to sign fledgling artist James Taylor to the label and produce his first album, 'James Taylor'. Two years later, both Peter and James left Apple and came to the US to continue working together.

Peter's interest in the artists he produces often goes beyond the main production chores and into management as well. His career in the music business has been phenomenal: as a producer he has been awarded 12 gold LPs and 10 platinum ones. Last year he was awarded a Grammy for 'Producer of the Year'.

According to the artists that Peter has helped to shape, Asher has gotten to where he is today by being fair and forthright. Says James Taylor, "When he wants something, he says he wants it. He doesn't feed you a line about how he deserves it or how it's done this or that. He just says, 'This is what I'm looking for'. That's not to say that we don't get fed up with each other now and then, 'cause that's also part of his job. But there's no doubt from either Linda's or my point of view, that working with Peter Asher is a totally positive thing."
MICHAEL GROSS

MIKE CHAPMAN

Mike Chapman first came to public attention in the early 1970's, when, along with his collaborator Nicky Chinn, he invented glitter pop and made it the predominant sound coming out of England. You remember The Sweet, Mud, The Glitter Band and Suzi Quatro?, 'Can The Can', 'Tiger Feet', 'I Didn't Know I Loved You (Till I saw You Rock and Roll)'? Chinnichap (as the collaboration was then known) had Lowest Common Denominator Pop (UK Division) down pat. For the Eighties, Mike's brought this vision to America.

Mike was the producer responsible for Blondie's 'Parallel Lines' disc. (Debbie Harry calls him "...a wild man. A piece of rock and roll". In cutting 'Heart of Glass' he probably cut his own throat with the Blondies. They took his disco hint straight to Giorgio Moroder, who's now signed up to followup 'Call Me' by producing their fifth album entirely.)

Mike was the producer responsible for Nick Gilder's wonderful 'Hot Child in the City', Exile's (co-written with Chapman) 'Kiss You All Over' and a little phenomenon known as The Knack. His choppy, simple sound is all over the radio.

The knack. That's what Mike's got. He reaches right out over those radio waves. He reaches teens. He gets their cash. He's known to be a little wild, but there's room in the music business for that. Room, hell, they encourage it. The music businessmen love Mike Chapman. He spins sound into gold.

He'll be doing it more now, as he's founded his own company, DREAMLAND RECORDS (distributed through RSO). His acts include Nervus Rex, Spider, Suzi Quatro, Consenting Adults, Shandi and one-time Silverhead vocalist Michael Des Barres.

Mike Chapman. Remember the name. You may not have heard of him, but you've heard from him if you've ever heard the radio. He's got the knack. There's no doubt about it. MICHAELGROSS

VIC COPPERSMITH -HEAVEN

The name of Vic Coppersmith-Heaven may not be one that has been too familiar until recently, when he became known as producer of both the Jam and the Vapors at a time when both bands had top three singles in this country. However, Vic has been helping to make records since 1962, when he joined DECCA RECORDS as a tape operator in their West Hampstead studios at the age of fifteen.

Vic's background was musical — his father was a classical/ jazz musician who worked with the Halle Orchestra and also with the orchestra led by Ted Heath and Ambrose. Vic often travelled round with his father, and the aura of recording studios fascinated him, so that when he left school, his father was persuaded to introduce him to his first employers. Initially, Vic worked on whatever was being recorded in the studio where he was based — he particularly recalls a celebrated recording of 'La Traviata' sung by Joan Sutherland. After some five months, he was working on a Billy Fury session, when the resident engineer gave him a chance to work the recording desk — this was the first time that Vic felt really involved. "I worked on such a great variety of records of so many different types that I can't really remember which tracks were hits, but one I do recall was 'One Other Guy' by the Big Three. I was the engineer on that".

Another involvement was with the legendary demo tapes which the Beatles recorded for Decca. "They put down thirteen tracks, and I was watching from the control room. They were very good, but the problem was that the Tremeloes were also auditioning at around the same time, and it came down to a straight choice between them and the Beatles, because the company were unwilling to invest in both bands".

By 1967, Vic was offered a job as staff producer by Don Arden, now head of JET RECORDS, but at that time fronting a company known as CONTEMPORARY MUSIC. As well as working with the Nashville Teens and Billy Fury, whose acquaintance he made during his days with Decca, Vic remembers particularly producing the LP by Skip Bifferty, the seminal band which produced Mickey Gallagher and John Turnbull, now members of the Blockheads. By 1969, however, Vic had grown both physically and emotionally tired, and left Arden, following which he took a long holiday for several months. On his return, he was offered a job as resident engineer at Olympic Studios — while this was on the face of it a backward step, engineering being a rung down the ladder from production, Vic decided to accept the offer — "Now I see that it was the best thing I could have done".

Apart from their use by such bands as the Rolling Stones and the Who, Olympic Studios were in some demand for the recording of film soundtracks, including those for 'The Prime Of Miss Jean Brodie', 'Hannibal Brooks' and 'The Ruling Class'. This provided the invaluable experience of working with 60 piece orchestras. Perhaps more relevant to his current work, however, was the experience of working with several musicians and producers whom Vic now feels were a source of inspiration to him (bearing in mind that he was in his early twenties at the time): Paul McCartney, for whom Vic engineered on a Mary Hopkin session which produced the top three single 'Goodbye', George Harrison, for whom Vic did likewise on Billy Preston's 'That's The Way God Planned It', Denny Cordell, with whom he worked on Joe Cockers's classic 'With A Little Help From My Friends', and Jimmy Miller and Mick Jagger. Vic worked on half of the Stones' 'Let It Bleed' LP (although he was not credited; something, he says, which happened a lot in those days). This was in 1970, when Vic remembers seeing numerous superstars passing through Olympic, which was one of the most highly rated British studios at the time — he watched several Jimmy Hendrix sessions ("he laid down hours and hours of stuff"), plus recordings by Steven Stills and the Who (although his involvement was as an interested observer rather than engineer) and engineered for several sessions involving Ginger Baker, Eric Clapton, Klaus Voormann and George Harrison. Of George, Vic remembers "He was great to work with — because he was often involved as both player and producer, he'd just let you get on with it". But Vic's greatest thrill of this era, and one of his proudest moments, concerned 'Honky Tonk Women' by the Rolling Stones. "They recorded three versions of the song, and when it came to mixing down, Jimmy Miller finished the stereo version, and when it came to the mono version, he said to me 'We've all heard this too much, and maybe you have too, but we're all going for a walk now. You can mix this one. So off they went on to Barnes Common for an hour or more, and I completely mixed that version, which became the single release, and it went to number one".

Vic stayed with Olympic until 1972 although he continued working at the studio in a freelance capacity for some time afterwards. During this period, he became greatly involved with Vinegar Joe, the band fronted by Elkie Brooks and Robert Palmer, for whom he produced their first two LPs, and also spent some time mixing their live sound. Of Vinegar Joe, Vic says "I loved that band, but after two LPs, Pete Gage decided that he'd like to produce the band. I think their problem was the diversity of the group members' musical directions — Elkie was into hard rock, while Robert was strongly influenced by Stevie Wonder,which sometimes meant they were working against each other." During this era (1972/4), Vic also produced an album for Snafu (whose live sound he also balanced for a while) and 'Black Sabbath Vol.4', which was recorded during a European tour on the Rolling Stones mobile facility.

Following this work, Vic returned partially to engineering, working as resident freelance engineer at Polydor's in-house recording studio, where he worked with several European bands, and later with Christopher Rainbow. As punk rock began to bite, Vic also produced demo sessions for Generation X and The Clash. "Their manager, Bernie Rhodes, spent hours talking to me about street credibility, trying to establish whether I knew what was what". Eventually, of course, both these bands signed to other labels, but Polydor were successful in signing the Jam, the act for which Vic has remained producer since their first hit."I was asked to go and see them playing live by Chris Parry (Polydor A&R man, who first spotted the band), who had originally been thinking of producing them by himself, but decided on a co-operation. I hadn't really been involved with anything like them before — I don't work on records if I don't like the material — but I saw lots of gigs and got really involved with them. The band worked very well on that first album — it was very much a question of transferring that raw energy to disc, because they were very impatient in the studio, aand I had to capture things quickly."

By the group's third LP, 'All Mod Cons', Vic was producing the band by himself. "Chris and I were feeling different things, and we may even have been working against each other." From the start of his involvement with The Jam, Vic devoted almost 100% of his time to the band for more than a year, his only other significant involvement being with Johnny Warman and Three Minutes, a band who remain virtually unknown in this country, although they released an album in Germany and were signed , somewhat abortively, to Ring 'O records. Vic has recently produced a new LP for the band, and hopes to be signing them to Rocket Records shortly.

More recently, and as a result of his Jam connection, Vic produced the debut album by the Vapors, who are managed jointly by Bruce Foxton of the Jam and Jam manager John Weller. The LP includes the bands top three hit single, "Turning Japanese' and their follow-up 'News At Ten'. Of 'Turning Japanese', Vic notes "I always knew it would be successful. There are certain records you can tell are going to happen, and this week is its second week at the top of the Australian charts". Currently, Vic is working on new albums for both the Jam and the Vapors, as well as with an American band called the Fools.

As far as his studio performances go, Vic says simply "I like studios with a natural acoustic sound, where you can hear yourself talking very clearly, such as Rak and Olympic. I also like the Townhouse, where you find a variety of acoustics — that's more important to me than a particular desk or speaker system. When we made the Johnny Warman LP which was only released in Germany, we were working at Ringo's house in Ascot, and the bass player was the only member of the group who was in the studio — we had the drummer in the hall, which was marble, and the acoustic guitar was recorded in a toilet. You can get much more variation from different acoustics than from equalisation in the studio."

Thinking back to his proudest moments, Vic's earliest treasured time was when he was left to mix 'Honky Tonk Women' by himself, as already described, but he also remembers working very vividly with Stanley Kubrick ("a very interesting, intense, dedicated man") on the soundtrack of 'A Clockwork Orange'. More recently, a more obvious choice was the moment when the Jam's 'Going Underground' went to the top of the British charts in its first week of release. "That was an ecstatic moment, although really my favorite track by the Jam is still 'Down In The Tube Station At Midnight', which should have got to number one. I just wish I'd been able to be with the band when that happened, but they were away on tour somewhere. Of course, that was nearly equalled for me a week or two later when the Jam were at number one and the Vapors at number three — that was a bit too much to cope with. And when all the early Jam singles were reissued simultaneously, I had something like 11 singles in the top 75. But maybe, thinking about it, I should feel more embarassed than proud about that".

When asked to name his favorite records, Vic reckons that he had been too busy with the acts he produces to have concentrated on any other music recently, but mentions golden goodies like 'Good Vibrations' by the Beach Boys, Revolver' and 'Sgt. Pepper', Elton John's eponymous LP, Stevie Wonder's work from the mid-'60s up to 'Music Of My Mind', Michael Jackson("because of the rhyme he uses"), 'Dark Side Of the Moon' by the Pink Floyd, and a selection of '60s singles including 'Itchycoo Park', 'My Generation', 'Penny Lane' and 'Eleanor Rigby'. His current listening, when time allows, might include the Pretenders, Michael Jackson, Pink Floyd, and early work by the Sex Pistols.

Talking about producers who inspired him, Vic claims to have been most influenced by people he has worked with, but reserves a special mention for George Martin together with the Beatles, Glyn Johns on his early recordings with the Faces, and Chris Thomas. He also cites Brian Wilson, Phil Spector ("for the Ronettes, but especially for 'River Deep, Mountain High' ") and credits Paul McCartney as being a great inspiration. "What I like about those people I've mentioned is that they always go for something different, and, never try to copy someone else's work. It's actually almost impossible to do anyway, but so many people seem to try. As far as I'm concerned, I'm always looking for a different sound, and I don't even try to reproduce what I've done myself before."

Ambitions? "Well without trying to go out after it, I think I'd enjoy working with Chrissie Hynde, although I must stress that I'm not looking for work. Maybe a very nice thing would be to work with Paul McCartney again. In the Mary Hopkin days, which was the last time I worked on one of his sessions, he'd ask my opinions and would really listen to what I'd said. I'd really like to work with him again."

JOHN TOBLER

MARTIN HANNETT

Martin Hannett aka Martin Zero, is undoubtedly the most celebrated British record producer outside London. After a career during the early '70s which combined playing bass with the Paul Young Band (Young is now lead singer of Sad Café) with working as a booking agent for a roster of bands which included Deaf School and the Albertos, Martin was invited by his friend and now colleague in the Invisible Girls, Steve Hopkins, to produce the music for a science fiction cartoon titled 'All Sorts Of Heroes'. His only previous production experience had been producing demos for a Manchester band known as Greasy Bear, for which he used the band's stereo stage mixer, as he was employed at the time as the band's road manager. Another early production job was with the Belt and Braces Show, but probably Martin's first significant production was on 'Spiral Scratch', the much admired EP by the Buzzcocks. Martin has noted that in many ways the record was unfinished — "when we went back to the studio to remix, we found that the sixteen track master tape had been wiped. It's the sort of thing that happens when you get a cheap recording deal, but we felt that they'd reused the tape rather more quickly than normal, because they thought it just contained a horrible noise". After this, Martin found himself in great demand as a producer for local (Manchester) bands, and among his productions can be found almost every New Wave type band from that part of the country, including Slaughter and The Dogs, A Certain Ratio, Joy Division, Durutti Column, Magazine and Orchestral Manoeuvres in the Dark, as well as better known work with artists like John Cooper Clarke, Ed Banger (Kintel Tommy) and Jilted John.

Apart from producing records, Martin also manages John Cooper Clarke when his other commitments allow: — "he doesn't take much managing. He got a television a couple of months ago, and now all he's doing is absorbing cultural input relentessly". Martin and Steve Hopkins, as already mentioned, are also the Invisible Girls, who function as JCC's instrumental backing group (for recording only) and help Clarke to provide tunes for his poetry. As Martin noted, "John's got two tunes, but they've both been written before. We have to help him with tunes to prevent him paying royalties to Buddy Holly and Lou Reed".

The vast majority of Martin's work is done at Strawberry Studios in Stockport, near Manchester, although he has worked in several London studios and has ventured as far afield as Dublin, where he produced the first single for Irish band U2. "I like Strawberry but perhaps it's mostly because it's very close to where I live, and I relate everything I do to being able to listen to it at home. I've got some flexibility here, and apart from the fact that I sometimes find the premises slightly small, it's fine — and that restriction makes me work in a more disciplined manner, which is good for me." Martin also enjoys working at Advision — "Studio One there is huge. It's perfect for lots of noise" — and the Townhouse — "I like that, but it's a bit inconsistent, I've found, and hard to relate to. Some mixes there get very exciting and others get out of control. Recently, I had to scrap some Buzzcock mixes, because it seemed as if the sound had changed again.

"Phil Spector was my first and only inspiration. I like the way he took a process and turned it into an art form — of mutilation! Once, the amount of distortion on his records used to horrify me, but not any more — I like it." Among Martin's favorite Spector items are 'You've Lost That Loving Feeling' by the Righteous Brothers, 'River Deep, Mountain High' by Ike and Tina Turner, and 'Instant Karma' by John Lennon. However, he also admits to liking George Martin's work with the Beatles, and the team of Paul Rothchild and Bruce Botnick, who produced numerous classic LPs in the '60s for bands like the Doors and Love. "My favourite active producers, apart from the ones I've already mentioned, are Lenny Waronker and Russ Titelman, who produced 'Little Criminals' for Randy Newman, and Ted Templeman, who worked on Captain Beefheart's 'Clear Spot' and Little Feat's 'Sailing Shoes'."

All those so far mentioned also qualify as his favorite records, along with 'Hot Rats' by Frank Zappa, and records by Abba — "They produce a flood of unreasonable optimism when you hear them".

Martin's immediate reaction when asked what his proudest moment was to recall an occasion from his years as a musician — "it was when Roger Eagle screamed, really screamed, at this reporter from MELODY MAKER, because she wouldn't leave the pub to review a gig when I was playing with this lunatic called Mike King". However a probably more accessible moment to the majority of readers might be "getting 56,000 people to buy John Cooper Clarke's 'Gimmix' record ".

Perhaps it would be best to quote from an interview in ZIGZAG with Martin to provide his epitaph — "I haven't actually done that much compared to a lot of people, but what I have done has all been a little odd, don't you think?"

JOHN TOBLER

JIMMY IOVINE

Jimmy Iovine was born March 11, 1953, son of middle-class Italian Americans from Red Hook, Brooklyn. his father was a longshoreman, his mother a secretary. He was as involved in sports as he was in music, and briefly, he played guitar.

At 18, Iovine quit his job in a clothing store and, through songwriter Ellie Greenwich, found work at A&R recording studios. Fired, he was given a first chance at engineering by the owner of New York's Record Plant, Roy Cicala.

At that time, Cicala was engineering for John Lennon. After only six months at Record Plant, Iovine became Lennon's assistant engineer. Then business took Cicala away from the sessions, but he'd already given young Iovine enough direction to take over the engineer's chair. At age 20, Iovine was working near the top of his professions. "I was so scared shit all the time that I never had time to think who he (Lennon) was", Jimmy told an interviewer.

Iovine's next engineering stint was with Jon Landau for Bruce Springsteen's 'Born To Run'. Through this job, he got the chance to engineer the first Southside Johnny album, premix the first Meat Loaf disc, and work with another E street-connected group, Flame. Then while engineering Springsteen's next, he got his first job at production and first taste of the top of the pops with Patti Smith's smash 'Easter' and the Smith/Springsteen collaboration 'Because The Night'. By 1980 Iovine was established as a man with the top-of-the-charts touch. And he still says his highest aim is to make records as exciting as those he heard on the radio growing up at Red Hook.

MICHAEL GROSS

STEVE LILLYWHITE

Steve Lillywhite entered the recording business at the age of eighteen, eight years ago, when he got a job as tape operator at PHONOGRAM's London studio. From there, he gradually progressed through engineering to co-production, also moving to

Island Studios, where he remained until the beginning of 1979. Currently, he works as a freelance producer, and is in great demand, especially since 'Peter Gabriel', that artist's third solo LP, which Steve produced, reached number one in the British charts in June 1980.

His first major co-production came late in 1976, when he worked on 'Ultravox!', along with the band and Brian Eno, and he has subsequently worked with numerous British name bands, including XTC ('Drums And Wires' LP, which included 'Making Plans For Nigel'), Penetration ('Coming Up For Air' LP), the Members ('At The Chelsea Nightclub' LP, which included 'The Song Of The Suburbs'), Siouxsie and the Banshees ('The Scream' LP) and Johnny Thunder (one of the few American stars Steve has produced).

What does Steve look for in a studio? "I look for the room first – it's got to be a nice recording area, and it's got to be live, or else you can't get a good drum sound. I reckon the best studio in London at the moment is the Townhouse. It's an

exceptionally live room made of stone, and every drummer can sound like John Bonham there." He's only really had one experience of working abroad in a foreign studio, in Atlanta, Georgia, where he produced and album for a little known US band The Brains. "I found it a lot slower and more laid back than working in England – people didn't necessarily arrive at the time when the session was supposed to start. I had to get them into a British way of thinking but it all worked out OK eventually."

Steve's recent work has included a spell when he produced Peter Gabriel's chart topping LP, but during the lengthy period that took to complete, he also worked concurrently with the Psychedelic Furs, the Brains and Tom Robinson's new band, Sector 27. His proudest moment was seeing the Gabriel album at the top of the album charts, although his ambitions include producing with David Bowie (his favorite artist), Talking Heads and Joan Armatrading ("she could do with a decent producer"). As far as the inspiration for his work goes, Steve mentions Phil Spector, Tony Visconti and Chris Thomas – "I'm definitely biased towards British producers, with the obvious exception of Phil Spector".

John Tobler

BOB SARGEANT

Unlike many of his current peers, Bob entered the music business as a musician initially with a band from his native Newcastle called Junco Partners, with whom he remained during the last four years of the '60s as lead singer doubling on keyboards and occasional guitar. After the band folded, Bob moved to London and helped form Everyone with Andy Roberts. After making an LP for B&C Records, Everyone collapsed after a tragic accident resulting in the death of the band's road manager, but only a week previously, Bob had been approached to join Mick Abrahams and Wommet (later the Mick Abrahams Band) who made two LPs for Chrysalis before splitting up in 1972. After some session work, including work on the final Curved Air LP, 'Airborne', and Al Stewart's 'Past, Present and Future', Bob acquired a recording contract with RCA, and released an album titled 'First Starring Role', also finding the time to work briefly with Mick Ronson, the major result being that the two wrote 'Play Don't Worry', the title track of Ronson's second solo LP.

After a lean year during 1976, Bob teamed up with Peter Ker to form Titanic Productions, and as a result of his work with Rat Scabies' ill-fated White Cats, was invited by BBC producer John Walters to work on sessions for BBC Radio One, which he has undertaken ever since. Among the artists for whom he has produced sessions broadcast on either the John Peel Show or the Mike Read Show are the Police, Joe Jackson, the Rezillos and the Selecter, among numerous others. Sessions like these led to outside production work, including the EP 'Flares and Slippers' for the Cockney Rejects, the Fall's first LP, 'Live At The Witch Trials', and the Monochrome Set's 'Strange Boutique' LP.

However, Bob is most celebrated for his work with The Beat. "John Peel saw them at a gig, and invited them to do a BBC session, which I produced. At the end of it, they asked me to produce their first single, 'Tears Of A Clown', which was a hit. We made that at the Sound Suite in Camden, and since then, I've produced everything they've released". That includes the two further single hits, 'Hands Off, She's Mine' and 'Mirror In The Bathroom', and the group's top five 'I Just Can't Stop It' LP. Currently, Bob is working with a heavy metal ska band called Headline ("an interesting concept") and also with soul revivalists the Q Tips.

As far as a preference for studios is concerned, Bob finds it difficult to be specific. "Until the end of 1979, it was really a question of budgets, and I had to work most of the time in mid-price sixteen track studios, but what I look for is a good engineer, effective monitoring and a good general atmosphere. Once I've found a studio I like, I tend to be very territorial about it – my favourite at the moment is the Roundhouse Studio, where they have two good engineers and a 3M digital machine. I think the Roundhouse is the first studio in Europe with digital facilities, which give you a lot of advantages. The purity and clarity of the sound, the lack of tape noise and a lot more facilities when it comes to mixing – when you go back to analogue recording, you really notice the different quality, and I prefer to use digital if possible, even though it's about one and a half times more expensive."

Bob's proudest moment was when 'Tears Of A Clown' achieved silver disc status and was an Xmas hit, and as far as his own taste in records goes, he describes himself as "cosmopolitan. I'm a big Presley fan, and I wouldn't miss a David Bowie record. From a sound point of view, I enjoy Earth, Wind and Fire, and even though he hasn't made a record for some time, I'm looking forward to whatever John Lennon comes up with".

Bob's favourite producers include David Bowie, Chris Thomas, Phil Spector ("you've got to say that, haven't you?"), Maurice White, Paul McCartney ("excellent"), Todd Rundgren ("he's a schizophrenic type that appeals to me – very unpredictable"), Nick Lowe and Ted Templeman.

CHRIS THOMAS

Without any doubt, there are few more experienced producers in the world today than Chris Thomas, who has been helping name bands to make generally ultra-successful albums since 1968. Prior to that, Chris had shown some musical promise at school, winning an Exhibition to the Royal Academy of Music, where he studied the violin, although he cheerfully admits "I can't play a note on it now". He was also in a rock band during the later '60s who were known as The Cat, and were signed to Robert Stigwood's Reaction label. Peter Townshend, who'll be appearing in this story a little later, wrote 'Run, Run Run' (which appeared on The Who's 'A Quick One' album) for the band, and it was recorded with a Speedy Keen track as the B side, but for reasons which have never been explained to Chris' satisfaction, the single was never released.

After leaving school in 1965, Chris decided that he wanted to become a record producer, and accordingly wrote a letter to George Martin ("the only producer whose name I really knew"). This led to an interview at EMI, for whom Martin was working, but it was unheard of for recruitment to be made directly into the company's A&R department at the time, and it was suggested to Chris that he become an accountant within the company for a while to 'learn about the business'. This was not an attractive proposition, and Chris pursued his musical career, before contacting Martin again at the end of 1967. By this time, George Martin, along with three partners, had established a production company, Air, and employed Chris as a talent scout.

His first signing was the Climax Blues Band, for whom he produced four albums over the next few years, although none were especially successful in commercial terms. However, while he was at Air, Chris found himself working with the Beatles on their 'white' double album, at times when George Martin was unavailable and the group wanted to work on something. At this point, Chris considered himself more or less George Martin's assistant, but in 1971 was given his first prestigious assignment, producing the 'Home' LP for Procol Harum, which became the group's first top thirty album. The relationship with Procol continued for some time, taking in several more LPs by the group, until at the end of 1971, Chris decided to leave Air and work on the road with Procol Harum, balancing their live sound until 1973, and producing all their LPs up to, and including 'Exotic Birds And Fruit', among them being what is probably their most successful LP, 'In Concert With the Edmonton Symphony Orchestra'. During this period, he also worked with Mick Abrahams, whose band, ironically, included Bob Sargeant, with Elton John and Caleb Quaye on a version of the 'Dick Barton' theme, and with John Cale, whose '1919' LP he produced during the same time as he was working on 'Grand Hotel' for Procol. "A guy I met spotted that they sounded very similar, almost as if they were the same album, and they are very similar in a lot of ways". Additionally, Chris found himself working simultaneously on mixing the Pink Floyd's 'Dark Side Of The Moon' album — a hectic five month period which resulted in a trio of influential records.

Further into 1973, Chris worked on Roxy Music's 'For Your Pleasure' LP, "It was strange, because they weren't like a band at all. And it wasn't because Bryan Ferry was a tyrant in the studio — everything seemed very democratic, and they all worked as individuals until the backing tracks were finished. Bryan's importance was when it came to the lyrics." After the success of 'For Your Pleasure', Chris worked with Roxy Music on 'Stranded', 'Siren' and the band's live album, and was also brought in at the end of 'Country Life', although he isn't credited on the record. This also led to work with Bryan Ferry during the latter's solo career. 1973 also saw work with Badfinger, whose last three LPs he produced. Of the final record of the three, Chris says "It was as if the album wasn't allowed to be successful. It got fantastic reviews in America, but it seemed as though there were never enough copies in the shops. We worked really hard on that one".

That was in 1974, when Chris also worked with Kilburn and the High Roads (featuring Ian Dury, of course) on a single of 'Rough Kids', which was somewhat different from the version which finally appeared on the group's LP. He also began a two LP relationship with the Sadistic Mika Band, a Japanese group whom Chris had met while holidaying in the Orient, and produced the first LP for Kokomo, of whom he says, "They were impossible to work with, like a football team. Half of them would like something, but when the other half heard it, they'd say they hated it. That was a band with terrible personality problems — they were built to self-destruct". After this, Chris spent time as part of John Cale's live band, for which he played keyboards, over four or five tours. Along with work for Roxy Music, the Mika Band and John Cale, Chris also mixed Ronnie Lane's 'One For The Road' album during 1975.

1976 saw more work with Bryan Ferry, who at one point invited Chris to collaborate with him in songwriting. Strangely, Chris had actually had a song recorded by the Everly Brothers during the '60s, although he describes it now as "diabolical". The partnership with Ferry was based around Ferry setting lyrics to Chris' chord sequences, but little of their mutual work has ever surfaced ...

After making an album with an obscure band called Krazy Kat ("it was terrible — I must have been ill at the time!"), Chris was invited by Malcolm McLaren to produce the Sex Pistols, and produced many of their most notorious songs, including 'Anarchy In The U.K.', 'God Save The Queen' and 'Pretty Vacant'. "The first session, Johnny Rotten was really difficult. There was no communication, and he was just screaming — I think he was pissed off because he wasn't allowed to be involved with the backing tracks but after that, he was fine. Contrary to rumour, the Pistols all worked hard in the studio, and were very serious about what they were doing".

After a number of singles with the Pistols, Chris was invited to work with Paul McCartney on the music for the TV Special, 'Wings Over The World'. That was difficult, because they were doing it the wrong way round — they chopped the film up first, then attempted to put music to it. But I was pleased with the way it turned out, although it was more of a technical exercise than a production job". This period also saw work with Frankie Miller (including the hit single 'Be Good To Yourself') and Chris Spedding, before Chris returned to the Sex Pistols to complete their 'Never Mind The Bollocks' LP, as the group apparently preferred working with Chris to their time with Bill Price, who Chris had suggested as his own replacement.

1977 and 1978 saw Chris working with Tom Robinson on his 'Glad To Be Gay' EP, and later on the second Robinson Band album, 'Power In The Darkness'. "That was a bit strange. I found the band a bit lackadaisical — Tom would shoot off to America for some kind of promotion, and without him being there, the rest of the band weren't sure what to do. I always work directly with the writer, and a lot of the time he wasn't there, which made it a very hard record to work on". The end of 1978, into 1979, saw work on the Wings LP 'Back To The Egg', and in May 1979, Chris began work with the Pretenders. "I'd known Chrissie (Hynde) for some time, and rather than just try and complete an album, we decided to record bits at a time, when the band felt like it, which made it much more enjoyable".

Concurrently, Chris was working on Pete Townshend's solo LP 'Empty Glass'. "It was difficult to get to know Pete — he was much harder to change than, say, the Pretenders, if he had an idea in his mind, but he did listen to what I suggested. Most people do listen". Following these two prestigious albums, Chris was forced to take a long holiday when he was afflicted by a virus, resulting in him not embarking on any new projects during the first half of 1980, although the latter part of the year will see him working again with both the Pretenders and Pete Townshend. There's also talk of a new LP with John Cale, for whom Chris has played more gigs with his keyboards hat on.

As far as studio preferences go, Chris is adamant that a particular studio is relatively unimportant compared to the rapport that can be achieved with an engineer. "Working closely with the man behind the desk is vital, and I've been lucky to have worked with three great engineers, John Punter, Steve Nye and Bill Price."

Who does he regard as his inspiration as a producer? "Originally, it was Phil Spector — everybody goes through that stage. George Martin? I suppose I'm too close to George to be able to really say, but he was certainly an influence in the way that he works with the bands he produces. I remember the Beatles asking his advice about things they weren't sure how to achieve, and he was probably a bigger subtle influence than I think. I've always been very interested in the production on records by the Beach Boys, and it's not just the stuff by Brian Wilson — I think some of Carl Wilson's work is tremendous. I enjoyed the early work by 10cc, and I love virtually everything by David Bowie. I also like a lot of Bob Dylan's records, which apprently weren't produced by anybody, and I thought 'Something /Anything' by Todd Rundgren was amazing. More recently, I've been impressed by Steve Lillywhite's work on the latest Peter Gabriel album".

Chris' personal musical tastes often coincide with the work of the producers mentioned above, but he reserves a special mention for Buddy Holly ("I had a big interest in him, which made the difference between the Royal Academy and what I've ended up doing") and for classical music, in particular Berlioz' 'Requiem' and Bruckner's '9th' ("a great turgid piece of music — I got into that from hanging around with John Cale").

AGREE OR DISAGREE

OUR TIPS FOR '81/'82

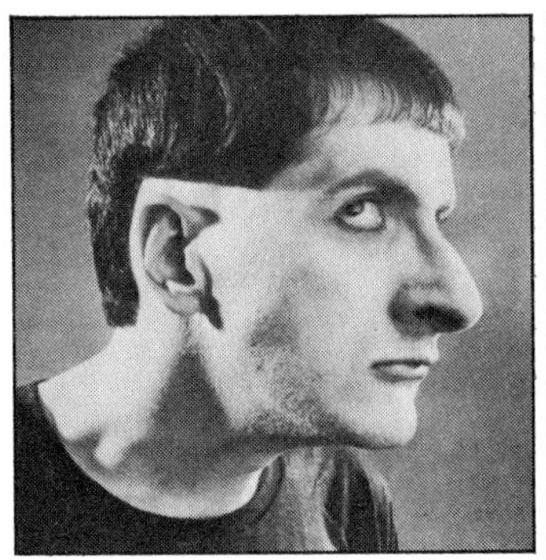

Skafish
The pose is the nose.

Def Leppard
Yet more heavy-metal hopefuls already well on the way to the rock Valhalla of the deaf.

Johnny G
Eclectic mystery man might not be mysterious much longer.

Inmates
Sleazy bar rhythm and blues music. Great Rolling Stones cover versions.

Willie Nile
Although mooted as this quarter's Bob Dylan, this New York songster is also in the Steve Forbert mould. Nice lyrics.

A Certain Ratio
Another offshoot of the Factory mafia. Could take over the, alas, fallen mantle of Joy Division.

Basement 5
Led by Dennis Morris, ex-Island art director and ace photographer, the epitome of reggae new wave.

Killing Joke
Modern band for the bleak modern world, blending punk, power and aggression.

F. Beat
Enterprising entrepreneur Jake Riviera's new label: Costello, Clive Langer, Carlene Carter. Everything he touches turns to gold.

Roky Erickson
A long-shot hot-shot courtesy of Pete Frame who's been known to be right.

Stiff
A label by and for eccentrics. Strangely enough, the formula works commercially: Lovich, Plasmatics, Jona Lewie, Rachel Sweet, Any Trouble, Graham Parker, Desmond Dekker and others adorn the roster.

Liverpool
Zoo and Eric's. The town of the 60's. The town of the 80's.

Original Mirrors
Ex-Deaf School. Better live than on vinyl. Melodies and impeccable musicianship.

Model Citizens
This band has splintered into any number of interesting offshoots including Two Yous, a multi-media group lead by a Bryan Ferry lookalike and Dance, whose 'Chandra' EP includes four tracks with vocals by 11 year-old Chandra Oppenheim.

Echo & The Bunnymen
And the psychedelic revival goes on and on and on, with heartfelt acknowledgement to The Doors.

Holly and The Italians
Thin Angeleno lady moves to London and rocks out with the power chords disregarding all fashions. Tough and melodic.

Krokus
Swiss heavy-metal rockers, which goes to show that no country is immune to the rising wail of the Stratocaster.

Toyah
Actress (Jubilee, The Tempest) with singing pretensions and gaudy-coloured hair. Devoted, very fanatical following, will impose her at the top.

Athletico Spizz 80
Previously known as Spizz Oil and Spizz Energi, high-energy combo who are A&M's hope for the future. Should not change name again.

Kirsty McColl
Folk-singer's daughter previously signed to Stiff and not content with being a Rachel Sweet understudy.

U2
Irish new wave pop and our editorial assistant says they're energetic and great and should be superstars.

Ultravox
A change of label has revitalized these synthesizer rockers whose main fault was to have been in advance of time and fashion.

Metal Boys
They're French; they're good; they're heavy.

UB40
The groups's name is inspired by a British unemployment application form and they play a blend of polished high energy, vindictive soul-come-reggae.

Synthetic Rock
Foxx, OMD, Ultravox, young Numan. Long live the microchip!

Expressos
Having a pretty lady in the line-up is, these days, halfways to success. But The Expressos have more than that. How can they fail?

Ron Alexenburg
Infinity Records' Mogul whose label was pulled out from under him bounces back with a new plastic disc company, 'Handshake', backed by deutschmarks from Germany's Hansa.

Spandau Ballet
Art school jumble sale chic. Style is of the essence.

B-Girls
A Debbie Harry production. Is this the second wave Stilletos?

Shakers
Percussionist Michael Shrieve's new band. Unsigned, but the buzz is on the streets.

Joe Ely
Pudgy country rocker charms the Clash and UK audiences. But no prophet in his own country.

Wesley Strick and the Stereotypes
The best looking pop band on the New York club circuit. Their gay sendup of 'My Boyfriend's Back' may have been 1980's most classic rare single.

Q-Tips
Close to the front of the pack of the many would-be soul revivalists.

Salsa
Year after year, the rhythm of the barrio has another go at getting the world to dance in frenzied abandon.

Motels
Atmospheric L.A. new wave band with sultry Martha Davis on vocals. Will be, must be, should be big.

Splodgenessabounds
How to make a career of idiosyncratic vulgarity. Dubious music but great entertainment.

Bridget St. John
Rural English folkie moves to Greenwich village and gets new, electric, lease of life.

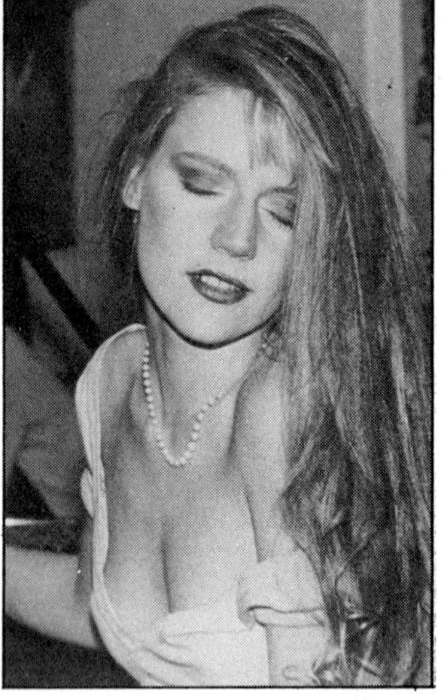

Phoebe Legere and Monad
The second bestlooking pop band on the New York club circuit. Very idionsyncratic. The boys don't know, but the little girls understand.

Terence Boylan
Boylan's unique ability as a lyricist has always been apparent, and his talent as a composer grows with each album. He avoids the trap of musical trends.

The Necessaries
Ernie Brooks (ex of the Modern Lovers) formed this combo on the New York new wave club circuit. When journeyman guitar virtuoso Chris Spedding joined up, attention began to be paid. With good reason.

One Trick Pony
Paul Simon goes Hollywood in his first big film, partially produced at the Concord Hotel, a singles Haven in New York's Catskill Mountains.

Hitmen
Bright and bouncy lightweight pop. So what's wrong with that, OK?

Art
We're all "Boat People" according to their dada-esque 45 about Vietnam and other things.

Times Square
The next big music film from the Robert Stigwood organization.

Lust/Unlust Music
Could become New York City's Stiff...current acts includes Love of Life Orchestra and Lydia Lunch (ex of Teenage Jesus and the Jerks).

Bodysnatchers
The ladies of Two-Tone go on the warpath for more than equal rights.

UT
All-girl polyrhythmic band led by Karen Ackenbach...a Rhode Island School of Design alum (just like Talking Heads), often described as "disturbed". She sleeps on a bed of rocks and thinks life is an adventure.

Bob Dylan by Robert Shelton
12 years in the making, this major biography will at last be seeing the light of day (Doubleday in the USA: NEL in the UK).

Any Trouble
Pub rock rises again (with sounds of Elvis Costello recognisable in the background).

Sterling
With songs like 'Robosexual', this is a band with its eye on the future and a lot of backing. Consistently uptempo and consistently excellent.

Rickie Lee Jones
Singer/Songwriter. New sounds get harder and harder to come by, but Rickie Lee's debut album proved that she's got something very special. 1981 is bound to be her year.

Jock McClean
Director of Artist Development, Columbia Records. McClean's ideas for the coming year include signing more artists on a singles (as opposed to albums) basis and staging events like last year's 'Rock Into the '80s' concert, with up to five bands on the program.

Michael McDonald
Keyboard player, singer/songwriter, Doobie Brother. Michael's solo album displayed his considerable talent as a musician and beyond the glimpses we were given by his work with the Doobies.

Wah Heat
Modern gothic best characterises their sound and image.

Polyrock
New-classical, new-wave fusion combo being produced by Philip Glass ('Einstein on the Beach').

Cure
Agressive new wave punkers slowly metamorphosing into spectral, atmospheric band, full of unknown promises of even better things to come.

Jimmy Destri
Producer, Member of Blondie. While Debbie Harry made her foray into the world of cinematography and jeans, Destri took some bands into his studio to test his mettle as producer. The results speak for themselves.

Ray Gomez
Ex-jazz fusion guitarist turns heavy and gives birth to an incredibly heavy over-produced version of 'Summer In the City'.

Moon Martin
Diminutive guitarist deserves megasuccess after providing hits for other, lesser performers.

Sting
The face from Police will hit the large screen with a vengeance and also publish a book for children (Message In A Bottle).

Roy Sundholm
Idiosyncratic British musicians with a knack for catchy melodies.

Chris Burden
Conceptual artist now performing 'Atomic Alphabet' at venues like the Mudd Club.

Rock Pool
Disc jockey heaven. Spinners from clubs all over the city can find any record they want thanks to this institution.

Martha and the Muffins
Canadian exports with two Marthas, two Ganes and two Muffins. In the art school mold.

The Maroons
Small NY band with one self-released single which should have been picked up by a major but wasn't. Time is on their side.

Pauline Murray
Lead singer with Penetration now on RSO whose golden touch hasn't until yet really succeeded with a girl singer. Could well be another Stigwood certainty. The lady has great eyes.

The Beat
Not Paul Collins' Beat, but the English Beat. Ska reigns supreme.

Bim
Bobbie Henry's (ex-Oval) new band. On the starting line ready to go.

Klaus Nomi
New age operatic soprano. His appearances at Xeon and Fiorucci's New York store have attracted the trendies in droves. Klaus is the bizarre character behind David Bowie in his recent Night Live appearance. Unclear commercial potential. Do you Nomi? Nomi does Lou Christie's 'Lightning Strikes'.

Container
Artist Jamie Dalglish and musician George Elliot's vehicle for "no wave music for children". Innocent rhythms. Multi-level performance with film, sound, video and femme fatale lead singer Jane Hamper.

Latoya Jackson
The Five's pretty sister is making tracks towards her first LP.

Love In Vain
Doubleday will publish this biography of bluesman Robert Johnson. Mick Jagger owns the film rights. Peter Guralnick contributes a learned introduction.

The Fabulous Thunderbirds
The best thing to happen to the electric blues since Paul Butterfield. Record for Takoma/Chrysalis.

Joe Perry
Aerosmith's guitarist goes solo. Perry deserves praise not only for coming to his senses and leaving Aerosmith but for his excellent guitar work on 'The Joe Perry Project'. No wonder Steve Tyler's been throwing more tantrums than usual.

Jimmy Pullis
Owner, JP's and Trax. Since the founding of JP's some five years ago, 'JP' has done his utmost to help new acts break into the record business. With the addition of Trax, a larger club more conducive to rock, music found a home away from the garage.

Regina Richards
Singer/Songwriter. With her 'Red Hot' band, Regina has only begun to rock, but her live performance is stunning. She has all the basics and no need for the frills.

20/20
Melodic rock at its very best. Ron Flynt and Steve Allen share forceful vocals and even stronger songwriting.

Girl Groups
So what's wrong about girls (The Raincoats, The Modettes, Girlschool, Slits, The Go Gos, The Orchids and they keep on coming)?

Psychedelic Furs
Resolutely out-of-fashion but pleasant nevertheless.

Suicide
The two man band whose second album, produced by The Cars' Ric Ocasek, has set the pace for where electronic/synthesizer music might go if the people playing it had taste.

Ze
New wave disco at its best on the Paris—New York axis.

OUR TIPS FOR '81/'82

Dead On Arrival
High Times magazine's Sex Pistols film. The title says it all.

Jim Steinman
Meat Loaf rejected his lyricist's second album, so Steinman is recording it himself.

Rock Gomorrah
Lester Bangs and Michael Ochs (Phil's brother) are co-producing this look at the sleazy side of rock, subtitled the music business' Hollywood Babylon. Coming soon from Virgin Books and Delilah.

Ellen Foley
The eyes of the year. Small lady with luscious big sound (courtesy of Mick Ronson) and hypnotizing (if brash) stage presence.

The Urban Verbs
Pretention unlimited from the little bro' of Talking Heads drummer Chris Frantz and his Washington D.C. combo. Crosses T-Heads with Doors. May be better than it sounds.

X
LA punk supremos. Darlings of some critics.

Jane Kennaway
A tough lady who has what it takes. Blondes always win out.

Walter Egan
Hasn't made it so far despite the Fleetwood Mac connection but every new platter is full of hidden treasures.

Paula Yates
More than just a pretty face, this model-journalist and wit must surely make it all the way to the silver screen.

Tommy Tutone
All of the advance press and publicity might have led to a let-down but this band deserved it. They've been described as the best thing to happen this year, and there is no evidence to the contrary.

Bebe Buell
The music world's Lily Langtree has been secretly planning a record since her days with Todd Rundgren. Including The Cars, Rick Derringer and other superstars (and dear old friends of Bebe's)..this may surprise some folks.

Jim Carroll
Pulitzer-nominated poet, author of the just re-released *Basketball Diaries*, close friend of Patti Smith, now on Rolling Stones Records with *Catholic Boy* ("redeemed through pain/not through joy"). About as hot as an unreleased act can get.

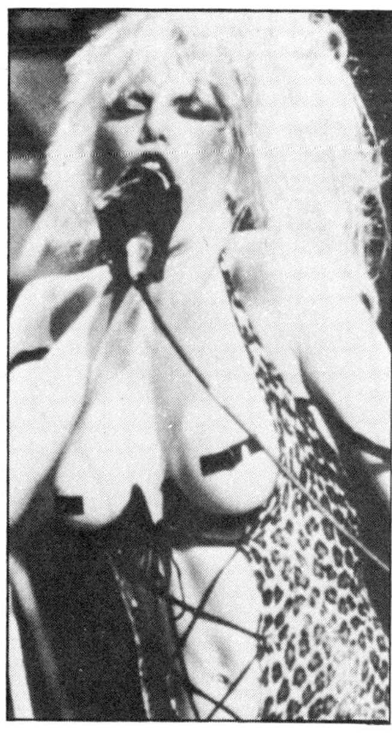

The Plasmatics
A female-fronted NYC band led by a woman who is rock's version of the Playboy centrespread. Sex and violence.

Richard Belzer
Comedian, Host of TV's 'It's Rock & Roll'. Now that music has really come into its own as a multi-media art, the obvious progression was a TV game show. Fortunately, Belzer has the talent to lift it above 'Gong Show' level and make it fun.

Joe 'King' Carrasco
Mexicali Punk Rocker from Austin, Texas with a sound that crosses Doug Sahm with Sam the Sham.

The Cretones
After scoring three songs on Linda Ronstadt's 'Mad Love' LP, The Cretones proves themselves as artists with their debut album, 'Thin Red Line'.

Danceteria
Clubmaker Jim Fouratt's latest venture opens late and has an admission price that rises as the evening wears on. Three floors, three sounds, exotic and out of town bands for the New York City scene.

The Vapours
One hit so far. Will they have others?

TOOLS OF THE TRADE

You probably see and/or hear your music in a wide variety of settings: on stage in outdoor giant ashtrays or inside sweaty cupboards, or on record from Indie 45s on ancient Dansettes to digitally-recorded albums on the highest-of-fi. Similarly, a huge variety of musical instruments, amplification and assorted ancillary equipment is used actually to *produce* all the music, so I'm offering here an haphazard glance at developments in

LES PAUL ARTIST GUITAR

these areas over the past year or so, coupled with a few guesses as to what might be used soon in the garages, basements, pubs, clubs, concert halls and auditoriums that host rock music.

Of course, different kinds of musicians have correspondingly different attitudes to the tools of their trade – there's the 'It-doesn't matter-what-guitar-I-use it's-the-feeling-that-counts' school, contrasted by the just as vehement 'My-instruments have-to-be-at-least-as complicated-as-my-music' club. Either way, an amplified rock band's instruments and equipment are usually an odd combination of old traditional crafts (especially in the guitarist's department, where carefully chosen woods may be used for the better instruments which can often be totally 'hand-made', or at least hand finished), and the newest of new scientific advances (especially in the keyboardist's department, with computer technology fast invading even the most basic synthesizer). But it's tension that makes good rock music, and musicians will argue forever over whether it's worth bothering about what particular instrument or amp you use and, if the conclusion to that one is yes, whether your 1958 Gibson **Les Paul** will automatically produce better music than my 1980 cheapo Taiwan-made electric guitar.

Talking of **Les Pauls**, any investigation of the instruments that guitarists are using these days would certainly come to the conclusion that these players are a conservative lot – the two most popular electric guitars would be the Gibson **Les Paul** (introduced in 1952 and still going strong) and the Fender **Stratocaster** (first issued in 1954 and ever-popular). So what's happening behind this front-stage group

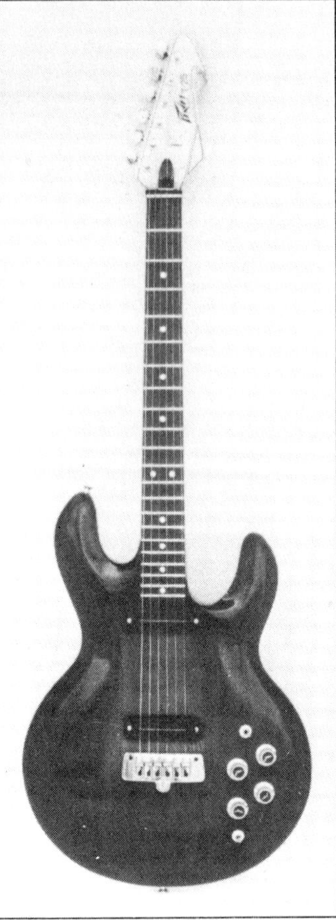

PEAVEY PROTOTYPE T-25 GUITAR

of seemingly unadventurous guitarists? Well, recently (although the process has taken a long ten to 15 years to bear good fruit) the Japanese threat to the previously undisputed American dominance of the electric guitar manufacturing industry has been becoming something like a parallel force, maybe even more. If Gibson and Fender are The Two Big Ones of US electric guitar, then the equivalent among the Japanese must be Ibanez and Yamaha.

And it's worth stressing that it *is* an *industry* with which we are dealing here – marketing strategy and business deals are inevitably going to play a part in what you see musicians using. The guitar which is currently sitting at the number three position in the Popular Japanese Electric Chart is Aria, and this is as much to do with the excellence and value-for-money of the first models available as it is to the extensive and efficient marketing policy adopted by the British importing firm – curiously, in the musical instrument fraternity, a small, healthy, new company.

But enough of high finance. What's been happening to electric guitars? I think two areas of interest recently have been active electronics and unconventional construction materials. Active electronics simply mean that the guitar in question has, on board, its own built-in, battery-powered pre-amp to allow the player (who, with the standard 'passive' tone controls, could only cut the tone already there) to add or subtract 12 or even 15dB to or from the bass and treble settings of the instrument. The idea's nothing *particularly* new (Gibson and Alembrics were among the American companies to encourage its introduction), but it's taken a while to be introduced on to normal production instruments. Some of the bigger manufacturers have, at last, issued guitars incorporating the circuits: Gibson have built on their original **RD Artist** innovations to launch, this year, a range of active-powered versions of their more successful models – most notably, of the **Les Paul** and the **ES335**. Fender, however, have only just got round to acknowledging the existence of active electronics: they showed an active-powered version of their extremely popular **Precision** bass guitar at a recent American trade show, so models will soon be reaching the music shops.

Materials for guitars other than wood (traditional woods

for electronics include ash for bodies, maple for necks and rosewood for fingerboards) have become more evident over the past few years—most known for this are probably Peavey, a Mississippi-based company making deserved inroads into all areas of the musician's stage, who have a 'Sustanite' plastic-type substance for the bodies of their (as yet unreleased) **T25** and **T15** guitars, and Ovation, another American company, who have their famous roundback acoustic guitars the backs of which are made from a synthetic fibreglass-like material called 'Lyrachord'. But Gibson have lately joined these two, with a body construction called 'Multi-Phonic', about which they are saying very little apart from the fact that it is a laminated material. At press time, guitars made from the 'Multi-Phonic' material had yet to appear on the market, but the models will be called the **Sonex-180** range.

Bass players are a conservative bunch too. The Fender **Precision**, mentioned earlier, has to be the most popular bass guitar in the world - it is a straightforward, no-nonsense, working instrument. It is also the original bass guitar first introduced in 1951, the design having changed very little over nearly thirty years of existence. Pro bassists have sometimes opted for a more expensive or prestigious American instrument, such as an Alembric or B C Rich model, later in their careers but nearly always returned to their Fender, who really do have the bass market sewn up. Even the enterprising Japanese have made few dents in the bass player's wallet—although the Aria **SB1000** is a bass that has drawn wide praise—and use—from a good number of bassists. Active electronics seem to be more at home in a bass guitar than a six-string electric, and, despite the developements noted earlier, it's the bass player who has seemed more willing to come to terms with the greater range offered from active-powered instruments. The Aria **SB1000** is one of this new breed of active basses, and as such finds particular favour in the studio, where the potential of active power can often be given the time to peak. Another active bass that has been winning over many studio musicians is the WAL bass guitar, made by Ian Waller in London.

GIBSON SONEX 180 RANGE OF GUITARS

Some bass players will be following the rest of the band in having synthesizers made especially to be controlled by their instrument when the Roland **GR33B** bass synthesiser finally becomes available later in the year. Roland are a Japanese company who have also had a profound effect on the instrument market of late and their keyboards, especially, will be seen in many a group's set-up. Roland, along with fellow Japs Yamaha and Korg, make a large range of (among other things) keyboard instruments for virtually every application: mono synths, poly-phonic synths, string machines, electronic pianos, organs, and combinations of most of these.

Moog started the whole synthesiser thing off in the early sixties and in particular with the launch of their **Minimoog** in 1971. But last year saw Moog issue a small performance synth called the **Prodigy**, which has two voltage controlled oscillators—the heart of the synthesiser's sound—compared to Moog's other budget synth the **Micromoog**'s one. The **Prodigy** was thus some competition for the battery of dual-VCO machines that were being shipped in by the ton from the land of the rising Yen. Arp, the other big mass-production US synth manufacturer with Moog, has also announced a (relatively) budget-priced two-oscillator synth, the **Solus**, and this should be on sale soon.

But guitars, keyboards and bass guitars all have to be amplified, of course; so what's been going on in the musician's backline? Fashion in amp set-ups has been evident for years to the keen observer who will have seen a move from 'stacks' (stacked up speaker cabinets with a separate amplifier on top) to 'combos' (combination amplifier and speaker(s) in

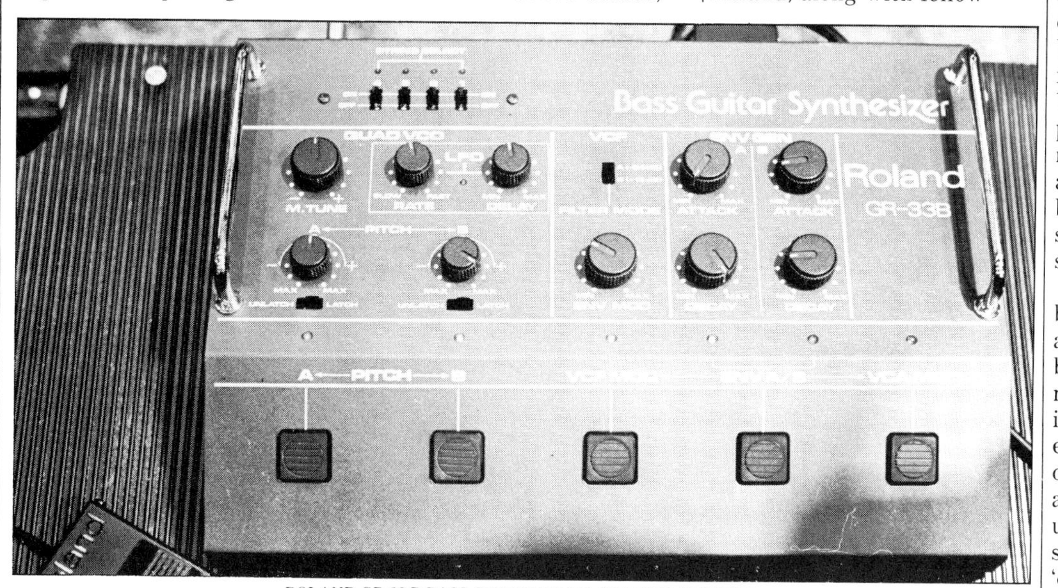

ROLAND GR 33-B BASS SYNTHESIZER CONTROL MODULE

BOLT 60 AND BOLT 30 AMPLIFIERS

one unit), and in the UK at least, the beginnings of a move back again, along with a continually changing picture on the preference of transistor amplifiers or valve amplifiers. Valves seem to be winning again – they have always been claimed to provide a raunchier, warmer sound – and some manufacturers who have always inisisted that transistors are best are even issuing valve combos for the first time, like Roland with their **Bolt-60** combo to be on sale later this year.

Amplification is one of the few areas of the stage where British-made products have any kind of impact, but the trusty duo of Marshall and Hiwatt (valves) have always been at home in rock. The later British contender, H/H (transistors), hasn't looked quite so world-dominating just lately as it did some years ago when the green-illuminated front panels of their amps were seen everywhere. But their new **Performer** series of amps are at least interesting, if not sitting on the end of every jack-to-jack lead in the land. More likely to become The Next Big Thing among British amplifiers is Burman, a Newcastle-based company doing good things in the loudness-with-quality department.

MOOG PRODIGY SYNTHESIZER

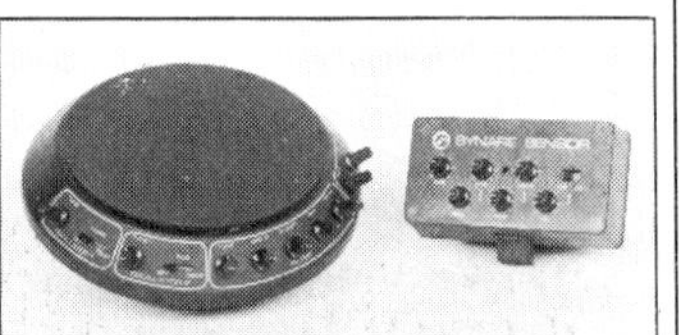

SYNARE 3 AND SYNARE SENSOR PERCUSSION SYNTHESIZERS

And so from wires to drums – in the traditional sense of bashing acoustic objects to make a noise and visiting the bar more often than other members of the band, the drummer has had little innovation to deal with, apart from a general move to tougher 'hardware' (that is, all the stands and pedals and bits and pieces the drummer carts around in addition to the drums and cymbals). These hardier parts came initially from Japanese makers, Tama in particular, and have slowly spread to (once again) the 'old guard' of American makers, like Gretsch and Ludwig. But the drummer can rely on most drums these days being of standard 5-ply construction; any changes from the manufacturers have been cosmetic rather than structural. Drum synthesizers however, have given some players a lot more scope (and some disco producers a repetition complex, it seems). Units most often seen in the studio or on stage are made by either Syndrum or Synare, although Synare have seemed the more innovative of the two just lately.

Many players consider drum synth sounds to be 'just an effect' – but effects units (small inter-connecting electronic boxes at a player's feet giving a certain sound effect and most commonly used by guitarists and key-boardists) have become an everyday tool for the rock musician and can be seen straddled across many a stage or studio floor. Once it was just wah-wah pedals and volume pedals; more recently everyone had phase pedals – now the range is incredible, and the choice offered to the effects-seeking musician is pretty mind-boggling. But, as in other areas, one or two names recur, with a New York company called MXR remaining a dominating force in effects, even though many more competitive (Electro-Harmonix, for example) and innovative manufacturers have come along in the meantime. Where batteries used to be the usual source of power for effects units, most now have mains-power option, and many makers (Multivox, H/H, Bell Electrolabs, Vox, Hohner, etc) are starting to offer linked 'systems' of interconnecting, uniform units, all powered by one master mains unit. The only trouble with this sort of system is that a musician might like the particular qualities of, say, an MXR **Phase 90** phaser, a Boss **BF-1** flanger and an old De Armond volume pedal, and be quite adamant on the merits of each unit: obviously one player who won't be interested in a linked system of one manufacturer's units.

One fact any member of a rock band can be *sure* of is that musical instrument and amplification manufacturers will be constantly tempting them with new products. Whether musicians see these as great developments in artistic and creative freedom or as attempts to part them with hard-earned appearance fees and royalties is another matter. Tony Bacon.

THE BEST (& WORST)

ALBUM COVERS OF THE YEAR

BEST

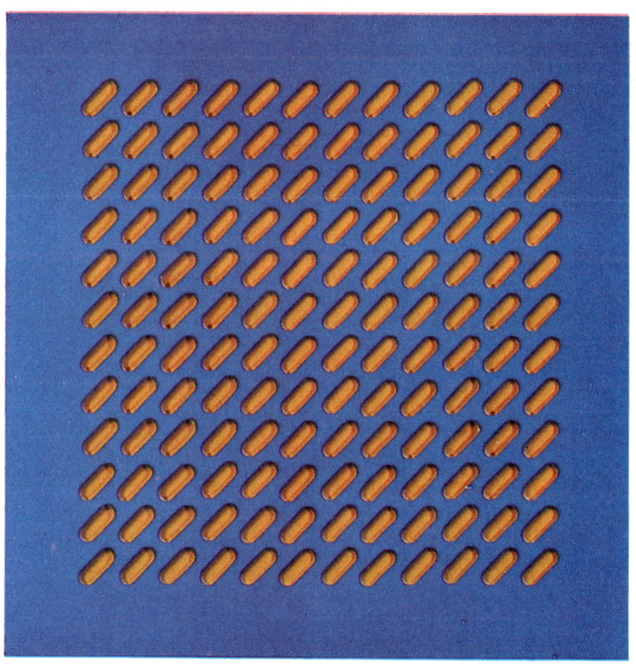

ORCHESTRAL MANOEUVRES IN THE DARK
ORCHESTRAL MANOEUVRES IN THE DARK (DINDISC)
Design
BEN KELLY/PETER SAVILLE

MADNESS
ONE STEP BEYOND (STIFF)
Design:
EDDIE/JULES/STIFF
Photography:
CAMERON McVEY

ALBUM COVERS BEST OF THE YEAR

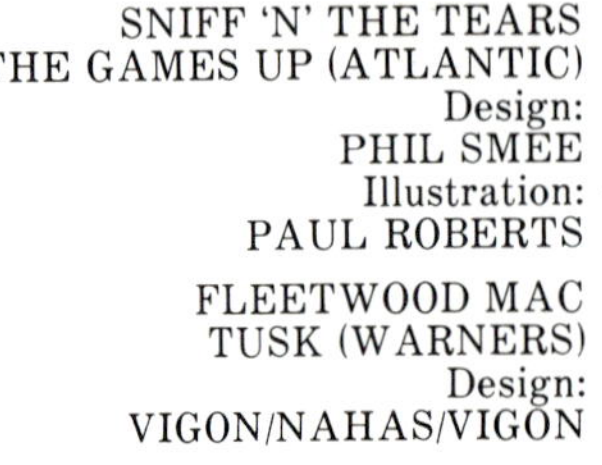

SNIFF 'N' THE TEARS
THE GAMES UP (ATLANTIC)
Design:
PHIL SMEE
Illustration:
PAUL ROBERTS

FLEETWOOD MAC
TUSK (WARNERS)
Design:
VIGON/NAHAS/VIGON

SNIFF 'N' THE TEARS
THE GAMES UP (CHISWICK)
Design:
PHIL SMEE
Illustration:
PAUL ROBERTS

THE DUGITES
THE DUGITES (DE LUXE)
Design:
JANICE HUNTER
Photography:
JANICE HUNTER

ALBUM CO BEST F THE YEAR

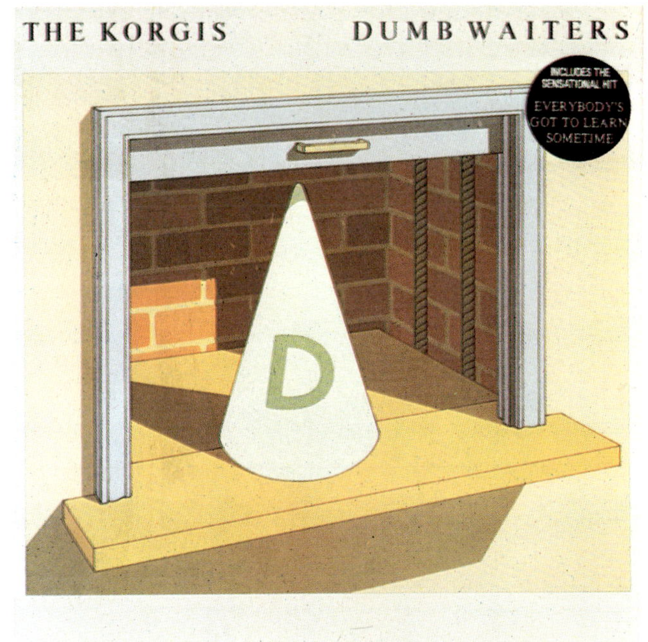

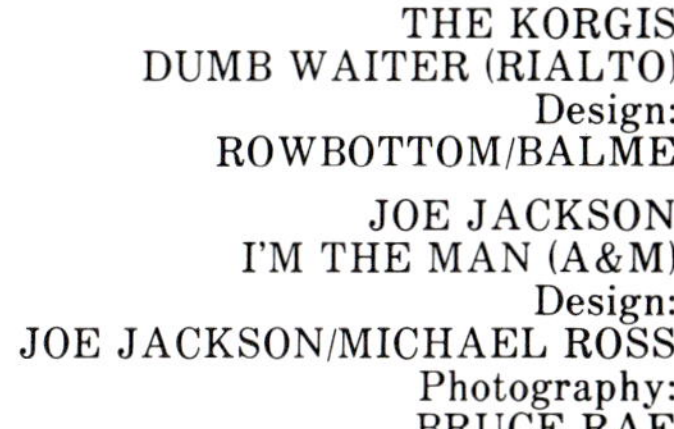

THE KORGIS
DUMB WAITER (RIALTO)
Design:
ROWBOTTOM/BALME

MAGAZINE
THE CORRECT USE OF SOAP (VIRGIN)
Design:
MALCOLM GARRET

JOE JACKSON
I'M THE MAN (A&M)
Design:
JOE JACKSON/MICHAEL ROSS
Photography:
BRUCE RAE

TUXEDO MOON
HALF MUTE (RALPH)
Illustration:
PATRICK ROQUES

ALBUM CO BEST F THE YEAR

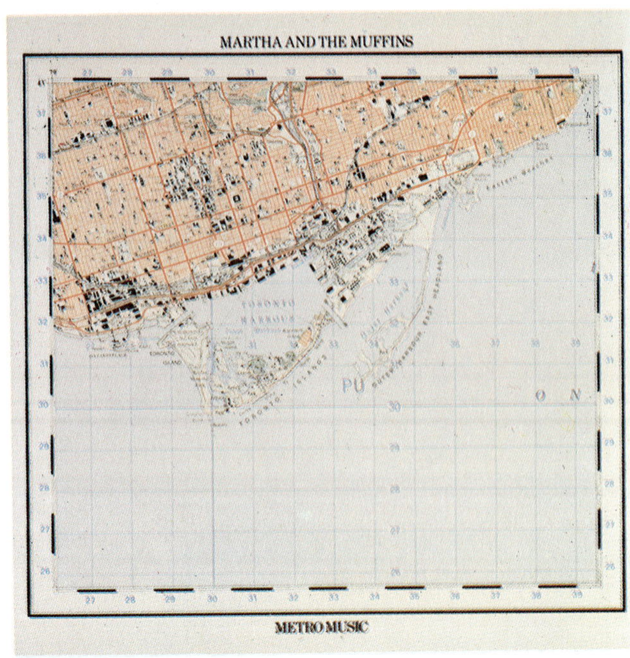

JOY DIVISION
CLOSER (FACTORY)
Design:
PETER SAVILLE/MARTYN ATKINS

CARLY SIMON
COME UPSTAIRS (WARNERS)
Design:
BILL GERBER
Photography:
MICK ROCK

MARTHA AND THE MUFFINS
METRO MUSIC (DINDISC)
Design:
MARTHA AND THE MUFFINS/
PETER SAVILLE

PHILIP GLASS
DANCES 1&3 (TOMATO)
Design:
MILTON GLASER

THE RAINCOATS
THE RAINCOATS (ROUGH TRADE)
Illustrations:
PANG HSIAO-LI

STEVIE WONDER
THE SECRET LIFE OF PLANTS (MOTOWN)
Design:
JOHN CABALKA
Illustrations:
MARGO NAHAS

JON HASSELL/BRIAN ENO
POSSIBLE MUSICS (EG)
©1980 EG RECORDS LTD
Design:
BRIAN ENO/JOHN HASSELL
Photography:
COURTESY OF NASA

GENESIS
DUKE (ATLANTIC/CHARISMA)
Illustration:
KOECHLIN

ALBUM CO BEST F THE YEAR

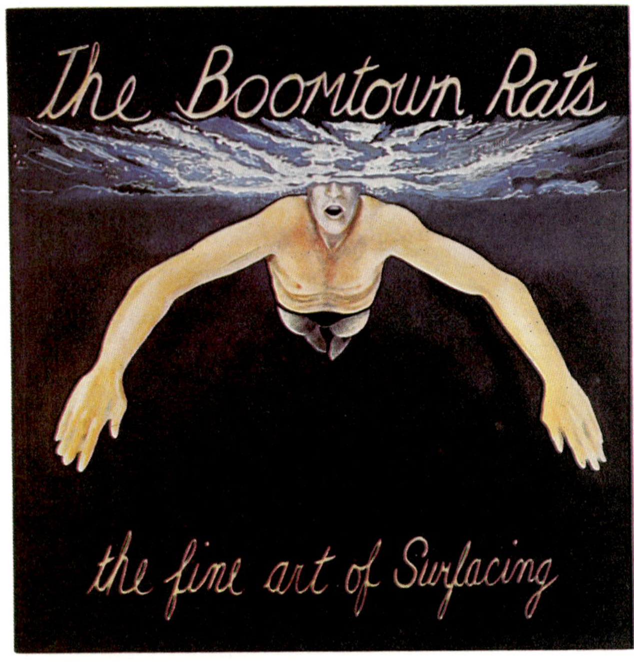

THE RUTS
THE CRACK (VIRGIN)
Design:
THE RUTS/HOTHOUSE
Illustration:
JOHN HOWARD

MOTELS
CAREFUL (CAPITOL)
Design:
ROY KOHARA/HENRY MARQUEZ
Illustration:
DUGGIE FIELDS

THE BOOMTOWN RATS
THE FINE ART OF SURFACING
(COLUMBIA/ENSIGN)
Design:
LORNE MILLER

THE SLITS
CUT (ISLAND)
Design:
BLOOMFIELD/TRAVIS
Photography:
PENNIE SMITH

ALBUM COVERS OF THE YEAR

BEST

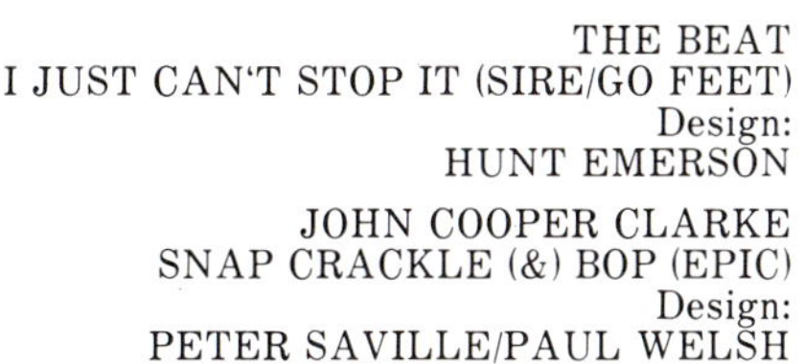

THE BEAT
I JUST CAN'T STOP IT (SIRE/GO FEET)
Design:
HUNT EMERSON

JOHN COOPER CLARKE
SNAP CRACKLE (&) BOP (EPIC)
Design:
PETER SAVILLE/PAUL WELSH

IAN LLOYD
GOOSE BUMPS (SCOTTI)
Design:
SANDI YOUNG
Photography:
CHRIS CALLIS

ANNETTE PEACOCK
THE PERFECT RELEASE (AURA)
Illustration:
CHLOE CHEESE

ALBUM CO BEST F THE YEAR

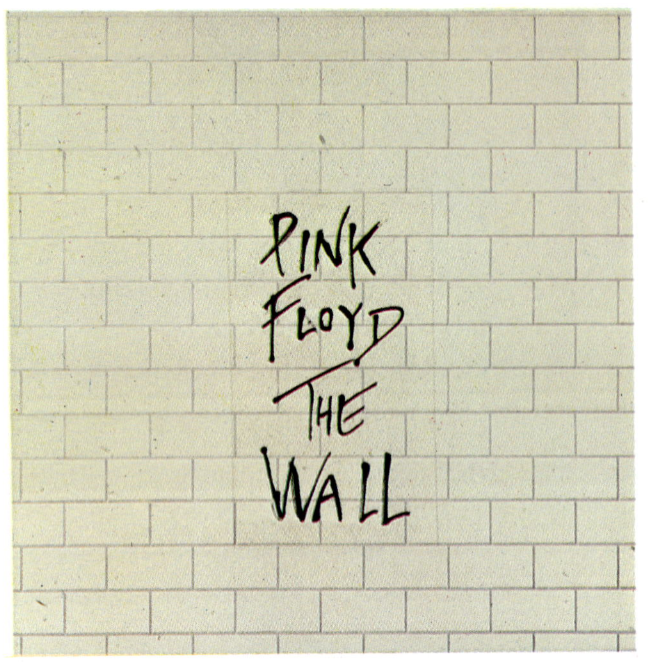

PINK FLOYD
THE WALL (HARVEST)
Design:
GERALD SCARFE/ROGER WATERS

THE MONOCHROME SET
STRANGE BOUTIQUE (DINDISC)
Design:
MONOCHROME SET/PETER SAVILLE

PIL
METAL BOX (VIRGIN)
Design:
PIL

STIFF LITTTLE FINGERS
NOBODY'S HEROES (CHRYSALIS)
Illustration:
GEOFF HALPIN

ALBUM WORST THE YEAR

GRACE SLICK
DREAMS (RCA)
Design:
GRACE SLICK/TIM BRYANT/
GRIBBITT/J.J. STELMACH/RCA
Photography:
RON SLENZAK

RACHEL SWEET
PROTECT THE INNOCENT (STIFF)
Photography:
BRIAN GRIFFIN

GARY NUMAN
THE PLEASURE PRINCIPLE
(ATLANTIC/BEGGARS BANQUET)
Design:
MALTI KIDIA
Photography:
GEOFF HOWES

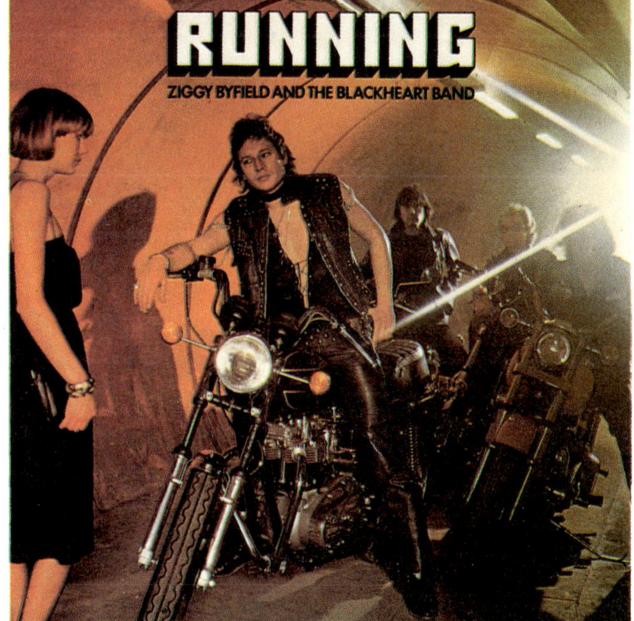

ZIGGY BYFIELD AND
THE BLACKHEART BAND
RUNNING (PVK)
Design:
CRAYON DESIGN
Photography:
MICHAEL TAYLOR

ALBUM COVERS OF THE YEAR

WORST

BOB SEGER
AGAINST THE WIND (CAPITOL)
Design:
ROY KOHARA
Illustration:
JIM WARREN

BOB DYLAN
SAVED (COLUMBIA/CBS)
Design:
TONY WRIGHT
Illustration:
BOB DYLAN

THE BEACH BOYS
KEEPING THE SUMMER ALIVE (CARIBOU/CBS)
Design:
TONY LANE
Illustration:
JOHN ALVIN

ELTON JOHN
21 at 33 (MCA/ROCKET)
Design:
NORMAN MOORE
Photography:
JIM SHEA

Attention all music heads, here is a little piece of technological wizardry which can shake, rattle and roll your brain cells wherever you go. It's your one and only Sony Walkman, a pocket-size stereo cassette player the like of which you've never heard before.

You can slip it in your pocket or, if you're the type who wears skin-tight jeans with no room in your pockets for your small change, let alone anything else, just clip your Walkman on your belt. Like the roller-skaters do.

You listen to your favourite sounds (on standard-size cassettes) through a set of hi-fi headphones, so light they almost float. Skipping the technical jargon, they're sensitive enough to tickle your eardrums with all the nuances of Tubular Bells in stereo, or scatter your mind to the four winds with Led Zep at full blast.

If you're a Doubting Thomas, put Walkman to the test yourself. Listen to one at your nearest Sony dealer.

The quality of sound is enough to make a lame man leap up and dance.

Honest. **SONY**®

Looking at distances, anyone can see we're miles apart. The Manor's at the heart of 50 acres of Oxfordshire countryside. The Town House only ten minutes away from the city centre.

Yet when you look at sound monitoring, the quality is indistinguishable. And that didn't happen by accident. Our nine years' experience in the sound business and Eastlake's philosophy of sound continuity made it happen by design.

Technically, this makes your choice rather difficult, especially since both studios can give you the complete service with accommodation and a relaxed, flexible atmosphere.

But what it really comes down to is whether you want the peace of the countryside to record or you need to be where everything's happening. In other words, the environment to suit your individuality.

And if you want to tack all this onto the side of your own house, take it halfway across Europe or anywhere else you have in mind, our two well-equipped Mobile recording units can handle it.

Ring Linda on 01-743 9313 for details on the Manor, Mobiles and the Town House.

Comparatively, we're less than

Both live-in studios have Eastlake monitoring, 24-track Ampex machines, 32-track Telefunken, 4/2 track Ampex ATR100's and consoles by Helios and Solid State Logic, (including S.S.L. Computer System). Outboard equipment includes EMT, Allison Research (including 65K programmers), Scamp, Teletronix, Urei, Eventide Clockworks, MXR, Lexicon and DBX, and microphones by Neumann, AKG, Beyer, Schoeps, Electrovoice, Shure, Calrec, STC and Sennheiser and every studio has C.C.T.V.

THE TOWN HOUSE

The Manor

a db apart...

GARY NUMAN

Throughout December, most Virgin Record Shops will be selling these four great Gary Numan albums at the amazing price of £3.25.
Cassettes will also be available at equally amazing prices.

TELEKON BEGA 19

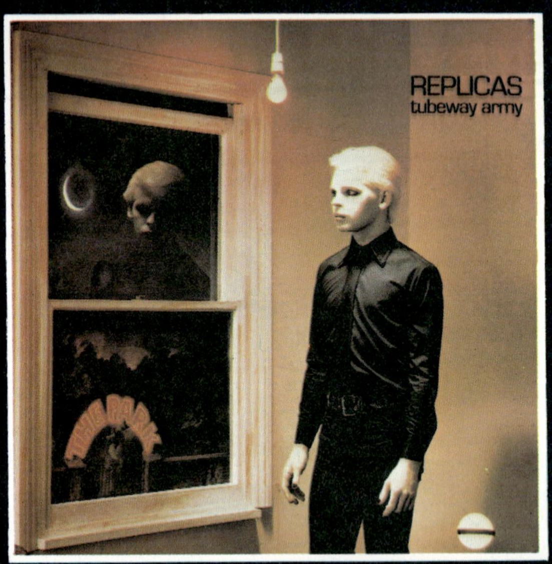

REPLICAS BEGA 7

THE PLEASURE PRINCIPLE BEGA 10

THE TUBEWAY ARMY BEGA 4

AC/DC
BACK IN TIME

Throughout December, most Virgin Record Shops will rip the price of these 5 AC/DC albums down to an amazing £3.25 each. The cassettes will also be available at equally amazing prices.

ONLY £3·25 EACH FROM VIRGIN

Back in Black K50735

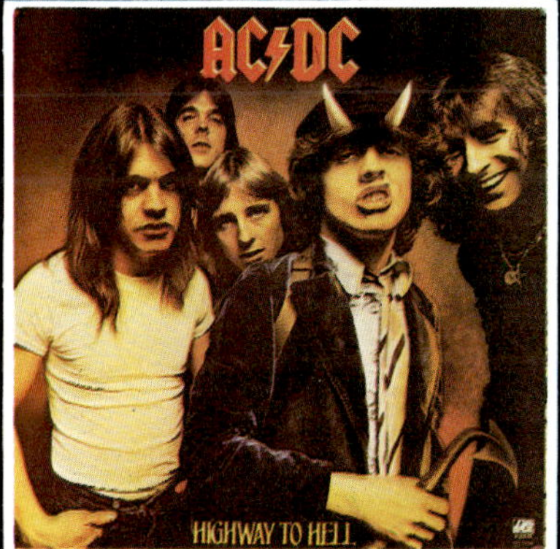

Highway to Hell K50628

If You Want Blood K50532

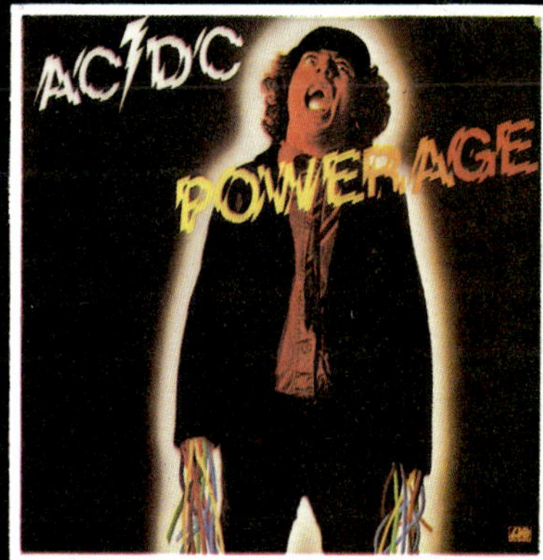

Powerage K50483

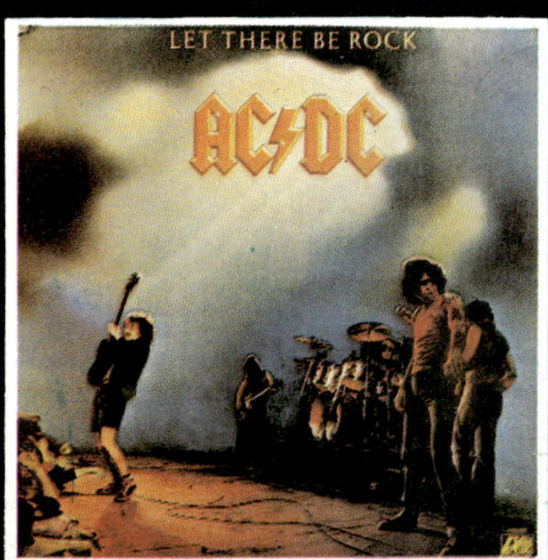

Let There Be Rock K50366

Flying High.
Robin Trower
Bridge of Sighs
Blondie
Jethro Tull
Living in the Past
Specials
Rory Gallagher
Stage Struck
recorded live
UFO
Steeleye Span
Original Masters

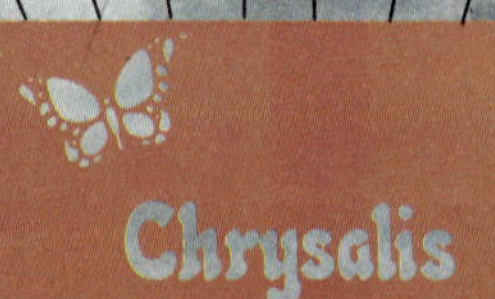
Chrysalis

INSIDE THE INDUSTRY

The art of making records made simple

THE STUDIO

HOW A TRACK IS RECORDED

NB: This breakdown is only one producer's approach ... methods vary with individuals. The drums, spread over 8 tracks or more, are most important: "drum sound dictates pop music".

Most producers prefer to spread piano across 2 tracks to achieve stereo effect (low notes one side, high notes the other).

The ambience track catches 'the sound of the studio', the natural reverberation, and is recorded on a boom mike situated as far from the drum kit as possible.

Cymbals and Tom Toms are given 2 tracks to achieve appropriate stereo effect.

Usual recording technique: bass/drums/rhythm guitar/guide vocal are recorded first, simultaneously. The rest of the parts are subsequently overdubbed. The guide vocal is retained until the backing track is complete, whereupon the vocal is usually re-recorded.

If all tracks are used and more are required — for instance, for strings and horns — the producer employs 'bounce-downs' i.e. makes intermediate mix-downs of certain sections: e.g. mixing the cymbals onto one track/mixing the tom toms onto one track/mixing the snare onto one track/mixing the bass onto one track/mixing two guitars onto one track creates 5 spare tracks.

Horns can then be recorded on 4 tracks: sax/sax/-trombone/trumpet and subsequently 'bounced' to 2, leaving 3 tracks for strings: violins/violas/cellos.

Studios

4 and 8 track studios are usually used to record demos; 16, 24 and 46 track studios are used for masters (i.e., tracks for public release).

1 BASS DRUM	2 SNARE DRUM MIXED OVERHEAD	3 SNARE DRUM MIXED UNDERNEATH	4 HIGH HAT
5 CYMBALS LEFT	6 CYMBALS RIGHT	7 TOM TOMS LEFT	8 TOM TOMS RIGHT
9 AMBIENCE (ROOM SOUND)	10 (DIRECT INJECTION INTO CONSOLE)	11 BASS (RECORDED THROUGH AMP AND SPEAKER)	12 RHYTHM GUITAR
13 SECOND RHYTHM GUITAR	14 LEAD GUITAR	15 LEAD GUITAR FILLS	16 PIANO
17 SYNTHESIZER	18 TAMBOURINE OR PERCUSSION	19 LEAD VOCAL	20 LEAD VOCAL
21 BACKING VOCALS	22 BACKING VOCALS	23 SMPTE CODE	24 SMPTE CODE

Typical breakdown showing how 24 tracks are deployed. SMPTE Code is a tone which enables 2 tape machines to be linked together to provide more tracks should the need arise.

One song takes 4 to 10 hours (including overdubs) to record — depending on the competence of the band and producer. Mixing time may be 2 to 10 hours or longer, depending on competence and clear sightedness of those involved. Therefore, a completed track-recording and mixing may take 20 hours at, say, £50/$125 an hour = £1,000/$2,500. "If you can bring in an album for around £10,000/$2,500, you're doing fine" says one noted producer. In fact the cost of one album may range from £3,000/$4,750 (as in the case of 'Outlandos d'Amour' by Police) to one million dollars (the alleged cost of 'Tusk' by Fleetwood Mac).

THE STUDIO

MIXING

The producer listens to each of the 24 tracks individually and sets the console controls to achieve the desired sound and effect. To do this he uses equalisers, which vary the amount of bass/middle/treble, and compressors and limiters, which squash and tighten the sound whilst retaining the full frequency.

At this stage, he may introduce certain 'toys' where appropriate. These modify the texture and dimension of the sound and include reverberation, echo, harmoniser, automatic double tracking, phasing and flanging.

He also uses 'noise gates' to remove unwanted sounds — e.g. squeaks from bass drum pedal, buzz from amplifier, etc.

When the sound of each instrument/voice is satisfactory, he adjusts their relative volume through the use of faders. This process establishes the rhythmic feel and sonic priorities. For example, he may accentuate the snare drum, or bring up the lead guitar for certain passages. Thus, some faders remain in the same position throughout the song, whilst others are continually being re-adjusted. On some recordings, sophisticated fader adjustments cannot be negotiated manually and require computerised controls.

The 24 individual tracks can be repositioned anywhere across the stereo spectrum — so the producer can pursue his preferred effect: stereo effects, sonic perfection, or a stage picture, where all the instruments are positioned as in a band onstage before the listener.

When all the adjustments have been satisfactorily concluded, the 24 track tape is 'recorded' — ie played back and recorded onto 2 tracks, the right and left channel which will be heard on the listener's stereo system.

This 2 track 'master' tape (¼" wide as opposed to the 2" wide 24 track tape) is then taken to the cutting room for the next process-mastering).

Whilst album tracks are usually mixed for expensive stereo systems, singles are often mixed with radio play in mind — to sound good through small speakers.

A Dolby noise reduction system may be used during the mixdown to remove tape hiss and other unwanted noises but most rock producers feel that, as certain frequencies are removed, this robs a record of some vitality. Its use on ballads and soft music is widespread, however.

An aural exciter is a gadget which brightens up the sound and gives extra top without sounding tinny. It costs £15 per recorded minute to hire. Though a fad about a year ago, their use seems to be on the decline.

Computer mixdown: if a track is particularly complicated in terms of adjusting the relative volumes of voices and instruments, computer mixdown may be used. A floppy disc records the details of each fader adjustment (so short passages can be done at different times) and when all adjustments are complete, the computer moves the faders automatically to provide the desired mix. Some producers think that computer mixing removes too much 'impulsiveness/spontaneity' from the mix.

THE CUTTING ROOM

MASTER TAPE TO LACQUER

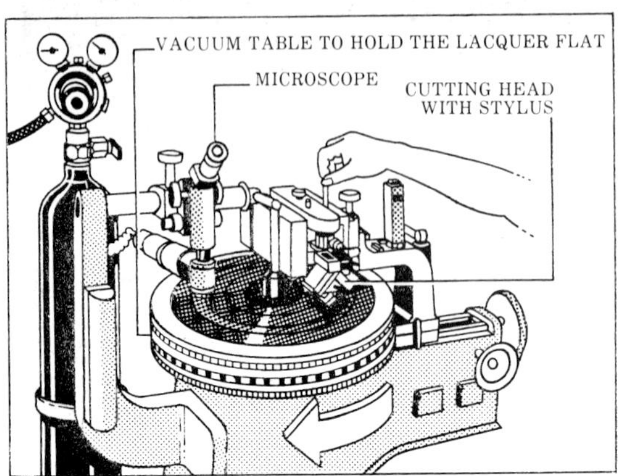

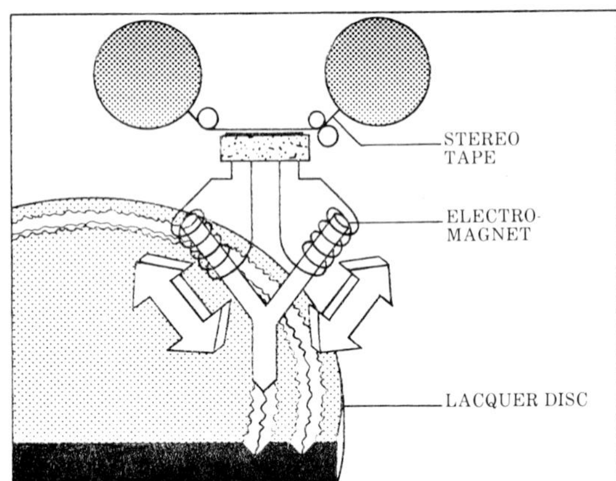

The process of transferring the finished sound from tape to disc is known as 'mastering' and is carried out by a highly skilled cutting engineer.

The cutting room contains a tape deck to play back the master tape, a console somewhat similar to those in studio control rooms, large speakers, small speakers (to create a 'radio sound'), and a cutting lathe equipped with a turntable and a cutting stylus.

A 12″ record is cut on a 14″ lacquer and a 7″ record on a 10″ lacquer, (to allow an outer rim for the various processes it will undergo) — a lacquer being an aluminium disc coated with nitro-cellulose lacquer.

The cutting engineer places a blank lacquer on the turntable, positions the stylus and plays the master tape, which then transmits signals to the cutting lathe. Heated automatically, the stylus cuts a groove which spirals inwards towards the centre of the disc. The waste material ('swarf') is sucked into a vacuum tube which

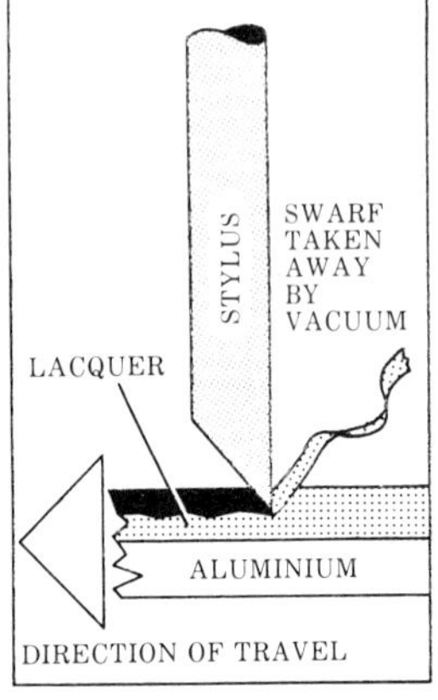

follows the stylus - so as not to leave any damaging matter wedged on the soft surface. The groove, which can be as long as a mile on an LP side, is narrower than a human hair.

As the cutting stylus moves across the disc, it vibrates subtly in response to the sounds being played on the tape, leaving a groove which wavers according to the tone and volume. During louder or bass heavy passages, the distance between the grooves are opened out to prevent intercutting.

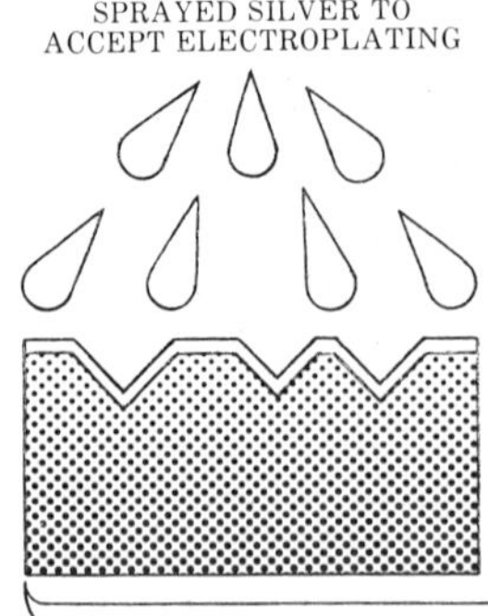

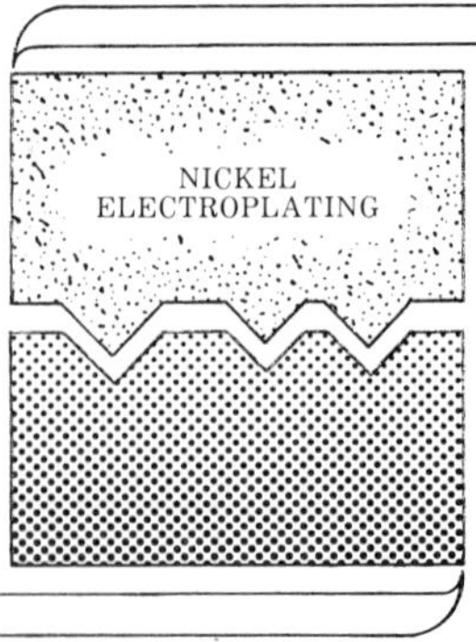

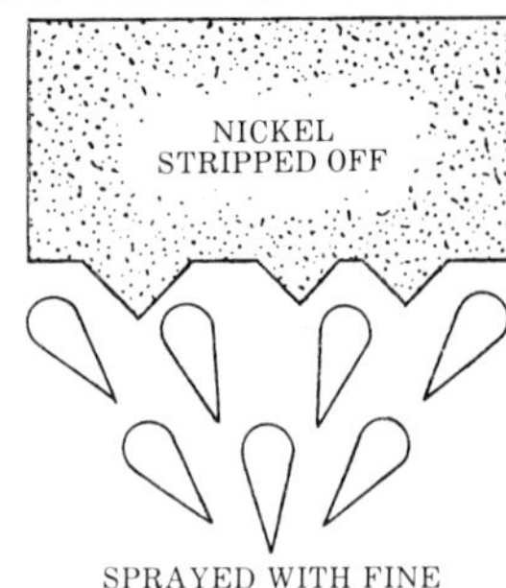

THE LABORATORY

LACQUER TO STAMPER

Lacquer arrives at factory laboratory, where high standard cleanliness is observed.

It is cleaned and rinsed thoroughly, and is then sprayed with solutions which react chemically to produce a thin coating of silver - to make it conductive to electricity. This process takes 3 minutes.

Lacquer is then placed in a bath of nickel sulphamate solution with an electric current running through it. The electricity causes a layer of nickel to form over the lacquer. It is left in a bath for 5 hours while the nickel 'grows' to a thickness of 0.018 inches — after which it is removed, rinsed and dried.

The master lacquer is now prised away from its nickel shell, which has become an exact replica of the original disc, except that it is in

12″ AUTOMATIC PRESS HALL, CBS AYLESBURY FACTORY

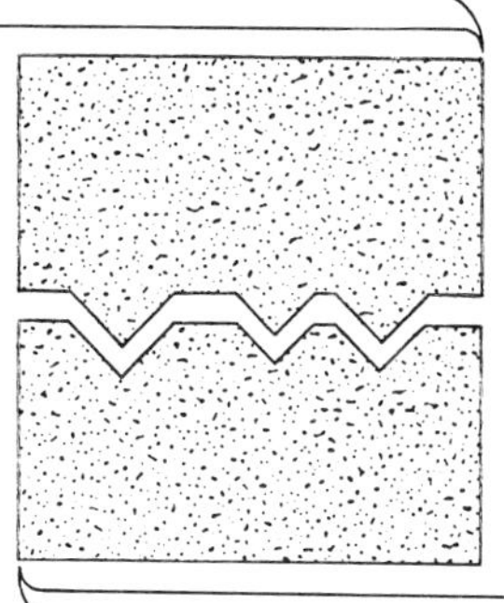

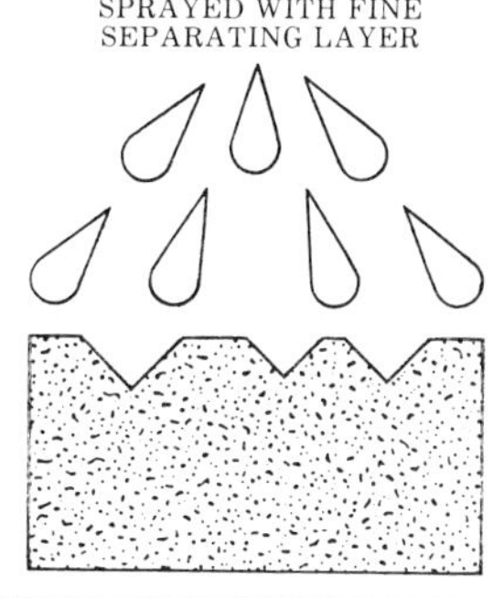

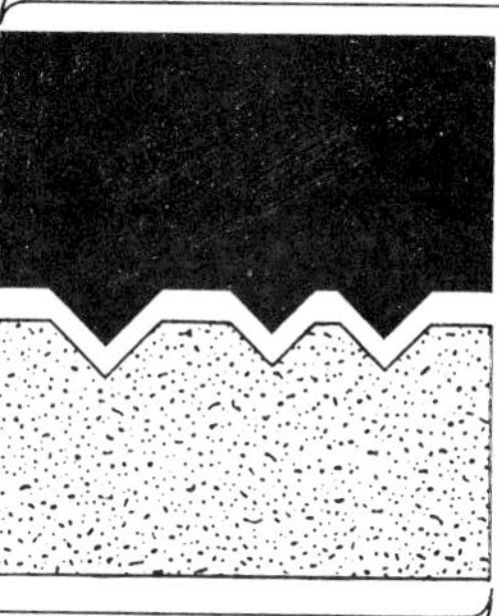

reverse or 'negative' form.

This new negative master is washed with nitro-cellulose solvent to remove all traces of the now redundant lacquer from its silver coating.

Master lacquer is thrown away.

Negative master is now treated with a colloidal preparation to form a separate layer before being placed in another electrolytic bath for 2½ hours to grow another coating for nickel.

Again the two shells are stripped apart and we now have, in addition to the negative master, a positive durable nickel replica of the original lacquer disc.

The negative master is stored away in case it is needed again.

The positive is often referred to as the 'posi' or 'mother'.

The positive is thoroughly cleaned before being immersed yet again in an electrolytic bath to grow the shell which on separation will be the 'matrix' or 'stamper' from which all the records will be pressed.

The stamper takes one hour to grow.

For a hit record, several stampers are grown from the positive -so that several presses can operate simultaneously.

Each stamper has a life of approx 4000 pressings. (It takes 2 stampers to make a record, of course -one each side).

At this point, an optical centering device puts a new hole in the centre of the stamper - working to an accuracy of two thousandths of an inch. The stampers edge is also lipped to fit into the press.

Test pressings are made — called white labels. These are checked for quality — and sent to the producer for final artistic approval — before the production run begins.

THE FACTORY

PRESSING, SLEEVING & DESPATCH

The stampers are mounted, facing each other, on the platens of a large automatic hydraulic press.

In a continuous operation, the machine places labels and the required amount of hot raw material between the stampers, then brings them together at a pressure of one ton per square inch and a temperature of 160°C.

Seconds later the platens are cooled and separated to reveal the pressed disc, which is then automatically and gently stacked in a pile at the end of the machine. Some of the machines also sleeve the disc automatically.

Entire process takes 25 seconds for an LP and 12 for a single.

Quality control. About 1 in every 200 classical records are checked, but only about 1 in every 3000 pop records.

Newly pressed records are placed on an overhead conveyor system to be sleeved (where not already done so) and packaged in boxes of 25, ready for despatch.

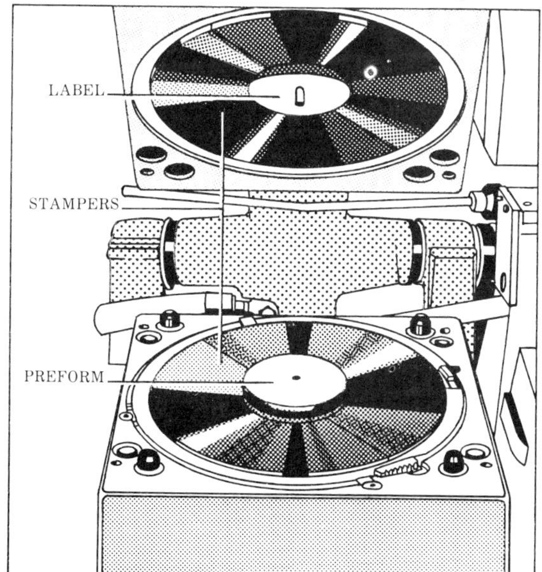

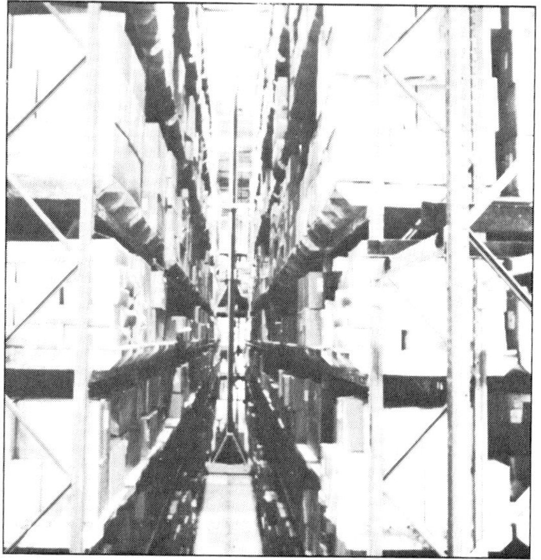

SLEEVE STORE, CBS AYLESBURY FACTORY

INSIDE THE INDUSTRY

THE BUSINESS YEAR UK

The last year has been a bad dream for the UK record industry. What happened was that several quite independent difficulties suddenly conflated to emerge as one enormous trading problem which one or two companies found insuperable.

The UK economic climate and the background of worldwide recession, were hardly healthy. Worse, when Britain's much-vaunted North Sea oil finally started flowing, it compounded, rather than alleviated, the country's financial burdens.

The oil ensured a strong currency – usually an indication of a buoyant economy. Not this time, however; Britain was placed in the virtually unique, and economically crippling, position of having a strong pound in conjunction with high interest rates and soaring inflation. Record companies (in common, of course, with all UK manufacturing industry) were incapacitated by the inevitable results – rising labour and production expenses, the high cost of borrowing and the relatively low cost of imports.

Certainly, imports were one problem. Some dealers began buying in albums from abroad – Canada and Portugal seemed favourite sources of supply – which could then be sold more cheaply that than UK – manufactured ones, even though the product was exactly the same.

Also, the British Phonographic Industry (BPI) was indefatigable in pointing to the debilitating effects of three associated problems – home-taping, piracy and bootlegging. Copying of recorded or live performance is technically illegal, but naturally very difficult to enforce.

In other respects, the record companies encountered problems for which they had no one to blame but themselves. Most of these were the long-term results of the needless extravagance and indulgent accounting which had characterised the years of plenty in the late '60s and early '70s.

One final problem was indigenous to the UK. The punk/new wave movement had been a watershed. It had eroded support for the established acts, and even toppled a few particularly recumbent superstars – but had replaced them with nothing of substance (commercially speaking, that is). Record companies had invested heavily in punk music, but only a few acts – the Sex Pistols, the Stranglers, for example – had paid their way.

At a time of such mounting difficulties, one might have expected industry casualties to be the smaller, under-capitalised companies. In the event, small proved not only beautiful, but also resilient. It was the larger concerns which went to the wall. EMI DECCA and PYE – the companies which, twenty years earlier, *were* the British record industry – failed to survive the crisis intact. All underwent metamorphoses.

In May 1979 Lord Delfont, upon his appointment as EMI's chief executive, announced that, trading difficulties notwithstanding, he did not intend to begin by dismantling the company. It was a salutary approach, but one which was quickly undermined by economic realities. The thunderbolt arrived in July. He agreed to sell a half-share in all EMI's music interests to Paramount for $70 million.

Paramount, a part of the US Gulf & Western conglomerate, had previously made one unsuccessful attempt to enter the record industry. This was destined to be their second. On September 13, to the relief of most EMI employees, the deal was called off – Delfont having adamantly refused either to negotiate much below the asking price, or to surrender vital areas of executive control.

Not that this resolved EMI's problems. On the contrary, they were only intensified with the publication of their trading account for 1978/9.

It should be noted that EMI while originally purely a record company, had developed into a sprawling conglomerate during the '60s and early '70s, with interests in fields such as defence and medical electronics. The latter division was losing money heavily because of the research costs involved in the pioneering development of brain-scanners. It had always been tacitly supposed that, in the years before the brain-scanner became commercially viable, the profitable music side would offset its losses.

Now it was revealed that EMI's profits had slumped 60% overall, and that during the second half of the year its record division had lost a staggering £14.6 million.

Hardly an opportune moment to launch a new label – and yet this is exactly what EMI did. Like a lung cancer patient who persists in smoking cigarettes, they responded to the crisis with perplexing stubbornness. Cobra, as it was called, was intended to be the house label of EMI's Licensed Repertoire Division (LRD), but the expense which the company incurred in launching it was money down the drain. Within a few months it was wound up – as was the entire LRD division – without having achieved any success at all.

By that time, though, EMI had lost its independence. The 1978/9 figures were virtually distress flares, and on October 14 rescue duly arrived when THORN, the electronics groups which had mushroomed out of a fluorescent tube business, bid £140 million for the company.

Although the position of EMI's position was so serious that one city wit – did you know there were any? – suggested that the THORN directors needed their brains scanning, the deal did make sense. The two concerns dovetailed nicely; THORN could match their hardware (television, video recorders, music centres) with EMI's software (records, cassettes, video tapes).

EMI rejected the initial offer, but on November 6 a revised THORN bid, worth about £169 million, was accepted. The final takeover took place on December 5; the new company was to be called THORN/EMI.

While the new arrangement did not result in any immediate loss of identity for EMI, the inevitable reorganisation encompassed staff cuts. Most significantly, Ramon Lopez, managing director of the records division, left at the end of April. Further, John Bush, his replacement, himself left within six weeks of taking up the appointment. As Oscar Wilde might have said, to lose one managing director may be regarded as a misfortune; to lose two looks like carelessness.

In fact, altogether EMI lost four. Leslie Hill, managing director of EMI Music Europe, also departed at the end of April. Roger Brooke, company MD until the takeover, had resigned in February. By July, still more redundancies appeared inevitable, as EMI's internal restructuring continued. For example, the hitherto separate organisations of EMI and UNITED ARTISTS (the US company which had been taken over in 1978) were amalgamated.

Ironically, the background to such drastic pruning was EMI's best period of chart success for some considerable time, with major hits from

Cliff Richard, Pink Floyd, Kenny Rogers, Paul McCartney and Don McLean, and in the US from Bob Seger also.

Unhappily, all that couldn't save the brain-scanner, which was sold to become another area of British expertise to be commercially exploited by the US.

DECCA's years of real commercial failure were 1974-8. During that time the company survived on its glorious past and could boast few contemporary achievements. The chickens inevitably came home to roast. In the second half of the 1978/9 financial year, DECCA, one of the great names in the history of British electronics, was the hapless victim of senility at management level. It is extraordinary to relate that at what transpired to be the company's last AGM in November 1979 (the one at which the above results were announced) Sir Edward Lewis, whose genius had established the company but who was then aged 79, blithely announced that he had no plans to retire.

Thus he came to preside over the destruction of the company he had created. At the end of October he had agreed to sell the recording and music publishing interests to POLYGRAM (the Dutch-German electronics company which already had two strings to its bow in the UK record industry — POLYDOR and PHONOGRAM).

In the event, DECCA RECORDS did not become part of POLYGRAM until March 1980, and the price negotiated was flexible — a basic £9.5 million, from which either £4 million would be withheld, or £6 million added, depending on the commercial strength of the catalogue in the early months. POLYGRAM could feel well satisfied; after all, DECCA's catalogue recordings included material by such disparate perennials as Mantovani and the Rolling Stones. For all record-buyers, however, this was a sad moment. DECCA's technical breakthroughs had been crucial in the development of the UK record industry, and the quality of the company's pressings had always been exemplary.

Initial redundancy costs for DECCA were estimated at £2.5 million, as the numbers thrown out of work exceeded 1,000. The records division's West End offices were closed down, and remaining personnel absorbed into the Albert Embankment head office. In March, the New Malden pressing plant closed — there was a wake, at which Rolling Stones records were played — and SELECTA, Decca's Lewisham distribution depot, was phased out in April.

The purchase of its consumer divisions paved the way for the sale of the entire company, with its valuable interests in radar and navigation. Decca thus became the object of the first great takeover contest of the '80s. Sadly, Sir Edward Lewis died on January 29, just as battle was about to commence between GEC and RACAL; appropriately, the winning party, RACAL, whose victory had cost them £104 million, was the one to which he had given his blessing.

PYE, too, though part of Lord Grade's ATV communications empire, had enjoyed little consistent success for some time. In June 1980, by which time it had been revamped as PRT (Precision Records & Tapes), a merger was agreed with RCA. The new company, to be known as RCA/PRT, was to be 51% owned by the former, and therefore represented yet another slice of the UK record industry no longer in British ownership.

While it was the affairs concerning those particular companies that made the headlines, throughout the year the BPI — which exists to protect and foster the interests of the record companies — was assiduously trying to ensure that all its members could operate in a less hazardous climate.

To try to combat bootlegging and piracy, the BPI had set up an investigative unit, which from 1979 onwards began to act with considerable zeal, bringing regular prosecutions against illegal operators — and invariably winning their cases. However, while this is something that can be controlled within the UK, piracy on a worldwide scale (and it is reckoned, for example, to account for 75% of the total market in Greece) will be more difficult to eradicate.

Naturally, the BPI was also concerned to stem the flow of imports. At the end of 1979, POLYDOR/RSO brought to court an unusual test case, surrounding the Bee Gees' 'Spirits Having Flown' album. As a result of this, they were granted an injunction banning the import and sales of records lawfully manufactured in Portugal by one of their associated companies. (Interestingly, this could not have applied to EEC countries, and Portugal is on the verge of becoming a member). It was also because of the hostile attitudes of the record industry towards import companies that, in January 1980, CHARMDALE RECORD DISTRIBUTORS ceased trading.

The BPI estimated that the total value in retail sales lost in 1979 because of home taping was £228 million. Their response to this has been to engage in discussions with the Board of Trade with a view to placing a levy on the sale of blank cassettes.

It is to be hoped that they do not succeed in this aim. There is a case for saying that home taping affects album sales, but it is one which the BPI have excessively overstated. basically, home taping is a symptom of the problem, rather than the problem itself — which is that people are now becoming reluctant to buy records. Sales of less than 75 million units were accumulated throughout 1979 — a figure which represented a drop of 11.5 million from the previous year. There are several explanations for this — the price of records, which went through the psychological £5 barrier at the precise moment that teenage unemployment was beginning to rise disturbingly; the appalling quality of many pressings; the recent improvements in BBC Radio 1, in both the quality and the extent of service, particularly in the evenings; and the belated effects of the abolition of resale price maintenance, which has put a premium on back-catalogue items. Thus, sales of records have become concentrated on fewer titles — and dealers have discovered their occupation to be a precarious one. Record companies hardly assisted the growing problems of the retail trade by cutting back on dealer margins throughout the year (from, on average, 35% to 30%).

The figures for market share did not especially reflect the individual difficulties of the companies, even though DECCA and PYE were sliding off the bottom of the league table. Despite increased pressure from the two US giants, CBS and WEA, EMI maintained its traditional lead throughout 1979, with 18.7% of the market. CBS (16.2%) came second and WEA (14.0%) third.

EMI, as we have said, vastly improved its performance in the first quarter of 1980, taking 20.9% of the market; WEA (13.9%) edged ahead of CBS (13.6%). It was no doubt a temporary setback for CBS who had invested heavily in their future, and in June opened what they described as the world's most advanced record factory in Aylesbury, Buckinghamshire; it had facilities for manufacturing 50 million records annually.

Meanwhile, two of the most buoyant independent companies took steps to diversify — VIRGIN moved into books and films, and CHRYSALIS lined up as a major shareholder of the 'Good Morning' consortium, one of eight bidding to bring breakfast television to the UK.

Everyone, however, expected the major development of the '80s to be the burgeoning of the domestic video market, and the major companies began to plan accordingly. THORN/EMI, which decided in April to adopt the JVC video system, looked well-placed to become the leading UK beneficiary of such market expansion. BOB WOFFINDEN.

THE BUSINESS YEAR

SUMMER 1979: It seems there's a new story every day of people losing their jobs in the music business. Hundreds of cuts take place in virtually every area of virtually every record company. The major labels are hurting the most. At upper levels the belt-tightening is visible through the loss of limousine privileges, an end to press junkets and lavish parties. Cocaine is still pervasive. It's coin-of-the-realm for the tenuously affluent and very, very nervous. At the bottom levels of the record companies the game is nearly over. People are on the street, lining up at Unemployment along with an ever-growing number of Americans who don't have the good, high times of the music biz to look back on.

SUMMER 1980: The only change is that the fat isn't missed quite as much. In New York City, the music's returned to the streets. It's happening all across America, if not on such a large scale. No one's been rehired in the music business and the fat keep getting fatter, if a little slower. As many as 2500 people have lost their jobs in the industry. No one's counting out-of-work musicians, soundmen and the peripherally unemployed. Every new music that's appeared over the commercial horizon has dropped back down. A few bands—The Clash, The Pretenders, and Talking Heads have survived. The rest die from lack of talent, promotion, tour support, publicity and/or advertising.

First of all, there's virtually nowhere left to advertise. Radio stations seek special markets with soft-rock and hit-rock programming marked by the consistency of processed cheese spread. "New Wave" stations exist with tiny audiences or fail. The rock press has all but disappeared. What's left no longer communicates to anyone. It's not that the stone has stopped rolling. It's just that no one cares.

ALL A MEGABOSS CARES ABOUT IS EVER-INCREASING PROFIT. THE MUSIC BUSINESS HAS BEEN STAGNANT FOR A YEAR

Have you noticed lately how many people in the record business are going bald and grey? All these leftovers from the gravy days. Do you think they've held onto their jobs by being avant-garde? They understand that that huge audience that created the American Rock Business is now too old to rock and roll. These days they rarely discover the sounds that will keep all these folks too young to die.

Fleetwood Mac, Saturday Night Fever and Peter Frampton are all homogenized music. Some is very good (the Mac), some not so good. What all 15-million selling albums share is an ability to reach several audiences at once. Once disco was no longer the exclusive preserve of blacks and gays, it was a mass-market music. Only the rarest star can generate huge amounts of coin anymore because the rock audience the companies are used to has scattered. Poof. Gone.

Several years ago an executive of Warner Brothers Records gave a prophetic speech that was duplicated and sent to many mailing lists. Luckily he did this before industry lists were cut, or his words might have reached very few. As it is, it's clear hardly anyone heard him. His point was simple—to keep a mass audience, you have to anticipate mass tastes. If you can't do that, appeal selectively to various factions of a splintered audience. Reggae for the rastas. Soul for the spades. Wimp-rock for whitey. The new young audience just isn't big enough to keep rock a mass music. When the rock audience was 15 in 1965, they had the numbers, but not the bucks, to make the business huge. When they were 22 in 1972 their word was law. Now, 30 years old in 1980, too many of them have drifted off to Manilowland, too few are willing to take the time to discover the truths offered by Costello, The Clash, and their own younger brothers.

So most record company investment and thinking these days is going into an expensive product meant to appeal to me—not some 14-year old rock fan. The videodisc is the wave of the future. Clive Davis, a man smart enough to have brought us both Barry Manilow and Patti Smith, just signed a film development deal. Who do you think is going to control rights to the videodisc? What will finally kill the radio star? Radicals blame it on conglomerate takeovers of record companies, and their fears are far from groundless. All a megaboss cares about is ever-increasing profit. The music business has been stagnant for a year. Art has nothing to do with this—it's a business deduction, something to hang on a waiting room wall. Nor will the conglomerate lords ultimately be mollified by excuses like recession, declines in multiple record purchases, high manufacturing costs passed along to reluctant consumers in the form of higher record prices or losses from wholesale counterfeiting and bootlegging. They won't stand for sixty percent return rates on superstar junk like solo Kiss albums. They won't be satisfied with hysterical campaigns against commercial free radio and the sale of blank recording tape. They will demand more new ideas like $5.98 introductory album prices on new bands and four-groups for the price of half-a-Rolling Stones concert ticket. And they will probably make the music business run better, smoother and leaner. It's been more than 25 years now since rock was born—time to shuck off those adolescent satin jackets and silver coke spoons disguised as quarter-notes.

And while the business retrenches, the music returns to the streets. New rock stars won't get quite so rich, quite so soon anymore. Old rock stars will adapt or their careers will end. Talent, as always, will out.

MICHAEL GROSS.

All you wanted to know about Digital Recording and were afraid to ask

THE FUTURE

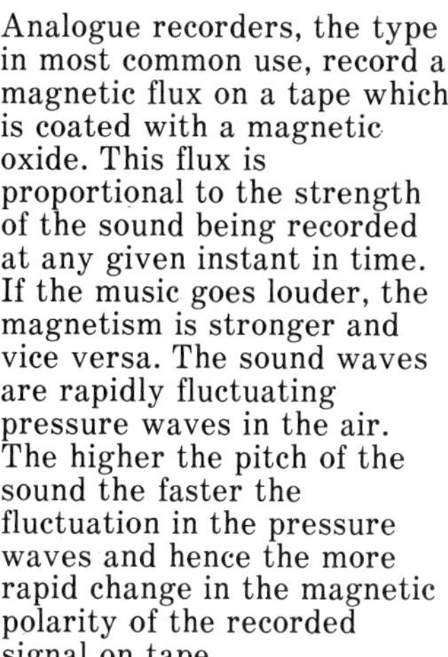

Analogue recorders, the type in most common use, record a magnetic flux on a tape which is coated with a magnetic oxide. This flux is proportional to the strength of the sound being recorded at any given instant in time. If the music goes louder, the magnetism is stronger and vice versa. The sound waves are rapidly fluctuating pressure waves in the air. The higher the pitch of the sound the faster the fluctuation in the pressure waves and hence the more rapid change in the magnetic polarity of the recorded signal on tape.

This principle is by no means as simple as it may seem as great care must be taken to ensure that the sensitivity of the recording sytem is equal over the entire frequency range of the sound. Should the recording be 2dB low at the high frequencies, there will be less brightness to the reproduced sound, and on each subsequent copy onto a similar system, this difficiency would increase. Likewise, should there be any instability in the speed of the tape, the pitch of the sound will vary accordingly, producing wow and flutter, depending upon the speed of the fluctuation. Another significant problem in analogue recording is tape hiss or noise. This is the result of imperfections in the oxide coating of the tape, superimposing their own random variations in the strength of the magnetic information on the tape.

All these effects are cumulative. Therefore, unless extreme care is taken in the design and maintenance of the recording equipment, by the fourth or fifth copy of a tape, the signal reproduced could be a very long way from the original signal that was recorded. Over the years, much has been done to improve both tape recorders and tape, but none of the above problems have been totally removed.

It was these seemingly insoluble problems that led to the search for an alternative recording system which was free of these inherent deficiencies. The current solution is digital recording. The fundamental difference is that the digital tape recorder records magnetic pulses. These are coded numbers, which relate to the intensity of the sound pressure waves. As long as these numbers are in any way discernable when reproduced, they will carry the precise information required to de-code them back to their original form. The best analogy would be an attempt to photocopy a picture. After several generations of copies, the picture would gradually fade into obscurity. By the time that you had a copy of a copy of a copy of a copy of a copy, it is probable that the information carried in the picture would be almost undiscernable. If, however, the light intensity at each point, of necessity smaller than the naked eye could see, was measured and stored with a grid reference, this information could then be re-created in a converter. Let's say that at a point 1″ down and 1″ from the left hand top corner, the light intensity was "27", we could write on a piece of paper the code "1,1,27". If this were then photocopied over and over again, although by the 20th copy of a copy of a copy, the numbers were very faint and blurred, as long as they could be recognised as "1,1,27", they would carry *precisely* the same information as the original. If this information was then passed into our converter, it would reproduce a spot intensity of "27" at the point 1″ down and 1″ in from the top left hand corner of our re-created picture.

From this, it can be deduced that with a digital sound recording system, the mechanical weak links are no longer a problem. As long as the tape is capable of storing a code, it will not in itself introduce any imperfections in the reproduced sound.

Unfortunately, you never seem to get anything for nothing. In order to be able to store these numbers quickly enough, the digital tape recorders must be capable of recording frequencies much higher than the human ear can hear. This is much more difficult than storing audio frequency information as with analogue tape recorders. Together with the development of the analogue to digital, and digital to analogue coverters these machines have become very complex and very expensive, currently three to four times the price of equivalent analogue machines.

Another problem has been flexibility. Analogue tape is very workable, it can be speeded up, slowed down, played backwards, cut up with razor blades and stuck back together again. This makes it a very useful tool for the recording engineer and producer, who may wish to doctor the tape to their specific requirements.

None of this is by any means as simple when dealing with the "numbers" of digital recording. With this system it is the electronic processing of the information which must be altered and not just the tape. These systems are still very much in their infancy and are by no means as flexible as their analogue counterparts. Cutting the tape with a razor blade may chop part way through a coded message which would produce totally random information and consequent peculiar and most unwanted noises.

Although free of many of the problems of analogue sound quality, the current generation of digital machines do have many restrictions of their own and it is currently up to the record producer to decide which system is of the greatest overall advantage to his particular type of recording. We have been operating digital and analogue systems side by side for some five month to date and although there is much interest in the digital system, there has still been no great rush towards it. These are however, still early days in the digital world. PHIL NEWELL

THE ROCK YEARBOOK 1981

ROCK REFERENCE

RECORD COMPANIES/US

A&M Records
(213) 469 3411
146 N. LaBrea, Los Angeles, California.
New York Offices
(212) 826 0477
595 Madison Avenue, New York.
Also ILLEGAL RECORDS, IRS RECORDS & HORIZON RECORDS.
Growing label in the mid-size range. They really do care.

Ariola Records
(213) 659 6530
8671 Wilshire Boulevard, Los Angeles, California.
Carries the meaning of the word "California" beyond laid-back.

Arista Records
(212) 489 7400
6 W. 57th Street, New York.
California Offices
(213) 553 1777
1888 Century Park East, Suite 1510, Los Angeles, California.
Also BUDDAH RECORDS.
Barry Manilow is this label's superstar, Iggy, Patti and Lou its street credibility.

Atlantic Records
(212) 484 6000
75 Rockefeller Plaza, New York.
California Offices
(213) 278 9230
9229 Sunset Boulevard, Los Angeles, California.
Atlanta Offices
(404) 344 4033
250 Villanova Drive, Atlanta, Georgia.
Also ATCO RECORDS, COTILLION RECORDS, ROLLING STONES RECORDS, MIDSONG RECORDS, SCOTTI BROTHERS RECORDS & SWAN SONG RECORDS.
Easy to get lost, but what a backlist!

Bearsville Records
(914) 679 7303
PO Box 135, Bearsville, New York.
This label seems to be retreating into the wilderness. Has Todd Rundgren found Utopia at last?

Blue Sky Records
(212) 751 3400
745 5th Avenue, New York.
Not bad for a blue suede shoestring operation. Owner Steve Paul is one of the greats.

Butterfly Records
(213) 273 9600
9000 Sunset Boulevard, Suite 617, Los Angeles, California.
Still trying to find their wings.

Capitol Records
(213) 462 6252
1750 N. Vine Street, Hollywood, California.
New York Offices
(212) 757 7470
1370 Avenue Of The Americas, New York.
Nashville Offices
(615) 244 1842
38 Music Square East, Nashville, Tennessee.
Still trying to recover from the rumor that Doug Fieger and Berton Averre aren't John Lennon and Paul McCartney in disguise.

Caribou Records
(303) 258 3215
Caribou Ranch, Nederland, Colorado.
Nearly extinct.

Casablanca Records
(213) 650 8300
8255 Sunset Boulevard, Los Angeles, California.
Trying to dodge their disco image.

Chrysalis Records
(213) 550 0171
9255 Sunset Boulevard, Los Angeles, California.
New York Offices
(212) 935 8750
115 E. 57th Street, New York.
Small but forceful. Distributes two-tone product in USA.

Columbia Records
(212) 975 4321
51 W. 52nd Street, New York.
California Offices
(213) 556 4700
1801 Century Park West, Los Angeles, California.
Nashville Offices
(615) 259 4321
49 Music Square West, Nashville, Tennessee.
Also ARC RECORDS and STIFF RECORDS and CBS RECORDS.
Best Of The Biggies.

Club 86 Records
(212) 799 6293
PO Box 73, Sewaren, New Jersey.
Best small label of 1980.

ECM Records
(212) 888 1122
509 Madison Avenue, Suite 512, New York.
Surprisingly well-known jazz talents do their own best work for this small label.

Elektra Records
(213) 655 8280
962 N. LaCienaga, Los Angeles, California.
New York Offices
(212) 355 7610
655 5th Avenue, New York.
Nashville Offices
(615) 320 7525
1201 16th Avenue South, Nashville, Tennessee.
Also ASYLUM RECORDS, NONESUCH RECORDS & BESERKLY RECORDS.
Best known as a singer-songwriter label with a heavy emphasis on California-style rock — but they're trying to change their image.

EMI-America Records
(213) 464 2488
6464 Sunset Boulevard, Penthouse Suite, Los Angeles, California.
New York Offices
(212) 757 7470
1370 Avenue Of The Americas, New York.
Small but forceful. EMI works hard at breaking new acts, breathing new life into old ones.

DIANA ROSS

Epic Records
(212) 975 4321
51 W. 52nd Street, New York.
California Offices
(213) 556 4700
1801 Century Park West, Los Angeles, California.
Nashville Offices
(615) 329 2134
49 Music Square West, Nashville, Tennessee.
Also NEMPEROR RECORDS, JET RECORDS & STIFF RECORDS.
Began as an off-shoot of Columbia, but now an entity in itself. Enthusiastic publicity department but sluggish backing from A&R.

Fantasy Records
(415) 549 2500
10th & Parker Street, Berkeley, California.
New York Office
(212) 757 2134
1775 Broadway, Suite 617, New York.
With artists like Sylvester, we have to wonder whose fantasy this is.

Island Records
(212) 355 6500
444 Madison Avenue, New York.
Highly respected.
Also ZE Records.
Low quantity, excellent quality.

Kirshner Records
(212) 489 0440
1370 Avenue Of The Americas, New York.
Don Kirshner is still trying to be the king of rock 'n' roll.

MCA Records
(213) 985 4321
100 Universal City Plaza, Universal City, California.
New York Offices
(212) 759 7500
445 Park Avenue, New York.
Nashville Offices
(615) 244 8944
27 Music Square East, Nashville, Tennessee.
Also BACKSTREET RECORDS & ABC RECORDS.
Low key promotion seems to work for them.

Mercury/Phonogram Records
(312) 645 6300
1 IBM Plaza, Chicago, Illinois.
New York Offices
(212) 399 7485
810 7th Avenue, New York.
California Offices
(213) 466 9771
6255 Sunset Boulevard, Los Angeles, California.
Nashville Offices
(615) 244 3776
10 Music Circle South, Nashville, Tennessee.

DEBBIE HARRY

Memphis Offices
(901) 726 6000
2000 Madison Avenue, Memphis, Tennessee.
Does okay in Europe, but no one seems to know what's going on in America. Last great moment: signing New York Dolls, circa 1974.

Motown Records
(213) 468 3500
6255 Sunset Boulevard, Los Angeles, California.
Also TAMLA RECORDS.
Had its heyday in the '50's & 60's, but Stevie Wonder lives on.

Nemperor Records
(212) 541 6210
888 7th Avenue, New York.
Still Epic's baby, but growing up fast.

PVC/Passport Records
(201) 753 6100
3619 Kennedy Rd, South Plainfield, New Jersey.
Main distributor of English imports — they Americanize with style.

Philadelphia International Records
(215) 985 0900
309 S. Broad Street, Philadelphia, Pennsylvania.
On the whole, we'd rather be in Pittsburgh.

Planet Records
(213) 275 4710
9120 Sunset Boulevard, Los Angeles, California.
President/producer Richard Perry is a dynamo with a good background of solid hit records.

Polydor Records
(212) 399 7100
810 7th Avenue, New York.
California Offices
(213) 466 9574
6255 Sunset Boulevard, Los Angeles, California.
Oh, are we in the music business?

RCA Records
(212) 930 4000
1133 Avenue Of The Americas, New York.
California Offices
(213) 468 4000
6363 Sunset Boulevard, Los Angeles, California.
Nashville Offices
(615) 244 9880
30 Music Square West, Nashville, Tennessee.
Also WINDSONG RECORDS & CHAMPION RECORDS.
Bring your own promotional team. These people can only deal with established acts — and even then it's shakey.

Rounder Records
(617) 354 0700
186 Willow Avenue, Somerville, Massachusetts.
No one told them that the '60's are over — they still believe in communes and living off the land.

RSO Records
(213) 650 1234
8335 Sunset Boulevard, Los Angeles, California.
New York Offices
(212) 975 0700
1775 Broadway, New York.
The Bee Gees and Andy Gibb are the label's hottest acts.

Salsoul Records
(212) 889 7340
240 Madison Avenue, New York.
Shoestring operation with possibilities.

Shadybrook Records
(213) 652 4782
8913 Sunset Boulevard, Los Angeles, California.
Mellow, man.

Sire Records
(212) 595 5000
165 W. 74th Street, New York.
Rising fast.

Solar Records
(213) 467 6527
6255 Sunset Boulevard, Los Angeles, California.
No, Jackson Browne and Bonnie Raitt don't own this label.

Source Records
(213) 731 0693
1902 5th Avenue, Second Floor, Los Angeles, California.
They try harder.

Stax Records
(901) 726 6360
Mid-Memphis tower, 1407 Union, Suite 600, Memphis, Tennessee.
This label is Fantasy's partner in crime.

T-Neck Records
(212) 582 5430
1650 Broadway, New York.
Small but growing.

TK Records
(305) 888 1685
495 SE 10th Court, Hialeah, Florida.
New York Offices
(212) 752 0160
65 E. 55th Street, New York.
Also DASH RECORDS and MARLIN RECORDS.
Terminally suntanned.

20th Century Fox Records
(213) 657 8310
8544 Sunset Boulevard, Los Angeles, California.
Should stick to soundtracks.

United Artists Records
(213) 461 9141
6920 Sunset Boulevard, Los Angeles, California.
New York Offices
(212) 757 7470
1370 Avenue Of The Americas, New York.
Nashville Offices
(615) 329 9356
50 Music Square West, Nashville, Tennessee.
Big but bewildered.

Unlimited Gold Records
(213) 877 0535
12403 Vetura Court, Studio City, California.
Hope they can live up to their name.

Virgin Records Inc.
(212) 620 7200
43 Perry Street, New York.
Our New York Office. What else can we say?

Warner Brothers Records
(213) 846 9090
3300 Warner Boulevard, Burbank, California.
New York Offices
(212) 832 0600
3 E. 54th Street, New York.
Nashville Offices
(615) 256 4282
1706 Grand Avenue, Nashville, Tennessee.
On a par with Columbia, but WB is everyone's favorite.

JOHNNY GUITAR WATSON

RECORD COMPANIES/UK

A&M Records
(01) 736 3311
136-140 Kings Road, London SW6
Their biggest acts are home grown — Police, Squeeze, Joe Jackson and Joan Armatrading — though founder Herb Alpert still has hits up his sleeve after almost 20 years.

Absurd Records
(061) 445 2661
20 Cotton Lane, Withington, Manchester 20
Also RABID.
Alarmingly idiosyncratic roster of local loonies including Naafi Sandwich and Bet Lynch's legs.

Ace Records
(01) 267 5192
3 Kentish Town Road, London NW1
Reissues from the noted Mississippi label, peppered with fifties oriented Brits. A branch of CHISWICK.

Affinity Records
(01) 741 0011
9 Beadon Road, London W6 OEA
An arm of CHARLY records specialising in modern jazz as dispensed by Mingus, Coltrane and the boys.

Albion Records
(01) 734 9072
147 Oxford Street, London W1
Expanding shrewdly, Ian Gomm and Hazel O'Connor are their brightest stars.

Alligator Records
Telephone number N/A
11 Ferndale Road, Birmingham B28
Local hillbillies.

Anti-Pop Records
Telephone numbeer N/A
20 Bigg Market, Newcastle-upon-Tyne
Bizarre locals, including Wavis O'Shave of 'Anna Ford's Bum' fame.

Ariola Records
(01) 408 1262
48 Maddox Street, London W1
Sky bring home the bacon, followed by the 3 Degrees.

Arista Records
(01) 491 3870
49 Upper Brook Street, London W1Y 2BT
Also I-SPY and GO-FEET . Cleaned up with cosmetic labels provided for Secret Affair and The Beat respectively. The Kinks are biggest export.

Attrix Records
(0273) 608941
3 Sydney Street, Brighton, Sussex
Local new wavers.

Aura Records
(01) 486 5288
1 Kendall Place, London W1H 3AG
Relatively new independent whose catalogue stretches from Annette Peacock to the Soft Boys and Alex Chilton.

Ballistic Records
(01) 961 3363
94 Craven Park Road, London NW10
Caribbean specialists.

B&C Records
(01) 969 6651
326 Kensal Road, London W10 5BL
Also MOONCREST and LOWBITE
Early Steeleye Span albums are consistent sellers.

Barn Records
(01) 637 2111
35 Portland Place, London W1
Also CHEAPSKATE and SIX OF THE BEST
Slade remain their most commercial act.

BBC Records
(01) 580 4468
Portland Place, London W1A 1AA
Pop compilations, sound effects, popular radio and TV shows.

GARY NUMAN

Beggars Banquet Records
(01) 370 6175
8 Hogarth Road, London SW.5
Also 4 A.D.
New wave indie which struck gold with Gary Numan. Other acts include Merton Parkas and Ivor Biggun.

Big Bear Records
(021) 454 7020
190 Monument Road, Birmingham B16 8VV
Strong American blues list interspersed with local punkos.

Billy Goat Records
(01) 657 3560
71 Benhurst Gardens, Selsdon, South Croydon, Surrey
Rockabilly.

Birds Nest Records
(0905) 820659
The Old Smithy, Post Office Lane, Kempsey, Worcs.
Something for everyone.

Blueport Records
(0632) 816855
81A Osborne Road, Jesmond, Newcastle-upon-Tyne
Local heroes.

Bridge House Records
(01) 476 2889
23 Barking Road, London E14 4HA
Metallurgists, mainstreamers, mods and other pub favorites.

Bronze Records
(01) 267 4499
100 Chalk Farm Road, London NW1 8EH
Uriah Heep provided financial stability, Motorhead do their best to shatter it.

Bulldog Records
(01) 839 4672
Broadhead House, 21 Panton Street, London SW1
Mixed bag of fifties Americans with the odd British folkie thrown in for good measure.

Casino Classics Records
(0942) 57430
3 Pennington Street, Hindley, Wigan, Lancs
Big in Wigan.

CBS Records
(01) 734 8181
17-19 Soho Square, London W1V 6HE
Also BLUE SKY, CARIBOU, EMBASSY, EPIC, FULL MOON, INVICTUS,KIRSHNER, MONUMENT, MUMS, ODE, PHILADELPHIA INT, TK, TABU, DIRECTION and UNLIMITED GOLD.
Dispirited major hoping for better times. Reliant on US heavies like Joel, Dylan, Springsteen, Mathis and Meatloaf. Of their domestic signings, only The Clash and Judas Priest have broken internationally.

Charisma Records
(01) 434 1351
90 Wardour Street, London W1
Also PRE
The success of Genesis and spin-offs allows for whimsical dabbling. A happy little label.

Charly Records
(01) 741 0011
9 Beadon Road, London W6 OEA
Also SUN and SMACK
Exceptional oldies catalogue ranging from Jerry Lee Lewis to the Shangri-Las. Newer signings are rather less spectacular.

Cherry Red Records
(01) 540 6831
199 Kingston Road, London SW19
Enterprising independent with a taste for the bizarre.

Chiswick Records
(01) 267 5192
3 Kentish Town Road, London NW1
Also ACE and BIG BEAT
Small label pioneers operating in controlled chaos, tempering reality with fun. The Damned and Sniff 'n' the Tears are principal chart acts.

Chrysalis Records
(01) 408 2355
12 Stratford Place, London W1N 9AF
Also TWO TONE
As mainstay Jethro Tull winds down, Blondie ascends. The Two Tone label was a sharp signing. On the case.

Creole Records
(01) 965 9223
4 Bank Buildings, High Street, Harlesden, London NW10
Also POLO and PVK
Hit single seekers with no obvious musical policy.

Criminal Records
(01) 960 5577
498-500 Harrow Road, London W9
Quirky label with folk leanings.

Dead Good Records
(0522) 38322
292 High Street, Lincoln, Lincs.
Local new wavers.

Decca Records
(01) 735 8111
Decca House, Albert Embankment, London SE1 7SW
Also DERAM, LONDON and UK
Scintillating in the sixties but now a sad PHONOGRAM adjunct, all but washed up by the new wave.

Dindisc Records
(01) 221 7535
61-63 Portobello Road, London W11 3DD
Recent Virgin birth, off to a good start with Orchestral Manoeuvres In The Dark and Martha & The Muffins. Manned (almost) exclusively by ladies!

Dingle's Records
(01) 903 4753/6
c/o Spartan, London Road, Wembley, Middlesex.
Fiddling folkies who soared on 'Daytrip To Bangor'.

DJM Records
(01) 242 6886
5 Theobalds Road, London WC1X 8SE
It's hardly the same without Elton.

Do It Records
(01) 267 0006
128b Camden Road, London NW1 9EE
From whence came M of 'Pop Music' fame. Current hopes hinge on Adam Ant.

Dread At The Controls Records
(01) 229 8235
The Basement, 32 Alexander Street, London W2
New reggae label, launched by Clash and Drury cohorts and starring Mikey Dread.

Earlobe Records
(01) 493 0270
c/o Precision Records, Great Cumberland Place, London W1
A new independent started by Larry Uttal, the man who started Bell and Private Stock in the States.

EMI Records
(01) 486 4488
EMI House, 20 Manchester Square, London W1A 1ES
Also CAPITOL, HARVEST, PARLOPHONE and ZONOPHONE (see also LIBERTY-UNITED and MOTOWN)
Formerly "The Greatest Recording Organisation in the World", they have been loosing heart and ground since the dissolution of the Beatles.

Ensign Records
(01) 723 8464
44 Seymour Place, London W1H 5WQ
The Boomtown Rats head a small but distinguished roster.

Eric's Records
(051) 733 5854
4 Rutland Avenue, Liverpool 17
Also INEVITABLE
Presenting some of the more interesting aspects of the burgeoning group scene in Liverpool.

Factory Records
(061) 434 3876
86 Palatine Road, Manchester 20
Presenting some of the more interesting aspects of the burgeoning group scene in Manchester.

Fast Product
(031) 229 3159
3-4 East Norton Place, Edinburgh
Also POP AURAL
Local New Wavers.

Faulty Products
(01) 727 0734
41b Blenheim Crescent, London W11 2EF
Also ILLEGAL, STEP FORWARD, DEPTFORD FUN CITY, BJ, & NIGHTHAWK.
Ramshackle premises belie intriguing catalogue which includes debut singles by The Police, Sham 69 and Squeeze. A hotbed of simmering talent.

Fresh Records
(01) 258 0572
359 Edgware Road, London W2
New wave mixture, but primarily distributors.

Graduate Records
(0384) 59048
1 Union Street, Dudley, West Midlands
Spread their wings to carry UB 40 into the top ten.

Grapevine Records
(0553) 840895
PO Box 3, Kings Lynn, Norfolk
Obscure American soul and R&B reissues.

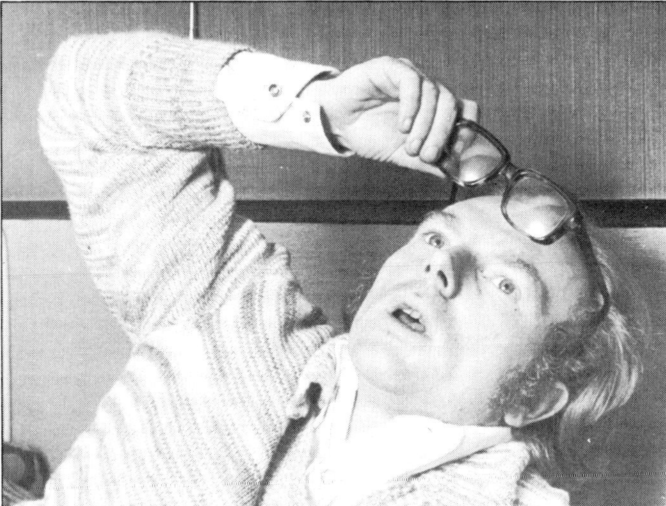
VAN MORRISON

F-Beat Records
(01) 993 4731
6 Horn Lane, Acton, London W3 9NJ
Enterprising indie founded by former Radar cohorts. Boasts a small but strong roster headed by Elvis Costello and Nick Lowe.

Fiction Records
(01) 459 8682
14-16 Chaplin Road, London NW2
Founded by Chris Parry, discoverer and first producer of The Jam. Small but growing. The Cure seem set to go.

Flyright Records
(0424) 214390
18 Endwell Road, Bexhill, Sussex
Mainly American R&B reissues.

Free Reed Records
(0773) 826264
Belper, Derbyshire
Folk specialists.

Greensleeves Records
(01) 749 3277
44 Uxbridge Road, London W12
Sounds of the Carribean, including Dr. Alimantado and Keith Hudson.

GTO Records
(01) 439 8971
37 Soho Square, London W1V 5DG
Also LIFESONG and OASIS.
Hit single oriented; currently hitting with the Dooleys.

Gull Records
(01) 459 8657
169 High Road, London NW10 2SG
Also MIRACLE and OVATION.
From early Judas Priest to Julie Felix, Kenneth More to Arthur Brown.

Heartbeat Records
(0272) 30458
4 Melrose Place, Clifton, Bristol BS8 2NQ.
Local new wavers including the Glaxo Babies.

Hurricane Records
(07) 573 5122
Damont Factory, Blythe Road, Hayes, Middlesex
Relatively new indie, yet to hit paydirt.

Industrial Records
(01) 254 9178
10 Martello Street, London E8
Home of Throbbing Gristle and The Leather Nun.

Inferno Records
(0922) 644225
37 Lichfield Street, Walsall, West Midlands
Potpourri of styles, mostly American reissues.

Island Records
(01) 741 1511
22 St Peters Square, London W6 9NW
Also BEARSVILLE, GROVE and ZE.
Pioneering independent which broke loose with Traffic in the mid-sixties. Their roster is never dull. Current inmates include Marianne Faithfull, Linton Kwesi Johnson and the B52s.

Jet Records
(01) 486 6040
102-104 Gloucester Place, London W1H 3PH
ELO guarantees this label a healthy slice of the market.

Kicking Mule Records
(01) 229 7267
121 Ledbury Road, London W11
Folk music and allied forms.

K-Tel Records
(01) 992 8000
620 Western Avenue, London W3
TV advertised chartbusters.

Laser Records
(01) 883 0674
20 Fitzroy Square, London W1P 6BB
Dennis Brown and Jimmy Tarbuck seem strange bedfellows.

Leader Records
(0422) 76161
209 Rochdale Road, Greetland, Halifax, West Yorks HX4 8JE.
Also TRAILER.
Folk.

Liberty United Records
(01) 580 4455
27-35 Mortimer Street,
London W1
Recently absorbed into EMI conglomerate. Also handles licensed labels: BRONZE, FANTASY, HURRICANE, MAM, MOTOWN, RAK, SOURCE and STAX.
Buzzcocks, Stranglers, Feelgoods and Whitesnake are home-grown heavies.

Lightning Records
(01) 969 5255
839-841 Harrow Road,
London NW10 5NH.
Primarily a distribution outfit. Associated label OLD GOLD has catalogue stuffed with US rock classics.

Logo Records
(01) 734 6710
119 Wardour Street,
London W1V 1FD
Backlist is predominantly ethnic; the Tourists are current rock spearhead.

Magnet Records
(01) 487 3650
22 York Street,
London W1H 1FD
Darts, Matchbox, Bad Manners and other exotic delights.

MCA Records
(01) 439 9951
1 Great Pulteney Street,
London W1R 3FW
Also ABC and BACKSTREET.
Tom Petty, M, the Crusaders and numerous country acts maintain their buoyancy.

Motown Records
(01) 580 4455
27-35 Mortimer Street,
London W1
Amazing back catalogue; few new breakers. All American.

Mountain Records
(01) 491 2904
49 Mount Street,
London W1.
Their heyday was with Alex Harvey and Nazareth.

New Hormones Records
(061) 236 9849
182 Oxford Street, Manchester 13.
Also OBJECT.
Small local concern which carried the Buzzcocks' first utterings.

Open Eye Records
(051) 709 9460
90-92 Whitechapel,
Liverpool L1 6EN.
Another local label to spread news of the proliferating group scene in Liverpool.

Oval Records
(01) 622 0111
11 Liston Road, London SW4
Small and select.

Phonogram Records
(01) 491 4600
129 Park Street,
London W1Y 3FA.
Also BACK DOOR, DE-LITE, MERCURY, PHILIPS & VERTIGO.
International major weathering recession storms with impressive roster of solid sellers.

Pinnacle Records
(0639) 73141
Electron House, Cray Avenue,
Orpington, Kent.
Idiosyncratic small label fostering Dansette Damage and Clive Pig & The Hopeful Chinamen among others.

Plastic Fantastic Records
(01) 836 1412
22 Tavistock Street,
London WC2A 7PH
Shrouds a plethora of ethnic labels.

Polydor Records
(01) 499 8686
17-19 Stratford Place,
London W1N OBL
Also handle EG, FICTION, PABLO, PHIL SPECTOR, RSO & VERVE.
James Last is their megastar but The Who, Roxy Music, The Jam and Siouxsie ensure sustained rock success.

Precision Records
(01) 262 5502
17 Great Cumberland Place,
London W1.
Also BLUEPRINT, CALIBRE, PICCADILLY & PYE.
As Pye they were sixties giants. Most of current income appears to derive from mass of licensed labels like BUDDAH and CASABLANCA. Seem to be totally bewildered in current rock market.

PVK Records
(0494) 36351
Unit 2, Hillbottom Road, Sands Industrial Estate, High Wycombe, Bucks.
Fleetwood Mac founder Peter Green is their rock star.

Rak Records
(01) 586 2010
42-48 Charlbert Street,
London NW8.
Hit single specialists. Most successful.

Rat Race Records.
(01) 267 2000
10a Belmont Street,
London NW1.
Small indie wielding Vibrators.

RCA Records
(01) 499 4100
1 Bedford Avenue,
London WC1B 3DT.
Also GEM and GRUNT.
Strong reliance on established or deceased Americans.

Recommended Records
(01) 622 8834
583 Wandsworth Road,
London SW8.
Restricted release sheet distinguished by Faust.

Red Records
(01) 624 8252
The Basement, 216 Randolph Avenue, London W9
"Your independent co-op label."

Red Lightning Records
(0379) 88693
The White House, The Street, North Lopham, Diss, Norfolk.
US R&B afficionados.

Red Rhino Records
(0904) 36499
9 Gillygate, York.
Local new wavers.

Refill Records
(01) 254 3631
78 Lenthall Road, London E8.
The Desperate Bicycles label.

Rialto Records
(01) 584 2441
4 Yeomans Row, London SW3
Small but growing; hit with the Korgis and the Regents.

Rip Off Records
(08494) 32711
c/o Emerald, 120 Coach Road, Templepatrick, Ballyclare, Antrim.
Disseminators of varied local talent.

Riva Records
(01) 731 4131
2 New Kings Road, London SW6
Rod Stewart's label. Not terribly adventurous.

Rocket Records
(01) 491 2777
40 South Audley Street,
London W1Y 5DH
Not only Elton John (the founding figurehead) but also Judie Tzuke and The Lambrettas, among others. Slow but sure.

Rockburgh Records
(01) 351 4333
134 Lots Road, London SW10
Imaginative independent. Ian Matthews is a major breaker so far.

Roller Coaster Records
(01) 942 7235
41 Elm Road, New Malden, Surrey
Rock 'n' rollers in the Haley/Crickets veins.

Rolling Stones Records
(01) 352 0005
2 Munro Terrace,
London SW10 ODL
Very exclusive. Only artist outside the Stones is Peter Tosh.

Ronco Records
(01) 876 8682
111 Mortlake Road, Kew, Richmond, Surrey.
TV advertised product.

Rough Trade Records
(01) 221 7355
202 Kensington Park Road,
London W11.
Also MUTE, PIANO, SPEC, RINKA & others.
A retail outlet which blossomed into a record company and national distributor for a wealth of interesting independents. Clever, caring and imbued with an integrity rare in the record biz.

RSO Records
(01) 629 9121
67 Brook Street,
London W1Y 1YD
Specialise in selling records by people called Gibb.

Rubber Records
(0632) 26461
11 Blackett Street, Newcastle-upon-Tyne.

Safari Records
(01) 486 6141
42 Manchester Square,
London W1M 5PE.
Expanding indie. Toyah is current hope.

Saydisc Records
(045) 424 266
The Barton, Inglestone Common, Badminton, Glos GL9 1BX
Also VILLAGE THING.
Various aspects of the folk and jazz spectra.

Silent Records
(01) 289 7952
c/o 118 Talbot Road,
London W11
"Silent Records speak for themselves" says equivocal man-about-town Jock Scot, who conceived this excellent new label.

Small Wonder Records
(01) 520 2727
162 Hoe Street, Walthamstow, London E17
The culprits who first unleashed the Cockney Rejects and the Angelic Upstarts.

Soho Records
(01) 240 0032
39 Hereford Road, London W12
Small independent: found the Inmates and the Nips.

Sonet Records
(01) 229 7267
121 Ledbury Road, London W11
Also SPECIALITY, KICKING MULE, ROUNDER & FLYING FISH.
Rooted in folk, country and blues but also come up with the odd pop hit.

Stiff Records
(01) 289 6221
9-11 Woodfield Road, London W9
The bane of the majors and the inspiration behind the small label boom. A short but extraordinarily illustrious history.

Swan Song Records
(01) 351 4151
484 Kings Road, London SW10
Led Zep and Bad Co consolidate; Dave Edmunds innovates.

The Label
(01) 385 6012
106 Dawes Road, London SW6 7EG
Early new wavers.

Topic Records
(01) 435 9983
27 Nassington Road, London NW3 2TX
Massive folk catalogue.

Trojan Records
(01) 961 4565
105 High Street, Harlesden, London NW10
Also ACTION, ATTACK, DRAGON & HORSE.
Early recordings by Toots and Bob Marley continue to sell.

Virgin Records
(01) 727 8070
2-4 Vernon Yard, Portobello Road, London W11
Also ICE & METALBEAT.
Home for Mike Oldfield, the Sex Pistols, Tangerine Dream, Ian Gillan, Sparks, Records, the Skids, many other hopefuls and indirectly responsible for the Rock Yearbook. Naturally, we're prejudiced.

Waldo's Records
(0727) 32109
4 Liverpool Road, St Albans, Herts
Local stuff of a peculiar nature.

Waterfront Records
(0702) 72281
74 High Street, Leigh-on-Sea, Essex
Folk, country and bluegrass.

WEA Records
(01) 434 3232
20 Broadwick Street, London W1V 2BH
Also ASYLUM, ATLANTIC, ATCO, CURB, ELEKTRA, HANSA, LASER, CARRERE, DARK HORSE, PLANET, SIRE, REAL, KOROVA, RADAR, SCOPE, STATE, SATRIL, PACIFIC, SCOTTI, REPRISE, AUTOMATIC, & WARNER BROTHERS.
American owned major. Gigantic roster and multitude of licensed labels ensure non-stop chart activity, though current recession has decimated sales.

Zoo Records
(051) 227 3343
1 Chicago Buildings, Whitechapel, Liverpool 1
Interesting independent nurturing cream of emerging local talent.

Zoom Records
(031) 229 3533
45 Shandwick Place, Edinburgh, EH2 4RG.
Springboard for bright local sparks.

VENUES/US

NEW YORK

ROCK CLUBS

Bottom Line
(212) 228 6300
15 W. 4th Street, New York.
Record companies use this club to showcase new acts.
Capacity: 400

Botany
(212) 741 9184
803 Sixth Avenue, New York.
Capacity: N/A

CBGB's
(212) 473 9763
315 Bowery Street, New York.
Springboard for many new wave acts.
Capacity: 350

Club 57
(212) 475 9671
17 Irving Plaza, New York.
New Jersey bar bands play here, but some of them are excellent.
Capacity: 600

Ear Inn
(212) 226 9060
326 Spring Street, New York.
Capacity: N/A

The 80's
(212) 348 4991
231 E. 86th Street, New York.
Capacity: N/A

The Electric Room
(212) 989 7457
100 Fifth Avenue, New York.
Capacity: N/A

Emerald City
(609) 488 0222
Cherry Hill, New Jersey
Frank Sinatra used to play here.
Capacity: N/A

Great Gildersleeves
(212) 533 3940
331 Bowery, New York.
Reasonably good sound system for loud new wave acts.
Capacity: 500

Heat
(212) 431 6955
10 Hubert Street, New York.
Huge club with a very small stage. Used to be a factory.
Capacity: 1,200

Home
(212) 876 0744
1748 Second Avenue, New York.
Good atmosphere.
Capacity: 70

Hurrah
(212) 586 2636
36 W. 62nd Street, New York.
New acts showcase here. Video taping and closed circuit TV are features.
Capacity: 500

JP's
(212) 288 1022
1471 First Avenue, New York.
Singer-songwriter heaven.
Capacity: 200

Kenny's Castaways
(212) 473 9870
157 Bleecker Street, New York.
Homely Greenwich Village joint. Willie Nile and Steve Forbert began here. One of our Editors worships the owner's lady.
Capacity: 180

Legz
(516) 561 7611
4th Street and Sunrise Highway, Valley Stream, New York.
Suburban new wave club.
Capacity: N/A

Lone Star Café
(212) 242 1664
61 Fifth Avenue, New York.
Usually showcases only established acts.
Capacity: 400

Max's Kansas City
(212) 777 7870
213 Park Avenue South, NewYork.
Two floors, with live music upstairs.
Capacity: 500

Mudd Club
(212) 227 7777
77 White Street, New York.
New wave club with occasional live acts. Upstairs used for celebrity parties.
Capacity: 400

Ones
(212) 925 0011
111 Hudson Street, New York.
Has single parents' nights, reggae nights, naughty nights.
Capacity: N/A

One Under
(212) 755 4990
1 E. 48th Street, New York.
Formerly The Rocker Room.
Capacity: N/A

The Other End
(212) 673 7030
149 Bleecker Street, New York.
Record company showcase.
Capacity: 200

Possible 20
(212) 558 1100
253 W. 55th Street, New York.
Session musicians hang out here. Best music around.
Capacity: 200

Snafu
(212) 691 3535
676 Sixth Avenue, New York.
Showcase for new bands.
Capacity: 175

Squat
(212) 691 1238
256 W. 23rd Street, New York.
Capacity: N/A

Tier 3
(212) 226 9299
225 West Broadway, New York.
Capacity: N/A

Tramps
(212) 777 5077
125 E. 15th Street, New York.
Interesting features include Mod Monday, reggae night and rock movies.
Capacity: N/A

Trax
(212) 799 1448
100 W. 72nd Street, New York.
Showcase for record companies. Also features a rock photography gallery.
Capacity: 280

UK Club
(212) 473 9647
106 Third Avenue, New York.
Capacity: N/A

The Village Gate
(212) 475 5120
Bleecker & Thompson Streets, New York.
A legend in its own time.
Two theatres with a capacity of 425 each.

Zzyzx
(212) 925 8788
64 North Moore Street, New York.
Capacity: N/A

LOS ANGELES

ROCK CLUBS

Backlot at Studio One
(213) 659 0472
657 N. Robertson Boulevard, Los Angeles, California.
Good all-purpose club. Parties held here.
Capacity: N/A

Blackie's Bar
(213) 932 8408
607 N. La Brea, Hollywood, California.
Capacity: N/A

Club 88
(213) 479 6923
11784 West Pico Boulevard, West Los Angeles, California.
Capacity: N/A

The Golden Bear
(714) 536 3192
306 Pacific Coast Highway, Huntington Beach, California.
Good place to play before or after playing L.A.
Capacity: 350

Madam Wong's West
(213) 624 5346
949 Sun Mun Way, Los Angeles, California.
Capacity: N/A

The Palomino
(213) 765 9256
6907 Lankershim Boulevard, Los Angeles, California.
Country-rock to Elvis Costello.
Capacity: 400

Pippin's Pub
(213) 394 8644
814 Broadway, Santa Monica, California.
Capacity: N/A

The Roxy
(213) 878 2222
9009 Sunset Boulevard, Los Angeles, California.
Star-studded audience. Everyone hangs out here.
Capacity: 500

The Starwood
(213) 656 2200
8151 Santa Monica Boulevard, Los Angeles, California.
Heavy metal rock is the norm, but reggae sneaks in once in a while.
Capacity: 600

The Whiskey
(213) 652 4202
8901 Sunset Boulevard, Los Angeles, California.
If they're not at the Roxy, they're here. And vice versa.
Capacity: 400

BEST OF THE REST
ROCK CLUBS

ATLANTA

The Agora
(404) 881 1301
655 Peachtree, Atlanta, Georgia.
Toned-down California-style rock is the norm.
Capacity: 1,300

Great Southerland Music Hall
(404) 261 2345
Broadview Plaza, Atlanta, Georgia.
Country-rock and jazz.
Capacity: 750

The Capri
(404) 281 9966
3110 Roswell Road, Atlanta.
Excellent sound system for new artists' showcases.
Capacity: 900

AUSTIN

Armadillo World Headquarters
(512) 477 3548
525 Barton Springs Road, Austin, Texas.
Capacity: 2,000

BOSTON

The Paradise Club
(617) 254 2052
967 Commonwealth Avenue, Boston, Massachusetts.
Owner Don Law has a lot of promotional power in the Northeast. Good venue for bands in all music categories.
Capacity: 500

Passim's
(617) 492 7679
47 Palmer Street, Boston, Massachusetts.
Coffeehouse setting for guitarists or small bands.
Capacity: 150

Modern Theater
(617) 426 8445
523 Washington Street, Boston, Massachusetts.
Comfortable club for fledgling bands.
Capacity: 628

CHICAGO

B'ginnings
(312) 882 8484
1227 E. Gulf Road, Shaumburg, Illinois
Popular press hang-out.
Capacity: 1,200

Gaspar's
(312) 871 6680
3159 Southport, Chicago, Illinois.
Elite but friendly.
Capacity: 200

Park West
(312) 929 5959
West Armitage Avenue, Chicago, Illinois.
Great lay-out, with good media connections.
Capacity: 750

CINCINNATI

Bogart's
(513) 281 8400
2621 Vine Street, Cincinnati, Ohio.
Live shows over the radio are often produced here.
Capacity: 600

CLEVELAND

The Agora
(216) 696 8833
1730 E. 24th Street, Cleveland,Ohio.
Major acts, like Bruce Springsteen and Meatloaf, have been broken here.
Capacity: 1,000

DALLAS

The Palladium Ballroom
(214) 363 4455
6532 E. NW Highway, Dallas, Texas.
Newly-signed rock bands test their tour acts here.
Capacity: 800

DETROIT

Center Stage
(313) 455 3010
39940 Ford Road, Detroit, Michigan.
Live shows and taped disco.
Capacity: 1,500

DENVER

The Blue Note
(303) 443 0523
116 Pearl, Boulder, Colorado.
Good atmosphere.
Capacity: 300

The Rainbow Music Hall
(303) 753 1252
6358 E. Evan, Denver, Colorado.
A musician's paradise.
Capacity: 1,400

DISTRICT OF COLUMBIA

The Cellar Door
(202) 337 3389
1201 34th Street NW, Washington, D.C.
A legend in its own time.
Capacity: 400

The Bayou
(202) 333 2898
3135 Kaye Street, Washington, D.C.
Shabby décor but some great rock 'n' roll.
Capacity: 500

HARTFORD

The Hard Rock Café
(203) 246 2602
165 Dexter Avenue, Hartford, Connecticut.
Sneak Press previews held here for bands at the starting gate.
Capacity: 1,000 – 3,000

Toad's Place
(203) 777 7431
300 York Street, New Haven, Connecticut.
Good atmosphere.
Capacity: 600

HOUSTON

Texas Opry House
(713) 524 4646
1416 Richmond Avenue, Houston, Texas.
Medium-priced rock 'n' roll.
Capacity: 700

MINNEAPOLIS

The Longhorn
(612) 333 8108
14 S. 5th Street, Minneapolis, Minnesota.
Showcase for signed acts.
Capacity: 400

Thumpers North
(612) 757 1720
2020 N. Dale Boulevard, Minneapolis, Minnesota.
Good atmosphere.
Capacity: 855

Thumpers South
(612) 457 2695
7884 Court House Boulevard, Minneapolis, Minnesota.
Ditto.
Capacity: 1,800

NASHVILLE

Exit In
(615) 327 2784
2208 Elliston Place, Nashville, Tennessee.
Superstars love to jam here.
Capacity: 248

PHILADELPHIA

The Bijou
(215) 735 4444
1409 Lombard Street, Philadelphia, Pennsylvania.
Preferred place to play in Philly.
Capacity: 250

BRUCE SPRINGSTEEN

Starrs Nightclub
(215) 627 8033
626 S. 2nd Street, Philadelphia, Pennsylvania.
Good atmosphere.
Capacity: 200

PHOENIX

Doolie's
(602) 968 2448
1216 E. Appache, Phoenix, Arizona.
Best club for miles (and miles, and miles).
Capacity: 650

SAN FRANCISCO

Back Door
(415) 391 7921
936 Montgomery, San Francisco, California.
Capacity: N/A

Berkley Square
(415) 849 3374
1333 University Avenue, Berkley, California.
Capacity: N/A

The Boarding House
(415) 441 4333
960 Bush, San Francisco, California.
No liquor license and shabby décor, but The Tubes emerged here.
Capacity: 280

The Old Waldorf
(415) 921 3050
2801 California, San Francisco, California.
Big club and popular hang-out.
Capacity: 600

Palms
(415) 673 7771
1406 Polk, San Francisco, California.
Capacity: N/A

Great American Music Hall
(415) 855 0750
859 O'Farrell, San Francisco, California.
Good atmosphere.
Capacity: 400

NEW YORK

VENUES

Brooklyn Academy Of Music, Inc.
(212) 636 4100
30 Lafayette Avenue, Brooklyn, New York.
Capacity: 2,000

Broome County Veterans Memorial Arena
(607) 772 2611
1 Stuart Place, Binghamton, New York.
Capacity: 7,200

Buffalo Convention Center
(716) 855 5555
Convention Center Plaza, Buffalo, New York.
Capacity: 8,000

Buffalo Memorial Auditorium
(716) 856 4200
Main & Terrace Streets, Buffalo, New York.
Capacity: 18,100

Carnegie Hall
(212) 397 8750
881 7th Avenue, New York.
Capacity, Main Hall: 2,800
Capacity, Recital Hall: 250

City Center
(212) 247 0430
131 W. 55th Street, New York.
Capacity: 2,930

Civic Center of Onondaga County
(315) 425 2155
411 Montgomery Street, Syracuse, New York.
Capacity: 2,120

Dome Center
(716) 334 4000
Box 22848, Rochester, New York.
Capacity: 4,700

Entermedia Theater
(212) 777 6230
187 2nd Avenue, New York.
Capacity: 1,140

Avery Fisher Hall
(212) 580 8700
Lincoln Center Plaza, New York.
Capacity: 2,720

Madison Square Garden
(212) 563 8000
4 Penn Plaza, New York.
Capacity: 19,680

Nassau Veterans Memorial Coliseum
(516) 794 9100
Hempstead Turnpike, Uniondale, New York.
Capacity: 16,500

Hofstra Stadium
(516) 292 1911
Hofstra College, Hempstead, New York.
Capacity: 9,000

Palladium
(212) 249 8870
126 E. 14th Street, New York.
Capacity: 3,387

Radio City Music Hall
(212) 246 4600
1260 Avenue of the Americas, New York.
Capacity: 5,880

Rochester Community War Memorial
(716) 546 2030
100 Exchange Street, Rochester, New York.
Capacity: 9,200

Saratoga Amphitheater
(518) 584 5000
Skidmore College, Saratoga Springs, New York.
Capacity: 33,000

Utica Memorial Auditorium
(315) 798 3356
400 Oriskany Street West, Utica, New York.
Capacity: 6,000

BEST OF THE REST

VENUES

ALABAMA

Auburn Memorial Coliseum
(205) 826 4564
Auburn University, Auburn, Alabama.
Capacity: 13,230

Birmingham-Jefferson Civic Center
(205) 328 8160
1 Civic Center Plaza, Birmingham, Alabama.
Coliseum Capacity: 19,000
Concert Hall Capacity: 1,000

Boutwell Auditorium
(205) 254 2820
1930 8th Avenue North, Birmingham, Alabama.
Capacity: 5,778

Denny Stadium
(205) 348 6010
University of Alabama, Tuscaloosa, Alabama.
Capacity: 56,000

Garrett Coliseum
(205) 832 6631
Federal Drive, Montgomery, Alabama.
Capacity: 12,528

Ladd Memorial Stadium
(205) 478 3344
Virginia Avenue, Mobile, Alabama.
Capacity: 40,646

Mobile Municipal Auditorium
(205) 438 7261
401 Auditorium Drive, PO Box 369, Mobile, Alabama.
Capacity: 14,000

Montgomery Civic Center
(205) 263 3886
300 Bibb Street, PO Box 4037, Montgomery, Alabama.
Capacity: 7,500

Ozark Civic Center
(205) 774 2543
Ozark, Alabama.
Capacity: 7,000

Rip Hewes Stadium
(205) 794 0361
Dothan, Alabama.
Capacity: 10,058

University of Alabama Memorial Coliseum
(205) 348 5984
University of Alabama, Tuscaloosa, Alabama.
Capacity: 16,546

Von Braun Civic Center
(205) 533 1953
700 Monroe Street, Huntsville, Alabama.
Capacity, Arena: 8,700 Capacity, Concert Hall: 2,200

ARIZONA

Arizona Veteran's Memorial Coliseum
(602) 252 6771
1826 W. McDowell, PO Box 6715, Phoenix, Arizona.
Capacity: 13,000

Pima Fairgrounds
(602) 624 1013
11300 S. Houghton Road, Yucson, Arizona.
Capacity: 10,000

Phoenix Civic Plaza
(602) 262 6225
225 E. Adams, Phoenix, Arizona.
Capacity: 7,500

Tucson Community Center
(602)791 4266
260 S. Church Avenue, Tucson, Arizona.
Capacity: 9,500

University Athletic Center
(602)965 2387
Arizona State University, Tempe, Arizona.
Capacity: 14,885

University of Arizona Stadium
(602) 626 0111
University of Arizona, Tucson, Arizona.
Capacity: 70,000

Yuma Civic & Convention Center
(602) 344 3800
PO Box 5653, Yuma, Arizona.
Capacity: 2,200

ARKANSAS

T.H. Barton Coliseum
(501) 372 8341
PO Box 907, Little Rock, Arkansas.
Capacity: 10,000

El Dorado Municipal Auditorium
(501) 862 1387
100 W. 8th Street, El Dorado, Arkansas.
Capacity: 1,900

Little Rock Convention Center
(501) 376 4781
PO Box 3232, Little Rock, Arkansas.
Capacity: 2,645

Pine Bluff Convention Center
(501) 534 3447
500 E. 8th St., Pine Bluff, Arkansas.
Capacity: 9,000

War Memorial Stadium
(501) 663 0775
West Markham & Van Buren, Little Rock, Arkansas.
Capacity: 54,000

CALIFORNIA

Anaheim Convention Center
(714) 533 5511
800 W. Katella Avenue, Anaheim, California.
Capacity: 9,000

Bakersfield Civic Auditorium
(805) 327 7550
1001 Truxtun Avenue, Bakersfield, California.
Capacity: 6,041

Century City Playhouse
(213) 839 3322
10508 W. Pico Boulevard, Los Angeles, California.
Capacity: 95

Circle Star Theater
(415) 364 2550
1717 Industrial Road, San Carlos, California.
Capacity: 3,700

Civic Auditorium
(408) 429 3655
307 Church Street, Santa Cruz, California.
Capacity: 1,952

Civic Memorial Auditorium
(209) 944 8223
525 N. Center Street, Stockton, California.
Capacity: 3,600

Community Convention Center
(916) 449 5324
14th and K Streets, Sacramento, California.
Capacity: 7,000

Concord Pavilion
(415) 798 3311
2974 Salvio Street, Concord, California.
Capacity: 9055

Cow Palace
(415) 584 2480
Geneva Avenue, PO Box 34206, San Francisco, California.
Capacity: 14,706

Dodger Stadium
(213) 224 1351 or (213) 224 1500
1000 Elysian Park Avenue, Los Angeles, California.
Capacity: 56,000 – 60,000

Embassy Auditorium
(213) 623 3261
8430 S. Grand Street, Los Angeles, Calilfornia.
Capacity: 18,000

The Forum
(213) 674 6000
3900 W. Manchester, Inglewood, California.
Capacity: 18,650

Fresno Convention Center
(209) 488 1511
700 M. Street, Fresno, California.
Capacity, Arena: 7,410
Capacity, Theater: 2,351

Hollywood Bowl
(213) 876 8742
2630 Cahuenga Boulevard East, Los Angeles, California.
Capacity: 17,680

Hollywood Pavilion
(213) 466 4311
6215 Sunset Boulevard, Hollywood, California.
Capacity: 2,200

Charles C. Hughes Stadium
(916) 442 0783
3835 Freeport Boulevard, Sacramento, California.
Capacity: 22,333

Great West Exhibition Center
(213) 873 8365
7703 Dinsmore Avenue, Van Nuys, California
Capacity: 25,300

Greek Theater
(213) 660 6302
2700 N. Vermont, Los Angeles, California.
Capacity: 4,600

Kern County Fairgrounds
(805) 831 8540
1142 S. P Street, Bakersfield, California.
Capacity: 8,000

Kezer Pavilion & Stadium
(415) 664 3200
Golden Gate Park, San Francisco, California.
Capacity, Pavilion: 5,500 – 71,000
Capacity, Stadium: 59,626

Ben Lewis Hall
(714) 787 7950
3443 Orange Street, Riverside, California.
Capacity: 2,724

Los Angeles Memorial Coliseum
(213) 747 7111
3911 S. Figueroa, Los Angeles, California.
Capacity: 92,604

Los Angeles County Fairgrounds
(714) 623 3111
Pomona, California.
Capacity: 12,000

Los Angeles Sports Arena
(213) 748 6131
3939 S. Figueroa, Los Angeles, California.
Capacity: 16,000

Long Beach Convention and Entertainment Center
(213) 436 3636
300 E. Ocean Boulevard, Long Beach, California.
Capacity, Arena: 6,200 – 9,200 – 13,933
Capacity, Terrace Theater: 3,141

Oakland-Alameda County Coliseum
(415) 569 2121
Nimitz Freeway & Hegenberger Road, Oakland, California.
Capacity, Stadium: 60,000
Capacity, Arena: 14,200

Oakland Municipal Auditorium
(415) 273 3186
10 Tenth Street, Oakland, California.
Capacity: 6,097

Ontario Motor Speedway
(714) 983 5811
3901 E. G Street, Ontario, California.
Capacity: 200,000

Oxnard Civic Auditorium
(805) 486 2424
800 Hobson Way, Oxnard, California.
Capacity: 1,600

La Paloma
(714) 436 7788
PO Box 41, Encinitas, California.
Capacity: 325

Paramount Theater
(415) 893 2300
2025 Broadway, Oakland, California.
Capacity: 2,998

Pasadena Civic Auditorium
(213) 577 4343
300 E. Green Street, Pasadena, California.
Capacity: 2,965

Rose Bowl Stadium
(213) 793 7193
Pasadena, California.
Capacity: 104,594

Sacramento Community Convention Center
(916) 449 5291
1100 14th Street, Sacramento, California.
Capacity, Exhibit Hall: 7,000
Capacity, Memorial Auditorium: 2,450

San Diego Sports Arena
(714) 224 4171
3500 Sports Arena Boulevard, San Diego, California.
Capacity: 15,000

San Diego Stadium
(714) 283 5503
9449 Friars Road, San Diego, California.
Capacity: 54,000

San Diego State University Amphitheater
(714) 286 6555
San Diego State University, San Diego, California.
Capacity: 3,800

San Francisco Civic Auditorium
(415) 558 5065
99 Grove Street, San Francisco, California.
Capacity: 7,500

Santa Barbara County Bowl
(805) 963 8634
1122 N. Milpas, Santa Barbara, California.
Capacity: 4,780

Santa Clara County Fairgrounds
(408) 295 3050
344 Tully Road, San Jose, California.
Capacity: 6,000

Santa Monica Civic Auditorium
(213) 451 1578
1855 Main Street, Santa Monica, California.
Capacity: 3,000

Shrine Auditorium
(213) 749 5123 or (213) 627 1248
3228 Royal, Los Angeles, California.
Capacity: 6,500

Sonoma County Fair Grandstand & Arena
(707) 545 0657
County Fairgrounds, Santa Rosa, California.
Capacity: 5,180

Universal Amphitheater
(213) 980 9421
100 Universal City Plaza, Universal City, California.
Capacity: 5,300

Winterland Arena
(415) 922 7000
1701 Steiner Street, San Francisco, California.
Capacity: 5,400

COLORADO

Colorado State Fairground Grandstand
(303) 561 8484
Fairgrounds, Pueblo, Colarado.
Capacity: 7,500

Denver Convention Complex Arena
(303) 575 2637
1323 Champa, Denver, Colorado.
Capacity: 7,387 – 11,110

MacKy Auditorium
(303) 492 6309
University of Colorado, Boulder, Colorado.
Capacity: 5,500 – 12,000

McNichols Sports Arena
(303) 575 3217
1635 Clay, Denver, Colorado.
Capacity: 19,100

Red Rock Amphitheater
(303) 575 2637
Morrison Street, Denver, Colorado.
Capacity: 9,000

Stauter Field Stadium
(303) 542 7424
600 E. Abriendo Avenue, Pueblo, California.
Capacity: 13,000

CONNECTICUT

Bushnell Memorial Hall
(203) 527 3123
166 Capitol Avenue, Hartford, Connecticut.
Capacity: 2,730

Hartford Civic Center
(203) 566 6588
1 Civic Centre Plaza, Hartford, Connecticut.
Capacity: 16,400

Hartford Jai Alai Fronton
(203) 566 6588
Hartford, Connecticut.
Capacity: 4,235 – 4,800

New Haven Veterans Memorial Coliseum
(203) 772 4200
275 S. Orange, New Haven, Connecticut.
Capacity: 10,889

DELAWARE

Grand Opera House
(302) 658 7897
818 Market Street Mall, Wilmington, Delaware.
Capacity: 1,100

DISTRICT OF COLUMBIA

Robert F. Kennedy Memorial Stadium
(202) 543 6465
2001 E. Capitol Street, Washington, D.C.
Capacity: 5,300

Warner Theater
(202) 347 7801
513 13th Street NW, Washington, D.C.
Capacity: 2,000

Washington Coliseum
(202) 547 5800
Washington, D.C.
Capacity: 7,347

FLORIDA

Bayfront Center
(813) 893 7251
400 First Street S., St. Petersburg, Florida
Capacity, Arena: 8,355
Capacity, Theater: 2,290

Mayor Bob Carr Municipal Auditorium
(305) 849 2185
401 W. Livingston Street, Orlando, Florida
Capacity: 2,540

Dade County Auditorium
(305) 547 5414 or (305) 547 5412
2901 W. Flagler Street, Miami, Florida
Capacity: 6,000

Florida State Fair Exposition Hall
(813) 621 7821
Administration Building, US. Highway 301, Tampa, Florida
Capacity: 12,000

Gator Bowl Stadium
(904) 633 2900
Jacksonville, Florida
Capacity: 70,000

Maurice Gusman Cultural Center
(305) 374 2444
174 E. Flagler Street, Miami, Florida
Capacity: 1,880

Curtis Hixon Convention Hall
(813) 223 8511
Ashley Street, Tampa, Florida.
Capacity: 7,400

Jacksonville Veterans Memorial Coliseum
(904) 633 2350
1145 E. Adams Street, Jacksonville, Florida
Capacity: 7,830 – 10,228

Lakeland Civic Center
(813) 686 7126
700 W. Lemon, PO Drawer Q, Lakeland, Florida.
Capacity, Arena: 8,136
Capacity, Theater: 2,282

Memorial Stadium
(904) 252 2371
Welch Area, Daytona Beach, Florida
Capacity: 7,101

Miami Beach Convention Center
(305) 673 7311
1901 Convention Drive, Miami Beach, Florida
Capacity, North Hall: 16,000
Capacity, South Hall: 12,000
Capacity, Theater: 3,000

Miami Hollywood Sportatorium
(305) 625 2900
16661 Hollywood Boulevard, Hollywood, Florida
Capacity: 17,300

Miami Jai-Alai Fronton
(305) 633 6400
3500 NW 37th Avenue, Miami, Florida.
Capacity: 6,000

Orlando Sports Stadium
(305) 277 8000
2285 N. Econ Trail, Orlando, Florida.
Capacity: 8,000 – 10,000

Palm Beach Fairgrounds Speedway
(305) 793 0551
9067 Southern Boulevard, West Palm Beach, Florida.
Capacity: 5,000

Swisher Gym
(904) 744 3950
Jacksonville University, 2800 University Boulevard North, Jacksonville, Florida.
Capacity: 1,500 – 2,500

Tampa Jai-Alai, Inc.
(813) 831 1411
5125 S. Delmabry Freeway, Tampa, Florida.
Capacity: 9,000

Tampa Stadium
(813) 872 7977
4201 S. Delmabry Freeway, Tampa, Florida.
Capacity: 72,000

Tangerine Bowl
(305) 849 2185
400 W. Livingston Street, Orlando, Florida.
Capacity: 60,000

Tinker Field Complex
(305) 849 6346
Tinker Field, Orlando, Florida.
Capacity: 6,000

West Palm Beach Auditorium:
(305) 683 6010
Palm Beach Lakes Boulevard, West Palm Beach, Florida.
Capacity: 5,895

GEORGIA

Atlanta Civic Center
(404) 523 1879
395 Piedmont Avenue, Atlanta, Georgia.
Capacity: 10,000

Augusta Civic Center
(404) 722 3521
601 7th Street, Augusta, Georgia.
Capacity: 10,000

Columbus Municipal Auditorium
(404) 323 3636
Fairgrounds, Columbus, Georgia.
Capacity: 5,265

Fox Theater
(404) 892 5685
660 Peachtree Street NE, Atlanta, Georgia.
Capacity: 3,930

Macon Coliseum
(912) 742 0901
200 Coliseum Drive, Macon, Georgia.
Capacity: 10,242

Maddox Hall
(404) 523 6275
Atlanta Civic Center, Atlanta, Georgia.
Capacity: 4,600

The Omni
(404) 681 2100
100 Techwood Drive NW, Atlanta, Georgia.
Capacity: 16,750

Savannah Civic Center
(912) 236 4275
Orleans Square, PO Box 726, Savannah, Georgia.
Capacity, Arena: 8,000
Capacity, Johnny Mercer Theater: 2,570

HAWAII

Aloha Stadium
(808) 487 3838
PO Box 30666, Honolulu, Hawaii.
Capacity: 40,000 – 50,000

Neal S. Blaisdell Center
(808) 521 2911
777 Ward Avenue, Honolulu, Hawaii.
Capacity: 8,805

Waikiki Shell
(808) 536 7333
2805 Monsarrat Avenue, Honolulu, Hawaii.
Capacity: 8,403

IDAHO

Bronco Stadium
(208) 385 1408
Boise, Idaho.
Capacity: 20,000

Fair Grandstand
(208) 384 8940
State Fairgrounds, Boise, Idaho.
Capacity: 5,300

Idaho State University Minidome
(208) 236 2831
Campus Box 8098, Pocatello, Idaho.
Capacity: 17,000

ILLINOIS

Assembly Hall
(217) 333 3141
University Of Illinois, Champaign, Illinois.
Capacity: 20,600

Chicago Stadium
(312) 733 5300
1800 W. Madison, Chicago, Illinois.
Capacity: 20,000

Comisky Park
(312) 924 1000
324 W. 35th Street, Chicago, Illinois.
Capacity: 60,000

Illinois State Fair Grandstand
(217) 782 6661
Fairgrounds, Springfield, Illinois.
Capacity: 12,266

International Amphitheater
(312) 927 5580
4300 S. Halsted Street, Chicago, Illinois.
Capacity: 11,956

Orchestra Hall
(312) 435 8122
200 S. Michigan Avenue, Chicago, Illinois.
Capacity: 2,566

Park West
(312) 929 1322
322 W. Armitage, Chicago, Illinois.
Capacity: 750 – 1,000

Prairie Capitol Convention Center
(217) 788 8800
Springfield, Illinois.
Capacity: 7,164

Robertson Memorial Field House
(309) 676 8242
1612 W. Main Street, Peoria, Illinois.
Capacity: 7,800

SIU Arena & Shylock Auditorium
(618) 453 5341
Southern Illinois University, Carbondale, Illinois.
Capacity: 11,000

Soldier Field
(312) 294 2309
425 E. McFetridge, Chicago, Illinois.
Capacity: 70,000

INDIANA

Clowes Memorial Hall
(317) 924 6321
4600 Sunset Avenue, Indianapolis, Indiana.
Capacity: 2,180

Coliseum
(317) 923 3431
Indianapolis, Indiana.
Capacity: 12,000 – 14,000

Hammond Civic Center
(219) 853 6387
5825 Sohl Avenue, Hammond, Indiana.
Capacity: 5,170

Hulman Civic University Center
(812) 232 6311
9th & Cherry Streets, Terre Haute, Indiana.
Capacity: 10,000

Indiana Convention Center
(317) 632 4321
100 S. Capitol, Indianapolis, Indiana.
Capacity: 10,536

Indianapolis Motor Speedway
(812) 337 5627
4790 W. 16th Street, Indianapolis, Indiana.
Capacity: 300,000

Indiana University Assembly Hall
(812) 337 5627
Indiana University, Bloomington, Indiana.
Capacity: 16,000

Market Square Arena
(317) 639 6411
300 E. Market Street, Indianapolis, Indiana.
Capacity: 18,250

Memorial Coliseum
(219) 482 9502
4000 Carnel, Fort Wayne, Indiana.
Capacity: 10,000

Morris Civic Auditorium
(219) 232 6954
211 N. Michigan Street, South Bend, Indiana.
Capacity: 2,490

Notre Dame Arena
(219) 283 6689
Illinois University, South Bend, Indiana.
Capacity: 12,000

Owen J. Bush Stadium
(317) 637 5371
1501 W. 16th Street, Indianapolis, Indiana.
Capacity: 12,934

Roberts Municipal Stadium
(812) 476 1383
2600 Division, Evansville, Indiana.
Capacity: 13,600

IOWA

All-Iowa Fair Grandstand
(515) 364 9097
Fairgrounds, Cedar Rapids, Iowa.
Capacity: 8,000

Five Seasons Center
(319) 398 5211
370 1st Avenue NE, Cedar Rapids, Iowa.
Capacity: 7,200

James H. Hilton Coliseum
(515) 294 3347
Iowa State Center, Ames, Iowa.
Capacity: 15,000

Kingston Stadium
(515) 362 1665
Cedar Rapids, Iowa.
Capacity: 15,500

Masonic Temple Auditorium
(319) 323 1874
115 W. 7th Street,
PO Box 3627, Davenport, Iowa.
Capacity: 2,700

McElroy Auditorium
(319) 291 4551
PO Box 622, Waterloo, Iowa.
Capacity: 7,200

John O'Donnell Stadium
(515) 324 2032
Davenport, Iowa.
Capacity: 8,500

Orpheum Theater
(319) 323 5314
116 E. 3rd Street, Davenport, Iowa.
Capacity: 2,700

Sioux City Auditorium
(712) 279 6157
401 Gordon Drive,
Sioux City, Iowa.
Capacity: 4,780 – 5,000

Uni-Dome Arena
(515) 273 6131
University of Northern Iowa, Cedar Rapids, Iowa.
Capacity: 25,000

Veterans Memorial Auditorium
(515) 283 4172
5th Avenue, Des Moines, Iowa.
Capacity: 12,216

Veterans Memorial Stadium
(515) 363 3887
Cedar Rapids, Iowa.
Capacity: 6,500

KANSAS

Cessna Stadium
(316) 689 3251
University Of Kansas, Wichita, Kansas.
Capacity: 31,500

Kansas Coliseum
(316) 755 1243
1229 E. 85th North, Wichita, Kansas.
Capacity: 12,200

Henry Levitt Arena
(316) 689 3250
1845 Fairmont, Wichita, Kansas.
Capacity: 11,235

KENTUCKY

Capitol Plaza Center
(502) 564 5589
Frankfort, Kentucky.
Capacity: 7,700

Commonwealth Convention Center
(502) 588 4381
221 River City Mall, Louisville, Kentucky.
Capacity: 3,000 – 8,250

Freedom Hall
(502) 366 9592
Kentucky Street Fairgrounds, Louisville, Kentucky.
Capacity: 19,400

Kentucky Fair & Exposition Center
(502) 366 9592
PO Box 21179, Louisville, Kentucky.
Capacity: 6,600

Louisville Gardens
(502) 582 2601
525 W. Muhammad Ali Boulevard, Louisville, Kentucky.
Capacity: 7,000

Memorial Coliseum
(606) 257 1818
800 S. Limestone, Lexington, Kentucky.
Capacity: 12,900

Owensboro Sportscenter
(502) 683 7347
12th & Hickman Avenue, Owensboro, Kentucky.
Capacity: 5,600

LOUISIANA

City Park Stadium
(504) 488 5563
City Park, New Orleans, Louisiana.
Capacity: 26,500

Hirsch Memorial Coliseum
(318) 635 1361
Louisiana State Fairgrounds, Shreveport, Louisiana.
Capacity: 10,360

LSU Assembly Center
(504) 388 8205
Louisiana State University, Baton Rouge, Louisiana.
Capacity: 15,327

Louisiana Superdome
(504) 587 3663
1500 Coydras, New Orleans, Louisiana.
Capacity: 35,000 – 76,000

Monroe Civic Center
(318) 387 4100
City Plaza, Monroe, Louisiana.
Capacity: 8,000

Municipal Auditorium
(504) 586 4314
1201 St. Peter, New Orleans, Louisiana.
Capacity: 8,000

Rapides Parish Coliseum
(318) 442 9581
5600 Highway 28 West, Alexandria, Louisiana.
Capacity: 10,090

Riverside Centroplex Arena
(504) 389 3030
275 S. River Road, Baton Rouge, Louisiana.
Capacity: 12,000

Thibodaux Civic Center
(504) 446 1570
PO Box 1178, Thibodaux, Louisiana.
Capacity: 4,500

The Warehouse
(504) 821 8211
323 Dauphine Street, New Orleans, Louisiana.
Capacity: 3,500

MAINE

Augusta Civic Center
(207) 622 4771
Community Drive, Augusta, Maine.
Capacity: 7,240

Bangor Municipal Auditorium
(207) 942 9000
Bangor, Maine.
Capacity: 6,932

Cumberland County Civic Center
(207) 775 3481
1 Civic Center Square, Portland, Maine.
Capacity: 9,000

MARYLAND

Baltimore Civic Center
(301) 837 0903
201 W. Baltimore Street, Baltimore, Maryland.
Capacity, Arena: 12,700
Capacity, Mini I: 4,310
Capacity, Mini II: 6,460

Baltimore Memorial Stadium
(301) 396 7111
33rd & Ellerslie Streets, Baltimore, Maryland.
Capacity: 60,762

Capital Center
(301) 350 3400
1 Harry S. Truman Drive, Landover, Maryland.
Capacity: 18,784

Cole Field House
(301) 454 4546
University of Maryland, College Park, Maryland.
Capacity: 14,500

Towson Center
(301) 321 2743
Towson, Maryland.
Capacity: 5,500

MASSACHUSETTS

Berklee Performance Center
(617) 266 7455
1140 Boylston Street, Boston, Massachusetts.
Capacity: 1,230

Boston Arena
(617) 437 3376
Boston, Massachusetts.
Capacity: 6,898

Music Hall Theater
(617) 423 3300
268 Tremont Street, Boston, Massachusetts.
Capacity: 4,225

The Music Inn
(413) 637 2200
Lenox, Massachusetts.
Capacity: 10,000

New Boston Garden Arena
(617) 227 3204
Causeway Street, Boston, Massachusetts.
Capacity: 15,510

New England Life Hall
(617) 266 7262
225 Clarendon Street, Boston, Massachusetts.
Capacity: 685

Springfield Civic Center
(413) 781 7080
1277 Main Street, Springfield, Massachusetts.
Capacity: 10,000

MICHIGAN

Aquinas College Fieldhouse
(616) 459 8281
1607 Robinson Road SE, Grand Rapids, Michigan.
Capacity: 4,500 – 5,000

Atwood Stadium
(313) 767 5650
Saginaw Avenue, Flint, Michigan.
Capacity: 11,000

Civic Center
(517) 485 2419
Lansing, Michigan.
Capacity: 5,376

Cobo Arena
(313) 962 1800
Detroit, Michigan.
Capacity: 11,957

Henry and Edsel Ford Auditorium
(313) 224 1055
20 Auditorium Drive, Detroit, Michigan.
Capacity: 2,870

IMA Sports Arena
(313) 234 4633
Flint, Michigan.
Capacity: 5,500

Marquette Lakeview Arena
(906) 228 7530
301 E. Fair Avenue, Marquette, Michigan.
Capacity: 5,400

Masonic Temple Auditorium
(313) 832 7100
500 Temple Avenue, Detroit, Michigan.
Capacity: 4,865

Olympia Stadium
(313) 895 7020
Detroit, Michigan.
Capacity: 16,500

Orchestra Hall, Paradise Theater
(313) 833 3700
3711 Woodward, Detroit, Michigan.
Capacity: 2,200

Pontiac Silverdome
(313) 857 7700
1200 Featherstone, Pontiac, Michigan.
Capacity: 15,000 – 80,600

Saginaw Civic Center
(517) 776 1320
303 Johnson Street, Saginaw, Michigan.
Capacity: 7,300

Tiger Stadium
(313) 962 4000
Detroit, Michigan.
Capacity: 58,000

Wings Stadium
(616) 345 5101
Kalamazoo, Michigan.
Capacity: 7,200

MINNESOTA

Duluth Arena-Auditorium
(218) 722 5573
350 S. 5th Avenue West, Duluth, Minnesota.
Capacity, Arena: 7,765
Capacity, Auditorium: 2,400

The Guthrie Theater
(612) 377 2824
Vineland Place, Minneapolis, Minnesota.
Capacity: 1,440

Mayo Civic Auditorium Arena
(507) 288 8475
30 SE 2nd Avenue, Rochester, Minnesota.
Capacity: 4,000

Met Center
(612) 854 4411
7901 Cedar Avenue South, Bloomington, Minnesota.
Capacity: 5,000 – 17,000

Midway Stadium
(612) 645 9500
1000 Snelling Avenue North, St. Paul, Minnesota.
Capacity: 26,000

Minneapolis Auditorium & Convention Hall
(612) 870 4436
1403 Stevens Avenue South, Minneapolis, Minnesota.
Capacity: 8,631 – 9,000

Northrop Memorial Auditorium
(612) 376 8378
84 Church Street SE, Minneapolis, Minnesota.
Capacity: 4,810

Orchestra Hall
(612) 371 5600
1111 Nicolett Mall, Minneapolis, Minnesota.
Capacity: 2,540

Orpheum Hall
(612) 338 7968
910 Hennepin Avenue, Minneapolis, Minnesota.
Capacity: 2,770

Parade Football Stadium
(612) 374 5996
600 Kenwood Avenue, Minneapolis, Minnesota.
Capacity: 16,560

Riverside Arena
(507) 437 7676
501 NE 2nd Avenue, Austin, Minnesota.
Capacity: 6,000

St, Paul Civic Center
(612) 224 7361
I.A. O'Shaughnessy Plaza, St. Paul, Minnesota.
Capacity: 5,000 – 17,500

MISSISSIPPI

Humphrey Coliseum
(601) 325 2743
PO Drawer HY, Mississippi State, Mississippi.
Capacity: 11,000

Memorial Stadium
(601) 354 5541
Jackson, Mississippi.
Capacity: 46,021

Mississippi Coast Coliseum & Convention Center
(601) 388 8010
3800 W. Beach Boulevard, Biloxi, Mississippi.
Capacity: 12,000

MISSOURI

Arrowhead Stadium
(816) 924 9300
1 Arrowhead Drive, Kansas City, Missouri.
Capacity: 80,000

Checkerdome
(314) 644 0900
5700 Oakland Avenue, St. Louis, Missouri.
Capacity: 19,230

Hearnes Multipurpose Arena
(314) 882 2056
University of Missouri, Columbia, Missouri.
Capacity: 13,795

Kansas City Convention Center
(816) 421 8000
301 W. 13th Street, Kansas City, Missouri.
Capacity: 10,429

Kemper Arena
(816) 421 6460
1800 Genesee Street, Kansas City, Missouri.
Capacity: 17,610

Henry W. Kiel Auditorium
(314) 241 1010
1400 Market, St. Louis, Missouri.
Capacity: 10,586

Jack Lawton Webb Convention Center
(417) 781 4000
5400 S. Range Line Road, Joplin, Missouri.
Capacity: 3,000

Memorial Hall
(417) 623 3254
212 W. 8th Street, Joplin, Missouri.
Capacity: 3,000

Royal Stadium
(816) 921 8000
PO Box 1969, Kansas City, Missouri.
Capacity: 40,000

St. Louis Convention Center
(314) 342 5000
801 Conventin Plaza, St. Louis, Missouri.
Capacity: 8,000

MONTANA

Yellowstone Media Arena
(406) 245 6561
Fairgrounds, Billings, Montana.
Capacity: 11,500

NEBRASKA

Omaha Civic Auditorium
(402) 346 1323
1804 Capitol Avenue, Omaha, Nebraska.
Capacity: 8,700 – 11,300

Omaha Stadium
(402) 731 8808
1200 Bart Murphy Avenue, Omaha, Nebraska.
Capacity: 12,132

Pershing Municipal Auditorium
(402) 477 3761
Lincoln, Nebraska.
Capacity: 7,500

University of Nebraska Sports Center
(402) 472 1132
University of Nebraska, Lincoln, Nebraska.
Capacity: 15,000

NEVADA

Aladdin Theater
(702) 736 0127
3667 Las Vegas Boulevard South, Las Vegas, Nevada.
Capacity: 7,416

Centennial Coliseum
(702) 825 6649
4590 S. Virginia, Reno, Nevada.
Capacity: 7,715

Las Vegas Convention Center
(702) 733 2323
3150 Paradise Road, Las Vegas, Nevada.
Capacity: 7,392

Pioneer Theater Auditorium
(702) 786 5105
100 S. Virginia, Reno, Nevada.
Capacity: 1,428

NEW HAMPSHIRE

Gill Stadium
(603) 623 9369
Valley Street, Manchester, New Hampshire.
Capacity: 7,300

NEW JERSEY

The Capitol Theater
(201) 778 2888
326 Monroe Street, Passaic, New Jersey.
Capacity: 3,250

Garden State Arts Center
(201) 264 9039
Box 116, Holmdel, New Jersey.
Capacity: 11,052

Giants Stadium
(201) 935 8500
The Meadowlands, East Rutherford, New Jersey.
Capacity: 65,000

NEW MEXICO

Johnson Gymnasium
(505) 277 5151
University of New Mexico, Albuquerque, New Mexico.
Capacity: 6,300

Pan American Center
(505) 645 4413
Las Cruces, New Mexico.
Capacity: 13,222

The Pit Arena
(505) 268 0393
300 San Mateo Boulevard NE, Albuquerque, New Mexico.
Capacity: 14,528

Tingley Coliseum
(505) 265 1791
State Fairground NE, Albuquerque, New Mexico.
Capacity: 15,800

NORTH CAROLINA

Asheville Civic Center
(204) 255 5736
Haywood Street, Asheville, North Carolina.
Capacity: 7,646

Charlotte Coliseum
(704) 372 3600
Independence Boulevard, Charlotte, North Carolina.
Capacity: 13,000

Cumberland County Memorial Coliseum
(919) 484 0161
Highway 301, Fayetteville, North Carolina.
Capacity: 7,000

J.S. Dorton Arena
(919) 733 2626
North Carolina State Fairgrounds, Raleigh, North Carolina.
Capacity: 7,000

Greensboro Coliseum Complex
(919) 294 2140
1921 W. Lee Street, Greensboro, North Carolina.
Capacity: 16,800

Raleigh Civic Center
(919) 755 6011
Raleigh, North Carolina.
Capacity: 6,000

Winston/Salem Memorial Colisuem
(919) 727 2759
Cherry Marshall Street, Winston, North Carolina.
Capacity: 8,500

World War Memorial Stadium
(919) 373 2123
510 Yanceyville Street, Greensboro, North Carolina.
Capacity: 17,000

NORTH DAKOTA

Bismarck Civic Center
(701) 222 6487
6th & Sweet, Bismarck, North Dakota.
Capacity: 7,850

Minot Municipal Auditorium & Arena
(701) 839 5420
515 2nd Avenue SW, Minot, North Dakota.
Capacity: 5,059

North Dakota State Fair Grandstand
(701) 852 3113
Fairgrounds, Minot, North Dakota.
Capacity: 5,600 – 6,200

Red River Valley Fair Pavilion
(701) 282 2200
The Fairgrounds, West Fargo, North Dakota.
Capacity: 8,000

OHIO

Akron Civic Center
(216) 535 3178
182 S. Main Street, Akron, Ohio.
Capacity: 2,918

Blossom Music Center
(216) 929 3048
1145 W. Steels Corners Road, Cuyahoga Falls, Ohio.
Capacity: 18,140

Cincinnati Gardens Roller Rink
(513) 731 1100
2250 Seymore Avenue, Cincinnati, Ohio.
Capacity: 14,000

Cincinnati Music Hall
(513) 621 1919
1243 Elm Street, Cincinnati, Ohio.
Capacity: 3,630

Cincinnati Riverfront Coliseum
(513) 241 1818
Cincinnati, Ohio.
Capacity: 18,348 – 58,000

Cleveland Convention Center
(216) 523 2200
1220 E. 6th Street, Cleveland, Ohio.
Capacity: 9,925

The Coliseum in Richfield
(216) 659 9100
2923 Streetsboro Road, Richfield, Ohio.
Capacity: 20,000

Dayton Hara Arena
(513) 278 4776
1001 Shiloh Springs Road, Dayton, Ohio.
Capacity: 7,500

Lucas County Recreational Center
(419) 893 9481
2910 Key Street, Toledo, Ohio.
Capacity: 11,000

Ohio Exposition Center
(614) 294 5441
State Fairgrounds, E. 11th Avenue, Columbus, Ohio.
Capacity: 6,000 – 10,000

Ohio Theater
(614) 469 1045
29 E. State Street, Columbus, Ohio.
Capacity: 2,900

H.H. Stambaugh Auditorium
(216) 747 5175
1000 5th Avenue, Youngstown, Ohio.
Capacity: 2,600

Toledo Masonic Auditorium
(419) 381 8851
4645 Heather Downs Boulevard, Toledo, Ohio.
Capacity: 2,520

Toledo Sports Arena
(419) 698 4545
1 Main Street, Toledo, Ohio.
Capacity: 7,500

OKLAHOMA

Comanche County Fairgrounds
(405) 357 1483
Great Plains Coliseum, 920 S. Sheridan Road, Lawton, Oklahoma.
Capacity: 3,500

Exposition Square Pavillion
(918) 936 1113
19th & New Haven, Tulsa, Oklahoma.
Capacity: 8,171

Indian Bowl
(918) 682 0431
402 N. S Street, Muskogee, Oklahoma.
Capacity: 7,000

Mabee Center
(918) 492 7545
8100 S. Lewis, Tulsa, Oklahoma.
Capacity: 11,575

Muskogee Civic Assembly Center
(918) 682 9131
425 Boston, Muskogee, Oklahoma.
Capacity: 3,710

Myriad Convention Center
(405) 232 8871
1 Myriad Gardens, Oklahoma City, Oklahoma.
Capacity: 15,634

Oklahoma City Fairgrounds Arena
(405) 947 5428
Fairgrounds, Oklahoma City, Oklahoma.
Capacity: 10,500

Tulsa Assembly Center
(918) 581 5521
100 Civic Center, Tulsa, Oklahoma.
Capacity: 8,994

Lloyd Noble Center
(405) 325 3838
2900 S. Jenkins, Norman, Oklahoma.
Capacity: 13,000

Tulsa Performing Arts Center
(918) 581 5641
2nd & Cincinnati, Tulsa, Oklahoma.
Capacity: 2,450

OREGON

Memorial Coliseum Complex
(503) 235 8771
PO Box 2746, Portland, Oregon.
Capacity: 13,200

Paramount Theater
(206) 682 1414
1037 SW Broadway, Portland, Oregon.
Capacity: 2,960

Portland Civic Stadium
(503) 248 4345
1844 SW Morrison, Portland, Oregon.
Capacity: 33,056

PENNSYLVANIA

Academy Of Music
(215) 893 1935
Broad & Locust Streets, Philadelphia, Pennsylvania.
Capacity: 2,930

Agricultural Hall
(215) 433 7541
Chew & 17th Streets, Allentown, Pennsylvania.
Capacity: 5,000

Albright College Stadium
(215) 921 2381
Albright College, Reading, Pennsylvania.
Capacity: N/A

Civic Arena
(412) 391 4545
Gate 8, Auditorium Place, Pittsburgh, Pennsylvania.
Capacity: 18,000

Erie County Fieldhouse
(814) 825 3333
5750 Wattsberg Road, Erie, Pennsylvania.
Capacity: 5,250

Hersheypark Arena
(717) 534 3900
Hershey, Pennsylvania.
Capacity, Arena: 10,000
Capacity, Stadium: 22,000

John F. Kennedy Stadium
(215) 561 5100
Broad Street & Terminal Avenue, Philadelphia, Pennsylvania.
Capacity: 90,400

109th Artillery Armory
(717) 288 6641
280 Market Street, Kingston, Pennsylvania.
Capacity: 6,800

Pennsylvania State Farm Show Arena
(717) 783 3071
Cameron & McClay Streets, Harrisburg, Pennsylvania.
Capacity: 11,000

Philadelphia Civic Center
(215) 823 7031
Civic Center Boulevard, Philadelphia, Pennsylvania.
Capacity: 11,005

Spectrum
(215) 336 3600
Philadelphia, Pennsylvania.
Capacity: 19,500

Stanley Theater
(412) 261 2800
207 7th Street, Pittsburgh, Pennsylvania.
Capacity: 3,500

Three Rivers Stadium
(412) 323 5000
700 Stadium Circle, Pittsburgh, Pennsylvania.
Capacity: 50,350 – 60,000

Tower Theater
(215) 352 0313
S. 69 Boulevard & Ludlow Street, Upper Darby, Pennsylvania.
Capacity: 3,000

RHODE ISLAND

Leroy Concert Theater
(401) 723 4745
66 Broad Street, Pawtucket, Rhode Island.
Capacity: 2,400

Ocean State Performing Arts Center
(401) 421 2997
220 Weybosset Street, Providence, Rhode Island.
Capacity: 3,230

Providence Civic Center
(401) 331 0700
1 LaSalle Square, Providence, Rhode Island.
Capacity: 14,000

SOUTH CAROLINA

Carolina Coliseum
(803) 777 5113
PO Box 11515, Columbia, South Carolina.
Capacity: 13,500

Spartanburg Memorial Auditorium
(803) 582 8107
385 N. Church Street, Spartanburg, South Carolina.
Capacity: 3,410

Textile Hall
(803) 233 2562
PO Box 5823, Greenville, South Carolina.
Capacity: 4,000

The Township
(803) 252 2032
1703 Taylor Street, Columbia, South Carolina.
Capacity: 3,200

SOUTH DAKOTA

Rushmore Plaza Civic Center
(605) 394 4115
444 Mt. Rushmore Road, Rapid City, South Dakota.
Capacity: 11,500

Sioux Falls Arena
(605) 336 3711
1201 W. Avenue North, Sioux Falls, South Dakota.
Capacity: 9,500

TENNESSEE

Coote Convention Center
(901) 523 2982
North Main Street, Memphis, Tennessee
Capacity: 18,500

Freedom Hall Civic Center
(615) 929 1171
PO Box 2836, CRS, Johnson City, Tennessee.
Capacity: 8,500

Jackson Civic Center
(901) 423 9404
400 S. Highland Avenue, Jackson, Tennessee.
Capacity: 2,200

Jackson Coliseum
(901) 427 3382
Highland Avenue, Jackson, Tennessee.
Capacity: 6,000

Liberty Bowl Memorial Stadium
(901) 272 1452
Hollywood Avenue, Memphis, Tennessee.
Capacity: 5,180

Mid-South Coliseum
(901) 274 3982
Mid-South Fairgrounds, Memphis, Tennessee.
Capacity: 12,000

Nashville Municipal Auditorium
(615) 259 5367
417 4th Avenue North, Nashville, Tennessee.
Capacity: 9,000

Stokely Athletic Center
(615) 974 2491
University of Tennessee, Knoxville, Tennessee.
Capacity: 14,712

TEXAS

Alamo Stadium
(512) 299 5781
110 Tuleta, San Antonio, Texas.
Capacity: 22,000

Amarillo Civic Center
(806) 378 3000
PO Box 1971, Amarillo, Texas.
Capacity, Coliseum: 7,040
Capacity, Auditorium: 2,430

Arlington Stadium
(817) 273 5100
Arlington, Texas.
Capacity: 35,682

Astrodome
(713) 749 9500
PO Box 288, Houston, Texas.
Capacity, Astrodome: 66,000
Capacity, Astroarena: 8,832

Austin Municipal Auditorium
(512) 476 5461
Riverside Drive, Austin, Texas.
Capacity: 6,000

Celebrity Civic Center
(713) 626 3520
7326 SW Freeway, Houston, Texas.
Capacity: 2,860

Chaparral Center
(915) 684 9811
3600 Garfield, Midland, Texas.
Capacity: 6,300

Civic Center Complex
(713) 838 0786
765 Pear Street, Beaumont, Texas.
Capacity: 7,500

Corpus Christi Memorial Coliseum & Exposition Hall
(512) 884 8228
402 S. Shoreline Drive, Corpus Christi, Texas.
Capacity: 6,000

Cotton Bowl
(214) 565 9931
Fair Park, Dallas, Texas.
Capacity: 72,000 – 82,000

Dallas Convention Center
(214) 658 7000
650 S. Griffin, Dallas, Texas.
Capacity, Arena: 9,820
Capacity, Theater: 1,770

El Paso County Coliseum
(915) 543 2961
PO Box 10697, El Paso, Texas.
Capacity: 10,000

Fairpark Coliseum
(713) 835 9430
Fairgrounds, Beaumont, Texas.
Capacity: 7,500

Joe Freeman Coliseum
(512) 224 6080
3201 E. Houston, San Antonio, Texas.
Capacity: 7,500

Houston Civic Center
(713) 222 3561
615 Louisiana, Houston, Texas.
Capacity, Coliseum: 12,000
Capacity, Music Hall: 3,000

Sam Houston Coliseum
(713) 222 3267
1810 Bagby, Houston, Texas.
Capacity: 11,500

Laurie Auditorium
(512) 736 8119
Trinity University, 715 Stadium Drive, San Antonio, Texas.
Capacity: 2,965

Lubbock Memorial Civic Center
(806) 762 6411
1501 6th Street, Lubbock, Texas.
Capacity: 6,271

Market Hall
(214) 655 6100
2200 Stemmons Highway, Dallas, Texas.
Capacity: 16,000

Lubbock Municipal Auditorium
(806) 762 6411
Lubbock, Texas.
Capacity: 9,809

Memorial Auditorium
(817) 322 5611
1300 7th Street, Wichita Falls, Texas.
Capacity: 2,720

Daniel Meyer Coliseum
(817) 921 7965
Texas Christian University, Fort Worth, Texas.
Capacity: 8,166

Moody Coliseum
(214) 692 2864
Southern Methodist University, Dallas, Texas.
Capacity: 7,000

Paramount Theater for the Performing Arts
(512) 472 5411
713 Congress, Austin, Texas.
Capacity: 1,320

Public School Stadium
(915) 653 4711
Fairgrounds, San Angelo, Texas.
Capacity: 17,200

Reunion Arena
(214) 651 1020
1507 Pacific Avenue, Dallas, Texas.
Capacity: 20,000

Will Rogers Memorial Center
(817) 335 0734
3301 W. Lancaster, Fort Worth, Texas.
Capacity: 9,917

San Antonio Convention Center
(512) 225 6351
PO Box 1898, San Antonio, Texas.
Capacity: 16,000

P.E. Shotwell Stadium
(915) 677 7181
E. Highway 36, Abilene, Texas.
Capacity: 20,042

State Fair of Texas Coliseum
(214) 565 1541
Fairpark, Dallas, Texas.
Capacity. 11,000

The Summit
(713) 627 9470
10 Greenway Plaza, Houston, Texas.
Capacity: 17,500

Tarrant County Convention Center
(817) 332 9222
1111 Houston Street, Fort Worth, Texas.
Capacity, Arena: 14,000
Capacity, Theater: 3,050

Taylor County Exposition Center
(915) 677 4376
West Texas Fairgrounds, Abilene, Texas.
Capacity: 7,943

Tri-State Fair Coliseum
(806) 376 7767 or
(806) 376 7922
Fairgrounds, Amarillo, Texas.
Capacity: 6,000

University of Houston
(713) 749 1011
4800 Calhoun, Houston, Texas.
Capacity: 10,731

University of Texas Special Events Center
(512) 477 6060
University of Texas, Austin, Texas.
Capacity: 7,950 – 18,000 – 76,524

UTAH

Capitol Theater
(801) 535 7916 or
(801) 535 7912
50 W. 200 South, Salt Lake City, Utah.
Capacity: 2,000

Cougar Stadium
(801) 378 1211
Brigham Young University, Provo, Utah.
Capacity: 32,000

Marriott Center
(801) 378 5666
Brigham Young University, Provo, Utah.
Capacity: 23,500

Special Events Center
(801) 581 8314
University of Utah, Salt Lake City, Utah.
Capacity: 15,400

VIRGINIA

Hampton Coliseum
(804) 838 5650
1000 Coliseum Drive, Hampton, Virginia.
Capacity: 12,075

Mosque Theater
(804) 780 8226
6 N. Laurel Street, Richmond, Virginia.
Capacity: 3,730

Richmond Coliseum
(804) 780 4956
601 E. Leigh Street, Richmond, Virginia.
Capacity: 11,800

Roanoke Civic Center
(703) 981 2241
710 Williamson Road NE, Roanoke, Virginia.
Capacity: 11,000

Scope Convention Hall
(804) 441 2161
PO Box 1808, Norfolk, Virginia.
Capacity: 12,100 – 13,000

Stadium
(804) 780 6170
3201 Maplewood Avenue, Richmond, Virginia.
Capacity: 22,611

Victory Stadium
(703) 981 2237
Roanoke, Virginia.
Capacity: 31,000

WASHINGTON

Joseph A. Albi Stadium
(509) 456 6000
W. 334 Spokane Falls Boulevard, Spokane, Washington.
Capacity: 37,500

Capitol Theater
(509) 575 6264
19 S. 3rd Street, Yakima, Washington.
Capacity: 1,529

Central Washington Fairground
(509) 248 7160
Fairgrounds, Yakima, Washington.
Capacity: 5,200

The Kingdom
(206) 628 3663
201 S. King Street, Seattle, Washington.
Capacity: 30,000 – 70,000

Paramount Northwest
(206) 682 1414
901 Pine Street, Seattle, Washington.
Capacity: 2,980

Performing Arts Coliseum
(509) 335 3525
Washington State University, Pullman, Washington.
Capacity: 13,000

Seattle Center
(206) 625 4254
305 Harrison Street, Seattle, Washington.
Capacity, Coliseum: 15,000
Capacity, Arena : 6200

Spokane Coliseum
(509) 328 4835
N. 1101 Howard, Spokane, Washington.
Capacity: 8,000

Spokane Riverpark Center Opera House
(509) 456 6000
W. 334 Spokane Falls Boulevard, Spokane, Washington.
Capacity: 2,700

UPS Memorial Fieldhouse
(206) 756 3143
1500 N. Warner, Tacoma, Washington.
Capacity: 5,500

WEST VIRGINIA

Charleston Center Auditorium
(304) 348 8148
Charleston, West Virginia.
Capacity: 9,500

Huntington Civic Center
(304) 696 4400
Huntington, West Virginia.
Capacity: 8,470

Memorial Field House
(304) 529 4124
5th Avenue & 26th Street, Huntington, West Virginia.
Capacity: 7,757

Wheeling Civic Center
(304) 233 7000
Wheeling, West Virginia.
Capacity: 7,500

WISCONSIN

Brown County Veterans Memorial Arena
(414) 494 3404
1901 S. Oneida Street, Green Bay, Wisconsin.
Capacity: 6,500

Dane County Memorial Coliseum
(608) 257 5681
1881 Expo Hall East, Madison, Wisconsin.
Capacity: 4,171 – 10,100

Mecca Arena
(414) 271 2750
500 W. Kilbourne, Milwaukee, Wisconsin.
Capacity: 12,000

Mecca Auditorium
(414) 271 2750
500 W. Kilbourne, Milwaukee, Wisconsin.
Capacity: 6,000

Milwaukee County Stadium
(414) 278 4380
210 S. 46th Street, Milwaukee, Wisconsin.
Capacity: 56,000

Milwaukee Summerfest Grounds
(414) 273 2680
200 N. Harbor Drive, Milwaukee, Wisconsin.
Capacity: 8,700

Performing Arts Center of Milwaukee
(414) 273 7121
929 N. Water Street, Milwaukee, Wisconsin.
Capacity: 2,330

Wisconsin State Fair Grandstand
(414) 257 8800
State Fair Park, Milwaukee, Wisconsin.
Capacity: 37,508.

WYOMING

Wyoming University Fieldhouse
(307) 766 2292
Laramie, Wyoming.
Capacity: 11,000

GANG OF FOUR

VENUES/UK

LONDON
CONCERT HALLS, THEATRES & CINEMAS

Albany Empire
(01) 692 0765
Creek Road, Deptford, SE8
Politically aware venue and mecca for South East London live music.

Drury Lane Theatre
(01) 836 3687
Catherine Street, WC2

Hammersmith Odeon
(01) 748 4081
Queen Caroline Street, W6
Spacious, seated, popular with big acts but ultimately impersonal.

London Palladium
(01) 437 7373
8 Argyll Street, W1
Anyone who likes to think they're anyone has played here.

Rainbow Theatre
(01) 272 9963
232 Seven Sisters Road, Finsbury Park, N4
London's old reliable rock venue. Frayed at the edges.

Royal Albert Hall
(01) 589 3203
Kensington Gore, SW7
An institution i.e. an establishment that intensely dislikes rock concerts.

Royal Festival Hall
(01) 928 3641
Belvedere Road, SE1
The sound is as near perfect as can be, but rock's only featured once every blue moon.

Tramshed Theatre
(01) 317 8687
51 Woolwich New Road, SE18

Theatre Royal
(01) 534 0310
Gerry Raffles Square, Angel Lane, E15

LONDON
ROCK PUBS

The Beckett (Thomas A. Beckett)
(01) 703 7334
320 Old Kent Road, SE1
Provides much needed venue in a barren area.

The Brecknock
(01) 485 3073
227 Camden Road, NW1

The Bridge House
(01) 476 2889
Barking Road, Canning Town, E16
Scene of mod revival but now expanding to cover all types of new bands.

The Cock Tavern
(01) 385 6021
360 North End Road, Fulham, SW6

Golden Lion
(01) 385 3942
490 Fulham Road, SW6
Pleasant but unadventurous venue.

Greyhound
(01) 385 0526
175 Fulham Palace Road, W6
Cavernous atmosphere but good grounding for many new bands.

Half Moon
(01) 737 4580
Half Moon Lane, Herne Hill, SE25

Half Moon
(01) 788 2387
93 Lower Richmond Road, Putney, SW15

Hope and Anchor
(01) 359 4510
207 Upper Street, N1
Basement with a reputation based on good music rather than comfort.

Kensington
(01) 603 3245
Russell Gardens, Holland Road, W14

Kings Head
(01) 226 1916
115 Upper Street, N1
Blues and folk.

Nashville
(01) 603 6071
171 North End Road, W14
Hopefully will have re-opened by the time this book is published. There are too few good venues in London as it is.

Pegasus
(01) 226 5930
109 Green Lanes, Stoke Newington, N16

Torrington
(01) 445 4710
4 Lodge Lane, High Road, N12

White Lion
(01) 870 3017
Putney High Street, SW15
Newly opened as a venue but is at least moderately spacious.

Windsor Castle
(01) 286 8403
309 Harrow Road, W9
Only for afficinados of bad music.

LONDON
CLUBS, BALLROOMS & MISCELLANEOUS VENUES

Acklam Hall
(01) 960 4590
Acklam Road, Portobello Road, W10
Community hall with occasional gigs.

Africa Centre
(01) 836 1973
38 King Street, WC2

Alexandra Palace
(01) 444 7203
Wood Green, N22

Clarendon Hotel
(01) 748 1454/568 0678
Hammersmith Broadway, W6

Dingwalls
(01) 267 4967
Camden Lock, Chalk Farm Road, NW1
Celebrated its seventh anniversary this year; seven day, late-night club.

Electric Ballroom
(01) 485 9006
184 Camden High Road, NW1
Largest new wave venue in London

Empire Ballroom
(01) 437 1446
Large disco for tourists with only very occasional concerts.

Hammersmith Palais
(01) 748 2812
242 Shepherds Bush Road, W6
Largest dance hall in Britain is now the scene of many fine concerts featuring the name acts who prefer this unseated venue to the Odeon just down the road.

Institute of Contemporary Arts
(01) 930 3647
ICA, The Mall, SW1
Slightly restrained atmosphere amongst the exhibitions.

Jacksons Rock Club
(01) 340 5226
Jacksons Lane Community Centre, 271 Archway Road, N6

The Lyceum
(01) 836 3715
Strand, WC2

The Marquee
(01) 437 6603
90 Wardour Street, W1
Has had its ups and downs over the years but the original home for The Who and the Rolling Stones is still going strong and remains the most important London venue for new bands.

The Moonlight Club
(01) 624 7611
100 West End Lane, West Hampstead, NW6
The most adventurous promoter of new bands in London with generally unerring taste.

The Music Machine
(01) 387 0428
Camden High Street, NW1
Rundown, ex-music hall with a regular punk clientele. Only go if you really want to see the band.

Notre Dame Hall
(01) 437 5571
Leicester Place, Leicester Square, WC2

Rock Garden
(01) 240 3916
King Street, Covent Garden, WC2
For all insomniacs: the music goes on to 2a.m., the restaurant stays open until 6a.m.

Roundhouse
(01) 267 2564
Chalk Farm Road, NW1

Royalty
(01) 886 4112
Winchmore Hill Road, Southgate, N14

Upstairs at Ronnie's
(01) 439 0747
47 Frith Street, W1
Unfortunately, nothing like the world-renowned jazz club downstairs; it features totally unknown bands.

The Venue
(01) 834 5882
160 Victoria Street, SW1
The largest rock club in London with erratic waitress service. Many visiting US artists and showcase gigs.

Wembley Arena
(01) 902 1234
Empire Way, Wembley, Middlesex.
7,000 capacity for the impersonal, superstar touch.

YMCA
(01) 636 7289
112 Great Russell Street, WC1

100 Club
(01) 636 0933
100 Oxford Street, W1
Mainly jazz and reggae bands

101 Club
(01) 223 8309
101 St. John's Hill, SW11
Small, upstairs room with little atmosphere.

PROVINCIAL ROCK VENUES

ABERDEEN

The Capitol
(0224) 23141
431 Union Street, Aberdeen
Capacity: 2010

Ruffles
(0224) 29092
13 Diamond Street, Aberdeen
Capacity: 1000

Aberdeen University
(0224) 572751
Students Union, Broad Street, Aberdeen
Capacity: 1000

AYLESBURY

Friars
(0296) 84568
Maxwell Hall, Market Square, Aylesbury
Capacity: 1250

AYR

Pavilion
(0292) 65489
Esplanade, Pavilion Road, Ayr
Capacity: 1000

BARNSTAPLE

Chequers
(0271) 2717
The Strand, Barnstaple
Capacity: 550

BARROW-IN-FURNESS

Civic Hall
(0229) 25500
Town Hall, Duke Street, Barrow-in-Furness
Capacity: N/A

BASILDON

Towngate Theatre
(0268) 22881
Towngate, Basildon, Essex
Capacity: N/A

BATH

Moles Club
(0225) 333423
14 George Street, Bath
Capacity: 130

Pavilion
(0225) 25628
North Parade, Bath
Capacity: N/A

Tiffanys
(0225) 65342
Kingsmead Square, Saw Close, Bath
Capacity: N/A

University
(0225) 63228
Claverton Road, Bath
Capacity: 600

BIRMINGHAM

Barrel Organ
(021) 622 1353
Digbeth, Birmingham
Capacity: N/A

Cedar Club
(021) 236 2454
Constitution Hill, Birmingham
Capacity: N/A

Digbeth Civic Hall
(021) 235 2434
Milk Street Entrance, Digbeth
Capacity: 400

Night Out
(021) 622 2233
Horsefair, Birmingham 1
Capacity: N/A

Odeon
(021) 643 6101
New Street, Birmingham 2
Capacity: 2551

Romeo & Juliet's
(021) 643 6696
Smallbrook Ringway, Birmingham
Capacity: 1330

Top Rank
(021) 236 3226
Dale End, Birmingham 3
Capacity: 2000

Town Hall
(021) 235 3942
Victoria Square, Birmingham 3
Capacity: 1450

University
(021) 472 1841
Edgbaston Park Road, Birmingham 15
Capacity: 1000

BLACKBURN

King George's Hall
(0254) 58424
Northgate, Blackburn
Capacity: N/A

BLACKPOOL

Norbreck Castle
(0253) 52341
Queens Promenade, Blackpool
Capacity: 600

Tiffanys
(0253) 21572
Central Drive, Blackpool
Capacity: 2800

BOURNEMOUTH

Pavilion
(0202) 28404
Westover Road, Bournemouth
Capacity: N/A

Stateside Centre
(0202) 26636
Glenfearn Road, Bournemouth
Capacity: N/A

Town Hall
(0202) 22066
St. Stevens Street, Bournemouth
Capacity: 1000

Winter Gardens
(0202) 27338
Exeter Road, Bournemouth
Capacity: 1818

BRACKNELL

Sports Centre
(0344) 54203
Bagshot Road, Bracknell
Capacity: 2000

BRADFORD

College
(0274) 392712
Vaults Bar, Great Horton, Bradford
Capacity: N/A

University
(0274) 33466
Great Hall, Students Union, Richmond Road, Bradford
Capacity: 1000

BRIDLINGTON

Royal Spa Pavilion
(0262) 78258
South Marine Drive, Bridlington
Capacity: N/A

BRIGHTON

Alhambra
(0273) 27874
24 Kings Road, Brighton
Capacity: N/A

Centre
(0273) 203131
Kings Road, Brighton
Capacity: 5000

Dome
(0273) 682046
29 New Road, Brighton
Capacity: 2100

Jenkinsons
(0273) 25897
Kings West (Seafront), Brighton
Capacity: 900

New Regent
(0273) 28757
West Street, Brighton
Capacity: N/A

Top Rank
(0273) 25895
Kings West, West Street, Brighton
Capacity: 2000

BRISTOL

Colston Hall
(0272) 293891
Colston Street, Bristol 1
Capacity: 2121

Granary
(0272) 28272
32 Welsh Back, Bristol
Capacity: 500

Locarno
(0272) 26193
Bristol New Centre, Frogmore Street, Bristol
Capacity: 2500

Polytechnic
(0272) 656261
Students Union, Coldharbour Lane, Frenchay, Bristol
Capacity: 450

Trinity Hall
(0272) 551544
Trinity Road, St, Philips, Bristol 1
Capacity: 400

University
(0272) 35035
Ansom Room, Queens Road, Clifton, Bristol
Capacity: 920

BURTON

76 Club
(0283) 61037
76 High Street, Burton-on-Trent
Capacity: 300

CAMBRIDGE

Corn Exchange
Telephone number N/A
Market Square, Cambridge
Capacity: 1000

CANTERBURY

Odeon
(0227) 62480
The Friars, Canterbury
Capacity: 1030

University
(0227) 65224
Elliot Masters House, Students Union, Kent University, Canterbury
Capacity: N/A

CARDIFF

Top Rank
(0222) 26538
43 Queen Street, Cardiff
Capacity: 1950

CHELMSFORD

Chancellor Hall
(0245) 65848
Market Road, Chelmsford
Capacity: 650

CHESTER

Deeside Leisure Centre
(0244) 817000
Queensferry, Deeside, Clywd
3 Halls. Capacities: 6000/2400/1000

CHESTERFIELD

Fusion
(0246) 32594
Holywell Street, Chesterfield
Capacity: 550

CLEETHORPES

Shakers
(0472) 67128
Grant Street, Cleethorpes
Capacity: 764

Winter Gardens
(0472) 62925
Kingsway, Cleethorpes
Capacity: 1150

COLCHESTER

Essex University
(0206) 863211
Wivenhoe Park, Colchester
Capacity: 900

COVENTRY

Lanchester Polytechnic
(0203) 21167
Students Union, Priory Street, Coventry
Capacity: N/A

Theatre
(0203) 23141
Hales Street, Coventry
Capacity: 2002

Tiffanys
(0203) 24570
Smithford Way, Coventry
Capacity: 770

University
(0203) 217406
Students Union, University of Warwick, Coventry
Capacity: 1500

CRAWLEY

Leisure Centre
(0293) 37431
Haslett Avenue, Crawley
Capacity: 1600

CROMER

West Runton Pavilion
(026 375) 203
West Runton, Norfolk
Capacity: 1200

CROYDON

Fairfield Hall
(01) 681 0821
Park Lane, Croydon, Surrey
Capacity: N/A

Greyhound
(01) 681 1445
Park Lane, Croydon, Surrey
Capacity: 1500

DERBY

Assembly Rooms
(0332) 3111
Market Place, Derby
Capacity: 1500

Ajanta Club
(0332) 32906
Sacheveral Street, Derby
Capacity: 700

DONCASTER

Rotters Club
(0302) 27448
Silver Street, Doncaster
Capacity: N/A

DUDLEY

JB's
(0384) 53597
King Street, Dudley
Capacity: 500

DUMFRIES

Stagecoach
(0387) 75493
Collin, Dumfries
Capacity: 300

DUNDEE

Barracuda
(0382) 27373
Marketgait, Dundee
Capacity: 700

Caird Hall
(0382) 28121
Caird Square, Dundee
Capacity: 2500

College of Technology
(0382) 27225
Marketgait, Dundee
Capacity: 550

Marryatt Hall
(0382) 28121
Caird Square, Dundee
Capacity: 400

University
(0382) 21841
Students Union, Airlie Place, Dundee
Capacity: 650

DUNSTABLE

Queensway Hall
(0582) 603326
Vernon Place, Queensway, Dunstable
Capacity: 1000

EDINBURGH

Astoria
(031) 661 1662
Abbey Mount, Edinburgh
Capacity: N/A

Claremont Hotel
(031) 556 1487
15 Claremont Crescent, Edinburgh 7
Capacity: N/A

Clouds
(031) 229 5753
3 West Tolcross, Edinburgh
Capacity: N/A

Nite Club
(031) 557 2590
The Playhouse, 20 Greenside Place, Leith Walk, Edinburgh
Capacity: 420

Odeon
(031) 667 3805
7 Clerk Street, Edinburgh 8
Capacity: 1894

Playhouse Theatre
(031) 557 2590
Greenside Place, Edinburgh
Capacity: 3000

Tiffanys
(031) 556 6292
St. Stephen Street, Edinburgh
Capacity: 800

Usher Hall
(031) 228 6611
Lothian Road, Edinburgh
Capacity: N/A

Valentinos
(031) 229 5151
3a East Fountain Bridge, Edinburgh
Capacity: N/A

EXETER

Routes
(0392) 58615
13 Okehampton Street, Exeter
Capacity: 1000

Tiffanys
(0392) 55679
The Quay, Exeter
Capacity: 1000

University
(0392) 75023
Great Hall, Stocker Road, Exeter
Capacity: 1800

GLASGOW

Apollo Theatre
(041) 332 9221
Renfield Street, Glasgow
Capacity: 3300

College of Technology
(041) 332 0681
70 Cowcaddens Road, Glasgow
Capacity: 600

Strathclyde University
(041) 552 1895
90 John Street, Glasgow
Capacity: 1000

Tiffanys
(041) 332 0992
Sauchiehall Street, Glasgow
Capacity: 1500

GLOUCESTER

Leisure Centre
(0452) 36498
Station Road, Gloucester
Capacity: N/A

GRANGEMOUTH

Town Hall
(032 44) 5133
Boness Road, Grangemouth
Capacity: 550

GRAVESEND

Woodville Halls
(0474) 4244
Windmill Street, Gravesend
Capacity: 1000

GREAT YARMOUTH

Tiffanys
(0493) 57018
Marine Parade, Great Yarmouth
Capacity: N/A

GRIMSBY

Central Halls
(0472) 55796
Duncombe Street, Grimsby
Capacity: 740

GUILDFORD

Civic Hall
(0483) 67314
London Road, Guildford
Capacity: N/A

HANLEY

Victoria Hall
(0782) 24641
Albion Square, Hanley, Stoke-on-Trent
Capacity: 1580

HEMEL HEMPSTEAD

Pavilion
(0442) 64451
Hemel Hempstead
Capacity: N/A

HIGH WYCOMBE

Nags Head
(0494) 21758
63 London Road, High Wycombe, Bucks
Capacity: N/A

Town Hall
(0494) 26100
Queen Victoria Road, High Wycombe, Bucks
Capacity: 880

HUDDERSFIELD

Coach House
(0484) 20930
Kings Street, Huddersfield
Capacity: 300

Polytechnic
(0484) 38156
Great Hall, Queensgate, Huddersfield
Capacity: 800

HULL

City Hall
(0482) 20123
Victoria Square, Hull
Capacity: N/A

Tiffanys
(0482) 28250
Ferensway, Hull
Capacity:N/A

University
(0482) 445361
Students Union, Cottingham Road, Hull
Capacity: 900

Wellington Club
(0482) 23262
105 Beverly Road, Hull
Capacity: N/A

IPSWICH

Gaumont
(0473) 53641
Majors Corner, 8 St. Helens Street, Ipswich
Capacity: 1666

KEELE

University
(0782) 625411
Keele, Staffs
Capacity: 770

LANCASTER

University
(0524) 63352
Great Hall, Bailirigg, Lancaster
Capacity: 1600

LEEDS

Fan Club
(0532) 663252
Brannigans, Call Lane, Leeds 8
Capacity: 450

Fforde Green Hotel
(0532) 490984
Roundhay Road, Harehills, Leeds
Capacity: 350

Grand Theatre
(0532) 456014
46 Briggate Street, Leeds
Capacity: 1554

Polytechnic
(0532) 30171
Assembly Hall, Calverley Street, Leeds
Capacity: 600

Queens Hall
(0532) 31961
Sovereign Street, Leeds
Capacity: 4000

University
(0532) 39071
Refectory, PO Box 157, Leeds
Capacity: 1500

LEICESTER

De Montfort Hall
(0533) 540396
Granville Road, Leicester
Capacity: 2536

University
(0533) 553760
Queens Hall, Percy Lee Building, University Road, Leicester
Capacity: 1630

LINCOLN

Drill Hall
(0522) 24393
Broadgate, Lincoln
Capacity: 1200

LIVERPOOL

Empire Theatre
(051) 709 1555
Lime Street, Liverpool
Capacity: 2550

Royal Court Theatre
(051) 708 7411
Roe Street, Liverpool 1
Capacity: 1500

University
2 Bedford Street North, Liverpool 7
Capacity: 1500

LOUGHBOROUGH

University
(0509) 66600
Students Union Building, Ashby Road, Loughborough
Capacity: 1100

MALVERN

Winter Gardens
(068 45) 66266
Grange Road, Malvern
Capacity: 1000

MANCHESTER

Apollo Theatre
(061) 273 6921
Ardwick Green, Manchester 12
Capacity: 2494

Free Trade Hall
(061) 834 3697
Peter Street, Manchester 2
Capacity: 2529

Osborne Club
(061) 205 1562
255 Oldham Road, Collyhurst, Manchester 10
Capacity: 900

Polytechnic
(061) 273 1162
Cavendish House, Cavendish Street, All Saints, Oxford Road, Manchester
Capacity: 650

Rafters
(061) 861 9610
65 Oxford Street
Manchester 1
Capacity: 600

Russell Club
(061) 226 6821/6366
Royce Road, Hulme, Manchester 15
Capacity: 1470

University
(061) 273 5111
Oxford Road, Charlton Upon Medlock, Manchester
Capacity: 1200

MIDDLESBROUGH

Rock Garden
(0642) 241995
208 Newport Road, Middlesbrough, Cleveland
Capacity: 450

Town Hall
(0642) 242561
Albert Road, Middlesbrough, Cleveland
Capacity: 400

NEWCASTLE-UPON-TYNE

City Hall
(0632) 20007
Northumberland Street, Newcastle
Capacity: 2168

Mayfair Ballroom
(0632) 23109
Newgate Street, Newcastle
Capacity: 2100

Polytechnic
(0632) 28761
Students Union, Education Precinct, 2 Sandyford Road, Newcastle
Capacity: 1500

University
(0632) 28402
King's Walk, Newcastle
Capacity: 1400

NEWPORT (GWENT)

The Stowaway
(0633) 50978
40 Stow Hill, Newport
Capacity: 600

NEWPORT (SALOP)

The Village
(0952) 811949
The Square, Newport
Capacity: N/A

NEWTON ABBOTT

Seale Hayne Agricultural College
(0626) 60557
Newton Abbott
Capacity: 550

NORTHAMPTON

Cricket Club
(0604) 32697
Wantage Road, Northampton
Capacity: 1000

NORWICH

Cromwells
(0603) 612909
Edward Street, Norwich
Capacity: 1500

University of East Anglia
(0603) 56161
The Plain, Norwich
Capacity: 920

NOTTINGHAM

Ad Lib Club
(0602) 51251
41 St. Marys Gate, Nottingham
Capacity: N/A

Albert Hall
(0602) 43921
Derby Road, Nottingham
Capacity: N/A

Boat Club
(0602) 869032
Trentside, Trent Bridge, Nottingham
Capacity: 500

Palais
(0602) 51075
Lower Parliament Street, Nottingham
Capacity: 2000

University
(0602) 55912
Portland Building, University Park, Nottingham
Capacity: 800

NUNEATON

77 Club
(0682) 386323
Queens Road, Nuneaton
Capacity: N/A

OXFORD

New Theatre
(0865) 44544
George Street, Oxford
Capacity: N/A

Polytechnic
(0865) 61998
Gypsy Lane, Headington, Oxford
Capacity: 1000

PAISLEY

Bungalow Bar
(041) 889 6667
9 Renfrew Road, Paisley
Capacity: N/A

PENZANCE

Demelza's
(0736) 2475
Penzance
Capacity: 600

PLYMOUTH

Fiesta
(0752) 25721
Mayflower Street, Plymouth
Capacity: 1100

POOLE

Arts Centre
(020 13) 70521
England Road, Poole, Dorset
Capacity: 1500

PORTSMOUTH

Guildhall
(0705) 834164
The Guildhall, Portsmouth
Capacity: 2017

PORT TALBOT

Troubadour
(063 96) 77968
Abervan Shopping Precinct, Port Talbot
Capacity: 600

PRESTON

Guildhall
(0772) 21921
Lancaster Road, Preston, Lancs.
Capacity: N/A

READING

Hexagon Theatre
(0734) 592397
PO Box 600, Civic Centre, Reading
Capacity: 1012

Target
(0734) 585887
Butto Centre, Reading
Capacity: 250

University
(0734) 64396
Upper Redlands Road, Reading
Capacity: 800

REDCAR

Coatham Bowl
(028 72) 2013
Majuba Street, Redcar
Capacity: 900

RETFORD

Porterhouse
(0777) 704981
20 Carolgate, Retford, Notts.
Capacity: 600

MOTORHEAD

SCARBOROUGH

Penthouse
(0723) 63204
35 St. Nicholas Street, Scarborough
Capacity: 308

SHEFFIELD

City Hall
(0742) 734550
Barker's Pool, Sheffield 1
Capacity: 2292

Limit Club
(0742) 730940
70-82 West Street, Sheffield 1
Capacity: 300

Polytechnic
(0742) 738934
The Phoenix Building, Pond Street, Sheffield
Capacity: 1200

Top Rank
(0742) 21927
Arundelgate, Sheffield
Capacity: 2500

SHREWSBURY

Tiffanys
(0743) 58786
Raven Meadows, Shrewsbury
Capacity: 1200

SLOUGH

College of Higher Education
(0753) 22338
Student's Union, Wellington Street, Slough
Capacity: 750

Fulcrum Theatre
(0753) 38669
Queensmere, Slough
Capacity: N/A

Langley College
(0753) 42203
Student's Union, Station Road, Langley, Slough
Capacity: 600

SOUTHAMPTON

Gaumont
(0703) 22001
Commercial Road, Southampton
Capacity: 2165

SOUTHEND

Zero 6
(0702) 546344
Aviation Way, Southend
Capacity: N/A

STAFFORD

Bingley Hall
(0785) 58060
Stafford
Capacity: N/A

ST.ALBANS

City Hall
(0727) 64511
Civic Centre, St. Albans
Capacity: 1000

ST. ANDREWS

University
(0334) 770000
St. Mary's Place, St. Andrews
Capacity: 1000

ST. AUSTELL

New Cornish Riviera Lido
(0726) 4261
Carlyon Bay, St. Austell, Cornwall
Capacity: 2000

STOKE

North Staffs Polytechnic
(0782) 412416
College Road, Stoke
Capacity: 450

Tiffanys
(0782) 614702
Crystal Buildings, Hasell Street, Newcastle-under-Lyme, Stoke
Capacity: N/A

SUNDERLAND

Mayfair Ballroom
(0783) 57568
Newcastle Road, Sunderland
Capacity: N/A

SWANSEA

University
(0792) 24851
College House, University College, Singleton Park
Capacity: 800

THE ROLLING STONES

SWINDON

Brunel Rooms
(0793) 31384
Havelock Square, Swindon
Capacity: 1000

TAUNTON

Odeon
(0823) 72283
Corporation Street, Taunton
Capacity: N/A

TORQUAY

Festival Theatre
(0803) 26244
The Esplanade, Paignton
Capacity: 1460

Town Hall
(0803) 26244
Castle Circus, Torquay
Capacity: 1200

400 Ballroom
(0803) 28103
Victoria Parade, Torquay
Capacity: 550

TOTNES

Civic Hall
(0803) 864499
Market Place, High Street, Totnes
Capacity: 400

UXBRIDGE

Brunel University
(0895) 5724
Kingston Lane, Uxbridge
Capacity: 400

WAKEFIELD

Unity Hall
(0924) 75719
Smythe Street, Wakefield
Capacity: 1000

WOLVERHAMPTON

Civic Hall
(0902) 20212
North Street, Wolverhampton
Capacity: 1697

Lafayette Club
(0902) 26285
Thornley Street, Wolverhampton
Capacity: 1000

YORK

University
(0904) 412328
Central Hall, Heslington, York
Capacity: 1326

Holly and The Italians

Professionals

Gillan

Skids

Devo

XTC

Headline

Roll into the TSB before you wreck into Rockless Eric

Dear TSB,

I'm a school leaver. One of the new wave. Heard you got the knack of opening cheque accounts for the under-twenties as well as the under-thirties. Also heard you play it straight, but unheavy.

Chances are, having my own cheque book would do me no harm. Sending me your special leaflet would do you some good and all. I have it in mind to get my pay put straight into my cheque account, too.

I might even drop in and see you. Heard you've got branches all over the place.

Sounds OK to me. And I get free banking for a year? Like it, like it.

To: TSB Information Service, FREEPOST, London EC2B 2AJ. **FREEPOST**

(You don't need a stamp.) Please send me your free brochure 'Your first job.'

Name ______________________

(BLOCK LETTERS, PLEASE)

Address ______________________

____

____

KG 16/1

TSB

We like to say YES to school leavers.

RADIO STATIONS/US

The following are many of the rock radio stations in America, including most major stations in the Top 50 markets (ranked by 1979 population) and the major Top 40 and Album-Oriented-Rock stations in many secondary markets, listed alphabetically by state.

ALABAMA

Birmingham
WENN-FM 107.7 Disco
WERC-AM 960 Top 40
WKXX-FM 106.9 Top 40
WSGN-AM 610 Top 40
WVOK-FM 99.5 AOR

Mobile
WABB-AM 1480 Top 40
WABB-FM 97.5 AOR
WKRG-FM 99.9 Sft Rk
WXLK-AM 1270 Top 40

Montgomery
WHHY-AM 1440 Top 40
WHHY-FM 101.9 AOR
WLSQ-AM 950 Tp40/Rk

ALASKA

Fairbanks
KFAR-AM 660 Top 40

ARIZONA

Phoenix
KBBC-FM 98/7 Sft Rk
KDKB-AM 1510 AOR
KDKB-FM 93.3 AOR
KIOG-FM 104.7 Sft Rk
KOOL-FM 94.7 Sft Rk
KQXE-AM 1310 Top 40
KRUX-AM 1360 Top 40
KSGR-AM 1440 Oldies
KUPD-AM 1060 Top 40
KUPD-FM 97.9 Top 40

Tucson
KWFM-FM 92.3 AOR

ARKANSAS

Little Rock
KAAY-AM 1090 Top 40

CALIFORNIA

Bakersfield
KAFY-AM 550 Top 40
KERN-AM 1410 Top 40

Fresno
KYNO-AM 1300 Top 40
KYNO-FM 95.5 AOR

Los Angeles Metropolitan Area
KEZY-AM 1190 Top 40
KEZY-FM 95.5 Sft Rk
KFI-AM 640 Top 40
KGIL-AM 1260 Sft Rk
KGIL-FM 94.3 AOR
KHJ-AM 930 Top 40
KHTZ-FM 97.1 Top 40
KIIS-AM 1150 Sft Rk
KIIS-FM 102.7 Sft Rk
KIQQ-FM 100.3 Top 40
KLOS-FM 95.5 AOR
KMET-FM* 94.7 AOR
KMPC-AM 710 Sft Rk
KNAC-FM 105.5 AOR
KNX-FM 93.1 Sft Rk
KPOL-FM 93.9 AOR
KRLA-AM 1110 Oldies
KROQ-AM* 1500 AOR
KROQ-FM* 106.7 AOR
KRTH-FM 101.1 Top 40
KWIZ-AM 1480 Sft Rk
KWIZ-FM 96.7 Sft Rk
KWST-FM 105.9 AOR
KWOW-AM 1600 Top 40

Ventura
KACY-AM 1520 Top 40

Sacramento
KNDE-AM 1470 Top 40
KROI-FM 96.9 AOR
KROY-AM 1240 Top 40
KSFM-FM 102.5 AOR
KZAP-FM 98.5 AOR

San Bernadino
KFXM-AM 590 Top 40
KMEN-AM 1290 Top 40
KOLA-FM 99.9 AOR
KSOM-FM 93.5 Oldies

San Diego
KCBQ-AM 1170 Top 40
KFMB-AM 760 Sft Rk
KGB-AM 1360 Top 40
KGB-FM 101.5 AOR
KMJC-AM 910 Top 40
KPRI-FM 106.5 AOR

San Francisco
KFRC-AM 610 Top 40
KMEL-FM 106.1 AOR
KSAN-FM* 94.9 AOR
KTIM-AM 1510 AOR
KTIM-FM 100.9 AOR
KYA-AM 1260 Top 40
KYA-FM 93.3 AOR
KYUU-FM 99.7 Oldies

San Jose
KARA-FM 105.7 Oldies
KLIV-AM 1590 Top 40
KOME-FM 98.5 AOR
KSJO-FM 92.3 AOR

Santa Barbara
KIST-AM 1340 Sft Rk
KTMS-FM 97.5 AOR
KTYD-AM 990 AOR
KTYD-FM 99.9 AOR

COLORADO

Aspen
KSPN-FM 97.7 AOR

Colorado Springs
KKFM-FM 96.5 AOR

Denver
KBCO-FM 97.3 AOR
KAZY-FM 106.7 AOR
KBPI-FM 105.9 AOR
KIMN-AM 950 Top 40
KIMN-FM 98.5 Top 40
KOAQ-FM 103.5 Top 40
KTLK-AM 1280 Top 40
KXKX-FM 95.7 AOR

CONNECTICUT

Hartford
WCCC-FM 106.9 AOR
WDRC-AM 1360 Top 40
WHCN-FM 105.9 AOR
WRCQ-AM 910 Oldies
WTIC-FM 96.5 Top 40

New Haven
WPLR-FM 99.1 AOR
WWOW-AM 1380 Oldies
WYBC-FM 94.3 AOR

DELAWARE

Wilmington
WAMS-AM 1380 Top 40

DISTRICT OF COLUMBIA (WASHINGTON)

WDON-AM 1540 Oldies
WHFS-FM 102.3 AOR
WPGC-FM 95.5 Top 40
WRQX-FM 107.3 AOR
WWDC-FM 101.1 AOR

FLORIDA

Daytona-Beach
WMFJ-AM 1450 Top 40

Ford Lauderdale Hollywood
WAXY-FM 105.9 Top 40
WHYI-FM 100.7 Top 40
WSRF-AM 1580 AOR
WSHE-FM 103.5 AOR

Gainesville
WGVL-FM 105.5 AOR

Jacksonville
WAIV-FM 96.9 AOR
WAPE-AM 690 Top 40
WIVY-FM 102.9 Top 40

Miami
WGBS-AM 710 Top 40
WINZ-FM 94.9 AOR
WMJX-FM 96.3 Top 40
WQAM-AM 560 Top 40
WWWL-FM 93.9 AOR

Orlando
WBJW-FM 105.1 Top 40
WDIZ-FM 100.3 Top 40
WLOF-AM 950 Top 40
WORJ-FM 107.7 AOR

Tallahassee
WGLF-FM 104.1 Sft Rk
WOWD-FM 103.1 AOR

Tampa-St. Petersburg
WAZE-AM 860 Oldies
WLCY-AM 1380 Top 40
WQSR-FM 102.5 AOR
WRBQ-FM 104.7 Top 40

GEORGIA

Athens
WRFC-AM 960 Top 40

Atlanta
WFOM-AM 1230 Top 40
WKLS-FM 96.1 AOR
WQXI-AM 790 Top 40
WQXI-FM 94.1 AOR
WRAS-FM 88.5 AOR
WREK-FM 91.1 AOR
WYZE-AM 1480 Oldies
WZGC-FM 92.9 Top 40

Savannah
WSGA-AM 1400 Top 40

HAWAII

Honolulu
KIKI-AM 830 AOR
KIOE-AM 1080 Top 40
KKUA-AM 690 Top 40
KORL-AM 650 Top 40
KQMQ-FM 93.3 AOR

IDAHO

Boise
KFXD-AM 580 Top 40

Lewiston
KOZE-AM 1300 Top 40

Moscow
KRPL-AM 1400 Top 40
KUID-FM 91.7 AOR

ILLINOIS

Chicago Metropolitan Area
WBBM-FM 96.3 Sft Rk
WDAI-FM 94.7 AOR
WEFM-FM 99.5 Top 40
WFYR-FM 103.5 Top 40
WVVX-FM 103.1 Oldies
WJKL-FM 94.3 AOR
WKQX-FM 101.1 AOR
WLS-AM* 890 Top 40
WLUP-FM 97.9 AOR
WMET-FM 95.5 Top 40
WXRT-FM 93.1 AOR

Peoria/Bloomington
WIRL-AM 1290 Top 40
WWCT-FM 105.7 AOR

Rockford
WROK-AM 1440 Top 40
WYFE-FM 95.3 AOR
WZOK-FM 97.5 AOR

INDIANA

Indianapolis
WFBQ-FM 94.7 AOR
WIBC-AM 1070 Sft Rk
WIFE-AM 1310 AOR
WNAP-FM 93.1 Top 40
WNDE-AM 1260 Top 40

IOWA

Cedar Rapids
KLWW-AM 1450 Top 40
KQCR-FM 102.9 Oldies

Davenport
KSTT-AM 1170 Top 40

Des Moines
KCBC-AM 1390 AOR
KGGO-FM 94.9 Top 40
KIOA-AM 940 Top 40
KRNQ-FM 102.5 AOR

Waterloo
KWWL-AM 1330 Top 40

KANSAS

Wichita
KEYN-FM 103.7 Top 40
KFDI-FM 101.3 AOR
KELO-AM 1480 Top 40

KENTUCKY

Lexington
WKQQ-FM 98.1 AOR
WLAP-FM 94.5 AOR
WVLK-AM 590 Top 40

Louisville
WAKY-AM 790 Top 40
WKLO-AM 1080 Top 40
WLRS-FM 102.3 AOR
WQHI-FM 95.7 AOR
WXVW-AM 1450 Oldies

LOUISANA

Baton Rouge
WAFB-FM 98.1 Oldies
WAIL-AM 1260 Sft Rk
WFMF-FM 102.5 AOR

Lake Charles
KGRA-FM 103.7 AOR

New Orleans
WNOE-AM 1060 Top40
WNOE-FM 101.1 AOR
WQUE-FM 93.3 Top 40
WRNO-FM 99.5 AOR
WTIX-AM 690 Top 40

Shreveport
KEEL-AM 710 Top 40
KROK-FM 94.5 Rock

MAINE

Bangor
WABI-AM 910 Top 40
WGUY-AM 1250 Top 40

Lewiston
WBLM-FM 107.5 AOR

MARYLAND

Baltimore
WAYE-AM 860 AOR
WBKZ-FM 95.9 Sft Rk
WCAO-AM 600 Top 40
WIYY-FM 97.9 AOR
WKTK-FM 105.7 AOR
WLPL-FM 92.3 Top 40

Hagerstown
WQCM-FM 96.7 AOR

MASSACHUSETTS

Boston Metropolitan Area
WACQ-AM 1150 Top 40
WBCN-FM* 104.1 AOR
WBZ-FM 106.7 Top 40
WCAS-AM 740 AOR
WCGY-FM 93.7 Top 40
WCOZ-FM 94.5 AOR
WEEI-FM 103.3 Sft Rk
WRKO-AM 680 Top 40
WROR-FM 98.5 Oldies
WVBF-FM 105.7 Top 40

Worcester
WAAF-FM 104.3 Top 40
WNCR-AM 1440 Top 40
WORC-AM 1310 Oldies

MICHIGAN

Ann Arbor
WCBN-FM 88.3 AOR
WIQB-FM 102.9 AOR

Detroit Metropolitan Area
CKLW-AM* 800 Top 40
WABX-FM 99.5 AOR
WDRQ-FM 93.1 Top 40
WHND-AM 560 Oldies
WRIF-FM 101.1 AOR
WWKR-AM 1310 Top 40
WWWW-FM 106.7 AOR
WXYZ-AM 1270 Top 40

Flint
WTAC-AM 600 Top 40
WWCK-FM 105.5 AOR

Grand Rapids
WGRD-AM 1410 Top 40
WGRD-FM 97.9 Top 40
WLAV-FM 96.9 AOR
WZZR-FM 95.7 Top 40

Saginaw
WIOG-FM 106.3 AOR
WSAM-AM 1400 Top 40

MINNESOTA

Duluth
WAKX-FM 98.9 Top 40
WEBC-AM 560 Top 40

MINNEAPOLIS

St. Paul
KQRS-AM 1440 AOR
WDWB-AM 630 AOR
WDWB-FM 101.3 AOR
KSTP-AM 1500 Top 40
WCCO-FM 102.9 AOR
WMIN-AM 1010 Top 40

Rochester
KWWK-FM 96.7 AOR
KWEB-AM 1270 Top 40

St. Cloud
WJON-AM 1240 Top40

MISSISSIPPI

Jackson
WJDX-AM 620 Rk/Tp40
WZZO-FM 102.9 Top 40

Tupelo
WTUP-AM 1490 Top 40

MISSOURI

Kansas City
KBEQ-FM 104.3 Top 40
KWKI-FM 93.3 AOR
KYYS-FM 102.1 AOR
WHB-AM 710 Top 40

St. Louis
KADI-FM 96.3 AOR
KKOJ-AM 1320 Top 40
KSD-AM 550 Sft Rk
KSHE-FM 94.7 AOR
KSLQ-FM 98.1 Top 40
KXOK-AM 630 Top 40

MONTANA

Great Falls
KEIN-AM 1310 Top 40

Missoula
KDXT-FM 93.3 AOR

NEBRASKA

Lincoln
KFMQ-FM 101.9 Adlt.Rk

Omaha
KGOR-FM 99.9 Top 40
KOIL-AM 1290 Top 40
KQKQ-FM 98.5 AOR
WOW-AM 590 Rk/Tp40

NEVADA

Las Vegas
KENO-AM 1460 Top 40
KENO-FM 92.3 AOR
KLUC-FM 98.5 Oldies

NEW HAMPSHIRE

Manchester
WFEA-AM 1370 Top 40

NEW JERSEY

Asbury Park
WJLK-FM 94.3 Oldies

Atlantic City
WMGM-FM 103.7 AOR

Trenton
WPRB-FM 103.3 AOR

NEW MEXICO

Albuquerque
KQEQ-AM 920 Top 40
KRKE-FM 94.1 AOR
KRST-FM 92.3 AOR

NEW YORK

Albany-Troy
WFLY-FM 92.3 Top 40
WGFM-FM 99.5 Top 40
WPTR-AM 1540 Top 40
WQBK-FM 103.9 AOR
WTRY-AM 980 Top 40
WWWD-AM 1240 AOR

Buffalo
WBEN-FM 102.5 AOR
WBUF-FM 92.9 AOR
WGRQ-FM 96.9 AOR
WKBW-AM* 1520 Top 40
WNIA-AM 1230 Top 40
WYSL-AM 1400 Top 40

New York City Metropolitan Area
WABC-AM 770 Top 40
WBAB-FM 102.2 AOR
WBLI-FM 106.1 Oldies
WBLS-FM 107.5 Black
WCBS-FM 101.1 Oldies
WFMU-FM 91.1 AOR
WKTU-FM 92.3 Disco
WLIB-AM* 1190 R&B
WLIR-FM* 92.7 AOR
WNBC-AM 660 Top 40
WNEW-FM 102.7 AOR
WPIX-FM 101.9 AOR
WPLJ-FM* 95.5 AOR
WRNW-FM 107.1 AOR
WRVR-FM 106.7 Jazz
WXLO-FM 98.7 Top 40
WYNY-FM 97.1 Adlt.Rk

Rochester
WWWG-AM 1460 Top 40
WBBF-AM 950 Top 40
WCMF-FM 96.5 AOR
WHFM-FM 98.9 Top 40
WVOR-FM 100.5 Oldies

Syracuse
WNDR-AM 1260 Oldies
WOLF-AM 1490 Top 40

Utica-Rome
WOUR-FM 96.9 AOR

NORTH CAROLINA

Asheville
WISE-AM 1310 Top 40

Charlotte
WAYS-AM 610 Top 40
WBT-AM 1110 Top 40
WIST-AM 1240 Oldies
WROQ-FM 95.1 AOR
WRLP-AM 1540 AOR

Greensboro
WBIG-AM 1470 Top 40
WCOG-AM 1320 Top 40
WRQK-FM 98.7 AOR

Raleigh
WKIX-AM 850 Top 40
WQDR-FM 94.7 AOR
WRAL-FM 101.5 Top 40

Winston-Salem
WAIR-AM 1340 Top 40
WBUY-AM 1440 Oldies
WLXN-FM 94.1 Oldies
WKZL-FM 107.5 AOR
WRQK-FM 98.7 Top 40
WTOB-AM 1380 Top 40

NORTH-DAKOTA

Bismarck
KFYR-AM 550 Top 40
KFYR-FM 92.9 OldTp40

Minot
KCJB-FM 97.1 AOR
KKOA-AM 1390 Top 40

OHIO

Akron/Canton
WCUE-AM 1150 Top 40
WKDD-FM 96.5 AOR
WQIQ-AM 1060 Oldies
WINW-AM 1520 Top 40

Cincinnati
WEBN-FM 102.7 AOR
WKRP* (CBS-TV)
WKRQ-FM 101.9 Top 40
WMOH-AM 1450 Top 40

Cleveland
WGCL-FM 98.5 Top 40
WWWE-AM 1100 Sft Rk
WMMS-FM* 100.7 AOR
WWWM-FM 105.7 AOR
WZZP-FM 106.5 Top 40

Columbus
WCOL-AM 1230 Top 40
WCOL-FM 92.3 AOR
WLVO-FM 96.3 AOR
WNCI-FM 97.9 Top 40
WRMZ-FM 99.7 Top 40

Dayton
WING-AM 1410
WTUE-FM 104.7 AOR
WVUD-FM 99.9 AOR

Toledo
WIOT-FM 104.7 AOR
WMHE-FM 92.5 AOR
WOHO-AM 1470 Top 40

Youngstown
WFMJ-AM 1390 Top 40
WHOT-AM 1330 Top 40
WHOT-FM 101.1 AOR

OKLAHOMA

Oklahoma City
KATT-FM 100.5 AOR
KGOU-FM 106.5 AOR
KOMA-AM 1520 Top 40
WKY-AM 930 Top 40
WKY-AM 930 Top 40

Tulsa
KAKC-AM 970 Top 40
KAKC-FM 92.9 Oldies
KELI-AM 1430 Top 40

OREGON

Eugene
KBDF-AM 1280 Top 40
KFMY-FM 97.9 AOR
KZEL-FM 96.1 AOR

Portland
KGON-FM 92.3 Top 40
KGW-AM 620 Top 40
KINK-FM 101.9 AOR
KMJK-FM 106.7 Top 40
KPAM-FM 97.1 Top 40
KVAN-AM 1480 AOR

PENNSYLVANIA

Allentown
WEEX-AM 1230 Oldies
WEZV-FM 95.1 AOR
WKAP-AM 1320 Top 40
WSAN-AM 1470 AOR

Harrisburg
WKBO-AM 1230 Top 40
WRHY-FM 92.7 AOR

Philadelphia
WFIL-AM 560 Top 40
WIFI-FM 92.5 Top 40
WIOQ-FM 102.1 AOR
WMMR-FM* 93.3 AOR
WYSR-FM 94.1 AOR
WZZD-AM 990 Top 40

Pittsburgh
WDVE-FM 102.5 AOR
WKTQ-AM 1320 Top 40
WPEZ-FM 94.5 Top 40
WWKS-FM 106.7 Top 40
WXKX-FM 96.1 Top 40
WYDD-FM 104.7 AOR

RHODE ISLAND

Providence
WBRU-FM 95.5 AOR
WPJB-FM 105.1 Top 40
WPRO-AM 630 Top 40
WPRO-FM 92.3 Top 40

SOUTH CAROLINA

Charleston
WCSC-AM 1390 Top 40
WKTM-FM 102.5 Top 40
WQSN-AM 1450 Oldies
WTMA-AM 1250 Top 40
WWWZ-FM 93.5 AOR

SOUTH DAKOTA

Rapid City
KKLS-AM 920 Top 40
KGGG-FM 100.8 Top 40

TENNESSEE

Memphis
WHBQ-AM 560 Top 40
WMC-FM 99.7 AOR
WMPS-AM 680 Country
WREC-AM 600 Sft Rk
WZXR-FM 102.7 AOR

Nashville
WIZO-FM 100.1 Top 40
SKDF-FM 103.3 AOR
WLAC-AM 1510 Top 40
WMAK-AM 1510 Top 40
WSM-FM 95.5 Sft Rk

TEXAS

Austin
KCSW-FM 103.7 Hits
KHFI-FM 98.3 Top 40
KLBJ-FM 93.7 AOR
KNOW-AM 1490 Top 40
KOKE-FM* 95.5 Country

Beaumont
KAYC-AM 1450 Top 40
KAYD-FM 97.5 Top 40
KOBS-FM 104.5 Top 40

Corpus Christi
KEYS-AM 1400 Top 40
KRYS-AM 1360 Top 40
KZFM-FM 95.5 AOR

Dallas/Fort Worth
KFJZ-FM 97.1 Top 40
KFWD-FM 102.1 AOR
KLIF-AM 1190 Top 40
KNUS-FM 98.7 Top 40
KZEW-FM* 97.9 AOR

Houston
KAUM-FM 96.5 AOR
KILT-AM 610 Top 40
KILT-FM 100.3 AOR
KLOL-FM 101.1 AOR
KRBE-FM 104.1 Top 40
KXYZ-AM 1320 Oldies

Lubbock
KLBK-AM 1340 Oldies
KLBK-FM 94.5 AOR
KSEL-AM 950 Top 40

San Antonio
KISS-FM 99.5 AOR
KITE-AM 930 Top 40
KITE-FM 104.5 Top 40
KTFM-FM 102.7 AOR
KTSA-AM 550 Top 40
KZZY-FM 100.3 Top 40

UTAH

Salt Lake City
KCPX-AM 1320 Top 40
KCPX-FM 98.7 AOR
KLO-AM 1430 Oldies
KRSP-AM 1060 Top 40
KRSP-FM 103.5 Top 40
KWHO-FM 93.3 Top 40

VERMONT

Burlington
WRUV-FM 90.1 AOR

VIRGINIA

Norfolk
WNOR-AM 1230 Top 40
WNOR-FM 98.7 AOR
WORK-FM 104.5 Top 40

Richmond
WGOE-AM 1590 AOR
WLEE-AM 1480 Top 40
WRVQ-FM 94.5 Top 40
WRXL-FM 102.1 AOR

Roanoke
WROV-AM 1240 Top 40
WSLQ-FM 99.1 Oldies

WASHINGTON

Seattle-Tacoma
KING-AM 1090 Top 40
KISW-FM 99.9 AOR
KJR-AM 950 Top 40
KLAY-FM 106.1 AOR
KRKO-AM 1380 Top 40
KTAC-AM 850 Top 40
KVI-FM 101.5 Top 40
KYYX-FM 96.5 Top 40
KZAM-AM 1540 AOR
KZAM-FM* 92.5 AOR
KZOK-AM 1590 AOR
KZOK-FM 102.5 AOR

Spokane
KHQ-FM 98.1 Top 40
KJRB-AM 790 Top 40
KREM-AM 970 Top 40
KREM-FM 92.9 AOR

WEST VIRGINIA

Charleston
WVAF-FM 99.9 AOR

Wheeling
WEIF-AM 1370 Oldies
WKWK-AM 1400 Top 40
WOMP-FM 100.5 AOR

WISCONSIN

Madison
WIBA-FM 101.5 AOR
WISM-AM 1480 Top 40
WISM-FM 98.1 Oldies
WYXE-FM 92.1 Top 40

Milwaukee
WLPX-FM 97.3 AOR
WOKY-AM 920 Top 40
WQFM-FM 93.3 AOR
WZMF-FM 98.3 AOR
WZUU-AM 1290 AOR
WZUU-FM 95.7 AOR

WYOMING

Caspar
KAWY-FM 94.5 AOR

Cheyenne
KFBC-AM 1240 Top 40
KFBC-FM 97.9 Top 40

EDITOR'S NOTE: Stations switch format in America suddenly. A mellow station goes disco, a progressive station suddenly goes very safe. More often than not the reason's in the ratings — the Arbitron book that gives jocks and station directors a statistical idea of how many households they reach. In a 1980 example, radio station WPIX-FM, owned by a Chicago company, switched formats because its low Arbitron rating in the New York market kept it from getting a high share of national advertiser dollars. Thus its risky, new-music format disappeared from the New York airways, replaced by a station that plays a lot of Eagles and Billy Joel.

These listings are thus subject to change without notice. SUPPORT AVANT-GARDE RADIO!

*Stations particularly recommended

KISS

RADIO STATIONS/UK

BBC RADIO

Radios 1, 2, 3 & 4
(01) 580 4468
Broadcasting House, Portland Place, London W1A 1AA

Radio Birmingham
(021) 472 5141
Broadcasting Centre, Pebble Mill Road, Birmingham.

Radio Blackburn
(0254) 62411
King Street, Blackburn, Lancs.

Radio Brighton
(0273) 680231
Marlborough Place, Brighton, Sussex.

Radio Bristol
(0272) 311111
3 Tyndalls Park Road, Bristol 8.

Radio Carlisle
(0228) 31661
Hilltop Heights, London Road, Carlisle

Radio Cleveland
(0642) 248491
91 Linthorpe Road, Middlesbrough, Cleveland.

Radio Derby
(0332) 361111
56 St Helens Street, Derby.

Radio Humberside
(0482) 23232
9 Chapel Street, Hull.

Radio Leeds
(0532) 42131
Broadcasting House, Woodhouse Lane, Leeds 2.

Radio Leicester
(0533) 27113
Epic House, Charles Street, Leicester.

Radio Lincolnshire
Due to begin broadcasting in late 1980.

Radio London
(01) 486 7611
35a Marylebone High Street, London W1.

Radio Manchester
(061) 228 3434
New Broadcasting House, Oxford Road, Manchester.

Radio Medway
(0634) 46284
30 High Street, Chatham, Kent.

Radio Merseyside
(051) 236 3355
Commerce House, 13/17 Sir Thomas Street, Liverpool L1.

Radio Newcastle
(0632) 814243
Crestine House, Archbold Terrace, Newcastle-upon-Tyne 2.

Radio Norfolk
(0603) 2884
St Catherine's Close, All Saints Green, Norwich.

Radio Nottingham
(0602) 47643
York House, York Street, Nottingham.

Radio Oxford
(0865) 53411
242/254 Banbury Road, Oxford.

Radio Scotland
(041) 339 8844
Broadcasting House, Queen Margaret Drive, Glasgow.

Radio Sheffield
(0742) 686185
Ashdell Grove, 60 Westbourne Road, Sheffield.

Radio Solent
(0703) 31311
South Western House, Canute Road, Southampton.

Radio Stoke
(0782) 24827
Conway House, Cheapside, Hanley, Stoke-on-Trent.

Radio Ulster
(0232) 44400
Broadcasting House, Ormeau Avenue, Belfast.

Radio Wales
(0222) 564888
Broadcasting House, Llandaff, Cardiff.

COMMERCIAL RADIO

Beacon Radio
(0902) 757211
PO Box 303, 247 Tettenhall Road, Wolverhampton.

BRMB Radio
(021) 359 4481
PO Box 555, Radio House, Aston Road North, Birmingham.

Capital Radio
(01) 388 1288
Euston Tower, London NW1.

CBC Radio
(0222) 384041
Radio House, West Canal Wharf, Cardiff.

Manx Radio
(0624) 3277
Douglas Head, Isle of Man.

Mercia Sound
(0203) 28451
Hartford Place, Coventry.

Metro Radio
(0632) 2884121
Radio House, Longrigg, Swalwell, Newcastle-Upon-Tyne.

Radio Orwell
(0473) 216971
Electric House, Lloyds Avenue, Ipswich.

Radio City
(051) 227 5100
8-10 Stanley Street, Liverpool.

Radio Clyde
(041) 204 2555
Ranken House, Anderston Cross Centre, Glasgow.

Downtown Radio
(0247) 815555
Kiltonga Radio Centre, PO Box 293, Newtonards, Co. Down.

Radio Forth
(031) 556 9255
Forth House, Forth Street, Edinburgh.

Radio Hallam
(0742) 71188
PO Box 194, Hartshead, Sheffield.

Hereward Radio
(0733) 40897
114 Bridge Street, Peterborough.

London Broadcasting (LBC)
(01) 353 1010
Gough Square, London EC4.

Radio Luxembourg
(01) 493 5961
38 Hertford Street, London W1.

Pennine Radio
(0274) 31521
PO Box 235, Pennine House, Forster Square, Bradford.

Piccadilly Radio
(061) 236 9913
Piccadilly Plaza, Manchester.

Plymouth Sound
(0752) 27272
Earl's Acre, Plymouth.

Swansea Sound
(0792) 893751
Victoria Road, Gowerton, Swansea.

Tay Radio
Due to begin broadcasting in late 1980.

Radio Tees
(0642) 615111
74 Dovecot Street, Stockton on Tees, Cleveland.

Thames Valley Radio
(0734) 413131
PO Box 210, Reading, Berks.

Radio Trent
(0602) 581731
29/31 Castlegate, Nottingham.

Two Counties Radio (2CR)
(0202) 294881
5-9 Southcote Road, Bournemouth.

Radio Victory
(0705) 27799
PO Box 257, Portsmouth.

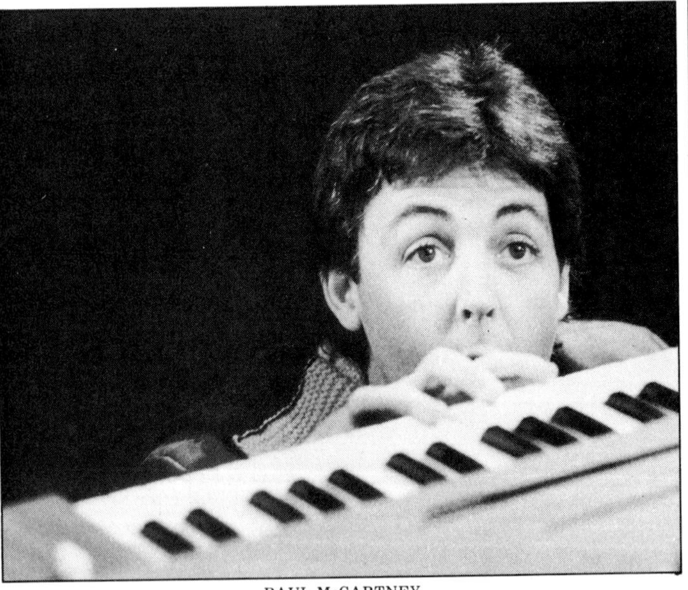

PAUL McCARTNEY

ROCK PUBLICATIONS/US

Ampersand
1680 Vine St., Suite 201, Hollywood, Calif. 90028
A student newspaper distributed on college campuses. Good-to-look-at, featuring much music and other arts coverage. Broad point-of-view. Doesn't take too many risks. Monthly during school year.

The Aquarian Weekly
One The Crescent, Montclair, New Jersey 07042
What's happening in the Northeast Metro area? Note especially columns by Bea Flatte and Charley Crespo.

Billboard
1515 Broadway, New York, NY 10036
The granddaddy of US trade magazines. BILLBOARD's charts are the most systematic, their coverage of all areas, the most respected. Weekly.

BOMP!
Box 7112, Burbank, CA 91510
The voice of West coast pop eccentricity. Publisher/Editor Greg Shaw also runs a record store known for its selection of rare and special, old and new discs. His magazine covers them, bimonthly, with style.

Boulevards
1008 Sutter Street, San Francisco, Calif. 94109
Superslick, trendy city magazine featuring but by no means limited to such mean writing machines as The Realist, Paul Krassner and (one of our favorites) R. Meltzer, author of *Gulcher*. Recent in-depth coverage of Public Image bodes well. Monthly.

Buddy
PO Box 8366, Dallas, Texas 75205
Subtitled "The Original Texas Music Magazine", Stoney Burns' journal is one of America's most singular. Many well-known critics began writing in its pages. Named after Mr. Holly, so you know you're they're in the right place. Biweekly.

Cashbox
6363 Sunset Blvd., Hollywood, Calif. 90028
The least necessary of America's three weekly trade magazines, Cashbox began covering the vending machine and juke box business — hence its name.

Circus
115 East 57th St., New York, NY 10022
Eager-to-please CIRCUS blows with the wind and consistently prints the highest quality, sexiest rock star pix in the biz. Still, how many articles can you read about Rush? Weekly — at the moment.

Contemporary Keyboard
Frets
Guitar Player
20605 Lazaneo, Cupertino, Calif. 95014
Magazines for players, by players and with players in mind. Every-so-often interviews with less-than-talkative stars. Too technical for the average reader, but check those coverlines! Each is a monthly.

Creem
187 South Woodward Ave., Birmingham, Michigan 48011
America's only rock magazine has survived a lot of challenges to its supremacy and has finally, seemingly settled into a predictably obstreperous rut. A letters column better than PENTHOUSE's and a quirky precociousness make it the only alternative to ROLLING STONE. Monthly.

Daily Dope
225 Lafayette St., New York 10012
A sex, rock and dope magazine for people who like sex and rock and dope — sometimes infantile, not likely to survive. Get it while you can. Monthly.

Downbeat
222 West Adams Street, Chicago, 111. 60606
All that jazz, from the experts. Monthly.

Ffanzeen
PO Box 109, Parkville Station, Brooklyn, NY 11204
Bimonthly. Very local, street level, by, for and about the fans magazine.

FMI (Friday Morning Quarterback)
Cherry Hill Plaza, 1415 East Marlton Pike, Cherry Hill, NJ 08034
The No. 1 most important radio tip sheet in the whole world. What publisher Kal Rudman says, goes on most of rock and roll radio. Watch the record execs get suddenly humble. Every week.

Goldmine
PO Box 187, Fraser, Michigan 48026
Rare stuff and old stuff only for those who like that stuff. Monthly.

Good Times
1619 East Sunrise Blvd., Ford Lauderdale, Fla. 33304
A biweekly newspaper covering local music scenes completely if not well. The New York version has lots of hot gossip from business regulars. Regional and biweekly.

High Fidelity
The Publishing House, Great Barrington, Mass. 01230
High-brow, serious coverage of music and hardware. Puts hard-to-interview acts like Steely Dan on the cover. Another one to check the coverlines on before you buy and buy before you buy a stereo.

High Times
Box 386, Cooper Station, New York, NY 10003
The first, best and always of drug magazines has seen its highs and lows of late. Fast to get into New Whatever You Want to Call It Music, they've since run an hilarious cover of Jagger with bare tits, disavowing any encouragement of drug use. Weekly, there are rumours the magazine will fold; yet it appears, monthly and a little confused.

Hollywood Reporter
6715 Sunset Blvd., Hollywood, Calif. 90028
Find out the latest on upwardly mobile rock stars, managers, sellouts and others. Wanna know where the money you spend on records is getting spent? Check it out, every day, just like every Hollywood mogul does. Diane Bennett covers music with a flair.

Hit Parader
Charlton Publications, Derby Conn. 06418
Lisa and Richard Robinson's magazine still looks like shit and smears ink onto your fingers while providing the most consistent photo and interview coverage of the rock world available in a magazine. Latest Top 40 song lyrics still fill the back-of-the-book so you can sing along with Michael Jackson. Monthly, in supermarkets everywhere.

International Musician
1500 Broadway, New York, NY 10036
The house organ of the American Federation of Musicians offers broad coverage of the music business from the artist's point of view. Monthly, not sold on newsstands.

Music City News
PO Box 22975, Nashville, Tenn. 37202
Down-home country coverage from the heart of twang-twang land. Monthly.

New York Rocker
166 Fifth Avenue, New York, NY 10010
America's most progressive music newspaper, where Richard Hell first appeared on a cover. Every six weeks or so.

Night
210 Fifth Avenue, New York, NY 10010
A monthly dedicated to the afterlife of New York's "don't have to disco but we do" set. Hot pictures of all year's models, sometimes without captions. Very in-crowd. Very amusing. Very large-format. Very black and white. Very monthly.

Punk
225 Lafayette St., New York, NY 10012
The source — the originators — where the comic book first went electric and the rock magazine first met the end of the century. Less sporadic than it used to be.

Radio & Records
1930 Century Park West, Los Angeles, Calif. 90067
The insider's choice among trade papers, lets you know who's on the air in Akron and whether disco's really dead. Weekly.

Record World
1700 Broadway, New York 10019
Most human and readable of the three major trade magazines. Some say their charts are a bit wishful at times. That's why we like them. Every week.

Relix
PO Box 94, Brooklyn, NY 11229
Rock coverage for hard-core American punters, Deadheads, electric blues freaks and down-eaters. Probably good from where they stand — but who cares anymore? Bimonthly, for the 20,000 or so readers who do.

Revue
900½ West Knoll Drive, Los Angeles, Calif. 90069
Edge-oriented fashion with lots of ads by LA clone photographers who all can do the perfect shoe. But chic. Really, darling.

Rock Love
515 Hempstead Turnpike, West Hempstead, NY 11552
Mainstream, Top-40 oriented teen magazine. Bimonthly.

Rock Scene
358 Fairwood Road, Bethany, Conn. 06525
The biggest hand job among American rock mags. This one's as addictive as onanism if you like to see funny pictures of people you've never heard of who happen to be in the music business and detailed-down-to-the-last-nose-pick coverage of the editor's fave raves. Anybody is a star. Sporadically.

Rolling Stone
745 Fifth Avenue, New York, NY 10022
Though its music coverage is as slow to react as a vegetable's nervous system and its reviews are the work of the world's most dedicated core of bellybutton watchers, STONE's saving grace is the fact that it is the only market left in America for intelligent, feature-length journalism. Buy it for that and forget that they didn't get around to covering The Clash until Spring 1980. Biweekly.

Rolling Stone College Papers
745 Fifth Avenue, New York, NY 10022
Edited by the boss' sister. An offshoot for the campus audience. More of the same but good stories and interviews, though irregular.

Slash
PO Box 48888, Los Angeles, Calif. 90048
New wave underground newspaper. Close your eyes, it's the Sixties, people are writing incoherent letters to the editor and everyone's trying to see who can curse the loudest. Ah, youth! Monthly.

Thunder Road
PO Box 171, Bogota, New Jersey 07603
This quarterly out of the swamps of Jersey covers Bruce Springsteen — who else? — and his friends with loving care. Quarterly.

Tiger Beat
7060 Hollywood Blvd., Hollywood. Calif. 90028
Heavy breathing heart-throb action for the sixteen and under set. Big on television hunks, Shaun Cassidy, Kiss and their ilk.

Trouser Press
Trouser Press Collector's Magazine
212 5th Avenue, Room 1310, New York, NY 10010
Now edited by Scott Isler, this is America's hottest young rock mag — not so young actually, but it takes a while to gain a rep like the PRESS has. No longer exclusively an Anglo-oriented mag, it cover-features bands from Talking Heads to The Clash, regularly and profiles and reviews them with intelligence and in-depth. Monthly. (The "collector's magazine" lists releases and auctions and comes out bimonthly).

Walrus
Box 35, Narberth, Penna 19072
Biweekly tip sheet with high subscription cost and high penetration among those in the know in rock and roll radio.

Other rock magazines come and go in America with startling regularity. The state of the American economy has lately dictated against record company advertising, thus the income base for many of the less secure magazines has disappeared, along with those magazines. Every so often a trash publisher will "discover" a band like Kiss and run them into the ground with one-shot personality magazines for teens, and, of course, new wave newsletters come and go in every form imaginable.

ROCK PUBLICATIONS/UK

Acoustic Music
28 Gordon Mansions, Torrington Place, London WC1
The successor to FOLK NEWS, this 55p monthly specialises in folk and bluegrass, but also takes in a spot of jazz. Varied, informative, and essential for folk buffs.

Beat Instrumental
1B Parkfield Street, London N1
"Written for musicians by musicians" is the boast of this 50p monthly. Articles span the entire rock spectrum but show a bias towards the heavy end. Its attitude and feel appear to have changed little over the past ten years. Superficial compared with others in the muso field.

Black Echoes
1B Parkfield Street, London N1
A somewhat insubstantial newspaper which lags behind its competitors (BLACK MUSIC and BLUES & SOUL) in terms of news, depth of coverage and enthusiasm. Weekly at 25p.

Black Music and Jazz Review
153 Praed Street, London W2
Concentrates on soul, reggae, jazz, rhythm 'n' blues (though not solely as dispensed by black artists) and covers its territories with authority and often dedication. Contributors list is peppered with respected scratchers. 50p monthly.

Blues & Soul
153 Praed Street, London W2
Put together by fanatics. Definitive in its fields. Packed solid every fortnight for 50p.

Blues Unlimited
36 Belmont Park, London SE13
The definitive blues encyclopaedia in unending bi-monthly parts.

Buy Gone
30 Radcliffe Road, West Bridgford, Nottingham
A 60p monthly for rock 'n' roll collectors, to advertise their auction/sales/wants lists. Where to pick up that rare Spector item.

Chart Songwords
23 Claremont, Hastings, E. Sussex
A market-milking clone of DISCO 45.

Comstock Lode
51 Bollo Lane, Chiswick, London W4
Early issues focused on the heydays of San Francisco but this literate if irregular fanzine has since moved towards uncharted territory and in doing so makes a worthwhile contribution to rock annals. 50p, whenever the editor can pull an issue together.

Country Music People
128a Lowfield Street, Dartford, Kent
Currently the best regular publication devoted to the Country & Western scene which it covers competently and exhaustively. Essential reading for the cowboy-hatted, gun-toting critters who fill Wembley every Easter. Monthly at 50p and throw.

Dark Star
58 Islip Manor Road, Northolt, Middlesex
Displaying an unswerving penchant for rock music born in California during the mid-sixties, this neat and compact bi-monthly is run by dedicated enthusiasts. 75p buys news, reviews and in-depth interviews, with an emphasis on fax and info.

Disco International
410 St John Street, London EC1
A fat, 60p monthly magazine as glossy as the music it explores, though its primary concern appears to be lights, turntables and other disco equipment. Thorough and authoritative. Conceived and run by rabid folkie Jerry Gilbert.

Disco 45
23 Claremont, Hastings, E. Sussex
At 16 sub-A4 pages for 20p, the self-styled "greatest pop songbook in the land" prints the lyrics of some 15 airplay hits every month, along with some cursory news and reviews.

The Face
Lisa House, 52-55 Carnaby Street, London W1
New 60p monthly edited by Nick Logan, who transformed the NME from a pile of shit in the early seventies. Concentrates on the more intelligent aspects of popular rock, with features, interviews and reviews by the best available freelancers. Packed with great pics too.

International Musician & Recording World
Grosvenor House, 141-143 Drury Lane, London WC2
Thick, but heavy on the ads. Comprehensive and scientific analyses of equipment, plus interviews with musos and token album reviews. Professional. 60p a month.

Melody Maker
24-34 Meymott Street, London SE1
It's been a bad year for the MM: plummeting circulation, strikes, union disputes, management hassles and staff problems. No wonder it's so slow, safe, stodgy, stuffy and supercilious. A handful of writers display flair and passion, but most seem to have lost their sparkle, their direction and their raison d'être. Needs a good kick up the pants and a bunch of enthusiasts who write from the heart, not the head. 25p a week.

Musicians Only
143 Charing Cross Road, London WC2
For 20p you get concise details of instruments, studios and amps. If you are a serious noodling musician requiring a more conservative weekly than even the MM, this is the paper for you. Lifted out of the gutters of snoozerama by Chris Welch's gentle humour.

Music Week
40 Long Acre, London WC2
Mandatory reading for retailers. Provides non-specialist shops with all the information they could need — including its most popular feature, the BMRB charts in removable poster form. 80p every week.

New Chartbusters
22 Offerton Road, London SW4
You always know a publication is dodgy when the names of editors and writers are entirely absent. Fifty pence buys a glossy cover shielding newsprint interior and open-out poster. Specialises in publicity shots and hack profiles of current megastars. A hotch potch of tat.

New Kommotion
3 Bowrons Avenue, Wembley, Middlesex.
The best of those mags catering for the rock 'n' roll collector. Stuffed with discographies, listings, reviews, interviews, facts and photos. Quarterly at 75p.

New Musical Express
5-7 Carnaby Street, London W1
Sex and drugs and rock 'n' roll, examined with cynical expertise. Currently the top selling weekly. First class news coverage, considered reviews, a bright tv and movie section, well written features, and a stimulating rapport with its readership (reflected on the letters page). Among its contributors are writers and cartoonists without peer...in fact, for 25p you get the best rock publication in the world.

QUEEN

New Music News
14 Rathbone Place, London W1
"Written by amateurs, ignored by intellectuals, inspired by greed, propelled by optimism." Originally rushed out by the opportunist Bunch publishing combine to scoop up unspent cash during the MM/NME strike, NMN quickly established itself as a viable weekly rat race competitor and stuck around. Knows its subject but doesn't take it too seriously. 25p.

Old Time Music
33 Brunswick Gardens, London W8
An excellent quarterly covering all aspects of old time and western swing music.

Omaha Rainbow
10 Lesley Court, Harcourt Road, Wallington, Surrey.
In continuous publication since November 1973, OR comes out as quarterly as possible. Carries long, erudite interviews with country and country-oriented musicians with a heavy emphasis on Texas and the so-called progressive country field. Narrow but non-pareil. 60p will secure a sample.

Record Business
Hyde House, 13 Langley Street, London WC2
Since the demise of RADIO and RECORD NEWS, MUSIC WEEK's only competitor in the retail/business market. Somewhat superior in terms of coverage, depth and potential but nonetheless doomed to remain second in importance unless the BBC decide to switch to their charts (which are more accurate in as much as they are unaffected by the widespread tamperings of hype artists). Weekly at 60p.

Record Mirror
40 Long Acre, London WC2
Tritest of all the weeklies it may be, but its chart surveys leave all the others at the post. Not as teenybop oriented as in the Bolan era but still follows trends and concentrates on the megastar. Goes in for lurid centrespread posters but is friendly and informative — and its circulation reflects rising popularity. 25p

Smash Hits
Lisa House, 52-55 Carnaby Street, London WI
Appearing fortnightly at 30p a time, this is a lively mag stuffed with informative interviews, the more articulate song lyrics, news, reviews, competitions, gig lists, letters, snippets and (some in colour) photos — all wrapped in non-patronising matiness. Vastly superior to anything else in the song-lyric field, mentally and physically.

Sound International
Link House, Dingwall Avenue, Croydon.
Most interesting of the gear/studio oriented mags. Technical pieces interspersed with rock star interviews (concentrating on music rather than drug habits and sexual proclivities). If you want to know about phasers, noise gates, binaural recordings, flangers and the like, SI is obtainable monthly for 60p.

Sounds
40 Long Acre, London WC2
Usually first on the case, irrespective of quality. Champions anything new, heavy or lewd and enjoys escalating sales as a result. Good on reggae, but wisely steers clear of disco and pop where possible. Plenty of gossip, rumour and tittle-tattle. If the NME is the GUARDIAN of rock weeklies, SOUNDS is the SUN. 25p per fat issue.

Zigzag
118 Talbot Road, London W11
Stumbling through its eleventh idiosyncratic year, examining the more interesting strata of the rock underground. Seems to run articles on whoever editor Kris Needs happens to bump into on his backstreet odysseys. Columnist John Walters is one of the wittiest in rock journalism. Colourful, erratic, optimistic, friendly and monthly at 50p.

Editors/publishers wishing entries in next year's Rock Year Book should forward copies of their works to Virgin Books.

RECORDING STUDIOS/US

NEW YORK

A & R Recording, Inc.
(212) 582 1070
322 W. 48th St., New York.

Atlantic Studios
(212) 484 8490
1841 Broadway, New York.

Bearsville Sound Studio
(914) 679 7303
Box 135, Speare Road, Bearsville, N.Y.

Blue Rock Studio, Inc.
(212) 925 2155
29 Greene St., New York.

CBS Recording Studios
(212) 975 5901
49 E. 52nd St., New York.

Electric Lady Studio
(212) 477 7500
52 W. 8th St., New York.

Hit Factory
(212) 581 9590
353 W. 48th St., New York.

Media Sound Studios
(212) 765 4700
311 W. 57th St., New York.

Paradise Studio
(212) 541 7920
1700 Broadway, New York.

Plaza Sound Studios
(212) 757 6111
55 W. 50th St., New York.

Power Station
(212) 246 2900
441 W. 53rd St., New York.

RPM Sound Studios
(212) 242 2100
12 E. 12th St., New York.

RCA Studios
(212) 598 5900
110 W. 44th St., New York.

Record Plant
(212) 581 6505
321 W. 44th St., New York.

Secret Sound Studio
(212) 691 7674
147 W. 24th St., New York.

Sigma Sound Studios
(212) 582 5055
1697 Broadway, New York.

Soundmixers
(212) 245 3100
1619 Broadway, New York.

Sound Palace
(212) 541 4870
37 W. 54th St., New York.

Sundragon Recording Studio
(212) 243 9000
9 W. 20th St., New York.

LOS ANGELES

A & M Recording Studios
(213) 469 2411
1416 North LaBrea, Hollywood, Ca.

ABC Recording Studios
(213) 658 5990
8255 Beverly Blvd., Los Angeles, Ca.

Brother Studio
(213) 451 5433
1454 Fifth St., Santa Monica, Ca.

The Burbank Studios
(213) 843 6000
4000 Warner Blvd., Burbank, Ca.

Capitol Recording Studios
(213) 462 6252
1750 North Vine St., Hollywood, Ca.

Chateau Recorders
(213) 769 3700
5500 Cahuenga, North Hollywood, Ca.

Cherokee Studios
(213) 653 3412
751 North Fairfax, Hollywood, Ca.

Conway Recording
(213) 463 2175
655 North St., Andrews Pl., Hollywood, Ca.

Crimson Sound
(213) 393 9444
1454 Fifth St., Santa Monica, Ca.

Crystal Sound Recording
(213) 466 6453
1014 North Vine St., Hollywood, Ca.

Custom Recorders
(213) 877 2557
PO Box 8045, Universal City, Ca.

Davlen Studios
(213) 980 8700
4162 Lankershim Blvd., Universal City, Ca.

Dawnbreaker Recording Studios
(213) 361 1283; (213) 875 0277
216 Chatsworth Dr., San Fernando, Ca.

Devonshire Sound Studios
(213) 985 1945
10729 Magnolia Blvd., North Hollywood, Ca.

Enactron Remote Recording Studios
(213) 271 9829
9500 Lania Lane, Beverly Hills, Ca.

Heider Recording Studio
(213) 466 5474
1604 North Cahuenga, Hollywood, Ca.

Gold Star Recording Studio
(213) 469 1173
6252 Santa Monica Blvd., Hollywood, Ca.

Golden Sound Studios
(213) 462 6688
7000 Santa Monica Blvd., Los Angeles, Ca.

Group IV Recording
(213) 462 6444
1541 North Wilcox Ave., Hollywood, Ca.

Hollywood Sound Recorders
(213) 467 1411
6367 Selma Ave., Hollywood, Ca.

Indigo Ranch Studio
(213) 456 9277
PO Box 24-A-14, Los Angeles, Ca.

Kendun Recorders
(213) 843 8096
619 South Glenwood Pl., Burbank, Ca.

Larrabee Sound
(213) 657 6750
8811 Santa Monica Blvd., Los Angeles, Ca.

MCA Whitney Recording Studios
(213) 245 6801
1516 Glenoaks Blvd., Glendale, Ca.

Mom & Pops Company Store
(213) 769 7282
4028 Colfax Ave., Studio City, Ca.

Motown Recording Studios
(213) 468 3500
6255 Sunset Blvd., Los Angeles, Ca.

Music Grinder Studios
(213) 655 2996
7460 Melrose Ave., Los Angeles, Ca.

The Pasha Music House
(213) 466 3507
5615 Melrose Ave., Hollywood, Ca.

Producer's Workshop
(213) 466 7766
6035 Hollywood Blvd., Hollywood, Ca.

Record Plant
(213) 653 0240
8456 West Third St., Los Angeles, Ca.

Rusk Sound Studios
(213) 462 6477
1556 North LaBrea, Hollywood, Ca.

Salty Dog Recording
(213) 994 9973
14511 Delano, Van Nuys, Ca.

Sound Arts
(213) 487 5148
2825 Hyans St., Los Angeles, Ca.

Sound City, Inc.
(213) 873 2842
15456 Cabrito Rd., Van Nuys, Ca.

Sound Factory
(213) 467 2500
6357 Selma Ave., Hollywood, Ca.

Sound Labs, Inc.
(213) 466 3463
1800 North Argyle, Los Angeles, Ca.

Sound Suite Recorders
(213) 649 3554
PO Box 66, Manhattan Beach, Ca.

Star Track Recording Studio
(213) 855 1171
8615 Santa Monica Blvd., West Hollywood, Ca.

Studio Masters
(213) 653 1988
8312 Beverly Blvd., Los Angeles, Ca.

Sunset Sound
(213) 469 1186
6650 Sunset Blvd., Hollywood, Ca.

Total Experience Recording Studio
(213) 462 6585
6226 Yucca St., Los Angeles, Ca.

United Western Studios
(213) 469 3983
6000 Sunset Blvd., Hollywood, Ca.

Village Recorders
(213) 478 8227
1616 Butler Ave., Hollywood, Ca.

Warner Bros. Recording Studios
(213) 980 5605
11114 Cumpston Ave., North Hollywood, Ca.

Westlake Audio
(213) 655 0303
6311 Wilshire Blvd., Los Angeles, Ca.

Westlake Studios
(213) 654 2155
8447 Beverly Blvd.,
Los Angeles, Ca;
6311 Wilshire Blvd.,
Los Angeles, Ca.

Whitney Studios
(213) 245 6801
1516 Glenoaks, Glendale, Ca.

Allen Zentz Recording
(213) 851 8300
1020 Sycamore Ave.,
Hollywood, Ca.

NASHVILLE

Jack Clement Recording Studio
(615) 383 1982
3102 Belmont Blvd., Nashville,
Tenn.

CBS Recording Studios
(615) 259 3434
34 Music Square East, Nashville,
Tenn.

Quadrafonic Sound Studio
(615) 327 4568
1802 Grand Ave., Nashville,
Tenn.

Sound Stage Studios
(615) 256 2676
10 Music Circle, Nashville, Tenn.

Woodland Sound Studios.
(615) 227 5027
1011 Woodland St., Nashville,
Tenn.

BEST OF THE REST

Air Studios
Montserrat 56-56/Montserrat
56-57
PO Box 94, Montserrat, West
Indies

Alpha International
(215) 271 7333
2001 W. Moyamensing Ave.,
Philadelphia, Pa. 19145

American Sound Studio
(901) 525 0540
827 Thomas St., Memphis, Tenn.,
38107

Apogee Recording Studios
(404) 522 8460
125 Simpson St., Atlanta, Ga.,
30313

Ardent Recordings, Inc.
(901) 725 0855
2000 Madison Ave., Memphis,
Tenn., 38104

The Automat
(415) 777 4111
827 Fulsom St., San Francisco,
Ca., 94107

Axis Sound Studios
(404) 355 8680
1314 Ellsworth Industrial Dr.,
Atlanta, Ga., 30318

Bayshore Recording Studios
(305) 856 5942
2665 S. Bayshore Dr., Coconut
Grove, Fla., 33133

Bear West Studios
(415) 543 2125
915 Howard St., San Francisco,
Ca., 94103

Bee Jay Recording Studios
(305) 293 1781
5000 Eggleston Ave., Orlando,
Fla., 32810

Capricorn Studio
(912) 745 8511
548 Broadway, Macon, Ga., 31201

Caribou Ranch Recording Studio
(303) 258 3215
Nederland, Co., 80466

Compass Point Studios
(809) 327 8282
Ocean Road, Nassau, The
Bahamas

Criteria Recording Studios
(305) 947 5611
1755 NE 149th St., Miami, Fla.,
33181

Dimension Sound Studios
(617) 522 3100
368 Centre St., Jamaica Plain,
Mass., 02130

**Dynamic Sounds Recording
Studio.**
923 9168
15 Bell Rd., Kingston 11, Jamaica

Eastern Sound Co.
(416) 920 2211
48 Yorkville Ave., Toronto,
Canada M4W-1LA

Fantasy Studios
(415) 549 2500
Tenth & Parker Streets,
Berkeley, Ca., 94710

Fifth Floor Studios
(513) 651 1871
517 W. 3rd St., Cincinnati, Ohio,
45202

**Filmways/Heider Recording
Studio**
(415) 771 5780
245 Hyde St., San Francisco, Ca.,
94102

Kaye-Smith Studios
(206) 624 8651
2212 4th Ave., Seattle, Wash.,
98121

Le Studio
(514) 226 2419
Morin Heights, PR 1, Quebec,
Canada, JOR-1HO

Long View Farm
(617) 867 7662
Stoddard Rd., North Brookfield,
Mass., 01535

Master Sound Studios
(404) 873 6425
1227 Spring St., NW, Atlanta,
Ga., 30309

Melody Recording Service
(404) 321 3886
2093 Faulkner Rd. NE, Atlanta,
Ga., 30324

Mountain Meadow Recording
(801) 394 3217
570 26th St., No. 1, Ogden, Utah,
84401

Muscle Shoals Sound Studios
(205) 381 2060
1000 Alabama Ave., Sheffield,
Ala., 35660

North Star Productions
(714) 365 7145
56624 Joshua Dr., Yucca Valley,
Ca., 92284

PS Recording Studios
(312) 225 2110
323 E. 23rd St., Chicago, Ill.,
60616

Paragon Recording Studios
(312) 664 2412
9 E. Huron St., Chicago, Ill.,
60611

Philadelphia Music Works
(215) 525 9873
PO Box 947, Bryn Mawr, Pa.,
19010

Record Plant
(415) 332 6100
2200 Bridgeway, Sausalito, Ca.,
94965

Santa Barbara Sound Recording
(805) 966 6630
33 W. Haley St., Santa Barbara,
Ca., 93101

Sigma Sound Studio
(215) 561 3660
212 N. 12th St., Philadelphia, Pa.,
19107

Stax Studios
(415) 549 2500
10 & Parker Streets, Berkeley,
Ca., 94710

Studio Center Sound Recordings
(305) 861 0756
14875 NE 20th Ave., North
Miami, Fla., 33181

Studio In The Country
(504) 735 8224
PO Box 490, Bogalusa, La., 70427

Studio One
(404) 447 9492
3864 Oakcliff Industrial Court,
Doraville, Ga., 30340

Studio One Inc.
(703) 988 4150
Box 69, Tazewell, Va., 24651

Studio Tempo, Inc.
(514) 937 9571
0707 Charlevoix St., Quebec
Canada, H3K-2Y1

Superdisc, Inc.
(313) 779 1380
14611 E. Nine Mile Rd., East
Detroit, Mich., 48021

Super Sound
(408) 649 4100
600 E. Franklin, Suite E.,
Monterey, Ca., 93940

United Sound Systems
(313) 871 2570
5840 2nd Blvd., Detroit, Mich.,
48202

Universal Recording
(312) 642 6465
46 E. Walton, Chicago, Ill., 60611

VILLAGE PEOPLE

RECORDING STUDIOS/UK

Abbey Road Studios (EMI)
(01) 286 1161
3 Abbey Road, London NW8.

Acorn Studios
(099 389) 324
Church Road, Stonesfield, Oxford.

Advision Studios
(01) 580 5707
23 Gosfield Street, London W1.

Air Recording Studios
(01) 637 2758
214 Oxford Street, London W1.

T.P. Alley Studios
(01) 836 1783
22 Denmark Street, London WC2.

Amazon Studios
(051) 546 6444
Stopgate Lane, Simonswood, Liverpool L33.

Audio International Studios
(01) 486 6466
18 Rodmarton Street, London W1.

Barn Studios
(01) 637 2111
35 Portland Place, London W1.

Basing Street Studios & Island Mobile
(01) 229 1229
8-10 Basing Street, London W11.

Berwick Street Recording Studio
(01) 734 5750
8 Berwick Street, London W1.

Britannia Row Studios
(01) 359 5275
35 Britannia Row, London N1 8QH.

CA VA Recording Studios
(041) 248 4561
201 St Vincent Street, Glasgow.

CBS Recording Studio
(01) 636 3434
31/37 Whitfield Street, London W1.

Central Recorders
(01) 836 6061
9 Denmark Street, London WC2.

Chalk Farm Studios
(01) 485 5798
1a Belmont Street, London NW1.

Chappell Recording Studios
(01) 629 3117
50 New Bond Street, London W1.

Chipping Norton Recording Studios
(0608) 3636
28-30 New Street, Chipping Norton, Oxfordshire.

Craighall Recording Studios
(031) 552 3685
68 Craighall Road, Edinburgh EH6.

Decca Recording Studios
(01) 624 7711
165 Broadhurst Gardens, London NW6.

Decibel Studios
(01) 802 7868
19 Stamford Hill, London N16.

DJM Studio
(01) 242 6886
5-11 Theobalds Road, London WC1.

Eden Studios
(01) 995 5432
20-24 Beaumont Road, London W4.

Essex Music
(01) 734 8121
19-20 Poland Street, London W1.

Fair Deal Recording Studios
(01) 573 8744
1 Gledwood Drive, Hayes, Middlesex.

Foel Studios
(093 882) 758
Foel, Llanfair, Caereinion, Powys, Wales.

Good Earth Studios
(01) 734 0864
59 Dean Street, London W1.

Grosvenor Studios
(021) 356 9639
16 Grosvenor Road, Handsworth Wood, Birmingham 20.

Hyde Park Recording Studios
(08494) 32711
120 Coach Road, Templepatrick, Ballyclare, Antrim.

Ice Recording Studios
(01) 806 3252
81a Osbaldeston Road, London N16.

Impulse Sound Studio
(063) 262 2499
71 High Street East, Wallsend, Newcastle-Upon-Tyne.

Independent Recording Studios
(0474) 65687
39 Hammer Street, Gravesend, Kent.

Island Studios
(01) 741 1511
22 St Peter's Square, London W6.

Jackson Studios
(09237) 72351
The Studios, Rickmansworth, Herts.

R.G. Jones Recording Studio
(01) 540 9882
Beulah Road, London SW19.

Kingsway Recorders
(01) 242 7245
129 Kingsway, London WC2.

Konk Studios
(01) 340 7873
84-86 Tottenham Lane, London N8.

Lansdowne Studios
(01) 727 0041
Lansdowne Road, London W11.

Leader Sound Studio
(0422) 76161
209 Rochdale Road, Greetland, Halifax, W. Yorks.

Lee Sound Recording Studios
(0922) 682961
158 Wolverhampton Road, Pelsall, Walsall.

Magritte Music Studios
(01) 897 9670
15 Holloway Lane, Harmondsworth, West Drayton, Middlesex.

Maison Rouge Studios
(01) 381 2001
2 Wansdown Place, Fulham Broadway, London SW6.

Manor Studios and Manor Mobile
(08675) 2128
Shipton Manor, Shipton-on-Cherwell, Kidlington, Oxford.

Marquee Studios
(01) 437 6731
10 Richmond Mews, Dean Street, London W1.

Mayfair Recording Studios
(01) 499 7173
64 South Molton Street, London W1.

Morgan Recording Studios
(01) 459 7244
169-171 High Street, London NW10.

Music Centre Studios
(01) 903 4611
(De Lane Lea and CTS Studios)
Engineers Way, Wembley, Middlesex.

Nova Sound Recording Studios
(01) 493 7403
27-31 Bryanston Street, London W1.

Odyssey Studios
(01) 402 2191
26-27 Castlereagh Street, London W1.

Old Smithy Recording Studios
(0905) 820659
The Old Smithy, Post Office Lane, Kempsey, Worcester.

Outlet Recording Studio
(0232) 22826
48 Smithfield Square West, Belfast, N. Ireland.

Pathway Studio
(01) 359 0970
2a Grosvenor Avenue, London N5.

Pebble Beach Sound Recorders
(0903) 201767
12 Southfarm Road, Worthing, West Sussex.

Phonogram Studios
(01) 402 6121
Stanhope House, Stanhope Place, London W1.

Pluto Recording Studios
(061) 228 2022
36 Granby Row, Manchester 1.

Polydor Recording Studios
(01) 499 8686
17-19 Stratford Place, London W1.

Pye Recording Studios
(01) 402 8114
ATV House, Bryanston Street, London W1.

RAK Recording Studios
(01) 586 2012
42-48 Charlbert Street, London NW8.

Ramport Studios
(01) 720 5066
115 Thessaly Road, London SW8.

Red Bus Recording Studios
(01) 402 9111
34 Salisbury Street, London NW8.

SPARKS

Rel Studios
(031) 229 9651
7a-10 Atholl Place,
Edinburgh EH3.

Rockstar Studios
(01) 379 7966
63 Charlotte Street, London W1.

Ridge Farm Studios
(0306) 711202
Ridge Farm, Capel, near Dorking, Surrey.

Riverside Recording Studios
(01) 994 3142
78 Church Path, Fletcher Road, London W4.

Roundhouse Recording Studios
(01) 485 0131
100 Chalk Farm Road,
London NW1.

Sain Recording Studios
(028 681) 732
Penygroes, Caernarfon,
Gwynedd, Wales.

Sarm Studios
(01) 247 1311
9-13 Osborn Street, London E1.

Satril Studio
(01) 435 8063
Satril House, 444 Finchley Road, London NW2.

Sawmills Studio
(072 683) 3337
Golant, Cornwall.

Scorpio Sound Studio
(01) 388 0263
19-20 Euston Centre,
London NW1.

September Sound Studios
(0484) 658895
38 Knoll Road, Golcar,
Huddersfield.

Sound Developments Studio
(01) 586 1271
Spencer Court, 7 Chalcott Road, London NW1.

Spaceward Studio
(0223) 64263
19 Victoria Street, Cambridge.

Startling Studios
(0990) 21184
Tittenhurst Park, London Road, Sunninghill, Berks.

Stiff Mobile (The China Shop)
(01) 289 6221
9-11 Woodfield Road, London W9.

Strawberry Recording Studios
(061) 480 9711
3 Waterloo Road, Stockport, Cheshire.

Strawberry South Studios
(0306) 87852
61 South Street, Dorking, Surrey.

Surrey Sound Studios
(03723) 79444
70 Kingston Road, Leatherhead, Surrey.

Sutton Sound Studios
(01) 262 9066
80 Queensway, London W2.

Townhouse Studios
(01) 743 9313
150 Goldhawk Road,
London W12.

Trend Studios
Dublin 760928
10 Hagan Court, Lad Lane,
Lower Baggot Street, Dublin 1.

Trident Recording Studios
(01) 734 9901
17 St. Anne's Court, Wardour Street, London W1.

Utopia Studios
(01) 586 3434
Unit 8, Spencer Court, 7 Chalcot Road, London NW1.

Wessex Sound Studios
(01) 359 0051
106a Highbury New Park,
London, N5.

The Workhouse Studio
(01) 237 1736
488-490 Old Kent Road,
London, SE1.

The above listings were compiled in June 1980 by our editorial team. Because of the transitory and volatile nature of the music business, addresses, telephone numbers and formats tend to change at very short notice.

Venues, studios and companies wishing to be added to our next edition should forward the necessary information to THE ROCK YEARBOOK, 61-63 Portobello Road, London W11 3DD.

CONTRIBUTORS

MICHAEL GROSS is the author of *Bob Dylan: An Illustrated History, I, A Groupie* and *Robert Plant*. His writing has appeared in more than 25 magazines around the world including *Crawdaddy*, the *Village Voice*, *Andy Warhol's Interview*, *Music Life* in Japan and England's *Melody Maker* and *New Musical Express*. he has reported Random Notes for *Rolling Stone* and was founding editor of *Rock*, a national music magazine. Over the years he has interviewed and profiled such artists as Brian Wilson, Brian Eno, The Rolling Stones, George Harrison, Talking Heads, The Allman Brothers, Rod Stewart, Kiss and Patti Smith.

MAXIM JAKUBOWSKI works for Virgin Books and is also known as a novelist in the SF and fantasy field, where his books have been translated into six languages (*Travelling Towards Epsilon, 20 Houses of the Zodiac, The Phosphorus War*, etc...). A contributor to many magazines (*New Scientist, SF Monthly, Fiction, Les Nouvelles Litteraires, New Behaviour, Foundation*), his fiction is generally recognized as being heavily influenced by rock music. He considers himself to be "an informed but opinionated fan who came to rock when Dylan went electric."

TONY BACON is a journalist specializing in musical instruments and associated equipment with *Sound International*. He has written about musicians and the tools that they use for nearly five years and has been known to lose the occasional wrestling match with a bass guitar.
ADAM BARNETT-FOSTER used to review rock records in, of all places, *Science Fiction Monthly*. He has also published short stories about the music scene.
JULIE BURCHILL reviews singles for *The Face* and *New Musical Express*. She is the author (with fellow writer – and husband – Tony Parsons) of the controversial book *The Boy Looked at Johnny*.
LINNET EVANS is a jazz and fusion music specialist and freelance writer. She lives in London.
PETE FRAME, founder of *Zigzag* magazine is the author of the recently published and critically acclaimed *Book of Family Trees*. He is one of the most respected rock historians in the world and lives in Buckinghamshire, in the English countryside.
COLIN IRWIN has, for many years now, been general writer and folk columnist for *Melody Maker*. He is now *MM* Features Editor.
PAUL KENDALL is a freelance music writer and contributor to *Zigzag*.
NICK KIMBERLEY is a London-based freelance journalist generally accepted as one of the foremost authorities on reggae music. He contributes to *Time Out, New Music News* and *New Musical Express*.
BARRY LAZELL works for trade magazine *Record Business* and is a connaisseur of soul.
PHILIPPE MANOEUVRE is among the leading French rock critics, as well as being the editor of the well-known comic strip magazine *Metal Hurlant*.
DREW MOSELEY is the rock correspondent for three American magazines based in New York City. She began her career in journalism as the Associate Editor of *Teen World* in 1978.
PHIL NEWELL is the Technical Director of Virgin Recording Studios *(The Manor, The Townhouse)*.
DAN NOOGER is a New York freelance writer who has contributed in the past to most of the leading US rock magazines.
ALEXEI PANSHIN lives on a Pennsylvania farm and is a double-Hugo award recipient SF writer (*Rite of Passage, Earth Magic, SF in Dimension*). He is also a self-confessed rockabilly freak.
ROB PARTRIDGE used to be a staffer on *Melody Maker* and is now Press Officer for *Island Records*.
TONY RUSSELL writes a column in *Jazz Journal* and edits/publishes *Old Time Music*. He is also Press Officer for folk-oriented label, *Topic*.
STEVE TAYLOR, joint-compiler (with David Marlow) of *The Small Labels Catalogue*, is a well-known music writer and frequent contributor to *The Face* and *NME*.
JOHN TOBLER is regularly featured on Radio One's *Rock On*. The author of many music books, he has also written for most of the major British newspapers and magazines in the rock field at one time or another.
MARK WILLIAMS shares his time between Los Angeles and London. At one time a *Melody Maker* correspondent, he was the founding editor of *New Music News* and is also on the team of *Slash Magazine*.
BOB WOFFINDEN, co-editor (with Nock Logan) of the best-selling *NME Encyclopedia of Rock* now works as a freelance journalist (*NME, AM, New Society*).
RICHARD WOOTTON is the author of *'Honky-Tonkin'*.

ACKNOWLEDGEMENTS

The ROCK YEARBOOK would not have been possible without the assistance, kindness and (often unpaid) collaboration of many people. We would therefore like to express our heartfelt thanks to our many contributors who often battled against unreasonable deadlines, to the many Press and Publicity Officers of record companies, publishing houses and film companies who supplied us with records, books, photographs and other assorted requirements during the compilation of the YEARBOOK. Many thanks also to the Virgin Megastore who provided record sleeves. A very special vote of gratefulness must also go to various persons without whom, it is fair to say, this book wouldn't even have existed: Pete Frame, Vivienne Haynes, Pearce Marchbank.

We end by issuing a conventional but in this case sincere apology and thanks to all those others who helped, whether knowingly or not, and cannot be correctly credited here; also, a friendly nod in the direction of all the critics, fans, musicians, friends and jolly liggers who took time to answer our questionnaire.

All photographs supplied by Chalkie Davies,
Andre Csillag and a host
of record company Press Officers.

'Fads 'n' Fashion' photos by Virginia Turbett

Illustrations pp. 210/211 by Richard Draper

Illustration p. 215 courtesy of Rolling Stone

Photoset by AGP (Typesetting) Ltd.